Attributes of
TREES AS CROP PLANTS

Attributes of

TREES AS CROP PLANTS

edited by

M. G. R. Cannell
and
J. E. Jackson

Institute of Terrestrial Ecology
Natural Environment Research Council

© NERC Copyright 1985

Published in 1985 by Institute of Terrestrial Ecology

Copies can be obtained from the ITE Administrative Headquarters, Monks Wood Experimental Station, Abbots Ripton, Huntingdon, PE17 2LS, England (Telex 32416).

BRITISH LIBRARY CATALOGUING-IN-PUBLICATION DATA
Attributes of trees as crop plants.
  1. Forests and forestry   2. Trees
    I. Cannell, M. G. R. (Melvin G. R.)
    II. Jackson, J. E. (John E.)
    III. Institute of Terrestrial Ecology
    634.9'5   SD391

ISBN 0–904282–83–X

Printed in Great Britain by
Titus Wilson & Son Ltd, Kendal, Cumbria

The cover design was drawn by Mr. R. H. F. Wilson, ITE, Edinburgh

The **Institute of Terrestrial Ecology (ITE)** was established in 1973, from the former Nature Conservancy's research stations and staff, joined later by the Institute of Tree Biology and the Culture Centre of Algae and Protozoa. ITE contributes to, and draws upon, the collective knowledge of the 13 sister institutes which make up the **Natural Environment Research Council**, spanning all the environmental sciences.

The Institute studies the factors determining the structure, composition and processes of land and freshwater systems, and of individual plant and animal species. It is developing a sounder scientific basis for predicting and modelling environmental trends arising from natural or man-made change. The results of this research are available to those responsible for the protection, management and wise use of our natural resources.

One quarter of ITE's work is research commissioned by customers, such as the Department of Environment, the European Economic Community, the Nature Conservancy Council and the Overseas Development Administration. The remainder is fundamental research supported by NERC.

ITE's expertise is widely used by international organizations in overseas projects and programmes of research.

Dr M. G. R. Cannell
Institute of Terrestrial Ecology
Bush Estate
Penicuik
Midlothian EH26 0QB
Scotland

Tel. 031 445 4343

Dr J. E. Jackson
East Malling Research Station
East Malling
Maidstone
Kent ME19 6BJ
England

Tel. 0732 843833

Contents

Flowering and fruiting

Trees in stands

Economic aspects

Participants

ALSTON, F. H.   East Malling Research Station, East Malling, Maidstone, Kent, ME19 6BJ, England.

AVERY, M. E.   School of Forestry and Environmental Studies, Yale University, New Haven, Connecticut 06511, USA.

BACHELARD, E. P.   Department of Forestry, Australian National University, PO Box 4, Canberra ACT 2600, Australia.

BARNES, R. D.   Department of Forestry, Commonwealth Forestry Institute, University of Oxford, South Parks Road, Oxford OX1 3RB, England.

BENTLEY, W. R.   The Ford Foundation, 55 Lodi Estate, New Delhi 110003, India.

BOWEN, G. D.   CSIRO Division of Soils, Private Bag No. 2, Glen Osmond, SA 5064, Australia.

BOWMAN, J. C.   Natural Environment Research Council, Polaris House, North Star Avenue, Swindon, Wilts SN2 1EU, England.

BRIDGWATER, F. E.   USDA Forest Service, Department of Forestry, North Carolina State University, Box 8002, Raleigh 27695, North Carolina, USA.

BROWN, M.   Forestry Commission, Northern Research Station, Roslin, Midlothian EH25 9SY, Scotland.

BROWNING, G.   East Malling Research Station, East Malling, Maidstone, Kent ME19 6BJ, England.

BURDEKIN, D. A.   Forestry Commission Research Station, Alice Holt Lodge, Wrecclesham, Farnham, Surrey GU10 4LH, England.

CAHALAN, C. M.   Department of Forestry and Wood Science, University College of North Wales, Bangor LL57 2UW, Wales.

CANNELL, M. G. R.   Institute of Terrestrial Ecology, Bush Estate, Penicuik, Midlothian EH26 0QB, Scotland.

CARLOWITZ, P. von.   International Council for Research in Agroforestry, PO Box 30677, Nairobi, Kenya.

CAUSTON, D. R.   Department of Botany and Microbiology, University College of Wales, Penglais, Aberystwyth SY23 3DA, Wales.

CEULEMANS, R.   Department of Biology, University of Antwerpen, Universiteitsplein 1, B-2610-Wilrijk/Antwerpen, Belgium.

COUPER, C.   Department of Botany, University of Edinburgh, King's Buildings, Mayfield Road, Edinburgh EH9 3JU, Scotland.

COUTTS, M. P.   Forestry Commission, Northern Research Station, Roslin, Midlothian EH25 9SY, Scotland.

CROZIER, A.   Department of Botany, University of Glasgow, Glasgow G12 8QQ, Scotland.

DEANS, J. D.   Institute of Terrestrial Ecology, Bush Estate, Penicuik, Midlothian EH26 0QB, Scotland.

DENNE, M. P.   Department of Forestry and Wood Science, University College of North Wales, Bangor LL57 2UW, Wales.

DICK, J.   Institute of Terrestrial Ecology, Bush Estate, Penicuik, Midlothian EH26 0QB, Scotland.

DICKMANN, D. I. Department of Forestry, Michigan State University, East Lansing, Michigan 48824, USA.

ELDRIDGE, K. G. CSIRO Division of Forest Research, PO Box 4008, Queen Victoria Terrace, Canberra ACT 2600, Australia.

ELLIOTT, G. K. Department of Forestry and Wood Science, University College of North Wales, Bangor LL57 2UW, Wales.

ELLIS, R. T. Tea Research Foundation of Central Africa, PO Box 51, Mulanje, Malawi.

FAULKNER, R. Forestry Commission, Northern Research Station, Roslin, Midlothian EH25 9SY, Scotland.

FAYLE, D. C. F. Ontario Tree Improvement and Forest Biomass Institute, Maple, Ontario L0J 1E0, Canada.

FLETCHER, A. M. Forestry Commission, Northern Research Station, Roslin, Midlothian EH25 9SY, Scotland.

FORD, E. D. (Institute of Terrestrial Ecology, Bush Estate, Penicuik, Midlothian EH26 0QB, Scotland.) New address: Center for Quantitative Science, University of Washington, Seattle, Washington 98195, USA.

FRANKLIN, E. C. School of Forest Resources, North Carolina State University, 103 Enterprise Street, Suite 200, Raleigh, North Carolina 27607, USA.

GIERTYCH, M. Institute of Dendrology, 62-035 Kornik, Poland.

GILL, G. Forestry Commission, Northern Research Station, Roslin, Midlothian EH25 9SY, Scotland.

GOLD, M. A. Department of Forestry, Michigan State University, 126 Natural Resources Building, East Lansing, Michigan 48824, USA.

GORDON, J. C. School of Forestry and Environmental Studies, Yale University, New Haven, Connecticut 06511, USA.

HARPER, P. C. Twyfords Plant Laboratories, Baltonsborough, Glastonbury, Somerset BA6 8QG, England.

HIBBS, D. E. Department of Forest Science, Oregon State University, Corvallis, Oregon 97331, USA.

HOOKER, J. E. Department of Botany, University of Glasgow, Glasgow G12 8QQ, Scotland.

HUXLEY, P. A. International Council for Research in Agroforestry, PO Box 30677, Nairobi, Kenya.

JACKSON, J. E. East Malling Research Station, East Malling, Maidstone, Kent ME19 6BJ, England.

JARVIS, P. G. Department of Forestry and Natural Resources, University of Edinburgh, King's Buildings, Mayfield Road, Edinburgh EH9 3JU, Scotland.

JONES, H. G. East Malling Research Station, East Malling, Maidstone, Kent ME19 6BJ, England.

KÄRKI, L. Foundation for Forest Tree Breeding, Alkutie 69, SF-0060 Helsinki 66, Finland.

KAUFMANN, M. R. USDA Forest Service, Rocky Mountain Forest and Range Experimental Station, Fort Collins, Colorado 80526, USA.

KENNEDY, D. Department of Forestry, University of Aberdeen, St Machar Drive, Aberdeen AB9 2UU, Scotland.

KOSKI, V. Department of Forest Genetics, Forest Research Institute, Box 18, SF-01301 Vantaa 30, Finland.

KOZLOWSKI, T. T. Director of the Biotron, University of Wisconsin, 2115 Observatory Drive, Madison, Wisconsin 53706, USA.

LANDSBERG, J. J. CSIRO Division of Forest Research, Banks Street, Yarralumla, Canberra ACT 2600, Australia.

LANNER, R. M. Department of Forestry and Outdoor Recreation, Utah State University, Logan, Utah 84322, USA.

LAST, F. T. Institute of Terrestrial Ecology, Bush Estate, Penicuik, Midlothian EH26 0QB, Scotland.

LEAKEY, R. R. B. Institute of Terrestrial Ecology, Bush Estate, Penicuik, Midlothian EH26 0QB, Scotland.

LENZ, F. Institute fur Obst-und Gemusebau der Universitat Bonn, Auf dem Hugel 6, Bonn 5300, West Germany.

LEMOINE, B. Recherches Forestieres, Domaine de l'Hermitage, Pierroton, 3361 Cestas Principal, France.

LEIKOLA, M. Department of Silviculture, University of Helsinki, Unionkatu 40 B, SF-00170 Helsinki 17, Finland.

LINDER, S. CSIRO Division of Forest Research, PO Box 4008, Queen Victoria Terrace, Canberra ACT 2600, Australia.

LINES, R. Forestry Commission, Northern Research Station, Roslin, Midlothian EH25 9SY, Scotland.

LONGMAN, K. A. Institute of Terrestrial Ecology, Bush Estate, Penicuik, Midlothian EH26 0QB, Scotland.

McMURTRIE, R. E. CSIRO Division of Forest Research, PO Box 4008, Queen Victoria Terrace, Canberra ACT 2600, Australia.

MALCOLM, D. C. Department of Forestry and Natural Resources, University of Edinburgh, King's Buildings, Mayfield Road, Edinburgh EH9 3JU, Scotland.

MOHREN, G. M. J. Department of Silviculture, Agricultural University, PO Box 342, 6700 AH Wageningen, The Netherlands.

MURRAY, M. B. Institute of Terrestrial Ecology, Bush Estate, Penicuik, Midlothian EH26 0QB, Scotland.

NEWMAN, S. M. Energy Research Group, Open University, Walton Hall, Milton Keynes MK7 6AA, England.

PALMER, J. W. East Malling Research Station, East Malling, Maidstone, Kent ME19 6BJ, England.

PERRY, D. A. Department of Forest Science, Oregon State University, Corvallis, Oregon 97331, USA.

PERRY, T. O. School of Forest Resources, Box 8002, North Carolina State University, Raleigh, North Carolina 27695, USA.

PHILIPSON, J. J. Forestry Commission, Northern Research Station, Roslin, Midlothian EH25 9SY, Scotland.

PLUMPTRE, R. A. Department of Forestry, Commonwealth Forestry Institute, University of Oxford, South Parks Road, Oxford OX1 3RB, England.

RAMOS-PRADO, J. M. 61 Reuglas Road, Edinburgh, Scotland.

RAVEN, J. A. Department of Biological Sciences, University of Dundee, Dundee DD1 4HN, Scotland.

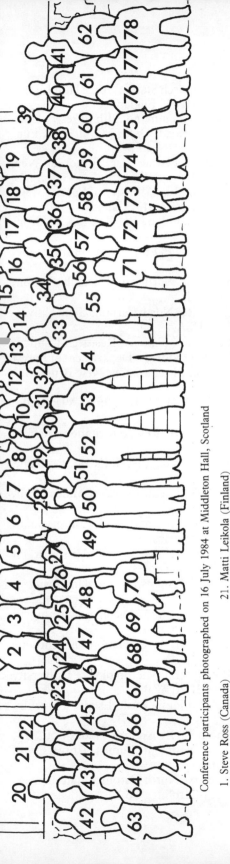

Conference participants photographed on 16 July 1984 at Middleton Hall, Scotland

1. Steve Ross (Canada)
2. Julian Philipson (Scotland)
3. Mike Coutts (Scotland)
4. Mike Gold (USA)
5. Bruce Rottink (USA)
6. Frank Alston (England)
7. Stan Thompson (Scotland)
8. Jan Dick (Scotland)
9. Carol Aitchison (Scotland)
10. Maureen Murray (Scotland)
11. Bernard Lemoine (France)
12. Hugh Miller (Scotland)
13. Bob Willey (India/England)
14. Yeang Hoong Yeet (Malaysia)
15. Maciej Giertych (Poland)
16. Lyn Jones (England)
17. David Causton (Wales)
18. John Palmer (England)
19. Alan Longman (Scotland)
20. Fritz Mohren (Netherlands)
21. Matti Leikola (Finland)
22. Veikko Koski (Finland)
23. Norman Simmonds (Scotland)
24. Peter Harper (Scotland)
25. Dave Hibbs (USA)
26. John Torrey (USA)
27. Julia Wilson (Scotland)
28. Irene Ellis (Malawi)
29. Rex Ellis (Malawi)
30. Richard Barnes (England)
31. Christine Cahalan (Wales)
32. Ken Eldridge (Australia)
33. Ross McMurtrie (Australia)
34. Gordon Browning (England)
35. Keith Rennolls (England)
36. Joe Landsberg (Australia)
37. Fritz Lenz (W. Germany)
38. Rod Savidge (Canada)
39. Mark Rutter (USA)
40. Peter von Carlowitz (Kenya)
41. Eric White (Scotland)
42. Fred Last (Scotland)
43. David Rook (New Zealand)
44. Derek Kennedy (Scotland)
45. Merrill Kaufmann (USA)
46. Pat Denne (Wales)
47. Roy Faulkner (Scotland)
48. John Bowman (England)
49. Dave Fayle (Canada)
50. Glyn Bowen (Australia)
51. Sune Linder (Australia)
52. Eric Bachelard (Australia)
53. Ron Lanner (USA)
54. Tom Perry (USA)
55. Roger Timmis (USA)
56. Peter Huxley (Kenya)
57. Lauri Kärki (Finland)
58. Reinhart Ceulemans (Belgium)
59. Pedro Sanchez (USA)
60. David Burdekin (England)
61. John Jackson (England)
62. Roger Leakey (Scotland)
63. Bill Bentley (India/USA)
64. Dave Perry (USA)
65. Lucy Sheppard (Scotland)
66. Roger Lines (Scotland)
67. Steve Newman (England)
68. Christine Couper (Scotland)
69. Don Dickmann (USA)
70. Peter Tigerstedt (Finland)
71. Jose Ramos-Prado (Scotland)
72. Melvin Cannell (Scotland)
73. Phillip Wareing (Wales)
74. Ted Kozlowski (USA)
75. Bob Plumptre (England)
76. Patrick Robinson (England)
77. Donald Thompson (Jamaica)
78. David Ford (Scotland/USA)

RENNOLLS, K.   Forestry Commission Research Station, Alice Holt Lodge, Wrecclesham, Farnham, Surrey GU10 4LH, England.

ROBINSON, P. J.   Department of Forestry, Commonwealth Forestry Institute, University of Oxford, South Parks Road, Oxford OX1 3RB, England.

ROOK, D. A.   Forest Research Institute, Private Bag, Rotorua, New Zealand.

ROSS, S. D.   Research Branch, British Columbia, Ministry of Forests, 4300 North Road, Victoria, British Columbia V8Z 5J3, Canada.

ROTTINK, B. A.   Crown Zellerbach Corporation, PO Box 368, Wilsonville, Oregon 97070, USA.

RUTTER, M. R.   Westvaco-Forest Research, PO Box 1950, Summerville, South Carolina 29484, USA.

SAMUEL, C. J. A.   Forestry Commission, Northern Research Station, Roslin, Midlothian EH25 9SY, Scotland.

SANCHEZ, P. A.   Department of Soil Science, North Carolina State University, Raleigh, North Carolina 27650, USA.

SAVIDGE, R. A. (Biological Sciences Division, National Research Council, Ottawa, Ontario K1A 0R6, Canada.) New address: Department of Forest Resources, University of New Brunswick, Fredericton, New Brunswick E3B 6C2, Canada.

SCARASCIA-MUGNOZZA, G.   Instituto di Bio-Selvicoltura, Via Riello, 001100 Viterbo, Italy.

SEAL, D. T.   Forestry Commission, Northern Research Station, Roslin, Midlothian EH25 9SY, Scotland.

SHEPPARD, L. J.   Institute of Terrestrial Ecology, Bush Estate, Penicuik, Midlothian EH26 0QB, Scotland.

SIMMONDS, N. W.   Edinburgh School of Agriculture, West Mains Road, Edinburgh EH9 3JG, Scotland.

THOMPSON, D. A.   Department of Forestry and Soil Conservation, 2 South Odeon Avenue, Kingston 10, Jamaica.

THOMPSON, S.   Department of Forestry, University of Aberdeen, St Machar Drive, Aberdeen AB9 2UU, Scotland.

TIGERSTEDT, P. M. A.   Department of Plant Breeding, University of Helsinki, 00710 Helsinki 71, Finland.

TIMMIS, R.   Weyerhaeuser Company, WTC 2B25, Tacoma, Washington 98477, USA.

TORREY, J. G.   Harvard University Forest, Petersham, Massachusetts 01366, USA.

WAREING, P. F.   Department of Botany and Microbiology, University College of Wales, Aberystwyth SY23 3DA, Wales.

WHITE, E. J.   Institute of Terrestrial Ecology, Bush Estate, Penicuik, Midlothian EH26 0QB, Scotland.

WILLEY, R. W.   (ICRISAT, Patancheru P.O., Andhra Pradesh 502324, India.) Present address: School of Development Studies, University of East Anglia, Norwich NR4 7TJ, England.

WILLIAMS, C. G.   Department of Forestry, North Carolina State University, Box 8002, Raleigh 27695, North Carolina, USA.

WILSON, J.   Institute of Terrestrial Ecology, Bush Estate, Penicuik, Mid-
lothian EH26 0QB, Scotland.
YEANG, H. Y.   Plant Science Division, Rubber Research Institute of
Malaysia, PO Box 10150, Kuala Lumpur 01-02, Malaysia.

Portraits of some of the participants, drawn by David Fayle. (Numbered as in the legend to the photograph.)

A. Geoff Elliott,   B. John Gordon,   C. Carlyle Franklin,   D. Floyd Bridgwater,
E. John Raven,   F. David Seal,   G. Paul Jarvis.

Preface

This book contains the proceedings of a conference held at Middleton Hall Conference Centre, Gorebridge, Midlothian, Scotland, between 15th and 21st July 1984. The conference was held under the auspices of the International Union of Forestry Research Organizations, working groups S2.01.00 (physiology) and S1.06.00 (biological productivity). The Institute of Terrestrial Ecology acted as host. The meeting was organized in liaison with Dr P. M. A. Tigerstedt of the University of Helsinki and Dr J. C. Gordon of Yale University, USA. The aim was to bring foresters, horticulturalists and agroforesters together to review the major characteristics of trees that influence the ways in which they have been, or could be, manipulated and exploited as crop plants.

The phrase 'attributes of trees' means that the focus was primarily on the trees themselves rather than on their roles in land use systems. The phrase 'as crop plants' means that the focus was on those attributes of trees that become important – as problems or advantages – when trees are domesticated or manipulated, both genetically and by management, to yield products of value to man. How do the size, longevity, life strategy, persistence and structure of trees and tree stands (forests and orchards) influence the ways in which they have been, and could be, exploited to yield wood, fruits, fodder and extractives? How could advantageous attributes of woody perennials be better exploited and what advances have been made to overcome disadvantageous attributes? It should not be forgotten, on the one hand, that many forest and multipurpose trees are still barely domesticated, and, on the other hand, that cotton, once grown as a small perennial tree, is now cropped as an annual and that, in tree fruit production and some types of forestry, there is a trend towards shorter rotations and smaller trees with simpler structures.

The intention of the conference was to provide a forum for an interchange of ideas, and perhaps a new synthesis of knowledge, rather than to elicit new information, although many new ideas were presented. Most contributors were assigned their topics, and were asked to give an overview of the current state of knowledge in their field, current thinking, key ideas or problems, and their views on the way ahead. Whole volumes could be, and in many cases have been, written on each topic covered, and contributors were forced to take a broad-brush approach. The result is a series of reviews in tree biology which will help teachers and researchers to keep abreast of developments in fields other than their own, and which might also be of value to students. An effort has been made to avoid or explain some of the jargon used by specialists to ensure that the book is of value to the widest possible readership.

The meeting brought together researchers who were concerned with various kinds of tree crops, including forest plantations, fuelwood trees, fodder trees, fruit trees, tea, rubber and tropical multipurpose trees. It therefore paralleled those meetings of agricultural scientists in which discussions automatically encompass crops as diverse as cereals, grain legumes, root crops and perennial herbage grasses. The outcome was an all-too-rare opportunity to pool ideas from horticulture, forestry and plantation crop research. Perhaps, inevitably, there was a bias towards the trees of coniferous plantations and much less emphasis on, for example, tropical plantation crops, but our approach was to focus on the *attributes* of tree crops important to all or many tree crop research scientists, rather than to attain complete coverage of each individual tree crop. This approach forced us to identify the key issues, and it put a heavy onus on the contributors. The topics we chose are divided here into six groups.

The first and largest group of topics concerned tree domestication, covering some thoughts on the evolutionary history and life strategy of trees, the domestication of multipurpose trees, forest and fruit tree breeding, vegetative propagation and some views on the selection criteria and 'ideotypes' that might be used by tree breeders. The second group concerned mainly the vegetative structure of trees – the relationships and distribution of dry matter among tree parts, cambial activity, branching structure, and the vegetative products of fuelwood, fodder and extractives. The third group of topics concerned tree root systems, mycorrhizas and N_2-fixing symbionts, and the important effects of trees on soils in the tropics. The fourth group concerned the attributes of trees as producers of fruits and seeds, covering flower induction, fruit set and the effects of flowering on the rest of the tree. The fifth group concerned the special attributes of tree communities or stands, including fruit orchard design, the characteristics of forest canopies and the process of inter-tree competition. And, finally, we invited two viewpoints, one from the developed and one from the developing world, on the economics of future forest design and future markets.

At the end of the conference, the participants were divided into five discussions groups which were asked to outline the main issues, any omissions in the review papers, points of contention, and priorities for future research. Their reports are given at the end of the book.

The meeting received generous financial support from the British Council and UNESCO that enabled many overseas participants to attend. It is also a pleasure to thank Professor F. T. Last, Dr J. C. Bowman, Dr J. G. Torrey, Dr P. A. Huxley, Dr R. Timmis, Dr D. T. Seal, Dr J. J. Landsberg and staff of the Forestry Commission Northern Research Station for contributing to the success of the conference. Special thanks are also due to our fellow organizers, Dr David Ford, Dr Alan Longman, Dr Roger Leakey, Dr Lucy Sheppard, Mrs Maureen Murray, Miss Carol Aitchison and Mr R. H. F. Wilson. Finally, we thank ITE's director, Mr J. N. R. Jeffers, and especially Mrs Penelope Ward and Mrs Jean King of ITE for their painstaking work in subediting and proof reading.

November 1984   *Melvin G. R. Cannell*
                                              John E. Jackson

DOMESTICATION

1

PERSPECTIVES ON THE EVOLUTIONARY HISTORY OF TREE CROPS

N. W. SIMMONDS
The Edinburgh School of Agriculture, Edinburgh, Scotland

I. INTRODUCTION

This meeting ranges widely, and most speakers have been assigned nice, clear subjects upon which to exercise their professional knowledge. I have not. The word 'perspectives' in a title is usually an indication of a vague essay to follow, and this paper is no exception. The fact is that our knowledge of the evolution of tree crops is generally poor, and often negligible, but I thought it better to try to generalize rather than merely to recite the better known cases.

II. WILD AND CULTIVATED

A crop is a plant cultivated to yield a useful product or products; likewise, if a plant is grown for such a purpose it is a crop. Thus, ornamental plants cannot reasonably be called crops, neither can wild plants of which parts are gathered. All crops, thus defined, are in some degree domesticated; that is, they have evolved under natural, semi-natural and human selection pressures in cultivation. The degree of genetic change, of course, varies profoundly from very slight (eg in timber trees just becoming crops, at the first step of domestication) to great (eg in some of the older fruit trees which may be far removed in many characters from their wild ancestors).

Characteristically, wild sources of a product and domesticated populations co-exist for a time (which may be long), but the normal final outcome is, one suspects, that the crop ousts the wild source economically, maybe even wholly replacing it as the wild sources are lost. Thus, a few decades ago, timbers such as many pines, spruces, eucalypts and teak were harvested from the wild; nowadays, wild stands and early domesticates co-exist and both are exploited; in another few decades, the products will probably be purely cultivated. Sugar and starch (sago) palms, some tannins (*Acacia*), and diverse fruit, nut and drug plants are probably in much the same position. If they survive at all it will probably be in cultivation. Likewise, many tropical hardwoods, now only gathered, will have to become crops if they are to survive in useful quantity.

The many tree crops that are further along the way to complete domestication yield a great diversity of products. They include, for example: a multitude of fruits and some nuts, temperate and tropical; oils from coconut and oil palm; flavours from clove, nutmeg, pimento and betel nut; stimulants from coffee, tea, cacao and coca; drugs from quinine and coca; fibres from coconut and kapok; and rubber from *Hevea*. These plants vary widely, from recent domesticates such as *Hevea* and *Elaeis* (which co-exist with well-defined wild sources, but have become dominant economically) to others which are sufficiently old, altered and widely travelled that their wild sources are quite doubtful. Thus, much uncertainty attaches to what wild plants gave rise to coconut, tea, breadfruit, citrus, mango, and even whether they still exist. The problems are exacerbated by bad taxonomy: up to 150 'species' have been proposed in *Citrus*, and even the more conservative 15 or so names which are commonly used contain some 'species' which are merely clonal cultivars. It is usually sensible and informative, when dealing with crops, to abandon conventional taxonomy, and to use Latin names only for unambiguous wild species, and an informal, genetically based terminology for the cultivars. To do so at least forces attention on the all-too-rarely asked question: what is truly wild and what is cultivated?

III. EVOLUTION

A. General

A list of what might be regarded as the main tree crops is given in Table I. It is based mainly on Simmonds (1976) and the contents are, to some extent, arbitrary. Many more minor crops might have been included, and I have not even tried to list the numerous tropical shade and browze trees which are nowadays exciting so much interest (eg *Gliricidia*, *Erythrina* and *Leucaena*). I have excluded, also, woody plants which can be tree-like but are more usually shrubby and/or short-lived (eg papaya, castor, cassava, cottons and coca).

To generalize rather widely (on what is admittedly often imperfect knowledge), nearly all are outbreeders, either wind or animal pollinated, and some are self-incompatible (eg cacao). The great majority are diploid by origin, and have remained so in cultivation. Exceptions are mulberry (with a spectacular $2n = 22x = 308$), the allotetraploid *Coffea arabica*, some kapok, some forms of *Prunus* (up to 6x), and odd polyploid clones of breadfruit and poplar. Arabica coffee is interesting, because it is one of the very few inbreeders

TABLE I.　Origins of some of the world's principal tree crops

Origins		Fruits and nuts	Drugs and stimulants	Spices	Timber trees	Industrial	Others
EURASIA	Temperate	Fig, olive, date, *Prunus*, apple, pear, nut trees, etc	—	—	Pines, spruces, larches, birches, beech, poplars, etc	—	—
	Tropical	Mango, citrus, durian, mangosteen, rambutan, litchi, *Artocarpus*	Tea	Nutmeg, betel nut, clove	Teak, dipterocarps and other hardwoods	Coconut, tungs	*Arenga, Borassus*, sago
AFRICA	Tropical	Tamarind, akee, shea butter	Coffees, kola	—	*Triplochiton*, mahoganies and other hardwoods	Oil palm, wattle, kapok	—
AMERICA	Temperate	*Prunus*, chestnut, pecan	—	—	Pines, spruces, firs, birches, poplars, etc	—	—
	Tropical	Avocado, cashew, *Annona*, guava, tree tomato, sapodilla, pechibaye	Quinine, cacao, mate, quassia	Pimento	*Pinus caribaea, Swietenia*, and other hardwoods	Rubber, kapok	Calabash
AUSTRALASIA	Tropical	*Artocarpus, Macadamia*	—	—	*Araucaria*, eucalypts	Black wattle	—

in the list – an allotetraploid relative of outbreeding (presumptively self-incompatible) diploids. That *C. arabica* is an inbreeder was a critical element in the history of the crop, enabling it to pass through the extreme bottleneck of one or a very few plants during its transmission to the New World. The peach is also tolerant of inbreeding, or at least much more tolerant than other *Prunus* 'species'.

B.   Places and times

Table I is set out geographically. Tropical outnumber temperate entries, and by a large margin if temperate plantation timber trees are excluded. All the continents have contributed, Eurasia and America the most, Australasia the least. Broadly the same is true for herbaceous crops. Centres of cultivation are sometimes far removed from origins, with coffee, oil palm and rubber being the most striking examples: in each of these cases, the main area of cultivation is in a different continent from the botanical source.

As to ages, some crops have certainly been in cultivation for several millennia (for example, the olive and many temperate Eurasian fruits and nuts) and many more probably have been (eg the leading tropical fruits). At the other extreme, rubber, oil palm and most of the timber trees are recent crops, all having been 100 years or less in cultivation. Among the timber trees, *Cryptomeria* and some poplars are exceptionally long established as crops.

C.   Selection pressures

Given that the tree crops yield very diverse products, it is certain that selection pressures during their evolution must also have been diverse. First, there must have been some natural selection for growth or even for survival in new habitats, for example tolerance of heat, cold, drought and wetness. Second, there must also have been semi-natural selection for survival in the socio-agricultural circumstances in which they were grown, for example ease of propagation, appropriate seed dormancy, wind-fastness, tolerance of fire and grazing animals, responsiveness to local soil conditions and competition. And third, there must have been conscious human selection for desired characters such as large, sweet fruits, non-toxic constituents (as in mango), high contents of desired constituents (such as oils, alkaloids, aromatics, latex), good flavours in the fruits, nuts and beverages, small size and non-spininess in fruit trees, but large, straight stems in timber trees. Finally, as a fourth category, we should add correlated responses to selection, which take the form of reduction of plant parts other than the desired part or parts. This idea is familiar and fairly well established for annual crops, and is of growing concern to students of trees. In the annuals, the effect is apparent as a changing harvest index (or partition ratio). Thus, in potatoes and cassava, flowering and fruiting have declined as tuber yield has risen while, in the small-grain cereals, a decline of straw from around 67% to about 50% (at roughly constant biomass) has occurred in recent decades. There must have been similar processes at work in the tree crops. Table II presents a rather speculative interpretation for a range of tree crop types.

TABLE II. Selection pressures in various tree crops

Examples	Root	Stem	Branch	Flower	Fruit	Seed
Coffee, cacao coconut	?	↓	↓	?	?	⋆
Oil palm	?	↓	—	?	⋆	⋆
Breadfruit, fig, pomes	?	↓	↓	?	⋆	↓
Tea	?	↓	⋆	↓	↓	↓
Rubber	?	latex⋆ ↓ wood ↓	↓	↓	↓	↓
Timber tree	?	⋆	↓	↓	↓	↓

Asterisks ⋆ indicate the desired product for which selection is practised. Arrows indicate probable directions of correlated responses in size or numbers of other plant parts.

We have a few concrete examples of correlated responses, as follows (and no doubt there are many more of which I am unaware). In coconuts, the trend is towards semi-dwarf, precocious high yielders, analogous with the cereals (although I have not been able to find estimates of partition ratios). Oil palm breeders are tending to favour a high bunch index, especially as it may favour growth in dense stands (Hardon et al. 1985). In rubber, there is evidence of reduced wood increment as rubber yields rise (Simmonds 1982) and evidence also that rubber (the material itself) is biologically far more costly than simple energetic considerations would suggest. Cannell (this volume) makes a similar point about tea. In cacao, Glendinning (1966) has shown that high-yielding families are those that grow fast when immature, but slowly when in full bearing, because fruits compete with vegetative growth. From Glendinning's data on two experiments in Ghana, we have, for example:

(1) $Y = 3·33 + 7·19D − 2·29G$ and (2) $Y = 10·99 + 2·21D − 1·34G$

where Y is yield of beans, D (positive coefficient) is immature stem diameter and G (negative coefficient) is growth increment of stem diameter in full bearing. Thus, harvest index has three interesting aspects: (a) it can be thought of usefully as an aspect of correlated response to selection, (b) once recognized, it must be of interest to both evolutionist and breeder, and (c) quantitative study should reveal useful ideas on the 'biological cost' of substituting some plant parts and constituents for others.

The term 'harvest index' nearly always refers to above-ground parts of plants, simply because these are relatively easy to measure. Our ignorance of

root systems is a recurrent theme in this book, and it will be noted that I had
to write queries in every cell of the first column of Table II. We simply do
not know whether root systems have shown correlated responses to selection
for above-ground plant parts. That the permanent roots of trees constitute a
substantial fraction of total biomass is certain, but the magnitude of turnover
of fine roots is usually unknown. To be able to include roots in an understanding of biomass partition, and correlated evolutionary response, would be a
valuable step. Reciprocal grafting experiments with phenotypically contrasted
genotypes, coupled with root studies, could be a useful point of entry into the
problem.

   Finally, I must mention an evolutionary trend among the fruits selected for
an edible pulp, a trend which may reflect conscious selection and/or correlated
response. I refer to a reduction of seediness, and a tendency to replace the
stimulus of developing seeds for fruit growth by an autonomous stimulus,
namely parthenocarpy (see Browning, this volume). The bananas are the best
example (Simmonds 1962) and in no other fruit (I think) is parthenocarpy so
highly developed. But it occurs, to some degree at least, in the pome fruits,
citrus and grape. In the fig and breadfruit, an analogous behaviour produces
seedless infructescences, which reflects a functional parthenocarpy (even if,
strictly, it should not be called parthenocarpy). Unfortunately, fruits, other
than the banana and fig, have been too little investigated to allow generalizations as to the kind of parthenocarpy encountered (vegetative or stimulative)
and its genetic control. Along with this tendency to reduced seed fertility in
fleshy fruits, there are various other reproductive derangements such as
apomixis/polyembryony in mango and citrus; their evolutionary status is
unknown. More generally (see Table II) some decline in flowering, fruiting
and seed fertility would be expected in any crop selected for a vegetative
product and, indeed, one encounters hints that just this occurs in tea and
rubber. In timber trees, where seed is taken from wild sources, there is, of
course, a risk of just the opposite effect, namely of selecting for seed fertility
to the disadvantage of subsequent wood production. Ultimately, breeders of
all crops that produce a vegetative product must be prepared to encounter
infertility problems as consequences of preceding success.

D.   Breeding

Plant breeding is the current phase of crop evolution, and the plant breeder
is, in effect, an applied evolutionist. The breeding plans of a crop are
dominated by the natural breeding system, and by the available modes of
reproduction. These factors circumscribe what the tree crop breeder can do,
because (a) tree crops are outbreeders (Arabica coffee excepted), so any high
degree of inbreeding is forbidden by inbreeding depression; (b) with trees
being perennials, clonal propagation is always a possibility which may or may
not be realizable in practice; and (c) if clones are not (or cannot) be adopted,
breeding must be carried on by one or other of the innumerable variants
of mass selection, parental selection with progeny testing, construction of
synthetics, interpopulation crossing and so on, that are available (Simmonds
1979; Bridgwater & Franklin, this volume).

Of the crops listed in Table I, the more important dicotyledonous agri-horticultural tree crops are often clonal (the fig, the rosaceous fruits, mango, citrus, avocado and breadfruit) or jointly seedling-clonal (tea, coffees, mango, avocado, cacao and rubber), and are rarely still wholly propagated by seed (olive). The lesser crops in this category (guava, cashew, and many other nuts) are mostly seedling propagated. The timber trees are, with the notable exceptions of some poplars, and some *Pinus radiata* and *Cryptomeria japonica*, still all seed propagated (but see below, and Leakey, this volume). The monocotyledonous tree crops, the palms, are (with the exception of the clonal date and sago, which sucker) perforce grown as seedlings.

The intensity of breeding effort varies very widely. The minor non-timber crops have had little or no attention beyond local selection of the odd favoured clone or mother tree. The rosaceous fruits have had a fair amount of effort put into them, but without much success: with few exceptions, old clones still dominate (Alston & Spiegel-Roy, this volume). Tea, coffee, quinine, cacao and coconut have all been the subjects of fairly effective breeding, but the real success stories have been oil palm and rubber in south-east Asia, both responsive to the powerful economic pull of efficient plantation industries.

Over the past decade or so, the opportunities inherent in *in vitro* multiplication of clones of trees have become apparent, though not yet, I think, adopted on any substantial practical scale. Such multiplication is, of course, well established and practised on an ever-increasing scale in diverse herbaceous crops and ornamentals. In essence, the prospect for trees is to generate *in vitro* large numbers of clonal propagules of plants that either cannot be cloned by conventional means (oil palm, coconut), or are difficult and/or slow and expensive to propagate in this way (many timber trees). The prospect is attractive, because good clones ought to be at least a little better than good seedling populations of outbreeders. The margin may not be great, however, (or easy to estimate), and one should be cautious of over-optimism. Further-more, mere clonal propagation is only the first step; most clones are poor or indifferent, and only intense selection among large numbers, and prolonged trials, will identify the really superior ones. It will be interesting to see whether the 30% yield advance predicted by Hardon et al. (1985) for oil palm clones is readily achieved. It may be that specification and uniformity of product are at least as important as yield, in this crop (and in others).

The technical problems of *in vitro* cloning are not easy to solve. In dicotyle-donous trees, the maintenance, rooting and multiplication of organized meris-tems *in vitro* are sometimes, for reasons yet unknown, rather difficult, but if/when achieved, the products should pose no problems of genetic integrity. In the unbranched palms, meristem culture is infeasible, and recourse must be had to multiplication through a disorderly callus phase which incurs the likelihood of induction of undesirable (and yet still mysterious) genetic changes, now generally referred to as 'somaclonal variation' (Larkin & Scow-croft, in Kosuge et al. 1983). The prospects for stable propagation of oil palm, however, seem to be good (Jones 1983) and, no doubt, refinements of technique will lead in time to clonal propagation on a commercial scale of both palms, and the timber trees, in which it has not previously been possible. The need for diversity of clones, as an escape from the pathological hazards of monoclonal planting, is widely accepted. But the important question – 'how many clones is enough?' – cannot yet be answered.

Finally, I wish to make a few points about breeding objectives and ideotypes. The object of all plant breeding programmes, without exception, is the production of populations that are more profitable to grow than their predecessors. Yield is an important, often dominant, component, but it is always accompanied by other characters which must, somehow, be integrated into the successful, economically and biologically 'balanced genotype'. This necessity suggests the use of economic index selection, which rarely appears explicitly, but is certainly inherently present in the intuitive indices that are universally adopted (Simmonds 1979).

Donald (1968) proposed the term 'ideotype' as a morphological (or morphophysiological) model of a small-grain cereal that should maximize yield. All plant breeders have some vision of the sort of plant they are trying to breed, and no knowledge of one's crop is ever amiss. But 'ideotypes', however interesting, have not been notably useful in practice. Intense selection for yield, and other characters, in diverse materials, generates complex correlated responses and diverse products. In general, there is no *one* 'ideotype'. At the component character level, again, none dominates, and numerous suggestions, to the effect that selection for this or that character should advance yield, have all failed. The only way so far known of advancing yield is to select for yield. The 'ideotype' is not the same as the breeding objective; this usage goes beyond Donald's and ignores the fact that several different plant forms may be successful. More generally, morpho-physiological ideas have been useful in interpreting *post hoc* what breeding has already achieved, but have not been notably successful in guiding breeding practice. Evans (in Gustafson 1984) goes so far as to describe crop physiology as 'the retrospective science'. This may yet change, of course. But, to be really useful, physiological parameters would have to be measured quickly and cheaply on very large numbers of plants, as well as be reasonably highly correlated with yield and devoid of undesirable negatively correlated responses. The harvest index certainly changes in many crops as a correlated response to yield selection, but it is harder to measure than yield itself, and of no evident use to the breeder. Perhaps tree physiologists could usefully take a retrospective look at contrasted high- and low-yielding tree populations (including their root systems).

Most agricultural crop breeding has a rather specific socio-agricultural environment and end use in view. The single purpose dominates, even if there are by-products. There are signs that tree breeding is moving the same way, for example to pulp, particles or sawnwood, as separate objectives in conifer improvement programmes. This must be economically sensible (Elliott, this volume). In the context of tropical agroforestry (Huxley, this volume), the multipurpose tree is prominent *at the species level*. But it cannot be doubted, I think, that, as agroforestry species are developed, divergence into populations specialized for specific end uses must emerge. Indeed, the trend is already evident in one of the most prominent agroforestry species, *Leucaena*, where the need for diverse plant forms adapted to hedges, browsing, fodder production and timber is already clear. The multipurpose tree will no doubt be with us for decades, but it must, in the longer run, be replaced by diverse, few- or one-purpose bred varieties adapted to socio-economic needs.

IV. THE FUTURE

It will be clear that our knowledge of the evolution of the tree crops is, with a few exceptions, still rather poor; annual crops are quicker and easier to study, have had far more attention, and are generally better known. We are now, however, at least far more conscious of trees, of their interest and importance, than we were only a decade or two ago. There are six points to make about current trends and likely future developments.

1. Improved evolutionary understanding must be based upon two things: (a) unambiguous identification of truly wild materials as reference points, and (b) comparison of wild with cultivated forms, in respect of diverse morphological, chemical and physiological characters. Only thus can we identify the critical correlated responses hinted at in Table II, which must also be useful elements in framing future breeding programmes.

2. In those relatively few tree crops which are already subject to breeding, refinements of technique (eg *in vitro* cloning), and the use of larger breeding populations, are likely to be important. The latter is so because genetic progress is roughly related to the log of the number of genetic entries – other things being equal, the bigger a programme, the better (but not linearly). Sugar cane breeders collectively raise several *million* seedlings per year.

3. No doubt more crops will be taken into breeding programmes and, trees being what they are, the sooner the better. Beyond a little bit of clonal selection, the tropical fruits have been sadly neglected, despite their socio-economic importance.

4. The general subject of tree crops is widening fast, not much maybe in the traditional fruits, nuts and spices, but rapidly in the timber trees, in the agroforestry species, and in that ill-defined group of plants that we hardly know we want (jojoba comes to mind). Agroforestry ideas (eg Huxley 1983) seem to be of peculiar importance for the development of stable farming systems in the wet tropics, yet much tropical agricultural research virtually ignores trees (Watson 1983).

5. Following from (4), I have frequently been impressed by how incompletely the tropical tree crops are distributed. One can travel in Asia without seeing avocados, in Africa without seeing breadfruit, and nearly everywhere without seeing pechibaye. A basic activity to exploit effectively these marvellous plants seems to me to be simply to set up a distribution programme so that, at many sites in every continent, a good range of genotypes of each of a hundred or two useful trees is actually *there and growing*. It is certain that useful research on exploitation cannot be done without such a resource. I am talking about old-fashioned botanic gardens kind of work – simply competent horticulture. The difficulties posed by plant quarantine obstruction should not be underestimated: it would be a difficult task, however worthwhile. Yet is would be immeasurably better to get the species and selected genotypes introduced widely on a systematic basis rather than *ad hoc*, with years of delay, when the needs were apparent. I can think of no simple activity more conducive to the beneficial evolution of tree crops.

6. The practical need to force the evolutionary pace of an ever-widening circle of tree crops by breeding is therefore plain. To back up the effort, in a time when natural vegetation is being destroyed, and the genetic base is being

narrowed in cultivation, there is plainly a need to conserve genetic resources, and this need is now widely accepted. To conserve existing crops is not difficult in principle, even if costly; methods are available and techniques are improving. But what of the prospective crops mentioned under (4): those plants that we do not yet really know we want, and for what purpose? *In situ* conservation may do something but, alas, probably not much. I think that, as a society, we have not yet properly understood the scale of need for genetic conservation of potentially useful plants, including the trees that are not yet crops. The activities outlined in (5) would themselves constitute a modest contribution to genetic resource conservation. The best place for conservation is in cultivation.

REFERENCES

Donald, C. M. (1968). The breeding of crop ideotypes. *Euphytica*, **17**, 385–403.
Glendinning, D. R. (1966). Further observations on the relationship between growth and yield in cocoa varieties. *Euphytica*, **15**, 116–127.
Gustafson, J. P., ed. (1984). *Gene manipulation in plant improvement.* (Proc. Stadler Genetics Symposium, 16th). New York; London: Plenum.
Hardon, J. J., Corley, R. H. V. & Lee, C. H. (1985). Breeding and selection for vegetative propagation in the oil palm. In: *Improvement of vegetatively propagated plants*, edited by A. I. Campbell, A. J. Abbott and R. K. Atkin. London: Academic Press. In press.
Huxley, P. A., ed. (1983). *Plant research and agroforestry.* Nairobi: International Council for Research in Agroforestry.
Jones, L. H. (1983). The oil palm and its clonal propagation by tissue culture. *Biologist*, **30**, 181–188.
Kosuge, T., Meredith, C. P. & Hollaender, A. (1983). *Genetic engineering of plants. An agricultural perspective.* New York; London: Plenum.
Simmonds, N. W. (1962). *The evolution of the bananas.* London: Longman.
Simmonds, N. W., ed. (1976). *The evolution of crop plants.* London: Longman.
Simmonds, N. W. (1979). *Principles of crop improvement.* London: Longman.
Simmonds, N. W. (1982). Some ideas on botanical research on rubber. *Trop. Agric., Trin.*, **59**, 2–8.
Watson, G. A. (1983). Development of mixed tree and food crop systems in the humid tropics: a response to population pressure and deforestation. *Exp. Agric.*, **19**, 311–332.

2

THE BASIS OF SELECTION, MANAGEMENT AND EVALUATION OF MULTIPURPOSE TREES – AN OVERVIEW

P. A. HUXLEY
International Council for Research in Agroforestry, Nairobi, Kenya

(An expanded text of this paper is contained in ICRAF's working paper no. 25, of the same title.)

I. INTRODUCTION

The term 'multipurpose tree' (MPT), in this paper, refers to woody perennials that are purposefully grown to provide more than one significant contribution to the production and/or service functions (eg shelter, shade and land sustainability) of the land use systems they occupy.

There are many similarities between the methods used to select, manage and evaluate MPTs for agroforestry and trees used in forestry or agriculture. There are, however, some differences that arise from the need to consider multiple outputs, and from the complexity of the plant associations. This paper concentrates on outlining the effects of these differences.

Ecologists, and those familiar with natural or integrated forms of land use, are well able to conceptualize the characteristics of complex systems involving species mixtures that include woody perennials. There are, however, many scientists and technologists trained in 'conventional' agriculture or 'industrial' forestry, who have now become interested in agroforestry, but who may not be so familiar with the problems involved. It is mainly to this audience that this overview is addressed.

There is a very wide range of uses for MPTs (von Carlowitz 1984) and a great diversity of agroforestry land use systems (Nair & Fernandes 1984). The selection, management and evaluation of MPTs for any one of these uses or systems always involve a consideration of the tree itself, sometimes the tree as a crop plant, and often its association with other species. Thus, the resolution of management alternatives and any research objectives requires answers to the following questions: (a) 'What species are most suitable for any *particular* agroforestry land use system?' (b) 'How many of them are required per unit area of land?' and (c) 'How should they be arranged and managed?' The subject areas concerned with finding the answers to these questions are discussed in the three sections that follow.

II.   KEY ISSUES IN SELECTING, MANAGING AND EVALUATING MULTIPURPOSE TREE SPECIES

A.   Some characteristics of the genotype

Choosing an MPT genotype for a particular agroforestry application often involves difficulties, owing to the need to rank the required outputs, as well as to consider potentials for environmental resource sharing with other kinds of crop species. As yet, some of the basic information on which to base a choice is little known for many, if not most, MPT species.

Some important characteristics to consider are: (a) general growth, flowering and fruiting attributes, which include specific morphological attributes, dry matter distribution as affected by genotype, fruiting and environment, and phenological characteristics; and (b) adaptability, which includes overall genetic fitness or flexibility, ecophysiological considerations, and genotype× environment interactions.

Some of these topics have been addressed fully elsewhere (eg Ledig 1983; Huxley 1983a,b, 1984) and only key topics will be dealt with here.

1.   *Specific morphological attributes*

Although general descriptions of growth and form are available for all MPT species, there is often inadequate information at the provenance level. Furthermore, no really detailed investigations have yet been carried out on the morphological basis of growth, in the way that has been so helpful for some of our more important tree cash crops. For example, in coffee, early studies on the different behaviour of particular buds provided a sound, predictive basis for shaping and pruning the tree (van der Meulen 1939). Only simple dissection techniques were needed to obtain this information.

2.   *Source-sink relationships and fruiting*

In woody perennials, the onset of a fruiting cycle (floral initiation to seed and fruit maturation) has effects on both the current and subsequent seasons' growth and development. It has long been known that the presence of fruits can enhance carbon assimilation (Neales & Incoll 1968) and that fruits and seeds are highly competitive sinks. Consequently, the manipulation of flowering and fruiting is a powerful tool to alter the distribution of dry matter in an MPT. The proportions of different outputs can be changed by encouraging, regulating or eliminating the fruiting process.

With the exception of some edible pod-bearing leguminous trees, such as *Prosopis* and *Acacia*, there are few species of MPTs that have been subjected so far to any intensive breeding in which fruiting has been a criterion. Most MPT genera have been selected using simple species and provenance trials. *Leucaena* has been subjected to fairly rigorous selection and, latterly, to interspecies crossing, in order to select fuelwood or fodder types (Brewbaker 1980, 1982) or genotypes that will grow in acid soils (Hutton 1981). A characteristic of *Leucaena* is its early and prolific flowering, yet *Leucaena* is not widely grown for its fruits. The litter of pods and seeds that form under *Leucaena* provides mainly a 'service' function which could better be provided by leaf litter, particularly as unwanted seedlings have to be removed. It might therefore be advantageous to select types which flowered less prolifically.

One scarcely studied aspect of source-sink relationships that warrants consideration is the spatial relationship between carbon assimilation sources (leaves or bracts) and fruits. C^{14}-tracer studies on woody plants have shown that assimilates can be transferred to developing fruits, not only from subtending leaves, but also from adjacent ones both up and down the stems (eg for coffee, Cannell & Huxley 1969). The extent to which this transfer occurs no doubt varies with species, the numbers of developing fruits at any site, and the stage of fruit growth. However, it seems a reasonable working hypothesis that fruits that are 'adequately provided' with source leaves might develop best and be less of a drain on stored carbohydrates and main canopy leaf sources. If we are choosing MPTs for their ability to provide fruits and/or seeds reliably, source-sink proximity might be a selection characteristic to consider. There are numerous ways in which flowers and fruits can be disposed in relation to the leaves (Fig. 1).

3. *Overall genetic fitness or flexibility*

When selecting MPT germplasm, we need to consider whether the objective is to satisfy a generally adaptive set of criteria, in a range of various types of agroforestry land use systems, situated perhaps in an environmentally diverse area, or whether the aim is to select critically for a particular system, in either one or a closely comparable set of systems.

Ecological flexibility is an attribute of a particular pool of germplasm, and individual genotypes may or may not have the ability to flourish outside the environments in which they are well adapted (Pickersgill 1983). Individual species or cultivars may exhibit a narrow or broad adaptive capacity, irrespective of how heterozygous they are. The ability of a genotype to grow in a range of different environments will depend on how far particular adaptive anatomical, morphological and physiological characters of the phenotype can be modified in response to changes in environmental variables.

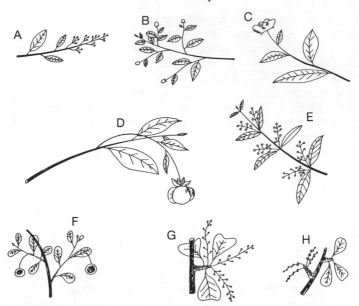

FIGURE 1. Different ways in which inflorescences and fruits (assimilate sinks) can be disposed relative to nearby leaves (assimilate sources) on woody plants.
A. Shoot apex ends in inflorescence without leaves.
B. Shoot apex vegetative, lateral inflorescences (single flowers) subtended by numerous leaves.
C. Single terminal flower, supplied by whole of leafy shoot below.
D. Single flower arising from a lateral, and supplied from leaves above and below a main shoot (*Monodora myristica*, Annonaceae).
E. Shoot apex vegetative, inflorescences many-flowered and lateral, each subtended by a single leaf only (*Combretum tenuipetiolatum*).
F. Single or few-flowered lateral inflorescences on lateral shoots that themselves remain vegetative (*Grewia*, Tiliaceae).
G. Inflorescences borne on 'short shoots' among leaves (*Terminalia*, Combretaceae).
H. Inflorescence borne alone on 'short shoots', leaves borne on other short shoots (some species in Anacardaceae and Burseraceae).

4. *Ecophysiological considerations*

(a) *Survival and resource sharing mechanisms.* Many of the attributes for adaptive change, and the capacity a plant has for expressing them in response to changes in the environment, will have evolved from a need both to ensure *survival* and to develop *competitively* in plant associations. Once an evolutionary trend has established some specialized plant modifications – in the form of either a survival mechanism, or an enhanced ability to compete – the plant's capacity to adapt to another set of environmental conditions may have been diminished.

For example, various adaptive structures have evolved to reduce water loss from leaves in arid environments, without which the plants would not survive prolonged periods of drought. Such leaves are very different in character from those of many plants which have evolved in wetter conditions, where plants can grow closer together, and where the major limiting resource may be light. In such circumstances leaves are aggressive organs, adapted to shade competitors, and the plants may respond rapidly to shading by producing leaves with greater specific leaf areas. This phenomenon is seen to a high degree in many species within the Cucurbitaceae, but it is clearly a feature which puts them at a disadvantage when water is in short supply. Conversely, arid land plants with thick leaves will be at a disadvantage in plant associations where the other species have leaves which readily respond to shading.

General adaptability, therefore, becomes a matter of being relatively non-specialized, as distinct from specific adaptability, which derives from morphological, anatomical and physiological specializations which are the result of evolution towards genetic fitness. When choosing MPT species, we need to be aware of their 'adaptability', and ideally to have some idea of the structural and physiological mechanisms which they have evolved to become adaptable in natural communities.

(b) *Potentials for exploitation.* 'Success' in any plant community can be defined as the ability of a genotype to increase in numbers. This ability may depend more on a plant's capacity to acquire a greater share of the available environmental resources than cohabiting species, rather than on its more positive modifications which fit it to a specific environment. The implications of this, in terms of selection for particular products or attributes, are rather important, and we need to apply the lessons learnt with other crop plants. For example, *Coffea arabica*, at its centre of origin (Ethiopia), is found as a successful understorey shrub, producing, under relatively shady conditions, only a modest number of fruits per tree. Removed from its natural habitat, it has been found to yield much more prolifically if grown in full sun, as long as it is provided with high levels of plant nutrients. There are many other examples of a similar nature in which the attributes for 'ecological success' tend to obscure the potentials for exploitation by man.

5.   *Genotype × environment interactions*

If the limits of, and reasons for, adaptive behaviour in MPT species are to be understood, a common set of critically evaluated MPT species/provenance trials, conducted in a suitable range of environments, is required. Experience to date with the major agricultural crops, and with provenance testing of forest tree species, establishes a clear indication of both the necessity and the magnitude of this task. Some attempts to undertake species/provenance testing are now being made by the Nitrogen Fixing Tree Association, the National Academy of Sciences, FAO, and others.

With MPTs, there is the added difficulty that a significant $G \times E$ interaction may be established for one yield output, but not for others, especially if two kinds of harvest come from competing sinks, such as fruits and wood. Plants may respond minimally in terms of overall vegetative growth to a small change in environment, but the flowering/fruiting process may be markedly affected (eg by a change in night temperature, Huxley & Summerfield 1976).

At present, the selection of MPT germplasm is done mainly at the species level. Selection on the basis of provenance trials is under way, but tree breeding programmes are needed to exploit the huge genetic variation that is available (Felker *et al.* 1981; Burley *et al.* 1984). The breeding programmes on *Leucaena leucocephala* (which is mainly inbreeding, unlike most MPT species) have provided two types of plants – mainly fuelwood types (eg cv 'K8') and mainly fodder types (eg cv 'Peruvian') (Brewbaker 1980). The extent to which different yield objectives are separated clearly affects the rate and degree of genetic gain, as well as the outcome of any G×E interactions.

6.   *Selection index procedures*

In the initial stages, it may be satisfactory to select MPTs subjectively by eye. But if we are objectively to select for several outputs simultaneously, it may become desirable to devise 'selection indices' like those used in agriculture (eg cotton, Manning 1956; Walker 1960; Arnold & Innes 1976). However, a lot of genetic information is needed to be able to weight each trait correctly. Simpler multitrait selection procedures could be used in which different end uses were listed against climatic designations or ecozones. Such two-way tables could include simple within-table ranking schemes, but they would have limited value where there was a high level of G×E interaction for particular traits. Furthermore, it must be remembered that the users themselves will establish a different ranking order, according to the land use systems in which the MPTs are grown. Therefore, a simple ranking scheme for user requirements will have to be incorporated. This could be done, at least partially objectively, by using a field diagnostic procedure such as ICRAF's 'Agroforestry diagnosis and design' procedure (Raintree 1985; ICRAF 1983).

Developments in vegetative and micro-propagation will clearly assist in the rapid dissemination of MPTs. Although foresters are wary of clonally established plantations, it should be remembered that most of the world's temperate and tropical tree fruit industries have been based on selected clones. MPTs may be used in lower-input land use systems than fruit trees, but many MPTs are fast-growing, and mature rapidly, and it would be possible to establish MPT breeding centres which could provide a succession of suitable germplasm (with pest and disease resistance) as needed.

B.   Attributes contributing to land sustainability

1.   *Soil changes at the microsite*

Species of woody perennials can differ very considerably in the extent to which they modify the soil, and in the time taken to bring any changes about. The tree's ability to change the microsite will itself be modified by management, particularly pruning, and by any removal of plant materials. A great number of variables, and their interactions, must be considered in order to estimate changes in the complex space-time arrangements of a mixed cropping agroforestry system (Huxley 1982).

Tropical broadleaved MPT species generally possess a potential for benefitting the microsite but, again, to various degrees. They may, therefore, be of differing values in agroforestry systems where land sustainability has a high priority. As yet, little is known about the tree characteristics that contribute to 'land sustainability'. For example, in India, the indigenous species *Prosopis cineraria* is commonly found on farmers' fields in Rajastan, where it is nurtured because of its favourable effects on the microsite, but the introduced species *Prosopis juliflora* is not so beneficial. In Africa, *Acacia albida* is similarly well known for its favourable effects (Felker 1978) and, in Central and South America, genera such as *Inga* and *Calliandra* behave similarly. Other examples are species of *Gliricidia*, *Erythrina*, *Acrocarpus* and *Sesbania*, as well as numerous other leguminous species, and non-legumes such as *Grevillea*, *Terminalia* and *Alnus*.

Not all woody species improve the status of the soil around them. Many gymnosperms, as we well know, produce a resinous and slowly decomposing leaf litter that can impede soil reactions. Eucalypts also deposit a litter of resinous leaves that can form a close-lying mat that may inhibit understorey growth and, on sloping land, encourage water runoff. A few species of higher plants are known to produce root secretions that inhibit the growth of associated plants (eg guayule produces trans-cinnamic acid, Bonner & Galston 1944). More obscurely, there are many different kinds of organic compounds that can accumulate from the decomposition of plant residues with adverse effects on associated species (Friedman 1983; Kozlowski & Huxley 1983; Shang-Shyng & Hsi-Hua 1983). There may also be specific replant problems following the cultivation of certain species, as have been reported for several fruit trees, *Stylosanthes* (a perennial fodder plant) and Arabica coffee.

Agroforestry systems are often promoted because of their implicit 'land sustainability' characteristics (Lundgren 1982). It seems essential, therefore, to establish the relative potentials for achieving this sustainability possessed by the 50 or 60 woody species that, at present, are considered to be highly promising candidates for different ecozones (from among the many hundreds of species that have so far been listed as 'possibles'; Burley *et al.* 1984).

2. *MPTs and land system sustainability*

The generalities, and sometimes illusions, that 'trees improve the soil' need to be replaced, for individual MPT species, by critical experimental evidence of the kind that facilitates extrapolation to other sites and management conditions (Young 1984). We need also to assess the effect of removing relatively large amounts of biomass from the site, because this is often implicit in many proposed agroforestry production systems.

Woody species are often (but not always) deeper rooted than forbs or grasses and may, therefore, be extracting nutrients from lower soil levels and recycling them in litter. This process has very significant ecological effects over long periods of time in natural ecosystems (eg Golley *et al.* 1975) and in systems of shifting cultivation (eg Kuile 1984). However, the timescales for any required improvements in most managed agroforestry systems are relatively short, and the nutrient cycles are not 'closed'. There is also considerable evidence in the tropics for an inexorable decline in soil fertility, under both continuous agricultural cropping and plantation forestry, which suggests that most high-output systems cannot provide sustained yields without the addition of nutrients. Agroforestry schemes which purport to be able to remove, annually, very large amounts of biomass from the sites, without the addition of nutrients, need to be treated with some scepticism. The amounts, location and rates of off-take and replenishment of nutrients need to be studied before such systems can be considered viable in the long term.

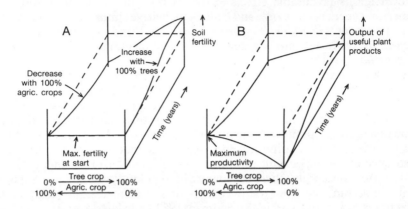

FIGURE 2.
A. Hypothetical response surface showing changes with time in soil fertility using cropping systems with different proportions of agricultural crops and soil-enriching multipurpose trees. The horizontal axis represents a 'replacement series'.
B. A similar hypothetical response surface showing the output of useful plant products (from Huxley 1983b).

3. *Sustainability in mixed cropping with MPTs*

When growing MPTs with agricultural crop species, there will be a compromise between the level of productivity (from all contributing species) and the sustainability of the system. In any system, the latter may depend predominantly on the tree species being used and their number per unit area. How then can we consider what proportions of tree and agricultural crops should be grown?

A model for evaluating existing data is given in Figure 2, which shows changes with time in soil status using tree/agricultural crop combinations, and corresponding changes in the output of useful plant products. Such a model can provide only conjectural solutions at present, because we can only guess at the values and, indeed, the shapes of the curves, but like most models, this one exposes the priorities for research.

C. Some tree management considerations

Cannell (1983a) has discussed a whole range of management options in agroforestry. What follows here is confined to some aspects of pruning.

1. *Pruning and the manipulation of vegetative growth and fruiting*

Woody perennials lend themselves to relatively precise forms of structural manipulation which are usually undertaken to (a) change or moderate stature and form, and (b) regulate the proportion of different parts such as fruits, foliage, wood and exudates. This manipulation has to be done with a knowledge of the vegetative condition and fruitfulness of the tree, as a consequence of previous growth and fruiting activities.

MPTs may or may not be purposefully grown for fruits or seeds. If not, the flowering process is usually just ignored, although the production of flowers, fruits and seeds will represent a waste of the plant's resources. So, whether flowers are wanted or not, a better understanding of the development processes involved may suggest ways of regulating them to advantage. The investigational requirements are not onerous. The first is to observe the type of stems on which flowering takes place (current or previous seasons' stems), and to note the sequences of flowering and shoot-flushing. These will be related – in as much as flowering, prior to a vegetative flush, must occur on stems produced in a previous season. Such information is essential for an effective pruning programme, as all fruit growers know.

When flowering occurs on 'old' wood, it may be from residual axillary buds which have remained dormant, or, more likely, it will be on some form of 'short shoot' – usually an axillary shoot with highly compressed internodes. Flowering on 'new' wood is not restricted to the periphery of a tree, because shoots can grow out from older stems. However, the supply of potentially active buds may rapidly be used up, and whole areas of older stems may become barren. Species or cultivars may exhibit a range of types, from those that flower mainly on old wood to those that flower mainly on new wood (in apple, the 'tip bearers'), each requiring different pruning treatments.

When an MPT is to provide browze, it may be feasible to impose browzing of newly developing shoots around the time at which flower initiation is occurring, in order to reduce flower numbers. If flowers (or inflorescence buds) have a dormant period, as in Arabica coffee, this may be some time before anthesis. To check the time, or part of the season, at which flower buds are initiated requires only a sequenced programme of bud dissection and examination using a binocular microscope.

2. *Pruning practices*

There are many forms of pruning (eg Cannell 1983a; von Carlowitz 1984), but only two basic pruning operations – 'thinning-out' and 'heading-back' (Fig. 3). Their skilled application can be used to change the overall size and shape of trees, to regulate growth and fruiting, and to modify the output of plant parts. The two operations can be carried out on stems of differing order – main stems, primary branches, secondaries, tertiaries, and so on (Fig. 3).

Although the overall effect on different species of either operation will be similar, the *precise* response will depend very much on the growth characteristics of the species concerned, the time at which the pruning operations take place, and the care and understanding with which the pruner selects which operation to use. Skilled pruning has reached a high degree of sophistication in many tree species grown for their fruits and/or seeds. Relatively simple

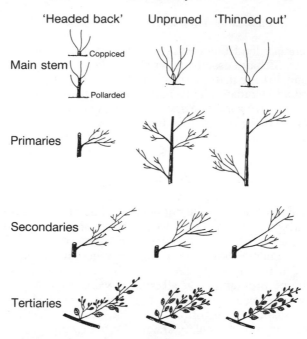

FIGURE 3.   A classification of tree pruning practices into 'heading-back' and 'thinning-out', which can be practised on the main stem, the primary, secondary or tertiary branches.

forms of pruning are likely to be used on MPTs, but we still need information of the same kind that exists for other trees.

III.   MULTIPURPOSE TREES AS CROPS

A.   Ideotypes

Up to the 1960s, plant breeders confined themselves, basically, to two types of breeding strategies – 'defect elimination' and 'selection for yield'. The development of crop physiology as a branch of plant science led Donald (1968; and see also Donald & Hamblin 1976) to propose that, if enough was known about the attributes that formed the basis of any set of breeding objectives, then a 'model' could be established, which could be used to make selection processes more exact. The term 'ideotype' was coined to describe this set of ideal plant characteristics. Three types of ideotype were envisaged, (a) those that do well as spaced individuals ('isolation' ideotypes) – often being widely branched and broadleaved, (b) those that do well in varietal mixtures ('competition' ideotypes) – having characteristics that tend to dominate less aggressive varieties, and (c) those that do well in crops consisting of single cultivars ('crop' ideotypes) – having forms and functions that enable them to share environmental resources in a community of their own kind. The validity of Donald's ideas has been well substantiated by agricultural crop breeders in the last two decades, particularly with regard to the selection of 'isolation' and 'crop' ideotypes. More recently, the concept has been taken up by forest tree researchers (Cannell 1979, 1982).

In agroforestry, and in systems consisting of mixtures of plant associates, we will mainly be concerned with 'associative' ideotypes. These will be selections of either woody perennials, or perennial or seasonal forbs and grasses, each of which can contribute to the fulfilment of the system's objectives, whilst maximizing environmental resource use by integrating and sharing resources in both space and time. Each kind of plant in such a system could be idealized in terms of a 'specification', based on the needs of the system and the technical requirements of available plant types.

ICRAF's procedures for 'Diagnosis and design' of agroforestry systems (Raintree 1985; ICRAF 1983) relate technical components to the requirements of the land user, and the land use system as a whole. The procedures now include a means of deriving a ranked list of 'specifications' of plant components as part of the process of defining any research needs, and this list can be considered as establishing a set of ideotypes for MPTs (Huxley & Wood 1984). Such specifications might include not only a set of required attributes associated with natural growth, but also those achievable under some form of management.

TABLE I.   A. Ranges of net biomass production of vegetation in different ecozones.
B. Expected ranges of plant dry matter ratios

	Semi-arid	Seasonally-arid	Highland tropics	Lowland wet tropics
A. Likely net biomass production $(t\,ha^{-1}\,yr^{-1})$	5–15	15–25	25–35	35–45
B. Expected range of plant dry matter ratios(%)	Roots	Stem*	Leaves	Fruits
(a) non-fruiting	15–30	25–40	20–35	Nil
(b) fruiting	11–22	18–30	15–26	up to 35

For any ecozone, values of (A×B) give an estimate of *potential* yields which incomplete ground cover, poor management, pests and diseases, bad weather, etc. will decrease. Data from Anon (1981) and Evans (1982).
* Of which 80% or so could be usable fuelwood.

B.   Planting density and rectangularity

The effects of manipulating planting density and rectangularity, for trees and herbaceous crops, have been well summarized and discussed by Cannell (1983a,b) and I intend to make only a few additional points here.

1. *Some general concepts*

The enthusiasm that has greeted the possibilities for improving the productivity and sustainability of land use systems by using MPTs has sometimes led to unthinking optimism with regard to the possible level of outputs. It pays to remind ourselves of the information that is available concerning potential biomass production in different ecozones, and the information on dry matter partitioning (Table I). Also, we should bear in mind that the 'good' seasonal yields of maize are $1 \cdot 3 – 3 \cdot 0 \, t \, ha^{-1}$, cassava $15 – 20 \, t \, ha^{-1}$, grain legumes $0 \cdot 5 – 1 \cdot 0 \, t \, ha^{-1}$; sugar cane $40 – 60 \, t \, ha^{-1}$ (10% of which is sugar), oranges $10 – 20 \, t \, ha^{-1}$ (fresh weight), cashew $1 \cdot 0 – 1 \cdot 5 \, t \, ha^{-1}$, coffee $1 \cdot 0 – 2 \cdot 0 \, t \, ha^{-1}$, tropical hardwood plantations $25 – 35 \, m^3 \, ha^{-1} \, yr^{-1}$ and tropical pines $15 – 45 \, m^3 \, ha^{-1} \, yr^{-1}$.

The very large differences between the potential and actual yields that always exist may encourage us to hope that a better use of the available environmental resources might ensue if a suitable MPT species were incorporated into a farming system, or if more productive MPTs were used. The possibility of improving the harvest index of MPTs is a less practical reality, because we are dealing with multipurpose plants, whose harvest indices may already be large, and whose outputs may often represent competing sinks.

The curve of a planting density/yield relationship can normally be approximated by a reciprocal yield equation:

$$\theta / \text{weight per plant} = (a + b \, (\text{plants}^{-ha}))$$

This expression can result in, basically, either an asymptotic (for biomass) or a parabolic relationship (for fruits and seeds, and perhaps other plant parts).

There are a number of practical issues relating to the choice of planting density with MPTs. The results of underpopulating a unit of land with herbaceous crops, which reach full structure during a single season, and which are grown for biomass, will be some loss of potential yield in average years, but no effective loss in good or poor years (because in below-average years the attainment of the curve's plateau is shifted to a lower plant population). Similarly, with herbaceous crops grown for a plant part, with a parabolic yield/planting density relationship, there will be little or no loss in poor years (as long as conditions are not severe), but there may be some loss in average or above-average years. In tropical regions the weather can vary markedly from year to year around the climatic mean, so there is an obvious difficulty in establishing an optimum planting density, and of regularly achieving optimum yields.

Even if there were a normal frequency distribution of years in which the growing conditions were optimal, most farmers in developing countries would be more concerned with avoiding crop failure than with optimizing yield. They fear the effects of a severe drought more than they covet the extra yield resulting from having a high plant population.

Trees are more expensive to plant and establish than herbaceous crops, so the losses following crop failure are greater. Furthermore, the result of plant stress in tree stands that are too closely planted is an increase in the proportion of small plants, and this effect is maintained over several or many years. The often-used practice of over-planting, and sequential thinning, gives an opportunity to remedy the effects of previous minor climatic disasters, but this opportunity is not available in fruit orchards, or in hedgerow or border plantings, where the intention is to maintain continuous lines of trees or shrubs.

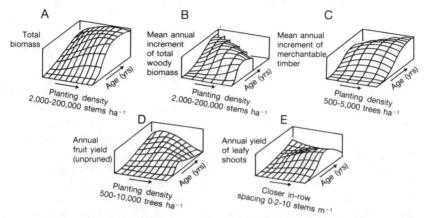

FIGURE 4. Suggested effects of planting densities on the yields of woody plant stands over time (from Cannell 1983b and Huxley 1983c).
A. Total biomass accumulation.
B. Woody biomass (branches and stems of any diameter).
C. Merchantable timber (stems above a given diameter).
D. Fruits on unpruned trees. Dense plantings can be productive early on, but pests, diseases and management problems make them unproductive in later years. Pruning will shift the response to the left.
E. Leafy shoots in hedgerows with different within-row spacings, assuming no over-browsing or excessive lopping, and assuming that hedge height is restricted to that achieved at age 4 to 5.

2. Effects of plant density on the harvest of plant parts over time

With MPTs it is necessary always to consider the effects of planting density on yields over time. In Figure 4, hypothetical situations are considered, for the mean annual increment of woody biomass and merchantable timber (from Cannell 1983b) and for total biomass, fruits/seeds, and leafy shoots or fodder (from Huxley 1983c).

3. Rectangularity

Crop plants which have the same stature share environmental resources most equitably when they are evenly spaced. In row-cropping this is represented by a rectangularity of one (the ratio of between-row to within-row spacing). However, large rectangularities are often used to facilitate management practices (drilling, weeding, spraying, etc), and there may be similar reasons for increasing the rectangularity of MPTs. But different MPT species have different capacities for branching and, also, there will be different effects of increasing rectangularity on the yield of different plant parts. We need, therefore, to explore the consequences of rectangularity changes on MPTs, at least at a few experimental sites.

C. Effects of the removal of plant parts on sustained yields

The effective handling of trees demands a clear perception of the way various management treatments will affect dry matter distribution. In particular, with MPTs, we need to know how harvesting the various products will influence future growth and development, in terms of total biomass production, partitioning between fruits and vegetative parts, partitioning among vegetative parts, and the entrainment of subsequent growth and flowering sequences.

We need to draw up sets of guidelines for field practitioners, using existing information, for plants in general and woody plants in particular; this is now far from just anecdotal. Appropriate field research can also quickly enhance our knowledge of the responses of particular MPT species, and it will be more widely applicable if it is crop physiologically – rather than purely management – orientated.

IV. MULTIPURPOSE TREES IN MANAGED MIXTURES OF SPECIES

A. Space-time considerations

1. *Dimensional opportunities*

The term 'multipurpose tree' is used to describe woody perennials of several kinds, including large and small trees, shrubs and bushes, palms, woody vines (lianes) and bamboos. Thus, the choice of natural dimensions and form available when selecting MPT species is much greater than one finds with agricultural plants or industrial forest tree species.

One group of agroforestry research workers is very much concerned with the study of natural vegetation, and with the transposition of concepts learned from such plant associations to the design of man-made plant communities, in which MPT species provide specifically required outputs. The first stage in this process is, indeed, just the partial replacement of existing vegetation by chosen MPTs which fit particular ecological niches.

A parallel approach is the study of complex man-made systems that involve multistoried mixtures of many species, such as Indonesian home and forest gardens (Michton *et al.* 1983). This is done in order to learn more about how groups of plants, including MPTs, can be associated and managed more efficiently. This work is now moving from the descriptive to the experimental phase (eg Oldeman 1983).

A common requirement is to understand how the associated plants can best share environmental resources in order to optimize their growth and development as individual species, in a way that provides the correct proportions of different outputs needed from the system as a whole. Such problems have been addressed by those concerned with intercropping herbaceous agricultural species, but with MPTs the space and time dimensions are larger and there are multiple products from individual plants.

The more 'permanent' nature of the MPT has a number of biological, economic and management implications, one set of which is related to the time at which events occur. In particular, there is a need to understand the phenological behaviour of the woody species, and to choose those kinds of MPTs that can best match the resource requirements of the lower storey plants, or can be entrained to do so by management (Huxley 1983a). We must, therefore, gain information on the phenophases of MPTs in their native habitats, and include phenological studies in trials of MPT species and provenances. Successful association in plant mixtures will depend very much on the stature, form and phenological behaviour of the MPT species.

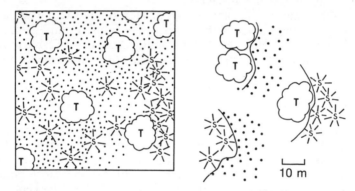

FIGURE 5.   Interfaces between crop types. Left: plan view of a three-component multistorey agroforest. Right: interfaces between pairs of the three components. T = tree; S = shrub; dots = agricultural crop (from Huxley 1983d).

2.   The tree-crop interface

Combinations of MPTs with herbaceous and other plant species must optimize the sharing of environment resources but, in practice, what can be done to discover how best to do this? With complex systems, we might begin by examining the mutual interactions of all species pairs at their interfaces (Fig. 5). Interactions will result in, and be a consequence of, changes in environmental resource pools at the interfaces. With MPTs, even a simple one tree/one crop association requires a large experimental area in order to test the range of management variables of interest, so, even here, it might be most cost-effective to examine the interface. Doing so can greatly simplify the design of field experiments (Huxley 1983d).

B.   Choice of 'optimum' populations and degrees of intimacy

1.   Planting density and intimacy in MPT-crop mixtures

The choice of planting density for MPTs in crop mixtures, apart from other considerations noted above, must involve decisions on how they are to be managed (eg pruned or lopped). The degree of intimacy of the mixture can then be controlled by manipulating the plant population, plant arrangement (ie whether species are arranged in some kind of mixture, or in strips, so as to maximize or minimize different tree/crop interfaces), by sequential thinning and by pruning.

Because we are concerned with the level of outputs from the whole mixture of species, any pruning regime must take into consideration the environmental resources required by the understorey crops. How should we prune the MPTs to maximize the tree outputs without detriment to long-term multiyield capacity, and how do we estimate the environmental resource needs of the other species in the mixture? Are periods of water stress to be avoided? How should we partition the light between upper and lower storey plants? What nutrient limitations might occur, and how can we best deal with their onset? These are difficult questions to answer separately, much less to resolve in terms of complete system's behaviour.

Clearly, the understanding and design of such systems require an aptitude for systems thinking, and an ability to perceive future events. If such skills are not available, and cannot easily be taught, it may be advisable to propose agroforestry systems that compromise efficiency for management simplicity.

2. *Rectangularity*

There is a growing interest in hedgerow intercropping ('alley cropping') as a way of introducing MPTs into tropical mixed cropping systems. There are various reasons for doing this, which need to be briefly explained, because they affect whether or not we are concerned with rectangularity ratios.

First, in most hedgerow-type situations, the MPTs will be kept short by some form of lopping or pollarding, which may be accompanied by side-pruning. This is done both to decrease mutual competition among the trees and to take harvests of leafy shoots, woody mulch materials and/or fuelwood. If the hedgerows are grown for other purposes (fruits/seeds, plant exudates, nectar sources, etc), then the pruning procedures will be different. Second, hedgerow intercropping may be practised in wet tropical regions (where it is already becoming well established) or in semi-arid areas. In the latter case, high rectangularity ratios might be a necessity to lessen 'competition' for available soil water, although this can be achieved by coppicing at the start of, or during, each growing season. Third, where a hedgerow is grown to provide woody mulch, or to conserve the soil, the choice of rectangularity may not depend entirely on attempts to optimize yields (of both the hedgerows and the inter-hedgerow crop plants).

Bearing these points in mind, we can limit ourselves here to discuss briefly the underlying principles of adjusting rectangularity ratios, in hedgerow intercropping, to those ecozones where water is not severely limiting. In such situations, manipulating the rectangularity is the key to successful intercropping of MPTs and agricultural crops. The first step is to consider the choice of MPT plant population per unit area in relation to environmental resources, and to assess the effects of management operations such as pruning and lopping. The choice of rectangularity also concerns the effects of shading from the hedgerow, and hence its orientation and height.

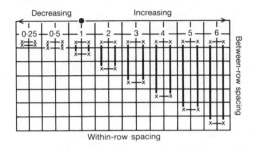

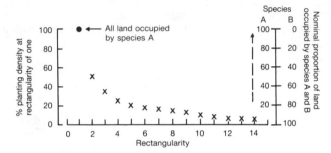

FIGURE 6. Different rectangularities (top) and the way in which plant population per unit area changes with a change in rectangularity, if the in-row spacing remains the same (bottom). Species A is assumed to be a tree which occupies all the land at its optimum planting density at a rectangularity of one. Then, changes in the nominal allocated area are as shown on the right-hand axis, but the actual area utilized by each species will be more in the direction of the dotted arrow as the trees mature, and their canopies and roots spread into the between-row space (from Huxley 1983c).

Figure 6 shows how the plant population decreases with increase in between-row spacing with constant in-row spacing (increasing rectangularity). In fact, rectangularities greater than about six have little subsequent effect on plant population, and relatively little interaction between hedgerows is to be expected at such large rectangularities. In some circumstances in the wet tropics, such as on hill slopes, rectangularities lower than six will often be of interest. In those circumstances, the next step is to consider how, as rectangularities change, we may adjust the basic in-row spacing so as to re-establish the optimum plant population. The way to approach this is shown in Figure 7.

3. Orientation

With MPT strips or hedgerows, orientation has to be considered, even in the tropics. Figure 8 shows the predicted light climate at ground level in 50 m wide alleys between strips of fuelwood trees (taken to be solid objects) modelled for latitude 3 °N (eg Malaysia) by Jackson (1983, and pers. comm.). Jackson's model can allow for different orientations, strip dimensions, and hedgerow heights. Although originally produced for fruit tree crops, this and

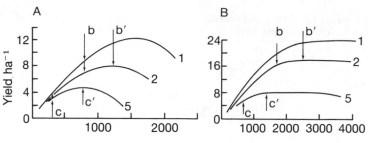

FIGURE 7.
A. Postulated parabolic yield/planting density response curves at rectangularities of 1, 2 and 5. b and c indicate the yields obtained when the plant population is decreased to a half or a fifth of the optimum (1600 plants ha^{-1}), respectively, when the in-row spacing is not changed to compensate for the increase in rectangularity. b' and c' indicate the scope there is for such compensation.
B. As for A, with asymptotic yield/planting density response curves, with less opportunity for compensation.

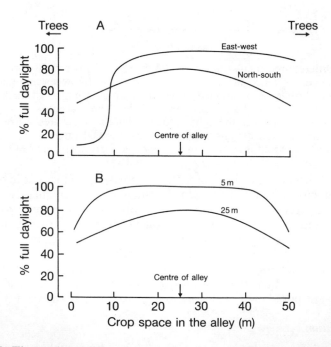

FIGURE 8. The predicted light climate at ground level in a 50 m wide alley between blocks of fuelwood trees (assumed to be solid objects) at latitude 3 °N.
A. Distribution of direct light when the tree strips are orientated E–W and N–S.
B. Distribution of diffuse light when the tree strips are 5 m or 25 m tall. (Data supplied by J. E. Jackson, using the model of Jackson 1983.)

similar computer models are likely to be useful in agroforestry research and design.

C.   Management in tree-crop mixtures

Unlike scientists, who are usually trying to *contain* variability in order to comprehend the complexities of biological systems, a tropical peasant farmer aims to *exploit* the heterogeneity inherent in his land use system, in both space and time (Huxley 1982). The opportunities to do this in agroforestry are very large in relation to the choice and management of MPTs, and they demand an appreciation of the 'environmental opportunities', and an understanding of how best to fill them.

1.   *Manipulating plant stress*

Connor (1983a) considered the ways in which different stresses will occur between the woody and herbaceous components in agroforestry systems. He described the characteristics of the 'resource pools' (light, water, nutrients) and emphasized the predictable ways in which suboptimal levels occur and can be replenished. An understanding of these 'pools' is essential for the good management of MPTs in mixtures.

Connor reminds us that, with light, preferential access relies on canopy display, in which stature is the most advantageous attribute, and differential response can be quantified in terms of the leaf photosynthesis/light response functions of different species. For water and nutrients in the soil, preferential access depends on root system profiles, with differential responses depending on efficiencies of extraction per unit of rooting volume. In fact, with relatively immobile nutrients, such as P, access depends on continued root growth into non-depleted soil volumes. Complementary use of resources is the key to successful cohabitation of a site.

If, in the tropics, agroforestry systems are more sustainable or productive than agricultural land use systems, then it is because they are better able to share the available environmental resources, or because they are less 'leaky' with regard to some, or all, of the resources pools. However, the hard evidence in terms of light interception, water use efficiencies, nutrient extraction rates, and so forth, is either unavailable or anecdotal. This ignorance exists largely because agroforestry systems are both subsistence-orientated and complex, so that they have neither attracted the experimental resources, nor have they been as easy to study as sole food or cash crops. Studies on plant-environment interactions in agroforestry are likely to demand a complex series of investigations, and it may be that approximations will have to suffice. Combinations of a pragmatic 'trial-and-error' approach, with existing conceptual ecophysiological models, might take us a long way (Loomis & Whitman 1983; Connor 1983b).

3.   *Entrainment*

Woody perennials proceed through a cyclic series of phenophases. Later steps are consequent upon the completion of earlier ones, and the start of each cycle can be influenced by both exogenous and endogenous controls (eg by the state of the leaf canopy, Huxley & van Eck 1974). The sequences of growth and development that normally occur under natural conditions can vary greatly among tropical woody perennial species. Within this wide range of plant behaviour, further variability can occur owing to weather variations about the climatic norm. Individual trees can be affected differently by site conditions and by pruning, irrigation and fertilization. Management practices have been shown to influence patterns of growth and development in tea and coffee (Carr 1974; Browning & Fisher 1975). In order to optimize both the design and management of MPTs in agroforestry, it is necessary to know the natural sequence of phenophases, as well as the opportunities for manipulating them.

V. CONCLUSIONS: RESEARCH PRIORITIES

There are clearly many research needs in evaluating MPTs, but perhaps the most urgent that arise from this discussion can be summarized as follows. Information is needed on:
— the location of buds and the growth and/or flowering potentials they possess;
— the effects of fruiting on vegetative growth;
— dry matter distribution;
— the relationship between morphological characteristics and functional performance (eg 'leafiness' and fruiting traits);
— the adaptability of species and provenances (and for the more important of these, some understanding of the mechanisms underlying adaptive responses);
— MPT breeding strategies (actual schemes for individual species), including the establishment of objective selection index procedures and $G \times E$ assessments;
— the capacity of individual species to enrich the microsite;
— the effects of tree-crop mixtures on soils and plant productivity (in relation to Fig. 2);
— the flowering characteristics of MPT species (flowering on new wood, old wood, short shoots, etc), with information on flower initiation times for important species;
— responses to pruning/lopping/browsing at different times and intensities;
— source-sink relationships of free-standing plants in order to examine the interactions between vegetative growth and flowering/fruiting;
— optimum pruning practices;
— the effects of changing the planting density and plant rectangularity on growth and yield;
— the effect of modifying source-sink relationships brought about by pruning and/or spacing;
— tree-crop interfaces with regard to resource sharing and plant stress effects;
— MPTs in hedgerows (including orientation aspects);

— the phenology of MPT species both (a) grown untouched (in different ecozones) and (b) after management by, say, pruning, including observations on entrainment.

REFERENCES

Anon. (1981). *Agricultural compendium – for rural development in the tropics and sub-tropics.* Amsterdam: Elsevier.

Arnold, M. H. & Innes, L. (1976). The BP52 Programme in Uganda. In: *Cotton Research Corporation in agricultural research for development – the Namulonge contribution*, edited by M. H. Arnold, 202–212. Cambridge: Cambridge University Press.

Bonner, J. & Galston, A. (1944). Toxic substances from the culture media of guayule which may inhibit growth. *Bot. Gaz.*, **106**, 188–198.

Brewbaker, J., ed. (1980). *Leucaena research reports.* Hawaii: Nitrogen Fixing Tree Association (published annually).

Brewbaker, J. (1982). Guide to the systematics of the genus *Leucaena* (Mimosoideae: Leguminosae). *Proc. Leucaena and other Nitrogen Fixing Trees Conf., Singapore.* Washington DC: USAID; Hawaii: Nitrogen Fixing Tree Association.

Browning, G. & Fisher, N. M. (1975). Shoot growth in *Coffea arabica* L., II. Growth flushing stimulated by irrigation. *J. hort. Sci.*, **50**, 207–218.

Brunig, E. F. & Sander, N. (1983). Ecosystem structure and functioning: some interactions of relevance to agroforestry. In: *Plant research and agroforestry*, edited by P. A. Huxley, 221–247. Nairobi: International Council for Research in Agroforestry.

Burley, J., Huxley, P. A. & Owino, F. (1984). Design, management and assessment of species, provenances and breeding trials of multipurpose trees. *Paper presented at Joint Meeting IUFRO working parties on Provenance and Genetic Improvement Strategies in Tropical Forest Trees, Mutare, Zimbabwe, 1984.*

Cannell, M. G. R. (1979). Biological opportunities for genetic improvement in forest productivity. In: *The ecology of even-aged forest plantations*, edited by E. D. Ford, D. C. Malcolm and J. Atterson, 119–144. Cambridge: Institute of Terrestrial Ecology.

Cannell, M. G. R. (1982). 'Crop' and 'isolation' ideotypes: evidence for progeny differences in nursery grown *Picea sitchensis*. *Silvae Genet.*, **31**, 60–66.

Cannell, M. G. R. (1983a). Plant management in agroforestry: manipulation of trees, population densities and mixtures of trees and herbaceous crops. In: *Plant research and agroforestry*, edited by P. A. Huxley, 455–487. Nairobi: International Council for Research in Agroforestry.

Cannell, M. G. R. (1983b). Plant population and yield of tree and herbaceous crops. In: *Plant research and agroforestry*, edited by P. A. Huxley, 489–502. Nairobi: International Council for Research in Agroforestry.

Cannell, M. G. R. & Huxley, P. A. (1969). Seasonal differences in the pattern of assimilate movement in branches of *Coffea arabica* L. *Ann. appl. Biol.*, **64**, 345–357.

Carlowitz, P. von. (1984). *Multipurpose trees and shrubs, opportunities and limitations. The establishment of a multipurpose tree database.* (ICRAF working paper no. 17). Nairobi: International Council for Research in Agroforestry. Mimeograph.

Carr, M. K. V. (1974). Irrigating seedling tea in Southern Tanzania: effects on total yields, distribution of yield and water use. *J. agric. Sci., Camb.*, **83**, 363–378.

Connor, D. J. (1983a). Plant stress factors and their influence on production of agroforestry plant associations. In: *Plant research and agroforestry*, edited by P. A. Huxley, 210–220. Nairobi: International Council for Research in Agroforestry.

Connor, D. J. (1983b). Crop models: components of and contributions to models of agroforestry plant associations. In: *Plant research and agroforestry*, edited by P. A. Huxley, 249–256. Nairobi: International Council for Research in Agroforestry.

Donald, C. M. (1968). The breeding of crop ideotypes. *Euphytica*, **17**, 385–403.

Donald, C. M. & Hamblin, J. (1976). The biological yield and harvest index of cereals as agronomic and plant breeding criteria. *Adv. Agron.*, **28**, 361–405.

Evans, J. (1982). *Plantation forestry in the tropics.* Oxford: Clarendon.

Felker, P. (1978). *State of the art:* Acacia albida *as a complementary permanent intercrop with annual crops.* (Rep. to USAID (Grant AID/afr-C-1361)). Washington DC: USAID.

Felker, P., Cannell, G. H. & Clark, P. R. (1981). Variation in growth among 13 *Prosopis* (mesquite) species. *Exp. Agric.*, **17**, 209–218.

Friedman, J. (1983). Allelopathy and antitoxicity in arid regions. *Proc. Seminar on Allelochemicals and Pheromones, 1982*, 97–106. Taipei: R.O.C.

Golley, F. B., McGinnis, J. T., Clement, R. G., Child, G. I. & Duever, M. J. (1975). *Mineral cycling in a tropical moist forest ecosystem.* Athens, GA: University of Georgia Press.

Hutton, M. (1981). Leucaena: *Leguminosa arborea promisoria para America de Sur.* (Eu-Boletin. Inf. de Pastos Tropicales). Colombia: Centro Internacional de Agricultura Tropical.

Huxley, P. A. (1982). Woody plants and land use. *Proc. FAO/IAEA Consult. Meeting on the Use of Nuclear Techniques in Improving Fertilizer and Water Management Practices for Tree Crops, Vienna, 1981*, 9–24. (IAEA technical document no. 270). Vienna: International Atomic Energy Agency.

Huxley, P. A. (1983a). Phenology of tropical woody perennials and seasonal crop plants with reference to their management in agroforestry systems. In: *Plant research and agroforestry*, edited by P. A. Huxley, 503–525. Nairobi: International Council for Research in Agroforestry.

Huxley, P. A. (1983b). The role of trees in agroforestry: some comments. In: *Plant research and agroforestry*, editied by P. A. Huxley, 257–276. Nairobi: International Council for Research in Agroforestry.

Huxley, P. A. (1983c). *Considerations when experimenting with changes in plant spacing.* (ICRAF working paper no. 15). Nairobi: International Council for Research in Agroforestry. Mimeograph.

Huxley, P. A. (1983d). *The tree-crop interface – simplifying the biological/environmental study of mixed cropping agroforestry systems.* (ICRAF working paper no. 13). Nairobi: International Council for Research in Agroforestry. (Also in *Agroforestry Systems*, in press).

Huxley, P. A., ed. (1984). *A manual of methodology for the exploration and assessment of multipurpose trees (MPTs).* (24 parts). Nairobi: International Council for Research in Agroforestry.

Huxley, P. A. & van Eck, W. A. (1974). Seasonal changes in growth and development of some woody perennials near Kampala. *J. Ecol.*, **62**, 579–592.

Huxley, P. A. & Summerfield, R. J. (1976). Effects of daylength and day/night temperatures on growth and seed yield of cowpea cv. K2809 grown in controlled environments. *Ann. appl. Biol.*, **83**, 259–271.

Huxley, P. A. & Wood, P. J. (1984). *The integration of technology and research considerations in ICRAF's landuse "Diagnosis and Design" procedures.* (ICRAF working paper no. 26). Nairobi: International Council for Research in Agroforestry.

International Council for Research in Agroforestry. (1983). *Draft guidelines for agroforestry diagnosis and design. Draft resources for agroforestry diagnosis and design.* Nairobi: ICRAF.

Jackson, J. E. (1983). Light climate and crop-tree mixtures. In: *Plant research and agroforestry*, edited by P. A. Huxley, 365–378. Nairobi: International Council for Research in Agroforestry.

Kozlowski, T. T. & Huxley, P. A. (1983). The role of controlled environments in agroforestry research. In: *Plant research and agroforestry*, edited by P. A. Huxley, 551–567. Nairobi: International Council for Research in Agroforestry.

Kuile, C. H. H. ter. (1984). The nature, extent and development problems of shifting cultivation. *Rep. FAO Tech. Consult. on Educ. Training and Extension Aspects of Shifting Cultivation, Rome, 1983.* Rome: FAO.

Ledig, F. T. (1983). The influence of genotype and environment on dry matter distribution in plants. In: *Plant research and agroforestry*, edited by P. A. Huxley, 427–454. Nairobi: International Council for Research in Agroforestry.

Loomis, R. S. & Whitman, C. E. (1983). Systems analysis in product ecology. In: *Plant research and agroforestry*, edited by P. A. Huxley, 210–220. Nairobi: International Council for Research in Agroforestry.

Lundgren, B. (1982). *The use of agroforestry to improve the productivity of converted tropical land.* (Report for the Office of Technology Assessment of the United States Congress). Nairobi: International Council for Research in Agroforestry.

Manning, H. L. (1956). Yield improvement from a selection index technique with cotton. *Heredity, Lond.*, **10**, 303–322.

Meulen, A. van der. (1939). *Over den bouw en de periodieke outuitikeling der bloemknoppen bij Coffea–sorten* (On the structure and periodical development of the flower buds in *Coffea* species). (English summary). Amsterdam: N.V. Noord-Hollandsche Uitgevers Maatschappij.

Michton, G., Bompard, J., Hecketsweiler, P. & Ducatillion, C. (1983). Tropical forest architectural analysis as applied to agroforestry in humid tropics: the examples of traditional village-agroforestry in West Java. *Agrofor. Syst.*, **1**, 117–129.

Nair, P. K. R. & Fernandes, E. (1984). Agroforestry as an alternative to shifting cultivation. *Proc. Expert Consultation on Alternatives to Shifting Cultivation, Rome, 1984*. Rome: FAO.

Neales, T. F. & Incoll, L. D. (1968). The control of leaf photosynthesis rate by the level of assimilate concentration in the leaf; a review of the hypothesis. *Bot. Rev.*, **34**, 107–125.

Oldeman, R. A. A. (1983). The design of ecologically sound agroforests. In: *Plant research and agroforestry*, edited by P. A. Huxley, 173–207. Nairobi: International Council for Research in Agroforestry.

Pickersgill, B. (1983). Aspects of evolution in herbaceous and tree crops relevant to agroforestry. In: *Plant research and agroforestry*, edited by P. A. Huxley, 309–321. Nairobi: International Council for Research in Agroforestry.

Raintree, J. B. (1985). A diagnostic approach to agroforestry design. In: *Let there be forest*. (Proc. int. Symp. on Strategies and Designs for Afforestation, Restoration and Tree Planting, Wageningen, 1983). In press.

Shang-Shyng, Y. & Hsi-Hua, W. (1983). The mechanism of action of suppressive soils and its effects on crop productivity. *Proc. Seminar on Allelochemicals and Pheromones, 1982*, 219–238. Taipei: R.O.C.

Walker, J. T. (1960). The use of a selection index technique in the analysis of progeny row data. *Emp. Cott. Grow. Rev.*, **37**, 81–107.

Young, A. (1984). *Site selection for multipurpose trees*. (ICRAF working paper no. 23). Nairobi: International Council for Research in Agroforestry. Mimeograph.

3

FOREST TREE BREEDING: STRATEGIES, ACHIEVEMENTS AND CONSTRAINTS

F. E. BRIDGWATER and E. C. FRANKLIN
USDA Forest Service, S.E. Forest Experiment Station and North Carolina State University, Raleigh, North Carolina, USA

I. INTRODUCTION

This review explains the main breeding strategies adopted by forest tree breeders, outlines some of the achievements made to date and some of the constraints on progress, and gives our view on current research priorities.

II. BREEDING STRATEGIES

Genotypic variance can be divided into additive and nonadditive components. Additive variance is the chief cause of resemblance among relatives, and is the part of the genotypic variance that is captured when selected individuals with a good general combining ability are allowed to interbreed at random. Nonadditive variance is due to 'dominance' and other interactions between genes or alleles, and can be captured by (a) cloning individuals with unique gene combinations, or (b) making single-parent crosses among individuals with a good specific combining ability.

The choice of breeding strategy is determined by the relative proportions of additive and nonadditive gene actions in the source or base populations available to the breeder. However, the breeder can search for new sources of genetic variation. If, for instance, the genetic variance within a local source population is largely additive, crosses with other provenances or species may reveal important sources of new genetic variance, which may be additive or nonadditive.

The cost of utilizing the genetic variance is directly influenced by several factors. These are the costs of making controlled pollinations, genetic testing, maintaining large breeding populations, and producing large numbers of propagules for forest planting.

The relative importance of additive and nonadditive genetic variance may differ, depending upon whether the source population is formed by interbreeding within species or by hybridization between species. More importantly, some peculiarities of seed production that arise when making hybrids can affect the choice of breeding strategy. Therefore, we will discuss intra- and interspecific methods separately.

A.   Intraspecific breeding strategies

1.   *Capturing additive genetic variance*

If only additive genetic variance is to be exploited, the breeding strategy can be as straightforward as simple mass selection. This breeding method consists of choosing the best phenotypes in stands, collecting open-pollinated seeds from them, and planting them in bulk without prior testing for the next cycle of selection. This method can be effective for single traits with a high heritability (McWilliam & Florence 1955). Heritability is that portion of the total phenotypic variation due to genetic as opposed to environmental factors. The proportion of additive genetic to total phenotypic variance among selected individuals (their 'narrow sense' heritability) is normally estimated from the performance of their open-pollinated seedling progenies, grown in 'genetic' or 'progeny tests'.

Most tree breeders, however, are concerned with improving several traits simultaneously, and among these will be vigour or other traits with a low heritability. Therefore, genetic testing is usually included as a component of a breeding strategy. The nearest tree breeders come to mass selection without separate progeny tests, as practised by breeders of other crops, is in open-pollinated seedling seed orchards (Goddard 1964). Such orchards arise from planting progeny tests with open-pollinated seeds from select trees. These plantings are then rogued, based on sibling performance, and become seed orchards.

Mass selection entails only selection of the maternal parent, while pollen may come from any male in the population. Selecting males, as well as females, and allowing pollination only among selects, increases the expected rate of genetic progress (Shelbourne 1969). This method was used to produce *Pinus elliottii* seedlings that are resistant to fusiform rust (*Cronartium quercuum* (Berk.) Miyabe ex Shirai f sp. *fusiforme*). Stands with high rust infections were thinned to leave only disease-free trees to intermate. Seedlings derived from this seed production area had improved rust resistance (Goddard *et al.* 1975).

Because most forest tree species can be vegetatively propagated, usually by grafting, selected males and females can be brought together to promote intermating among selects in recurrent selection schemes. Recurrent selection is the planned selection of individuals and/or families, repeated over several generations within a base or source population. Simple recurrent selection schemes rely upon open-pollinations among selected trees. This breeding method has been proposed for *Juglans nigra* and *Quercus* spp., where the cost of producing large numbers of seeds from controlled matings is prohibitive (McKeand & Beineke 1980).

Where controlled pollinations are practical, forest tree breeders invariably chose that option, combined with genetic testing. In fact, most intraspecific forest tree breeding programmes (particularly those for conifers) have incorporated both controlled pollinations, and genetic testing, into recurrent selection methods to improve general combining ability (Stonecypher 1969). There have been three primary reasons for this approach. First, the relative proportions of additive and nonadditive genetic variances within the source populations were largely unknown when tree breeding programmes began. Genetic tests using controlled matings were required to determine this ratio. Recurrent methods for improving general combining ability were chosen because the ratio of additive to nonadditive genetic variances was unknown and breeding methods to improve specific combining ability were more complicated and costly. Second, from studies on the effects of self-pollinations in forest trees, and evidence from other crops, breeders anticipated that inbreeding depression might present problems. By keeping complete pedigrees, co-ancestry would be known and managed. Third, the only hope of utilizing nonadditive variance through sexual (as opposed to vegetative) propagation was to keep track of male and female parents, so that good specific crosses could be repeated.

2. *Capturing additive and nonadditive genetic variation*

Many species of forest trees have significant amounts of nonadditive as well as additive genetic variation, and suffer from inbreeding depression in fecundity and metrical traits. The presence of inbreeding depression is evidence that there is nonadditive variance, because if there is no dominance there should be no inbreeding depression. Severe inbreeding depression after self-fertilization has been found in many species, particularly the conifers (Franklin 1970; Sorensen & Miles 1982); the depression seems to lessen linearly with milder inbreeding (Gansel 1971). Furthermore, it was found that relatedness could increase rapidly under selection, where complete pedigrees were not known (Zobel *et al.* 1972).

The deleterious effects of inbreeding can be avoided in two ways. First, co-ancestry can be managed in the breeding population if pedigrees are known, by adopting some controlled system of mating. Ultimately, any closed population must become completely inbred, but the rate at which that occurs is under the breeder's control if pedigrees are known. Second, breeding of multiple sublines can be incorporated as part of the breeding strategy (Burdon *et al.* 1978). This method requires that all matings occur within sublines, and that trees for forest planting be derived from crosses among individuals from different sublines. Thus, all individuals in plantations will be derived from crosses among unrelated individuals. There has been considerable interest in sublining recently, and it has been incorporated into some large tree breeding programmes (van Buijtenen & Lowe 1979; McKeand & Beineke 1980; Matheson 1983; Purnell & Kellison 1983). Co-ancestry control within sublines may still be necessary, however, because inbreeding depression may reduce the size and fecundity of individuals within sublines so much that seed production costs become prohibitive.

Controlled pollinations and genetic testing are also necessary components of a breeding strategy, if nonadditive genetic variance is to be utilized by sexual methods in the short term. Specific combining ability can be exploited only if specific crosses can be recreated at acceptable cost. Large amounts of controlled-cross seeds can be produced from large-scale controlled pollinations, by establishing two-clone seed orchards, or by supplemental mass pollination (that is, artificial pollination without isolating females from wind-borne pollen).

Large numbers of interspecific crosses of *Pinus rigida* × *Pinus taeda* seedlings were produced by controlled crossing for afforestation in Korea (Hyun 1969). However, rising labour costs soon outweighed the benefits derived from these interspecific hybrids (Hyun 1976). For two-clone seed orchards to be successful, the parents must not only be good specific combiners, they must also have synchronous flowering and be either self-sterile or unaffected by inbreeding depression. As these conditions are rarely met, two-clone seed orchards have not been successful (Kellison 1971). Only recently has the feasibility of supplemental mass pollination for producing good specific combinations on a large scale been demonstrated (Bridgwater & Williams 1983). Further trials are necessary to determine whether the method is practical on a large scale.

Whatever the method for producing large numbers of controlled-cross seeds, the added benefits from utilizing specific combining abilities (capturing nonadditive genetic variance) must outweigh the added cost of production.

If large numbers of propagules can be produced at a reasonable cost through vegetative propagation, good specific combinations can be produced simply and immediately, whether they arise from good chance matings of individuals within populations, between populations, or even between species. The widest use of vegetative propagation for afforestation is found in several *Populus* and *Salix* species which are relatively easy to propagate vegetatively (Zsuffa 1973).

Vegetative propagules may not perform as well as sexual propagules (Burdon & Shelbourne 1974). In these cases, vegetative propagules are of doubtful utility in realizing genetic gains from specific combining ability. For example, in Australia, *Pinus radiata* cuttings from trees older than four to five years from seed are not easily rooted in large numbers, and the vigour of propagules is inversely related to age of ortet (Matheson 1983). New propagation methods must be found to overcome these effects, if vegetative propagation is to be a viable option for *P. radiata*, or ways must be found to predict the performance of trees when they are still young enough to propagate vegetatively.

If short-term methods for utilizing specific combining ability are impractical, one may consider methods to utilize specific combining ability in the long term. These methods involve developing lines or populations for subsequent outcrossing. They have not been widely used in forest tree breeding.

Heterotic F_1 crosses among inbred lines offer a method for utilizing specific combining ability. This method typically requires several cycles of inbreeding with selection, which produces individuals within lines with like alleles at corresponding chromosome loci. These homozygous individuals yield a uniform genetic contribution when mated, so that mean progeny performance is repeatable. The mean performance of offspring from some crosses exceeds the parental values, ie exhibits heterosis. This method has not been used in forestry because generation cycles are long and it is necessary to inbreed for several generations before outcrossing (Orr-Ewing 1976). In addition, it is difficult to produce inbred lines due to inbreeding depression in traits affecting fecundity (Franklin 1969).

Reciprocal recurrent selection utilizes both general and specific combining ability (Comstock *et al*. 1949). The method employs two populations that exhibit racial heterosis. Concurrent but separate selections are made in both populations, pairs of parents from different populations are intermated, and parents of the best hybrid progenies are intermated within populations to form the basis for the next generation. Inter-racial heterosis has been demonstrated in forest trees (Fowler 1978), but reciprocal recurrent selection is being used only on an experimental basis (Yeh *et al*. 1980; Riemenschneider 1980). The reluctance to utilize reciprocal recurrent selection arises from the necessity of maintaining two separate breeding populations, and the fact that several cycles could be required before maximum heterosis is reached in the hybrid population.

B.   Interspecific hybridization

Interspecific hybrids may be useful because they are heterotic, or because they combine traits that previously were not found together in either parental species, ie 'combinatorial' hybrids (Fowler 1978).

If vegetative propagation is viable, then heterotic or combinatorial hybrids can be immediately useful. Interspecific hybrids of *Populus* and *Salix* have been used successfully in this way (Zsuffa 1973), because both genera include several species that are easily crossed and vegetatively propagated. However, this approach is a 'dead-end' in terms of continuing genetic improvement, unless a breeding programme is carried out from which new hybrids can be derived (Brune & Zobel 1981).

The production of interspecific hybrids requires breeding in two parental populations to emphasize specific combining abilities. Costs are greater than for single population methods, but interspecific reciprocal recurrent selection programmes have been suggested for *P. radiata*×*P. attenuata* (Conkle 1970) and *P. rigida*×*P. taeda* (Hyun 1973).

Breeding methods for combinatorial hybrids do not necessarily require maintaining multiple populations. F_1 hybrid populations can serve as the foundation for single population breeds using simpler breeding methods. If gene action is largely additive, single population methods may be as effective as, and less expensive than, hybrid methods.

Combinatorial hybrids can also be improved by backcrossing to the most desirable parental species. Backcrossing has been used to combine resistance to fusiform rust in *Pinus echinata* with the faster growth rates of *Pinus taeda* (LaFarge & Kraus 1980). Backcrossing requires maintaining both the backcross population and the parental population.

Problems often arise when attempting to produce large numbers of hybrids. Barriers to successful seed production exist between many species (Zobel & Talbert 1984), and, even when controlled pollination is possible, it may be impractical to produce sufficient hybrids for forest planting. Open-pollinated seed orchards composed of two species are seldom practical. The species may or may not flower synchronously, and, even if they do, some seeds would still be of the parental species. It is expensive to identify and segregate hybrids from parental species. Supplemental mass pollination has been used to overcome problems of producing hybrid seeds with variable success (Hadders 1978; Bridgwater & Trew 1981).

Because of the difficulty of producing hybrid seeds, and the expense of maintaining two parental species lines, some breeders have resorted to the use of open-pollinated seed orchards composed of F_1 hybrids (Hyun 1976; Nikles 1981). F_2 progenies of inbred lines are much more variable than the F_1 hybrids. If F_1 hybrids of forest trees are heterotic, the F_2 progenies of these noninbred lines should also show some increased variability. Uniformity in forest plantations is generally desirable. If there is little or no heterosis, as in combinatorial hybrids, there may be no increase in variability among F_2 progenies (Hyun 1976; LaFarge & Kraus 1980).

III.   ACHIEVEMENTS AND CONSTRAINTS ON PROGRESS

Significant gains in tree improvement to date have resulted from utilizing genetic variation that could be readily captured by the simplest means available for producing large numbers of propagules.

In *Populus*, vegetative propagation was relatively easy and the growth of propagules equalled or exceeded that of seedlings. Many interspecific crosses were easily made (Zsuffa 1973), so gains were quickly obtained. Resistance to diseases was easily found and incorporated into forest plantations. For example, screening *Populus deltoides* clones and interspecific hybrids provided immediately useful sources of resistance to rusts (*Melampsora* spp.) (Steenackers 1972). When hybrids are more vigorous than the parents, yields from plantations can be increased markedly through vegetative propagation, as in Brazil, where rooted cuttings of natural *Eucalyptus* hybrids possess both good growth and high wood density (Campinhos 1980).

Progress with vegetatively propagated species is influenced by the strategy for deploying clones. A big question is whether single-clone or multiple-clone mixtures will give maximum genetic gains in vigour, while minimizing risks of disaster from insects or diseases. An analysis of factors bearing on these questions indicated that mixtures of 7 to 25 clones may be a robust, perhaps optimum, strategy (Libby 1980). Such strategies should be tested in the field.

Even though it is tempting to emphasize hybridization and clonal selection, rather than line breeding (Zsuffa 1979), the parental population(s) must be improved through breeding and selection if there is to be progress in the future (Brune & Zobel 1981). Nowhere is this point more emphatically made than with the redirection of national tree improvement programmes in Japan. After centuries of practising clonal forestry, the Japanese have begun to establish seed orchards and breeding programmes to create new variability for continued improvement (Toda 1974).

Early selection shortens the interval between the identification and utilization of new clones, providing increased financial returns from these programmes. Early screening for resistance to pests is particularly valuable to minimize the risk of catastrophic losses. In this manner, release of the *Cryptomeria* cultivar 'Kumotoosi' might have been forestalled before widespread plantings were found to be susceptible to both a disease and an insect pest (Toda 1974). Early evaluation of growth potential may be particularly difficult for clones selected to perform well over a broad range of sites, because genotype×environment interaction effects should be more pronounced in clones than in genetically diverse plantations.

Coniferous species are difficult to propagate vegetatively in large numbers, but some flower relatively early and consistently. *Pinus taeda* and *Pseudotsuga menziesii* are good examples because these species have great commercial importance, and are the subject of large tree breeding programmes. For these species, the strategy used to deploy the improved genetic material is of primary importance. In the south-eastern USA, most forestry industry plantations are now established with bulked seedlots using first-generation, genetically improved, seed orchards. However, there may be advantages in planting half- or full-sib families in large (20 ha) family blocks. Plantations of individual half-sib families of *P. taeda* are planted operationally by a few companies in the south-eastern USA. One company has been planting in this manner since 1975, with the intention that management regimes be customized, to take advantage of the different attributes of each family to maximize profitability (Gladstone 1975). Early results of empirical trials suggest that the growth of half-sib families in pure stands is better than in mixtures of the same families. The average volume of 15 families in pure stands was 8% greater than the average volume of the same 15 families planted in mixtures after 4 years in the field (Williams *et al.* 1983). There were no differences between pure and mixed stands in percentages of trees infected with fusiform rust or in straightness scores. The relative performance of pure versus mixed stands may change as competition increases (Cannell 1978).

If half-sib families change rank when planted in pure rather than mixed blocks, genetic test designs will have to be altered. Entries will have to be tested in the configuration in which they will be deployed. In addition, predicted gains from first-generation seeds must be re-evaluated, because genetic performance will have been predicted from row-plot tests, not bulk- or pure-family blocks.

If two-clone seed orchards, or supplemental mass pollination, become popular for the short-term utilization of specific combining ability, the performance of full-sib family blocks and mixtures must be evaluated. Competition effects between full-sib families are more likely to be important than those among half-sib families. Such effects have been demonstrated among full-sib seedling families of *P. taeda* (Adams *et al.* 1973), but not for half-sib families. Even greater is the need to evaluate inter-genotypic competition effects for clonal mixtures. The higher the genetic purity of the propagules, the more likely it is that there will be important differences between mixed and pure stands.

Another primary constraint on progress in most coniferous tree improvement programmes is the length of the breeding cycle. Reducing the time required to cross, test, and achieve flowering to cross again would increase the genetic gain per unit time. Procedures for producing strobili on trees only a few years old from seed have been worked out for some important conifers. Notable examples are in *P. taeda* (Greenwood 1978) and *P. menziesii* (Ross *et al.* 1980; Ross & Pharis, this volume). The ability to promote early flowering in these species has spurred interest in developing reliable early genetic evaluation procedures, and some promising results have been obtained. Several analyses with conifers have suggested that selection at age five to ten years of age is most efficient for improving growth traits (Nanson 1969; Squillace & Gansel 1974; Lambeth 1980; Lambeth *et al.* 1983). Several studies have shown promising results that may lead to the ability to select at even younger ages (Cannell *et al.* 1978; Cotterill & Nambiar 1981; Waxler & van Buijtenen 1981). Work on early evaluation of other important traits is beginning to pay dividends. Histological examination of loblolly pine embryos infected with fusiform rust basidiospores may give an accurate assessment of susceptibility of sibs in field experiments (Frampton *et al.* 1983).

A third constraint on progress in these programmes is not knowing how best to deal with the effects of related matings. There is always a trade-off between the genetic gain that may be obtained in one cycle of breeding and selection, and the degree to which co-ancestry will be allowed to increase. Intensive family selection will result in the most rapid gains for traits with low heritability, such as growth rate. However, rapidly reducing the numbers of families in a closed breeding population quickly leads to the necessity of making related matings. Tree breeders can make the correct decisions only if the consequences of mating sibs, cousins, and other relatives are understood.

Species that are not easy to propagate vegetatively or sexually present an obvious challenge. Ways must be found to produce large numbers of propagules at an acceptable cost before gains from breeding and selection can be realized. For example, tree breeding programmes on some of the spruces (*Picea* spp.) have been constrained by difficulties with propagation. These species produce seeds, but they often have not done so on a schedule that meets needs. For example, *Picea sitchensis* seed orchards established in Britain in the 1970s are not expected to meet forecast seed requirements until about 2010 (Gill 1983). Delayed seed production, in large part, has led to a great deal of effort in the attempt to produce rooted cuttings for forestry planting in several spruce programmes.

Operational use of rooted spruce cuttings is fraught with problems (Roulund 1981). Cuttings from older trees root and grow less well than cuttings from young trees, so selections must be made among young trees. But selection at young ages means that expected genetic gains are reduced, especially as there is a need to apply some selection pressure to improve rootability as well as other traits. This problem is exacerbated by the fact that ortets selected at young ages continue to age and, therefore, root less well over time. Research is under way to study, and perhaps retard, this ontogenetic ageing process, but this significant problem has not yet been solved. The conclusions from at least one study with eight-year-old *Picea abies* was that clonal forestry was not viable, because of the ineffectiveness of juvenile selection, and the poor repeatability of performance among successive generations of clones (Dietrichson & Kierulf 1982).

Rooting cuttings, without clonal selection, might be a reasonable option to rapidly increase genetically improved sexual propagules in short supply, even though costs are greater than for seedlings (Gill 1983). If the problems described above are not solved before seed orchards begin to produce large numbers of seeds, then operational programmes using rooted cuttings (Rauter 1974; Kleinschmit & Schmidt 1977) may be relegated to a minor role. If the problems of vegetative propagation are solved, the future problems will be those of easily rooted species.

IV. RESEARCH PRIORITIES

A. Utilizing nonadditive genetic variance

The best way to capture nonadditive, in addition to additive, genetic variance is through vegetative propagation. For species that are easily propagated vegetatively, the research priority should be to test empirically strategies for deploying clones. Where vegetative propagation is not simple, but seeds can be produced with relative ease, more research should be done to find ways to capture nonadditive variation using sexual methods. This is not to say that research on ways to propagate these species vegetatively should not be continued. However, the problems of producing large numbers of vegetative propagules for forest planting have proved to be more recalcitrant than originally hoped. It is time to accept that the methodology to make vegetative propagation practical may take longer to produce than once hoped. Other methods, like supplemental mass pollination, should be employed now to increase genetic gains until vegetative propagation methods are worked out.

As with clonal deployment, the use of sexual propagules in deployment strategies, other than bulked seed orchard mixes, raises questions of gain and risk. Empirical trials with half- and full-sib family plantings should receive more emphasis.

For species that are not easy to propagate vegetatively, and do not produce abundant seeds in seed orchards, research emphasis should be placed on improving seed production. Seed orchard research seems to have languished in some species, under the assumption that vegetative propagation techniques will be practical in the short term.

B. Early genetic evaluation

Learning to evaluate genetic entries earlier will be of value in all breeding programmes. Early evaluation may become more critical as less genetically diverse entities are planted. For example, plantings of single clones are less well buffered against environmental changes than mixed seedling populations. Important genotype×environment interactions are more likely in clonal plantings. Testing each clone for performance over a broad range of sites will be expensive.

More research emphasis should be given to ways to incorporate early genetic evaluation procedures into current breeding programmes.

C. Dealing with the effects of inbreeding

The question of how best to deal with inbreeding influences every type of programme mentioned above. Every species, regardless of the method of reproduction used for afforestation, or the method used for deployment, depends upon a programme of controlled crossing and progeny testing for continuing genetic improvement. The rate at which gains can be made will be indirectly determined by the degree to which inbreeding depression is manifested under different levels of inbreeding. Empirical studies to determine this relationship should be high priorities for research in every breeding programme.

V. CONCLUSIONS

Significant genetic gains have been made to date by using the easiest propagation methods available.

Breeders working with easily rooted species have used vegetative propagation to capitalize upon good individual genotypes, hybrid vigour, and combinatorial hybrids. The ease with which dramatic improvements have been made may have reduced the emphasis being given to sexual methods of reproduction and to breeding. Breeders working with species that are not easily propagated vegetatively, but which produce seeds relatively easily and consistently, have used seed orchards to capture additive genetic variance by selecting parents with improved general combining ability. More expensive breeding methods to utilize nonadditive genetic variance have not been used widely. Rather, ways to utilize the nonadditive genetic variance in the short term are being sought. Those working with species that are difficult to propagate economically, by either sexual or asexual means, have elected to pursue vegetative propagation methods.

Problems associated with the short-term use of nonadditive genetic variation are different for sexual and asexual propagation systems, but both are more expensive than methods to utilize general combining abilities. To be worthwhile, the additional expense must be offset by increased genetic gains or increased efficiency.

Whatever the breeding strategy, the ability to evaluate accurately selections at earlier ages would increase the efficiency of breeding programmes. Similarly, all programmes would benefit from knowledge on how best to deal with the effects of inbreeding.

REFERENCES

Adams, W. T., Roberds, J. H. & Zobel, B. J. (1973). Intergenotypic interactions among families of loblolly pine (*Pinus taeda* L.). *Theor. appl. Genet.*, **43**, 319–322.

Bridgwater, F. E. & Trew, I. F. (1981). Supplemental mass pollination. In: *Pollen management handbook*, 52–57. (Agriculture handbook no. 587). Washington DC: USDA Forest Service.

Bridgwater, F. E. & Williams, C. G. (1983). Feasibility of supplemental mass pollination to increase genetic gains from seed orchards. *Proc. Southern Forest Tree Improvement Conf., 17th, Athens, 6A,* 78–83. Springfield, VA: National Technical Information Service.

Brune, A. & Zobel, B. J. (1981). Genetic base populations, gene pools and breeding populations for *Eucalyptus* in Brazil. *Silvae Genet.*, **30**, 146–149.

Buijtenen van, J. P. & Lowe, W. J. (1979). The use of breeding groups in advanced generation breeding *Proc. Southern Forest Tree Improvement Conf., 15th,* 59–65. Mississippi State University.

Burdon, R. D. & Shelbourne, C. J. A. (1974). The use of vegetative propagules for obtaining genetic information. *N.Z. J. For. Sci.*, **4**, 418–425.

Burdon, R. D., Shelbourne, C. J. A. & Wilcox, M. D. (1978). Advanced selection strategies. *Proc. Third World Consultation on Forest Tree Breeding, Canberra, 1977,* 1133–1147. Canberra: CSIRO.

Campinhos, E., jr. (1980). More wood of better quality: intensive silviculture with rapid-growth improved *Eucalyptus* spp. for pulpwood. *Proc. TAPPI Annual Meeting,* 351–357.

Cannell, M. G. R. (1978). Improving per hectare forest productivity. *Proc. North American Forest Biology Workshop, 5th,* edited by C. A. Hollis and A. E. Squillace, 120–148. Gainesville, FLA: University of Florida, School of Forest Resources.

Cannell, M. G. R., Bridgwater, F. E. & Greenwood, M. S. (1978). Seedling growth rates, water stress responses and root-shoot relationships related to eight-year volumes among families of *Pinus taeda* L. *Silvae Genet.*, **27**, 237–248.

Comstock, R. E., Robinson, H. F. & Harvey, P. H. (1949). A breeding procedure designed to make maximum use of both general and specific combining ability. *Agron. J.*, **41**, 360–367.

Conkle, M. T. (1970). Hybridization: application to pine populations. *Proc. Working Group on Quantitative Genetics, Section 22, IUFRO, 1969,* 131–133. New Orleans, LA: USDA Forest Service, S.E. Exp. Stn.

Cotterill, P. O. & Nambiar, E. K. S., (1981). Seedling physiology of three radiata pine families with parents of contrasting growth. *Aust. For. Resour.*, **11**, 13–22.

Dietrichson, J. & Kierulf, C. (1982). Selection of eight-year-old Norway spruce (*Picea abies* [L.] Karst.) plants in a progeny trial and mass production by cuttings. *Rep. Norw. For. Inst.,* 38.1.

Fowler, D. P. (1978). Population improvement and hybridization. *Proc. Third World Consultation on Forest Tree Breeding, Canberra, 1977.* Canberra: CSIRO. Also *Unasylva* (1978), **30**, 21–26.

Frampton, L. J., Amerson, H. V. & Weir, R. J. (1983). Potential of *in vitro* screening of loblolly pine for fusiform rust resistance. *Proc. Southern Forest Tree Improvement Conf., 17th, Athens, 6A,* 325–331. Springfield, VA: National Technical Information Service.

Franklin, E. C. (1969). Inbreeding as a means of genetic improvement of loblolly pine. *Proc. Southern Forest Tree Improvement Conf., 10th,* 107–115. Texas Forest Service.

Franklin, E. C. (1970). Survey of mutant forms and inbreeding depression in species of the family *Pinaceae. Res. Pap. S.E. For. Exp. Stn (US)*, SE-61.

Gansel, C. R. (1971). Effects of several levels of inbreeding on growth and oleoresin yield in slash pine. *Proc. Southern Forest Tree Improvement Conf., 11th,* 173–177. Atlanta, GA: USDA Forest Service.

Gill, J. G. S. (1983). Comparisons of production costs and genetic benefits of transplants and rooted cuttings of *Picea sitchensis. Forestry*, **56**, 61–73.

Gladstone, W. T. (1975). Tree improvement programmes of forest industries. In: *Forest tree improvement: the third decade*, edited by B. A. Thielges, 65–74. Baton Rouge, LA: University of Louisiana.

Goddard, R. E. (1964). Tree distribution in a seedling seed orchard following between and within family selection. *Silvae Genet.*, **13**, 17–21.

Goddard, R. E., Schmidt, R. A. & Vande Linde, F. (1975). Immediate gains in fusiform rust resistance in slash pine from rogued seed production areas in severely diseased plantations. *Proc. Southern Forest Tree Improvement Conf., 13th, Raleigh, N.C.*, 177–203. Macon, GA: Tree Seed Laboratory.

Greenwood, M. S. (1978). Flower stimulation techniques for loblolly pine (*Pinus taeda* L.). *Proc. Third World Consultation on Forest Tree Breeding, Canberra, 1977*, 1031–1042. Canberra: CSIRO.

Hadders, G. (1978). Experiments with supplemental mass pollination in seed orchards of Scots pine (*Pinus sylvestris*). *Proc. Third World Consultation on Forest Tree Breeding, Canberra, 1977*, 967–979. Canberra: CSIRO.

Hyun, S. K. (1969). Mass controlled pollination. *Proc. Second World Consultation on Forest Tree Breeding*, 1341–1354. Washington DC.

Hyun, S. K. (1973). Developing an advanced generation breeding population for a hybrid breeding programme. In: *Selection and breeding to improve some tropical conifers*, edited by J. Burley and D. G. Nikles, 439–448. Oxford: Commonwealth Forestry Institute, and Queensland: Department of Forestry.

Hyun, S. K. (1976). Interspecific hybridization in pines with special reference to *Pinus rigida×taeda*. *Silvae Genet.*, **25**, 188–191.

Kellison, R. C. (1971). Seed orchard management. *Proc. Southern Forest Tree Improvement Conf., 11th*, 166–172. Atlanta, GA: USDA Forest Service.

Kleinschmit, J. & Schmidt, J. (1977). Experiences with *Picea abies* cuttings propagation in Germany and problems connected with large scale application. *Silvae Genet.*, **26**, 197–203.

LaFarge, T. & Kraus, J. F. (1980). A progeny test of (shortleaf×loblolly)×loblolly hybrids to produce rapid-growing hybrids resistant to fusiform rust. *Silvae Genet.*, **29**, 197–200.

Lambeth, C. C. (1980). Juvenile-mature correlations in *Pinaceae* and implications for early selection. *Forest Sci.*, **26**, 571–580.

Lambeth, C. C., Buijtenen, J. P. van, Duke, S. D. & McCullough, R. B., (1983). Early selection is effective in 20–year-old genetic tests of loblolly pine. *Silvae Genet.*, **32**, 137–228.

Libby, W. J. (1980). What is a safe number of clones per plantation? In: *Resistance to disease and pests in forest trees*, 342–360. (Proc. International Workshop on the Genetics of Host-parasite Interactions in Forestry, 3rd, Wageningen).

Matheson, A. C. (1983). Strategy and tactics. In: *Radiata pine breeding manual*, edited by A. C. Matheson and A. G. Brown, sections 4.1–4.13. Canberra: Division of Forest Research, CSIRO.

McKeand, S. E. & Beineke, W. (1980). Sublining for half-sib breeding populations of forest trees. *Silvae Genet.*, **29**, 14–17.

McWilliam, J. R. & Florence, R. G. (1955). The improvement in quality of slash pine plantations by means of selection and cross breeding. *Aust. For.*, **19**, 8–12.

Nanson, A. (1969). Juvenile and correlated trait selection. *Proc. IUFRO Meeting of the Working Group on Quantitative Genetics, 2nd*, 17–25. Raleigh, NC.

Nikles, D. G. (1981). Some successful hybrid breeds of forest trees and need for further developments in Australia. *Proc. 7th Meeting RWG No. 1 – Forest Genetics*. Traralgon, Victoria.

Orr-Ewing, A. L. (1976). Inbreeding Douglas-fir to the S_3 generation. *Silvae Genet.*, **25**, 179–183.

Purnell, R. C. & Kellison, R. C. (1983). A tree improvement programme for southern hardwoods. *Proc. Southern Forest Tree Improvement Conf., 17th, Athens, GA*, 90–98. Springfield, VA: National Technical Information Service.

Rauter, R. M. (1974). A short-term tree improvement programme through vegetative propagation. *N.Z. J. For. Sci.*, **4**, 373–379.

Riemenschneider, D. E. (1980). The Lake States jack pine breeding programme. In: *Research needs in tree breeding*, 110–121. (Proc. North American Quantitive Forest Genetics Group Workshop, 15th, edited by R. P. Guries and H. Kang). Coeur d'Alene, Idaho.

Ross, S. D., Pharis, R. P. & Heaman, J. C. (1980). Promotion of cone and seed production in grafted and seedling Douglas-fir seed orchards by application of gibberellin $A_{4/7}$ mixture. *Can. J. For. Res.*, **10**, 464–469.

Roulund, H. (1981). Problems of clonal forestry in spruce and their influence on breeding strategy. *For. Abstr.*, **42**, 457–471.

Shelbourne, C. J. A. (1969). *Tree breeding methods*. (Technical paper no. 55). Wellington: Forest Research Institute, New Zealand Forestry Service.

Sorensen, F. C. & Miles, R. S. (1982). Inbreeding depression in height, height growth, and survival of Douglas-fir, ponderosa pine, and noble fir to 10 years of age. *Forest Sci.*, **28**, 283–292.

Squillace, A. E. & Gansel, C. R. (1974). Juvenile-mature correlations in slash pine. *Forest Sci.*, **20**, 225–229.

Steenackers, V. (1972). The state of knowledge in breeding rust resistant poplars. In: *Biology of rust resistance in forest trees*, 419–430. (Miscellaneous publication no. 1221). Washington DC: USDA Forest Service.

Stonecypher, R. W. (1969). Recurrent selection in forest tree breeding. *Proc. Southern Forest Tree Improvement Conf., 10th*, 7–16. Texas Forest Service.

Toda, R. (1974). Vegetative propagation in relation to Japanese forest tree improvement. *N.Z. J. For. Sci.*, **4**, 410–417.

Waxler, M. S. & Buijtenen, J. P. van. (1981). Early genetic evaluation of loblolly pine. *Can. J. For. Res.*, **11**, 351–355.

Williams, C. G., Bridgwater, F. E. & Lambeth, C. C. (1983). Performance of single family versus mixed family plantation blocks of loblolly pine. *Proc. Southern Forest Tree Improvement Conf., 17th, Athens, GA*, 194–201. Springfield, VA: National Technical Information Service.

Yeh, F. C., Crown, M. & Bower, R. C. (1980). British Columbia Cooperative Coastal Tree Improvement Programme. In: *Research needs in tree breeding*, 1–15. (Proc. North American Quantitative Forest Genetics Group Workshop, 15th, edited by R. P. Guries and H. Kang). Coeur d'Alene, Idaho.

Zobel, B. J. & Talbert, J. T. (1984). Hybrids in tree improvement, In: *Applied tree improvement*, 346–373. New York: John Wiley.

Zobel, B. J., Weir, R. J. & Jett, J. B. (1972). Breeding methods to produce progeny for advanced-generation selection and to evaluate parent trees. *Can. J. For. Res.*, **2**, 399–345.

Zsuffa, L. (1973). A summary review of interspecific breeding in the genus *Populus*. *Proc. Canadian Tree Improvement Association, 14th*, 107–123. Fredericton.

Zsuffa, L. (1979). The breeding of *Populus* species in Ontario. *Proc. Tree Improvement Symposium*, 153–160. Ottawa: Canadian Forestry Service.

4

FRUIT TREE BREEDING: STRATEGIES, ACHIEVEMENTS AND CONSTRAINTS

F. H. ALSTON
East Malling Research Station, Maidstone, Kent, England

P. SPIEGEL-ROY
Institute of Horticulture, Volcani Centre, Bet-Dagan, Israel

I. INTRODUCTION

Fruit tree species are mostly outbreeding and largely heterozygous being hermaphrodite and most often self-incompatible. Notable exceptions are the peach (*Prunus persica*, which although often outbreeding is self-compatible), the fig (*Ficus carica*, dioecious) and the avocado (*Persea americana*, which has a special system of synchronous dichogamy). Clonal propagation is widespread, and new varieties are commonly derived from segregating F_1 generations. The fruit tree breeder aims to select compact precocious good flowering varieties which have a high fruit/shoot ratio. By contrast, the forest tree breeder favours sparsely flowering, fast-growing, tall trees, which are usually seed-propagated. A further refinement usually available to the fruit tree industry is the production of composite plants, through the use of rootstocks and interstocks. In this way, plants can be produced which carry characters derived from four or six parental varieties, thus providing a means of combining characters from several widely different parents after only one generation of breeding. Developments in genetic manipulation techniques promise the means of further modifying varieties and selections, through induced mutations and gene modification and transference.

Fruit tree plantations become established as production units over a shorter period than most forests. Fifteen to thirty years cover the life span of most fruit tree plantations, much of which is spent in full production. One of the main breeding aims is to maximize the period of full production by selecting for precocity, which is closely correlated with yield.

Market and consumer requirements have special effects on fruit tree breeding policy. As well as flavour and appearance, season of harvest, storage period, shelf life and durability during transport have to be taken into account. Furthermore, most markets require a standard product for most fruits, according to type and season. Marketing is even more specialized for fruits like apples and pears, where the name of the variety has become an important aspect of consumer recognition. There is, therefore, a natural reluctance to grow new varieties – growers are not prepared to plant large areas without first being assured of markets for the produce. A period of consumer and market testing is usually necessary before varieties can enter large-scale production.

Early selection techniques have been developed for yield, disease and pest resistance, and tree type, during the first two years after germination, and for yield and quality features in the first or second years of fruiting. The use of such techniques has shortened the period from germination to release of new genotypes, and has decreased the amount of land and labour needed for seedling assessment and orchard trials.

Apples (*Malus pumila*) are the most widely grown of the commercial tree fruits, and have received the most attention from breeders. Experience in apple breeding can be applied to most other tree fruit crops because the breeding methods have much in common (Janick & Moore 1975; Moore & Janick 1983).

II. BREEDING SYSTEMS

A. Crossing and selection

For most tree fruit crops, the selection of superior phenotypes and their subsequent random mating, followed by mass selection, is the most effective means of increasing the number of favourable alleles, because there is a relatively high additive variance governing the inheritance of most traits. However, several important commercial characters are determined by single dominant or recessive genes (Knight 1969; Alston 1975; Alston & Watkins 1975), thus justifying the careful matching of parents according to genotype where dominant genes are concerned. In apples, desirable parental combinations are determined from the results of previous progeny and variety trials, as well as from genotypic details (Alston 1985).

Tree fruit breeders usually select individuals which are exceptional members of a progeny. Such plants are not representative of a progeny because they often exhibit, in the F_1, a heterotic type of effect. Clonal propagation of élite selections enables the total genetic variance, including that due to dominance and epistasis, to be exploited, and, because clones are uniform in performance, there is no need to breed seed-propagated hybrid varieties. Clonal propagation largely offsets the slow pace of genetic gain which is a consequence of the long juvenile phase of most tree crops. However, long periods are needed to assess the field and market performance of new varieties, using trial orchards and grower plantings, which often delays the inclusion of new selections in crossing programmes. Thus, in some crops, such as apple, there has been a slow build up of generations in breeding programmes, until recently, although this has not been the case in peaches, where many new varieties are now being produced from the fourth or fifth generation.

B.   Inbreeding

In order to produce superior phenotypes in which desirable characters are fully expressed, some degree of inbreeding is desirable. Such an approach has been very successful in peach, which lacks any marked inbreeding depression (Lesley 1957) – possibly because of intense selection during the development of the crop from an area of origin where inbreeding was favoured. In apple breeding, it is usual to avoid any degree of inbreeding. Inbreeding depression has been associated with a lengthening of the average progeny juvenile phase (Brown 1975). However, apple varieties vary in sensitivity to inbreeding, and severe inbreeding depression can be avoided by selection for vigour and precocity. Indeed, a slight loss in vigour, combined with precocity, can be of considerable benefit when dwarf or semi-dwarf trees are required, as experienced with the avocado (Bergh 1975). Bell *et al.* (1981) observed that fruit quality improved with a degree of inbreeding in pear (*Pyrus communis*) progenies. The recently released high quality 'Bartlett-like', fireblight-resistant, pear variety, 'Harvest Queen', is the result of such an approach (Quamme & Spearman 1983). Another approach is to make crosses between superior siblings in order to maximize the expression of characters determined by recessive genes, as well as to obtain a greater genetic gain by the F_2 than is usually possible from a backcross. However, sib-cross progenies are often small, and it can take up to six years to establish enough fruiting trees to produce sufficient seed for effective selection.

C. Backcrossing

Backcrossing is the usual means of transferring characters from wild species or primitive varieties to fruit tree crops. It commonly takes the form of a series of crosses at each generation back to the cultivated species. A different cultivated species parent is used in each generation to avoid excessive inbreeding. In apple, backcrossing programmes of this type have resulted in successful commercial selections (carrying disease resistance from wild species) by the second backcross generation (Alston 1983a).

III. YIELD AND PRECOCITY

A. Shortening the juvenile phase

The length of the juvenile phase is a major factor affecting the breeding of tree crops. Amongst the tree fruits, this period varies from two years in lime (*Citrus aurantifolia*) to over 14 years in some pears. There are considerable environmental (Jonkers 1971; Aldwinkle & Lamb 1976) as well as genetic effects (Visser 1976; Thibault 1979; Alston & Bates 1979) on the length of the juvenile phase in apples and pears. Full sunlight, long days and long growing seasons tend to shorten the juvenile phase (promote early fruiting). Genetically, the juvenile phase can be significantly shortened by selecting precocious parents, and this is a major aspect of most tree fruit breeding programmes. Zimmerman (1977) reported flowering as early as two years after germination in some seedlings of pear, while Potapov (1971) found individuals of this species with a juvenile phase of 15 years.

One widely practised means of hastening flowering in fruit trees is to select seedlings which grow rapidly on their own roots (eg apple, Zimmerman 1972; and peach, Sherman *et al.* 1973). Alternatively, seedlings can be budded on to dwarfing rootstocks. In apple, the very dwarfing rootstock M.27 can reduce the juvenile phase from 9–10 years to 6–7 years (Tydeman & Alston 1965), whereas in pears the most dwarfing commercial rootstock (Quince C, *Cydonia oblonga*) is only moderately effective in shortening the juvenile phase (Alston 1983b).

B. Early selection for high yield

In apple, there is a close relationship between the length of the juvenile period in seedlings, and the period to initiation of cropping on orchard trees (Visser & De Vries 1970), and precocious apples (Alston & Bates 1979) and avocados (Bergh 1976) tend to be high-yielding. In apple, preselection for precocity, and hence high yield, is possible 18 months after germination (Alston & Bates 1979). Seedlings are selected which have the attributes of the pomologists' ideal maiden tree, with many side branches or feathers and wide branch angles. Such selections can yield up to 300% more than their siblings, and they have been the means of producing new varieties at East Malling which yield twice the crop of the existing main crop variety. These selections are budded on to M.27, principally to shorten the juvenile phase, but the yield of young apple seedlings grown on this very dwarfing rootstock is closely correlated with their later performance as orchard trees (Alston & Bates 1979). There is considerable variation in cropping due to factors not directly related to precocity – such as flower and pollen fertility, flowering date, and the density and position of flower trusses – so, at this stage, it is usual to select apple seedlings which yield more than a predetermined level over a specific period. Significant improvements in yield have been achieved in the English walnut (*Juglans regia*) by selecting for a lateral fruiting habit, with fruits borne in clusters, instead of the normal types which have single fruits at the ends of the shoots.

C. Breeding trees for very intensive growing systems

Commercial systems of producing tree fruits range from intensive systems, used for peach and nectarine, in which each tree has a single one-year-old shoot about one metre tall, to avocado orchards, in which the trees usually grow seven to nine metres tall. When breeding for high yield, the breeder selects the most 'efficient' trees – those which maximize fruit production at the expense of shoot production – and it is therefore essential to select a dwarf or spurred habit. In many cases, these types of habit are under simple genetic control, such as in the compact columnar apple mutant 'McIntosh Wijcik' (Lapins 1969), the compact sweet cherry (*Prunus avium*) 'Compact Lambert' (Lapins 1963), and the brachytic dwarf in peach (Lammerts 1945).

New apple varieties have been produced at East Malling, combining the compact columnar habit of 'Wijcik' with a range of improved fruit types (Tobutt 1985). Trees of this type, grown as unpruned natural cordons less than one metre apart, have produced yields in the second year equal to those normally expected eight years after planting a conventional orchard. The future development of this type of orchard depends on the production of varieties which can be propagated cheaply, and which can be grown on their own roots as easily as on established rootstocks. Elsewhere, encouraging results have been obtained using brachytic dwarf peach selections in closely planted orchards (3,750 trees ha^{-1}); at age four yields were four times those normally expected at age seven from standard plantings with 270 trees ha^{-1} (Hansche & Beres 1980). Also, a new compact variety of avocado has been selected from a seedling population, and there are good prospects of combining the compact habit with high fruit quality (Barrientos-Perez & Sanchez-Colin 1983).

D. Selection for improved fertility in regions with low spring temperatures

Responses to specific climatic conditions can be important determinants of yield, particularly responses to low temperatures at flowering time. But, rather than select for low temperature tolerance, a common approach has been to select for late flowering. This can be achieved by selecting for late vegetative bud-burst on one-year-old apple and pear seedlings, because dates of flowering and vegetative bud-burst are correlated (Tydeman 1964; Thibault 1979). Differences in flowering time are largely determined by differences in winter chilling requirement in temperate fruit tree crops (high requirements leading to late flowering); this fact was recognized by Wilson *et al.* (1975) when selecting for late flowering in plums (*Prunus domestica*) and by Spiegel-Roy and Alston (1979) for pears. There is, however, a risk of selecting varieties with such high chilling requirements that they cannot be satisfied in some seasons. This risk is much greater in apples than in plums (which naturally flower four to five weeks earlier), and results in sparse spasmodic flowering and poor fruit set. It is also necessary to avoid the deleterious effect on cropping of shorter leaf area durations and fruit developmental periods. A further problem with apples and pears arises from delaying blossom time to a later, warmer period, when the risk of infection from fireblight (*Erwinia amylovora*) is increased. Blossoms are the main sites for fireblight infection. To achieve maximum fruit set in apples and pears, it is best to select varieties with frost- or cold-resistant blossoms, which flower either at the normal time or only slightly later than normal. The rate of pollen tube growth differs in response to temperature in different varieties of apple (Petropoulou 1984) and peach (Holub 1981), which suggests that there are good prospects of genetically improving fruit set in areas liable to experience cold spring temperatures.

The degree of self-compatibility is another determinant of yield. Orchards with self-compatible fruit trees need not contain low value pollinators, and so can give greater economic yields. The main English plum variety, 'Victoria', and most of the sour cherries (*Prunus cerasus*) are self-fertile. The sweet cherry 'Stella' was specifically bred for self-fertility (Lapins 1971), while at least partially self-fertile mutants of the apple 'Cox's Orange Pippin' have been produced by irradiation (Campbell & Lacy 1982).

There are prospects of developing parthenocarpic varieties of some fruits, particularly pear, fig and citrus. This development would not only remove the need for separate pollinators, but would also, in many cases, reduce dependence on critical temperatures for fertilization.

E. Chilling requirements and cold hardiness

Two factors which affect the productivity of fruit trees when they are grown outside their normal climatic limits are their winter chilling requirements and their cold hardiness. Low chilling requirements are essential for varieties of temperate fruit crops grown in subtropical regions. Successful varieties of peach (Bowen 1971), pear (Sherman *et al.* 1982) and apple (Oppenheimer & Slor 1968), with low chilling requirements, have been bred for these regions. Clearly, cold hardiness is essential when extending fruit growing to colder regions, and this has been achieved by using wild species as donors of cold hardiness, eg *Pyrus ussuriensis* for pear (Stushnoff & Garley 1980), *Malus baccata* for apple (Macoun 1928) and *Poncirus trifoliata* for citrus (Goliadaze 1980).

F. Economic yield

An important distinction exists in fruit tree crops between biological yield and economic yield. High yields are required of high quality fruits of the right size, free from blemish or damage due to pests and diseases. Thus, pest and disease resistance is an important determinant of yield, as also is a natural propensity to thin fruits from fully set trusses to single fruits (which will attain a good commercial size), as occurs in the apple 'Malling Jester'.

IV. PEST AND DISEASE RESISTANCE

Resistance breeding must be concentrated on those pests and diseases of greatest economic importance in order to justify the long-term programmes needed, often involving the transfer of high levels of resistance from wild species. The pests and diseases of greatest importance are those (a) which are difficult or impossible to control chemically, (b) which are expensive to control chemically, and (c) for which chemical control presents serious spray residue problems, contravening food regulations or interfering with the biological control of other pests and diseases.

A. Foliar diseases

The fungal foliar diseases apple scab (*Ventura inaequalis*) and apple mildew (*Podosphaera leucotricha*) account for the largest part of the pesticide costs in apple growing. To achieve good control of apple mildew, up to 17 spray applications are necessary in English orchards during the growing season. Most new European apple varieties carry a higher level of mildew resistance than the main commercial varieties Golden Delicious and Cox's Orange Pippin. This resistance has been achieved by stringent field selection in the second or third growing seasons after germination. Mildew resistance is under polygenic control (Brown 1959) and is rarely sufficient to permit a complete relaxation of the spraying programme. Such polygenic resistance is transmitted to only a small proportion of seedlings in progenies. Attempts to incorporate such low levels of resistance can drastically handicap breeding progress in complex breeding programmes designed primarily to produce high yields of high quality fruits. However, high levels of simply inherited mildew resistance, sufficient to allow a complete relaxation of spraying programmes, have been found amongst *Malus* species and introduced into commercial breeding programmes. Second backcross derivatives from the resistant, small-fruited species *M. robusta* and *M. zumi* have good commercial fruit size, good skin finish, and good flavour and texture, as well as resistance to mildew. In addition, they are precocious and therefore potentially high-yielding (Alston 1983a). Very high levels of resistance, derived from these two *Malus* species, have remained effective in unsprayed plots for nearly 20 years. However, care is taken to combine both simply inherited and polygenetically inherited resistance in mildew resistance selection programmes (Alston 1977). A similar approach has proved effective in programmes incorporating monogenic resistance to apple scab derived from *Malus floribunda*, and several good scab-resistant apple varieties have been released. This source of resistance has remained effective in unsprayed conditions for over 40 years. But, again, it is probable that the stability of the single major gene resistance can be very significantly enhanced by polygenes (Rouselle *et al.* 1975).

B.   Root and shoot diseases

Most diseases which affect the roots or shoots of fruit trees are difficult to control chemically. Sources of resistance to apple canker (*Nectria galligena*) have been identified (Alston 1970a; Kruger 1983) and selection techniques involving wound inoculations have been used on young seedlings (Alston & Bates 1978). Cut-shoot tests on one-year-old wood have proved effective as an initial screen for resistance to collar rot (*Phytophthora cactorum*) among apple scion selections (Alston 1970b).

Three new commercial sweet cherry varieties resulted from a programme that combined resistance to bacterial canker (*Pseudomonas morsprunorum*) with high yield and good fruit quality (Matthews 1979). Selection was based on leaf scar inoculation of five-month-old pot-grown seedlings, followed by re-inoculation into the bark parenchyma of seedlings that showed no signs of infection. The appearance of a more virulent strain of the bacterial canker pathogen posed a serious threat to this programme (Freigoun & Crosse 1975). However, resistance to both races is now combined in the newer varieties.

The bacterial disease fireblight (*Erwinia amylovora*) is the most serious disease of pear. High levels of resistance have been transferred from *P. ussuriensis* and *P. serotina*, but the most promising commercial selections are derived from cultivated varieties (Zwet & Keil 1979). Seedling selection techniques involving whole plants (Zwet & Keil 1979) or cut shoots (Alston 1973) have been developed. Resistant selections are normally verified by inoculating shoots on young trees, either in the field (Zwet 1977) or in a cool glasshouse (Alston 1983c). Although resistance in cultivated varieties is found in only a small proportion of the seedlings, the level of resistance can be very high, justifying stringent screening of large populations. Another approach is to breed for fireblight avoidance concurrently with selection for high yield and precocity. This approach involves selecting types with a low incidence of secondary blossom (the prime site for infection in areas with low spring temperatures).

C.   Pest resistance

Striking examples of strong, simply inherited resistance to aphids occur in apple, to both the rosy leaf-curling aphid (*Dysaphis devecta*) and the rosy apple aphid (*Dysaphis plantaginea*) (Alston & Briggs 1968, 1970). It takes no more than five days to screen selections for resistance to these two pests among two-month-old seedlings growing in a glasshouse. The virus-induced disease, sharka, of peach could potentially be controlled by selecting for known resistance to its polyphagous aphid vector, *Myzus persicae* (Maison *et al.* 1983).

Pest and disease resistance is important when breeding new rootstocks and, as mentioned, is a component of fruit quality in scion varieties. At present, resistance is generally regarded as a bonus in new scion varieties bred primarily for improved horticultural and market qualities.

V. FRUIT QUALITY

There are four broad quality categories: appearance, eating quality, storage quality and processing quality. Appearance usually involves fruit size and shape, as well as colour and skin finish. Eating quality covers all aspects of flavour, flesh colour and texture. Storage quality depends on a number of factors, including resistance to physiological disorders and those caused by pathogens. In all crops, shelf life and transport performance are important – in most *Prunus* crops, these are critical components of quality. Processing quality depends on canning and cooking performance, ease of peeling, fruit size, flesh colour and juice quality.

In nearly all tree fruits grown for fresh consumption the sugar/acid balance is the critical component of flavour, the most favoured combination being a moderate to low acidity combined with a high sugar content. The texture and colour of the fruits also affect sensory appreciation; in apples, in particular, crispness is an important aspect of texture. Other examples of specific features important in quality selection are seedlessness in citrus, absence of stone cells in pears, and absence of astringency in persimmons (*Diospyros virginiana*). Selection for flavour in apples is practised by the breeder, within well-defined limits, for texture, acidity and sugar content (Alston & Watkins 1984), followed by critical tasting by panels and consumers when sufficient fruits are available. After preliminary selection for storage and transport qualities, it is necessary for sufficient quantities of élite selections to be grown to enable large-scale experiments to be conducted using fruit from a range of sites, before definite recommendations can be made on their commercial value.

The nutritive value of tree fruits has received little attention in breeding programmes, although a wide varietal variation in vitamin C content has been reported for many fruits, including the apple (Knight 1963). In addition, varietal differences have been reported in the dietary fibre content of apples (Gormley 1981).

There are many instances of major quality characters being under simple genetic control. Single dominant genes control acidity, fruit colour and flesh colour in apples (Alston 1981), flesh colour in *Prunus salicina*, the Japanese plum (Hurter 1962), and skin hairiness, stone attachment and flesh colour in peaches (Hesse 1975).

Although direct assessments of fruit quality must necessarily await the end of the juvenile phase, attempts have been made to correlate subsequent fruit characters with the vegetative characters of one- or two-year-old seedlings. While correlations are not high, there are good prospects of selecting for fruit acidity within large populations of apples, on the basis of seedling leaf pH (Visser & Verhaegh 1978), provided information is available on the parental genotypes. In addition, the proportion of apple trees that produce small fruits can be substantially decreased by the routine of discarding small-leaved seedlings at age 18 months.

As mentioned, resistance breeding is an important aspect of quality improvement. Many fruit storage disorders can be controlled by post-harvest dips, but these are now forbidden in many European countries. Also, it is likely that increasingly stringent regulations will be introduced to control the sale of fruit from sprayed plantations; some large retailers already prefer to sell fruit from plantations with limited spray programmes.

VI.   ROOTSTOCKS

In all fruit tree crops, breeders are aiming to select new rootstocks with particular attributes, additional to their role as vehicles for the multiplication and establishment of scion varieties. The most important attribute of rootstocks is an ability to control the size and fruit productivity of the scion. A further important attribute – uniformity of tree size and performance – is usually met by clonal multiplication, although selected seedling provenances and hybrid lines are also used in some crops such as apple (Spangelo 1971) and apricot (*Prunus armeniaca*) (Layne & Harrison 1975). In addition, apomictic seedling rootstocks of apple are being developed (Schmidt & Kruger 1983) and in citrus and mango (*Mangifera indica*) crops are propagated on nucellar seedlings derived from selected clones. Selection and breeding for resistance to root and stem diseases, especially those caused by *Phytophthora* sp., resistance to drought, waterlogging, salt tolerance and lime-induced chlorosis, are more important than size control in some areas. Mass selection techniques are used wherever possible; for instance, young apple rootstock seedlings can be screened in seed trays for resistance to *Phytophthora cactorum* (Watkins & Werts 1971). Selection for improved nutrient uptake by rootstocks is a means of improving fruit storage quality in some scion varieties. In pears, clonal rootstocks of quince are frequently used, because they control tree size, they root easily, and they have a beneficial effect on fruit quality in some regions. Considerable variation exists amongst pear scion varieties in their compatibility with quince stocks. Pear/quince compatibility is controlled by a single gene in derivatives of the incompatible species *Pyrus ussuriensis* (Alston 1975).

The apple rootstock M.9 is outstanding in that it reduces growth in the scions, and induces them to produce a high yield of fruits with good size. At East Malling, where a gene pool of between 60 and 70 rootstock parents has been investigated, most élite selections have M.9, M.27 and/or MM.106 in their parentage. M.9 and MM.106 are the most widely used clonal rootstocks, and M.27 is a seedling from M.9. MM.106 and M.27 were bred at East Malling.

Apple seedlings can be preselected for their ability to control scion size on the basis of the percentage of bark present in their roots (positively correlated with the dwarfing effect, Beakbane & Thompson 1939) and the number of stomata per unit area on their leaves (negatively correlated with the dwarfing effect, Beakbane & Majumder 1975). Apple seedlings can also be preselected for their rate of nutrient uptake during their first three years of growth – high foliar calcium levels being a prime target (Kennedy *et al.* 1982). Most apple varieties grown on the established dwarfing rootstocks need to be staked, so new dwarfing rootstocks with improved anchorage would considerably reduce orchard establishment and maintenance costs. A wide range of root structures are found among seedling selections (Tydeman 1933) and there are good prospects of selecting well-anchored dwarfing rootstocks (Tydeman 1943). Selecting for a dwarf habit among young seedlings is itself insufficient; new selections must also be inherently precocious; indeed, the natural vigour of one-year layers of M.9 suggests that precocity is the prime factor distinguishing this rootstock from the more vigorous MM.106. The ability to root easily – an essential character in a rootstock – is assessed in apple rootstocks at East Malling from the amount of roots produced by hardwood cuttings, taken after the second or subsequent growing seasons. It is now usual to discard seedlings showing burr-knots, which produce rootstocks that sucker prolifically and are thus more easily infected by trunk and root pests and diseases.

Many pest-resistant rootstocks have been successfully selected. The MM series of apple rootstocks has been bred specifically for resistance to woolly aphid (*Eriosoma lanigerum*) (Preston 1966), and peach rootstocks for resistance to the root-knot nematodes (*Meloidogyne incognita* and *M. javanica*) (Sharpe *et al.* 1969), while an apple rootstock has been selected for resistance to the pine vole (*Micrototus pinetorum*) and the meadow vole (*M. pennsylvanicus*) (Cummins *et al.* 1983). The two latter examples included wild species derivatives (*Prunus persica*×*P. davidiana* for nematode resistance and *Malus prunifolia* for vole resistance). Other successful rootstocks derived from interspecific hybrids, or seed collected in the wild, include (a) citrus rootstocks with resistance to *Phytophthora*, tristeza virus, and the citrus nematode (*Tylenchulus semipenetrans*) from *Poncirus trifoliata*, (b) chlorosis-resistant rootstocks for peach from *P. persica*×*P. amygdalus*, and (c) semi-dwarfing plum and cherry stocks including the cherry stock 'Colt', from *P. avium*×*P. pseudocerasus*, and 'Cob', a more vigorous stock of the same parentage, which is resistant to the cherry replant disease (*Thevialiopsis basicola*). Thus, useful first generation progenies from open-pollination or interspecific crosses can provide valuable new rootstock varieties, without the necessity to pass through lengthy back-crossing programmes.

VII. POLYPLOIDY AND APOMIXIS

A wide range of ploidy levels is represented amongst fruit tree species, varying from simple diploids like the peach ($2n = 16$, $n = 8$) to multipolyploids like the black mulberry (*Morus nigra*, $2n = 308$, $n = 14$). The European plum ($2n = 48$, $n = 8$) is probably an allopolyploid, derived from a natural hybrid of *Prunus cerasifera* ($2n = 16$) and *Prunus spinosa* ($2n = 32$). The European plum has a good fruit size and wide environmental adaptability, while the Japanese plum, a diploid ($2n = 16$) with a similar fruit size, is less adaptable and is restricted to the warm temperate and subtropical regions. *Citrus* species are consistently diploid, but a low frequency of triploid and tetraploid seedlings occur in their progenies – triploids being particularly important because they are seedless.

In north-western Europe, apple and pear fruits can be small in areas with low temperatures and short growing seasons, and in such conditions the gigantism or 'gigas effect' of polyploidy is an advantage, particularly in triploids. The most promising triploids are those which occur by chance in about one in 300 apple seedlings derived from diploid×diploid crosses (Einset 1947; Knight 1966). These 'natural' triploids normally arise from the fertilization of an unreduced diploid egg cell by a normal haploid pollen grain. In this way, two-thirds of the genetic constitution of the resulting triploid is derived almost unchanged from the female parent. 'Mutsu' ('Golden Delicious'דIndo') and 'Malling Jupiter' ('Cox's Orange Pippin'דStarking') are examples of such triploids, which produce a much higher proportion of good sized fruits than their maternal parents, but retain many of their eating quality, shape and colour features. Triploids can be preselected among 18–month-old seedlings by retaining the most vigorous, large-leaved plants. Screening on the basis of leaf stomatal size or, as recently demonstrated, on stomatal chloroplast number (Solovyeva 1982) might be applied as a further selection sieve prior to chromosome counting.

In citrus, triploids do not have large cells or fruits, but they can be identified from their seeds, which are characteristically small owing to their small embryo/endosperm ratios (Esen & Soost 1972). In contrast, triploid seeds of apples are usually large. Valuable citrus varieties have resulted from diploid×tetraploid crosses, such as the seedless 'Oroblanco' grapefruit, but spontaneous triploids are also common (Speigel-Roy & Vardi 1983). Triploid citrus varieties tend to have low fruit yields, but triploid apple varieties can give high yields provided there is adequate pollination in the orchards. In both groups of fruits, triploids produce vigorously growing trees, possibly because of their hybrid origin.

In contrast, some spontaneous tetraploids of apple and citrus appear to be slow growing, possibly because their autotetraploid origin has an inbreeding type of effect. Their leaves and fruits have large cells, but their shoots have relatively short internodes. In apples, tetraploids derived from crosses (as opposed to spontaneous ones) are often as vigorous as diploids, but they do not show the same heterotic effect as triploids. One example of reduced vigour in an autotetraploid is a dwarfing tetraploid clone of the moderately vigorous rootstock M.13 (Beakbane 1967).

Apomictic reproduction is facilitated by polyploidy, but it is also common in some diploids (Stebbins 1980) and it is particularly important in citrus. In many citrus species, apomictic seed formation occurs by means of adventitious embryony, giving nucellar seedlings, which are raised as genetically uniform, virus-free rootstocks from selected parents. A similar situation exists in the mango. Small numbers of nucellar seedlings also occur in some varieties of apple as a result of fertilization failure, but techniques for seed production are not yet available. Gametophytic apomixis is found in some polyploid *Malus* species where cells surrounding the embryo-sac mother cell develop into unreduced embryo-sacs (apospory). Such *Malus* species have been tested as sources of seed-propagated apple rootstocks, but they were not sufficiently dwarfing or productive to be of commercial value (Luckwill & Campbell 1954). Dwarfing rootstocks have been selected from hybrids of apomictic

Malus species and are under test (Schmidt & Kruger 1983). Clonal propagation, either vegetatively or by apomixis, facilitates the maintenance of polyploidy in plantation crops, providing a means of exploiting and maintaining heterosis or similar genetic effects.

VIII. GENETIC MANIPULATION

The selection of improved clones – which may be natural mutants or the result of genetic manipulation – has an important part to play in maintaining established varieties in cultivation. The major North American apple variety 'Delicious' has been almost entirely replaced over the past 50 years by natural colour and semi-dwarf mutants. A glabrous mutant of peach was selected to give rise to a new fruit, the nectarine. The success of natural mutants has encouraged work on the induction of mutants in fruit tree crops by irradiation and chemical means. However, the time needed to select and establish the stability of induced mutants can be as long as that taken to conduct a hybridization and selection programme, while usually producing a much smaller genetic gain involving only one or two characters. Nevertheless, promising induced mutants have been released of established varieties, including semi-dwarf mutants of the vigorous triploid apple 'Bramley's Seedling' (Lacy 1982), a russet-free mutant of the apple 'Golden Delicious' (Le Lezec 1973), a compact cherry (Lapins 1963) and a seedless red grapefruit (Hensz 1971). These are mainly chimaeric mutants, resulting from indiscriminate chromosome breakages rather than point mutations, and they can be accompanied by many deleterious effects – hence the need to select them carefully and to test their stability.

There are, however, prospects of selecting more precise genetic modifications, using cell and tissue culture techniques to exploit the re-arrangement of genetic material that occurs spontaneously during plant regeneration (somaclonal variation). Also, mutations can be induced more readily in cell and tissue culture than in whole plant parts, and procedures are being developed to facilitate rapid and efficient screening of cell and tissue culture material. Tolerance to both the herbicide 2–4–D (Spiegel-Roy *et al.* 1983) and high salt concentrations (Kochba *et al.* 1982) has been selected for in *Citrus* callus.

Most of the techniques so far considered offer the potential of selecting new varieties which differ from established varieties in only one or two significant characters. Such transformed or mutated varieties would probably be accepted more easily by established markets than completely new varieties derived from crossing programmes.

However, in the long term, there is no doubt that new and novel forms are required which are quite different to those in current culture. Considerable changes are necessary in most crops to respond to changes in environment, growing systems and market trends. While hybridization programmes are likely to generate most variation, the techniques of transformation and mutation will be invaluable as a means of adding to the crop breeding material and providing the fine-tuning necessary in the commercial varieties.

New techniques to enable the transfer of polygenic characters between distantly related species are being developed in fruit crops, such as protoplast fusion (Vardi *et al.* 1975; James *et al.* 1984). Interesting developments may also stem from anther culture (Hidaka *et al.* 1979; Fei & Xue 1981). A further possibility is the use of gene transfer techniques, including specific DNA vectors such as *Agrobacterium tumefaciens*, which are being investigated as a means of introducing 'key' genes controlling specific enzyme systems in other crops.

IX. BREEDING PRIORITIES

Attempts to rapidly combine the desirable resistance, growth habit, yield and shelf life characteristics with all the important quality characteristics of fruit tree crops are hampered by the highly heterozygous nature of the parents, the long juvenile phase, and the necessity to make several crosses to combine all desirable features. Priorities have to be carefully decided, on the basis of feasibility and the prospects of producing new varieties which will make an early impact on the fruit industry. In apples, optimum values have been assigned to the main selection criteria which are used at the first fruiting stage (Alston 1985), and market demands have been considered by selecting fruits of specific types (Alston 1981).

High quality, high yield, low unit costs and easy harvesting (including tree size control) must remain the first priorities. Also, markets require a continuous supply of fruits, so it is desirable to extend the harvest period, by selecting for earlier or later maturity, and to select for storage ability.

Rootstocks should be bred primarily for better control of tree size and precocity (affecting yield) and improved nutrient uptake (affecting storage). There are also special cases where rootstock resistance to specific soil or site problems is recognizably a first priority.

It is vital that specific priorities are defined at the start. The greatest chances of success occur in programmes with limited aims involving large progenies and efficient selection procedures.

X. ACHIEVEMENTS

Outstanding advances have been made in tree fruit breeding. Selection within the MM series of apple rootstocks, bred specifically for woolly aphid resistance, resulted in the rootstock MM.106, which has become the standard semi-dwarfing apple rootstock in most of the world's apple-growing regions. Initial selection for woolly aphid resistance was followed by extensive pomological trialling before this rootstock was released. The release, more recently, of similar semi-dwarfing rootstocks of plum ('Pixy') and cherry ('Colt') promises to have a similar effect on those crops. The introduction of a rootstock for peach with nematode resistance (Nemaguard) is another significant achievement.

Breeding and selection have extended the peach marketing period, and the selection of varieties with low chilling requirements has enabled commercial peach production to be extended to warmer regions. The development of new easy peeling and seedless varieties has been an important factor in the citrus industry.

Examples of successfully introduced mutants include the nectarine, the Washington navel orange, and the red mutants of the apple variety 'Delicious'.

New, high-yielding, apple and pear varieties have been produced at East Malling which produce fruits with a high quality and storage potential; the new apple varieties can produce double the yield of top quality fruit compared with the present main English variety 'Cox's Orange Pippin'. Very promising disease-resistant apple and pear varieties have resulted from breeding programmes in North America, in particular those at Geneva, New York and Harrow, Ontario.

XI. CONCLUSIONS

Using the various techniques of plant breeding, there is considerable potential in all fruit tree crops to significantly increase the yield and profitability of plantations, providing regular supplies of high quality fruit and extending consumer choice. The importance of concentrated marketing campaigns to establish new varieties cannot be overlooked, particularly in the case of crops like apple where varieties are recognized not only by their fruit type but also by their name. Thus, the main English variety, 'Cox's Orange Pippin', is established with an individual 'brand image'.

The quality and disease resistance of fruits are likely to become an increasingly important breeding concern, following steps to limit spray residues and to improve nutritive values.

Breeding has often enabled fruit tree crops to spread to new environments, by introducing such features as *Phytophthora* resistance, chlorosis resistance, frost resistance and adaptation to warm winters. Present trends suggest an emphasis on apples as a world-wide fruit tree crop, as its cultivation spreads to new areas, including the tropics. Such developments must be supported by well-planned breeding programmes.

Continued progress in understanding and shortening the juvenile phase of fruit trees is of crucial importance for future progress. Preselection techniques, both in *in vitro* culture and in seedling nurseries, together with selection of precocious dwarf trees for use in intensive plantations, will also improve the efficiency and economy of most selection programmes.

Genetic manipulation techniques offer the possibility of introducing valuable characters into established varieties, but only rarely will such 'single step' improvements remove all the commercial and developmental limitations of established varieties. Improvement should proceed on a broad front, in which mutation and gene transformation techniques provide valuable aids in breeding programmes.

REFERENCES

Aldwinkle, H. S. & Lamb, R. C. (1976). Greenhouse forced flowering as a tool for resistance breeding. *Fruit Var. J.*, **30**, 11.

Alston, F. H. (1970a). Response of apple cultivars to canker, *Nectria galligena. Rep. E. Malling Res. Stn 1969*, 147–148.

Alston, F. H. (1970b). Resistance to collar rot *Phytophthora cactorum* (Leb. and Cohn.) Schroet., in apple. *Rep. E. Malling Res. Stn 1969*, 143–145.

Alston, F. H. (1973). Pear breeding at East Malling. *Proc. Symp. int. Soc. hort. Sci., Pear Growing, Angers, 1972*, 41–50.

Alston, F. H. (1975). Early stages in pear breeding at East Malling. *Proc. Eucarpia Fruit Sec. Symp., Top Fruit Breed., 5th, Canterbury, 1973*, 14–29.

Alston, F. H. (1977). Practical aspects of breeding for mildew (*Podosphaera leucotricha*) resistance in apples. *Proc. Eucarpia Fruit Sec. Symp., Top Fruit Breed., 6th, Wageningen, 1976*, 4–17.

Alston, F. H. (1981). Breeding high quality high yielding apples. In: *Quality in stored and processed vegetables and fruit*, edited by P. W. Goodenough and R. K. Atkin, 93–102. London: Academic Press.

Alston, F. H. (1983a). Progress in transferring mildew (*Podosphaera leucotricha*) resistance from *Malus* species to cultivated apple. *Bull. SROP/WPRS*, **6**(4), 87–95.

Alston, F. H. (1983b). Pear breeding, progress and prospects. *Proc. int. hort. Congr., 21st, Hamburg, 1982*, 127–137.

Alston, F. H. (1983c). Fireblight (*Erwinia amylovora*) resistance in the East Malling pear breeding programme. *Bull. SROP/WPRS*, **6**(4), 165–170.

Alston, F. H. (1985). Apple and pear breeding strategy. In: *The improvement of vegetatively propagated plants*, edited by A. I. Campbell, A. J. Abbot, and R. K. Atkin. London: Academic Press. In press.

Alston, F. H. & Bates, J. W. (1978). Apple canker (*Nectria galligena*). *Rep. E. Malling Res. Stn 1977*, 126.

Alston, F. H. & Bates, J. W. (1979). Selection for yield in apple progenies. *Proc. Eucarpia Fruit Sec. Symp., Tree Fruit Breed., Angers*, 15–27.

Alston, F. H. & Briggs, J. B. (1968). Resistance to *Sappaphis devecta* in apple. *Euphytica*, **13**, 468–472.

Alston, F. H. & Briggs, J. B. (1970). Inheritance of hyper-sensitivity to rosy apple aphis *Dysaphis plantaginea* in apple. *Can. J. Genet. Cytol.*, **12**, 257–258.

Alston, F. H. & Watkins, R. (1975). Apple breeding at East Malling. *Proc. Eucarpia Fruit Sec. Symp., Top Fruit Breed., 5th, Canterbury, 1973*, 1–13.

Alston, F. H. & Watkins, R. (1984). Future apple and pear cultivars – quality, techniques, testing. In: *Apples and pears*, edited by Elspeth Napier, 97–105. London: Royal Horticultural Society.

Barrientos-Perez, F. & Sanchez-Colin, S. (1983). Height variability obtained from a new dwarf avocado tree population. *Acta Hortic.*, **140**, 163–165.

Beakbane, A. B. (1967). The dwarfing effect of a tetraploid sport of M.XIII apple rootstock. *Rep. E. Malling Res. Stn 1966*, 96–97.

Beakbane, A. B. & Majumder, P. K. (1975). A relationship between stomatal density and growth potential in apple rootstocks. *J. hort. Sci.*, **50**, 285–289.

Beakbane, A. B. & Thompson, E. C. (1939). Anatomical studies of stems and roots of hardy fruit trees. II. The internal structure of the roots of some vigorous and some dwarfing apple rootstocks and the correlation of structure with vigour. *J. Pomol.*, **17**, 141–149.

Bell, R. L., Janick, J., Zimmerman, R. H., Zwet, T. van der & Blake, R. C. (1981). Response of pear to inbreeding. *J. Am. Soc. hort. Sci.*, **106**, 584–589.

Bergh, B. O. (1975). Avocados. In: *Advances in fruit breeding*, edited by J. Janick and J. N. Moore, 541–567. West Lafayette, IN: Purdue University Press.

Bergh, B. O. (1976). Avocado breeding and selection. *Proc. int. Trop. Fruit short course, The Avocado, 1st, Gainesville*, 24–32.

Bowen, H. H. (1971). Breeding peaches for warm climates. *HortScience*, **6**, 153–157.

Brown, A. G. (1959). The inheritance of mildew resistance in progenies of the cultivated apple. *Euphytica*, **8**, 81–88.

Brown, A. G. (1975). The effect of inbreeding on vigour and the length of juvenile period in apples. *Proc. Eucarpia Fruit Sec. Symp., Top Fruit Breed., 5th, Canterbury, 1973*, 30–39.

Campbell, A. I. & Lacy, C. N. D. (1982). Induced mutants of Cox's Orange Pippin apple with increased self-compatibility. I. Production and selection. *Euphytica*, **31**, 469–475.

Cummins, J. N., Aldwinkle, H. S. & Byers, R. E. (1983). Novole apple. *HortScience*, **18**, 772–774.

Einset, J. (1947). Apple breeding enters a new era. *Fm Res., N.Y.*, **13**(2), 5.

Esen, A. & Soost, R. K. (1972). Unexpected triploids in *Citrus*, their origin, identification and possible use. *J. Hered.*, **62**, 329–333.

Fei, K. W. & Xue, G. R. (1981). (Induction of haploid plantlets by anther culture in the apple variety Delicious). *Sci. Agric. Sin.*, **44**, 41–47.

Freigoun, S. O. & Crosse, J. E. (1975). Host relations and distribution of a physiological and pathological variant of *Pseudomonas morsprunorum*. *Ann. appl. Biol.*, **81**, 317–330.

Goliadaze, S. K. (1980). (Problems of breeding citrus crops for resistance to frost and *Deuterophoma tracheiphila*). *Subtrop. Kult.*, no. 3/4, 111–115.

Gormley, R. (1981). Dietary fibre – some properties of alcohol-insoluble solids residues from apples. *J. Sci. Fd Agric.*, **32**, 392–398.

Hansche, P. E. & Beres, W. (1980). Genetic remodelling of fruit and nut trees to facilitate cultivar improvement. *HortScience*, **15**, 710–715.

Hensz, R. A. (1971). Star Ruby, a new deep red-fleshed grapefruit variety with distinct tree characteristics. *J. Rio Grande Vall. hort. Soc.*, **25**, 54–58.

Hesse, C. O. (1975). Peaches. In: *Advances in fruit breeding*, edited by J. Janick and J. N. Moore, 285–335. West Lafayette, IN: Purdue University Press.

Hidaka, T., Yamada, Y. & Shichijo, T. (1979). *In vitro* differentiation of haploid plants by anther culture in *Poncirus trifoliata* (L.) Raf. *Jap. J. Breed.*, **29**, 248–254.

Holub, J. (1981). (Pollen germination and pollen tube growth in selected peach varieties, in relation to temperature). *Sb. vys. Sk. Zeměd. Praze*, A, **34**, 235–249.

Hurter, N. (1962). Inheritance of flesh colour in the fruit of the Japanese plum, *Prunus salicina*. *S. Afr. J. agric. Sci.*, **5**, 673–674.

James, D. J., Passey, A. J. & Malhotra, S. B. (1984). Isolation and fusion of protoplasts. *Rep. E. Malling Res. Stn 1983*, 63.

Janick, J. & Moore, J. N., eds. (1975). *Advances in fruit breeding*. West Lafayette, IN: Purdue University Press.

Jonkers, H. (1971). An international experiment on juvenility in apple. *Euphytica*, **20**, 57–59.

Kennedy, A. J., Werts, J. M. & Watkins, R. (1982). An analysis of mineral uptake in apple rootstock seedlings. *Theoret. appl. Genet.*, **61**, 141–144.

Knight, R. L. (1963). Abstract bibliography of fruit breeding and genetics to 1960, *Malus* and *Pyrus*. *Tech. Commun. Commonw. Bur. Hort. Plantn Crops*, no. 29.

Knight, R. L. (1966). Progress in breeding apples and pears. *Proc. Balsgard Fruit Breed. Symp.*, *1964*,129–146.

Knight, R. L. (1969). Abstract bibliography of fruit breeding and genetics to 1965, *Prunus*. *Tech. Commun. Commonw. Bur. Hort. Plantn Crops*, no. 31.

Kochba, J., Ben-Hayyim, G., Spiegel-Roy, P., Saad, S. & Neumann, H. (1982). Selection of stable salt-tolerant callus cell lines and embryos in *Citrus sinensis* and *C. aurantium*. *Z. PflPhysiol.*, **106**, 111–118.

Kruger, J. (1983). Anfälligkeiten von Apfelsorten und Kreuzungsnachkommenshaften für den Obstbaumkrebs nach natürlicher und künstlicher Infektion. *Erwerbsobstbau*, **25**, 114–116.

Lacy, C. N. D. (1982). The stability of induced compact mutant clones of Bramley's Seedling apple. *Euphytica*, **31**, 451–459.

Lammerts, W. E. (1945). The breeding of ornamental edible peaches for mild climates. I. Inheritance of tree and flower characters. *Am. J. Bot.*, **32**, 53–61.

Lapins, K. O. (1963). Compact mutants of Lambert cherry produced by ionizing radiation. *Can. J. Pl. Sci.*, **43**, 424–425.

Lapins, K. O. (1969). Segregation of compact growth types in certain apple seedling progenies. *Can. J. Pl. Sci.*, **49**, 765–768.

Lapins, K. O. (1971). Stella, a self-fruitful sweet cherry. *Can. J. Pl. Sci.*, **51**, 252–253.

Layne, R. E. C. & Harrison, T. B. (1975). 'Haggith' apricot: rootstock seed source. *HortScience*, **10**, 428.

Le Lezec, M. (1973). Quelques variétés de pommier pour un renouvellement du verger Français. *Pomol. fr.*, **15**, 111–115.

Lesley, J. W. (1957). A genetic study of inbreeding and of crossing inbred lines in peaches. *Proc. Am. Soc. hort. Sci.*, **70**, 93–103.

Luckwill, L. C. & Campbell, A. I. (1954). The use of apomictic seedling rootstocks for apples. Progress report. *Rep. Long Ashton Res. Stn 1953*, 47–52.

Macoun, W. T. (1928). Progress in apple breeding in Canada. *Proc. Am. Soc. hort. Sci.*, **25**, 117–122.

Maison, P., Kerlan, C. & Massonié, G. (1983). Sélection de semis *Prunus persica* (L.) Batsch résistants à la transmission du virus de la sharka par la virginopares aptères de *Myzus persicae* Sulzer. *C.r. hebd. Séanc. Acad. Agric. Fr.*, **69**, 337–346.

Matthews, P. (1979). Progress in breeding cherries for resistance to bacterial canker. *Proc. Eucarpia Fruit Sec. Symp., Tree Fruit Breed., Angers*, 157–163.

Moore, J. N. & Janick, J., eds. (1983). *Methods in fruit breeding.* West Lafayette, IN: Purdue University Press.

Oppenheimer, C. H. & Slor, E. (1968). Breeding apples for a subtropical climate. II. Analysis of two F_2 and nine backcross populations. *Theoret. appl. Genet.,* **38**, 97–102.

Petropoulou, S. P. (1984). Selection for temperature tolerance. *Rep. E. Malling Res. Stn 1983,* 135.

Potapov, S. P. (1971). (Inheritance of earliness in pear seedlings). *Izv. Timiryazev. sel'.-hoz. Akad.,* **6**, 124–134.

Preston, A. P. (1966). Apple rootstock studies: fifteen years' results with Malling-Merton clones. *J. hort. Sci.,* **41**, 349–360.

Quamme, H. A. & Spearman, G. A. (1983). Harvest Queen and Harrow Delight pear. *HortScience,* **18**, 770–772.

Rouselle, G. L., Williams, E. B. & Hough, L. F. (1975). Modification of the level of resistance to apple scab from the V_f gene. *Proc. int. hort. Congr., 19th, Warsaw, 1974,* **3**, 193–195.

Schmidt, H. & Kruger, J. (1983). Fruit Breeding at the Federal Research Centre for Horticultural Plant Breeding, Ahrensburg/Holstein. *Acta Hortic.,* **140**, 15–33.

Sharpe, R. H., Hesse, C. O., Lownsberry, B. F., Perry, V. G. & Hansen, C. J. (1969). Breeding peaches for root-knot nematode resistance. *J. Am. Soc. hort. Sci.,* **94**, 209–212.

Sherman, W. B., Sharpe, R. H. & Janick, J. (1973). The fruiting nursery: ultrahigh density for evaluation of blueberry and peach seedlings. *HortScience,* **8**, 170–172.

Sherman, W. B., Andrews, C. P., Lyrene, P. M. & Sharpe, R. H. (1982). Flordahome, a pear for home owners in north and central Florida. *Circ. Fla Univ. agric. Exp. Stn,* no. S–287.

Solovyeva, L. V. (1982). The number of chloroplasts in stomata guard cells as a ploidy test in apple. *Abstr int. hort. Congr., 21st, Hamburg,* **1**, 1044.

Spangelo, L. P. S. (1971). Hybrid seedling rootstocks for apple. *Publs Can. Dep. Agric.,* no. 1431.

Spiegel-Roy, P. & Alston, F. H. (1979). Chilling and post dormant heat requirement as selection criteria for late flowering pears. *J. hort. Sci.,* **54**, 115–120.

Spiegel-Roy, P. & Vardi, A. (1983). Citrus breeding and genetics. *Proc. int. hort. Congr., 21st, Hamburg, 1982,* 407–414.

Spiegel-Roy, P., Kochba, J. & Saad, S. (1983). Selection for tolerance to 2–4–dichlorophenoxyacetic acid in ovular callus of orange (*Citrus sinensis*). *Z. Pflanzenphysiol.,* **109**, 41–48.

Stebbins, G. L. (1980). Polyploidy in plants unsolved problems and prospects. In: *Polyploidy, biological relevance,* edited by W. H. Lewis, 495–520. New York: Plenum.

Stushnoff, C. & Garley, B. (1980). Breeding for cold hardiness. In: *The pear,* edited by T. van der Zwet and N. F. Childers, 189–199. Gainesville, FLA.

Tobutt, K. R. (1985). Breeding columnar apples. *Acta Hortic.* In press.

Thibault, B. (1979). Étude de la transmission de quelques caractères dans la descendances de poirier. *Proc. Eucarpia Fruit Sec. Symp., Tree Fruit Breed., Angers,* 47–58.

Tydeman, H. M. (1933). Breeding experiments with 'paradise' apple rootstocks. *J. Pomol.,* **9**, 214–236.

Tydeman, H. M. (1943). Further studies on new varieties of apple rootstocks. *J. Pomol.,* **20**, 116–126.

Tydeman, H. M. (1964). The relation between time of leaf break and of flowering in seedling apples. *Rep. E. Malling Res. Stn 1963,* 70–72.

Tydeman, H. M. & Alston, F. H. (1965). The influence of dwarfing rootstocks in shortening the juvenile phase of apple seedlings. *Rep. E. Malling Res. Stn 1964,* 97–98.

Vardi, A., Spiegel-Roy, P. & Galun, E. (1975). *Citrus* cell culture: isolation of protoplasts, planting densities, effect of mutagens and regeneration of embryoids. *Plant Sci. Lett.,* **4**, 231–236.

Visser, T. (1976). A comparison of apple and pear seedlings with reference to the juvenile period. II. Mode of inheritance. *Euphytica,* **25**, 339–342.

Visser, T. & De Vries, D. P. (1970). Precocity and productivity of propagated apple and pear seedlings dependent on the juvenile period. *Euphytica,* **19**, 141–144.

Visser, T. & Verhaegh, J. J. (1978). Inheritance of some fruit characters of apple. II. The relationship between leaf and fruit pH as a basis for pre-selection. *Euphytica,* **27**, 761–765.

Watkins, R. & Werts, J. M. (1971). Preselection for *Phytophthora cactorum* (Leb. and Cohn.) Schroet., resistance in apple seedlings. *Ann. appl. Biol.,* **67**, 153–156.

Wilson, D., Jones, R. P. & Reeves, J. (1975). Selection for prolonged winter dormancy as a possible aid to improving yield stability in European plum (*Prunus domestica* L.). *Euphytica*, **24**, 815–819.

Zimmerman, R. H. (1972). Juvenility and flowering in woody plants: a review. *HortScience*, **7**, 447–455.

Zimmerman, R. H. (1977). Relation of pear seedling size to length of juvenile period. *J. Am. Soc. hort. Sci.*, **102**, 443–447.

Zwet, T. van der. (1977). Comparative sensitivity and response of various *Pyrus* tissues to infection by *Erwinia amylovora*. (Current topics in plant pathology). *Symp. Hung. Acad. Sci., Budapest, 1976,* 263–276.

Zwet, T. van der & Keil, H. L. (1979). *Fireblight, a bacterial disease of rosaceous plants.* (Handbk Science and Education Administration, no. 510). Washington DC: United States Department of Agriculture.

5

STRATEGIES FOR OPTIMIZING THE YIELD OF TREE CROPS IN SUBOPTIMAL ENVIRONMENTS

H. G. JONES
East Malling Research Station, Maidstone, Kent, England

I. INTRODUCTION

This paper presents a broad introduction to the principles that must be considered when attempting to improve yields of tree crops in suboptimal environments, and highlights those ways in which the special features of trees are likely to result in approaches that are different from those appropriate to other crops. More detailed discussion of some of the specific points raised will be presented in succeeding chapters of this book.

The economic yield of tree crops can vary from only a very small proportion of net primary production (eg in sugar maple the yield of syrup may be less than 1% of primary production), through fruit crops (where 60% or more of annual dry matter production may end up in fruit – eg Avery 1975) and conventional forestry, to systems where almost all production is used, as for example in biomass production (see Cannell, this volume). It is therefore difficult to generalize about methods to improve yields. In all cases, however, the economic yield can be regarded as the product of three components: (a) the net primary production, (b) the proportion of assimilate that is converted to useful yield (ie the harvest index), and (c) the quality of the product. Although methods for improving the harvest index and quality are very crop-specific, it is possible to make useful generalizations concerning primary production, so I shall concentrate on this aspect.

Before proceeding further, it is necessary to consider what is meant by a suboptimal environment. Although one may have a general idea of an 'ideal' environment, with fertile soil, moderate temperatures and ample water and radiation, many crops have evolved in, and become adapted to, environments very far from this ideal. In terms of primary productivity of the best-adapted species growing under natural conditions, there are great differences between trees in the poorest climates (polar areas, cold deserts and hot arid deserts) and those found in warm-temperate to tropical regions, with long growing seasons and ample rainfall. For example, many coniferous forest species evolved in the subarctic, with its characteristically short season, low temperatures and nutrient-deficient soils, while other species are adapted to Mediterranean (eg citrus and olive), semi-arid (eg apricot) or even arid (eg date palm) climates where lack of water is the major factor limiting yields and even plant survival. Yet other species (eg coffee and cacao) have evolved in the shady understorey of tropical forests, where low light limits potential yields. A wide range of other factors, including soil problems such as salinity, water-logging and metal toxicities (eg aluminium toxicity), and aerial factors such as fire and high windspeeds, can also restrict the yields of tree crops.

Within each climatic zone, certain plant species may be particularly well adapted and may have a competitive advantage. The actual productivity of a plant in any particular environment is a function both of the climatic potential and of the degree of adaptation.

Although indigenous species may be adapted to these non-ideal environments, in that they are successful competitors in such situations, it does not follow that they will perform best there. When transferred to 'better' environments, productivity and yield may increase dramatically, particularly if interspecific competition and certain pathogens are eliminated or reduced – as they usually are in managed horticultural or forestry plantations. A well-known example is *Pinus radiata*, which is extremely productive when grown, for instance, in New Zealand, but is not so productive over its native range in California.

It follows from the above discussion that even the natural habitat of a species is usually suboptimal to some extent, so that the problem of yield improvement is, at least partially, a question of improving 'stress tolerance'. Even in those cases where a genotype has evolved in a particular environment and actually grows best there, that environment may still be limiting, and hence suboptimal. Related species or ecotypes from elsewhere may have fewer specific adaptations (which frequently have some yield penalty), and thus may have a greater yield potential.

It is possible, at least in principle, to determine experimentally the optimal conditions for any one species. We can then regard any deviation from that environment as suboptimal for that species. Clearly, a particular environment may be suboptimal for one species because, for example, temperatures may be too low, and suboptimal for another because temperatures are too high.

A further point that needs explaining is the use in the title of the term 'optimizing yield' rather than 'maximizing yield'. Although the long-term objective, where trees are grown as crop plants, is generally to maximize the total long-term yield, it does not follow that the way to achieve this objective is to maximize the yield in each year. For example, too much early seed production, as often occurs in response to stresses such as drought, flooding, disease, insect attacks or nutrient deficiencies (see Wolgast & Zeide 1983),

limits vegetative growth and delays the attainment of maximum production
(see below).

II. SPECIAL FEATURES OF TREES

Rational manipulation of tree morphology or physiology, and rational management require an understanding of the special features of trees, the reasons for
the evolution of this life form, and of those situations where trees are particularly well adapted. This knowledge is valuable when determining the ideal
plant types (ideotypes) for particular environments, particularly if one is to
make the most of the existing genetic base. Furthermore, the differences
between trees and herbaceous crops, both in their physiology and in the
ways in which they interact with the environment (eg coupling through the
boundary layer – see below), can mean that the approaches to yield improvement in stress conditions that are used for field crops may not be appropriate
for trees.

It can be argued that the primary factor determining the evolution of the
tree life form has been the competitive advantage of growing tall and intercepting light at the expense of other vegetation (see Walter 1973; Newman 1983;
Schulze 1982). This advantage, together with the extreme longevity of trees,
enables them to form the climax vegetation in many environments. Other
factors, such as resistance to grazing, may also be important (Walter 1973).
The evolution of the perennial habit, and of the massive woody stem, has
been necessary for the development of adequate height. Because the mass of
the necessary supporting structure increases approximately with the cube of
plant height, the assimilate available in one year usually limits the height of
annual plants to about two or three metres. Even the size of a perennial herb
is limited, by the fact that the assimilate available from a given leaf area is
adequate to support the maintenance respiration of only a limited amount of
non-photosynthetic tissue. The factor that enables trees to grow so much
larger than even perennial herbs is that much of the support and transport
function is provided by non-living woody tissue, with zero respiratory
demand.

It is relevant to consider how far this evolutionary background constrains
tree crop yield. In many managed systems, such as fruit orchards, the
competitive advantage conferred by height is no longer needed, because in a
closely planted, even-sized monoculture, height would not be expected to
influence radiation interception. (It is worth noting here that, in practice,
there is a slight tendency for radiation absorption by crop canopies to increase
with height, though the effect is small (at most a few per cent) and inconsistent
– see Stanhill 1981). Another potential advantage conferred by height –
resistance to grazing – is also unlikely to be as important in cultivation as in
the wild. In fact, height may be a positive disadvantage for high productivity,
because leaf water potential decreases with increasing height as a result of the
increasing frictional resistance to transpiration (eg Paltridge 1973). It is only
in forestry, where the height and mass of large stems is a component of yield,
that there is a good argument for retaining the traditional tree form.

The long period of growth required before a tree can achieve a mature size has the corollary that it would normally be advantageous in the wild to possess a long juvenile period before flowering occurs. One reason for this is the obvious competitive advantage conferred where all assimilate is used for growth in the crucial early years of establishment, leaving none available for reproductive development. Another argument has been suggested by Cohen (1971) (see also Paltridge & Denholm 1974), who presented a simple proof that, for a fixed environment, seed yield is maximal when the life cycle is partitioned into a wholly vegetative phase followed by a reproductive phase, with a complete switch between the two at an appropriate time. This behaviour is common in determinate annual species (eg wheat) and is found in monocarpic perennials (eg bamboo). In most trees, however, the reproductive phase, once started, continues for many years, along with some vegetative growth. This is what might be called a 'pessimistic' adaptation (see Jones 1979) in that it allows some reproduction, even if conditions are not good enough to enable the tree to reach full maturity. The possession of a drawn-out flowering period is particularly important as a pessimistic or conservative response for plants growing in very variable climates, especially where conditions are marginal and there is a significant probability of a plant dying in any one year (Jones 1981).

In most trees, there is a general tendency for stress to increase the proportion of effort devoted to reproduction (eg Grierson et al. 1982; Wolgast & Zeide 1983), presumably improving the chance of genetic survival. This trend can, however, be reversed in mature trees (once enough seed production has occurred to ensure survival of the genes). For example, irrigation of mature fruit trees is necessary to maintain maximum fruit yield in many situations (see, eg, Kriedemann & Barrs 1981; Landsberg & Jones 1981; Chalmers et al. 1983) while Wolgast and Zeide (1983) showed that, in contrast to the effect in young trees, a decrease of nutrient stress by fertilizer application to older oak trees (more than 13 years old) led to an increased reproductive effort in both absolute and relative terms.

Elimination or reduction of the juvenile period has particular value in speeding the process of tree breeding, while in fruit crops early fruiting can have large economic benefits, particularly where high-density planting systems are adopted, so that the initial establishment of a large flower-bearing framework is not required. The use of smaller plants, with shorter life cycles, grown at high densities, also means that the 'cost' of losing individuals is less significant than for plants with long juvenile periods. This suggests that, at least for horticultural applications, it is likely that a useful approach would be to breed more 'optimistic' genotypes, that divert a greater proportion of resources to reproduction, rather than those having the characteristic pessimistic tree trait of partitioning carbohydrate so as to ensure survival of the individual in the worst conditions likely to occur.

Another pessimistic characteristic of trees is their tendency to favour stress tolerance or survival mechanisms at the expense of high productivity. For example, some tree species tend to have a particularly marked stomatal closure in response to increased humidity deficits in the air (see Bradford & Hsiao 1982), which may help to stabilize transpiration rates from forests (Roberts 1983).

Two other relevant biological features of the tree life form are as follows. First, the large environmental buffering capacity that it confers, particularly in terms of the capacity for damping rapid environmental changes (eg short-term temperature and water status fluctuations are damped within tree tissues as a result of the large thermal mass and water content of the trunk); longer-term buffering is provided by the tree's capacity to withstand relatively long stress periods, partly by using the substantial carbohydrate reserves that can build up in woody tissues (eg Priestley 1970). Second, the perennial framework (taken to an extreme in evergreen species) provides a mechanism allowing almost complete utilization of short growing season environments.

Another important feature of trees is the effect that plant height has on heat and mass transfer through the crop boundary layer and on the 'coupling' between plant and atmosphere (Jarvis 1981, and this volume). The aero-dynamic roughness of a plant canopy, and hence the canopy conductance for heat and mass transfer, increases with crop height and is probably also enhanced for spaced plants, as in many orchards (Monteith 1973). The high boundary layer conductance of tree crops results in their evaporation rates being much more closely determined by changes in stomatal conductance than is the case in field crops (Jarvis 1981, and this volume). These effects can have important implications for optimization of water use efficiency in tree crops, in comparison with herbaceous plants (eg Jones 1976).

In the remainder of this paper, I shall consider how far it may be possible to make the most of specific features of trees, or to overcome some of their special disadvantages, when attempting to improve yields in marginal environments.

III. METHODS AVAILABLE FOR IMPROVING YIELD

Techniques available for obtaining yield improvements include (a) the use of improved management systems, (b) the breeding or introduction of new, specifically adapted cultivars, and (c) the use of different, better-adapted species. Management approaches can include those that attempt to eliminate or reduce specific environmental constraints, such as the use of irrigation where water is limiting, frost protection (eg by heating or water sprinkling), fertilizer application, and even manipulation of the light environment (eg the use of shade trees). However, I shall not consider such environmental manipulations further, and shall concentrate on those methods that affect the plant or its response.

Appropriate management procedures include the use of artificial growth regulators to modify tree growth, flowering, fruit set, tree size, stomatal behaviour, etc, and the use of different planting systems, as well as pruning, thinning and training practices to optimize yield production or light intercep-tion.

Whether yield improvements are to be achieved by breeding, or by changes in management practices, depends on the relative ease of making the required changes in plant type by each approach. Although some yield improvements can be, and have been, obtained from entirely empirical studies where only final yields are studied, there is enormous potential for a more physiological approach based on improvement of particular components of the yield process. The determination of the particular character required is a process that is common to both breeding and management approaches and will be discussed in the next section.

IV. DETERMINATION OF OPTIMUM PLANT TYPES

The elucidation of optimal plant types or ideotypes for high yield (whether to be achieved by breeding or by management) is a difficult problem, not least because of the complex interactions and internal compensations and feedbacks involved in the yield process (Jones 1983). The best plant for any particular situation involves a series of compromises between conflicting requirements. For example, if one considers a case where drought is the main limiting factor, the partitioning of carbohydrate between root and shoot, or between yield and continued root growth, must be optimized, as must the degree of stomatal opening (Jones 1981).

The procedures for determining ideotypes in trees are the same as those available for other crops, though the constraints upon the chosen combination of characters are going to be different. It is probably true to say that, in the past, most advances have relied on empiricism, and what might be called 'inspired guesswork' (usually based on long experience), and that there has been relatively little successful application of the physiological or reductionist approach. In some cases, particularly when concerned with stress tolerance, it is possible to use an intermediate approach, and screen for the character without attempting to determine the precise physiological mechanism involved. For example, improvements in stress tolerance can be achieved by selecting seedlings for survival at high temperatures or high salinity, while similar screens can also be applied to populations of cells in culture. Because stress tolerance (in terms of survival) is usually negatively related to yield, it is necessary to combine this type of screen with one for yield.

Perhaps the most powerful tool for identifying appropriate ideotypes is the mathematical model, which enables one to investigate the consequences of possible alterations in plant characters, both to determine the optimum combination of characters for any environment, and to identify those characters where greatest yield improvements could be achieved with least effort (eg Brunig 1976; Rose & Charles-Edwards 1981; Jones 1983). Effective modelling requires (a) a knowledge of the environment, including the probability distributions for different weather conditions, (b) a knowledge of the particular environmental factors limiting yield, (c) an understanding of the way each character considered contributes to yield, and the control mechanisms involved, and (d) – as an essential final step before large-scale application of the results to management or breeding – a validation of the chosen ideotype or management strategy. One technique is to use isogenic lines, but the long generation time in most tree crops, coupled with the extensive backcrossing required, limits its value in tree crops. In such cases, use of naturally occurring sports or artificially induced mutants may be more practical.

I shall now illustrate the application of modelling to the identification of frost- or drought-tolerant genotypes.

A.   Avoidance of spring frosts

The use of modelling can be demonstrated by using a very simple model to investigate the ideal time for flowering in fruit crops so as to maximize production. The ideal flowering date should be late enough to escape damage by late spring frosts in most years, yet early enough to allow sufficient time for fruit growth. Using a knowledge of the sensitivity of flower buds to freezing temperatures at various stages in their development, and of the normal rate

TABLE I.   Stages of apple fruit bud development, the normal date each stage is reached (mean for the years 1955-64 for Cox's Orange Pippin at East Malling, from Hamer 1980), and critical temperatures at which 50% of the buds are killed (Richardson *et al.* 1976)

Development stage	Normal date	Critical temperature (°C)
Bud burst	1 April	−10·0
Mouse ear (3–4 leaves)	6 April	−7·2
Green cluster (5+ leaves)	16 April	−4·4
Pink bud (half buds coloured)	24 April	−3·3
Open flower (first open)	2 May	−2·8

of flower bud development (Table I), together with a meteorological record of the occurrence of frosts over many years at a particular site, it is possible to calculate the earliest date, in each of those years, when the plant of interest could have flowered without significant frost damage. This enables one to determine the probability (f(d)) of at least 50% of flower buds surviving for plants flowering on any date (d) (Fig. 1). At East Malling, there are about 60

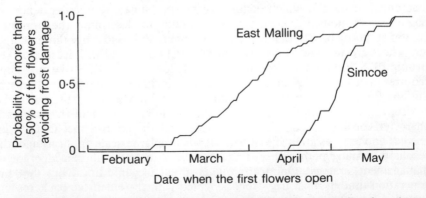

FIGURE 1.   Probability of more than 50% of apple flower buds avoiding frost damage on trees flowering on different dates at East Malling, England, and Simcoe, Ontario. Distributions were calculated using the developmental sequence and frost sensitivities given in Table I, and frost records for 1925–83 (East Malling) and 1953–79 (Simcoe).

days between the dates when there are 90% and 10% probabilities of damaging frosts. In the more continental climate of Simcoe, Ontario, the corresponding period is about 25 days. The simple calculation used to obtain Figure 1 could be improved by modifying the rate of bud development according to prevailing temperatures (Hamer, unpublished data); this narrows the range of dates where damage is uncertain, but it has only a small effect on the final conclusions.

The relationship between the average annual yield ($\bar{Y}$) and the flowering date (d) can be expressed as

$$\bar{Y}=f(d).Y(d)$$

where $Y(d)$ is the expected yield in the absence of frost damage. Unfortunately, our understanding of how $Y(d)$ varies with flowering date is incomplete; many factors such as the effects of fruit set on fruit size, and environmental effects on fruit growth and maturity, need to be considered in a complete model. However, it is instructive to consider some possible extremes. One extreme is that the potential yield is not affected by flowering date: this gives a yield probability distribution of the same form as Figure 1, where the long-term average yield would increase to a maximum with later flowering. This would imply that the genotypes that flowered latest would be the best. In practice, however, there is likely to be some decrease in yield potential with later flowering, though the magnitude of this effect is uncertain. In a rather similar model, used to estimate the optimum date on which frost-sensitive shoot buds should initiate growth, Lockhart (1983) assumed that $Y(d)$ was simply proportional to the length of the growing season. Although useful, this is clearly too simplistic, because radiation and temperature are also important, especially in the spring.

For apple, the date of fruit maturity is relatively little affected, for any cultivar, when flowering is delayed or advanced by altered temperatures (Luton & Hamer 1983), so that we can assume a fixed date of maturity as another extreme, and make the extreme assumption that potential fruit yield is proportional to the radiation receipt between flowering and maturity. (This assumption is clearly unrealistic, because the time between flowering and maturity is a function of summer temperature (Denne 1963), and probably also of other climatic factors.) The yield probability distributions calculated on this basis for fruits with two different maturity dates at East Malling are presented in Figure 2. This extreme calculation is likely to over-estimate, significantly, the effect of flowering date on potential yield, but, as the precise effect is not known, we shall have to assume a real result somewhere between the two extremes.

Notwithstanding the uncertainty, it is clear from Figure 2 that there is only a slight disadvantage in delaying flowering until all risk of frost is over. This is true for plants with either short or long fruit growth periods, as long as the available growing period (before the onset of autumn frosts or severe water stress) is long enough. As a final general point, it should be noted that the best flowering date may also depend on the economic situation of the farmer concerned. Some farmers may be more concerned with avoiding serious frost damage every year, even if that prevented them from obtaining the maximum possible yield, while others may wish to maximize the long-term average yield (or, more likely, the long-term average income).

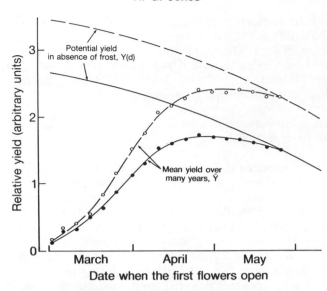

FIGURE 2.   The effect of flowering time on the relative yield of apple trees growing at East Malling. The solid lines refer to fruit maturing on 15 August, and the dashed lines to fruit maturing on 31 October. The upper line in each case represents the potential yield in the absence of frost damage (assumed proportional to total incident radiation over the period), while the lower line is the mean yield over many years.

B.   Drought tolerance

Because of the widespread importance of drought to crop production, there have been many attempts to define characters that confer drought tolerance, but those characters generally conflict with those required for high yield, so that optimization is necessary for any particular crop and environment combination.

Optimization theory has been used, for example, to investigate the optimal partitioning of carbohydrates between root and shoot. Schulze *et al.* (1983) showed that, when water is not limiting, maximum biomass is achieved by a plant that partitions the minimum amount of carbohydrate to new roots required to maintain its leaf water status. Unfortunately, this model does not consider the situation where soil water becomes limiting, in which case a more pessimistic behaviour would be better, with the degree of pessimism depending on the probability of future rainfall (Jones 1981). Other models have been used to investigate optimal root system form (Landsberg & Fowkes 1978) and especially stomatal behaviour (Jones 1976, 1981; Cowan & Farquhar 1977; Cowan 1982). It is, however, only in relation to stomatal behaviour that attempts have been made to extend the models to more realistic variable climates (Jones 1981; Cowan 1982). In general, the more variable the climate, the greater the advantage of the more pessimistic responses. Unfortunately, this type of approach has not yet been applied explicitly to tree crops, which are frequently better able to survive periods of severe drought (eg by going dormant) than annual crops, though the models (particularly that of Cowan 1982) could be applied to perennial plants.

The main considerations relating to optimal water use (whether controlled by stomatal movements or by leaf area changes) are illustrated in Figure 3. This figure shows how the optimum assimilation rate (assumed to be closely related to the evaporation rate) changes during a rain-free period. All curves indicate that the rate of water use should ideally decline with time during a rainless period (when the length of that period varies randomly), with the

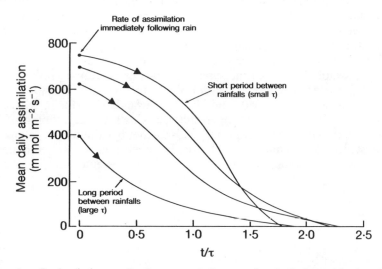

FIGURE 3. Optimal changes in the mean daily rate of assimilation with t/τ, where t is the time since it last rained, and τ is the average interval between rainfalls. The different curves represent the optimal sequences for different initial rates of water use (and hence assimilation), and depend, among other things, on τ, with low initial rates being necessary if the expected wait until the next rainfall is long (after Cowan 1982).

exact shape of the curves depending on the probability of rainfall (represented by τ – the average time between rainfalls) and on processes that compete for water (eg soil evaporation) (Cowan 1982). Where the average time between rainfalls is short (the upper curves), higher mean rates of assimilation (and of water use) can be sustained without the plants being likely to die from drought. The lower curves represent the more conservative behaviour necessary when the period between rainfalls is long. This information can help in the definition of ideal patterns of stomatal behaviour or leaf area development for specific environments.

V. CONCLUSIONS

It has not been possible, in a paper of this length, to discuss in detail all the ways in which yields of different tree crops can be optimized in all types of suboptimal environment. What I have attempted to do is highlight those ways in which trees differ from many agricultural crops, and to illustrate the ways in which this information can be used in studies to identify the appropriate crop ideotypes for specific situations. In particular, it is clear that it is necessary to identify those features of any environment that are most limiting. It is also worth remembering that both breeding and management approaches to yield improvement in managed crops need not be constrained by those characteristics of trees that have evolved solely as an adaptation to natural environments (eg competitive ability).

Despite the tremendous potential for improvement that exists in tree crops, the advances that have been made to date have been attributable largely to improved management and not to improved genotypes. A major factor contributing to the slow genetic improvement of tree crops is the extremely long-term nature of a tree breeding programme. The magnitude of improvements achievable by altered management practice is clear from the fact that mean apple yields have more than doubled since the early 1950s in both the UK (Jackson & Hamer 1980) and the Netherlands (Wertheim 1980). The data for the UK apply to a single cultivar (Cox's Orange Pippin). There remains enormous scope to improve yields further by adopting novel management systems (such as meadow orchards, Luckwill et al. 1972), increasing the use of growth regulators, and making genetic improvements.

REFERENCES

Avery, D. J. (1975). Reduction in growth increments by crop competition. In: *Climate and the orchard*, edited by H. C. Pereira, 103–106. (Research review no. 5). Farnham Royal: Commonwealth Bureau of Horticulture and Plantation Crops.

Bradford, K. J. & Hsiao, T. C. (1982). Physiological responses to moderate stress. In: *Physiological plant ecology*, vol. 2, edited by O. L. Lange et al., 263–324. (Encyclopedia of plant physiology, vol. 12B). Berlin: Springer.

Brunig, E. F. (1976). Tree forms in relation to environmental conditions: an ecological viewpoint. In: *Tree physiology and yield improvement*, edited by M. G. R. Cannell and F. T. Last, 139–156. London: Academic Press.

Chalmers, D. J., Olsson, K. A. & Jones, T. R. (1983). Water relations of peach trees and orchards. In: *Water deficits and plant growth*, vol. 7, edited by T. T. Kozlowski, 197–232. London: Academic Press.

Cohen, D. (1971). Maximizing final yield when growth is limited by time or by limiting resources. *J. theor. Biol.*, **33**, 299–307.

Cowan, I. R. (1982). Regulation of water use in relation to carbon gain in higher plants. In: *Physiological plant ecology*, vol. 2, edited by O. L. Lange et al., 589–613. (Encyclopedia of plant physiology, vol. 12B). Berlin: Springer.

Cowan, I. R. & Farquhar, G. D. (1977). Stomatal function in relation to leaf metabolism and environment. In: *Integration of activity in the higher plant*, edited by D. H. Jennings, 471–505. Cambridge: Cambridge University Press.

Denne, M. P. (1963). A comparison between fruits of Cox's Orange Pippin from Kent, England and Auckland, New Zealand. *N.Z. J. Bot.*, **1**, 295–300.

Grierson, W., Soule, J. & Kawada, K. (1982). Beneficial aspects of physiological stress. *Hort. Rev.*, **4**, 247–271.

Hamer, P. J. C. (1980). A model to evaluate evaporative cooling of apple buds as a frost protection technique. *J. hort. Sci.*, **55**, 157–163.

Jackson, J. E. & Hamer, P. J. C. (1980). The causes of year-to-year variation in the average yield of Cox's Orange Pippin apple in England. *J. hort. Sci.*, **55**, 149–156.

Jarvis, P. G. (1981). Stomatal conductance, gaseous exchange and transpiration. In: *Plants and their atmospheric environment*, edited by J. Grace *et al.*, 175–204. Oxford: Blackwell.

Jones, H. G. (1976). Crop characteristics and the ratio between assimilation and transpiration. *J. appl. Ecol.*, **13**, 605–622.

Jones, H. G. (1979). Stomatal behaviour and breeding for drought resistance. In: *Stress physiology of crop plants*, edited by H. Mussell and R. C. Staples, 408–428. New York: Wiley.

Jones, H. G. (1981). The use of stochastic modelling to study the influence of stomatal behaviour on yield-climate relationships. In: *Mathematics and plant physiology*, edited by D. A. Rose and D. A. Charles-Edwards, 231–244. London: Academic Press.

Jones, H. G. (1983). *Plants and microclimate*. Cambridge: Cambridge University Press.

Kriedemann, P. E. & Barrs, H. D. (1981). Citrus orchards. In: *Water deficits and plant growth*, vol. 6, edited by T. T. Kozlowski, 325–417. London: Academic Press.

Landsberg, J. J. & Fowkes, N. D. (1978). Water movement through plant roots. *Ann. Bot.*, **42**, 493–508.

Landsberg, J. J. & Jones, H. G. (1981). Apple orchards. In: *Water deficits and plant growth*, vol. 6, edited by T. T. Kozlowski, 419–469. London: Academic Press.

Lockhart, J. A. (1983). Optimum growth initiation time for shoot buds of deciduous plants in a temperate climate. *Oecologia*, **60**, 34–37.

Luckwill, L. C., Child, R. D., Webster, A. & Campbell, H. (1972). Meadow orchards. *Rep. Long Ashton Res. Stn 1971*, 34–36.

Luton, M. T. & Hamer, P. J. C. (1983). Predicting the optimum harvest dates for apples using temperature and full-bloom records. *J. hort. Sci.*, **58**, 37–44.

Monteith, J. L. (1973). *Principles of environmental physics*. London: Edward Arnold.

Newman, E. I. (1983). Interactions between plants. In: *Physiological plant ecology*, vol. 3, edited by O. L. Lange *et al.*, 679–710. (Encyclopedia of plant physiology, vol. 12C). Berlin: Springer.

Paltridge, G. W. (1973). On the shape of trees. *J. theor. Biol.*, **38**, 111–137.

Paltridge, G. W. & Denholm, J. V. (1974). Plant yield and the switch from vegetative to reproductive growth. *J. theor. Biol.*, **44**, 23–34.

Priestley, C. A. (1970). Carbohydrate storage and utilization. In: *Physiology of tree crops*, edited by L. C. Luckwill and C. V. Cutting, 113–126. London: Academic Press.

Richardson, E. A., Ashcroft, G. L., Anderson, J. L., Seeley, S. D., Walker, D. R., Alfaro, J. F., Griffin, R. E. & Keller, J. (1976). *Pheno-climatography of selected fruit trees used in programming sprinkling for bloom delay.* (Paper no. 75-4053). Davis, CA: American Soc. of Agric. Engineers.

Roberts, J. (1983). Forest transpiration: a conservative hydrological process? *J. Hydrol. (Amst.)*, **66**, 133–141.

Rose, D. A. & Charles-Edwards, D. A. (1981). *Mathematics and plant physiology*. London: Academic Press.

Schulze, E.-D. (1982). Plant lifeforms and their carbon, water and nutrient relations. In: *Physiological plant ecology*, vol. 2, edited by O. L. Lange *et al.*, 615–676. (Encyclopedia of plant physiology, vol. 12B). Berlin: Springer.

Schulze, E.-D., Schilling, K. & Nagarajah, S. (1983). Carbohydrate partitioning in relation to whole plant production and water use of *Vigna unguiculata* (L.) Walp. *Oecologia*, **58**, 169–177.

Stanhill, G. (1981). The size and significance of differences in the radiation balance of plants and plant communities. In: *Plants and their atmospheric environment*, edited by J. Grace *et al.*, 57–73. Oxford: Blackwell.

Walter, H. (1973). *Die Vegetation der Erde. I. Tropische und subtropische Zonen.* 3rd ed. Stuttgart: Fischer, Jena.

Wertheim, S. J. (1980). High-density planting: development and current achievements in the Netherlands, Belgium and West Germany. *Acta Hortic.*, **114**, 318–327.

Wolgast, L. J. & Zeide, B. (1983). Reproduction of trees in a variable environment. *Bot. Gaz.*, **144**, 260–262.

6

TREE GROWTH AT COOL TEMPERATURES AND PROSPECTS FOR IMPROVEMENT BY BREEDING

P. F. WAREING

Department of Botany and Microbiology, University College of Wales, Aberystwyth, Wales

I. LIGHT INTERCEPTION AND LEAF DEVELOPMENT

There is often a linear relationship between annual dry matter production and the amount of solar radiation intercepted by the crop. Furthermore, the relationship between quantity of intercepted radiation and annual production of dry matter is closely similar for crops as different as apples, barley, potatoes and sugar beet (Monteith 1977).

The amount of light intercepted by a crop during its growing season is a function of the seasonal distribution of its *leaf area index*. But ever since the pioneering work of Watson (1952), it has been recognized that, in temperate climates, one of the major factors limiting annual dry matter production in arable crops, such as sugar beet, is the slow development of a leaf canopy in the spring.

The situation is similar in late-flushing deciduous trees, although the presence of preformed leaf primordia in the resting buds ensures that a high leaf area index can be achieved in a few days, once flushing commences. A considerable amount of potential dry matter production is lost in the spring if bud-break and flushing do not occur until considerably later than the improvement in light conditions. Light conditions improve rapidly in late March and April, whereas some broadleaved deciduous species, such as *Quercus* and *Fraxinus*, may not flush until well into June. However, early flushing incurs the risk of damage by spring frosts, which has to be set against the advantages accruing from a longer growing season. A mathematical approach to this problem has been adopted by Lockhart (1983), who has developed a model predicting optimum growth initiation times for buds of deciduous plants based on maximizing average annual photosynthesis as a function of photosynthetic rates, length of growing season and the probability of late frost. A different approach has been adopted by Cannell and Smith (1984), who have carried out a detailed study of the probability of spring frost damage in young trees of *Picea sitchensis* in Britain, based upon predicted dates of bud-burst in relation to meteorological records of spring frosts.

Detailed studies have been carried out on the factors determining the time of bud-break in *Pseudotsuga menziesii* (Campbell & Sugano 1975, 1979) and *Picea sitchensis* (Cannell & Smith 1983). Bud-burst in these, and other conifers of the temperate zone, requires a period of winter chilling, followed by warmer temperatures in the post-dormancy period, but there is an interaction between these two requirements, and an absence of winter chilling can sometimes be replaced by long photoperiods in late spring. There appear to be no corresponding detailed studies on deciduous hardwood species.

There is evidence of considerable intraspecific genetic variation in the time of bud-burst, within both evergreen conifers such as *Picea abies* (eg Worrall & Mergen 1967), and broadleaved species (Kozlowski 1964), so there may be considerable scope for achieving earlier flushing by breeding. However, the risk of damage by spring frosts is a major problem, and probably prevents any major advancement of flushing dates in sensitive species, but, with very late flushing deciduous species, some advancement of flushing time by selection seems feasible.

II.   TEMPERATURE AS A FACTOR LIMITING TREE GROWTH

Apart from the effects of temperature on the time of bud-break and the growth of preformed leaf primordia in the bud, temperature will affect tree growth throughout the growing season. This discussion will be confined to the effects of temperature on height growth and dry weight increase – the interaction between temperature and photoperiod on the time of growth cessation will not be considered. Even so, the effects of temperature on growth rate will be highly complex, because it directly affects the rate of almost every process in the plant. As well as affecting general metabolism, temperature also affects the rates of cell division and cell expansion which underlie the overall growth processes. Moreover, temperature affects the photosynthetic rate and hence the supply of assimilates available for growth (ie *source activity*'), as well as the rate of utilization of assimilates in growth and storage of reserves ('*sink activity*'). Dry matter allocated to the formation of new leaves will, of course, increase the *photosynthetic capacity* of the tree, as a 'positive feedback' process, and hence will promote a greater absolute growth rate.

The rise in mean temperatures in the spring lags behind the improvement in light conditions by several weeks. Growth processes, such as leaf initiation and leaf growth, generally show higher temperature minima and higher temperature coefficients than does photosynthesis (Monteith & Elston 1971), so that under cool conditions the growth rate of arable crops (and presumably of trees, also) is frequently limited by the rate at which assimilates can be utilized in growth, rather than by the rate of assimilate production in photosynthesis. Consequently, in many temperate regions, low temperature may constitute the major factor limiting plant growth, even during late spring.

What evidence is there that tree growth may be limited by temperature during the growing season, and to what regions does this apply?

There are accurate data for the effects of temperature on photosynthetic rates in trees (Neilson *et al.* 1972), but, bearing in mind the complexity of temperature effects, together with the difficulty of growing sizeable trees in controlled environments, it is not surprising that, except for small seedlings, the available information on the effects of temperature on tree growth (as measured by dry matter production) is very sparse and lacking precision. However, the temperature responses of older trees are likely to be closely related to those of younger ones, because the same processes of cell division and cell expansion underlie the growth processes, irrespective of age.

Studies on seedlings and young trees indicate that the optimum temperature for height growth in *Picea abies*, *Pinus sylvestris* and *Betula pubescens* is in the region of 20–25 °C (Håbjørg 1972), and the same temperature range appears to apply to dry matter production in *Pinus resinosa* (Kozlowski & Borger 1971). When these temperature optima are related to the mean summer temperatures in the northern boreal forest zone (or in the British uplands), it is clear that temperature must be a major limiting factor to tree growth in those areas for most of the growing season. Thus, on *a priori* grounds, it is highly likely that tree growth is limited by temperature in such areas (in addition, very often, to mineral nutrient deficiency and water stress).

Indirect evidence in support of this conclusion comes from a number of studies on shoot growth in trees (Miller 1965; Lavender 1980). In Finland, a model was applied to a study of height growth in *Picea abies*, *Pinus sylvestris* and *Betula* spp. under field conditions (Hari & Leikola 1974). Tree heights and temperatures were recorded at frequent intervals, and the effects of temperature on growth were assumed to be closely correlated with its effects on respiration. With this assumption, there was close agreement between the observed and the predicted increments in height throughout the season. Similar results were obtained in a further study with *Pinus sylvestris*, using a modification of the earlier model (Pietarinen *et al.* 1982). These findings provide indirect evidence that temperature was, indeed, a major limiting factor for tree growth under the environmental conditions of southern Finland.

Patterns of shoot growth in trees vary considerably and may be either 'free' or 'episodic'. In species with a period of free growth (such as *Betula* and *Populus*), the temperature throughout the growth period will directly affect the rate of shoot growth, including leaf initiation and expansion and internode elongation. In species with episodic growth (such as *Quercus* and *Pinus*), shoot growth in the spring involves the expansion of primordia laid down in the resting bud during the previous year, and temperature will affect both the rate of current elongation growth and leaf expansion, and also the rate at which primordia are laid down in the bud (and hence the growth in the subsequent year).

If we are correct in concluding that temperature may be a major factor limiting tree growth in some areas, what scope is there for increasing the growth rate at cool temperatures by selection and breeding? That is to say, what evidence is there that there is genetic variation within tree species with respect to growth responses to temperature, and what would be the prospects for achieving higher growth rates at cool temperatures by selection and breeding? There is very little information on variation in temperature responses within species of woody plants, but there is considerable evidence for such variation in herbaceous species.

III. GENETIC VARIATION IN TEMPERATURE RESPONSES

It is common knowledge that there are marked differences between species in their ability to grow at cool temperatures, but there have been relatively few studies on the extent of genetic variation in temperature responses within a single species. However, it has been shown that there is considerable ecotypic variation in growth/temperature responses within various grass species, including *Dactylis glomerata*, *Lolium perenne* and *Festuca arundinacea* (Cooper 1964; Eagles 1967). Mediterranean races of these species show higher leaf growth rates during the winter months than do Scandinavian races, and studies in controlled environments have shown that there are marked differences between populations of different origins in their ability to grow at cool temperatures. Similar genetic variation in growth responses to temperature have been shown for *Festuca rubra* (Ollerenshaw *et al.* 1976).

Håbjørg (1972) studied the effects of photoperiod and temperature on growth and development of three latitudinal and three altitudinal populations of *Betula pubescens*. In an experiment under controlled environmental conditions, in which the photoperiod was constant and temperature was varied, significant differences were observed between the populations in the optimum temperature for growth.

Very little is known about the special aspects of metabolism which confer the ability to grow at cool temperatures, although there is an increasing body of information on genetic variation within species with respect to the effects of temperature on metabolism, especially on photosynthesis (see Berry & Björkman 1980; Berry & Raison 1981; Graham & Patterson 1982).

Oxyria digyna is a species with a wide circumpolar distribution, but also with a wide latitudinal distribution at high altitude sites in North America. Studies on northern and southern populations of the species showed the optimum temperature for photosynthesis in plants from Alaska was in the region of 15–19 °C, whereas in alpine populations from Colorado it was in the region of 30–35 °C (Mooney & Billings 1961). Moreover, the respiration rates at cool temperatures were significantly higher in plants from the northern population, as might be expected for plants adapted to grow at low temperatures. Other studies on *Oxyria digyna* have shown that the photosynthetic rate of plants from some European populations reaches half the maximum at temperatures as low as 0 °C (Pisek *et al.* 1973). Trees of *Picea excelsa* and *Pinus cembra* from the timberline in Europe have lower temperature optima for photosynthesis than those from lower altitudes (see Pisek *et al. loc. cit*).

Slatyer and his associates have carried out extensive studies on altitudinal variation in the photosynthetic characteristics of *Eucalyptus pauciflora* in Australia (Slatyer 1977a, b; Slatyer & Ferrar 1977). There were marked differences between populations in the optimum temperature for photosynthesis, the material from the lowest elevation (warmest) site showing the highest temperature optimum and significantly higher rates of net photosynthesis at the highest growth temperature, while the material from the highest elevation (coldest) site showed the lowest temperature optimum, and higher rates of photosynthesis, at the lowest growth temperature.

The thermal characteristics of photosynthesis are markedly affected by the temperatures at which the plants are grown. In general, plants grown at cool temperatures show a higher rate of photosynthesis at low temperatures than do plants grown at higher temperatures, and are hence said to show 'acclimation'. Acclimation has been shown for the photosynthetic rates of high and low altitude populations of *Eucalyptus pauciflora* (Slatyer 1977a, b). Moreover, the temperature optima at given sites vary with the season, indicating acclimation to the prevailing seasonal temperature regime (Slatyer & Morrow 1977).

It is clear that, as well as being able to carry on active photosynthesis at low temperatures, plants adapted to cool conditions must be able to maintain active metabolism, if they are to be able to grow under these conditions. It has, indeed, been known for many years that the rate of respiration at 20 °C is higher in plants native to cold climates than in those from warm climates (Forward 1960). Stocker (1935) observed that the average rate of respiration for three tropical species at 30 °C was the same as that for three arctic species at 10 °C. The respiration rates of plants of *Oxyria digyna* were found to be significantly higher at low temperatures in plants from arctic populations than in those from alpine sites (Mooney & Billings 1961). Higher respiration rates in cold-adapted populations have been reported for *Festuca rubra* (Ollerenshaw *et al.* 1976; Stewart & Ollerenshaw 1977). The application of normal temperature coefficients of two to three would lead one to expect that the metabolic rates of plants would be greatly decreased at low temperatures, but the finding that this is not the case in cold-adapted species raises the interesting question as to how this temperature adaptation is achieved at the molecular level.

IV. VARIATION IN THERMAL PROPERTIES OF ENZYMES

The chilling injury shown by tropical and subtropical species when they are exposed to low, non-freezing temperatures has been attributed to a change in the cell membranes from the fluid to the gel state, as indicated by a change in the slope of the Arrhenius plot for certain enzymes (Lyons 1973). By contrast, in temperate species adapted to cool temperatures, this phase transition in cell membranes does not occur at non-freezing temperatures. Thus, the ability to grow at cool temperatures must depend upon the ability to maintain the membranes in a fluid state.

However, there is increasing evidence, particularly from studies on cold-blooded ('ectothermic') animal species, that adaptation to cool temperatures also involves evolutionary changes in the thermal properties of their enzymes (Hochachka & Somero 1973). Several strategies are open to an organism to increase the rate at which an enzyme-controlled reaction proceeds at a lower temperature. One way would be to increase the *amount* of enzyme present at the lower temperature. There is good evidence that the *activities* of several enzymes in ectothermic animals are higher at lower temperatures, but whether this is due to higher concentrations of the enzyme is not known. In some plant species there appears to be a strong correlation between the activity of the photosynthetic enzyme, ribulose-1,5,bisphosphate (RuBP) carboxylase, in extracts of leaves and their photosynthetic rates at suboptimal temperatures (Berry & Raison 1981). Arctic populations of *Oxyria digyna* have high RuBP carboxylase activity when compared to alpine ecotypes from warmer sites (Chabot *et al.* 1972). Moreover, increases in the level of enzymes involved in photosynthesis, such as RuBP carboxylase, are apparently important in acclimation to lower temperatures (Berry & Björkman 1980).

Another possible strategy would be to produce enzymes which function more efficiently at cool temperatures. There are two major characteristics of an enzyme which affect its effectiveness at any given temperature: (a) the *affinity* between the enzyme and the molecules of its substrate, and (b) the *free energy of activation* for the reaction catalyzed.

The affinity between enzyme and substrate is given by the value of the Michaelis constant (Km), which is defined as half the saturating concentration of substrate – a low value of Km indicating a high affinity. The value of Km falls with temperature, indicating that the affinity increases at lower temperatures, but with some enzymes there is a temperature at which the Km is a minimum, and below this the affinity decreases. Studies on various animal species indicate, for several enzymes, that binding affinity is high at the temperature to which the organism is adapted.

Enzymes act by reducing the activation energy required for a given chemical reaction to occur. The question arises as to whether enzymes in organisms adapted to cold conditions can be made more efficient by lowering the threshold energy of activation further. There appears to be good evidence that this does occur in several cold-blooded animal species.

Comparable studies on plants are much less advanced than for animals, although there is increasing interest in the subject. There are several studies which point to lower Km values in cold-adapted plant species (see Graham & Patterson 1982). The activation energy of RuBP carboxylase, extracted from *Caltha intraloba* plants which had adapted to low temperatures, was lower than that of species from warmer environments (Phillips & McWilliam 1971). Studies on widely distributed ecotypes of *Typha latifolia* provided evidence for differences in NAD malate dehydrogenase (MDH) properties in clonal populations from different climates. Genotypes could be differentiated and ordered according to the apparent energies of activation, thermostabilities and activity levels of MDH on a pattern related to climatic origin (McNaughton 1974). It was suggested that differences in thermal properties found in ecotypes of *T. latifolia* may be due to differential synthesis of MDH isozymes differing in thermal properties.

A recent study was carried out on *Lathyrus japonicus*, which has a wide geographical distribution in eastern North America, and in which there is evidence of ecotypic variation in the properties of certain enzymes (Simon 1979a, b). The thermal properties of NAD malate dehydrogenase were investigated in eight clonal populations. Clones from cooler sites had consistently lower activation energies under three contrasting growth temperature regimes. The Km values at different substrate concentrations indicated that enzyme-substrate affinity was temperature-dependent and decreased at the higher temperatures, with distinct differences between populations from northern and southern sites. Similar differences were found in a comparison of the kinetic properties of MDH in clones of *L. japonicus* from a cold maritime site (Hudson Bay) and a warm summer continental site (Lake Michigan) (Simon 1979c).

V. CONCLUSIONS

Hitherto, although it was self-evident that plant species differed in their adaptation to environmental temperature conditions, we knew nothing of the physiological and metabolic basis of these differences, and the possibility of breeding for higher growth rates at cool temperatures appeared a very formidable and extremely long-term task. However, the demonstration that there is considerable intraspecific genetic variation in growth/temperature responses, involving the thermal properties of various enzymes, and that such variation seems to underlie natural adaptation to different environmental conditions, opens up the prospect that significant progress could be achieved by breeding. Variation in growth/temperature responses is a very easy character for which to select. Moreover, it is likely that such variation in the properties of metabolic enzymes will be expressed at an early stage of seedling growth, as well as in older trees, because we have found that the temperature responses of young grass seedlings of diverse origins are closely correlated with those of older plants of the same populations under field conditions (Elias & Wareing, unpublished). Thus, intense selection for growth at low temperatures could be carried out on large numbers of seedlings at an early stage of growth. Such selection would need to be carried out at upland sites, where environmental conditions would be similar to those under which the mature trees would have to grow.

It might be objected that, if we select for higher growth rates at cooler temperatures, it would lead to earlier flushing, and hence to a greater risk of frost damage. However, as mentioned, the time of bud-burst is determined by the chilling requirement and by the 'thermal-time' requirements during the post-dormancy period and it seems very probable that the biochemical basis of the chilling requirement is different from that determining the growth rate after bud-burst, so that the genetic control of these two processes is likely to be independent.

The prospects for significantly improving dry matter production in agricultural crops by increasing the rate of photosynthesis do not appear to be very promising in the short term (Monteith 1977), and indeed the photosynthetic rates of highly productive modern varieties of wheat appear to be no higher than those of their wild ancestors (Evans 1975). It has long been recognized that the most promising approach for increasing biomass production in agricultural crops lies in improving the efficiency of light interception and the 'harvest index'. The same argument has been advanced for improving the growth rate of trees (Wareing 1964), but an undue amount of attention continues to be paid to studies on photosynthesis, as against studies of the effects of temperature on growth (Monteith 1981). Attention to this matter has recently been drawn again by Jarvis and Leverenz (1983), who emphasize the need for studies on the influence of temperature on leaf growth in forest trees.

REFERENCES

Berry, J. & Björkman, O. (1980). Photosynthetic response and adaptation to temperature in higher plants. *A. Rev. Pl. Physiol.*, **31**, 491–543.

Berry, J. A. & Raison, J. K. (1981). Responses of macrophytes to temperature. In: *Physiological plant ecology. 1. Responses to the physical environment*, edited by O. L. Lange, P. S. Nobel, C. B. Osmond and H. Ziegler, 277–338. (Encyclopedia of plant physiology, n.s. vol. 12a). Berlin: Springer.

Campbell, R. K. & Sugano, A. J. (1975). Phenology of bud burst in Douglas fir related to provenance, photoperiod, chilling and flushing temperature. *Bot. Gaz.*, **136**, 290–298.

Campbell, R. K. & Sugano, A. J. (1979). Genecology of bud burst phenology in Douglas fir: response to flushing temperature and chilling. *Bot. Gaz.*, **140**, 223–231.

Cannell, M. G. R. & Smith, R. J. (1983). Thermal time, chill days and prediction of bud burst in *Picea sitchensis*. *J. appl. Ecol.*, **20**, 951–963.

Cannell, M. G. R. & Smith, R. I. (1984). Spring frost damage on young *Picea sitchensis*. 2. Predicted dates of budburst and probability of frost damage. *Forestry*, **57**, 61–81.

Chabot, B. F., Chabot, J. F. & Billings, W. D. (1972). Ribulose-1,5,biphosphate carboxylase activity in arctic and alpine populations of *Oxyria digyna*. *Photosynthetica*, **6**, 364–369.

Cooper, J. P. (1964). Climatic variation in grasses. I. Leaf development in climatic races of *Dactylis glomerata* in controlled environments. *Ann. Bot.*, n.s. **31**, 31–39.

Eagles, C. F. (1967). The effect of temperature on vegetative growth in climatic races of *Lolium* and *Dactylis*. *J. appl. Ecol.*, **1**, 45–61.

Evans, L. T. (1975). The physiological basis of crop yield. In: *Crop physiology*, edited by L. T. Evans, 327–355. Cambridge: Cambridge University Press.

Forward, D. F. (1960). Effect of temperature on respiration. In: *Encyclopedia of plant physiology*, edited by W. Ruhland, vol. 12(2), 234–258. Berlin: Springer.

Graham, D. & Patterson, B. D. (1982). Responses of plants to low, non-freezing temperatures: proteins, metabolism and acclimation. *A. Rev. Pl. Physiol.*, **33**, 347–372.

Håbjørg, A. (1972). Effects of photoperiod and temperature on growth and development of three latitudinal and three altitudinal populations of *Betula pubescens* Ehrh. *Meld. Norg. LandbrHogsk.*, **51**, 1–27.

Hari, P. & Leikola, M. (1974). Further development of the dynamic growth model of plant height growth. *Flora, Jena*, **163**, 357–370.

Hochachka, P. W. & Somero, G. L. (1973). *Strategies of biochemical adaptation*. Philadelphia, PA: W. B. Saunders & Co.

Jarvis, P. G. & Leverenz, J. W. (1983). Productivity of temperate, deciduous and evergreen forests. In: *Physiological plant ecology. 4. Ecosystem processes: mineral cycling, productivity and man's influence*, edited by O. L. Lange, P. S. Nobel, C. B. Osmond and H. Ziegler, 233–280. (Encyclopedia of plant physiology, vol. 12D). Berlin: Springer.

Koslowski, T. T. (1964). Shoot growth in woody plants. *Bot. Rev.*, **30**, 335–392.

Kozlowski, T. T. & Borger, G. A. (1971). Effect of temperature and light intensity early in ontogeny on growth of *Pinus resinosa* seedlings. *Can. J. For. Res.*, **1**, 57–65.

Lavender, D. P. (1980). Effects of the environment upon the shoot growth of woody plants. In: *Control of shoot growth in trees*, edited by C. H. A. Little, 76–106. Fredericton, NB: Maritimes Forest Research Centre.

Lockhart, J. A. (1983). Optimum growth initiation time for shoot buds of deciduous plants in a temperate climate. *Oecologia*, **60**, 34–37.

Lyons, J. M. (1973). Chilling injury in plants. *A. Rev. Pl. Physiol.*, **45**, 386–389.

McNaughton, S. J. (1974). Natural selection at the enzyme level. *Am. Nat.*, **108**, 616–624.

Miller, A. (1965). The effect of temperature and daylength on the height growth of birch (*Betula pubescens*) at 1900 feet in the northern Pennines. *J. appl. Ecol.*, **2**, 17–29.

Monteith, J. L. (1977). Climate and efficiency of crop production in Britain. *Phil. Trans. R. Soc.*, **218B**, 277–294.

Monteith, J. L. (1981). Does light limit crop production? In: *Physiological processes limiting plant productivity*, edited by C. B. Johnson, 23–38. London: Butterworth.

Monteith, H. A. & Elston, J. F. (1971). Microclimatology and crop production. In: *Potential crop production*, edited by P. F. Wareing and J. P. Cooper, 23–42. London: Heinemann Educational.

Mooney, H. A. & Billings, W. D. (1961). Comparative physiological ecology of arctic and alpine populations of *Oxyria digyna*. *Ecol. Monogr.*, **31**, 1–29.

Neilson, R. E., Ludlow, M. M. & Jarvis, P. G. (1972). Photosynthesis in Sitka spruce (*Picea sitchensis* (Bong.) Carr.). II. Response to temperature. *J. appl. Ecol.*, **9**, 721–745.

Ollerenshaw, J. H., Stewart, W. S., Gallimore, J. & Baker, R. H. (1976). Low temperature growth in grasses from northern latitudes. *J. agric. Sci., Camb.*, **87**, 237–239.

Phillips, P. J. & McWilliam, J. R. (1971). Thermal responses of the primary carboxylating enzymes from C_3 and C_4 plants adapted to contrasting temperature environments. In: *Photosynthesis and photorespiration*, edited by M. D. Hatch, C. B. Osmond and R. O. Slatyer, 97–104. New York: Wiley Interscience.

Pisek, A., Larcher, W., Vegis, A. & Knapp-Zinn, K. (1973). The normal temperature range. In: *Temperature and life*, edited by H. Precht, J. Christophersen, H. Hensel and W. Larcher, 102–143. Berlin: Springer.

Pietarinen, I., Kanninen, M., Hari, P. & Kellomäki, S. (1982). A simulation model for daily growth of shoots, needles and stem diameter in Scots pine trees. *Forest Sci.*, **28**, 573–581.

Simon, J.-P. (1979a). Adaptation and acclimation of higher plants at the enzyme level: latitudinal variations of thermal properties of NAD malate dehydrogenase in *Lathyrus japonicus* Willd. (Leguminosae). *Oecologia*, **56**, 273–287.

Simon, J.-P. (1979b). Adaptation and acclimation of higher plants at the enzyme level: temperature-dependent substrate binding ability of NAD malate dehydrogenase in four populations of *Lathyrus japonicus* Willd. (Leguminosae). *Plant Sci. Lett.*, **14**, 113–120.

Simon, J.-P. (1979c). Differences in thermal properties of NAD malate dehydrogenase in genotypes of *Lathyrus japonicus* Willd. (Leguminosae) from maritime and continental sites. *Plant, Cell Environ.*, **2**, 23–33.

Slatyer, R. O. (1977a). Altitudinal variation in the photosynthetic characteristics of snow gum, *Eucalyptus pauciflora* Sieb. ex Streng. III. Temperature response of material grown in contrasting thermal environments. *Aust. J. Plant Physiol.*, **4**, 301–312.

Slatyer, R. O. (1977b). Altitudinal variation characteristics of snow gum, *Eucalyptus pauciflora* Sieb. ex Streng. IV. Temperature response of four populations grown at different temperatures. *Aust. J. Plant Physiol.*, **4**, 583–594.

Slatyer, R. O. & Ferrar, P. J. (1977). Altitudinal variation in the photosynthetic characteristics of snow gum, *Eucalyptus pauciflora* Sieb. ex Spreng. II. Effects of growth temperature under controlled conditions. *Aust. J. Plant. Physiol.*, **4**, 289–299.

Slatyer, R. O. & Morrow, P. A. (1977). Altitudinal variation in the photosynthetic characteristics of snow gum, *Eucalyptus pauciflora* Sieb. ex Spreng. I. Seasonal changes under field conditions in the Snowy Mountains area of south-eastern Australia. *Aust. J. Bot.*, **25**, 1–20.

Stewart, W. S. & Ollerenshaw, J. H. (1977). Intra-specific variation in rates of dark respiration and photosynthesis at low positive temperatures in *Festuca rubra* L. *Proc. int. Grassl. Congr.*, 419–426.

Stocker, O. (1935). Assimilation und Atmung Westjavanischer Tropenbäume. *Planta*, **24**, 402–445.

Wareing, P. F. (1964). Tree physiology in relation to genetics and breeding. *Unasylva*, **18**, 1–10.

Watson, D. J. (1952). The physiological basis of variation in yield. *Adv. Agron.*, **4**, 101–145.

Worrall, J. & Mergen, F. (1967). Environmental and genetic control of dormancy in *Picea abies*. *Physiologia Pl.*, **20**, 733–745.

7

THE IDEOTYPE CONCEPT APPLIED TO FOREST TREES

D. I. DICKMANN
Department of Forestry, Michigan State University, East Lansing, Michigan, USA

I. INTRODUCTION

There are many avenues along which forest plantations might be directed toward the goal of increased productivity (DeBell *et al.* 1977). Some involve the silvicultural manipulation of the stand trees and their competitors; others involve enhancement of site productivity by fertilization, site preparation, drainage and irrigation; another concerns the control of insects, diseases, fire, and other destructive agents; and a fourth involves the genetic manipulation of the trees. All approaches are interrelated, and usually will be applied in concert. To cite an example of the potential pay-offs, Farnum *et al.* (1983) reported that, using the four avenues cited above, the productivity of plantations of *Pseudotsuga menziesii* and *Pinus taeda* in the United States can be increased up to 70% and 300% respectively, compared with natural forests on the same sites. Similar gains have been realized, or could be expected, in other important species.

This discussion will focus on one aspect of tree genetic improvement, namely the specific goal toward which a tree breeder should strive. In a broad sense, this goal is to increase tree or stand growth, while minimizing losses to injurious agents. But a breeder needs a much more specific, highly focused goal, so that progress can be more easily measured.

It should be emphasized at the outset that the primary unit of genetic manipulation is the tree, not the stand. Although the plantation is the basis of increased forest productivity, it is the creation of the silviculturist. Breeders select and breed individual trees and, at the start of any tree improvement programme, they must ask this question: in a particular environment (or on a certain type of site), using a prescribed silvicultural system, and assuming a well-defined end use of the harvested trees, what are the precise traits of a tree of the species under consideration that will produce a yield that approaches maximum? The answer to this rather complex question is a model tree, an 'ideotype', and is the first step towards bioengineering an improved tree species.

II. THE CONCEPT OF THE IDEOTYPE

C. M. Donald developed the idea of breeding model plants or ideotypes in a now-classic paper (Donald 1968). The term ideotype literally means 'a form denoting an idea', but Donald went on to define it in a more precise, biological way. In its broadest sense, an ideotype is a biological model which is expected to perform or behave in a predictable manner within a defined environment. More specifically, a crop ideotype is a plant model which will yield a greater quantity or quality of useful products than conventional cultivars or wild plants. The formulation of an ideotype is a truly practical step, because it provides a clear, workable goal toward which plant breeders can work. The use of ideotypes has begun to infiltrate the field of agronomic crop genetics (eg Adams 1982), but it has not become an operational part of most tree breeding programmes.

A. Why an ideotype?

Aside from providing a clear, well-defined goal for a breeder, there are other reasons for spending time and resources in the formulation of ideotypes. Donald (1968) suggested that ideotypes provide an opportunity to devise and examine a combination of characters that otherwise may not appear in breeders' plots for centuries. A corollary, more relevant to tree breeders, is that an ideotype provides a guide to the selection of potential breeding stock from wild populations. Individual trees in a natural forest community have evolved to survive and reproduce – a quite different strategy from that required of trees in an intensively managed plantation. Thus, a tree that is ideally adapted for fast growth in an intensively managed plantation could be at a competitive disadvantage in a natural forest community, and could easily be overlooked. It is well known that high-yielding cultivars of agronomic crop plants are unsuited for survival in the wild.

Another justification for the use of ideotypes is that they can be used as a basis for understanding the physiology of the crop (Donald 1968). The initial design of a crop ideotype is, in essence, a framework to build upon physiologically, an opportunity to eventually arrive at a synthesis that leads to greater understanding of the whole plant. Such syntheses are rare for forest trees. Furthermore, wood yield is a polygenic character; only by breaking yield down into its components, and systematically dealing with them one by one can major break-throughs be made in tree improvement (Ford 1976). Significantly, the ideotype can provide a working link between physiologists and breeders, a union with much potential synergism.

The ideotype concept is, perhaps, best justified by giving an example from field crop breeding. In Michigan, slow progress was made towards increased yields of *Phaseolus vulgaris*, using the conventional 'selection for yield' approach (Donald 1968). Then, in 1972-73 an ideotype was formulated. Selection for the ideotype within the available population proved to be unprofitable, but, by screening mutants from atomic-irradiated seed, and by introducing genes from the tropical black bean, several promising genotypes were identified which conformed to the hypothesized ideotype (Adams 1982). Recent independent field tests by commercial growers showed that the new varieties have outyielded standard varieties by 20–40%. The potential for similar success surely exists in many tree species, although progress may be slower.

B. Construction of an ideotype

An ideotype is not a wistful construction born of unproven assumptions or opinions; it is rather a deductive product founded on a detailed understanding of plant morphology and physiology. Donald (1968) proposed that the design of crop ideotypes will depend on knowledge and experimental data in several areas, such as photosynthesis, sink dynamics, and competition, and for woody perennials one might add phenology and ageing. Several authors have discussed yield components in trees (Wareing & Matthews 1973; Gordon 1975; Cannell 1978; Farmer 1978; Dickmann 1979), but not in the context of ideotype construction, and for many major tree species knowledge of the components of yield is still sketchy.

1. *Photosynthesis*

The success that plant breeders have enjoyed in increasing crop yields has not stemmed from modifications in the basic chemistry of the photosynthetic process (Evans 1980). However, the efficiency with which photosynthesis occurs in individual plants or stands has been increased by manipulating plant structure or by improving the environment for plant growth (eg by applying fertilizers or irrigation). Nevertheless, Evans (1980) does add that further increases in the yield of agronomic crops will depend heavily on raising the inherent photosynthetic potential of leaf chloroplasts. There may be several approaches to this end, including regulating photorespiration (Zelitch 1975) or dark respiration (Gifford & Evans 1981), reducing the size of the photosynthetic unit (Radmer & Kok 1977), or increasing the capacity of chloroplasts to acclimatize to low leaf water potentials (Matthews & Boyer 1984). Progress in these areas will probably be enhanced by employing the techniques of biotechnology. However, heavy investment in research to increase the photosynthetic potential of tree crops is probably unwarranted at this time, because more tractable approaches to yield improvement have yet to be fully exploited.

A more practical way to increase photosynthetic productivity is to alter leaf characteristics and crown architecture, to enhance light interception and to optimize the environment for photosynthesis within the stand. Genetic variation has been shown to exist in many tree crown characteristics such as (a) specific leaf weight, (b) stomatal responses, leaf fluttering, and other adaptations that minimize the adverse effects of high heat loads and water stress, (c) leaf orientation, shape, size, and duration, and (d) branch number, angle, length, arrangement and longevity. Analyses of tree form (Horn 1971; Tomlinson 1983; White 1983a, b) suggest that certain architectural models, defined by fairly rigid empirical rules, prevail in nature; these models should be studied before the crown of a tree ideotype is designed.

As is true with most ideotype characteristics, the crown structure prescribed will depend strongly on the growth environment of the tree (Brunig 1976). Compare, for example, the branching of the ideal *Pinus sylvestris* tree proposed by workers in Finland (Kärki 1983; Kärki & Tigerstedt, this volume) and Poland (Jankiewicz & Stecki 1976): the Finnish tree has short, thin branches inserted at a 90° angle, whereas the Polish ideotype has thin, short, upright branches inserted at acute angles. Branches that arise at a 90° angle, or even droop, are better able to shed the heavy snow loads that are common in Scandinavia, thus preventing breakage, whereas snow loading is not such an important problem in the Polish environment. Plantation spacing also is a factor that will strongly influence the conception of an ideal tree crown. Densely spaced, short-rotation, intensively cultured plantations call for narrow-crowned trees (Isebrands *et al.* 1983), whereas a broad-crowned tree may be the prescription for a nut orchard, or a widely spaced plantation grown for sawlogs. Utilization objectives also will affect the branching characteristics of an ideotype. In the case of trees grown for high-grade lumber or veneer, branches are a major degrading factor and should be small and predisposed to early abscission.

2. Sink dynamics

Perhaps the most fruitful avenue in agricultural crop improvement has been the alteration of assimilate partitioning to increase the harvest index (Donald 1962; Evans 1980; Gifford & Evans 1981) – defined as the proportion of the total dry matter of a crop that comprises the economic product.

Conceptually, a plant can be viewed as a network of competing sinks; those sinks that are the largest and most active physiologically at a particular time attract the most photosynthate and grow most rapidly. The 'strength' of the cambium compared with other sinks determines the harvest index of a tree. Variation in cambial sink strength relative to other sinks, and resultant differences in harvest index, may exist in all tree species, and this variation could be exploited. In terms of an ideotype, Adams (1982) suggested that a plant should be engineered to consist of as many phytomeric (source-sink) units as possible, with each phytomeric unit high in functional efficiency. Perhaps, then, a forest tree should consist of a long crown to maximize phytomeric (branch source/stem cambium sink) units, with branches that are spatially arranged to intercept light efficiently, yet not so numerous as to induce 'feedback' inhibition of photosynthesis because of a high branch source/stem sink ratio.

A tree is an integrated unit; any attempt to improve the harvest index will probably produce compensatory changes which might reduce yields or lead to excessive mortality in certain situations. Therefore, a partitioning 'balance' must be achieved for each species in a given environment. The data of Keyes and Grier (1981) illustrate this point. On a good site in western Washington (USA), 46% of the net primary production of *Pseudotsuga menziesii* trees went to stemwood but only 8% went to fine roots, whereas on a poor site only 27% of net primary production was apportioned to stemwood, with fine roots receiving a substantial 36% (see Cannell, this volume). The survival implications of these differences in partitioning are obvious. If such partitioning responses are at least partially under genetic control (Isebrands & Nelson 1983), then there is potential for developing high-yielding ideotypes whose harvest index is optimized at a particular site. Clearly, there is a concomitant danger of growing such an ideotype at the wrong site.

3.   *Competition*

Intensive competition for available resources is the basic fact of life in forest stands. The finite supply of these resources, both above and below ground, is insufficient to meet potential demand, and so in closed forest stands there are individual 'winners' and 'losers'. The winners are assured continued survival; the losers face suppression and death. Yet there is great inter- and intraspecific variation in competitiveness. The forest ecologists' division of species into 'tolerant' and 'intolerant' is nothing more than a reflection of the competitive niche of the species. Donald and Hamblin (1976) defined competitiveness in a manner more appropriate to this discussion. They proposed that plants could be divided into 'isolation', 'competition' (here referred to as 'dominating'), and 'crop' ideotypes, each with a distinct competitive strategy, and each one appropriate for a particular cultural system.

The 'isolation' ideotype is a free-standing tree which is able to exploit its environment as extensively as possible. It produces a tall, dense and broad crown which displays foliage over a broad area (Cannell 1978), and presumably has a deep and spreading root system. Although the growth and development of an 'isolation' ideotype may be limited by the environment (for instance in the dry savanna), it is nevertheless a strong competitor, able to suppress surrounding vegetation. In terms of tree crops, the 'isolation' ideotype would be appropriate for a fruit, nut or pasture tree.

The 'dominating' ideotype tends to overtop neighbouring trees, becoming large at their expense. Stands comprised of this ideotype soon break into crown classes – dominant, codominant, intermediate, and suppressed – and display a wide range of stem diameters. The 'dominating' ideotype would be the model most appropriate for plantations of high-value species, such as *Juglans nigra* and *Quercus robur*, where the aim is to produce large-diametered trees yielding high-grade logs. Mortality of suppressed trees is of little consequence in this situation, if the remaining trees are of the highest quality and are growing rapidly. The silvicultural goal may be just a few exceptionally valuable trees per hectare at the end of the rotation.

Finally, the 'crop' ideotype is the model appropriate for the fibre or biomass plantation. Individuals of the crop ideotype are not strong competitors, and make efficient use of that portion of the basic site resources to which they have access in a forest community (Cannell 1978). They typically have a dense, narrow crown, with strong apical control, and produce stands with a narrow range of stem diameters. Mortality, and the concomitant loss of accumulated biomass, is not excessive and per-hectare productivity is potentially high. Trees of this ideotype are the forestry equivalents of agricultural field crops, and, like their agronomic counterparts, they require a high level of inputs. Control of weeds during establishment, and the period prior to stand closure, is particularly important. Once established, resources must not become limiting in stands comprised of 'crop' ideotypes, otherwise stagnation may occur and productivity may drop markedly. Therefore, thinning may be necessary in long rotations, because natural thinning would not readily occur, and would not be desirable economically.

The preceding discussion of ideotypes for stand conditions has assumed that the trees are established in pure species plantings. What about mixed stands? Although not all species mixtures are compatible, and do not produce synergistic responses (Trenbath 1974), mixtures may be desirable in certain situations. For example, mixed plantations of nitrogen-fixing and non-fixing species can have a greater productivity than pure stands on nitrogen-deficient sites (Gordon & Dawson 1979; Binkley 1983). Again, the choice of competitive ideotypes depends on the particular silvicultural system employed. If the two species are both managed as part of the overstorey, both should be 'crop' ideotypes. If, on the other hand, only one species is managed as the overstorey component (eg autumn olive, *Elaegnus umbellata* planted with *Juglans nigra*; Funk *et al.* 1979), then the overstorey species should conform to the 'dominating' ideotype. Many other silvicultural scenarios could be envisaged for mixed planting, each with its appropriate ideotypes.

Cannell (1978) cautioned that breeders may not want to adhere to a single ideotype, because trees need, on the one hand, to capture the site rapidly after planting, release or thinning (requiring an 'isolation' or 'dominating' ideotype), and, on the other hand, to utilize the site efficiently (requiring a 'crop' ideotype). Cannell goes on to suggest that phenotypically 'plastic' genotypes, which can modify their physiology and morphology in different competitive environments, might be desirable. This is a genetic solution to a problem that can also be addressed silviculturally. Proper site preparation and weed management can ensure that a weakly competitive ideotype quickly captures a site. Clones of *Populus* species and hybrids, for example, are notoriously weak competitors, but poplar plantations can be readily established if weeds are controlled during the first few years after planting (Dickmann & Stuart 1983). This requirement for weed control argues for consideration of another ideotypic trait – tolerance to commonly used pre- and post-emergent herbicides. Inter- and intraspecific variation in herbicide tolerance exists in poplars (Akinyemiju & Dickmann 1982), and probably occurs in other tree species as well.

The degree to which phenotypic plasticity is needed depends greatly upon the conditions under which a tree will be grown, and the type of wood products required. Trees destined for a general market must, of necessity, be plastic, because they will be grown under a range of silvicultural situations. Such trees must be more flexible than fit; that is, they must perform well over a range of sites and silvicultural systems, rather than perform outstandingly in a specific situation. Conversely, trees designed for a particular wood product could be quite rigid phenotypically, and may be engineered for particular planting sites and silvicultural systems.

4. *Phenology*

Seasonal physiological and morphological changes in trees are timed so as to maximize their 'fitness', in terms of survival and growth, during an often marginally favourable growing season, sandwiched between successive cold- or drought-induced dormant seasons. A wide range of phenological patterns exists within most commercially important tree species, which can be exploited to ensure that selected ideotypes make the best use of given growing seasons (Nienstaedt 1974). Here, the breeder cuts across the grain of evolution, because trees tend to be very conservative in their exploitation of environmental resources, sacrificing rapid growth for stress tolerance and survival (Cannell 1979). The tendency for local provenances to under-utilize the growing season is a reflection of this conservation, and is the basis for some successes in moving provenances of certain species to higher latitudes (*Juglans nigra*, Bey 1980; *Pinus strobus*, Wright *et al.* 1976).

Not only can commonly recognized phenological traits, such as time of bud-break and leafing out, shoot extension, bud formation and leaf abscission, be specified in an ideotype, but also the timing of internal physiological changes. For example, the seasonal timing of shifts in photosynthate flows to various sinks (Isebrands & Nelson 1983), or the time of cessation of photosynthesis in the autumn (Nelson *et al.* 1982) may be important. As our knowledge of the phenology of internal processes expands, so will our ability to precisely define these traits in a tree ideotype.

5. *Ageing effects*

During rotations lasting several decades, substantial changes occur in the physiology and morphology of the trees, as they age (Hackett 1980; Hanover 1980). These changes pose a special challenge because certain ideotypic characters will change, so that the ideotype for a 5-year-old tree may be quite different from that of a 40-year-old tree. Unfortunately, our present understanding of the physiology of older trees is not sufficient for us to construct late-rotation ideotypes for many species. Even if appropriate ideotypes could be devised, it would be difficult to select and breed trees that conformed to these ideotypes as they aged. It will be essential to test selections in stand conditions for a period that encompasses most of the anticipated rotation, particularly as juvenile-mature correlations are low for many traits (eg LaFarge 1975; Wilkinson 1974).

Two traits of older trees require special mention. First, to maximize the harvest index, the onset of reproductive maturity should occur late in the rotation. Tree fruits are strong sinks for available photosynthate (Dickmann & Kozlowski 1970), and heavy fruiting has been shown to depress vegetative growth in fruit and forest trees (Kozlowski 1971). An interesting side issue here is the effect that selection for early fruiting in forest tree seed orchard stock will have on the reproductive characteristics of their offspring; hopefully, genes controlling growth and those regulating flowering will segregate independently. Second, the duration of the exponential height growth phase should extend to the end of the rotation (Farmer 1978). Given the large inherent variability in shoot growth patterns that exists within tree species, and the trend towards shorter rotations, this objective should not be difficult to achieve.

C. Some cautions

While the ideotype concept presents many opportunities to tree breeders, implementation of this concept is not without risk. Experience to date with tree ideotypes has been limited, so there is reason to proceed with caution. Donald (1968) raised some questions concerning the use of model plants, while other doubts arise in forestry because of the unique character of trees and some peculiarities of the forestry enterprise.

1. Good physiological data may be lacking

An ideotype, like any other model, will be no better than the data upon which it is built. The recent trend towards ecophysiological studies, where trees (often mature trees) are monitored in their natural environment (eg Helms 1976; Hinckley et al. 1978), is heartening in this regard. For a long time, our knowledge of tree physiology was based either on data collected from seedlings grown in controlled environments, or on crude field studies of larger trees. Future progress must be built upon long-term in situ studies of trees in a silvicultural setting, even though the logistic, technological and financial problems of conducting such studies will be formidable. Studies which compare trees with contrasting phenotypic characteristics will be particularly valuable (Isebrands et al. 1983).

2. A breeding programme may become unduly narrowed

The definition of a model plant is potentially dangerous, because it could result in restricted vision and a disregard for alternative models that could produce equal or greater gains. Extreme narrowing of genetic variability that would result from adherence to a single ideotype could invite disaster from pest and pathogen epidemics.

Fortunately, tree breeders have the great advantage of a large and diverse gene pool from which ideotypes can be selected – perhaps in only one or two generations of recurrent selection, if large-scale surveys of existing populations were made. But to ensure that sufficient genetic diversity is built into a tree crop, several alternative ideotypes should be employed.

3. Ideotypes must be dynamic

By definition, an ideotype is a 'stop-frame' in the process of evolution, a prototype into which refinement and improvements can be built as new information becomes available. Certainly, there will be a lag between model construction and its realization in a plantation, but the breeder should not wait for this realization before revising the initial model.

Cropping systems and silvicultural technologies evolve, so those who construct ideotypes must be forward-looking and anticipate future environments (Frey 1970). This anticipation is not without its hazards, of course, and has always been the bane of forestry. We may safely assume that demand for wood will continue to increase, so that any step towards increased productivity will be welcomed, but we should not select single, specialized ideotypes based only on present silvicultural technologies.

4. *Ideotypes can limit silvicultural options*

Just as modern agronomic crop varieties are unable to compete and survive without intensive cultural inputs, so may the concept of tree ideotypes imply intensive silvicultural systems. For instance, a typical conifer ideotype has a long narrow crown, and stands of these trees can grow to harvest age without thinning (Kärki 1983); but weed control will be necessary well into the rotation, because the canopy may never fully close. Phenotypically plastic phenotypes (Cannell 1978) could increase flexibility in developing silvicultural prescriptions.

III. A CASE STUDY OF IDEOTYPE DEVELOPMENT

An example of ideotype development may be given from a co-operative research programme among scientists at the North Central Forest Experiment Station of the US Forest Service at Rhinelander, Wisconsin, the Department of Forestry at Michigan State University and other universities in the north central United States.

A. Background

The programme began in the early 1970s and was designed to provide physiological criteria for improving short-rotation, intensively cultured poplars. The goal was to obtain baseline morphological and physiological data on poplar trees grown in the field. Integrated studies, of crown morphology, photosynthesis, stomatal physiology and photosynthate distribution, were conducted in relation to biomass yield using traditional growth analysis (Isebrands *et al.* 1983). The philosophy was that detailed physiological data on a few representative poplar clones would be valuable at the early stage of the research programme. Studies of the few selected clones were also designed to enable baseline physiological data, derived from trees grown in controlled environments, to be extended to trees growing in the field.

B.   A short-rotation, intensive-culture poplar ideotype

The ideotype, outlined in Table I, assumed the following silvicultural system and product utilization: (a) a clone of a *Populus* species or hybrid would be

TABLE I.   Characteristics of a short-rotation, intensive-culture poplar ideotype

---

Growth and phenology
  Fast yearly shoot growth rate (>2 m yr^{-1}).
  Rapid height growth early in the growing season to quickly maximize the leaf area index, and slower growth later in the season to minimize vessel formation.
  Indeterminate growth habit with bud-set just prior to first frosts.
  High shoot/root ratio.
  Rapid shift of photosynthate flow to roots after bud-set.
  Weak competitor ('crop' ideotype).
  Efficient use of soil nutrients.
  Vigorous stump/stool sprouting, but weak root sprouting; sprouts few in number with strong apical control.
  Tolerance to pre- and post-emergent herbicides.
  Resistance to major pathogens (eg *Septoria musiva*, *Cytospora chrysosperma*, *Melampsora medusae*, and *Marssonina brunnea*) and insects (especially defoliators and borers).

Crown and leaves
  Large, vertically oriented leaves in the upper crown grading to smaller, horizontally oriented leaves in the lower crown.
  Leaves with a large photosynthetic rate, specific leaf weight, ratio of net photosynthesis to dark respiration, and water use efficiency.
  Leaves, especially in the upper crown, retained until late autumn to maximize the period of photosynthate production.
  Relatively few, vigorous but thin lateral branches (to maximize the harvest index).
  Branches borne at an acute angle from the main stem to produce a long, narrow crown.
  Short internodes on currently expanding shoot axes to maximize the number of 'phytomeric' units.
  High ratio of long (indeterminate) to short (determinate) shoots in the lower crown.

Stem and wood properties
  Excurrent growth habit with straight central stem.
  Cambium active until late in the growing season.
  Bark thin, low in stone cell content, and with over 20% fibre content.
  Small pith.
  Wood low in gelatinous fibres and extractives, with vessel content <20%.
  Specific gravity c 0.4 g cm^3, fibre length >0.8 mm.

Roots
  Vigorous rooting along the entire length of hardwood cuttings.
  Strongly developed taproot for anchorage and exploitation of soil water and nutrients.
  Dense fibrous root mass in the upper 10 cm of soil.
  Predisposed to infection by endomycorrhizas.
  Strong sink for photosynthates late in the growing season.

grown from unrooted cuttings on a moist, well-drained, cultivated, fertile site located in the northern Lake States (USA); (b) spacing would be approximately 2×2 m; (c) weeds would be controlled for the first two years; (d) the rotation would be six to eight years; (e) mechanical harvesting would be employed, with on-site chipping; (f) whole-tree chips would be pulped for production of linerboard; and (g) stand regeneration would be by stump coppicing.

The attributes of the ideotype for this system (Table I) were largely morphological, but physiological and phenological characters were also defined. This ideotype represents a refinement of the models first proposed by Dickmann (1975) and Larson et al. (1976), and is our current conception of an ideal tree for short-rotation, intensive culture (Hansen 1983).

IV.   CONCLUSIONS

In the future, forest management will be viewed as another form of intensive cropping, differing from agriculture mainly in the length of the rotation and the nature of the economic end product. To fully exploit the potential of intensive cropping systems, trees must be genetically engineered for these systems. Implementation of the ideotype concept can provide precise descriptive models, which tree breeders can work towards, and thereby increase the efficiency of tree improvement programmes. Although problems exist in the design and implementation of ideotypes, the potential benefits of using them are great.

ACKNOWLEDGMENTS

Special thanks are due to Drs M. W. Adams, J. W. Hanover, J. G. Isebrands and D. A. Michael for reviewing the draft of the manuscript.

REFERENCES

Adams, M. W. (1982). Plant architecture and yield breeding. *Iowa State J. Res.*, **56**, 225–254.
Akinyemiju, O. A. & Dickmann, D. I. (1982). Variation among 21 *Populus* clones in tolerance to simazine and diuron. *Can. J. For. Res.*, **12**, 708–712.
Bey, C. F. (1980). Growth gains from moving black walnut provenances northward. *J. For.*, **78**, 640–641, 645.
Binkley, D. (1983). Ecosystem production in Douglas-fir plantations: interactions of red alder and site fertility. *For. Ecol. Manage.*, **5**, 215–227.
Brunig, E. F. (1976). Tree forms in relation to environmental conditions: an ecological viewpoint. In: *Tree physiology and yield improvement*, edited by M. G. R. Cannell and F. T. Last, 139–156. London: Academic Press.
Cannell, M. G. R. (1978). Improving per hectare forest productivity. *Proc. North American Forest Biology Workshop, 5th*, edited by C. A. Hollis and A. E. Squillace, 120–148. Gainesville, FLA: University of Florida, School of Forest Resources.
Cannell, M. G. R. (1979). Biological opportunities for genetic improvement in forest productivity. In: *The ecology of even-aged forest plantations*, edited by E. D. Ford, D. C. Malcolm and J. Atterson, 119–144. Cambridge: Institute of Terrestrial Ecology.
DeBell, D. S., Brunette, A. P. & Schweitzer, D. L. (1977). Expectations from intensive culture on industrial lands. *J. For.*, **75**, 10–13.

Dickmann, D. I. (1975). Plant materials appropriate for intensive culture of wood-fiber in the North Central Region. *Iowa State J. Res.*, **49**, 281–286.

Dickmann, D. I. (1979). Physiological determinants of poplar growth under intensive culture. In: *Poplar research management and utilization in Canada*, edited by D. C. F. Fayle, L. Zsuffa and H. W. Anderson, 12–1 to 12–12. (Forest research information paper no. 102). Ontario: Ministry of Natural Resources.

Dickmann, D. I. & Kozlowski, T. T. (1970). Mobilization and incorporation of photoassimilated ^{14}C by growing vegetative and reproductive tissues of adult *Pinus resinosa* Ait. trees. *Pl. Physiol.*, *Lancaster*, **45**, 284–288.

Dickmann, D. I. & Stuart, K. W. (1983). *The culture of poplars in eastern North America*. East Lansing, MI: Michigan State University.

Donald, C. M. (1962). In search of yield. *J. Aust. Inst. agric. Sci.*, **28**, 171–178.

Donald, C. M. (1968). The breeding of crop ideotypes. *Euphytica*, **17**, 385–403.

Donald, C. M. & Hamblin, J. (1976). The biological yield and harvest index of cereals as agronomic and plant breeding criteria. *Adv. Agron.*, **28**, 361–405.

Evans, L. T. (1980). The natural history of crop yield. *Am. Scient.*, **68**, 388–397.

Farmer, R. E., jr. (1978). Yield components in forest trees. *Proc. North American Forest Biology Workshop, 5th*, edited by C. A. Hollis and A. E. Squillace, 99–119. Gainesville, FLA: University of Florida, School of Forest Resources.

Farnum, P., Timmis, R. & Kulp, J. L. (1983). Biotechnology of forest yield. *Science, N.Y.*, **219**, 694–702.

Ford, E. D. (1976). Competition, genetic systems and improvement of forest yield. In: *Tree physiology and yield improvement*, edited by M. G. R. Cannell and F. T. Last, 463–472. London: Academic Press.

Frey, K. J. (1970). Improving crop yields through crop breeding. In: *Moving off the yield plateau*, 15–58. (Special publication no. 20). Madison, WI: American Society of Agronomy.

Funk, D. T., Schlesinger, R. C. & Ponder, F., jr. (1979). Autumn-olive as a nurse plant for black walnut. *Bot. Gaz.*, **140**, S110–S114.

Gifford, R. M. & Evans, L. T. (1981). Photosynthesis, carbon partitioning, and yield. *A. Rev. Pl. Physiol.*, **32**, 485–509.

Gordon, J. C. (1975). The productive potential of woody plants. *Iowa State J. Res.*, **49**, 267–274.

Gordon, J. C. & Dawson, J. O. (1979). Potential uses of nitrogen fixing trees and shrubs in commercial forestry. *Bot. Gaz.*, **140**, S88–S90.

Hackett, W. P. (1980). Control of phase change in woody plants. In: *Control of shoot growth in trees*, edited by C. H. A. Little, 257–272. (Proc. Joint IUFRO Workshop S2.01–10 and S2.01–11). Fredericton, NB: Maritimes Forest Research Centre.

Hanover, J. W. (1980). Control of tree growth. *BioScience*, **30**, 756–762.

Hansen, E. A., compiler. (1983). *Intensive plantation culture: 12 years research*. (General technical report NC–91). USDA Forest Service.

Helms, J. A. (1976). Factors influencing net photosynthesis in trees: an ecological viewpoint. In: *Tree physiology and yield improvement*, edited by M. G. R. Cannell and F. T. Last, 55–78. London: Academic Press.

Hinckley, T. M., Lassoie, J. P. & Running, S. W. (1978). Temporal and spatial variations in the water status of forest trees. *Forest Sci. Monogr.* no. 20.

Horn, H. S. (1971). *The adaptive geometry of trees*. (Monographs in population biology no. 3). Princeton, NJ: Princeton University Press.

Isebrands, J. G. & Nelson, N. D. (1983). Distribution of ^{14}C-labelled photosynthates within intensively cultured *Populus* clones during the establishment year. *Physiologia Pl.*, **59**, 9–18.

Isebrands, J. G., Nelson, N. D., Dickmann, D. I. & Michael, D. A. (1983). Yield physiology of short rotation intensively cultured poplars. In: *Intensive plantation culture: 12 years research*, compiled by E. A. Hansen, 77–93. (General technical report NC-91). USDA Forest Service.

Jankiewicz, L. S. & Stecki, Z. J. (1976). Some mechanisms responsible for differences in tree form. In: *Tree physiology and yield improvement*, edited by M. G. R. Cannell and F. T. Last, 155–172. London: Academic Press.

Kärki, L. (1983). *Forest tree breeding combines the highest timber quality and the highest stem wood production per hectare*. (Information report no. 1.) Foundation for Forest Tree Breeding in Finland.

Keyes, M. R. & Grier, C. C. (1981). Above- and below-ground net production in 40-year-old Douglas-fir stands on low and high productivity sites. *Can. J. For. Res.*, **11**, 599–605.

Kozlowski, T. T. (1971). *Growth and development of trees*, vol. 2. New York: Academic Press.
LaFarge, T. (1975). Correlations between nursery and plantation height growth in slash and loblolly pine. *Forest Sci.*, **21**, 197–200.
Larson, P. R., Dickson, R. E. & Isebrands, J. G. (1976). Some physiological applications for intensive culture. In: *Intensive plantation culture: 5 years research*, 10–18. (General technical report NC-21). USDA Forest Service.
Matthews, M. A. & Boyer, J. S. (1984). Acclimation of photosynthesis to low leaf water potentials. *Pl. Physiol., Lancaster*, **74**, 161–166.
Nelson, N. D., Dickmann, D. I. & Gottschalk, K. W. (1982). Autumnal photosynthesis in short-rotation intensively cultured *Populus* clones. *Photosynthetica*, **16**, 321–333.
Nienstaedt, H. (1974). Genetic variations in some phenological characteristics of forest trees. In: *Phenology and seasonality modelling*, edited by H. Leith, 389–400. New York: Springer.
Radmer, R. & Kok, B. (1977). Photosynthesis: unlimited yields, unlimited dreams. *BioScience*, **27**, 599–605.
Tomlinson, P. B. (1983). Tree architecture. *Am. Scient.*, **71**, 141–149.
Trenbath, B. R. (1974). Biomass productivity of mixtures. *Adv. Agron.*, **26**, 177–210.
Wareing, P. F. & Matthews, J. D. (1973). Physiological and genetic factors determining productivity of species. *Proc. IUFRO Congress, 15th, Gainesville, Fla, 1971*, 136–143.
White, P. S. (1983a). Evidence that temperate east North American evergreen woody plants follow Corner's rules. *New Phytol.*, **95**, 139–145.
White, P. S. (1983b). Corner's rules in eastern deciduous trees: allometry and its implications for the adaptive architecture of trees. *Bull. Torrey bot. Club*, **110**, 203–212.
Wilkinson, R. C. (1974). Realized and estimated efficiency of early selection in hybrid poplar clonal tests. *Proc. Northeastern Forest Tree Improvement Conf., 21st*, 26–32.
Wright, J. W., Lemmien, W. A., Bright, J. N. & Kowalewski, G. (1976). Rapid growth of southern Appalachian white pine in southern Michigan. *Res. Rep. Michigan agric. Exp. Stn*, no. 307.
Zelitch, I. (1975). Improving the efficiency of photosynthesis. *Science, N.Y.*, **188**, 626–633.

8

DEFINITION AND EXPLOITATION OF FOREST TREE IDEOTYPES IN FINLAND

L. KÄRKI
Foundation for Forest Tree Breeding, Helsinki, Finland

P. M. A. TIGERSTEDT
Department of Plant Breeding, University of Helsinki, Helsinki, Finland

I. DEFINITION OF FOREST TREE IDEOTYPE

Although the term ideotype is derived from agriculture (Donald 1962, 1968), the notion of an ideotype is not new to forest tree breeding. When selecting 'plus' trees, conifer breeders have long favoured trees with narrow crowns, thin short branches and 'good' stem form (eg Lindquist 1938, 1946). However, tree breeders have usually focused on the attributes of individual trees rather than on stand performance, and some have distinguished 'quality trees' from 'volume-producing trees'. In Finland we have suggested that *extremely narrow-crowned trees* can produce both high-quality timber and a high yield per hectare, irrespective of whether the timber is to be utilized as fibre or lumber (Kärki 1965, 1971, 1980a and b, 1983). However, we would emphasize that high yields may be realized only when new stand management regimes are devised, based on analyses of yield-density relationships using the new ideotypes (Drew & Flewelling 1977, 1979).

We venture to suggest that the conifer 'crop' tree ideotype (for Finland, and perhaps elsewhere) has *stems* which are straight, have small taper, thin bark, good-quality timber and rapid height and diameter growth, and *branches* which are slow-growing, are consequently small in length and diameter, subtend angles of about 90 degrees with the stems, have few flowers, have large leaf areas per unit branchwood weight, retain their foliage, and produce long, green, very narrow (columnar or pendulous) crowns (Fig. 1; also illustrated by Kärki 1985). Also, the trees should be wind-firm and tolerant of snow loads. Many of these characteristics are positively correlated in closed stands (see below). We suggest that this morphology and many of the character correlations are due to *strong, genetically determined apical dominance* (or, strictly, apical control, Ford, this volume).

Some of the reasons why we believe that such narrow-crowned trees may be capable of producing high stemwood yields per hectare are as follows: (a) a large proportion of the biomass is allocated to stemwood rather than to branches, bark and reproductive organs; that is, there is a high harvest index; (b) there may be less competitive suppression of neighbouring small trees; (c) there may be more effective light interception, because of the large foliage/branchwood ratio and the large vertical crown depth (Oker-Blom & Kellomäki 1982); (d) there will be more direct precipitation to ground level, and less ground freezing owing to better snow cover; (e) there may be a smaller nutrient demand, because stems have a smaller nutrient concentration per unit weight than branches (Mälkönen 1974; Kärki 1985; see Cannell, this volume); and (f) there will be a greater leaf area duration, and less loss due to death of branch 'modular units' (Saarnijoki 1954; Harper 1978).

We foresee three disadvantages of the narrow-crowned tree form. First, our crop ideotypes would lack some of the attributes of 'isolation/competition' ideotypes as described by Cannell (1979a, b), and so might be less efficient at 'site capture' (ie capture of nutrients and light) than normal, spreading trees. Second, the low competitive ability of crop ideotypes may exacerbate the amount of interference from unwanted weeds during early stand development. And third, silvicultural systems giving the largest stemwood production within desirable rotations might yield trees with relatively small individual diameters. The first two disadvantages might be minimized by establishing the trees at high population densities, while the third disadvantage needs to be analysed with regard to yield-density relationships, as mentioned above.

We have identified some economic and management advantages of narrow-crowned trees, apart from our assumption of high yield per hectare of valuable stemwood. First, expensive thinning operations may be minimized, and in some cases eliminated. Second, pruning, if desirable, is easier and cheaper when branches are thin and at 90 degrees to the stems. Third, good bole form makes cutting more economical, as there is more stemwood per unit basal area (Kärki 1985). Fourth, a large proportion of the trees yield fairly uniform timber. Fifth, whole tree harvesting is easier. Finally, logging residues are small-sized and so are easy to handle.

In Finland, several hundred narrow-crowned trees have been selected in natural stands of *Pinus sylvestris* and *Picea abies*. Many of them have been progeny tested, and it has been shown that breeding values for harvest index can be established at age 15 (Velling & Tigerstedt 1984). Many thousands of grafts have been placed in clone banks, and in seed orchards which are now producing seed.

In *Pinus sylvestris*, special attention has been given to a genotype (a single tree) called E1101 (Fig. 1D), where the narrow-crowned habit seems to be determined by a single, dominant gene, as revealed by segregation in F_1 and F_2 progenies. In *Picea abies*, special attention has been given to the 'pendula' types (Fig. 1A), using open-pollinated progenies and clones (see below).

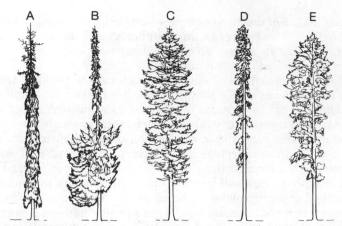

FIGURE 1.   Crown forms of *Picea abies* and *Pinus sylvestris* found in Finland.

A. Pendulous *P. abies*, found at Mäntsälä (an ideotype), described by Saarnijoki (1954) (*P. abies* f. *pendula*). Two open-pollinated progeny tests (16 and 33 years old) and a controlled cross all show about 50:50 segregation of pendulous:non-pendulous crown forms.

B. A dichotype *P. abies* (both broad and narrow-crowned on the same tree) found in southern Finland.

C. A 'normal' *P. abies*.

D. The very narrow-crowned *P. sylvestris*, tree E1101, growing at Punkaharju (an ideotype). This tree is about 100 years old, 32 m tall and 44 cm in diameter at breast height. Progeny tests indicate about 50:50 segregation of 'normal':E1101-type crown forms.

E. A 'normal' *P. sylvestris*.

II.   INHERITANCE OF CROWN FORM

Variations in branching habit, such as 'fastigiata', 'pendula' and 'columnaris', are known within coniferous and deciduous tree species throughout the world. Genetically, such variation forms a homologous series, and if a series is found in one species it is likely to exist in another species. Variation of this kind is due to rare mutations and may, in fact, arise during the development of a tree, as occurs in the 'dichotype pendulous' form of *Picea abies* (Fig. 1B).

As mentioned, the inheritance of a particular very narrow-crowned form can sometimes be attributable to a single, dominant gene, as has been demonstrated for a few pendulous forms of *Picea abies* (Lepistö 1984) as well as for *Pinus sylvestris* genotype E1101 (see Fig. 1). The naturally occuring genotypes must then be regarded as heterozygous carriers of the mutation. However, in most of our spruce material, the inheritance pattern is additive, although there are maternal effects, and pendulous parents exist which produce few pendulous individuals among their young progenies (Lepistö 1984).

Apical mutation which gives rise to 'dichotypes' (Fig. 1B) is often unstable, sometimes reverting to normal when propagated from seed, like the chimeric thornless brambles. In such cases, the breeding approach must be based on asexual multiplication. Young pendulous spruce can be propagated vegetatively, but there are problems of rejuvenation and somatic variation in tissue cultures. However, pendulous spruce also has a low female flowering capacity, which makes it difficult to multiply by seed. Clearly, with non-uniform patterns of genetic inheritance, the breeding strategy may be complicated.

In *Pinus sylvestris*, crown form can be both mono- and polygenically inherited. Single gene inheritance in E1101 was suggested by segregation approaching 50:50 among open-pollinated progenies at age 23. We suggest that, in both E1101 and in some of the pendulous spruces, a dominant gene controls apical dominance.

TABLE I. Narrow-sense heritabilities, and significant genetic correlations (P< 0·05) among morphological traits in a 16-year-old progeny test of 68 full-sib families of *Pinus sylvestris* in Finland

Character	Heritability	Positively correlated with	Negatively correlated with
Height (H)	0·14	D, CW, SW	BD/D
Diameter at breast height (D)	0·37	NB, HI, SW	H/D, BD/D
Slenderness (H/D)	—	BD/D	BD, NB, SW
Crown width (CW)	0·26	CW/H, BA	—
Crown form (CW/H)	—	—	HI
Branch diameter (BD)	0·05	BD/D	—
Relative branch diameter (BD/D)	0·17	—	HI, SW
Numbers of branches per whorl (NB)	0·18	SW	—
Stemwood fresh weight (SW)[1]	—	—	—
Harvest index (HI)[1]	0·52	—	—
Branch angle (BA)	0·22	—	—

[1] Based on destructive analysis of five trees of each of 30 full-sib families, where harvest index is stemwood fresh weight/total above-ground fresh weight.

The narrow-sense heritabilities (additive genetic/total phenotypic variances) of eight crown form and related traits were derived for *P. sylvestris* from a field trial of 68 full-sib families (7 randomized blocks, 9-tree plots, 2·5 m spacing) resulting from controlled crosses among 22 'plus' trees using 4 pollinators in a factorial mating design (Tigerstedt 1969). Measurements were made in 1982 at age 16 years from seed; the trees averaged 6·4 m in height and the canopy had closed (Velling & Tigerstedt 1984).

The most strongly inherited characters were (a) harvest index, measured as standing stemwood/total above-ground fresh weight ($h^2 = 0·52$, Table I), (b) diameter at breast height ($h^2 = 0·37$) and (c) crown width ($h^2 = 0·26$). We therefore concluded that a combination of these three traits would be the best selection criteria to use when breeding *P. sylvestris*. Total height was poorly inherited (Table I), as is often the case, although many tree breeding programmes are based on this trait. Branch diameter was poorly inherited in this study, which may be understood by regarding branches as 'modular units' affected by competition (Harper 1978). The inheritance of branching characteristics was quite different in progeny tests involving E1101 or the pendulous forms of *P. abies*, because these types remain narrow-crowned even when grown as isolated individuals. Thus, the heritability of branch diameter in one study including progenies of E1101 was 0·74 (Pöykkö 1982). We concluded that the most effective way to decrease branch size is to exploit single-gene effects. 'Number of branches per whorl' was poorly inherited (Table I); however, studies including E1101 progenies showed that branch numbers and branch diameters were negatively correlated (Velling 1982).

III. CORRELATION BETWEEN MORPHOLOGICAL TRAITS AND YIELD

Correlations, like variances, may be genetic (r_G) or environmental (r_E), and phenotypic correlations (r_P) are the sum of $r_G + r_E$. Phenotypic character correlations may be positive, while genetic correlations are negative. From a tree breeder's point of view, only genetic correlations, derived from progeny tests, are useful. The test material may be full- or half-sib families, or clones, but clones will give broad-sense heritabilities (total genetic/total phenotypic variances), and imply that vegetative propagation will be used for afforestation.

Genetic correlations among the traits measured in the 16-year-old trial discussed above showed that increased breast height diameter meant more branches per whorl, greater stemwood fresh weight and a high harvest index (Table I). Also, trees with a large volume tended to have a small ratio of branch to stem diameter (BD/D). Negative correlations existed between breast height diameter and stem slenderness (height/diameter) reflecting larger variation in diameter than in height, and resulting in more tapering in the high-volume trees. Most importantly, we found that trees with a high harvest index tended to be narrow-crowned, and to have relatively small branches. Similar relationships were reported by Cannell *et al.* (1983) among clones of *Picea sitchensis* and *Pinus contorta*. In our trial, the harvest index of different full-sib families ranged from 0·43 to 0·57, and families with high harvest indices varied greatly in stemwood fresh weight: that is, these two traits were not significantly correlated.

IV. SUGGESTIONS FOR THE EXPLOITATION OF FOREST TREE IDEOTYPES

A. Selection procedures

'Plus' tree selections in Finland were initially made among the phenotypic variants within natural stands, assuming polygenic inheritance. Comparisons between four 'plus' tree progenies and unselected controls at age 20 have shown that such selection increased breast height diameter by 2·3%, height by 6·8%, branch angle by 3·6%, number of branches per whorl by 8·6%, stem volume by 12·9%, and decreased branch thickness by 10·0% (Velling

1982). Thus, conventional 'plus' tree selection has improved the ideotypic traits listed above.

The results of artificial selection suggest that *natural* selection does not favour the crop tree ideotype, but rather a type that is more spreading and competitive. The tree E1101 (at Punkaharju; Fig. 1D) has been growing free from competition for 50 years, while the very narrow-crowned pendulous spruces (at Mäntsälä; Fig. 1A) have been repeatedly freed from competition by thinning during the past 40 years. We suggest that crop tree ideotypes should be selected in open stands, or before severe competition begins, but at an age when the crown form traits are expressed (from about age 15 in our field trials). In birch (*Betula pendula*), where genetic gains have been shown to be much greater than in conifers, selection can be done from about age 10 onwards.

In Finland, the conservative selection and breeding strategy based on polygenes will continue, but an alternative 'progressive' breeding strategy has begun based on monogenic inheritance of strong apical dominance in pine and spruce.

B. Silvicultural aspects

The 'crop' ideotype concept must include crop physiological and crop ecological aspects of forest trees. Crop physiological aspects include crown form, branch and stem characteristics, stemwood growth and the harvest index, while crop ecological aspects include competition and phenotypic plasticity. We would draw attention to the concept of 'ecological combining ability' (Harper 1967), the ability of different genotypes to interact in mixtures, and to two empirical 'laws' of plant communities: (a) the 3/2 power law of self-thinning (Yoda *et al.* 1963) and (b) the reciprocal yield law (Shinozaki & Kira 1956; Perry, this volume). These laws have recently been applied as forest management models for *Pinus radiata* and *Pseudotsuga menziesii* (Drew & Flewelling 1977, 1979), and similar attempts are being made in Finland for *Pinus sylvestris*, *Picea abies* and *Betula pendula* (Kellomäki & Nevalainen 1983). This is a new attempt at constructing yield models, recognizing that population structures are both density-dependent and genetically regulated. Pendulous spruces and E1101-type pines need to be fitted into these new models. At present, conclusions concerning their yield are largely speculative, and have to be verified in large silvicultural experiments. In such experiments, we need to study the effects of different initial planting densities and different thinning regimes. We also need to study the effects of genotype and species mixtures, possibly combining narrow-crowned conifers with fast-growing deciduous tree species, exploiting differences in 'ecological combining ability'.

Forest tree breeding to produce 'trees as crop plants' can be efficient only if it is closely followed by research on silvicultural management systems. We believe that a fundamentally new approach is needed to make full use of the potentials. Ideotype development in agricultural plants during this century has resulted in increased harvest indices in almost all cases, from tubers to beans and cereals. The harvest index has often been improved by 20–40%. This change has usually been based on intuitive selection for types that allocate more of their biomass to the valuable parts of the plant. But yield increases by using crop ideotypes in cereals have nearly always been accompanied by an increase in stand density. The ideology in this case has been that every individual in the stand must produce a valuable yield. We suggest that this should also be taken as a goal in the exploitation of forest trees.

REFERENCES

Cannell, M. G. R. (1979a). Biological opportunities of genetic improvement in forest productivity. In: *The ecology of even-aged forest plantations*, edited by E. D. Ford, D. C. Malcolm and J. Atterson, 119–144. Cambridge: Institute of Terrestrial Ecology.

Cannell, M. G. R. (1979b). Improving per hectare forest productivity. *Proc. North American Forest Biology Workshop, 5th*, edited by C. A. Hollis and A. E. Squillace, 120–148. Gainesville, FLA: University of Florida, School of Forest Resources.

Cannell, M. G. R., Sheppard, L. J., Ford, E. D. & Wilson, R. H. F. (1983). Clonal differences in dry matter distribution, wood specific gravity and foliage 'efficiency' in *Picea sitchensis* and *Pinus contorta*. *Silvae Genet.*, **32**, 195–202.

Donald, C. M. (1962). In search of yield. *J. Aust. Inst. agric. Sci.*, **29**, 171–178.

Donald, C. M. (1968). The breeding of crop ideotypes. *Euphytica*, **17**, 385–403.

Drew, J. T. & Flewelling, J. (1977). Some recent Japanese theories of yield-density relationships and their application to Monterey pine plantations. *Forest Sci.*, **23**, 517–534.

Drew, J. T. & Flewelling, J. (1979). Stand density management: an alternative approach and its application to Douglas fir plantations. *Forest Sci.*, **25**, 518–532.

Harper, J. L. (1967). A Darwinian approach to plant ecology. *J. Ecol.*, **55**, 247–270.

Harper, J. L. (1978). The demography of plants with clonal growth. In: *Structure and functioning of plant populations*, edited by A. H. J. Freysen and J. W. Woldendrop, 27–48. Amsterdam: North-Holland.

Kärki, L. (1965). Kuusi jalostuksen kohteena. (Tree breeding of spruce). *Pellervo*, **4–5**, 202–205.

Kärki, L. (1971). Solakan aidin sutjakat lapset. (The slender children of slim mothers). *Metsä ja Puu*, **11**, 16–17.

Kärki, L. (1980a). Breeding the timber quality of Norway spruce. *Proc. Scandinavian Seed Orchard Tree Breeding Group Meeting*. Mimeograph.

Kärki, L. (1980b). *Genetically narrow-crowned and fine-branched trees are valuable in forestry.* (Information note no. 1). Foundation for Forest Tree Breeding in Finland.

Kärki, L. (1983). *Forest tree breeding combines the highest timber quality and the highest stem wood production per hectare.* (Information note no. 3). Foundation for Forest Tree Breeding in Finland.

Kärki, L. (1985). Crop tree ideotypes and harvest index should be the basis of selection in cultivated trees. *Annu. Rep. Found. For. Tree breed. Finl. 1984*, 20–23.

Kellomäki, S. & Nevalainen, T. (1983). On relationship between stand density and tree size. *Silva fenn.*, **17**, 389–402.

Lepistö, M. (1984). *Pendulaominaisuuden periytyminen kuusella* (Picea abies *(L.) Karst.) (The inheritance of the pendula-trait in spruce)*. M.Sc. thesis, University of Helsinki.

Lindquist, B. (1938). Virkeskvalitet och rotnettovärde hos smalkronig och bredkronig tall. *Svenska SkogsvFör. Tidskr.*, **37**, 1–119.

Lindquist, B. (1946)). Den skogliga rasforskningen och praktiken. *Sv. Skogsf. Forl.* Stockholm. (*Genetics in Swedish forestry practice* (1948). Waltham, MA: Chronica Botanica Co.).

Mälkönen, E. (1974). Annual primary production and nutrient cycle in some Scots pine stands. *Metsäntutkimuslaitoksen Julkaisuja*, **84**, (5).

Oker-Blom, P. & Kellomäki, S. (1982). Effect of stand density on the within-crown light regime and dying off of branches. *Folia For.*, **509**, 1–14.

Pöykkö, T. (1982). Genetic variation in quality characters of Scots pine. An evaluation by means of the heritability concept. *Silva fenn.*, **16**, 135–140.

Saarnijoki, S. (1954). Uber ein Gruppenvorkommen von Trauerfichten, *Picea abies* (L.) H. Karst. f. *pendula* Jacq. & Herincq. *Commun. Inst. for. fenn.*, **42**(3).

Shinozaki, K. & Kira, T. (1956). Intraspecfic competition among higher plants. VII. Logistic theory of the C–D effect. *J. Inst. Polytech. Osaka Cy. Univ.*, Ser. D **7**, 35–72.

Tigerstedt, P. M. A. (1969). Progeny tests in a *Pinus sylvestris* (L.) seed orchard in Finland. *Acta for. fenn.*, **99**, 1–17.

Velling, P. (1982). Genetic variation in quality characteristics of Scots pine. *Silva fenn.*, **16**, 129–134.

Velling, P. & Tigerstedt, P. M. A. (1984). Harvest index in a progeny test of Scots pine with reference to the model of selection. *Silva fenn.*, **18**, 21–32.

Yoda, K., Kira, T., Ogawa, H. & Hozumi, K. (1963). Intraspecific competition among higher plants. XI. Self thinning in over-crowded pure stands under cultivated and natural conditions. *J. Biol. (Osaka City Univ.)*, **14**, 107–129.

9

THE CAPACITY FOR VEGETATIVE PROPAGATION IN TREES

R. R. B. LEAKEY

Institute of Terrestrial Ecology, Bush Estate, Midlothian, Scotland

I. INTRODUCTION

The roots and shoots of plants are capable of growth throughout their lives, owing to the presence of relatively undifferentiated cells with unrestricted developmental potential (Wareing & Graham 1976). The classic work of Steward (1970), in which whole carrot plants were grow from single cells, clearly demonstrated the totipotency of parenchyma cells, which in many species can dedifferentiate and develop into new plants (Street 1976). For centuries, horticulturists, botanists and foresters have exploited this capacity of plant cells to multiply and differentiate in a variety of propagation techniques.

The capacity of trees to be propagated vegetatively ought in theory to be similar to that of herbaceous plants; however, their greater size and structural complexity at maturity result in a loss in rooting ability which has to be avoided or overcome by using young plants, coppice or 'rejuvenated' shoots (Zimmermann 1976). Also, the capacity for vegetative propagation in trees varies greatly between species and genotypes, and is affected by both their environment and physiological state. Some examples of these influences will be described in this chapter (see also Komissarov 1969; Bonga & Durzan 1982; Hartmann & Kester 1983).

II. VEGETATIVE REGENERATION IN NATURAL STANDS

Many plants, notably weed species, have evolved the ability to regenerate vegetatively from intact or detached plant parts, some of which are specialized organs (Leakey 1981). In trees, this form of vegetative propagation is relatively uncommon, but a few examples are given below.

Sucker shoots grow from intact root systems in a number of genera, including *Ulmus, Robinia, Prunus, Malus, Populus* and *Liquidambar*. Suckers normally develop either from newly initiated meristems on young roots with a developed bark layer and some secondary thickening (Eliasson 1971a), or from preformed shoot primordia developing as protuberances in the phellogen of older roots up to about 2·5 cm in diameter (Schier 1973a). Suckers are apparently prevented from developing, at least in *Populus tremula*, by the accumulation of auxins in the roots, and are stimulated by treatments or events interrupting their translocation from the shoots (Eliasson 1971b, c). Apart from the regeneration of cut aspen and other poplar stands in the USA, little practical use is made of suckering on intact root systems, although sucker shoots could be collected and planted. In a few instances, techniques have been developed to increase the incidence of suckering, as in potted seedlings of *Agathis robusta* (Whitmore 1977) and in natural stands of *Santalum album* (Mahmood Husain & Ponnuswamy 1982).

In the annually burned zone of tropical Australia, rhizomes and lignotubers provide a survival mechanism for a range of *Eucalyptus* species, which maintain a subterranean 'bank' of viable, dormant buds for root and shoot production (Lacey *et al.* 1982). In a somewhat similar way, old and isolated trees of *Doryphora sassafras* and *Eucryphia moorei*, in the cool temperate rainforests of Australia, are adapted to regenerate by producing new shoots from their swollen stem bases (Johnson & Lacey 1983). In North America, *Quercus gambelii* and *Prunus virginiana* produce a shallow network of rhizomes, bearing some large roots which extend vertically downwards to a deep-feeding root system (Schier 1983).

Some intact prostrate branches or buried stems are able to produce roots when in contact with damp ground. This natural 'layering' ability is particularly well seen in some tropical species (Hall & Swaine 1981) and it is exploited in the propagation of various fruit and ornamental tree species (see IIIB, below).

Adventive polyembryony (the asexual multiplication of seeds by agamospermy or apomixis) occurs in *Shorea agami* and *Shorea ovalis* – emergent trees of the Malaysian tropical forests – and it may be common in the Dipterocarpaceae (Kaur *et al.* 1978; Jong 1980). It also occurs in apple, and is well known in cultivated fruit trees like *Citrus, Eugenia, Garcinia* and *Lansium*, originating from the tropical forest understorey.

III.   VEGETATIVE PROPAGATION IN ARTIFICIAL SYSTEMS

A.   Graft formation

Scion/rootstock grafting is an age-old practice, and numerous techniques have been developed by horticulturists and foresters (Garner 1979; Hartmann & Kester 1983). They all exploit the ability of cambial cells, placed and held firmly in close contact, to produce callus, uniting the graft, and subsequently differentiating new vascular tissues. The ability to produce a graft union, which will not disintegrate or break, is a composite function of many genetic, environmental, anatomical and physiological factors.

1. Genetic factors

Plants with continuous cambial layers which can readily be placed in direct contact are easiest to graft; they include all true woody species. Grafting success is greatest between closely related plants (Hartmann & Kester 1983); *heteroplastic* grafts between plants of different families and genera are rare, and different species within a genus can be difficult to intergraft, although over 800 combinations are known (Sziklai 1967). Among the spruces, *Picea abies* and *P. glauca* are used as rootstocks for at least six other species (Holst *et al.* 1956). Compatibility in interspecific grafts is sometimes successful only when using specific clonal combinations, as with peach and almond scions on plum rootstocks, in which even reciprocal clonal combinations can fail (Hartmann & Kester 1983). Very easy and compatible unions often result from *homeoplastic* graftings between clones of the same species, as they do from *autoplastic* grafts within a clone. In a few instances, as in peaches, certain species will graft better on to other species than on to themselves.

2. Environmental factors

Probably the most common environmental causes of grafting failure are losses of cell turgidity and desiccation, sub- or supra-optimal temperatures for rapid cell growth, the incidence of disease (particularly virus infections) and movement of the scion on the stock. Great care has to be taken to protect the thin-walled, tender parenchyma cells from water stress, which might arise internally through excessive transpiration from the scion and/or externally by inadequate protection of the graft itself.

The need for rapid cell division in the cambium means that grafting should be done at a time of year when temperatures are favourable and the tissues are active or breaking dormancy. In temperate zones, these conditions often occur in spring when, for example, grafting success in *Pseudotsuga menziesii* can exceed 90% (Copes 1970). In the tropics, the equivalent situation occurs prior to the transition from dry to rainy seasons (Okoro 1976). In hot climates, it is often necessary to shade the grafts – this provides a cool, moist environment and can considerably extend the grafting period (Hearne 1971).

3. Anatomical factors

The capacity to develop a compatible union is greatly dependent on the close juxtaposition of the cambium across the graft, giving direct and functional connections within the xylem and phloem. Cell recognition, callus formation and differentiation are critical steps in graft formation (Hartmann & Kester 1983). In *Pinus sylvestris* and *Picea abies*, cell division first occurs most vigorously in those regions of the stock that act as storage places for nutrients, like the parenchyma cells of the rays (Dormling 1963), but, in well-matched grafts, tissues external to the cambium produce the most callus.

4.   *Physiological factors*

Normally, it is essential for vigorous growth that the stock and scion are correctly orientated. Thus, in stem grafts, the proximal end of scions are inserted into the distal ends of stocks, and, when shoots are grafted on to roots, their proximal ends are brought together (Hartmann & Kester 1983).

Despite a considerable body of practical evidence suggesting that the condition of the stocks and scions is important for the successful development of a graft union, there are few physiological data indicating which aspects are important. Seasonal variation has been demonstrated in apple, by comparing field-grown micro-grafted scions *in vitro* with those grown *in vitro*: consistent year-round success was achieved in the latter but not the former (Huang & Millikan 1980). Greatest success with field-grown material is usually achieved when the scion is dormant, but has been chilled, and when the stock is beginning to make active growth (Holst *et al*. 1956). However, there are few data to explain why this is so. Furthermore, little is known about the role of plant hormones in the development of a graft union.

The compatibility of graft unions is ultimately a function of biochemical events. Two types of incompatibility have been observed: those that are translocated and those that are localized; only the latter can be overcome by the insertion of a compatible interstock or incompatibility bridge. Translocated incompatibilities involve phloem degeneration and necrosis, while localized incompatibilities often result from translocation difficulties, such as the abnormally early termination of xylem growth (Copes 1975).

Biochemically, the compatibility of a graft union may depend on recognition events between the division products of cells within the vascular tissue and cortex, but little work has been done using tree species. In autoplastic grafts of tomato, a pectinaceous common wall complex is produced between stock and scion, which subsequently becomes thin in places to allow the development of plasmodesmatal connections between cells that are in contact. Jeffree and Yeoman (1983) suggested that the cell walls become thin in response to an exchange of diffusible messenger molecules, providing a direct structural linkage between membranes of opposing cells and a pathway for molecules with a recognition function. This may be a critical step in a hierarchy of recognition events, determining the capacity of a graft to form a compatible union. However, incompatibility between pear (*Pyrus communis*) and quince (*Cydonia oblonga*), in warm climates, is attributed to the catabolism of a cyanogenic glycoside (prunasin) ascending into the pear scion from the quince stock (Gur *et al*. 1968). Other evidence on the causes of incompatibility implicates peroxidase activity in the phloem. Thus, grafts between *Prunus* cultivars produce quantitatively more, and qualitatively different, peroxidases above and below the union (Schmid & Feucht 1982), and peroxidase activity is negatively correlated with *in vitro* micro-grafting success in peach (*Prunus persica*) (Pöessel *et al*. 1980).

B.   Layering

The stimulation of rooting on intact stems (layering) has traditionally been used in several forms. Mound layering or stooling has been used to propagate apple and pear rootstocks, where success can depend on the size of the plants established in the stoolbed (Howard 1977). Simple layering is used to propagate filberts (*Corylus maxima*) and air layering, or marcottage, is used on litchi (*Nephelium litchi*) and mature pines (Hartmann & Kester 1983). In all these circumstances, the part of the shoot to be rooted is kept in the dark under the soil or enclosed in a polythene-covered bundle of moss. The bark may be removed or cut, to promote the accumulation of carbohydrates and endogenous hormones, and auxins may be applied to the wound. The greatest success is achieved in spring, using vigorously leafy shoots. In the tropical hardwood *Triplochiton scleroxylon*, root formation was greatest on leading shoot internodes and declined with increasing order of branching. Auxins were beneficial and disbudding was detrimental to rooting (Okoro & Omokaro 1975). Marcotts were more successful on large trees than on saplings, and the capacity to form roots was greatest in August, at the end of the growing season. By contrast, air layering of *Morus alba*, *Ficus carica*, *Grewia optiva* and *Acacia catechu* is most successful before the Indian monsoon (Khosla *et al.* 1982).

C. Propagation from root and rhizome fragments

As mentioned above, shoot bud primordia can form on intact roots (in *Populus*, *Salix*, *Prunus*, etc). The initiation and development of these buds can be stimulated in summer by artificial fragmentation, which releases them from the effects of high levels of endogenous auxin and β inhibitor (Eliasson 1971c). In *Populus tremula*, the levels of β inhibitor were ten times greater in root fragments in the light than in the dark, but shoot growth was unaffected. The absence of β inhibitor in dark shoots may enable suckers to emerge on roots at great depths in the soil (Eliasson 1971b).

In *Populus tremuloides*, sucker production was increased by treating root fragments with (a) ethylene-releasing 'Ethepon' at $100 \, mg \, l^{-1}$ (Schier & Campbell 1978), (b) the anti-auxin α-(p-chlorophenoxy)isobutyric acid (CPIBA) in June, when their auxin content was greatest (Schier 1975), and (c) gibberellic acid (GA_3) in July, applied to visible buds (Schier 1973b). Clones differed considerably, with an average of 6 to 24 sucker shoots forming on root fragments of different genotypes (Schier 1974). The use of long root fragments (up to 1 m) did not increase the total number of shoots formed or the numbers overwintering (Perala 1978).

In apple cultivars, adventitious shoots form only after root fragmentation. The greatest number of shoots formed on root cuttings collected in early winter, when they were rich in stored polysaccharides (Robinson & Schwabe 1977b). Shoot formation was enhanced by cold storage and cytokinin application, and shoot cuttings from them were subsequently rooted easily with applied auxins (Robinson & Schwabe 1977a).

In contrast to the development of sucker shoots from *Populus* root fragments, shoot production by oak (*Quercus gambelii*) and chokecherry (*Prunus virginiana*) rhizomes was greater in the light than in darkness (Schier 1983). Rhizome fragments of both species produced similar numbers of shoots, perhaps owing to the development of dominance (Leakey 1981), although chilling dormant rhizomes of *Q. gambelii* enhanced sprouting. It appears that these shoots, from underground stems, have topophytic variation similar to that in aerial shoots. This variation is not found in sucker shoots from roots (Schier 1983).

D.   Bud formation *in vitro*

Few plant tissues are completely unsuitable as the starting point for *in vitro* culture. The capacity for propagation by *in vitro* culture is limited by the establishment and maintenance of the tissue in an appropriate condition to induce the rapid division and subsequent differentiation of cells. The explant must be kept in sterile conditions, and provided with (a) macro- and micro-nutrients, (b) a source of energy, usually sucrose, (c) vitamins, amino-acids, etc, and (d) the correct balance and sequence of plant growth regulators, co-factors, etc, to regulate the subcellular and cellular processes of cell division and differentiation of shoot, root, or embryo. Success will also depend on the osmotic pressure and pH of the medium, which can be a solid or liquid, and the physical environment. The details of these requirements are presented in many books on this subject and will not be considered further here.

Three *in vitro* propagation systems have evolved: organogenesis, embryo-genesis and meristem proliferation or micro-propagation. A problem common to these methods is the exudation of toxic phenolic compounds into the medium. Various techniques have been used to reduce this problem, including the use of only a short period of sterilization in sodium hypochlorite rather than alcohol (Staritsky & van Hasselt 1980), soaking the explants in sterile water for 3 h prior to culturing them (Chevre *et al.* 1983; Vieitez *et al.* 1983), culturing in the dark, and using activated charcoal (Monaco *et al.* 1977).

1.   *Organogenesis*

Although a number of tree species have been successfully propagated by organogenesis from callus culture (see David 1982; Brown & Sommer 1982), this approach has been relatively unsuccessful in trees (Jones 1983). It remains important, however, because the rates of multiplication from individual cells are very great. On the other hand, there is a risk that genetic changes will occur.

In forest trees, successful organogenesis has usually occurred in callus cultures derived from embryos, or from hypocotyl and cotyledon explants, although tissues from large trees have also been found to be capable of developing adventitious primordia (Biondi & Thorpe 1982). Seed or seedling-derived material is generally recommended, and attention should be paid to their physiological state, including the conditions of germination and seed stratification (Sommer & Caldas 1981).

Differences in media composition cannot be considered here, except to say that, with various modifications, the Murashige and Skoog basal medium (M & S) is the most commonly used. The performance of species and cultivars differs on media with different mineral composition, with high levels of organogenesis in *Picea abies* occurring on media with slow callus formation (Bornman 1983). Generally, the differentiation of shoot primordia from callus requires higher concentrations of cytokinins than auxins, but the relative levels of these have to be determined for each species, and possibly modified for different clones. The different auxins (Durzan 1982) and cytokinins (von Arnold 1982) used can have varying optimal concentrations, depending on the production system. Organogenesis in *Pinus radiata* is promoted by withdrawing cytokinins after a 21-day bud initiation phase (Biondi & Thorpe 1982). In *Picea abies*, the cytokinin requirement for organogenesis can best be met by a short-duration (3 h), high-concentration (125 μM) pulse, or by lower concentrations (5 μM) with vacuum infusion (Bornman 1983). Other advances in the generally poor performance of *P. abies* have resulted from attention to the details of basal media concentration, to the optimal balance of different cytokinins, and to photoperiod (von Arnold 1982).

The culture of protoplasts – the living parts of plant cells removed from their cell walls by enzymatic digestion – is a necessary prerequisite to the production of somatic hybrids by the fusion of cells from different plant species, and their subsequent regeneration by callus culture. In trees, protoplasts have been isolated and cultured for a number of species (reviewed by Ahuja 1982), but their capacity for propagation remains virtually unknown, as this technique is still in its infancy. The main exception to this generalization is the *Citrus sinensis* cultivar Shamouti, which has a high optimal plating density (4×10⁻⁵ cells ml⁻¹) for cell division with a lower optimum (10⁵ cells ml⁻¹) for colony formation, and active callus colonies free from protoplasts subjected to X-ray treatments have subsequently formed embryoids (Vardi *et al.* 1975).

In common with the previously mentioned *in vitro* techniques, the physiological condition of the starting material for protoplast isolation is critical, with seedling material, particularly that already cultured with auxins and cytokinins *in vitro*, being the most amenable. In *Betula*, the yield of protoplasts from 3- to 4-week-old seedling shoot cultures exceeded, by 30 times, that from 12- to 16-week-old cultures (Smith & McCown 1983). The reformation of cell walls in culture is prevented by the inclusion of cellulase and pectinase in the liquid media, together with osmotic stabilizing agents like 0·4–0·8 M mannitol (see Kirby 1982). *Pinus taeda* protoplasts can form cell walls in 48 h, divide every four to nine days, and produce numerous callus colonies in three weeks (Teasdale & Rugini 1983). The future prospects for long-term culture, and probably protoplast fusion, are reasonably good. Furthermore, the occurrence of genetic variability in rapidly dividing single-cell cultures may be a source of somaclonal variation of benefit to future tree improvement programmes (Larkin & Scowcroft 1981).

2. *Embryogenesis*

Cells can form somatic embryos, under basically similar conditions to the above, as in internode and leaf explants of coffee (*Coffea arabica*) (Monaco *et al.* 1977), nucellus tissues of citrus fruits (Button & Kochba 1977) and immature embryos of cacao (*Theobroma cacao*) (Pence *et al.* 1979). In coffee, different combinations of auxins and cytokinins seem to determine both the speed with which embryo initiation occurs and the final extent of multiplication (Staritsky & van Hasselt 1980). In four *Citrus* cultivars, the carbohydrate source is thought to be important for embryo formation, with galactose in particular enhancing embryogenesis (Kochba *et al.* 1982). Mango (*Mangifera indica*), like *Citrus*, is a naturally polyembryonic species (Rangaswamy 1982), and seems to be highly amenable to embryogenesis *in vitro* (Litz *et al.* 1984). In mango, success followed a series of media transfers, in which auxin (2, 4–D) replaced coconut milk, and was then omitted, leaving the basal medium free from plant growth regulators. Similarly, auxins, cytokinins and gibberellins inhibited embryogenesis of *Citrus* on a galactose-containing medium (Kochba *et al.* 1982), although benzyladenine was later needed for embryo germination. Contrary to these experiences, the capacity for embryogenesis in forest trees has been stimulated by the addition of gibberellic acid to the medium, both with and without cytokinins, in *Santalum album* and *Eucalyptus citriodira* (Sita *et al.* 1980; Sita 1982). We now know that a number of tropical tree species are naturally polyembryonic, so the prospects look encouraging for further exploitation of embryogenesis.

3.   Meristem proliferation of shoot cultures

This technique starts with an organized meristematic explant – normally a shoot tip or axillary bud (preferably with little callus) containing a terminal bud and many lateral buds. The objective is to stimulate the continued growth of all these meristems by enhancing the capacity for sylleptic branching (as defined by Tomlinson & Gill 1973) and preventing the establishment of apical dominance. Large multiplication rates (4- to 10-fold every four to six weeks) have been achieved by regularly subculturing and cropping the shoots for subsequent rooting. Over the last eight years, this approach has been applied successfully to an increasing range of tree species, notably apple and some other horticultural and plantation crops (Jones 1983).

As in material for all forms of propagation, the state of the explant is important, but a year-round supply of young apple shoots has been successfully achieved by removing leafless winter shoots from cold storage at regular intervals. Although successful proliferation occurs most frequently from vigorous young shoots, explants from mature trees of *Tectona grandis*, *Tamarindus indica*, *Punica granatum* and *Eucalyptus citriodora* have been cultured and rooted (Mascarenhas *et al.* 1982). Similarly, successful propagation has occurred using explants from 4-year-old apple scion cultivars (Jones *et al.* 1979).

Not surprisingly, clones vary in their media requirements, and in their capacity to proliferate, perhaps reflecting differing degrees of apical dominance. For instance, whereas shoot proliferation of apple rootstocks M7 and M26 and several scion cultivars was greatly enhanced by phloridzin and phloroglucinol (PG) in the presence of $0·5$ mg l^{-1} 6-benzlaminopurine (BAP) (Jones 1976; Jones *et al.* 1979), cytokinin-induced proliferation in M9 was not enhanced by PG, although it did improve subsequent rooting (James & Thurbon 1981). Cytokinins alone ($0·5–1·0$ mg l^{-1}) were similarly found to be sufficient for proliferation of M27, M26 and the scion cultivar Macspur (Lane & McDougald 1982).

Beneficial effects of PG have been reported in plum and cherry (Jones & Hopgood 1979). In plum, it enhanced shoot numbers three-fold in BAP-treated cultures of the cultivar Pixy, but it had no additive effect in the cherry rootstock F12/1, while in the Myrobalan plum rootstock cytokinin was effective on its own (Hammerschlag 1982). In cacao, on PG-free media, zeatin and zeatin-riboside (10^{-5} M) were equally as effective as BAP (10^{-6} M), but the cultures died after 12 to 14 months (Passey & Jones 1983). In *Pistacia vera*, on the other hand, kinetin was not as effective as BAP, and gibberellins improved neither proliferation nor shoot growth (Barghchi & Alderson 1983).

In chestnut (*Castanea* spp.), the number of shoots formed per culture, and the elongation of the longest shoots were affected by the nutrient content of the media (Vieitez *et al.* 1983), and in common with some forest trees the M & S medium was not found to be the best. Chevre *et al.* (1983) overcame this difficulty by lowering the pH to 4, doubling the Ca and Mg concentrations and adding ascorbic acid. However, cultures derived from mature trees had to be subcultured to a BAP-free, auxin-containing medium for elongation to occur prior to rooting.

Among the forest tree species, shoots of *Eucalyptus* spp. have proliferated on various media. *E. citriodora* was successfully propagated on media similar to those used on horticultural crops, except that phloroglucinol was not tried (Sita & Vaidyanathan 1979; Mascarenhas *et al.* 1982). In *E. ficifolia*, on the other hand, proliferation of explants occurred on media in which the auxin concentration exceeded the cytokinin concentration, although only seedling origin cultures produced rooted plantlets (de Fossard *et al.* 1977).

Clonal variation in growth and proliferation in culture have been observed in *Populus* spp. (Ahuja 1983) and in a preliminary study of African mahogany (*Khaya ivorensis*). In the former species, 26 out of 48 clones failed to grow in culture, while, in the latter, shoots of different clones proliferated on an NAA-containing medium with BAP ranging from 0·9 to 1·5 mg l^{-1} (England & Leakey, unpublished).

Similar success has been achieved in coniferous trees, for example in *Sequoia sempervirens* where activated charcoal enhanced shoot elongation (Boulay 1977). Explant origin affected the level of success in *Pinus radiata*, a species now reliably propagated *in vitro*, with cultures of embryo origin rapidly producing an average of nine shoots each, while those from seedling shoot tips took longer to produce 25 shoots each (Horgan & Aitken 1981).

E. Rooting stem cuttings and *in vitro* shootlets

The capacity of stem cuttings to form roots can be assessed by (a) the percentage of cuttings rooted, (b) the number of roots per rooted cutting, and (c) the speed with which roots emerge and grow. These three criteria are not necessarily related, although generally the longer a cutting takes to root the fewer roots develop. It is also important commercially that there are at least three or more well-branched roots dispersed on all sides of the cuttings. In African mahogany (*Khaya ivorensis*), the form of the root system is affected by the slope of the cutting base (Leakey, unpublished), and the number of roots formed on apple winter cuttings can be increased by splitting the base of the cutting (Howard *et al.* 1984).

The rooting process can be divided into four stages: (a) dedifferentiation, which, in woody plants, usually occurs in cells close to the central core of vascular tissue, often in parenchyma cells near immature or secondary xylem and phloem (see Haissig 1974a), (b) the formation of root initial cells in these newly meristematic areas, (c) the organization of these cells into root primordia, and (d) their subsequent growth and emergence. It should be remembered that the requirements for root initiation and root elongation often differ, the former being particularly influenced by the genetic and physiological state of the plant, while the latter is more sensitive to environmental factors.

Rooting ability varies between tree species, between clones within species, and among plants within clones. The genetic component of this variability may sometimes be attributed to (a) a lack of endogenous auxins, phenolic or other rooting co-factors, (b) a lack of enzymes or their activators for synthesis of auxin-phenol complexes, (c) the presence of inhibitors, or (d) the presence of enzymes that oxidize or degrade auxins or their co-factors. Variation among plants within clones is attributable mainly to the physiological condition of the stockplant. This condition can be affected by (a) the environment and season, (b) the position of the harvested shoots on the plants, (c) the age and size of the tree, and (d) the incidence of pathogens, virus particles and mycorrhizal organisms (Howard 1972; Hartmann & Kester 1983; Leakey 1983). Additionally, and very importantly, the capacity to develop roots is strongly influenced by the propagator's treatment of the cuttings, (a) chemically, by the application of auxins, other growth regulators, rooting co-factors, minerals and fungicides, (b) physically, either by influencing the size of the cutting, its leaf area, or by wounding or splitting the base, and (c) environmentally, by manipulation of moisture/humidity, light, temperature and the type of rooting medium used.

Clearly, the capacity of cuttings to root is influenced by many factors, so it is perhaps not surprising that tree breeders have sometimes been disappointed by the slow progress made towards large-scale mass propagation (see Bridgwater and Franklin, this volume). This viewpoint is especially strong in forestry, because of the importance attached to conifers, which until recently have been relatively difficult to root, particularly *in vitro* (Jones 1983).

Among broadleaved species, there are differences in ability to root, but experience suggests that most species can be rooted easily (Leakey *et al.* 1982b) although detailed studies are necessary to overcome specific problems in a few difficult-to-root species.

The choice of propagation technique has been extended in recent years by the development of *in vitro* systems. Although technologically more difficult than traditional systems of propagation, an increasing number of species are being successfully cultured *in vitro*; however, few species have yet been propagated commercially *in vitro*. Explants collected from large mature trees are particularly difficult to propagate. Space does not allow a full discussion of the many factors influencing rooting of stem cuttings, but a brief synopsis follows, using examples from recent work (see also Haissig 1985).

1.   *The role of auxins*

Auxins are basipetally translocated in plant stems, and are largely responsible for the polarity of shoots. Since the discovery fifty years ago that auxins greatly increased the capacity of cuttings to produce roots in most plant species, auxins have become universally used alone, or in combination with other chemicals, as an aid to propagation in horticulture and forestry.

Synthetic auxins are now usually preferred to endogenous indoleacetic acid (IAA). Indole-3-butyric acid (IBA) is the most commonly used, often combined with α-napthalene acetic acid (NAA) or one of the phenoxyacetic acids. Recently, equimolar concentrations of aryl- and phenyl-esters of IAA and IBA have been reported to outperform the unmodified acids in *Pinus banksiana* (Haissig 1979, 1983).

The effects of auxins on rooting capacity may depend on the method of application (Howard 1973). Common forms of treatment include (a) a quick dip in relatively concentrated solution, in which a proportion of the solvent, if not all, is an alcohol, and (b) a soak in relatively weak aqueous solutions. In both cases, the amount of auxin taken up is unknown and a more precise approach would be to apply known weights of auxin to cuttings of known sizes and sensitivities (Bowen *et al.* 1975; Leakey *et al.* 1982a; Amerson & Mott 1982; James 1983a).

Differing responses to auxins between species are well known (Nanda *et al.* 1970), but there can also be within-species variation in auxin preference, as in *Triplochiton scleroxylon* (Leakey *et al.* 1982a). In apples, scion cultivars are generally more difficult to root than the clonal rootstocks, although there is considerable variation between rootstocks (Delargy & Wright 1979; James 1983b).

In addition to species and clone, auxin applications also commonly interact with season of treatment (eg *Pinus sylvestris*, Eliasson *et al.* 1977) and age and size of the stockplant (eg *Olea europaea*, Portlingis & Therios 1976).

2. The role of co-factors

Although auxins play an important role in the rooting process, there are many occasions when a range of other substances are required to enhance auxin activity. A major group of these has been called the 'rooting co-factors' (Haissig 1974b) which are a complex of indole and phenolic substances, together with their oxidative enzymes that may directly affect the initiation of root primordia. However, there may be intricate interactions between these co-factors, auxins and other substances. In pear (*Pyrus communis*) there is evidence that indole-phenolic complexes exist (Fadl & Hartmann 1967), while in hardwood cuttings of the apple rootstock M26 no such evidence has been found (Bassuk *et al.* 1981), although polyphenyl oxidase (PPO) activity, and levels of phloridzin (a phenolic glycoside), increased prior to increases of a number of endogenous co-factors, which in turn were related to improvements in rooting ability (Bassuk & Howard 1981). The importance of phenols is emphasized by the enhanced rooting *in vitro* of apples (Jones & Hatfield 1976; James & Thurbon 1981), plums (Jones & Hopgood 1979) and cacao (Passey & Jones 1983), following the addition of phloroglucinol to the culture medium.

Cytokinins are involved in cellular differentiation processes, but there are only a few reports of cytokinin-enhanced rooting. More commonly, applied cytokinins inhibit rooting. Higher levels of endogenous cytokinins were found in difficult-to-root *Populus tremula*, than in easy-to-root *Populus × euramericana*

(Okoro & Grace 1978). It appears, however, that the balance of enzymes important to the formation of indole-phenolic complexes may sometimes by complicated by sensitivity to plant growth regulators (*Rhododendron*, Foong & Barnes 1981; *Mangifera indica*, Sadhu *et al.* 1978). As will be seen later, these balances can also be affected by the environment and stockplant condition.

3. Role of the leaf

It is common experience that leafless summer cuttings rarely root, while leafless winter cuttings root well, especially at the end of the winter. This difference exists because winter cuttings have greater amounts of stored reserves and endogenous co-factors than summer cuttings, and winter cuttings can have preformed root initials (Cheffins & Howard 1982a, b). Winter cuttings are, however, dependent on the rapid emergence of new shoots to replenish dwindling carbohydrate reserves (*Populus* spp., Okoro & Grace 1976). Summer cuttings, by contrast, are entirely dependent on the leaf for photosynthates. Hence, the carbohydrate content of leafy cuttings of *Triplochiton scleroxylon* almost doubled in nine days, whereas carbohydrate reserves in leafless cuttings were virtually depleted over the same period (Leakey *et al.* 1982a). However, not all the effects of leaves are beneficial (Reuveni & Raviv 1980), and there is evidence for optimal leaf areas per cutting. For instance, leaf areas greater than 50 cm² per cutting were detrimental in *T. scleroxylon* and *Cleistopholis glauca*, but not in *Terminalia ivorensis*

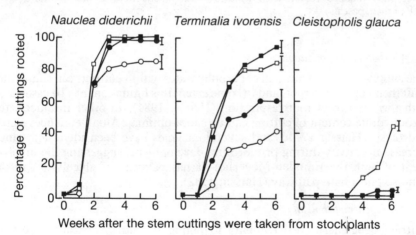

FIGURE 1. Differences in the rooting ability of leafy stem cuttings of three tropical hardwood species, and the effects of different leaf areas per cutting. O=5 cm², ●=10 cm², □=50 cm² and ■=100 cm². The cuttings were treated with 20 μg indole-3-butyric acid, and were rooted under intermittent mist. The vertical bars denote ± one standard error.

and *Nauclea diderrichii* (Fig. 1; Leakey *et al.* 1982a). The deleterious effects of sub- or supra-optimal leaf areas seem therefore to be greater in difficult-to-root species. In *T. scleroxylon* the optimum leaf area was shown to represent a balance between photosynthetic gains and transpirational losses (Fig. 2).

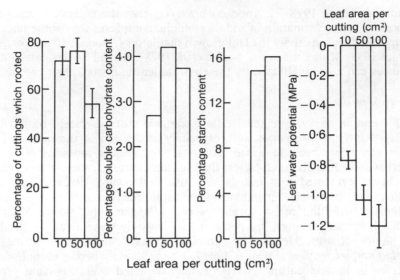

Leaf area per cutting (cm²)

FIGURE 2.   Effects of leaf area on the percentage rooting, stem-soluble carbohydrate and starch contents, and leaf water potential of *Triplochiton scleroxylon* leafy stem cuttings after 28 days under intermittent mist. Note that cuttings with 100 cm² of leaf had the largest total (non-structural) carbohydrate content, but suffered the greatest water stress and so rooted least well. Vertical bars denote ± one standard error (MPa=megapascals).

4.   *Carbohydrate metabolism*

The supply and redistribution of carbohydrates within cuttings can sometimes limit their capacity to root, and to some extent this limitation may be associated with the absence of root respiration (Haissig 1984). In other instances, the carbohydrate content of cutting can be supra-optimal. Auxin enhances starch hydrolysis (Haissig 1974c) and several enzymes have been identified which increase in activity during primordium development, suggesting the involvement of both the Embden-Meyerhof-Parnas pathway of glycolysis and the pentose phosphate pathway (Haissig 1982).

5.   *Nitrogen metabolism*

Nutrient deficiencies are detrimental to rooting, presumably because threshold levels are necessary for such processes as protein and nucleic acid synthesis (Hartmann & Kester 1983). Responses to nutrients are not always predictable; for example, when given to *Triplochiton scleroxylon* stockplants, complete fertilizers enhanced the rooting ability of only suppressed basal shoots (Leakey 1983), while halving the macro-nutrient content of the culture medium enhanced rooting *in vitro* of *Pistacia vera* (Barghchi & Alderson 1983).

A considerable body of evidence suggests that high carbohydrate/nitrogen ratios in cuttings favour root initiation, but this evidence can be misleading because the C/N ratio at the base of cuttings can become very different from that in the cuttings as a whole (Haissig 1974c).

6. *Water relations*

The rooting capacity of cuttings is frequently related to the water balance. Experimentally, rooting has been shown to suffer when leaf water potentials fall to about -0.8 to -1.0 MPa (Loach 1977; Loach & Gay 1979), below which there is a linear relationship between declining leaf water potential and decreased rooting.

The water balance of cuttings is governed by the rate of uptake, principally through the cut basal ends, but sometimes also through the leaf, and the rate of transpirational losses. With increased duration in the propagation bed a resistance to water uptake develops, which is apparently unrelated to callus formation or embolism in the vascular tissues. Water losses are affected by the vapour pressure deficit of the air, radiation levels and leaf resistances to water loss. Stomatal conductance typically drops rapidly in fresh cuttings and rises again as roots develop (Gay & Loach 1977). Rooting can normally be enhanced by shading and by maintaining a water film over the leaves, often associated with a lowering in leaf temperature (Loach & Gay 1979). The effects of different propagation systems and media on the water balance of leafy cuttings have been discussed by Grange and Loach (1983).

In leafless winter cuttings, one might expect that the water balance might not be too critical. However, root formation on hardwood plum and apple cuttings can be greatly influenced by applying antidesiccants to the cut ends, increasing the humidity of the rooting environment, and by preventing water stress (Howard 1980; Howard *et al.* 1983).

7. *Light*

Cuttings from conifers and deciduous trees of temperate and tropical origin root more readily after the stockplants have been kept in light levels well below the photosynthesis saturation point (*Pinus sylvestris*, Hansen *et al.* 1978; *Populus* and *Salix*, Eliasson & Brunes 1980; apple, Christensen *et al.* 1980). However, in *P. sylvestris*, the beneficial effects of applied auxins were enhanced by keeping the stockplants under high irradiances, suggesting that light changed either the auxin or co-factor content of the shoots (Strömquist & Hansen 1980).

In *Triplochiton scleroxylon*, low stockplant irradiances enhanced rooting and changed the dominance relationships between the shoots of 2-shoot stockplants (Fig. 3). This result supported earlier findings that competition between shoots decreased the rooting ability of cuttings taken from dominant shoots (Leakey 1983). Additionally, four weeks' growth of *T. scleroxylon* at $155 \text{W m}^{-2}\text{s}^{-1}$ for 19.5 h day^{-1} resulted in lower rates of net photosynthesis than at $75 \text{W m}^{-2}\text{s}^{-1}$, perhaps owing to end product inhibition; in this instance, rooting was greatest in cuttings taken from stockplants grown at the low irradiances and seemed to be related to the fact that they had low starch contents. In contrast, increased illumination has enhanced rooting in apple explants *in vitro* (25 to $100 \mu\text{E m}^{-2}\text{s}^{-1}$, Sriskandarajah *et al.* 1982). It is possible, however, that the importance of light environments *in vitro* may change at different stages in the growth and development of explants. The effects of different levels of irradiance on the cuttings themselves during the rooting phase have been found to be relatively minor, provided that water

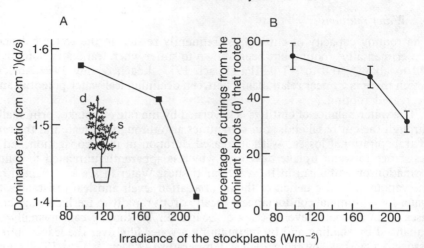

FIGURE 3.
A. Relationship between the light intensity, given for 19·5 h to stock-plants of *Triplochiton scleroxylon* at 30 °C and 80% relative humidity, and the ratio of the length of the dominant/suppressed shoots (d/s, on potted plants with two shoots). Note that dominance was greatest at the low light intensities.
B. The percentage of cuttings from the dominant shoots that rooted. Note that the poorly illuminated, most dominant, shoots rooted best.

stress was prevented, presumably because of the limited photosynthetic activity of detached cuttings (Hansen *et al.* 1978; Strömquist & Hansen 1980). However, irradiation of the basal ends of *Populus* and *Salix* cuttings can inhibit rooting (Eliasson & Brunes 1980). Thus, it is important to keep cutting bases in the dark.

Etiolation and/or blanching the stockplants in complete darkness can enhance rooting, for instance in difficult-to-root apple cultivars (Delargy & Wright 1979). Similarly, the *in vitro* rooting ability of M9 apple rootstocks can be enhanced by a period of darkness prior to severance (James 1983a), and in the variety 'Jonagold' this was associated with an increased phenol content and decreased peroxidase activity (Druart *et al.* 1982). Similar benefits of darkness in plum were offset by the application of the phenolic compound, chlorogenic acid (Hammerschlag 1982). Some recent evidence suggests that the etiolation effect is due to a mobile factor from the shoot apex, and that the enhanced rooting is closely related to the irradiance effects mentioned above (Harrison-Murray 1984).

8. *Temperature*

Temperature influences cambial activity and could therefore be expected to be important in propagation, especially in winter, as demonstrated in leafless apple cuttings (Cheffins & Howard 1982a), where warm temperatures enhanced rooting, but increased respiration losses, and so hampered successful establishment. In *Larix*, early rooting was best at 27 °C, but maximum rooting occurred at 15 °C (John 1977) emphasizing the importance of minimizing respiratory losses.

9. *Season*

The date at which both leafy softwood cuttings, and leafless hardwood cuttings are collected can markedly affect their rooting ability. Softwood cuttings often decrease in rooting ability during the summer (Klahr & Still 1979), while hardwood cuttings increase in rooting ability during the winter (Lux 1982). There are, however, exceptions to this generalization (eg *Olea europaea* can root well throughout the year, Portlingis & Therios 1976). *Pseudotsuga menziesii* cuttings were unrootable in September, and became progressively more rootable, without auxins, as winter dormancy declined, principally in response to winter chilling (Roberts *et al.* 1974). Applications of auxin to *P. menziesii* in winter, and artificial chilling of *Larix*, have enhanced the rooting of dormant shoots (John 1979).

Seasonal variations in rooting of leafy cuttings are less well understood, but high summer levels of irradiance, water stress, and the incidence of flowering may all contribute to decreased rooting ability. In non-dormant plants, it is difficult to obtain truly comparable cuttings at different times throughout the growing season.

10. *Gravity*

Cuttings taken from vertical *Populus* plants produced more roots than cuttings taken from horizontal plants, although the number of newly initiated wound roots were the same in both treatments (Smith & Wareing 1971). In *Triplochiton scleroxylon*, the overall percentage of cuttings rooted per stockplant was unaffected by different orientation treatments, but basal shoots rooted better than apical shoots when taken from vertical plants (Leakey 1983).

11. *Mycorrhizal fungi*

In some woody plants, the addition of mycorrhizal inoculum to the propagation medium enhances rooting (Linderman & Call 1977; Navratil & Rochon 1981), possibly because growth regulators are exuded into the medium prior to the development of mycorrhizal associations.

12. *Stockplant factors*

Some important differences in the capacity to root can be traced to differences in the physiological condition of different parts of the stockplants, and to their interactions with the environment.

(a) *Within-shoot variables.* In *Triplochiton scleroxylon*, the rooting ability of single-node leafy cuttings decreased markedly down the stockplant shoots (Leakey 1983), which could be due to any of the many differences between them, such as leaf age, internode length, extent of lignification and secondary thickening, gradients in carbohydrate, nitrogen and auxin contents, etc. Currrent experiments indicate that, like carbohydrate contents, the gradient in leaf water potential down the shoot is reversed in the cuttings after two weeks' propagation, and so may not be too important (Leakey & Coutts, unpublished). Perhaps more relevantly, cutting size, as determined by the normal pattern of internode lengths, was closely correlated with percentage cuttings rooted – the longer cuttings at the apical end rooting best (Leakey 1983). Interestingly, when all cuttings were cut to the same length, basal cuttings rooted best, and hence the normal gradient in rooting ability was reversed (Leakey & Mohammed 1985). The benefits of using large cuttings have also been reported for multi-node cuttings of leafless and winter cuttings (Richardson *et al.* 1979; John 1977). In apple, and other fruit trees, the swollen shoot base with many short internodes is a favoured site for root development (Howard 1981).

(b) *Between-shoot variables*. Cuttings from main stems and branches have different rooting abilities, the latter being best in plum, pine, spruce (Hartmann & Kester 1983) and fir (Miller *et al.* 1982). A comparison, using different *T. scleroxylon* plants of identical size, form and growth rate, has confirmed this intrinsically higher rooting ability of lateral cuttings, although many factors affect their rooting ability (Leakey 1983). For example, there was a negative correlation between the numbers of shoots per plant and the rooting ability of the uppermost shoot, with two shoots per potted stockplant being optimal. The rooting ability of cuttings from these shoots was strongly affected by the application of nutrients and the extent of mutual shading; heavy shading was detrimental, but some shading was beneficial. Thus, much of the between-shoot variation in rooting ability appeared to be attributable to competition between shoots and to their different light environments.

Bearing the above in mind, it is not surprising that there are topophytic effects of cutting origin on the rooting ability of cuttings collected from different parts of tree crowns. For example, in 6- and 21-year-old *Picea abies*, rooting decreased by 2·5% with each successive branch whorl up the trees (Roulund 1973). Commonly, throughout the propagation literature, the very low rooting ability of crown shoots from large trees is attributed to the attainment of the reproductive or mature phase ('phase-change'). While this may be so, many of the comparative studies between juvenile and mature shoots make no attempt to distinguish between 'phase-change' *per se*, and the numerous other differences between cuttings collected from seedlings or coppice shoots and those from the structurally complex crowns of large trees (eg Morgan & McWilliams 1976). In particular, attention should be paid to: internode length, rates and periodicity of growth, leaf size, frequency of branching, and differences in light environments, leaf water potential, carbohydrate and nutrient contents. Some studies do partially offset this criticism by using cuttings from mature shoots grafted on to juvenile rootstocks; significantly, the rooting ability of the cuttings from these more vigorous and comparable shoots is often considerably improved, and such material has been said to be 'rejuvenated' (eg *Eucalyptus grandis*, Paton *et al.* 1981), although 'reinvigorated' may be a more appropriate term. In a similar way, mature, second-generation cuttings (cuttings from cuttings) of *Triplochiton scleroxylon* have rooted well, even following flowering, and despite persistent plagiotropism (Leakey, unpublished). Reinvigoration has also enhanced rooting of shoots on large, but heavily pruned trees of *Artocarpus heterophyllus* (Mukherjee & Chatterjee 1979). Similar changes may also account for the reported 'rejuvenation' by successive subculturing of apple shoots *in vitro* (Sriskandarajah *et al.* 1982).

Accepting the above-mentioned difficulties, it is clear that cuttings from crown shoots do differ from seedling or coppice shoots in their content of inhibitors (Vieitez & Vieitez 1976), various growth regulators, nucleic acids and rooting co-factors (Heuser 1976; Paton *et al.* 1981). Additionally, as in chestnut (*Castanea sativa*) and avocado (*Persea americana*), there can be differences in anatomy or leaf retention which may limit rooting (Vieitez & Vieitez 1976; Reuveni & Raviv 1980).

To minimize topophytic variation in rooting ability, horticulturists and foresters have developed methods of stockplant management which encourage the continued formation of young vigorous shoots, Traditionally, some fruit rootstocks are propagated by stooling, and stone fruits by layering (Howard 1981). However, recent improvements in the techniques for rooting winter cuttings of apple, plum and cherry have led to the increased use of more productive 'hedged' stockplants. These stockplants have also been developed with some success for *Pinus radiata*, yielding more than 100 shoots per square metre (Libby *et al.* 1972).

Recently, there has been evidence that rooting can be enhanced by pre-conditioning *in vitro* explants, either by changing the medium (Horgan & Aitken 1981) or the light environment (Druart *et al.* 1982).

IV. CONCLUSIONS

In recent years, rapid progress has been made in developing and refining a range of vegetative propagation techniques. These techniques exploit numerous facets of tree physiology that centre around the inherent totipotency of many plant cells. Provided with appropriate environmental and hormonal stimuli to prevent physiological stresses, promote division, and activate differentiation, the cells of most tree species will multiply and organize new tissues to form grafts, develop root initials, proliferate shoot apices, or even produce whole new plantlets from single cells. While the techniques used on trees are basically similar to those developed for herbaceous plants, horticulturists and foresters have had to overcome the within-plant difficulties associated with both the greater age, size and complexity of trees, and the effects of season on their patterns of growth.

Despite the large number of variables presented in this review, many tree species are easily propagated, provided that physiological stresses are avoided and appropriate material is used. For example, using the techniques and regimes developed for rooting *Triplochiton scleroxylon* stem cuttings, over 90% of 50 other tree species have been successfully rooted (Leakey *et al.* 1982b). Experience suggests, moreover, that even species considered difficult to propagate may become relatively easy following detailed study, as has been demonstrated for hardwood cuttings of apple (*Malus* spp.) by Howard *et al.* (1983), softwood cuttings of *Triplochiton scleroxylon* by Leakey *et al.* (1982a), and *Pinus sylvestris* by Whitehill and Schwabe (1975).

REFERENCES

Ahuja, M. R. (1982). Isolation culture and fusion of protoplasts: problems and prospects. *Silvae Genet.*, **31**, 66–77.

Ahuja, M. R. (1983). Somatic cell differentiation and rapid clonal propagation of aspen. *Silvae Genet.*, **32**, 131–135.

Amerson, H. V. & Mott, R. L. (1982). Improved rooting of western white pine shoots from tissue culture. *Forest Sci.*, **28**, 822–825.

Barghchi, M. & Alderson, P. G. (1983). *In vitro* propagation of *Pistacia vera* L. from seedling tissues. *J. hort. Sci.*, **58**, 435–445.

Bassuk, N. L., Hunter, L. D. & Howard, B. H. (1981). The apparent involvement of polyphenol oxidase and phloridzin in the production of apple rooting co-factors. *J. hort. Sci.*, **56**, 313–322.

Bassuk, N. L. & Howard, B. H. (1981). A positive correlation between endogenous root-inducing co-factor activity in vacuum extracted sap and seasonal changes in M26 winter apple cuttings. *J. hort. Sci.*, **56**, 301–312.

Biondi, S. & Thorpe, T. A. (1982). Clonal propagation of forest tree species. In: *Tissue culture of economically important plants*, edited by A. N. Rao, 197–204. Singapore: Committee on Science and Technology in Developing Countries, and Asian Network for Biological Sciences.

Bonga, J. M. & Durzan, D. J., eds. (1982). *Tissue culture in forestry*. The Hague; London: Martinus Nijhoff/Junk.

Bornman, C. H. (1983). Possibilities and constraints in the regeneration of trees from cotyledonary needles of *Picea abies in vitro*. *Physiologia Pl.*, **57**, 5–16.

Boulay, M. (1977). Multiplication rapide du *Sequoia sempervirens* en culture *in vitro*. *Ann. Rech. sylvic.*, 37–67.

Bowen, M. R., Howarth, J. & Longman, K. A. (1975). Effects of auxins and other factors on the rooting of *Pinus contorta* Dougl. cuttings. *Ann. Bot.*, **39**, 647–656.

Brown, C. L. & Sommer, H. E. (1982). Vegetative propagation of dicotyledonous trees. In: *Tissue culture in forestry*, edited by J. M. Bonga and D. J. Durzan, 109–149. The Hague; London: Martinus Nijhoff/Junk.

Button, J. & Kochba, J. (1977). Tissue culture in the citrus industry. In: *Applied and fundamental aspects of plant cell, tissue and organ culture*, edited by J. Reinert and Y. B. S. Bajaj, 70–92. Berlin; New York: Springer.

Cheffins, N. J. & Howard, B. H. (1982a). Carbohydrate changes in leafless winter apple cuttings. I. The influence of level and duration of bottom leaf. *J. hort. Sci.*, **57**, 1–8.

Cheffins, N. J. & Howard, B. H. (1982b). Carbohydrate changes in leafless winter apple cuttings. II. Effects of ambient air temperature during rooting. *J. hort. Sci.*, **57**, 9–15.

Chevre, A. M., Gill, S. S., Mouras, A. & Salesses, G. (1983). *In vitro* vegetative multiplication of chestnut. *J. hort. Sci.*, **58**, 23–29.

Christensen, M. V., Eriksen, E. N. & Andersen, A. S. (1980). Interactions of stockplant irradiance and auxin in the propagation of apple rootstocks by cuttings. *Sci. Hortic. (Neth.)*, **12**, 11–17.

Copes, D. L. (1970). Effect of date of grafting on survival in Douglas-fir. *Res. Note Pacif. NW Forest Range Exp. Stn*, PNW–135.

Copes, D. L. (1975). Graft incompatibility in *Pinus contorta*. *Res. Note Pacif. NW Forest Range Exp. Stn*, PNW–260.

David, A. (1982). *In vitro* propagation of gymnosperms. In: *Tissue culture in forestry*, edited by J. M. Bonga and D. J. Durzan, 72–108. The Hague; London: Martinus Nijhoff/Junk.

Delargy, J. A. & Wright, C. E. (1979). Root formation in cuttings of apple in relation to auxin application and to etiolation. *New Phytol.*, **82**, 341–347.

De Fossard, R. A., Barker, P. K. & Bourne, R. A. (1977). The organ culture of nodes of four species of *Eucalyptus*. *Acta Hortic.*, **78**, 157–165.

Dormling, I. (1963). Anatomical and histological examinations of the union of scion and stock in grafts of Scots pine (*Pinus sylvestris* L.) and Norway spruce (*Picea abies* (L.) Karst.). *Stud. for. suec.*, **13**, 1–136.

Druart, P., Kevers, C., Boxus, P. & Gaspar, T. (1982). *In vitro* promotion of root formation by apple shoots through darkness effect on endogenous phenols and peroxidase. *Z. Pflanzenphysiol.*, **108**, 429–436.

Durzan, D. J. (1982). Cell and tissue culture in forest industry. In: *Tissue culture in forestry*, edited by J. M. Bonga and D. J. Durzan, 36–71. The Hague; London: Martinus Nijhoff/Junk.

Eliasson, L. (1971a). Growth regulators in *Populus tremula*. IV. Apical dominance and suckering in young plants. *Physiologia Pl.*, **25**, 263–267.

Eliasson, L. (1971b). Growth regulators in *Populus tremula*. II. Effect of light on inhibitor content of root suckers. *Physiologia Pl.*, **24**, 205–208.

Eliasson, L. (1971c). Growth regulators in *Populus tremula*. III. Variation of auxin and inhibitor level in roots in relation to root sucker formation. *Physiologia Pl.*, **25**, 118-121.

Eliasson, L. & Brunes, L. (1980). Light effects on root formation in aspen and willow cuttings. *Physiologia Pl.*, **48**, 261–265.

Eliasson, L., Strömquist, L.-H. & Brunes, L. (1977). Influence of light, nutrients and plant hormones on root formation in woody cuttings. In: *Vegetative propagation of forest trees – physiology and practice*, 43–54. Garpenburg: Swedish Institute for Forest Improvement, College of Forestry and University of Agricultural Sciences.

Fadl, M. S. & Hartmann, T. H. (1967). Isolation, purification and characterization of an endogenous root-promotion factor obtained from basal sections of pear hardwood cuttings. *Pl. Physiol., Lancaster*, **42**, 541–549.

Foong, T. W. & Barnes, M. F. (1981). Rooting 'co-factors' in *Rhododendron*: the fractionation and activity of components from an easy-to-root and a difficult-to-root variety. *Biochem. Physiol. Pflanz.*, **176**, 507–523.

Garner, R. J. (1979). *Grafter's handbook*. 4th ed. London: Faber.

Gay, A. P. & Loach, K. (1977). Leaf conductance changes on leafy cuttings of *Cornus* and *Rhododendron* during propagation. *J. hort. Sci.*, **52**, 509–516.

Grange, R. I. & Loach, K. (1983). Environmental factors affecting water loss from leafy cuttings in different propagation systems. *J. hort. Sci.*, **58**, 1–7.

Gur, A., Samish, R. M. & Lifshitz, E. (1968). The role of cyanogenic glycoside of the quince in the incompatibility between pear cultivars and quince rootstocks. *Hort. Res.*, **8**, 113–134.

Haissig, B. E. (1974a). Origins of adventitious roots. *N.Z. J. For. Sci.*, **4**, 299–310.

Haissig, B. E. (1974b). Influences of auxins and auxin synergists on adventitious root primordium initiation and development. *N.Z. J. For. Sci.*, **4**, 311–323.

Haissig, B. E. (1974c). Metabolism during adventitious root primordium initiation and development. *N.Z. J. For. Sci.*, **4**, 324–337.

Haissig, B. E. (1979). Influence of aryl-esters of indole-3-acetic and indole-3-butyric acids on adventitious root primordium initiation and development. *Physiologia Pl.*, **47**, 29–33.

Haissig, B. E. (1982). Activity of some glycolytic and pentose phosphate pathway enzymes during the development of adventitious roots. *Physiologia Pl.*, **55**, 261–272.

Haissig, B. E. (1983). N-phenyl indolyl-3-butyramide and phenyl indole-3-thiolobutyrate enhance adventitious root primordium development. *Physiologia Pl.*, **57**, 435-440.

Haissig, B. E. (1984). Carbohydrate accumulation and partitioning in *Pinus banksiana* seedlings and seedling cuttings. *Physiologia Pl.*, **61**, 13–19.

Haissig, B. E. (1985). Metabolic processes in adventitious rooting. In: *New root formation in plants and cuttings*, edited by M. B. Jackson. The Hague: Martinus Nijhoff/Junk. In press.

Hall, J. B. & Swaine, M. D. (1981). *Distribution and ecology of vascular plants in a tropical rain forest – forest vegetation in Ghana*. Geobotany 1. The Hague: Junk.

Hammerschlag, F. (1982). Factors influencing *in vitro* multiplication and rooting of the plum rootstock 'Myrobalan' (*Prunus cerasifera* Ehrh.). *J. Am. Soc. hort. Sci.*, **107**, 44–47.

Hansen, J., Strömquist, L. H. & Ericsson, A. (1978). Influence of the irradiance on carbohydrate content and rooting of cuttings of pine seedlings (*Pinus sylvestris* L.). *Pl. Physiol., Lancaster*, **61**, 975–979.

Harrison-Murray, R. S. (1984). Light intensity and site of sensitivity. *Rep. E. Malling Res. Stn 1983*, 77–79.

Hartmann, H. T. & Kester, D. E. (1983). *Plant propagation: principles and practices*. 4th ed. New Jersey: Prentice Hall.

Hearne, D. A. (1971). The development of grafting techniques for *Pinus caribaea* in the northern territory of Australia. *Proc. IUFRO Meeting, Gainesville, Florida, USA, March 1971*, 220–225. Oxford: Commonwealth Forestry Institute.

Heuser, C. W. (1976). Juvenility and rooting co-factors. *Acta Hortic.*, **56**, 251–261.

Holst, J. J., Santon, J. A. & Yeatman, C. W. (1956). Greenhouse grafting of spruce and hard pine at the Petawawa Forest Experiment Station, Chalk River, Ontario. *Tech. Notes Forest Res. Div. Can.*, no. 33.

Horgan, K. & Aitken, J. (1981). Reliable plantlet formation from embryos and seedling shoot tips of radiata pine. *Physiologia Pl.*, **53**, 170–175.

Howard, B. H. (1971). Propagation techniques. *Scient. Hort.*, **23**, 116–126.

Howard, B. H. (1972). Depressing effects of virus infection on adventitious root production in apple hardwood cuttings. *J. hort. Sci.*, **47**, 255–258.

Howard, B. H. (1973). Factors affecting the rooting response of plants to growth regulator application. *Acta Hortic.*, **34**, 93–105.

Howard, B. H. (1977). Effects of initial establishment practice on the subsequent productivity of apple stoolbeds. *J. hort. Sci.*, **52**, 437–446.

Howard, B. H. (1980). Moisture change as a component of disbudding responses in studies of supposed relationships between bud activity and rooting in leafless cuttings. *J. hort. Sci.*, **55**, 171–180.

Howard, B. H. (1981). Propagation of fruit and other broadleaved trees. *Jl R. agric. Soc.*, **142**, 110–128.

Howard, B. H., Harrison-Murray, R. S. & Fenlon, C. A. (1983). Effective auxin treatment of leafless winter cuttings. In: *Growth regulators in root development*, edited by M. B. Jackson and A. D. Stead, 73–85. (Monograph 10). Wantage: British Plant Growth Regulator Group, Letcombe Laboratory.

Howard, B. H., Harrison-Murray, R. S. & Mackenzie, K. A. D. (1984). Rooting responses to wounding winter cuttings of M26 apple rootstock. *J. hort. Sci.*, **59**, 131–139.

Huang, S.-C. & Millikan, D. F. (1980). *In vitro* micrografting of apple shoot tips. *HortScience*, **15**, 741–743.

James, D. J. (1983a). Adventitious root formation *in vitro* in apple rootstocks (*Malus pumila*). I. Factors affecting the length of the auxin-sensitive phase in M9. *Physiologia Pl.*, **57**, 149–153.

James, D. J. (1983b). Adventitious root formation *in vitro* in apple rootstocks (*Malus pumila*). II. Uptake and distribution of indol-3yl-acetic acid during the auxin-sensitive phase in M9 and M26. *Physiologia Pl.*, **57**, 154–158.

James, D. J. & Thurbon, I. J. (1981). Shoot and root initiation *in vitro* in the apple rootstock M9 and the promotive effects of phloroglucinol. *J. hort. Sci.*, **56**, 15–20.

Jeffree, C. E. & Yeoman, M. M. (1983). Development of intercellular connections between opposing cells in a graft union. *New Phytol.*, **93**, 481–509.

John, A. (1977). Vegetative propagation in hybrid larch (*Larix × eurolepsis* Henry) in Scotland. In: *Vegetative propagation of forest trees – physiology and practice*, 129–136. Garpenburg: Swedish Institute for Forest Improvement, College of Forestry and University of Agricultural Sciences.

John, A. (1979). Propagation of hybrid larch by summer and winter cuttings. *Silvae Genet.*, **28**, 220–225.

Johnson, R. D. & Lacey, C. J. (1983). Multi-stemmed trees in rainforest. *Aust. J. Bot.*, **31**, 189–195.

Jones, O. P. (1976). Effect of phloridzin and phloroglucinol on apple shoots. *Nature, Lond.*, **262**, 392-395, with Erratum. *Nature, Lond.*, **262**, 724.

Jones, O. P. (1983). *In vitro* propagation of tree crops. In: *Plant biotechnology*, edited by S. H. Mantell and H. Smith, 139–159. (S.E.B. seminar series 18). Cambridge: Cambridge University Press.

Jones, O. P. & Hatfield, S. G. S. (1976). Root initiation in apple shoots cultured *in vitro* with auxins and phenolic compounds. *J. hort. Sci.*, **51**, 495-499.

Jones, O. P. & Hopgood, M. E. (1979). The successful propagation *in vitro* of two rootstocks of *Prunus*: the plum rootstock Pixy (*P. insititia*) and the cherry rootstock F12/1 (*P. avium*). *J. hort. Sci.*, **54**, 63–66.

Jones, O. P., Pontikis, C. A. & Hopgood, M. E. (1979). Propagation *in vitro* of five apple scion cultivars. *J. hort. Sci.*, **54**, 155–158.

Jong, K. (1980). A cytoembryological approach to the study of variation and evolution in rainforest tree species. In: *Tropical ecology and development*, edited by J. I. Furtado, 213–218. (*Proc. int. Symp. on Tropical Ecology, Kuala Lumpur, Malaysia, 16–21 April, 1979*).

Kaur, A., Ha, C. O., Jong, K., Sands, V. E., Chan, H. T., Soepadmo, E. & Ashton, P. S. (1978). Apomixis may be widespread among trees of the climax rain forest. *Nature, Lond.*, **271**, 440–442.

Khosla, P. K., Nagpal, R. & Puri, S. (1982). Propagation of some forestry species by air-layering. *Indian J. For.*, **5**, 171–174.

Kirby, E. G. (1982). The use of *in vitro* techniques for genetic modification of forest trees. In: *Tissue culture in forestry*, edited by J. M. Bonga and D. J. Durzan, 369-386. The Hague; London: Martinus Nijhoff/Junk.

Klahr, M. & Still, S. M. (1979). Effect of indole-butyric acid and sampling-dates on the rooting of four *Tilia* taxa. *Sci. Hortic. (Neth.)*, **11**, 391–397.

Kochba, J., Spiegel-Roy, P., Neumann, H. & Saad, S. (1982). Effect of carbohydrates on somatic embryogenesis in subcultured nucellar callus of *Citrus* cultivars. *Z. Pflanzenphysiol.*, **105**, 359–368.

Komissarov, D. A. (1969). *Biological basis for the propagation of woody plants by cutting.* Jerusalem: Israel Programme for Scientific Translations.

Lacey, C. J., Gillson, A. N. & Whitecross, M. I. (1982). Root formation by stems of *Eucalyptus botryoides* Sm. in natural stands. *Aust. J. Bot.*, **30**, 147–159.

Lane, W. D. & McDougald, J. M. (1982). Shoot tissue culture of apple: comparative response of five cultivars to cytokinin and auxin. *Can. J. Pl. Sci.*, **62**, 689–694.

Larkin, P. J. & Scowcroft, W. R. (1981). Somaclonal variation – a novel source of variability from cell cultures for plant improvement. *Theor. appl. Genet.*, **60**, 197-214.

Leakey, R. R. B. (1981). Adaptive biology of vegetatively regenerating weeds. *Adv. appl. Biol.*, **6**, 57–90.

Leakey, R. R. B. (1983). Stockplant factors affecting root initiation in cuttings of *Triplochiton scleroxylon* K. Schum., an indigenous hardwood of West Africa. *J. hort. Sci.*, **58**, 277–290.

Leakey, R. R. B. & Mohammed, H. R. S. (1985). Effects of stem length on root initiation in sequential single-node cuttings of *Triplochiton scleroxylon* K. Schum. *J. hort. Sci.*, **60**. In press.

Leakey, R. R. B., Chapman, V. R. & Longman, K. A. (1982a). Physiological studies for tropical tree improvement and conservation. Factors affecting root initiation in cuttings of *Triplochiton scleroxylon* K. Schum. *For. Ecol. Manage.*, **4**, 53–66.

Leakey, R. R. B., Last, F. T. & Longman, K. A. (1982b). Domestication of tropical trees: an approach in securing future productivity and diversity in managed ecosystems. *Commonw. Forest. Rev.*, **61**, 33–42.

Libby, W. J., Brown A. G. & Fielding, J. M. (1972). Effects of hedging radiata pine on production, rooting and early growth of cuttings. *N.Z. J. For. Sci.*, **2**, 263–283.

Lindermann, R. G. & Call, C. A. (1977). Enhanced rooting of woody plant cuttings by mycorrhizal fungi. *J. Am. Soc. hort. Sci.*, **102**, 629–632.

Litz, R. E., Knight, R. J. & Gazit, S. (1984). *In vitro* somatic embryogenesis from *Mangifera indica* L. callus. *Sci. Hortic.*, **22**, 233–240.

Loach, K. (1977). Leaf water potential and the rooting of cuttings under mist and polythene. *Physiologia Pl.*, **40**, 191–197.

Loach, K. & Gay, A. P. (1979). The light requirements for propagating hardy ornamental species from leafy cuttings. *Sci. Hortic. (Neth.)*, **10**, 217–230.

Lux, A. (1982). The annual cycle of rhizogenesis of poplar stem cuttings. *Biologia (Bratisl.)*, **37**, 31–41.

Mahmood Husain, A. M. & Ponnuswamy, P. K. (1982). An innovation in the vegetative propagation of Sandal (*Santalum album* Linn.). *Indian J. For.*, **5**, 1–7.

Mascarenhas, A. F., Gupta, P. K., Kulkarni, V. M., Mehta, U., Iyer, R. S., Khuspe, S. S. & Jagannathan, V. (1982). Propagation of trees by tissue culture. In: *Tissue culture of economically important plants*, edited by A. N. Rao, 175–179. Singapore: Committee on Science and Technology in Developing Countries, and Asian Network for Biological Sciences.

Miller, N. F., Hinesley, L. E. & Blazich, F. A. (1982). Propagation of Fraser fir by stem cuttings: effects of type of cutting, length of cutting and genotype. *HortScience*, **17**, 827-829.

Monaco, L. C., Söndahl, M. R., Carvalho, A., Crocomo, O. J. & Sharp, W. R. (1977). Applications of tissue culture in the improvement of coffee. In: *Applied and fundamental aspects of plant cell, tissue and organ culture*, edited by J. Reinert and Y. R. S. Bajaj, 109–129. Berlin; New York: Springer.

Morgan, D. L. & McWilliams, E. L. (1976). Juvenility as a factor in propagating *Quercus virginiana* Mill. *Acta Hortic.*, **56**, 263–268.

Mukherjee, S. K. & Chatterjee, B. K. (1979). Effects of forcing etiolation and indolebutyric acid on rooting of cuttings of *Artoearpus heterophyllus* Lam. *Sci. Hortic. (Neth.)*, **10**, 295–300.

Nanda, K., Anand, V. K. & Kumar, P. (1970). Some investigations of auxin effects on rooting of stem cuttings of forest plants. *Indian Forester*, **96**, 171–187.

Navratil, S. & Rochon, G. C. (1981). Enhanced root and shoot development of poplar cuttings induced by *Pisolithus* inoculum. *Can. J. For. Res.*, **11**, 844–847.

Okoro, O. O. (1976). Some factors affecting successful 'take' of *Pinus caribaea* grafts. *Niger. J. For.*, **6**, 20–23.

Okoro, O. O. & Grace, J. (1976). The physiology of rooting *Populus* cuttings. I. Carbohydrates and photosynthesis. *Physiologia Pl.*, **36**, 133–138.

Okoro, O. O. & Grace, J. (1978). The physiology of rooting *Populus* cuttings. II. Cytokinin activity in leafless hardwood cuttings. *Physiologia Pl.*, **44**, 167–170.

Okoro, O. O. & Omokaro, D. N. (1975). Marcotting *Triplochiton scleroxylon* K. Schum. *Proc. Symp. Variation and Breeding Systems of* Triplochiton scleroxylon *(K. Schum.), Ibadan, Nigeria, 1975*, 93–98.

Passey, A. J. & Jones, O. P. (1983). Shoot proliferation and rooting *in vitro* of *Theobroma cacao* L. type Amelonado. *J. hort. Sci.*, **58**, 589–592.

Paton, D. M., Willing, R. R. & Pryor, L. D. (1981). Root-shoot gradients in *Eucalyptus* ontogeny. *Ann. Bot.*, **47**, 835–838.

Pence, V. C., Hasegawa, P. M. & Janick, J. (1979). Asexual embryogenesis in *Theobroma cacao* L. *J. Am. Soc. hort. Sci.*, **104**, 145–148.

Perala, D. A. (1978). Aspen sucker production and growth from outplanted root cuttings. *Res. Note N. Cent. For. Exp. Stn*, NC-241.

Pöessel, J.-L., Martinez, J., Macheix, J.-J. & Jonard, R. (1980). Variations saisonnières de l'aptitude au greffage *in vitro* d'apex de Pêcher (*Prunus persica* Batsch). Relations avec les teneurs en composés phénoliques endogènes et les activités peroxydasique et polyphenol-oxydasique. *Physiol. Vég.*, **18**, 665–675.

Portlingis, I. C. & Therios, I. (1976). Rooting response of juvenile and adult leafy olive cuttings to various factors. *J. hort. Sci.*, **51**, 31–39.

Rangaswamy, N. S. (1982). Nucellus as an experimental system in basic and applied tissue culture research. In: *Tissue culture of economically important plants*, edited by A. N. Rao, 269–286. Singapore: Committee on Science and Technology in Developing Countries, and Asian Network for Biological Sciences.

Reuveni, O. & Raviv, M. (1980). Importance of leaf retention to rooting of avocado cuttings. *J. Am. Soc. hort. Sci.*, **106**, 127–130.

Richardson, S. G., Barker, J. R., Crofts, K. A. & van Epps, G. A. (1979). Factors affecting rooting of stem cuttings of salt desert shrubs. *J. Range Mgmt*, **32**, 280–283.

Roberts, A. N., Tomasovic, B. J. & Fuchigami, L. H. (1974). Intensity of bud dormancy in Douglas-fir and its relation to scale removal and rooting ability. *Physiologia Pl.*, **31**, 211–216.

Robinson, J. C. & Schwabe, W. W. (1977a). Studies on the regeneration of apple cultivars from root cuttings. I. Propagation aspects. *J. hort. Sci.*, **52**, 205–220.

Robinson, J. C. & Schwabe, W. W. (1977b). Studies on the regeneration of apple cultivars from root cuttings. II. Carbohydrate and auxin relations. *J. hort. Sci.*, **52**, 221–233.

Roulund, H. (1973). The effect of cyclophysis and topophysis on the rooting ability of Norway spruce cuttings. *For. Tree Improv.*, **5**, 21–41.

Sadhu, M. K., Bose, S. & Saha, L. (1978). Auxin synergists in the rooting of mango cuttings. *Sci. Hortic. (Neth.)*, **9**, 381–387.

Schier, G. A. (1973a). Origin and development of Aspen root suckers. *Can. J. For. Res.*, **3**, 45–53.

Schier, G. A. (1973b). Effects of gibberellic acid and an inhibitor of gibberellin action on suckering from aspen root cuttings. *Can. J. For. Res.*, **3**, 39–44.

Schier, G. A. (1974). Vegetative propagation of aspen: clonal variation in suckering from root cuttings and in rooting of sucker cuttings. *Can. J. For. Res.*, **4**, 565–567.

Schier, G. A. (1975). Promotion of sucker development on *Populus tremuloides* root cuttings by an antiauxin. *Can. J. For. Res.*, **5**, 338–340.

Schier, G. A. (1983). Vegetative regeneration of Gambel oak and chokecherry from excised rhizomes. *Forest Sci.*, **29**, 499–502.

Schier, G. A. & Campbell, R. B. (1978). Effect of ethephon on suckering of excised roots and rooting of cuttings in trembling aspen. *Forest Sci.*, **24**, 66–72.

Schmid, P. P. S. & Feucht, W. (1982). Changes in peroxidases in the phloem of *Prunus avium/Prunus cerasus* graftings during the initial stage of the union formation. *Angew. Bot.*, **56**, 93–98.

Sita, G. L. (1982). Tissue culture of *Eucalyptus* species. In: *Tissue culture of economically important plants*, edited by A. N. Rao, 180–184. Singapore: Committee on Science and Technology in Developing Countries, and Asian Network for Biological Sciences.

Sita, G. L. & Vaidyanathan, C. S. (1979). Rapid multiplication of *Eucalyptus* by multiple shoot production. *Curr. Sci.*, **48**, 350–352.

Sita, G. L., Shobha, J. & Vaidyanathan, C. S. (1980). Regeneration of whole plants by embryogenesis from cell suspension cultures of sandalwood. *Curr. Sci.*, **49**, 196–198.

Smith, M. A. L. & McCown, B. H. (1983). A comparison of source tissue for protoplast isolation from three woody plant species. *Plant Sci. Lett.*, **28**, 149–156.

Smith, N. G. & Wareing, P. F. (1971). The effect of gravity on root emergence from cuttings of some tree species. *Forestry*, **44**, 177–187.

Sommer, H. E. & Caldas, L. S. (1981). *In vitro* methods applied to forest trees. In: *Plant tissue culture: methods and applications in agriculture*, edited by T. A. Thorpe, 349–358. New York: Academic Press.

Sriskandarajah, S., Mullins, M. G. & Nair, Y. (1982). Induction of adventitious rooting *in vitro* in difficult-to-propagate cultivars of apple. *Plant Sci. Lett.*, **24**, 1–9.

Staritsky, G. & van Hasselt, G. A. M. (1980). The synchronised mass propagation of *Coffea canephora* in vitro. *Proc. int. Colloq. Coffee, 9th, London*, vol. 2, 597–602.

Steward, F. C. (1970). From cultured cells to whole plants: the induction and control of their growth and differentiation. *Proc. R. Soc.*, **175B**, 1–30.

Street, H. E. (1976). Experimental embryogenesis – the totipotency of cultured plant cells. In: *The developmental biology of plants and animals*, edited by C. F. Graham and P. F. Wareing, 73–89. Oxford: Blackwell Scientific.

Strömquist, L.-H. & Hansen, J. (1980). Effects of auxin and irradiance on the rooting of cuttings of *Pinus sylvestris*. *Physiologia Pl.*, **49**, 346–350.

Sziklai, O. (1967). Grafting techniques in forestry. *Comb. Proc. I.P.P.S.*, **17**, 124–129.

Teasdale, R. D. & Rugini, E. (1983). Preparation of viable protoplasts from suspension-cultured loblolly pine (*Pinus taeda*) cells and subsequent regeneration to callus. *Plant Cell, Tissue and Organ Cult.*, **2**, 253–261.

Tomlinson, P. B. & Gill, A. M. (1973). Growth habits of tropical trees: some guiding principles. In: *Tropical forest ecosystems in Africa and South America: a comparative review*, edited by B. J. Meggers, E. S. Ayensu and W. D. Duckworth, 124–143. Washington: Smithsonian Institute.

Vardi, A., Spiegel-Roy, P. & Galun, E. (1975). Citrus cell culture: isolation of protoplasts, plating densities, effects of mutagens and regeneration of embryos. *Plant Sci. Lett.*, **4**, 231–236.

Vieitez, E. & Vieitez, A. M. (1976). Juvenility factors related to the rootability of chestnut cuttings. *Acta Hortic.*, **56**, 269–273.

Vieitez, A. M., Ballester, A., Vieitez, M. L. & Vieitez, E. (1983). *In vitro* plantlet regeneration of mature chestnut. *J. hort. Sci.*, **58**, 457–463.

Von Arnold, S. (1982). Factors influencing formation, development and rooting of adventitious shoots from embryos of *Picea abies* L. Karst. *Plant Sci. Lett.*, **27**, 275–287.

Wareing, P. F. & Graham, C. F. (1976). Problems of development. In: *The developmental biology of plants and animals*, edited by C. F. Graham and P. F. Wareing, 3–4. Oxford: Blackwell Scientific.

Whitehill, S. J. & Schwabe, W. W. (1975). Vegetative propagation of *Pinus sylvestris*. *Physiologia Pl.*, **35**, 66–71.

Whitmore, T. C. (1977). *A first look at Agathis*. (Tropical forestry papers no. 11). Oxford: Commonwealth Forestry Institute.

Zimmerman, R. H., ed. (1976). Juvenility in woody perennials. *Acta Hortic.*, **56**, 3–317. (Proc. int. Soc. for Hort. Sci. Symp., Maryland and West Berlin, 1975).

The vegetative structure

10

BIOMETRICAL, STRUCTURAL AND PHYSIOLOGICAL RELATIONSHIPS AMONG TREE PARTS

D. R. CAUSTON
Department of Botany and Microbiology, University College of Wales, Aberystwyth, Wales

ABBREVIATIONS

dbh	diameter at breast height
PCA	principal component analysis

NOTATION

Any symbol not appearing in this list, and not defined when used in the text, is a constant.

A	cross-sectional area of stem at height h
B_o	basal area
C	non-photosynthetic tissue biomass at height h
d	diameter at height h
d_K	diameter at relative height K
D	dbh
D_o	basal diameter
D_B	branch basal diameter

D_M	asymptotic maximum diameter
$f(x)$	a mathematical function of x
F	cumulative foliage biomass over distance $(H - h)$
g	root biomass
G	foliage biomass at height h (in practice, over a small vertical distance, δh)
h	height above ground on the stem
h_o	height to crown base
h_B	height to the base of a branch
H	total stem height
K	h/H (relative height)
$\bar{K}$	relative height of centre of gravity of a stem
l	crown length
L	specific pipe length
L_A	foliage area
L_F	foliage fresh weight
L_W	foliage biomass
n	number of trees per unit area (tree density)
P_i	proportion of currently produced photosynthate directed to plant part i
P	net photosynthetic rate per unit leaf weight per unit time
r	radius of stem at height h
R	radius of stem at breast height
R_i	relative growth rate of plant part i
s	shoot biomass
S_i	dark respiration rate of plant part i
t	time
T	cumulative total biomass over distance $(H - h)$
V	total stem volume or biomass
V_B	branchwood volume or biomass
w	crown width at height h
W	whole plant biomass
W_i	biomass of plant part i
W_B	branch foliage, or branchwood, biomass
$\Gamma(x) = \int_0^\infty x^{n-1}e^{-x}dx$	(gamma function of x)
ε	error term in a regression model
ϱ	specific gravity of wood
σ	stress per unit volume of wood
σ^2	variance

I. INTRODUCTION – MATHEMATICAL MODELS

A forester is interested largely in the growth and dimensions of the main stem (trunk or bole), whereas a tree biologist is concerned with the growth of all the tree parts and their mode of interaction. These twin interests underlie the development and subject matter of this paper.

First, I shall consider relationships between the dimensions of the stem, such as those that underlie timber production volume tables. Second, I shall review the more biologically relevant relationships between stemwood (particularly sapwood) and the foliage it supports, both mechanically and physiologically. Third, features of the crown structure itself will be examined in relation to foliage mass and age; and finally, some attention is given to ideas of modelling assimilate partitioning in plants.

Thornley (1976) has divided mathematical descriptions, or models, into two categories: empirical and mechanistic. In reality, though, there is a continuum of model types from the very empirical, which merely fits a simple mathematical curve to data purely for smoothing purposes, to the highly mechanistic, involving realistic basic mechanisms and more difficult mathematics (Causton 1986). In general, models directed towards the estimation of timber volume are empirical, whereas those developed as an aid to studies in tree physiology are more mechanistic, and aim to develop a theoretical framework which explains existing observations and enables predictions to be made.

II. DIMENSIONAL RELATIONSHIPS IN THE STEM

A. Relationships between volume or biomass and diameter and height

1. *Polynomials*

Prior to the work of Schumacher and Hall (1933), volume tables were constructed either by correlating tree volume with diameter and height, or by constructing eye-fitted curves to such data. Occasionally, simple correlations alone are still used, implying linear relationships (Tamm & Ross 1980; Rathinam *et al.* 1982). Occasionally, polynomial functions (usually of the second degree) have been employed: Landis and Mogren (1975) used the restricted form $V = a + bD^2$ for *Picea engelmanii*; Voronchikhin and Druzhinin (1978) employed a second degree polynomial relating volume to dbh in *Pinus sylvestris*; and Kr"stanov (1978) employed the form $V_B = aD + bD^2$. These models are highly empirical.

Spurr (1952) suggested the use of D^2H as a composite independent variable to estimate volume, in the linear form:

$$V = a + b(D^2H) \tag{1}$$

while, more recently, Edminster *et al.* (1980) used this equation, both with and without constant a, in a study on *Pinus ponderosa*. Alemdag (1982) also applied this equation to *Pinus banksiana*, *Picea mariana*, *Picea glauca*, and *Abies balsamea*. Avery and Burkhart (1983) argue that, for total volume, $a = 0$, while, if V represents merchantable volume only, $a < 0$. As will be seen later, models using D^2H in the form of equation (1) are rather less empirical than are polynomial models (see Section II.B.2).

2. *Allometry*

When a mathematical relationship is fitted to data, of the form $V = f(D)$, the regression of V on D assumes homoscedasticity[1] of V over the range of D. If volume data are collected from a stand of trees over a prolonged time, it will be found that the variance of V increases as V itself increases. Although a weighted regression could be (and has been) used, in which each volume observation is weighted inversely to its variance, a more satisfactory and biologically relevant approach is to use logarithms of the quantities concerned. The equation of this form (for V and D) is:

$$\log_e V = \log_e a + b \log_e D \tag{2}$$

and is known as the (linear) allometric relationship. The fact that the variance of $\log_e V$ (and of $\log_e D$ also) is constant indicates that these growth attributes are lognormally distributed. This is what one would expect, because growth is a multiplicative rather than an additive process, and so the result of the central limit theorem leads to the lognormal rather than the normal distribution.

In 'unlogged' form, equation (2) becomes:

$$V = aD^b \tag{3}$$

and is known as the power function. Pearsall (1927) first demonstrated this relationship between the dry weights of the major organ systems of growing herbaceous plants, and Schumacher and Hall (1933) were the first to introduce it into forest mensuration.

Many authors have used the allometric relationship between volume (or weight) of tree stem and dbh (eg, in conifers, Hegyi 1972; Grier & Milne 1981; in hardwoods, Harrington 1979; Nwoboshi 1983), and Mikhov and Lazarov (1979) used $V = aH^b$ to estimate stem volumes in several conifers and hardwoods.

Other workers have based an allometric relationship on D^2H, in the forms:

$$V = b(D^2H)^c \tag{4}$$
$$V = a + b(D^2H)^c \tag{5}$$

Equation (5) has been applied, for instance, by Edwards and McNab (1981) to *Pinus* species and by Clark and Schroeder (1977) to *Liriodendron tulipifera*. Equation (4) has mainly been used by Japanese workers (see Ogawa & Kira 1977).

A generalization of equation (4) is:

$$V = aD^b H^c \tag{6}$$

which was used by Schumacher and Hall (1933). More recently, this function has been applied by, for instance, Maezawa and Haga (1977) to *Cryptomeria japonica*, Schmitt and Grigal (1981) to *Betula papyrifera*, and Spank (1982) to *Pinus sylvestris*. The obvious popularity of equation (6) is undoubtedly due to the greater flexibility of treating dbh and tree height as two separate variables, rather than combining them in a single composite variable as in D^2H.

---

[1] Homoscedastic means 'of uniform variance', literally 'of equal scatter'. Heteroscedastic means 'of non-uniform variance'.

3. Miscellaneous functional relationships

Various other empirical relationships linking volume, height and dbh have been proposed, often with little or no justification. The more recent examples are:

$$\frac{D^2H}{V} = a + \frac{b}{c+D^2} \tag{7}$$

(Opie 1976), which was developed from an earlier model:

$$V = (D^2H)(a+bD) \tag{8}$$

(Webb 1969); both models were applied to *Eucalyptus regnans*. Ker and Raalte (1981) used the following multiple regression model:

$$V = a + b(D^2H) + cH + eD^2 + gD + iw + jl \tag{9}$$

in a stepwise approach to obtain the best combination of variables for each of the two species *Abies balsamea* and *Picea glauca*. Finally, Alemdag and Stiell (1982) added spacing and age effects in a stepwise fashion to a linear relationship of biomass to dbh applied to trees in a *Pinus resinosa* plantation:

$$V = a + b(D^2H) + c/n + et \tag{10}$$

4. Comparisons between function types

Many authors have made comparisons between different equations. Egunjobi (1976) compared most of the allometric-type equations on trees in an even-aged plantation of *Pinus caribaea*, and found that $V = a(D^2H)$ and $V = aB_oH$ provided the best fits; but there was little difference in goodness-of-fit among a whole range of function types.

Crow and Laidly (1980) applied a range of models to *Betula papyrifera*, *Pinus resinosa* and *Ilex verticillata*. The models included relationships of the form given in equations (1), (2), (3) and (6). Weighted linear, and some weighted nonlinear, models were acceptable alternatives to the logarithmic form of the allometric function. Weighted models accommodate hetero-scedastic data, and also avoid transformation bias (see below).

Rencz and Auclair (1980) compared parabolic and logarithmic regressions to quantify the relationship between dbh and the biomass of roots, root crown, bole, branches and cones on *Picea mariana*. The logarithmic models appeared to be the more appropriate. Payandeh (1981) compared a logarithmic and two simple nonlinear power functions for $V = f(D)$ in *Betula alleghaniensis* and *Acer saccharum*. The power functions provided the best fit, and the addition of height in a multiple regression model did not significantly improve the fit. Lavigne and Nostrand (1981) tested a number of models of the form $V = f(D,H)$ on several conifers and hardwoods, and found that a weighted regression, using D^2H as the independent variable, provided the best fit.

5. Methodological difficulties in allometry implementation

Methodology has concerned several workers in forestry. Finney (1941) and Aitchison and Brown (1957) have described the lognormal distribution.

Zar (1968; see also Hafley 1969) pointed out that, although $\log_e V = \log_e a + b \log_e D$ is *mathematically* equivalent to $V = aD^b$, the two forms are not *statistically* equivalent. Different values of the constants a and b will be obtained if one uses least squares regression with the usual error structure for each form, ie:

$$\log_e V = \log_e a + b \log_e D + \varepsilon \qquad (11)$$

$$V = aD^b + \varepsilon \qquad (12)$$

where ε is $N(0,\sigma^2)$ in each case. More recently, Flewelling and Pienaar (1981) reviewed the properties of the lognormal distribution and considered the fitting of the logarithmic form of the allometric function.

The main problem in using the logarithmic form of the allometric function in the construction of volume tables is that the regression value of volume, that is the expected value of $\log_e V$ at any given dbh (or other independent variable), gives an expected value of V itself, $\hat{V}$, which has a downward bias. This value of $\hat{V}$ is an estimate of the geometric mean, that is the arithmetic mean of the logarithm of volume. If volume really is lognormally distributed – and there are good biological reasons for supposing that it is – then the geometric mean is a valid quantity. Foresters, however, require volume tables which estimate arithmetic mean volumes. For this requirement, either a weighted form of regression model (12) can be used, in which ε is not distributed throughout simply as $N(0,\sigma^2)$, or regression model (11) can be employed, with subsequent adjustments for the downward bias of V given by the expected value of $\log_e V$.

Several authors have suggested ways of adjusting the expected value of $\log_e V$ (eg Finney 1941; Baskerville 1972; Wiant & Harner 1979). Yandle and Wiant (1981) concluded that Finney's estimator should be used in preference to Baskerville's when dealing with small, highly variable data sets, whereas Lee (1982) advocated Baskerville's method rather than Finney's in all circumstances, on both theoretical grounds and ease of computation.

B. Stem form

1. *Empirical relationships between total height and dbh*

In young trees, height and diameter increase together in a roughly proportional manner; but as trees age, height growth eventually ceases, while diameter continues to increase. A rectangular hyperbola of the form:

$$H = a + b/D \qquad b < 0 \qquad (13)$$

where the constant a is the asymptotic maximum of height, seems appropriate as an empirical model (Dimitrov 1978; Avery & Burkhart 1983). West (1979) used the form $H = D/(a+bD)$, where b is the asymptote, in investigations on three species of *Eucalyptus*, while Wensel and Schöenheide (1971) used $\log_e H$ instead of H in equation (13) in a study of *Sequoia gigantea*. Each form of relationship seemed appropriate to the data.

Other total height/dbh relationships have been used. Donald (1976) and Snowdon (1981) employed the second degree polynomial $H = a + bD + cD^2$, presumably with $c < 0$, when the ascending portion of the curve bears a superficial resemblance to the above rectangular hyperbola; but the maximum here is not asymptotic.

2. *Models based on solids of revolution*

In addition to estimates of volume and mass of a tree stem, foresters need to know something of its shape. Mechanisms responsible for the observed form of tree stems have been interpreted as (1) physiological – the necessary structure and function to support the transpiring canopy of foliage, and (2) mechanical – the necessary structure to provide a uniform resistance along the stem to bending by wind (Assman 1970). Metzger (1893) showed theoretically that requirement (2) is met when:

$$h = a - bd^3 \qquad (14)$$

where a is the height of the centre of crown mass, and b is an expression of stem form. Equation (14) is called a 'cubic paraboloid' in the forestry literature.

Closer analysis shows that only the central stem section conforms to a cubic paraboloid, which, in mature plantation conifers, is the longest part of the stem. The base of the stem is convex to the axis (buttswell), and is often modelled as a frustum of a neiloid[2], while the upper part of the stem within the crown takes the form of an ordinary paraboloid (or quadratic paraboloid, to distinguish it from the cubic paraboloid). Gray (1956), however, envisaged the situation literally one degree simpler; he considered the main part of the stem to be adequately represented by an ordinary paraboloid, and the top by a cone.

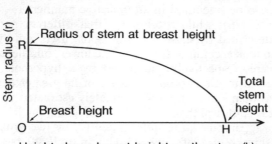

FIGURE 1. The 'cubic paraboloid', which may describe the shape of a tree stem above breast height. See text equation (15).

If the whole of the stem down to breast height could be considered as a cubic paraboloid, equation (14) may be written as:

$$r = R(1 - h/H)^{\frac{1}{3}} \qquad (15)$$

(Fig. 1) where height is measured from breast height rather than the ground. The volume of the stem is then given by:

$$V = \pi R^2 \int_0^H (1 - h/H)^{\frac{2}{3}} dh$$

which, on evaluation yields:

$$V = \frac{3\pi}{20} D^2 H$$

where $D = 2R$. If the whole stem could be modelled as a quadratic paraboloid, then:

[2] A neiloid is the solid of revolution of Neil's parabola: $y = ax^{3/2}$.

$$V = \frac{\pi}{8} D^2 H$$

Clearly, in both cases volume is proportional to D^2H, with only the constant of proportionality changing, according to whether the taper curve is assumed to be a cubic or quadratic paraboloid.

3. Empirical models of stem form

In reality, a single model is unlikely to be found which would adequately describe the form of the whole stem, and a huge literature, based on a plethora of methods, has evolved in recent years. When it is realized that the errors involved in measuring the height and diameter of a tree are large compared with the small differences predicted by a range of empirical models, one wonders if all the effort has been worthwhile. I shall mention only a few of the more interesting approaches here.

Scrinzi and Tabacchi (1981) used a polynomial model incorporating submodels for *Picea abies*; their best result was given by utilizing three quadratic submodels corresponding to the butt, central, and top stem sections. Max and Burkhart (1976) adopted a similar approach; but Lahtinen and Laasasenaho (1979) working with *Picea abies*, and Liu (1983) with *Liriodendron tulipifera*, used splined polynomials which enable the transitions between the different curves to be smoothed in an objective manner.

Roiko-Jokela (1976), while recognizing that different parts of the stem needed to be described by dissimilar functions, used more unconventional models and also took account of tree age. The lower, middle, and upper parts of the stem were, respectively, described by a hyperbola, a logarithmic function (preferred to the parabola because of its greater flexibility), and a cone. Trees less than 7 m high were adequately estimated by a cone.

Somewhat less empirical than most of the foregoing models are approaches recently made, apparently quite independently, by two groups of Japanese workers (Nagashima *et al.* 1980; Sweda & Umemura 1980), based on Mitscherlich growth curves for height and diameter growth. Assuming that height at time t is given by $h = H(1-e^{-at})$ and $d = D_M(1-e^{-bt})$, where H and D_M are asymptotic maxima, then:

$$f(h,d) = D_M \left\{ 1 - \left(\frac{H-h}{H-d} \right)^{b/a} \right\} \qquad (16)$$

(Nagashima *et al.* 1980). Sweda and Umemura's (1980) result was slightly different.

4. Centre of gravity and stem form

One interesting modern development for investigating volume equations and tree form is through a consideration of the stem moments (Nagashima & Yamamoto 1981).

Forslund (1982), however, found that a revealing analysis could be made by using just the first moment about the base (the centre of gravity), and a general profile equation of the form:

$$d = \{1-(h/H)^b\}^{1/a} D_o \qquad (17)$$

From this equation, Forslund (1982) deduced that stem volume was given by:

$$V = \frac{\Gamma(2/a+1)\cdot\Gamma(1/b+1)}{\Gamma(2/a+1/b+1)}\left(\frac{1}{1-K^b}\right)^{2/a}\cdot\frac{\pi d_K^2 H}{4} \tag{18}$$

and that the centre of gravity is at the relative height, $\bar{K}$ ($= h/H$), given by:

$$\bar{K} = \frac{\Gamma(2/b)\cdot\Gamma(2/a+1/b+1)}{\Gamma(1/b)\cdot\Gamma(2/a+2/b+1)} \tag{19}$$

Because the centre of gravity was the only physical property being considered, it was necessary to eliminate one unknown parameter. The special case of $b = 1$ was selected because it resulted in the conic sections commonly used to describe tree form. Then, by changing the value of a, a continuum of forms resulted, including the following familiar solids: neiloid ($a = 0.6$, $\bar{K} = 0.2$), cone ($a = 1$, $\bar{K} = 0.25$), paraboloid ($a = 2$, $\bar{K} = 0.3$) and cylinder (a infinite, $\bar{K} = 0.5$) (Fig. 2).

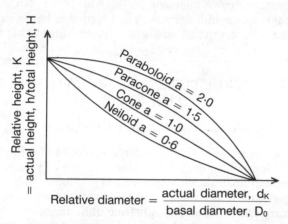

FIGURE 2. Relationships between the relative height and relative diameter of four solids (after Forslund 1982). The curves describe text equation (17) with $b = 1$ and the given values of a. Tree stems may approximate to paracones.

Applying the above to a sample of widely different tree heights of *Populus tremuloides*, Forslund (1982) found $\bar{K} \simeq 0.03$, giving $a = 1.5$. This value of a, lying between 1 (cone) and 2 (paraboloid), supports an earlier observation (Honer 1965) 'that trees are neither paraboloids nor cones but something in between'. Forslund called this shape the 'paracone'. By substituting $a = 1.5$ and $b = 1$, equation (18) becomes:

$$V = \frac{3}{7}\left(\frac{1}{1-K}\right)^{4/3}\cdot\frac{\pi d_K^2 H}{4} \tag{20}$$

It was also noted that the volume estimate was very much more sensitive to errors in diameter than in height.

Finally, if $K = 0$ in equation (20), ie $d_K = D_o$ we have:

$$V = \frac{3\pi}{28} D_o^2 H$$

and so, as before, volume is essentially proportional to D^2H.

5. *A multivariate model*

The multivariate method of PCA has been used by a few workers to characterize stem form. Liu and Keister (1978) used 14 relative height positions on the stems of *Pinus taeda* and *Pinus elliottii* as variates. In all data sets examined, the first component accounted for more than 99% of the total variability: in other words, the stem taper curve was almost completely described by the first principal component. Furthermore, because the variates were all of the same kind – diameters – and measured on the same scale, a graph of the 14 elements of the first eigenvector plotted against relative height position defined the stem profile.

6. *Stem eccentricity*

Most mensurational formulae used to estimate stem volume assume that the cross-sectional area is circular. However, stems are commonly eccentric, for a variety of reasons (eg Williamson 1975; Kio 1976). No simple way of incorporating this factor into mensurational formulae has been devised, but the close fits between estimated and actual values suggest that the errors are minimal.

III. CROWN STRUCTURE AND RELATIONSHIPS WITH THE STEM

A. Foliage/stem relationships

The underlying concept here is that a certain amount of foliage is supported physiologically and mechanically by a given amount of xylem or wood. The first part of this section deals with dimensional relationships involving the tree crown, and particularly the foliage. The major component quantities of the crown, which are estimated empirically from dbh, diameter at base of crown, or diameter at branch base, are branchwood mass, foliage mass, and foliage area.

1. *General*

The first application of a relationship between dbh and foliage weight was to *Pinus ponderosa* by Kittredge (1944) using the simple allometry, already discussed:

$$\log_e L_W = \log_e a + b \log_e D \qquad (21)$$

By using the method of Kozlowski and Schumacher (1943) to estimate the surface area of a pine needle, Cable (1958) established a linear relationship between foliage area and weight for *Pinus ponderosa*:

$$L_A = a' + b' L_W \qquad (22)$$

By substituting (22) into (21), we have:

$$\log_e \left(\frac{1}{b'} L_A - \frac{a'}{b'} \right) = \log_e a + b \log_e D \qquad (23)$$

If a' is small, and can be neglected, equation (23) becomes:

$$\log_e L_A = (\log_e a + \log_e b') + b \log_e D \qquad (24)$$

a linear function. Within the (wide) limits of variability of the data, this approximation is acceptable.

Various authors have investigated the applicability of crown component estimation from dbh (Attiwill 1966, in *Eucalyptus obliqua*; Snell & Anholt 1981, in *Pseudotsuga menziesii*; and Vasenkov 1982, in *Pinus sylvestris*). Other easily measured features have also been used. Carbon *et al.* (1979) compared the following allometric regressions: L_A on H, L_A on D, L_A on DH and L_A on D^2H in several *Eucalyptus* species, and found the second pair of variables to have the highest correlation. Snell and Anholt (1981), in addition to using dbh alone, also introduced height as a second regressor variable; while Kurvits (1981), in a study on *Pinus sylvestris*, investigated relationships between foliage weight and both height and dbh.

Relatively early, Attiwill (1962) working on *Eucalyptus obliqua* found that simple allometric functions adequately described the relationships between (a) foliage weight on a branch or the branchwood weight itself, and (b) the basal diameter of the branch. Loomis *et al.* (1966) investigated allometric relationships between foliage and branchwood weights on various other tree attributes in *Pinus echinata*. Bole diameter at the base of the crown was the best single estimator of foliage and branchwood weights, but dbh and crown ratio (crown length/total stem length) used together were satisfactory. Interestingly, none of the relationships appeared to be affected by stand density. More recently, Ek (1979) used a model of the form:

$$W_B = aD_B^b(H - h_B)^c(H/D)^e \qquad (25)$$

in hybrid poplar in a stepwise nonlinear multiple regression model.

2. Foliage/sapwood relationships

Except for Huber (1928), the first report of a relationship between foliage mass and sapwood cross-sectional area at breast height appears to be that of Grier and Waring (1974), who found that a linear function adequately described the situation in *Pseudotsuga menziesii*, *Abies procera*, and *Pinus ponderosa*. Snell and Brown (1978) compared dbh and sapwood area as estimators of crown biomass in seven conifer species. For *Pseudotsuga menziesii*, *Pinus monticola*, and *Pinus ponderosa*, sapwood area was a significantly better estimator than dbh, whereas in *Thuja plicata*, *Abies grandis*, *Abies lasiocarpa*, and *Larix occidentalis* there was no significant difference between dbh and sapwood area as estimators. However, Snell and Brown used young trees, and there may have been little heartwood in the latter group of species. Several other workers have reported linear relationships between sapwood area and foliage biomass (eg Whitehead 1978; Kaufmann & Troendle 1981; Waring *et al.* 1982).

Waring *et al.* (1977) examined four contrasting broadleaved species: *Castanopsis chrysophylla*, an evergreen tree, *Acer macrophyllum*, a deciduous tree, *Rhododendron macrophyllum*, an evergreen shrub, and *Acer circinatum*, a deciduous shrub. The authors found well-defined linear relationships in all but *Acer circinatum* where, despite increased variability, an allometric function was required. It can be argued that an allometric function is preferable in all cases for reasons already discussed. On the other hand, Rogers and Hinckley (1979) argued that in *Quercus* species only the most recent one or two annual rings actively conduct water, because in older xylem the large vessels cavitate relatively easily, and tylose formation tends to block them.

The most detailed analysis of this kind was made by Long *et al.* (1981) in *Pseudotsuga menziesii*. They found that sapwood cross-sectional area was linearly related to foliage mass above the point of measurement, for any height up the stem. This meant that, while sapwood area changed with height within the crown, beneath the crown sapwood cross-sectional area remained constant with height (while heartwood area increased).

B. Distribution of foliage within the crown

1. General crown characteristics

Much detailed work on crown structure has been done in Japan on *Cryptomeria japonica* (Kajihara 1976, 1980; Satoo & Imoto 1979), on *Chamaecyparis obtusa* (Kajihara 1981) and on *Abies sachalinensis* (Inose 1982).

In *Cryptomeria japonica* stands, three developmental stages of trees were recognized. In trees up to 6 m height, the whole crown was exposed to sunlight, and crown length, diameter, and slenderness ratio (crown length/ crown diameter) increased with tree height. In trees about 7 to 12 m tall, these three characters decreased slightly with increasing tree height, in that part of the crown exposed to sunlight, while the length and slenderness ratio of the whole crown increased. In trees over 12 m tall, the slenderness ratio of both parts of the crown remained constant, while crown length and diameter showed a small linear increase with increasing height.

In sample trees ranging from nine to 58 years old, crown mantle volume (the outer part of the crown containing foliage) and surface area seemed to correspond better with leaf fresh weight than with total crown volume. Using the allometric relationship $\log_e y = \log_e a + b\log_e L_F$, where y is crown mantle volume, crown mantle surface area, total crown volume, or crown basal area, strong correlations were found between $\log_e y$ and $\log_e L_F$. Similar relationships were found in *Chamaecyparis obtusa*.

2. Observational studies on foliage distribution

Most studies on foliage distribution within the crown have also considered the effects of tree population densities within stands, and irradiance levels within crowns. Strong and Zavitkovski (1978) examined needles from different parts of the crowns of six-year-old *Pinus banksiana* and *Larix laricina* growing at different densities. Needles from the lower third of the crowns were shorter, and had smaller surface areas and dry weights, than those from the upper third, and these within-crown differences were greatest in samples from trees grown at a high density. Schmid and Morton (1981) found that needle area and biomass were distributed in the ratio $1·0:3·5:2·0$ (top/middle/bottom) for open-grown *Pseudotsuga menziesii*, and $1:2:1$ for *Abies concolor*. They also found that current year new growth, expressed as a percentage of total needle weight per branch, decreased from the top of the crown to the bottom in *Pseudotsuga menziesii*, and from the top to the middle in *Abies concolor*.

Siemon *et al.* (1980) studied the distribution of foliage age in *Pinus radiata*. In the upper third of the crown the percentage of one-year-old foliage increased acropetally from 52% to 75%, whereas that of two- and three-year-old needles decreased from 28% to 22%, and 20% to 3% respectively. In the middle and lower crown, the distribution of foliage was constant at 37% (one-year-old), 27% (two-year-old) and 36% (three-year-old and more). Stand density had little effect on the distribution of foliage by crown position or leaf age.

Ilonen *et al.* (1979), examining *Pinus sylvestris*, found that there was a linear decrease in bud number per whorl, and a curvilinear decrease in shoot growth, with increase in whorl number counting from the apex. Shoot growth was linearly related to the prevailing light conditions within the crowns, but differences existed between dominant and suppressed trees.

According to Kellomäki (1981), light affects the partitioning of growth in the crowns of *Pinus sylvestris*, poor light conditions favouring needle growth at the expense of stem and branchwood growth, and stemwood production being maximal in moderate shade (about 60-70% of full daylight).

3. *Probability density models of foliage distribution*

Several authors have attempted to describe the vertical distribution of foliage biomass and area within tree canopies empirically, by means of probability densities. Gary (1978) applied the Weibull distribution to 80-year-old *Pinus contorta*; Kellomäki *et al.* (1980) used the beta distribution in young *Pinus sylvestris*; while Beadle *et al.* (1982) used the normal distribution, with the inclusion of a term to accommodate the significant skewness which they found in the vertical distribution of foliage in mature *Pinus sylvestris*. Massman (1982) compared a range of probability densities describing the distribution of foliage with height in *Pseudotsuga menziesii* and *Pinus lambertiana*; beta and chi-squared distributions fitted almost as well. The Weibull distribution is described, in relation to another use in forestry, by Bailey and Dell (1973), who also gave a useful list of references to papers describing some of the other distributions mentioned above.

C. The pipe model and its theory

1. *Foliage sapwood model*

Prior to the investigations described above, similar concepts had been developed in Japan. The culmination of these developments was an integrated model of certain aspects of tree growth and form – the pipe model theory – the basic analysis of which was done by Shinozaki *et al.* (1964a).

Figure 3A shows curves of foliage biomass with stem height, $G(h)$, on the left-hand side of the vertical axis, and of non-photosynthetic tissue biomass, $C(h)$, on the right. Non-photosynthetic organs – stem and branches – at height h are considered to support, both mechanically and physiologically, all the foliage above h whose amount is given by:

$$F(h) = \int_H^h G(h)dh \tag{26}$$

The corresponding curve of $F(h)$ is shown in Figure 3B (in other words, the cumulative foliage biomass from the top downwards). There is then a relationship *observed* between $F(h)$ and $C(h)$ illustrated in Figure 3C. Over the length of the crown:

$$F(h) = L \cdot C(h) \tag{27}$$

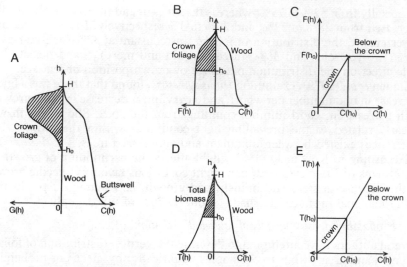

FIGURE 3. The pipe model theory of Shinozaki *et al.* (1964a) and the stem form theory of Oohata and Shinozaki (1979).
A. Vertical profiles of the biomasses of foliage, G, and woody tissues, C (stem and branches) on a tree. H = total tree height, h_o = height at the base of the crown, h = height above the ground.
B. Vertical profile of the biomass of woody tissues (as in A), and the cumulative biomass of foliage, F (accumulated from the top to the bottom of the tree).
C. The relationship between F and C.
D. As in B, but showing, on the left, the cumulative total biomass, T (accumulated from the top to the bottom of the tree).
E. The relationship between T and C.

but beneath the crown $F(h)$ is constant while $C(h)$ continues to increase. (L is defined below.) Differentiation of (27) with respect to h gives:

$$\frac{\mathrm{d}F(h)}{\mathrm{d}h} = \mathrm{L} \cdot \frac{\mathrm{d}C(h)}{\mathrm{d}h}$$

and from (26) we have:

$$G(h) = \mathrm{L} \cdot \frac{\mathrm{d}C(h)}{\mathrm{d}h} \qquad (28)$$

This implies that, at a particular height, the rate of change of non-photosynthetic tissue with increase in height is proportional to the amount of foliage at that height. Another form of (28) is:

$$C(h) = \frac{1}{L} \int_{H}^{h} G(h)\mathrm{d}h \qquad (29)$$

which shows the relationship of non-photosynthetic tissue with integrated foliage biomass at different heights.

At first, seemingly divorced from the mathematical model, Shinozaki *et al.* (1964a) postulated that, 'a unit amount of leaves is associated with the downward continuation of non-photosynthetic tissue that has a constant cross-sectional area. [In other words] a unit amount of leaves is provided with a *pipe* . . . . The pipe serves both as the vascular passage and as mechanical support, and runs from the leaves to the stem base'.

As far as foliage on *living* branches is concerned, the 'pipes' correspond to the sapwood xylem; the heartwood represents the pipes to foliage on dead or pre-existing branches. Accordingly, $C(h)$ in the above equations cannot represent total non-photosynthetic tissue but only sapwood, because the $G(h)$ function represents merely the existing foliage. However, the pipe model theory accommodates the heartwood as the pipes going to pre-existing branches.

The link between the mathematical and descriptive models comes in the constant L, which has the dimension of length, and is known as the *specific pipe length*. From equation (28), the larger L is, the smaller the amount of sapwood at height h that supports a given foliage mass at that height and above. In other words, the larger the specific pipe length, the more efficient is the sapwood in supporting foliage. Hence, a high value of L can be equated with high conductivity and rigid support.

In addition to the examples supplied by Shinozaki *et al.* (1964a), Waring *et al.* (1982) provided further evidence of the value of the pipe model theory in examining foliage distribution within a canopy.

2. Stem, root and branch analysis

In a second paper, Shinozaki *et al.* (1964b) used their model to examine the frequency distribution of diameters measured at 10 cm intervals along the trunk, branches, and roots of a tree. Their analyses showed that roots and branches represent simple pipe assemblages. The trunk, however, gave quite a different pattern indicating that it could be approximated by a combination of three cones: the stem within the crown, the branchless part of the stem, and the buttswell. The model also predicted that a better estimate of total foliage biomass would be obtained from trunk diameter just beneath the lowest branch rather than at breast height, and this was shown to be the case by measurement.

3. A model of stem size beneath the crown

Fifteen years elapsed before the pipe model was developed further, by Oohata and Shinozaki (1979). From Figure 3A it is evident that cumulative total biomass (of foliage and wood) from any height h to the tree top is given by:

$$T(h) = \int_H^h \{G(h)+C(h)\}dh \qquad (30)$$

as shown on the left of Figure 3D. It is also *observed* that, in the leafless part of the trunk (below the crown, $h<h_o$), a linear relationship exists between $C(h)$ and $T(h)$, ie,

$$T(h) = a+b \cdot C(h) \qquad (31)$$

as shown in Figure 3E. From equation (30),

$$\frac{dT(h)}{dh} = -\{G(h)+C(h)\} \qquad (32)$$

and from (31),

$$\frac{dT(h)}{dh} = b \cdot \frac{dC(h)}{dh} \tag{33}$$

The negative sign in equation (32) appears because integration starts from the top of the tree, H, down to any other height, h; and $h < H$. Over the linear range of $T(h)$, when $h < h_o$, $G(h) = 0$, thus putting $G(h) = 0$ in equation (32) and eliminating the derivative between (32) and (33), we have:

$$\frac{dC(h)}{dh} = -\frac{1}{b} \cdot C(h)$$

which, on integrating and rearranging, gives:

$$C(h) = ce^{-h/b}$$

where c is the constant of integration which, when evaluated, gives the final relationship:

$$C(h) = C(h_o)e^{(h_o - h)/b} \tag{34}$$

thus the relationship between $C(h)$ and h is exponential.

In a similar manner, Oohata and Shinozaki (1979) developed a stress model, giving the result:

$$A(h) = A(h_o)e^{\varrho(h_o - h)/\sigma} \tag{35}$$

Because, for a vanishingly small length of stem, $C(h) = \varrho A(h)$, substitution into (35) yields:

$$C(h) = \varrho A(h_o)e^{\varrho(h_o - h)/\sigma} \tag{36}$$

Comparing equations (36) and (34), we may conclude that $b = \varrho/\sigma$; b has the dimensions of length, and is called the *specific stress length*.

IV. QUANTITATIVE ASPECTS OF ASSIMILATE PARTITIONING

Any discussion of relationships between tree parts must take cognisance of assimilate partitioning, but the present coverage will be confined to some aspects of modelling the phenomenon.

A. The relevance of allometry

Let the biomasses of two plant parts be allometrically related, ie,

$$\log_e W_i = \log_e a + b \log_e W_j \tag{37}$$

Differentiation with respect to time gives:

$$\frac{d(\log_e W_i)}{dt} = b \cdot \frac{d(\log_e W_j)}{dt}$$

and so:

$$b = R_i/R_j \tag{38}$$

Warren Wilson (1972) has suggested, for actively growing tissue, the whole of which may be regarded as a sink for assimilates, that relative growth rate could be regarded as a measure of sink activity; thus, b may be interpreted as the ratio of the two sink activities. Note that this is a mechanistic model; even if there is some unknown nonlinear relationship between $\log_e W_i$ and

$\log_e W_j$, the gradient at any point of this relationship is still the ratio of relative growth rates at that particular time (Causton & Venus 1981).

Naturally, only in young seedlings can the whole of the foliage, stem and roots be regarded as consisting of actively growing tissue. Here, the relative growth rate ratios of the different organs can be regarded as ratios of the sink activities of the two organs. Data of this kind are given by Causton (1970) for *Acer pseudoplatanus* and *Betula pubescens*. A similar analysis could be made on older trees if attention were confined to actively growing parts, such as expanding buds or vascular cambium.

B.   Models of assimilate partitioning

1.   *Empirical models*

An early model, primarily describing the effect of photosynthetic rate on growth, is that of Ledig (1969). Starting with the relationship:

$$\frac{dW(t)}{dt} = kP(t)L_W(t) \qquad (39)$$

and invoking the allometric form:

$$L_W = aW^b \qquad (40)$$

equation (39) becomes:

$$\frac{dW(t)}{dt} = kaP(t)\{W(t)\}^b \qquad (41)$$

Integration from the start of growth to time τ yields:

$$W(t) = ka\int_0^\tau P(t)\{W(t)\}^b dt \qquad (42)$$

By assuming a combination of two logistic functions for $kP(t)$ – assumptions unexplained (but see Ledig & Perry 1969) – Ledig was able to solve equation (42) numerically to obtain a growth curve for $W(t)$. This curve was validated against growth data in *Pinus taeda*. However, the essential feature of this model, for our purposes, is that assimilate partitioning is described empirically by linear allometry.

Promnitz (1975) took a somewhat more mechanistic approach, starting from a series of equations of the form:

$$\frac{dW_i(t)}{dt} = p_i(t)P(t)W_4(t) - S_i(t)$$

$$i = 1, \ldots, 4 \qquad (43)$$

where $i = 1$ refers to stem elongation material, $i = 2$ to stem thickening material, $i = 3$ to root material, and $i = 4$ to leaf material. All quantities are regarded as functions of time. However, when it comes to describing the partitioning of assimilates, the formula is based entirely on experimental data (an empirical attribute) and is:

$$\frac{W_i(t_j) - W_i(t_j-1)}{\sum\limits_{i=1}^{4} W_i(t_j) - \sum\limits_{i=1}^{4} W_i(t_j-1)} = p_i(t_j) + \frac{p_i(t_j)\sum\limits_{i=1}^{4} S_i(t_j) - S_i(t_j)}{P(t_j) - \sum\limits_{i=1}^{4} S_i(t_j)} \qquad (44)$$

for the ith plant part and time interval from t_{j-1} to t_j (ie from some previous time to present time). Assimilate partitioning is thus based on observation over a time period. This model was applied to a *Populus* clone.

2. *Mechanistic models*

Two models of assimilate partitioning, including shoot/root ratios, were developed by Thornley (1972a,b) and Reynolds and Thornley (1982). Both models were almost wholly mechanistic, in that only the modes of substrate utilization and translocation were specified: the former by the Michaelis-Menten function, and the latter by a basic flow equation (based on concentration differences and resistances to flow).

Barnes (1979) developed a wholly mechanistic model of assimilate partitioning in carrot. His resulting expression is:

$$\log_e s = \log_e a + b\log_e g + ct \qquad (45)$$

A plot of $\log_e s$ against $\log_e g$ over a long period of time is thus curvilinear, which is true for the carrot. Constants b and c are made up of 'internal' characteristics – ratios of shoot and root sink activities, conversion efficiencies of assimilated carbon in the production of new dry matter, and maintenance respiration rates per unit of shoot and root tissue. There is no reason why this model cannot be applied to any species, but many plants show linear allometry between their parts over prolonged periods of time, implying $c = 0$. In Barnes' model, it would take a particular balance of the above internal characteristics to ensure this situation obtained.

V.   CONCLUSIONS

My impression, gained from the forestry literature on dimensional relationships, is that of excessive devotion to the task of formulating quantitative criteria to estimate stem volume or mass using a range of empirical models. Very rarely have attempts been made to compare models; indeed there seems to be much replication in the use of models, sometimes involving different species, with a minimum of reference to similar work. With such a mass of 'isolated' papers in the literature, generalization is difficult; however, the following points can be made.

When attempts have been made to take a more mechanistic approach (eg volume of a solid of revolution, and Forslund's centre of gravity analysis), the simple equation $V = a(D^2H)$ results. However, this function implies that the tree stem consists of a single simple solid; this is unlikely, and it is more realistic to divide the stem into several sections (three have often been suggested), each consisting of a single solid. Thus, the allometric variants of the above equation $V = a(D^2H)^b$ or $V = aD^bH^c$ probably give the best general estimate of stem volume from height and dbh measurements that one can expect.

Similarly, the cubic paraboloid (14), relating height and diameter of the stem, was derived from mechanistic considerations; but again this can really be applied only to a section of the stem, albeit a long section, and it cannot be applied to an old tree when height growth has ceased. Consequently, the rectangular hyperbola (13) provides the best height/diameter relationship.

However, from the comments made above, more rigorous comparisons of empirical models of tree form are desirable.

Although the idea of 'pipes' in a woody stem is a straightforward concept, some of the mathematics of the Japanese pipe model theory usefully quantifies, and also slightly predates, work in the West. Thus, apart from introductory ideas by Huber (1928), Kittredge (1944) and Cable (1958), the idea of a relationship between the foliar and non-foliar biomasses has only really developed during the last two decades. Furthermore, practical application of the concept of a relationship involving foliage biomass at height h in the crown, $G(h)$, requires at least an empirical model for $G(h)$, such as the probability densities in Section III.B.3. The mathematics of the theory is partly based on mechanistic models – the integral equations – and partly on empirical models of observations – the linear equations; there seems to be considerable scope for further development of this theory.

While the modelling of tree form (the result of *many* processes) has hitherto been mainly empirical, mechanistic models of *one* of the main underlying processes which determines tree morphology – assimilate partitioning – are somewhat more feasible to construct. Some headway has been made in this direction in herbaceous plants in recent years, but little has yet been achieved for trees. If one assumes a 'demand limited' situation, where the photosynthetic rates of leaves are below their potential rates, owing to some negative feedback mechanism from the sinks to the sources (leaves), then the rate of assimilate usage would depend on the rate of sink activity, and the rate at which assimilates could be translocated from source to sink. These two processes should therefore be the focus of attention in the construction of mechanistic models of assimilate partitioning in the future.

All the topics covered in this paper are aimed at describing and understanding tree form. Evidently, the biometrician must continue to play a crucial role in these activities alongside the forester and tree biologist.

ACKNOWLEDGEMENT

I am grateful to Keith Rennolls for drawing my attention to an error in the derivation of equation (34).

REFERENCES

Aitchison, J. & Brown, J. A. C. (1957). *The lognormal distribution*. Cambridge: Cambridge University Press.

Alemdag, I. S. (1982). Aboveground dry matter of jack pine, black spruce, white spruce and balsam fir trees at two localities in Ontario. *For. Chron.*, **58**, 26–30.

Alemdag, I. S. & Stiell, W. M. (1982). Spacing and age effects on biomass production in red pine plantations. *For. Chron.*, **58**, 220–224.

Assman, E. (1970). *The principles of forest yield study*. Oxford: Pergamon.

Attiwill, P. M. (1962). Estimating branch dry weight and leaf area from measurements of branch girth in *Eucalyptus*. *Forest Sci.*, **8**, 132–141.

Attiwill, P. M. (1966). A method for estimating crown weight in *Eucalyptus* and some implications of relationships between crown weight and stem diameter. *Ecology*, **47**, 795–804.

Avery, T. E. & Burkhart, H. E. (1983). *Forest measurement*. 3rd ed. New York: McGraw-Hill.

Bailey, R. L. & Dell, T. R. (1973). Quantifying diameter distributions with the Weibull function. *Forest Sci.*, **19**, 97–104.

Barnes, A. (1979). Vegetable plant part relationships. II. A quantitative hypothesis of shoot/storage root development. *Ann. Bot.*, **43**, 487–499.

Baskerville, G. L. (1972). Use of logarithmic regression in the estimation of plant biomass. *Can. J. For. Res.*, **2**, 49–53.

Beadle, C. L., Talbot, H. & Jarvis, P. G. (1982). Canopy structure and leaf area index in a mature Scots pine forest. *Forestry*, **55**, 105–123.

Cable, D. R. (1958). Estimating surface area of ponderosa pine foliage in central Arizona. *Forest Sci.*, **4**, 45–49.

Carbon, B. A., Bartle, G. A. & Murray, A. M. (1979). Leaf area index of some eucalypt forests in south-west Australia. *Aust. For. Res.*, **9**, 323–326.

Causton, D. R. (1970). *Growth functions, growth analysis, and plant physiology*. (Statistics section paper no. 151.) Alice Holt: Forestry Commission Research Division.

Causton, D. R. (1986). *A biologist's advanced mathematics*. London: George Allen & Unwin. In press.

Causton, D. R. & Venus, J. C. (1981). *The biometry of plant growth*. London: Edward Arnold.

Clark, A. III & Schroeder, J. G. (1977). Biomass of yellow-poplar in natural stands in western North Carolina. *Res. Pap. S.E. For. Exp. Stn (US)*, SE-165.

Crow, T. R. & Laidly, P. R. (1980). Alternative models for estimating woody plant biomass. *Can. J. For. Res.*, **10**, 367–370.

Dimitrov, E. T. (1978). Use of mathematical modelling for analytical representation of the relation between height and diameter in spruce (*Picea abies*) trees. (In Bulgarian). *Gorsko Stop.*, **15**, 27–33.

Donald, D. G. M. (1976). The measurement of height in fertiliser trials. *S. Afr. For. J.*, no. 98, 6–11.

Edminster, C. B., Beeson, R. T. & Metcalf, G. E. (1980). Volume tables and point-sampling factors for ponderosa pine in the Front Range of Colorado. *Res. Pap. Rocky Mt. For. Range Exp. Stn*, RM–218.

Edwards, M. B. & McNab, W. H. (1981). Biomass prediction for young southern pines. *J. For.*, **79**, 291.

Egunjobi, J. K. (1976). An evaluation of five methods for estimating biomass of an even-aged plantation of *Pinus caribaea* L. *Oecol. Plant.*, **11**, 109–116.

Ek, A. R. (1979). A model for estimating branch weight and branch leaf weight in biomass studies. *Forest Sci.*, **25**, 303–306.

Finney, D. J. (1941). On the distribution of a variate whose logarithm is normally distributed. *Suppl. Jl R. statist. Soc.*, **7**, 155–161.

Flewelling, J. W. & Pienaar, L. V. (1981). Multiplicative regression with lognormal errors. *Forest Sci.*, **27**, 281–289.

Forslund, R. R. (1982). A geometrical tree volume model based on the location of the centre of gravity of the bole. *Can. J. For. Res.*, **12**, 215–221.

Gary, H. L. (1978). The vertical distribution of needles and branchwood in thinned and unthinned 80–year-old lodgepole pine. *N.W. Sci.*, **52**, 303–309.

Gray, H. R. (1956). The form and taper of forest tree stems. *Imp. For. Inst. Pap.*, no. 32.

Grier, C. C. & Milne, W. A. (1981). Regression equations for calculating component biomass of young *Abies amabilis* (Dougl.) Forbes. *Can. J. For. Res.*, **11**, 184–187.

Grier, C. C. & Waring, R. H. (1974). Conifer foliage mass related to sapwood area. *Forest Sci.*, **20**, 205–206.

Hafley, W. L. (1969). Calculation and miscalculation of the allometric equation reconsidered. *BioScience*, **19**, 974–975, 983.

Harrington, G. (1979). Estimation of above-ground biomass of trees and shrubs in a *Eucalyptus populnea* F. Muell. woodland by regression of mass on trunk diameter and plant height. *Aust. J. Bot.*, **27**, 135–143.

Hegyi, F. (1972). Dry matter distribution in jack pine stands in northern Ontario. *For. Chron.*, **48**, 193–197.

Honer, T. G. (1965). Volume distribution in individual trees. *Pulp Pap. Mag. Can.*, **66**, 499–508.

Huber, B. (1928). Weitere quantitative Untersuchungen über das Wasserleitungssystem der Pflanzen. *Jb. Wiss. Bot.*, **67**, 877–959.

Ilonen, P., Kellomäki, S., Hari, P. & Kanninen, M. (1979). On distribution of growth in crown system of some young Scots pine stands. *Silva fenn.*, **13**, 316–326.

Inose, M. (1982). A tree growth model based on crown competition in todomatsu (*Abies sachalinensis*). I. The relationship between crown development and volume increment. (In Japanese). *Bull. For. For. Prod. Res. Inst. Ibaraki*, no. 318, 103–127.

Kajihara, M. (1976). Studies on the morphology and dimensions of tree crowns in even-aged stand of sugi. III. Development of crown morphology with growing stage. (In Japanese). *J. Jap. For. Soc.*, **58**, 313–320.

Kajihara, M. (1980). Crown structure of sugi (*Cryptomeria japonica*) and the relationship between crown dimensions and leaf fresh weight. (In Japanese). *Bull. Kyoto Prefect. Univ. For.*, no. 24, 49–63.

Kajihara, M. (1981). Crown form, crown structure, and the relationship between crown dimensions and leaf fresh weight of hinoki (*Chamaecyparis obtusa*). (In Japanese). *Bull. Kyoto Prefect. Univ. For.*, no. 25, 11–28.

Kaufmann, M. R. & Troendle, C. A. (1981). The relationship of leaf area and foliage biomass to sapwood conducting area in four subalpine forest tree species. *Forest Sci.*, **27**, 477–482.

Kellomäki, S. (1981). Effect of the within-stand light conditions on the share of stem, branch and needle growth in a twenty-year-old Scots pine stand. *Silva fenn.*, **15**, 130–139.

Kellomäki, S., Hari, P., Kanninen, M. & Ilonen, P. (1980). Eco-physiological studies on young Scots pine stands. II. Distribution of needle biomass and its application in approximating light conditions inside the canopy. *Silva fenn.*, **14**, 243–257.

Ker, M. F. & Raalte, G. D. van. (1981). Tree biomass equations for *Abies balsamea* and *Picea glauca* in northwestern New Brunswick. *Can. J. For. Res.*, **11**, 13–17.

Kio, P. R. O. (1976). Uneven crown loading and the regulation of tree form in tropical trees. *Niger. J. For.*, **6**, 15–19.

Kittredge, J. (1944). Estimation of the amount of foliage on trees and stands. *J. For.*, **42**, 905–912.

Kozlowski, T. T. & Schumacher, F. X. (1943). Estimation of stomated foliar surface of pines. *Pl. Physiol., Lancaster*, **18**, 122–127.

Kr"stanov, K. (1978). Form heights, form factors, and branch volume in *Pinus leucodermis*. (In Bulgarian). *Gorsko Stop.*, **34**(8), 35–38.

Kurvits, P. T. (1981). The optimum dimensions of tree foliage and the amounts actually available. (In Russian). *Les. Khoz.*, no 3, 44–45.

Lahtinen, A. & Laasasenaho, J. (1979). On the construction of taper curves by using spline functions. *Metsätiet. Tutkimuslait. Julk.*, **95**(8).

Landis, T. D. & Mogren, E. W. (1975). Tree strata biomass of subalpine spruce-fir stands in south-western Colorado. *Forest Sci.*, **21**, 9–12.

Lavigne, M. B. & Nostrand, R. S. van. (1981). *Biomass equations for six tree species in central Newfoundland.* (Information report no. N-X-199). Newfoundland Forest Research Centre.

Ledig, F. T. (1969). A growth model for tree seedlings based on the rate of photosynthesis and the distribution of photosynthate. *Photosynthetica*, **3**, 263–275.

Ledig, F. T. & Perry, T. O. (1969). Net assimilation rate and growth in loblolly pine seedlings. *Forest Sci.*, **15**, 431–438.

Lee, C. Y. (1982). Comparison of two correction methods for the bias due to the logarithmic transformation in the estimation of biomass. *Can. J. For. Res.*, **12**, 326–331.

Liu, C. J. (1983). Stem profile analysis. In: *Planning, performance and evaluation of growth and yield studies*, edited by H. L. Wright, 62–73. (Occasional papers no. 20). Oxford: Commonwealth Forestry Institute.

Liu, C. J. & Keister, T. D. (1978). Southern pine stem form defined through principal component analysis. *Can. J. For. Res.*, **8**, 188–197.

Long, J. N., Smith, F. W. & Scott, D. R. M. (1981). The role of Douglas-fir stem sapwood and heartwood in the mechanical and physiological support of crowns and development of stem form. *Can. J. For. Res.*, **11**, 459–464.

Loomis, R. M., Phares, R. E. & Crosby, J. S. (1966). Estimating foliage and branchwood quantities in shortleaf pine. *Forest Sci.*, **12**, 30–39.

Maezawa, K. & Haga, T. (1977). Method of estimating parameters in volume equations. (In Japanese). *J. Jap. For. Soc.*, **59**, 245–252.

Massman, W. J. (1982). Foliage distribution in old-growth coniferous tree canopies. *Can. J. For. Res.*, **12**, 10–17.

158 D. R. Causton

Max, T. A. & Burkhart, H. E. (1976). Segmented polynomial regression applied to taper equations. *Forest Sci.*, **22**, 283–289.

Metzger, K. (1893). Der Wind als massgebender Faktor für das Wachstum der Bäume. *Mündener Forstl.*, **3**, 35–62.

Mikhov, I. & Lazarov, E. (1979). Mathematical models of the yield tables used in Bulgaria for the main tree species. (in Bulgarian). *Nauchni Trud. vissh lesotekh. Inst.*, **24**, 13–17.

Nagashima, I. & Yamamoto, M. (1981). An expression of stem-form by moments. (In Japanese). *J. Jap. For. Soc.*, **63**, 354–358.

Nagashima, I., Yamamoto, M. & Sweda, T. (1980). A theoretical stem taper curve (I). *J. Jap. For. Soc.*, **62**, 217–226.

Nwoboshi, L. C. (1983). Growth and nutrient requirements in a teak plantation age series in Nigeria. I. Linear growth and biomass production. *Forest Sci.*, **29**, 159–165.

Ogawa, H. & Kira, T. (1977). Methodology. (Chapter 2). In: *Primary productivity of Japanese forests*, edited by T. Shidei and T. Kira, 15–37. Tokyo: University of Tokyo Press.

Oohata, S. & Shinozaki, K. (1979). A statistical model of plant form – further analysis of the pipe model theory. *Jap. J. Ecol.*, **29**, 323–335.

Opie, J. E. (1976). Volume functions for trees of all sizes. *For. tech. Pap.*, no. 25, 27–30. Forestry Commission, Victoria.

Payandeh, P. (1981). Choosing regression models for biomass prediction equations. *For. Chron.*, **57**, 229–232.

Pearsall, W. H. (1927). Growth studies. VI. On the relative sizes of growing plant organs. *Ann. Bot.*, **41**, 549–556.

Promnitz, L. C. (1975). A photosynthate allocation model for tree growth. *Photosynthetica*, **9**, 1–15.

Rathinam, M., Surendran, C. & Kondas, S. (1982). Inter-relationship of wood yield components in *Eucalyptus tereticornis*. *Indian Forester*, **108**, 465–470.

Rencz, A. N. & Auclair, A. N. (1980). Dimension analysis of various components of black spruce in subarctic lichen woodland. *Can. J. For. Res.*, **10**, 491–497.

Reynolds, J. F. & Thornley, J. H. M. (1982). A root:shoot partitioning model. *Ann. Bot.*, **49**, 585–597.

Rogers, R. & Hinckley, T. M. (1979). Foliar weight and area related to current sapwood area in oak. *Forest Sci.*, **25**, 298–303.

Roiko-Jokela, P. (1976). Die Schaftformfunktion der Fichte und die Bestimmung der Sortimentsanteile am stehenden Baum. *Mitt. Eidg. Anst. forstl. Versuchswes.*, **52**, 1–84.

Satoo, T. & Imoto, H. (1979). Modelling crown canopy of an even-aged stand of *Cryptomeria japonica* from measurement of leaf mass – a new approach to the morphology of forest crown. *J. Jap. For. Soc.*, **61**, 127–134.

Schmid, J. M. & Morton, M. B. (1981). Distribution of foliage on open-grown white fir and Douglas-fir in northern New Mexico, U.S.A. *Can. J. For. Res.*, **11**, 615–619.

Schmitt, M. D. C. & Grigal, D. F. (1981). General biomass estimation equations for *Betula papyrifera* Marsh. *Can. J. For. Res.*, **11**, 837–840.

Schumacher, F. X. & Hall, F. D. S. (1933). Logarithmic expression of timber-tree volume. *J. agric. Res.*, **47**, 719–734.

Scrinzi, G. & Tabacchi, G. (1981). Interpretazione matematica del fenomeno formale nell'abete rosso (*Picea abies* Karst.) del centro-Cadore. *Ann. Ist. sper. Assestamento For. Alpicolt.*, **7**, 147–186.

Shinozaki, K. K., Hozumi, Y. K. & Kira, T. (1964a). A quantitative analysis of plant form – the pipe model theory. I. Basic analysis. *Jap. J. Ecol.*, **14**, 97–105.

Shinozaki, K. K., Hozumi, Y. K. & Kira, T. (1964b). A quantitative analysis of plant form – the pipe model theory. II. Further evidence of the theory and its application in forest ecology. *Jap. J. Ecol.*, **14**, 133–139.

Siemon, G. R., Müller, W. J., Wood, G. B. & Forrest, W. G. (1980). Effect of thinning on the distribution and biomass of foliage in the crown of radiata pine. *N.Z. J. For. Sci.*, **10**, 461–475.

Snell, J. A. K. & Anholt, B. F. (1981). Predicting crown weight of coast Douglas-fir and western hemlock. *Res. Pap. Pacif. NW Forest Range Exp. Stn*, PNW-281.

Snell, J. A. K. & Brown, J. K. (1978). Comparison of tree biomass estimators – DBH and sapwood area. *Forest Sci.*, **24**, 455–457.

Snowdon, P. (1981). Estimation of height from diameter measurements in fertiliser trials. *Aust. For. Res.*, **11**, 223–230.

Spank, G. (1982). Zur Schätzung der Kronen- und Nadelmasse in Reinbeständen der Baumart Kiefer (*Pinus sylvestris* L.). *Beitr. Forstwirtsch.*, **16**, 129–139.

Spurr, S. H. (1952). *Forest inventory*. New York: Ronald Press.

Strong, T. F. & Zavitkovski, J. (1978). Morphology of jack pine and tamarack needles in dense stands. *Res. Pap. N. Cent. For. Exp. Stn*, NC-153.

Sweda, T. & Umemura, T. (1980). A theoretical height-diameter curve. I. Derivation and characteristics. *J. Jap. For. Soc.*, **62**, 459–464.

Tamm, Y. A. & Ross, V. A. (1980). Patterns in the distribution of the aerial biomass of aspen in stands in Estonia. (In Russian). *Lesovedenie*, no. 1, 42–51.

Thornley, J. H. M. (1972a). A model to describe the partitioning of photosynthate during vegetative plant growth. *Ann. Bot.*, **36**, 419–430.

Thornley, J. H. M. (1972b). A balanced quantitative model for root:shoot ratios in vegetative plants. *Ann. Bot.*, **36**, 431–441.

Thornley, J. H. M. (1976). *Mathematical models in plant physiology*. London: Academic Press.

Vasenkov, G. I. (1982). Determination of crown biomass in Scots pine plantations. (In Russian). *Les. Khoz.*, no. 1, 46–48.

Voronchikhin, N. Z. & Druzhinin, N. A. (1978). Determining the effectiveness of drainage by the dimensions of trees. (In Russian). *Les. Khoz.*, no. 6, 26–29.

Waring, R. H., Gholz, H. L., Grier, C. C. & Plummer, M. L. (1977). Evaluating stem conducting tissue as an estimator of leaf area in four woody angiosperms. *Can. J. Bot.*, **55**, 1474–1477.

Waring, R. H., Schroeder, P. E. & Oren, R. (1982). Application of the pipe model theory to predict canopy leaf area. *Can. J. For. Res.*, **12**, 556–560.

Warren Wilson, J. (1972). Control of crop processes. In: *Crop processes in controlled environments* edited by A. R. Rees, K. E. Cockshull, D. W. Hand and R. G. Hurd, 7–30. London: Academic Press.

Webb, A. W. (1969). A formula for estimating total volume of individual trees of mountain ash. *For. tech. Pap.*, no. 20, 17–19. Forestry Commission, Victoria.

Wensel, L. C. & Schöenheide, R. L. (1971). Young growth gross volume tables for Sierra redwood (*Sequoia gigantea* (Lindl.) Decne). *Hilgardia*, **41**, 65–76.

West, P. W. (1979). Estimation of height, bark thickness and plot volume in regrowth eucalypt forest. *Aust. For. Res.*, **9**, 295–308.

Whitehead, D. (1978). The estimation of foliage area from sapwood basal area in Scots pine. *Forestry*, **51**, 137–149.

Wiant, H. V., jr & Harner, E. J. (1979). Percent bias and standard error in logarithmic regression. *Forest Sci.*, **25**, 167–168.

Williamson, R. L. (1975). Out-of-roundness in Douglas-fir stems. *Forest Sci.*, **21**, 365–370.

Yandle, D. O. & Wiant, H. V., jr. (1981). Estimation of plant biomass based on the allometric equation. *Can. J. For. Res.*, **11**. 833–834.

Zar, J. H. (1968). Calculation and miscalculation of the allometric equation as a model in biological data. *BioScience*, **18**, 1118–1120.

11

DRY MATTER PARTITIONING IN TREE CROPS

M. G. R. CANNELL
Institute of Terrestrial Ecology, Bush Estate, Penicuik, Midlothian, Scotland

I. INTRODUCTION

It is now a truism of crop physiology that, during crop evolution and domestication, yield has been increased mainly by increasing the proportion of assimilates partitioned to the harvested parts of the plants, and much less (or not at all) by increasing total biomass production (Evans 1976). Indeed, it has proved very difficult to find evidence for an increase, during domestication in the maximum light-saturated CO_2 exchange rate per unit leaf area of wheat, maize, sorghum, sugar cane, cotton, cowpea and pearl millet (Gifford & Evans 1981). In all these crops, genetic improvement in yield has generally been achieved by altering the size of plant parts, developmental processes, and adaption to the 'agronomic' environment, all resulting in increased partitioning of dry matter to the organs that are harvested (Evans 1975).

The purpose of this review is to consider the opportunities that exist in tree crops to increase yield by changing the partitioning of dry matter. These opportunities are sought in part empirically, by reviewing widely scattered information on dry matter partitioning in trees, and in part by considering the factors that influence or control assimilate partitioning. McMurtrie (this volume) extends our understanding further, by using conceptual models to explore the effects on tree growth of changes in assimilate partitioning. It is important to consider some aspects of mineral nutrient, as well as carbon, partitioning. However, no attempt is made to cover the extensive literature on source-path-sink relationships (see Warren-Wilson 1972; Wareing & Patrick 1975; Moorby 1977; Thornley 1977; Gifford & Evans 1981).

The framework of this review is to consider (a) the relevance to tree crops of the notion of 'harvest index', (b) the limited factual information on carbon budgets of whole trees and forests, (c) root/shoot interactions, (d) the effects of fruiting on dry matter partitioning, and (e) partitioning between leaves, branches and stems.

II. HARVEST INDEX

The notion of harvest index ($H.I.$) was devised primarily to assess dry matter partitioning in annual grain crops, defined as: dry weight of harvested part/total above-ground dry weight at harvest. Let us consider this concept with respect to tree crops.

A. Defining yield

A premise of the $H.I.$ concept, and indeed of this review, is that yield can be adequately defined in terms of dry weight. However, different harvested parts can have greatly different values. The most lucrative aspects of harvest index to explore are often the opportunities to increase the proportion of dry matter partitioned to the highest value products. However, it is beyond the scope of this review to consider, for instance, factors affecting the relative value of fruits and fuelwood, or the quality and size distributions of forest tree boles.

A second aspect of harvest index to explore is the possibility of increasing the size or number of tree parts that can be removed as yield. The extreme example of this is the multipurpose tree, where even the litterfall might be of value for soil improvement. A less extreme example is whole-tree harvesting in forestry (eg Keays 1971). A further example occurs in tea (*Camellia sinensis*), where yield consists of young shoots with 'two-leaves-and-a-bud'. These are the only parts which make good quality beverage. Each shoot is plucked at the end of a period of slow exponential growth lasting about 35 days. If the shoots were allowed to grow to 'three-leaves-and-a-bud', they would double their dry weights, and take only a further 7 days to do so (Tanton 1979). Thus, if tea bushes were selected in which this third leaf could be used to make good quality tea, yield might be substantially increased. There are, perhaps, other instances in which *H.I.* could be increased, not by changing dry matter partitioning, but by redefining yield.

B. Harvest index and yield

There is a considerable literature in the agricultural sciences showing that there is a strong association between *H.I.* and yield, and it has been suggested that measurement of *H.I.* might advance our understanding of crop performance (eg Singh & Stoskopf 1971; Donald & Hamblin 1976). However, Charles-Edwards (1982) warns against this suggestion, on two grounds: (a) correlations between a ratio (*H.I.*) and a measurement from which that ratio is derived (yield) are 'false' and can be obtained using random numbers, and (b) *H.I.* is actually a complex measure of performance which integrates phenological, physiological and environmental factors affecting yield. Thus, genetic improvements in the yield of cereals in Britain during the period 1900 to 1980 were accompanied by a large increase in *H.I.* (Austin *et al.* 1980), but the true determinants of increased yields were probably a decline in the duration of the vegetative growth phase, and an increase in the amount of light intercepted during the grain-filling phase (Charles-Edwards 1982). Thus, when looking for ways of increasing the yield of tree crops, we should examine the whole-plant processes that determine *H.I.*; it is not sufficient to say that yield increase is associated with an increase in *H.I.*

Finally, we should recognize that the relationship between yield and *H.I.* is always likely to be parabolic; that is, there will be an optimum value beyond which continued increase in the proportion of assimilates devoted to the yielded part occurs at the expense of new light-intercepting foliage, new roots, or essential structural parts.

C. Harvest increment of tree crops

The harvest indices of annual crops are calculated over their lifetimes, so for the purposes of comparison the same should be done for perennials (eg Pritts & Hancock 1983). However, in tree crops, we are also interested in the increment apportioned to a harvested part over a period of years within the lifespan, which we may call the harvest increment (*H.Incr.*)[1]. Clearly, the value of *H.Incr.* will depend on the age of the trees and span of years chosen.

The *H.Incr.* values of forest trees and most fruit trees are, in fact, quite high. Thus, Cannell's (1982) 'forest production data set' shows that the stems took 40–60% of the current annual above-ground dry matter increment in a large number of both broadleaved and coniferous stands around the world

[1] *H.Incr.* = Increment in harvested part/total above-ground increment; where the interval may be one or several years during the life of the trees.

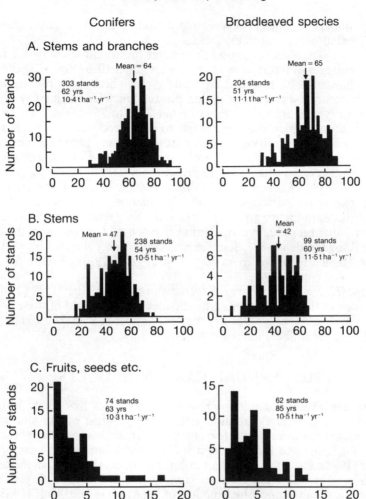

FIGURE 1. Percentage of the current annual increment in above-ground dry matter of forest stands taken by: A. stems and branches, including bark, B. stems only, including bark, and C. reproductive structures (fruits, seeds, etc).

Values were taken from Cannell (1982), using all data sets in which estimates had been made of foliage, branch and stem production. C does not include those stands that had zero values for reproductive structures. Many studies did not include good estimates of tree mortality or woody litterfall. Each histogram gives the number of stands, the average age of the stands, and their average current above-ground dry matter production.

(Fig. 1B). If branches are included with stems, then the *H.Incr.* of many stands are in the range 60–80% (Fig. 1A). Furthermore, these values are probably under-estimates, because many studies failed to give values for woody litterfall or tree mortality.

The proportion of above-ground dry matter increment taken by the reproductive structures of forest trees is usually less than 10% (Fig. 1C), although higher values may be recorded in 'mast' years, heavy coning years, and perhaps if accurate estimates of pollen production were made. The $H.Incr.$ measured on young fruit trees ranges from 23% to 75% (Table I). Despite biennial bearing (which may be related to seed-produced hormones rather than to shortage of assimilates), mature fruit trees may have average $H.Incr.$ values exceeding 60%, which is considered to be near the maximum $H.I.$ ($= H.Incr.$) of cereals, which have to produce new structural tissues each year (Austin et al. 1980). Carbon allocation models for wild annual species suggest that the maximum reproductive yield is obtained when the switch from vegetative to reproductive growth occurs at the time when the vegetative mass is equal to final reproductive yield, that is when $H.I.$ is no more than 50% (King & Roughgarden 1983). Selected progenies of oil palm are able to sustain a $H.Incr.$ (bunch index) of about 50% (Corley et al. 1971b; Breure & Corley 1983).

Tea and *Hevea* rubber have $H.Incr.$ values of less than 15% (Table I), which is one of the main reasons why the mean annual yield of these crops is usually only 1 to 3 t ha^{-1}yr^{-1} of dry matter, compared with 5 to 15 t ha^{-1}yr^{-1} in many tropical timber, fuelwood and fruit trees.

III. ANNUAL CARBON BUDGETS

The first step to understanding whole-plant processes that might influence the $H.Incr.$ of trees is to examine yield in the context of the total annual carbon budget. Unfortunately, few complete carbon budgets have been constructed for trees, and most of them suffer serious limitations (see Jarvis & Leverenz 1983). However, sufficient information exists to establish the relative magnitude of the different biomass components and carbon fluxes, which form a basis for the conceptual models of McMurtrie and Wolf (1983) and McMurtrie (this volume).

Figure 2 presents two carbon budgets for forest trees, in which attempts were made to determine all the components by measurement. However, there was considerable uncertainty about the magnitude of root respiration and woody litterfall (Agren et al. 1980; Edwards et al. 1981). Also note that the two stands differed markedly in age, size and site conditions. Two further budgets are presented later (Fig. 7, for the same stands as Fig. 2A), but other published budgets for trees are incomplete, or were balanced by assigning a remainder to one of the processes (Schulze 1970; Schulze et al. 1977; Kinerson et al. 1977; Kira & Yabuki 1978).

In the absence of other data, Figure 3 presents four of the best current net-dry-matter-production budgets published for forests (that is, omitting respiration), in which good estimates were made of each component, including fine root turnover.

The most striking feature of all these budgets is the high proportion of dry matter allocated to root respiration and fine root turnover. Thus, in Figures

TABLE I. Harvest increment[1] of some tree crops

Tree crop	Yield	Age (years)	Increment period (years)	Harvest increment (%)	Source
Forest trees	Stems and branches	Average 57	1 to 10	40–85	Cannell 1982; Fig. 1A
	Stems	Average 57	1 to 10	20–70	Cannell 1982; Fig. 1B
Apple	Fruits	2	0·5	40	Maggs 1963
	Fruits	2	0·6	44	Avery 1969
	Fruits	2–5	3	23–74	Avery 1970
	Fruits	3–4	1	53	Hansen 1971a
	Fruits	3–4	1	27–72	Heim et al. 1979
Peach	Fruits	4–15	1	35–70	Chalmers & Ende 1975
Citrus	Fruits	2–3	1	up to 52	Lenz 1979
Coffee	Fruits (seeds)	3–4	1·3	44(30)	Cannell 1971
	Fruits (seeds)	4	0·3	75(50)	Cannell 1971
Oil palm	Bunch (oil)	17–22	5	27(11)	Rees & Tinker 1963
	Bunch (oil)	7–18	11	43(17)	Corley et al. 1971a
	Bunch (oil)	10	1	25–54(10–22)	Corley et al. 1971b
Tea	Young shoots	6	1	11	Magambo & Cannell 1981
Hevea rubber	Latex	6	1	3–11	Templeton 1969

[1] Dry weight increment in the harvested part/dry weight increment in all above-ground parts.

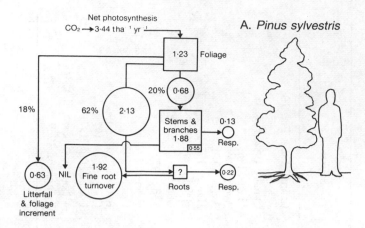

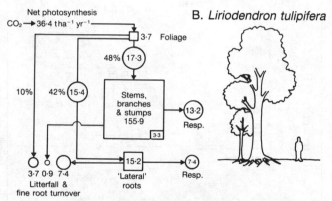

FIGURE 2. Current annual dry matter budgets of two contrasting forests. Both budgets were balanced using measurements of net photosynthesis, biomass increments, respiration, litterfall and fine root turnover.

A. *Pinus sylvestris*, 14 years old, 60°49′N in Sweden, poor sandy iron-podzol (Ågren *et al.* 1980).

B. *Liriodendron tulipifera*, broadleaved woodland, up to 50 years old, 35°58′N in Tennessee, deep alluvial silt-loam (Edwards *et al.* 1981).

Squares: biomass $(t\,ha^{-1})$; circles: fluxes $(t\,ha^{-1}yr^{-1})$. Values can be converted to $g\,C\,m^{-2}yr^{-1}$ by multiplying by 50. The areas of the squares and circles are proportional to the values, but the scales differ in A and B. The small boxes within the woody biomass squares give the annual net wood increments $(t\,ha^{-1}yr^{-1})$. The budget for B includes the understorey canopy, but omits the ground flora, and small losses from predators and herbivores. Note that the percentage dry matter going to foliage is equal to the litterfall plus the increment in living foliage.

2A and 2B the roots took 62% and 42%, respectively, of the total carbon, while in Figure 3 they took between 24% and 66% of the current net dry matter production. These percentages represented 2·1 to 16·8 $t\,ha^{-1}yr^{-1}$ of dry matter, often exceeding the dry matter used each year to produce new foliage. The second feature to note is that, whereas the *H.Incr.* values for

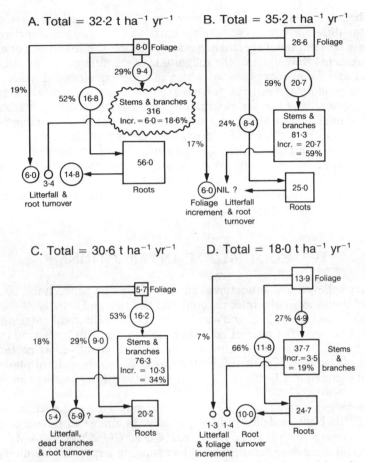

FIGURE 3. Current annual net dry matter production budgets of four forest stands (excluding respiration).

A. Tropical rainforest, Venezuela, on infertile leached lateritic soil (see Cannell 1982, p. 372). (A fairly complete budget also exists for the Pasoh tropical rainforest, Malaysia; see Cannell 1982, p. 196.)

B. *Picea sitchensis*, Scotland, aged 17, peaty gley soil (see Cannell 1982, p. 242).

C. *Pinus taeda*, North Carolina, aged 14, sandy loam (see Cannell 1982, p. 326, assuming $5 \cdot 5 \, t \, ha^{-1} yr^{-1}$ increment in dead branches).

D. *Abies amabilis*, Washington State, aged 23, sandy, gravelly clay loam (see Cannell 1982, p. 289).

Squares: biomass $(t \, ha^{-1})$; circles: fluxes $(t \, ha^{-1} yr^{-1})$. The large biomass of stems and branches in A $(316 \, t \, ha^{-1})$ is not drawn to scale, but all other biomass and flux values are represented by squares or circles on the same scale. See legend to Fig. 2.

woody parts in these stands were quite high, the net increment of woody parts often represented a small part of the total carbon budget. For instance, the *H.Incr.* of woody parts in Figure 2A was 47% $[0 \cdot 55/(0 \cdot 55 + 0 \cdot 63)]$, whereas the annual net increment of woody parts represented only 16% of the total fixed carbon (0·55/3·44). Third, note how very different the allocation patterns were in the different stands. We do not know to what extent the differences were due to species, stand age, management, climate, site conditions or errors in measurement. Nevertheless, the magnitude of the differences suggests that important variation exists, some of which may be exploitable. Finally, note that the respiratory losses from foliage and fine roots were proportional to their biomasses, whereas the respiratory losses from woody parts were a function of their surface areas, and so were small relative to their biomasses (Butler & Landsberg 1981). However, whereas the surface area of woody parts increases with tree size, the biomass and respiratory burden of foliage and fine roots remain relatively constant after canopy closure (Rauner 1976; McMurtrie, this volume). This fact means that the *net* dry matter increment of woody parts represents a decreasing proportion of the total net increment with increase in the tree size.

IV. ROOT/SHOOT INTERACTIONS

It is widely believed that a functional equilibrium exists between the size and activity of the shoots (which fix carbon) and the size and activity of the fine roots (which take up nutrients and water). In a constant environment favouring continuous growth, the ratio of root/shoot relative growth rates tends to be constant. The root/shoot equilibrium tends to be adaptive; in particular, assimilates are used preferentially by the shoots if conditions limit photosynthesis, and preferentially by the roots if conditions limit nutrient or water uptake.

The root/shoot equilibrium is virtually the only aspect of partitioning in plants that has been modelled non-empirically. In almost all the major plant and crop growth models (ELCROS, SIMCOT, GOSSYM, SIMAIZ, etc) carbon partitioning has been simulated by assuming a specified allometry, by predefining patterns of partitioning, or by pre-assigning priorities to different sinks (Hesketh & Jones 1976; Loomis *et al.* 1979; Penning de Vries & Laar 1982).

Here, I shall briefly consider the predictions of different approaches to modelling root/shoot interactions, and then describe the observed effects on root/shoot partitioning of some environmental, management and plant factors.

A. Root/shoot models

There have been basically three approaches to modelling root/shoot assimilate partitioning: (a) the 'whole-plant view' proposed by Davidson (1969) and extended by Thornley (1977) and Charles-Edwards (1976, 1981, 1982), (b) the 'resistance-utilization' approach of Thornley (1977), and (c) a 'storage-pool' model proposed by Reynolds and Thornley (1982). All of them are relevant to trees if we redefine roots as only the fine roots, and shoots as the foliage.

The whole-plant view is based on the relationship:

$$W_R \sigma_R / f_m = W_S \sigma_S / f_c \qquad (1)$$

where W_R is the root mass, W_S is the shoot mass, σ_R is the specific activity of the roots (eg the rate of nitrogen uptake per unit root mass), σ_S is the specific activity of the shoots (normally the rate of carbon assimilation per unit shoot mass), f_m is the nutrient composition of an increment of new plant dry matter (eg percentage nitrogen), and f_c is its carbon composition. The root/shoot ratio $W_R / W_S = f_m \sigma_S / f_c \sigma_R$ and the proportion partitioned to roots becomes:

$$\text{root fraction} = f_m \sigma_S / (f_c \sigma_R + f_m \sigma_S) \qquad (2)$$

Equation (2) states that the proportion of new plant dry matter partitioned to roots will decrease if (a) the root specific activity, σ_R, increases (eg with improved nutrition, see below), (b) the nutrient composition of new plant dry matter, f_m, decreases (eg with increased partitioning to wood, see below), and (c) the rate of carbon assimilation by the shoots, σ_S, decreases (eg as a result of shading) (see Fig. 4A).

The balanced 'resistance-utilization' model of Thornley (1977) makes the assumptions that (a) carbon, C, and nitrogen, N, are transported passively, at rates dependent upon concentration gradients divided by resistances in the pathway, and (b) the rates at which C and N are utilized by the shoots and roots depend upon their masses and the concentrations of C and N in the substrate (Fig. 4B). This model predicts similar changes in partitioning to those expressed in Figure 4A, resulting from changes in substrate C/N ratio. Under steady-state conditions, the relative growth rates of shoots and roots are in constant ratio to each other, and if the root/shoot ratio is perturbed, this brings about changes in C and N substrate concentrations that lead to a return to steady-state conditions (Fig. 4B).

The 'storage-pool' model proposed by Reynolds and Thornley (1982) does not invoke assimilate transport resistances, which cannot easily be measured, but instead supposes that there are two storage pools, one for C and one for N (Fig. 4C). The model is a further advance, in that it allows suboptimal and optimal partitioning strategies to be compared, assuming that an optimal strategy is one giving the greatest plant relative growth rate. The model suggests that, when σ_R is low (in nutrient-poor conditions), the root/shoot ratio will be lower with an optimal strategy than with a fixed or suboptimal strategy, but the situation will be reversed when σ_R is high. Trees, which must endure a range of environments, may not adopt optimal partitioning strategies in their native environments. They may, for instance, partition less to foliage and more to roots than would be needed to maximize their relative growth rates, and hence to perform well as crop plants (see Bowen, this volume).

B. Effects of nutrition

There are numerous papers, on woody and herbaceous species, showing that high levels of nutrient supply increase shoot growth relative to root growth (Ledig 1983 lists 24 papers). A few papers give sufficient information to allow estimates to be made of specific root activity in relation to nutrient supply, elemental composition and root/shoot partitioning. Two examples are given

A. Whole plant view

Root fraction = $f_m \sigma_s/(f_c \sigma_R + f_m \sigma_s)$

σ_R, σ_s = root and shoot
    specific activities

f_c, f_m = carbon and nutrient
    elemental composition

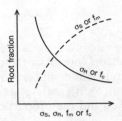

B. Resistance-utilization model

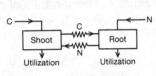

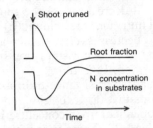

C. Storage-pool model

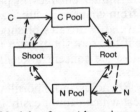

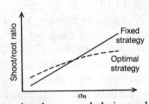

FIGURE 4. Models of root/shoot interactions in plants, and their predictions.
A. Whole-plant view of Davidson (1969), modified by Thornley (1977) and Charles-Edwards (1982).
B. Resistance-utilization model (balanced version) of Thornley (1977).
C. Storage-pool model of Reynolds and Thornley (1982).

in Figure 5. In both instances, specific root activity (σ_R), percentage N content of the tissues, and partitioning to shoots increased with increase in N supply. Also, the form of the relationships between σ_R and the proportion of dry matter partitioned to roots and shoots was similar to that expressed in equation (2) (Fig. 4A). Furthermore, Ingestad's experiments showed that birch seedlings adapted rapidly to changes in rate of N supply so that tissue concentrations of N and growth rates were balanced in the manner predicted by Thornley's models. Also, it should be noted that increased N supply increased the proportion of dry matter partitioned to stems (Fig. 5B).

In the past, explanations for increased above-ground dry matter production in trees in response to improved nutrition have been sought mainly in terms of increased foliage biomass and/or photosynthetic rates. But, bearing in mind the high carbon cost of fine roots, more researchers are realizing that greater

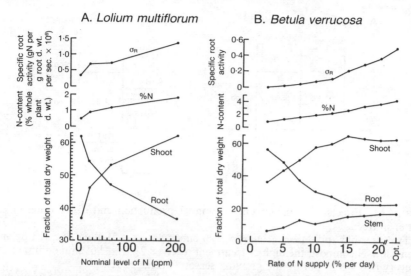

FIGURE 5.   Effects of differences in N level or supply rate on the specific root activity, the percentage N in plant dry matter, and the proportion of dry matter in plant parts.
A. *Lolium multiflorum* grown in sand culture with different nominal levels of N provided in watering solutions (Charles-Edwards 1982).
B. *Betula verrucosa* seedlings grown with their roots in a nutrient mist, supplying N at different rates according to demand for 80 days, maintaining constant N concentrations in the tissues (Ingestad & Lund 1979; Ingestad 1979).

weight must be given to the effect of improved nutrition on root/shoot partitioning (Linder & Rook 1984).

Maggs (1961) showed that N nutrition of young pot-grown apple trees increased the total annual dry matter production per tree by only 1·3%, but it altered root/shoot partitioning so as to increase above-ground dry matter production by 5·9% (Fig. 6A). More dramatically, Keyes and Grier (1981), working on 40-year-old stands of *Pseudotsuga menziesii* in Washington State, showed that trees growing in a fertile soil produced only about 17% more total dry matter per hectare per year than similar trees growing in an infertile soil, but the former were producing about 88% more dry matter above-ground, largely owing to decreased fine root turnover (Fig. 6B).

However, the best data on the effects of improved nutrition on assimilate partitioning in trees were reported by Linder and Axelsson (1982), who supplied a complete nutrient solution, daily from mid-May to mid-September for six years, to plots of the *Pinus sylvestris* trees illustrated in Figure 2A. Figure 7 shows the measured annual carbon budget of the trees at age 20 compared with untreated controls. The treated trees were over twice as large in dry biomass as the untreated trees, and were fixing over twice as much dry matter per year (22·24 compared with 11·60 t ha^{-1}yr^{-1}, with leaf area index 3·0 compared with 1·4). Most importantly, the treated trees partitioned only about 31% of their assimilates to roots, compared with 59% in the untreated trees – representing a similar dry weight of 6·9 t ha^{-1}yr^{-1} in both cases. Fine

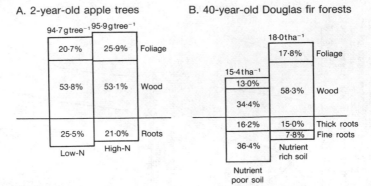

FIGURE 6. Effects of nutrition on the annual production and distribution of dry matter in trees.

A. Two-year-old apple trees grown in pots outside at East Malling, Kent, England, in a low-N compost; the high-N treatment received 2 g tree^{-1} of ammonium nitrate every two weeks during the growing season (Maggs 1961).

B. Forty-year-old stands of *Pseudotsuga menziesii* in Washington State, USA, growing either in infertile loam-sand, low in N, and with a low base saturation, or in fertile colluvial soil, with 33% base saturation (Keyes & Grier 1981). Fine root increments were estimated by soil core sampling and root observations through underground windows.

root turnover, derived as the residual term needed to balance the budgets, was only 2·48 t ha^{-1}yr^{-1} on the treated trees compared with 4·00 t ha^{-1}yr^{-1} on the untreated trees. In consequence, improved nutrition greatly increased partitioning to foliage (from 12% to 20%) and to wood (28% to 49%) and increased the proportion of assimilates used in stem growth from 8% to 14%.

If we look again at the dry matter increment budgets for the three conifer plantations given in Figure 3B, C and D, we find that the stands that produced most above-ground and total dry matter (B = 35·2 t ha^{-1}yr^{-1}, C = 30·6 t ha^{-1}yr^{-1}, D = 18·0 t ha^{-1}yr^{-1}) also partitioned least to roots (B = 24%, C = 42%, D = 66%). It is tempting to suggest that one of the factors involved was a difference in soil fertility, although differences also existed in age, species and water relations.

In conclusion, there is growing evidence that decreased partitioning to fine roots is one of the most important mechanisms by which improved nutrition increases above-ground dry matter production. This fact could not have been appreciated in tree nutrition studies that did not include estimates of fine root turnover (eg Brix & Ebell 1969; Miller & Miller 1976).

C. Effects of water stress and shade

Root/shoot models predict that a drought-induced decrease in root-specific activity with respect to water uptake would increase root relative to shoot growth. Gales (1979) found 19 papers which reported this predicted effect,

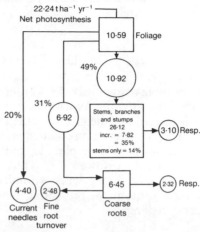

A. Untreated

11·60 t ha⁻¹ yr⁻¹
Net photosynthesis

B. Nutrient solution

22·24 t ha⁻¹ yr⁻¹
Net photosynthesis

FIGURE 7. Current annual dry matter budgets of 20-year-old *Pinus sylvestris* trees, A untreated, and B supplied for 6 years with a complete nutrient solution from mid-May to mid-September representing 3 mm of water per day. The trees were in the same location as those illustrated in Fig. 2A, at age 14. Squares: biomass (t ha⁻¹); circles: fluxes (t ha⁻¹yr⁻¹). The areas of the squares and circles are proportional to the values. These values can be converted to kg C ha⁻¹yr⁻¹, as given by Linder and Axelsson (1982), by multiplying by 500.

and nine which did not. It appeared that, where levels of soil nutrients were low (especially P), drought could exacerbate nutrient deficiency as well as induce water stress, and the net effect was increased or unchanged root/shoot relative growth rates. However, when P levels were high, water stress generally increased the root/shoot ratio, and indeed it is often recommended practice to withhold irrigation to promote deep rooting when establishing tropical trees in drought-prone areas. Conversely, if irrigation can be maintained throughout the year, this may decrease the carbon demand of the roots, and, like nutrition, increase above-ground dry matter production (Evans 1980).

Numerous shading experiments have shown that the resulting decrease in shoot-specific activity (net photosynthetic rate) is accompanied by greater partitioning to the shoots (see Ledig 1983). Where this effect has not been found, the results can often be explained by confounding with nutrient levels, water stress or ontogenetic drifts in root/shoot relative growth rates. Increased shoot growth in shade argues in favour of growing shoot- or leaf-yielding plants such as forage crops, spinach or tea in the understorey of agroforests (Cannell 1983). One may also speculate that high levels of solar radiation and seasonal droughts in the tropics would favour higher root/shoot relative growth rates than in temperate regions. Cripps (1971) noted that the root/shoot ratios of young apple trees in Western Australia were about 1:1, whereas similar trees in England had root/shoot ratios of about 1:2. He suggested that this was why reduced shoot growth and early cropping occurred naturally in

Western Australia, but has to be induced by using dwarfing rootstocks or chemicals in England.

D.   Effects of pruning

Shoot pruning temporarily checks root growth, while root pruning temporarily checks shoot growth. As would be predicted using Thornley's models, the more is pruned off, the greater is the check in growth; and the longer it takes for the plants to recover the root/shoot relationship that existed before pruning (beans, Brouwer 1962; apple, Maggs 1965; orange, Alexander & Maggs 1971; peach, Richards & Rowe 1977). Thus, shoot pruning is a means of promoting new shoot growth (eg when stimulating a 'pruning response'), and root pruning is a means of promoting new root growth (eg when undercutting nursery seedlings).

E.   Seasonal and plant factors

In trees, the functional balance between roots and shoots is normally perturbed by changes in the environment, and by periodicity in the activity of the shoot meristems. In temperate regions, assimilates are usually used preferentially by the shoots during elongation or 'flushing' in spring or early summer, and preferentially by the roots in autumn (Fig. 8A; Cannell & Willett 1976; McLaughlin et al. 1979; Isebrands & Nelson 1983). Work on conifer seedlings showed that, over a succession of seasons, the root/shoot relationship remained in balance, but within any season the trees developed a relatively high root/shoot ratio in the autumn, which was restored to equilibrium when shoot elongation occurred the following spring (Cannell & Willett 1976). Furthermore, the shorter the period of shoot elongation, the greater the root/shoot ratio each autumn (Fig. 8A comparing Oregon and Alaskan provenances). In tropical regions, we would expect assimilates to be used preferentially by the shoots during periods of rapid shoot growth at the start of (or during) each rainy season, and preferentially by the roots during dry and/or cool seasons, as is roughly the case for coffee in Kenya (Fig. 8B). There are, of course, numerous variations on the two partitioning patterns shown in Figure 8, and neither describes the movement of storage carbohydrates.

Tree shoot growth is often intermittent, even in constant environments. In seedlings of temperate-zone pines and oaks, intermittent shoot growth is often paralleled by equal and opposite fluctuations in root growth (eg pines, Drew & Ledig 1980; Drew 1982; oaks, Reich et al. 1980). Similar fluctuations may also occur in tropical trees with periodic shoot growth. Alternatively, Borchert (1973, 1976) suggested that root growth may be constant, but that rapid shoot growth periodically outstrips the ability of the roots to supply the shoots with water, thereby inducing water stress, checking leaf expansion, and producing intermittent shoot elongation.

Whatever the mechanism, endogenously or environmentally induced perturbations in root/shoot relationships seem eventually to be restored by

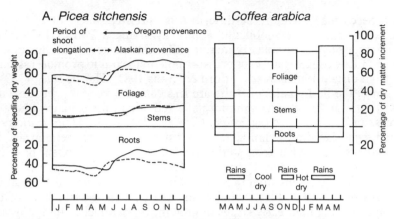

FIGURE 8.   Seasonal changes in the distribution of dry matter in trees.
A. *Picea sitchensis* seedlings of Denmark, Oregon (42°51′N) and Cordova, Alaska (60°30′N) provenance, during their second year, growing in pots in a nursery at Bush, Midlothian, Scotland (Cannell & Willett 1976; from their Fig. 3).
B. *Coffea arabica* trees, during their fourth year, growing in deep loam at Ruiru, Kenya. The leaf fraction includes flower buds, but there were no fruits because the trees were deblossomed (Cannell 1971). Note that this figure shows the distribution of *increment*, whereas A shows the distribution of *biomass*.

feedback mechanisms as predicted in root/shoot models. When examining root/shoot ratios in trees, it is important to distinguish the long-term equilibrium from the short-term fluctuations (Cannell & Willett 1976).

To complete this account, attention should be drawn to the genetic differences in root/shoot balance that exist between and within tree species. Ledig (1983) suggested that species of early seral stages have smaller root/shoot relative growth rates than those from later seral stages. There has also been debate about the optimal root/shoot investment strategy of trees and other plants in xeric and mesic habits with regard to survival, growth and the carbon cost of constructing and maintaining mesophytic and xerophytic leaves (see Orians & Solbrig 1977; Mooney *et al.* 1978). Clearly, within-species variation in root/shoot relationships may offer important opportunities for genetic advance in yield.

V.   FRUITING

A.   Fruits and seeds as priority sinks

Whereas the growth rates of roots and shoots may fluctuate with time, and may often be below their potential rates, the growth rates of seeds tend to be constant during the period of endosperm filling (eg cereals, Biscoe & Gallagher 1977; Martinez-Carrasco & Thorne 1979; coffee, Cannell 1974). Within limits, the final weights of seeds (beans, grains and nuts) are often inherently fixed, and are less variable than other components of seed or fruit yield (Harper

1977). Seeds may therefore be described as 'priority sinks', or as having a large 'sink strength' or 'mobilizing ability' (Wareing & Patrick 1975). More exactly, they seem to be able to generate and maintain steep gradients in sieve-tube assimilate concentrations or pressure potentials so as to promote assimilate flow from distant leaf sources (Gifford & Evans 1981; Thorpe et al. 1983). In this sense, the fleshy parts of fruits are less competitive sinks, because their growth rates and final sizes are more affected when, for instance, there is a decrease in leaf/fruit ratio (eg coffee, Cannell 1974; apple, Heim et al. 1979). Seeded fruits can draw assimilates from leaves at least one metre away, so it is possible to manipulate trees so that the fruits are to some extent physically separated from the foliage (Parry 1974; Hansen 1977). We may expect that fruits of different species differ in 'sink strength', depending upon the numbers and sizes of the seeds they contain, and perhaps on the numbers of cells developed during their early stages of growth. Golden Delicious apples seem to be weaker sinks than Graasten apples, in that their growth rates are lower at a given leaf/fruit ratio, and they are less able to attract assimilates from distant leaves (Hansen 1977).

The total assimilate demand per tree of the seeds and fruits depends on their number. Most mature trees are capable of producing more flowers, in some years, than they can sustain to fruit maturity. Their strategy is to adjust fruit numbers to match assimilate and nutrient resources by flower or fruit abortion. June drop of apples in Europe has counterparts in cherelle wilt of cacao, abortion of button coconuts, and citrus and coffee fruit drop two to four months after anthesis. Young fruits often seem, at some stage, to be weak sinks compared with the shoot tips, especially when there is environmental stress (eg Quinlan & Preston 1971). Lloyd (1980) suggested that the optimal strategy to produce full-sized fruits and seeds was to initiate the maximum number of flowers that could be supported; then, if future resources were certain to be limiting, abortion would occur early, whereas if resources were less certain to be limiting, or if there was a high risk that fruits would be lost later on from pests, pathogens or predators, abortion would be delayed. In Arabica coffee, fruit drop rarely occurs after the stage of fruit expansion (before endosperm filling) possibly because, in its native shady habitat, coffee initiates relatively few flowers, so that it is likely that all can be sustained to produce full-sized seeds (Cannell 1974). By contrast, mango can drop its fruits at any time during their development, possibly because such large fruits are likely to be attacked at any stage by pests, pathogens or predators. It might be argued that, when fruit or nut trees are brought into cultivation, we increase the certainty of resources being adequate to sustain fruit and seed growth, and so we need to decrease the trees' susceptibility to flower or fruit abortion. Conversely, if the trees bear irregularly in nature, and we manage them to bear fruits every year, some propensity for flower or fruit abortion might be desirable.

Oil palm is an interesting special case, in which the single, large vegetative apex seems to take precedence over the fruit bunches for carbohydrates and nutrients. Defoliation decreases fruit production by increasing abortion of young inflorescences or by restricting fruit growth, but it rarely decreases the growth rate of the vegetative growing points (Corley 1973).

So far, I have assumed that carbon is the resource limiting fruit and seed growth, but very often it is a mineral element (Harper 1977; Thompson & Stewart 1981; Swank *et al.* 1982). The mineral content of seeds is four to seven times greater than that of wood. In Arabica coffee in Kenya, the flower buds alone took nearly 40% of the total P uptake of the trees during a dry season and, during an 87-day period, the fruits on heavily fruiting trees took 89%, 95%, 98% and 99% of the total tree uptake of Mg, K, N and P, respectively, compared with 72% of the dry matter (Cannell 1971; Cannell & Kimeu 1971).

B.   Effects of fruits on partitioning

In forest trees, it might be argued that fruiting has little effect on vegetative growth because (a) the reproductive parts represent a relatively small proportion of the total above-ground dry matter increment (Fig. 1C); (b) green fruits photosynthesize and refix respiratory CO_2, and (c) fruiting often enhances leaf photosynthesis. However, there is ample evidence that cone and seed production can reduce wood and/or foliage production (conifers, Danilow 1953; Eis *et al.* 1965; broadleaves, Harper 1977; Tuomi *et al.* 1982).

The production of 75 cones tree^{-1}yr^{-1} on the 14-year-old *Pinus sylvestris* trees illustrated in Figure 2A would represent 6% of the annual photosynthetic production (Linder & Troeng 1981). In 120-year-old *P. sylvestris* stands in Sweden, cone production of $0 \cdot 21$ t ha^{-1}yr^{-1} dry weight, with an additional estimated respiratory cost equal to 50% of the cone dry weight, was estimated to represent 10–15% of the carbon cost of stemwood production (Linder & Troeng 1981). Earlier, Fielding (1960) reached a similar conclusion for *Pinus radiata* in Australia, but ignoring respiratory costs; over a 40-year rotation, trees produced about $1 \cdot 1$ t ha^{-1}yr^{-1} of cones and pollen, which was equivalent to about $3 \cdot 0$ m^{3}ha^{-1}yr^{-3} of stemwood, or 16% of the mean annual increment on medium-quality sites. In both the *P. sylvestris* and *P. radiata* studies, the mineral nutrient cost of cone production might well have been 40–50% of the mineral cost of stemwood production (Matthews 1963).

Clearly, the carbon and mineral costs of fruiting will not be solely at the expense of wood production, but, even so, selection for non-fruiting forest trees could enhance stemwood production by several per cent. Conversely, inadvertent selection by tree breeders for enhanced fruiting at maturity might cancel out a significant proportion of the genetic gain observed within juvenile progeny tests.

In dioecious species (eg *Populus* spp. and *Fraxinus excelsior*), it has been suggested that male trees grow faster than females, because they carry a smaller reproductive burden (Matthews 1963; Harper 1977), and this is often the case if the females have a consistently large percentage fruit set (Grant & Mitton 1979). However, in other cases, the males may grow slower than the females, because the expenditure on male reproductive structures is concentrated in the spring and so reduces or delays foliage development (Gross & Soule 1981).

In fruit trees, the heavy demands of the fruits greatly distort the pattern of carbon partitioning among vegetative parts, including the root/shoot balance.

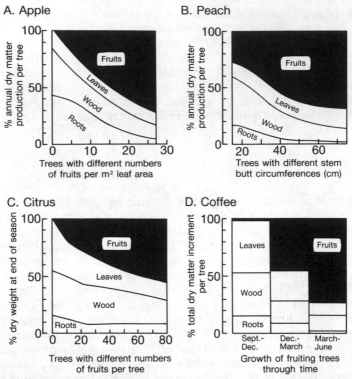

FIGURE 9.   Partitioning of dry matter in fruit trees.
A. Apple (Golden Delicious), 3–4 years old, growing in pots in England and France (Heim *et al.* 1979).
B. Peach (Golden Queen), 4–15 years old, growing in Australia (Chalmers & Ende 1975).
C. *Citrus madurensis* (Lenz 1979).
D. *Coffea arabica*, 4 years old, growing in Kenya (Cannell 1971).

Studies on apple, peach and coffee have all shown that root growth suffers most (Fig. 9, also Maggs 1963; Avery 1970; Hansen 1971a). In England, relatively light crops of fruits greatly reduce new root growth on apple trees during July to October (Head 1969). The explanation usually given is that the roots are furthest from the leaves, and that over such long distances there is a path resistance to assimilate movement (Heim *et al.* 1979), although the resistance to assimilate flow in both angiosperm and gymnosperm phloem is very low (Watson 1980). An alternative explanation is that the root apices are inherently 'weak' sinks compared with the shoot apices, but there is no evidence for this in the vegetative plant (Warren-Wilson 1972). Stem and branch growth is less restricted by fruiting than root growth, and, in apple and peach, the proportion of the total dry matter increment taken by leaves is relatively constant, irrespective of fruiting level (Fig. 9). Fruiting, therefore, reveals an order of priority among the carbon sinks which may be expressed as differences in their growth rates at different leaf/fruit ratios; the order is usually seeds>fleshy fruit parts = shoot apices and leaves>cambium>roots>storage. If true, this will also be the sequence in which vegetative parts are first affected by fruiting; that is, assimilates will be withdrawn from storage first, then withheld from roots, and so on.

If fruiting greatly decreases the mass of fine roots, W_R, relative to the foliage mass, W_S, and equation (2) is to hold, then there must be a corresponding increase in specific root activity, σ_R, or a decrease in plant elemental composition, f_m. (There is ample evidence that σ_S does not decrease.) Studies on apple (Hansen 1971a, b), coffee (Cannell & Kimeu 1971), and tomato (Richards *et al.* 1979) have shown that, at moderate fruiting levels, the main change in

TABLE II. Rate of uptake of nutrients per unit of root dry weight ($mg\,g^{-1}$harvest interval^{-1}) in 4-year-old Golden Delicious apple and Arabica coffee trees, expressed as a percentage of that in non-fruiting trees

Crop	Fruiting level	N	P	K	Ca	Mg
Apple	Heavy[1]	146	170	299	166	157
Coffee	Moderate[2]	165	500	216	176	150
Coffee	Very heavy[3]	101	86	162	86	110

[1] Derived from Hansen (1971a and b), for the period of one year, assuming the fruiting and non-fruiting trees had an average of 1,000 g and 350 g roots tree^{-1} respectively during the year. The fruits took 53% of the total dry matter increment. The trees were grown in containers outdoors in Denmark.
[2] From Cannell (1971) and Cannell and Kimeu (1974) for an 82-day period. Root weight included only those roots <1 mm diameter. The fruits took 29% of the total dry weight increment. The trees were growing in a plantation in Kenya.
[3] As for 2, for an 87-day period during which the fruits took 72% of the total dry matter increment.

equation (2) is a large increase in σ_R (Table II). In tomato, the overall plant f_m, including fruits, remains relatively constant, while in apple and coffee, fruiting trees can have higher concentrations of some nutrients (eg Ca) in their leaves than non-fruiting trees (Hansen 1971b; Cannell & Kimeu 1971). However, at very high fruiting levels, σ_R values in coffee can fall below those in non-fruiting trees (Table II), associated with almost zero root growth and 'dieback' of the shoots. Thus, 'overbearing dieback' may be due more to the high demand of the fruits for mineral nutrients, combined with the distance of the roots from assimilate sources, rather than to direct diversion of assimilates from shoots to fruits.

VI. ABOVE-GROUND VEGETATIVE PARTS

A. Effect of harvesting vegetative parts

Whereas the removal of fruits from trees *increases* vegetative growth and the potential to produce future fruit yield, the removal of vegetative parts such as foliage, fuelwood or extractives *decreases* vegetative growth and the potential to produce future vegetative yield. Thus, in tea, the plucking of young shoots, representing only 8·3% of the total annual dry matter production, decreased total dry matter production by 35·7%, compared with unplucked bushes (Fig.10A). And, in rubber, the removal of latex, representing only 7·2% of the total annual dry matter production above-ground, decreased total dry matter production by 29·6%, compared with untapped trees (Fig. 10B). Thus, the energy cost of vegetative yield is much greater (about 4 times) than the energy content of the parts that are harvested.

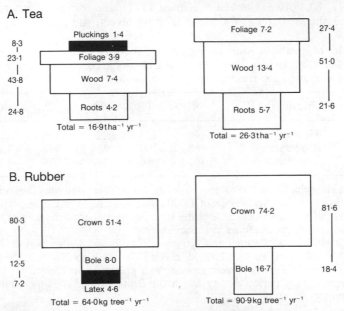

FIGURE 10.   Effect of removing vegetative yield on the current annual production and distribution of dry matter in trees (t ha⁻¹yr⁻¹). Marginal numbers are percentages.
A. Tea, plucked and unplucked bushes in Kenya (Magambo & Cannell 1981).
B. *Hevea* rubber, tapped and untapped trees in Malaysia, means of six clones (Templeton 1969).

Simmonds (1982) suggested that high-yielding rubber clones might be selected by looking for clonal differences in the inverse relationship between the amount of latex removed and the decrement in total tree dry matter production (see Raven, this volume). Templeton (1969) had earlier shown that the removal of latex from rubber had less effect on total dry matter production in some clones than others. A similar approach could be adopted in the selection of high-yielding fodder and fuelwood trees.

B.   Partitioning between wood and foliage

In Figure 1A, it was shown that the proportion of the above-ground dry matter increment allocated to wood, as opposed to foliage, varied greatly among forest stands. Some of this variation will be due to environmental, management and exploitable genetic variation, although, as discussed below, we know surprisingly little about how these factors influence wood/foliage partitioning.

Wood/foliage partitioning is important, partly because it influences wood yield, but also because it influences the parameters in equation (2). New woody tissues have a lower nutrient content than foliage, so increased partitioning to wood decreases the average nutrient content of new dry matter increment (f_m). This decreased nutrient demand should lessen the proportion of assimilates taken by roots (Fig. 5A), and increase the amount of new dry matter that can be produced per unit of nutrient.

Let us consider some of the factors that might influence wood/foliage partitioning.

1.   *Variation with latitude*

Jordan (1971) postulated that trees adapted to low light intensities at high latitudes might devote more carbon to structural tissues, and less to foliage, than trees adapted to more equatorial conditions. He reasoned that, at low light intensities, there would be a greater selective pressure to produce stemwood, in order to overtop competitors, than at high light intensities. In support of this contention, he reported a decrease in the ratio of annual wood production to annual litterfall with increase in total possible incident solar radiation during the growing season, using data for 26 forest stands spanning cold temperate to tropical regions. In other words, proportionately more carbon was allocated to wood at high latitudes. This was not clearly the case among the 28 forest stands studied in the International Biological Programme (O'Neill & DeAngelis 1981), but the 204 broadleaved forest stands in the 'forest production data set' (Fig. 1; Cannell 1982) showed a significant, although weak, positive relationship between the percentage of the current above-ground dry matter increment allocated to wood and latitude ($r = 0.28$). No such relationship existed for the 303 conifer stands, because no values existed for stands at latitudes less than 31°N or S.

2.   *Relationship with 'vigour'*

Several authors have suggested that the cambium has a lesser priority for assimilates than the fine roots or foliage, so that the proportion of carbon allocated to wood might increase with increase in net photosynthesis or total net dry matter production per tree or per hectare (eg Gordon & Larson 1968; Rangnekar & Forward 1973; Waring *et al.* 1980). In support of this argument, the 'forest production data set' revealed a significant trend towards greater allocation to wood with increase in total dry matter production, accounting for 14% and 18% of the variation in percentage allocation to wood among the 204 broadleaved and 303 coniferous stands, respectively (Fig. 11). The IBP woodland data set revealed a similar trend, expressed by O'Neill and DeAngelis (1981) as an increase in current annual wood increment per unit of annual litterfall with increase in total above-ground dry matter production.

Among the studies in the 'forest production data set' there were four in which current net dry matter production had been estimated for comparable

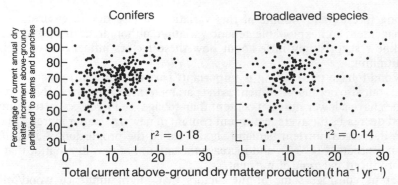

FIGURE 11.   Percentage of the current annual dry matter increment above-ground taken by the woody parts (stems and branches, and including cones and fruits) in stands of conifers and broadleaved forest trees, as a function of their total current annual above-ground dry matter production.

Data are for forest stands of all types, ages, planting densities, etc, at various sites throughout the world, from Cannell (1982), as in Fig. 1A. Outlying values in the bottom-right of the graphs probably indicate failure to fully account for woody litterfall and/or tree mortality.

forests growing on neighbouring infertile and fertile sites. In all four studies, a smaller proportion of the above-ground dry matter increment was allocated to wood on infertile sites than on fertile sites, but only by a few per cent (Table III, average difference 5·5%; see also Satoo & Madgwick 1982, their p. 106). No consistent difference in wood/foliage partitioning existed between stands with and without fertilizers (Table III). The Swedish experiment, illustrated in Figure 7, on the effects of applying a nutrient solution to mature *Pinus sylvestris*, showed only a small effect on wood/foliage partitioning. Thus, on untreated trees, the $4·74 \, t \, ha^{-1} yr^{-1}$ $(3·28+1·46)$ of above-ground dry matter increment was partitioned 30·8% to foliage and 69·2% to wood, whereas in treated trees the $15·32 \, t \, ha^{-1} yr^{-1}$ $(10·92+4·40)$ of above-ground dry matter increment was partitioned 28·7% to foliage and 71·3% to wood (Fig. 7; see also Waring 1983; Linder & Rook 1984). Further support for slightly increased partitioning to wood with increase in nutrient supply comes from Ingestad's studies on *Betula verrucosa* seedlings illustrated in Figure 5B. However, the abundant evidence that fertilization increases ring widths, wood production and wood production per unit leaf area does not, of itself, provide any information on wood/foliage partitioning (cf Waring 1980).

Overall, the evidence strongly supports the conclusions that foliage and wood production are closely coupled, and that any effects of fertilization on increasing wood/foliage partitioning are much less important than its effects on increasing shoot/root partitioning.

3.   Effect of tree age and size

Within the 'forest production data set', stand age accounted for only 6% and 3% of the variation in percentage of current net above-ground dry matter increment partitioned to wood in broadleaved and coniferous forest stands,

TABLE III. Effects of site 'quality' and fertilizer application on the proportion of the current net dry matter increment above-ground allocated to wood (stems and branches) as opposed to foliage (data from Cannell 1982)

Species	Country	Net dry matter increment above-ground (incl. litterfall) allocated to wood (%)		Reference	Page number in Cannell (1982)
		Infertile sites	Fertile sites		
Picea abies	Japan	70	73	Satoo 1971	169
Pinus banksiana	Canada	65	70	Doucet *et al.* 1976	48–49
Populus grandidentata	USA	67	78	Koerper & Richardson 1980	268
Pseudotsuga menziesii	USA	73	76	Keyes & Grier 1981	333
		No fertilizer	Fertilizer applied[1]		
Pinus nigra	Scotland	68	66	Miller & Miller 1976	246
Pinus sylvestris	Finland	80	77	Paavilainen 1980	64
Eucalyptus globulus	Australia	60	64	Cromer *et al.* 1980	10

[1] Means of all fertilizer treatments.

respectively. Closer examination of particular studies showed that partitioning to wood was usually constant, or declined, with age after canopy closure, but in some studies there was an increase in partitioning to wood during the years before canopy closure (Fig. 12). It is tempting to conclude that, in young trees, the proportion of dry matter taken by the cambium is limited by the size of the cambial sink. If this is so, then the greatest *H.Incr.* of wood will be obtained when the trees are allowed to grow moderately tall. There is some suggestion of this in the literature on mini-rotation forestry (Cannell & Smith 1980; Heilman & Peabody 1981). Conversely, the greatest *H.Incr.* of *foliage* will be obtained when the trees are kept small, by pruning or coppicing, and

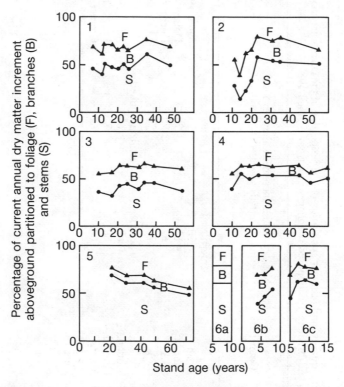

FIGURE 12.   Age trends in the percentage distribution of annual above-ground dry matter increment in coniferous forest stands (including litterfall). F = foliage; B = branches and cones; S = stems.
1. *Pinus densiflora*, Japan (quoted by Satoo & Madgwick 1982).
2. *Pinus sylvestris*, England (Ovington 1957).
3. *Cryptomeria japonica*, Japan, Obi, at wide spacings (435 trees ha^{-1} at age 45) (Ando et al. 1968, see Cannell 1982).
4. As above, at close spacings (1,557 trees ha^{-1} at age 45).
5. *Pseudotsuga menziesii*, Washington, USA; averages have been taken of duplicate estimates for ages 30 and 42 years (Turner & Long 1975).
6. *Pinus radiata*. (a) Closely planted in New Zealand (Madgwick 1981); (b) New Zealand (Madgwick et al. 1977); (c) Australia (Forrest & Ovington 1970).

there is some evidence for this in the study on plucked and unplucked tea bushes (Fig. 10A).

However, in most forests, the size of the cambial sink, expressed as stem surface area, cannot be said to be limiting wood production, or partitioning to wood, for most of the rotation. This fact is self-evident when one realizes that the annual activity of the cambium, in terms of wood volume produced per unit surface area of cambium, is manifestly equal to the width of an annual ring (Duff & Nolan 1957), and, as forests increase in size beyond canopy closure, stem surface area (cambial sink size) increases, while mean ring width (cambial sink activity) decreases. At their maximum, mean ring widths in unthinned stands are below their potential value, as shown by the increase in ring width when forests are thinned. Even in thinned forests, which may have an almost constant stem surface area, there is a decrease in mean ring width with increase in tree size.

4. Other factors

Many factors affect cambial activity, as expressed in mean annual ring widths and variation in ring widths along tree boles, but, on this evidence alone, it cannot be said that these factors affect dry matter partitioning. Thus, improved nutrition greatly increases ring widths, but, as we have seen, it may have only a small effect on wood/foliage partitioning. Similarly, thinning increases ring widths, but this increase occurs overwhelmingly because the total dry matter partitioned to wood within the stand is spread over a smaller cambial surface area, without necessarily any change in assimilate partitioning. This point may be illustrated by plotting mean ring widths against total cambial surface area for stands subjected to different degrees of thinning. There is invariably a strong inverse relationship, and, when one considers that there are accompanying changes in stem/branch ratio and mean wood density, it is impossible to conclude from any non-linearity in the relationship that thinning has any effect on wood/foliage partitioning (Hamilton 1976).

Mitchell (1975) was able to model the volume growth of thinned and unthinned forest stands on the assumption that the total wood increment of each tree was a simple function of its foliar volume. Furthermore, changes in ring width and stem basal area could be simulated on the assumption that the annual wood increment was disposed along each bole so as to maintain a constant cross-sectional area increment from the base of the crown to ground level (Pressler's Law, Larson 1963). Inevitably, ring widths decreased (a) from the base of the crown to ground level, with increase in bole circumference, (b) with increase in tree size, and (c) with decrease in crown size, as shown in other studies (Larson 1963; Denne 1979). In other words, variation in ring widths (cambial activity) results from geometrical factors and differences in assimilate supply, and against this background it is difficult to detect effects of management or the environment on the 'sink-strength' of the cambium itself.

Mechanical stress, in the form of bending, wind sway or stem rubbing, is known to stimulate cambial activity, and these treatments can alter the disposition of cambial activity around the bole, and can increase the ratio of radial/height growth. Several studies have shown that total plant dry matter production is decreased, but there seems to be no quantitative evidence for a change in dry matter partitioning (Jacobs 1954; Larson 1965; Jaffe 1976; Mitchell *et al*. 1977; Rees & Grace 1980; and see Pressman *et al*. 1983).

C. Partitioning between stems and branches

Numerous estimates have been made of the proportion of stems to branches in the standing woody biomass of forests, but relatively few estimates have been made of the distribution of current net dry matter increment, much less of the allocation of carbon, between stems and branches. Within the 'forest production data set', there were only 44 broadleaved and 47 coniferous stands in which reasonable estimates had been made of branch increments and woody litterfall from stems and branches. Whereas the stems formed, on average, about 79% of the above-ground woody biomass, they took only 57% and 68% of the current above-ground woody increment in the broadleaved and

TABLE IV.   Distribution of (a) above-ground woody increment and (b) above-ground standing woody biomass in broadleaved and coniferous forest stands

	44 broadleaved forests (%±SD)	47 coniferous forests (%±SD)
Age in years	73±37·0	56±56·2
(a) Percentage of above-ground woody increment taken by stems	57±14·9	68±13·4
(b) Percentage of above-ground standing woody biomass in stems	78± 9·8	79±10·2

Means of all stands in Cannell (1982) for which estimates existed for woody biomass, increment and litterfall, partitioned to stems and branches. The woody biomass and stem biomass values include bark.

coniferous stands, respectively (Table IV; cf Fig. 1 which gives percentages of the total increment including foliage). However, the estimates of woody litterfall were highly variable, and no significant relationship could be found between the percentage of above-ground woody increment taken by stems and stand age, basal area, height, or total wood increment per hectare.

The carbon budget of Linder and Axelsson (1982) for 20-year-old *Pinus sylvestris* in Sweden (Fig. 7) suggested that the stems (excluding the branches) took only about 40% of the net, and about 28% of the gross (including respiration) carbon allocated to above-ground woody parts, irrespective of treatment. (Stems on untreated and treated trees increased by 0·88 and $3·16 t ha^{-1} yr^{-1}$, respectively.)

It is often assumed that, because inter-tree competition suppresses branch growth, there is a corresponding increase in carbon partitioning to stems. However, the evidence for this fact in widely spaced or conventionally thinned forest stands is rather weak (see age trends in Fig. 12). The clearest evidence comes from studies on very closely planted stands. Thus, in studies on closely spaced poplars, it was shown that the proportion of above-ground woody increment taken by stems increased with increasing population density, and this proportion increased with increasing inter-tree competition from the first

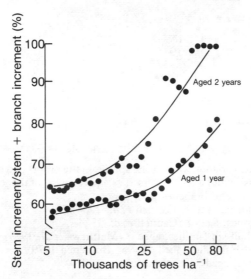

FIGURE 13. Percentage of the net above-ground woody biomass increment allocated to stems (as opposed to branches) in *Populus trichocarpa* grown at a range of close spacings (Cannell 1980).

to the second year of growth (Fig. 13). Satoo and Madgwick (1982) reported increased partitioning to stems in stands of *Pinus densiflora* with over 2,500 stems ha^{-1}, and Madgwick (1981) found that more dry matter was allocated to stems in *Pinus radiata* planted with over 6,000 trees ha^{-1}, compared with stands at wider spacing (2,500 trees ha^{-1}, Madgwick et al. 1977; 1,500 trees ha^{-1}, Forrest & Ovington 1970; see Fig. 12).

Genetic differences in branchiness are well known, and there are now several studies in which they have been quantified in terms of the proportion of stem- to branchwood in the standing biomass. In young or small trees, which have not yet shed branches, these proportions may satisfactorily reflect differences in dry matter partitioning (Fig. 14A), but in larger trees these proportions may be confounded with differences in branch retention (Fig. 14B). Nevertheless, there are clearly very large differences in stem/branch partitioning within species, which could be exploited to greatly increase stemwood production per unit of foliage on young trees (Cannell et al. 1984; Ford, Kärki & Tigerstedt, and Dickmann, this volume).

VII. CONCLUSIONS

The purpose of this review was to highlight the opportunities to increase tree crop yields by altering dry matter partitioning. In trees yielding vegetative

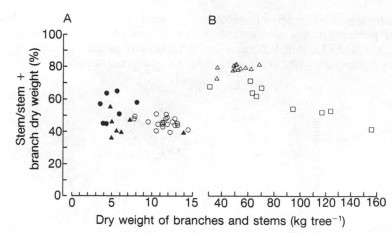

FIGURE 14.   Genetic variation within pine species in the proportion of standing woody biomass in the stems (with bark), expressed as a percentage of the total above-ground woody biomass (stems and branches with bark).
● Picea sitchensis clones, aged 8 (Cannell et al. 1984).
▲ Pinus contorta clones, aged 8 (Cannell et al. 1984).
○ Pinus virginiana half-sib families, aged 8 (Matthews et al. 1975).
△ Pinus taeda half-sib families, aged 14 (van Buijtenen 1979).
□ Pinus elliotti clones, aged 7-11 (van Buijtenen 1979).

products, the main opportunities seem to be to increase (a) the proportion of dry matter defined as yield, (b) the long-term foliage/fine root equilibrium, by altering the parameters in Equation 2, and (c) stem/branch partitioning in timber trees. There would seem to be less opportunity to substantially alter wood/foliage partitioning, although we know very little about what controls this, or how to lessen the high cost of the removal of vegetative parts. In fruit trees which are capable of a high fruit set every year, yields seem to be limited ultimately by root growth and nutrient supply.

It became clear, while writing this review, that our thinking on partitioning in tree crops could be very misleading if it is restricted to the ideas of harvest index and harvest increment of above-ground parts. In both management and genetic studies, we need more information on the total integrated carbon and nutrient budgets of whole trees over time.

REFERENCES

Ågren, G. I., Axelsson, B., Flower-Ellis, J. G. K., Linder, S., Persson, H., Staaf, H. & Troeng, E. (1980). Annual carbon budget for a young Scots pine. In: Structure and function of northern coniferous forests, edited by T. Persson, 307-313. (Ecological bulletin no. 32). Stockholm: Swedish Natural Science Research Council.
Alexander, D. McE. & Maggs, D. H. (1971). Growth responses of sweet orange seedlings to shoot and root pruning. Ann. Bot., 35, 109–115.
Ando, T., Hatiya, K., Doi, K., Kataoka, H., Kato, Y. & Sakaguchi, K. (1968). Studies on the system of density control of Sugi (Cryptomeria japonica) stand. Bull. Govt Forest Exp. Stn, Meguro, 209, 1–76.

Austin, R. B., Bingham, J., Blackwell, R. D., Evans, L. T., Ford, M. A., Morgan, C. L. & Taylor, M. (1980). Genetic improvements in winter wheat yields since 1900 and associated physiological changes. *J. Agric. Sci., Camb.*, **94**, 675–689.

Avery, D. J. (1969). Comparisons of fruiting and deblossomed maiden apple trees, and of non-fruiting trees on a dwarfing and an invigorating rootstock. *New Phytol.*, **68**, 323–336.

Avery, D. J. (1970). Effects of fruiting on the growth of apple trees on four rootstock varieties. *New Phytol.*, **69**, 19–30.

Biscoe, P. V. & Gallagher, J. N. (1977). Weather, dry matter production and yield. In: *Environmental effects on crop physiology*, edited by J. J. Landsberg and C. V. Cutting, 75–100. London: Academic Press.

Borchert, R. (1973). Simulation of rhythmic tree growth under constant conditions. *Physiologia Pl.*, **29**, 173–180.

Borchert, R. (1976). Feedback control and age-related changes of shoot growth in seasonal and non-seasonal climates. In: *Tropical trees as living systems*, edited by P. B. Tomlinson and M. H. Zimmermann, 497–515. Cambridge: Cambridge University Press.

Breure, C. J. & Corley, R. H. V. (1983). Selection of oil palms for high density planting. *Euphytica*, **32**, 177–186.

Brix, H. & Ebell, L. F. (1969). Effects of nitrogen fertilization on growth, leaf area, and photosynthesis rate in Douglas fir. *Forest Sci.*, **15**, 189–196.

Brouwer, R. (1962). Distribution of dry matter in the plant. *Neth. J. agric. Sci.*, **10**, 361–376.

Buijtenen, J. P. van. (1979). Genetic differences in dry matter distribution within stems, branches and foliage in loblolly and slash pine. *Proc. North American Forest Biology Workshop, 5th*, edited by C. A. Hollis and A. E. Squillace, 235–241. Gainesville, FLA: University of Florida, School of Forest Resources.

Butler, D. R. & Landsberg, J. J. (1981). Respiration rates of apple trees, estimated by CO_2-efflux measurements. *Plant, Cell Environ.*, **4**, 153–159.

Cannell, M. G. R. (1971). Production and distribution of dry matter in trees of *Coffea arabica* L. in Kenya as affected by seasonal climatic differences and the presence of fruits. *Ann. appl. Biol.*, **67**, 99–120.

Cannell, M. G. R. (1974). Factors affecting Arabica coffee bean size in Kenya. *J. hort. Sci.*, **49**, 65–76.

Cannell, M. G. R. (1980). Productivity of closely-spaced young poplar on agricultural soils in Britain. *Forestry*, **53**, 1–21.

Cannell, M. G. R. (1982). *World forest biomass and primary production data*. London: Academic Press.

Cannell, M. G. R. (1983). Plant management in agroforestry: manipulation of trees, population densities and mixtures of trees and herbaceous crops. In: *Plant research and agroforestry*, edited by P. A. Huxley, 455–487. Nairobi: International Council for Research in Agroforestry.

Cannell, M. G. R. & Kimeu, B. S. (1971). Uptake and distribution of macro-nutrients in trees of *Coffea arabica* L. in Kenya as affected by seasonal climatic differences and the presence of fruits. *Ann. appl. Biol.*, **68**, 213–230.

Cannell, M. G. R. & Smith R. I. (1980). Yields of mini-rotation, closely spaced hardwoods in temperate regions: review and appraisal. *Forest Sci.*, **26**, 415–428.

Cannell, M. G. R. & Willett, S. C. (1976). Shoot growth phenology, dry matter distribution and root: shoot ratios of provenances of *Populus trichocarpa*, *Picea sitchensis* and *Pinus contorta* growing in Scotland. *Silvae Genet.*, **25**, 49–58.

Cannell, M. G. R, Sheppard, L. J., Ford, E. D. & Wilson, R. H. F. (1984). Clonal differences in dry matter distribution, wood specific gravity and foliage 'efficiency' in *Picea sitchensis* and *Pinus contorta*. *Silvae Genet.*, **32**, 195–202.

Chalmers, D. J. & Ende, B. van den. (1975). Productivity of peach trees: factors affecting dry weight distribution during tree growth. *Ann. Bot.*, **39**, 423–432.

Charles-Edwards, D. A. (1976). Shoot and root activities during steady-state plant growth. *Ann. Bot.*, **40**, 767–772.

Charles-Edwards, D. A. (1981). *The mathematics of photosynthesis and productivity*. London: Academic Press.

Charles-Edwards, D. A. (1982). *Physiological determinants of crop growth*. London: Academic Press.

Corley, R. H. V. (1973). Effects of planting density on growth and yield of oil palm. *Exp. Agric.*, **9**, 169–180.

Corley, R. H. V., Gray, B. S. & Kee, Ng S. (1971a). Productivity of the oil palm (*Elaeis guineensis* Jacq.) in Malaysia. *Exp. Agric.*, **7**, 129–136.

Corley, R. H. V., Hardon, J. J. & Tan, G. Y. (1971b). Analysis of growth of the oil palm (*Elaeis guineensis* Jacq.). 1. Estimation of growth parameters and application in breeding. *Euphytica*, **20**, 304–315.

Cripps, J. E. L. (1971). The influence of soil moisture on apple root growth and root:shoot ratio. *J. hort. Sci.*, **46**, 121–130.

Cromer, R. N., Williams, E. & Tompkins, D. (1980). Biomass and nutrient uptake in fertilized *E. globulus. Proc. IUFRO Symp. and Workshop on Genetic Improvement and Productivity of Fast-growing Trees*. Sao Pedro, Sao Paulo, Brazil.

Danilow, D. (1953). Einfluss der Samenerzeugung auf die Struktur der Jahrringe. *Allg. Forstz.*, **8**, 454–455.

Davidson, R. L. (1969). Effect of root/leaf temperature on root/shoot ratios in some pasture grasses and clover. *Ann. Bot.*, **33**, 561–569.

Denne, M. P. (1979). Wood structure and production within the trunk and branches of *Picea sitchensis* in relation to canopy formation. *Can. J. For. Res.*, **9**, 406–427.

Donald, C. M. & Hamblin, J. (1976). Biological yield and harvest index of cereals as agronomic and plant breeding criteria. *Adv. Agron.*, **28**, 361–405.

Doucet, R., Berglund, J. V. & Farnsworth, C. E. (1976). Dry matter production in 40-year-old *Pinus banksiana* stands in Quebec. *Can. J. For. Res.*, **6**, 357–367.

Drew, A. P. (1982). Shoot-root plasticity and episodic growth in red pine seedlings. *Ann. Bot.*, **49**, 347–357.

Drew, A. P. & Ledig, F. T. (1980). Episodic growth and relative shoot:root balance in loblolly pine seedlings. *Ann. Bot.*, **45**, 143–148.

Duff, G. H. & Nolan, N. J. (1957). Growth and morphogenesis in the Canadian forest species. II. Specific increments and their relation to the quantity and activity of growth in *Pinus resinosa* Ait. *Can. J. Bot.*, **35**, 527–572.

Edwards, N. T., Shugart, H. H., McLaughlin, S. B., Harris, W. F. & Reichle, D. E. (1981). Carbon metabolism in terrestrial ecosystems. In: *Dynamic properties of forest ecosystems*, edited by D. E. Reichle, 499–536. Cambridge: Cambridge University Press.

Eis, S., Garman, E. H. & Ebell, L. F. (1965). Relation between cone production and diameter increment in Douglas fir (*Pseudotsuga menziesii* (Mirb.) Franco), grand fir (*Abies grandis* (Dougl.) Lindl.), and western white pine (*Picea monticola* Dougl.). *Can. J. Bot.*, **43**, 1553–1559.

Evans, L. T. (1975). *Crop physiology*. Cambridge: Cambridge University Press.

Evans, L. T. (1976). Physiological adaptation to performance as crop plants. *Phil. Trans. R. Soc.*, **275B**, 71–83.

Evans, L. T. (1980). The natural history of crop yield. *Am. Scient.*, **68**, 388–397.

Fielding, J. M. (1960). Branching and flowering characteristics of Monterey pine. *Bull. Commonw. For. Timb. Bur. Aust.*, no. 37.

Forrest, W. G. & Ovington, J. D. (1970). Organic matter changes in an age series of *Pinus radiata* plantations. *J. appl. Ecol.*, **7**, 177–186.

Gales, K. (1979). Effects of water supply on partitioning of dry matter between roots and shoots in *Lolium perenne. J. appl. Ecol.*, **16**, 863–877.

Gifford, R. M. & Evans, L. T. (1981). Photosynthesis, carbon partitioning, and yield. *A. Rev. Pl. Physiol.*, **32**, 485–509.

Gordon, J. C. & Larson, P. R. (1968). Seasonal course of photosynthesis, respiration, and distribution of ^{14}C in young *Pinus resinosa* trees as related to wood formation. *Pl. Physiol.*, *Lancaster*, **43**, 1617–1624.

Grant, M. C. & Mitton, J. D. (1979). Elevational gradients in adult sex ratios and sexual differentiation in vegetative growth rate of *Populus tremuloides* Michx. *Evolution, Lancaster, Pa*, **33**, 914–918.

Gross, K. L. & Soule, J. D. (1981). Differences in biomass allocation to reproductive and vegetative structures of male and female plants of a dioecious perennial herb, *Silene alba* (Miller) Krause. *Am. J. Bot.*, **68**, 801–807.

Hamilton, G. J. (1976). The Bowmont Norway spruce thinning experiment 1930–1974. *Forestry*, **49**, 109–121.

Hansen, P. (1971a). The effect of cropping on the distribution of growth in apple trees. *Tidsskr. PlAvl.*, **75**, 119-127.

Hansen, P. (1971b). The effects of cropping on uptake, content, and distribution of nutrients in apple trees. *Tidsskr. PlAvl.*, **75**, 615–625.

Hansen, P. (1977). The relative importance of fruits and leaves for cultivar-specific growth rates of apple fruits. *J. hort. Sci.*, **52**, 501–508.

Harper, J. L. (1977). *Population biology of plants*. London: Academic Press.

Head, G. C. (1969). The effects of fruiting and defoliation on seasonal trends in new root production on apple trees. *J. hort. Sci.*, **44**, 175–181.

Heilman, P. & Peabody, D. V. (1981). Effect of harvest cycle and spacing on productivity of black cottonwood in intensive culture. *Can. J. For. Res.*, **11**, 118–123.

Heim, G., Landsberg, J. J., Watson, R. L. & Brain, P. (1979). Eco-physiology of apple trees: dry matter production and partitioning by young Golden Delicious trees in France and England. *J. appl. Ecol.*, **16**, 179–194.

Hesketh, J. D. & Jones, J. W. (1976). Some comments on computer simulators for plant growth – 1975. *Ecol. Modell.*, **2**, 235–247.

Ingestad, T. (1979). Nitrogen stress in birch seedlings. II. N, K, P, Ca and Mg nutrition. *Physiologia Pl.*, **45**, 149–157.

Ingestad, T. & Lund, A. B. (1979). Nitrogen stress in birch seedlings. I. Growth technique and growth. *Physiologia Pl.*, **45**, 137–148.

Isebrands, I. & Nelson, N. D. (1983). Distribution of ^{14}C-labelled photosynthates within intensively cultured *Populus* clones during the establishment year. *Physiologia Pl.*, **59**, 9–18.

Jacobs, M. R. (1954). The effect of wind sway on the form and development of *Pinus radiata* D. Don. *Aust. J. Bot.*, **2**, 35–51.

Jaffe, M. J. (1976). Thigmomorphogenesis: a detailed characterization of the response of beans (*Phaseolus vulgaris* L.) to mechanical stimulation. *Z. Pflanzenphysiol.*, **77**, 437–453.

Jarvis, P. G. & Leverenz, J. W. (1983). Productivity of temperate, deciduous and evergreen forests. In: *Physiological plant ecology 4*, edited by O. L. Lange, P. S. Nobel, C. B. Osmond and H. Ziegler, 233–280. (Encyclopedia of plant physiology, vol. 12D). Berlin: Springer.

Jordan, C. F. (1971). A world pattern in plant energetics. *Am. Scient.*, **59**, 425–433.

Keays, J. L. (1971). *Complete tree utilization. An analysis of the literature*, vols I–V. Vancouver: Canadian Forestry Service, Forest Products Laboratory.

Keyes, M. R. & Grier, C. C. (1981). Above- and below-ground net production in 40-year-old Douglas fir stands on low and high productivity sites. *Can. J. For. Res.*, **11**, 599–605.

Kinerson, R. S., Ralston, C. W. & Wells, C. G. (1977). Carbon cycling in a loblolly pine plantation. *Oecologia*, **29**, 1–10.

King, D. & Roughgarden, J. (1983). Energy allocation patterns of the California grassland annuals *Plantago erecta* and *Clarkia rubicunda*. *Ecology*, **64**, 16–24.

Kira, T. & Yabuki, K. (1978). Primary production rates in the minamata forest. In: *Biological production in a warm-temperate evergreen oak forest of Japan*, edited by T. Kira, Y. Ono and T. Hosokawa, 131–139. (JIBP Synthesis vol. 18). Tokyo: University of Tokyo Press.

Koerper, G. J. & Richardson, C. J. (1980). Biomass and net primary production regressions for *Populus grandidentata* on three sites in northern lower Michigan. *Can. J. For. Res.*, **10**, 92–101.

Larson, P. R. (1963). Stem form development in forest trees. *Forest Sci. Monogr.*, no. 5.

Larson, P. R. (1965). Stem form of young *Larix* as influenced by wind and pruning. *Forest Sci.*, **11**, 412–424.

Ledig, F. T. (1983). The influence of genotype and environment on dry matter distribution in plants. In: *Plant research and agroforestry*, edited by P. A. Huxley, 427–454. Nairobi: International Council for Research in Agroforestry.

Lenz, F. (1979). Fruit effects on photosynthesis, light- and dark-respiration. In: *Photosynthesis and plant development*, edited by R. Marcelle, H. Clijsters and M. van Poucke, 271–281. The Hague: Junk.

Linder, S. & Axelsson, B. (1982). Changes in carbon uptake and allocation patterns as a result of irrigation and fertilization in a young *Pinus sylvestris* stand. In: *Carbon uptake and allocation in sub-alpine ecosystems as a key to management*, edited by R. H. Waring, 38–44. Corvallis, OR: Oregon State University, Forest Research Laboratory.

Linder, S. & Rook, D. A. (1984). Effects of mineral nutrition on the carbon dioxide exchange of trees. In: *Nutrition of forest trees in plantations*, edited by G. D. Bowen and E. K. S. Nambiar, 211–236. London: Academic Press.

Linder, S. & Troeng, E. (1981). The seasonal course of respiration and photosynthesis in strobili of Scots pine. *Forest Sci.*, **27**, 267–276.

Lloyd, D. G. (1980). Sexual strategies in plants. I. An hypothesis of serial adjustment of maternal investment during one reproductive season. *New Phytol.*, **86**, 69–79.

Loomis, R. S., Rabbinge, R. & Ng, E. (1979). Explanatory models in crop physiology. *A. Rev. Pl. Physiol.*, **30**, 339–367.

McLaughlin, S. B., McConathy, R. K. & Bate, B. (1979). Seasonal changes in within-canopy allocation of ^{14}C-photosynthate by white oak. *Forest Sci.*, **25**, 361–370.

McMurtrie, R. & Wolf, L. (1983). Above- and below-ground growth of forest stands: a carbon budget model. *Ann. Bot.*, **52**, 437–448.

Madgwick, H. A. I. (1981). Above-ground dry matter content of a young close-spaced *Pinus radiata* stand. *N.Z. J. For. Sci.*, **11**, 203–209.

Madgwick, H. A. I., Jackson, D. S. & Knight, P. J. (1977). Above-ground dry matter, energy and nutrient contents of trees in an age series of *Pinus radiata* plantations. *N.Z. J. For. Sci.*, **7**, 445–468.

Magambo, M. J. S. & Cannell, M. G. R. (1981). Dry matter production and partition in relation to yield of tea. *Exp. Agric.*, **17**, 33–38.

Maggs, D. H. (1961). Changes in the amount and distribution of increment induced by contrasting watering, nitrogen and environmental regimes. *Ann. Bot.*, **25**, 353–361.

Maggs, D. H. (1963). The reduction in growth of apple trees brought about by fruiting. *J. hort. Sci.*, **38**, 119–128.

Maggs, D. H. (1965). Growth rates in relation to assimilate supply and demand. II. The effect of particular leaves and growing regions in determining the dry matter distribution in young apple trees. *J. exp. Bot.*, **16**, 387–404.

Martinez-Carrasco, R. & Thorne, G. N. (1979). Physiological factors limiting grain size in wheat. *J. exp. Bot.*, **30**, 669–679.

Matthews, J. D. (1963). Factors affecting the production of seed by forest trees. *For. Abstr.*, **24**, 1–13.

Matthews, J. A., Feret, P. P., Madgwick, H. A. I. & Bramlett, D. C. (1975). Genetic control of dry matter distribution in twenty half-sib families of Virginia pine. In: *Proc. Southern Forest Tree Improvement Conference, 13th, Raleigh, NC*, 234–241. Macon, GA: Eastern Tree Seed Laboratory.

Miller, H. G. & Miller, J. D. (1976). Effect of nitrogen supply on net primary production in Corsican pine. *J. appl. Ecol.*, **13**, 249–256.

Mitchell, K. J. (1975). Dynamics and simulated yield of Douglas fir. *Forest Sci. Monogr.*, no. 17.

Mitchell, C. A., Dostal, H. C. & Seipal, T. M. (1977). Dry weight reduction in mechanically dwarfed tomato plants. *J. Am. Soc. hort. Sci.*, **102**, 605–608.

Mooney, H. A., Ferrar, P. J. & Slatyer, R. O. (1978). Photosynthetic capacity and carbon allocation patterns in diverse growth forms of *Eucalyptus*. *Oecologia*, **36**, 103–111.

Moorby, J. (1977). Integration and regulation of translocation within the whole plant. In: *Integration of activity in the higher plant*, 425–454. (Symp. Soc. Exp. Biol. 31). Cambridge: Cambridge University Press.

O'Neill, R. V. & DeAngelis, D. L. (1981). Comparative productivity and biomass relations of forest ecosystems. In: *Dynamic properties of forest ecosystems*, edited by D. E. Reichle, 411–449. Cambridge: Cambridge University Press.

Orians, G. H. & Solbrig, O. J. (1977). A cost-income model of leaves and roots with special reference to arid and semi-arid areas. *Am. Nat.*, **111**, 677–690.

Ovington, J. D. (1957). Dry matter production of *Pinus sylvestris* L. *Ann. Bot.*, **21**, 287–316.

Paavilainen, E. (1980). Effect of fertilization on plant biomass and nutrient cycle on a drained dwarf shrub pine swamp. *Commun. Inst. for. fenn.*, no. 98.

Parry, M. S. (1974). The control of biennial bearing of Laxton's Superb apple trees. *J. hort. Sci.*, **49**, 123–130.

Penning de Vries, F. W. T. & Laar, H. H. van, eds. (1982). *Simulation of plant growth and crop production*. Wageningen: Centre for Agricultural Publishing and Documentation.

Persson, H. (1980). Fine-root dynamics in a Scots pine stand with and without near-optimum nutrient regimes. *Acta phytogeogr. suec.*, **68**, 101–110.

Pressman, E., Huberman, M., Aloni, B. & Jaffe, M. J. (1983). Thigmomorphogenesis: the effect of mechanical perturbation and ethrel on stem pithiness in tomato (*Lycopersicum esculentum* (Mill.)) plants. *Ann. Bot.*, **52**, 93–100.

Pritts, M. P. & Hancock, J. F. (1983). Seasonal and lifetime allocation patterns of the woody golden rod, *Solidago pauciflosculosa* Michaux (Compositae). *Am. J. Bot.*, **70**, 216–221.

Quinlan, J. D. & Preston, A. P. (1971). The influence of shoot competition on fruit retention and cropping of apple trees. *J. hort. Sci.*, **46**, 525–534.

Rangnekar, P. V. & Forward, D. F. (1973). Foliar nutrition and wood growth in red pine: effects of darkening and defoliation on the distribution of ^{14}C-photosynthate in young trees. *Can. J. Bot.*, **51**, 103–108.

Rauner, J. L. (1976). Deciduous forests. In: *Vegetation and the atmosphere*, vol. 2, edited by J. L. Monteith, 241–264. London: Academic Press.

Rees, D. J. & Grace, J. (1980). The effects of shaking on the extension growth of *Pinus contorta* Dougl. *Forestry*, **53**, 154–166.

Rees, A. R. & Tinker, P. B. H. (1963). Dry-matter production and nutrient content of plantation oil palms in Nigeria. I. Growth and dry-matter production. *Pl. Soil*, **19**, 19–32.

Reich, P. B., Teskey, R. O., Johnson, P. S. & Hinckley, T. M. (1980). Periodic root and shoot growth in oak. *Forest Sci.*, **26**, 590–598.

Reynolds, J. F. & Thornley, J. H. M. (1982). A shoot:root partitioning model. *Ann. Bot.*, **49**, 585–597.

Richards, D. & Rowe, R. N. (1977). Effects of root restriction, root pruning and 6-benzlamino-purine on the growth of peach seedlings. *Ann. Bot.*, **41**, 729–740.

Richards, D., Goubran, F. H. & Collins, K. E. (1979). Root-shoot equilibria in fruiting tomato plants. *Ann. Bot.*, **43**, 401–404.

Satoo, T. (1971). Materials for the studies of growth in stands. VIII. Primary production relations in plantations of Norway spruce in Japan. *Bull. Tokyo Univ. Forests*, **65**, 125–142.

Satoo T. & Madgwick, H. A. I. (1982). *Forest biomass.* The Hague; London: Martinus Nijhoff/Junk.

Schulze, E.-D. (1970). Der CO$_2$-Gaswechsel der Buche (*Fagus sylvatica* L.) in Abhängigkeit von den Klimafaktoren im Freiland. *Flora, Jena*, **159**, 177–232.

Schulze, E.-D., Fuchs, M. I. & Fuch, M. (1977). Spatial distribution of photosynthetic capacity and performance in a mountain spruce forest of northern Germany. I. Biomass distribution and daily CO$_2$ uptake in different crown layers. *Oecologia*, **29**, 43–61.

Simmonds, N. W. (1982). Some ideas on botanical research on rubber. *Trop. Agric., Trin.*, **59**, 2–8.

Singh, I. D. & Stoskopf, N. C. (1971). Harvest index of cereals. *Agron. J.*, **63**, 224–226.

Swank, J. C., Below, F. E., Lambert, R. J. & Hageman, R. H. (1982). Interaction of carbon and nitrogen metabolism in the productivity of maize. *Pl. Physiol., Lancaster*, **70**, 1185–1190.

Tanton, T. W. (1979). Some factors limiting yields of tea (*Camellia sinensis*). *Exp. Agric.*, **15**, 187–191.

Templeton, J. K. (1969). Partition of assimilates. *J. Rubb. Res. Inst. Malaya*, **21**, 259–263.

Thompson, K. & Stewart, A. J. A. (1981). The measurement and meaning of reproductive effort in plants. *Am. Nat.*, **177**, 205–211.

Thornley, J. H. M. (1976). *Mathematical models in plant physiology.* London: Academic Press.

Thornley, J. H. M. (1977). Root:shoot interactions. In: *Integration of activity in the higher plants*, edited by D. M. Jennings, 367–389. Cambridge: Cambridge University Press.

Thorpe, M. R., Lang, A. & Michin, P. E. H. (1983). Short-term interactions between flows of photosynthate. *J. exp. Bot.*, **34**, 10–19.

Tuomi, J., Niemela, P. & Mannila, R. (1982). Resource allocation on dwarf shoots of birch (*Betula pendula*): reproduction and leaf growth. *New Phytol.*, **91**, 483–487.

Turner, J. & Long, J. N. (1975). Accumulation of organic matter in a series of Douglas fir stands. *Can. J. For. Res.*, **5**, 681–690.

Wareing, P. F. & Patrick, J. (1975). Source–sink relations and the partition of assimilates in the plant. In: *Photosynthesis and productivity in different environments*, edited by J. P. Cooper, 481–499. Cambridge: Cambridge University Press.

Waring, R. H. (1983). Estimating forest growth and efficiency in relation to canopy leaf area. *Adv. ecol. Res.*, **13**, 327–353.

Waring, R. H., Thies, W. G. & Muscato, D. (1980). Stem growth per unit of leaf area: a measure of tree vigor. *Forest Sci.*, **26**, 112–117.

Warren-Wilson, J. (1972). Control of crop processes. In: *Crop processes in controlled environments*, edited by A. R. Rees, K. E. Cockshull, D. W. Hand and R. G. Hurd, 7–30. London: Academic Press.

Watson, B. T. (1980). The effect of cooling on the rate of phloem translocation in the stems of two angiosperms, *Picea sitchensis* and *Abies procera*. *Ann. Bot.*, **45**, 219–223.

12

FOREST PRODUCTIVITY IN RELATION TO CARBON PARTITIONING AND NUTRIENT CYCLING: A MATHEMATICAL MODEL

R. E. McMURTRIE

CSIRO, Division of Forest Research, Canberra, Australia

I. INTRODUCTION

In several recent studies, large differences in partitioning to above- versus below-ground production have been observed for forests on highly productive versus poorly productive sites (Miller & Miller 1976; Keyes & Grier 1981; Linder & Axelsson 1982). Keyes and Grier (1981), studying a 40-year-old *Pseudotsuga menziesii* forest in Oregon, contrasted stands with annual above-ground net primary production of 13·7 and 7·3 t ha^{-1} and annual below-ground net primary productions of 4·1 and 8·1 t ha^{-1}, respectively. The difference in total net primary production between the two stands was small (2·4 t ha^{-1} yr^{-1}); but partitioning to roots on the poor site represented 53% of dry matter production compared to 23% on the highly productive site. Similar trends were observed by Linder and Axelsson (1982), who compared the growth of an irrigated/fertilized plot and a control plot of 20-year-old *Pinus sylvestris* (see Cannell's Fig. 7, this volume).

These results suggest that substantial gains in forest productivity might be achieved if it were possible to manipulate partitioning of biomass, and that one of the key factors influencing partitioning is forest nutrition. What is needed is a synthesis of our knowledge of how the nutrient status of soils affects tree nutrition, productivity and partitioning. Such a synthesis would

shed light on the relationship between management practices and forest
productivity, including questions of when to fertilize, how much to apply,
when to thin, how to preserve site fertility, what is appropriate management
practice following harvest, and which species or family within a given species
is best suited to a particular site.

In this paper, a relatively simple dynamic model of the growth and nutrient
cycling of evergreen forests is constructed to explore the relationship between
nutrient cycling and carbon partitioning. In Section II, which describes the
carbon budget and partitioning model, I estimate the upper limit to productivity for a given environment, and determine how partitioning of biomass
will change with age in a forest which maximizes productivity. This optimal
partitioning strategy predicted by the model is compared with data on partitioning in forest stands.

In Section III, the model is extended to consider how nutrient cycling
affects growth. I explore how partitioning of biomass to roots versus tops
determines whether growth is nutrient-limited or assimilate-limited, and I
estimate the upper limit to productivity for a given environment, by asking
what partitioning strategy will maximize productivity.

II. FOREST PRODUCTIVITY VERSUS CARBON ALLOCATION

A. The carbon balance model

McMurtrie and Wolf (1983) describe a simple dynamic model of assimilate
production and allocation in forest stands. Following Charles-Edwards (1981,
1982), they calculate assimilate production from radiation interception by the
forest canopy. According to the Lambert-Beer's law (Monsi & Saeki 1953),
the fraction of incident radiant energy intercepted by the canopy is
$(1-\exp(-kL^\star))$ where k is a canopy light extinction coefficient and $L^\star$ is the
leaf area index. Here $L^\star = (\sigma_F w_F/10)$ where σ_F is specific leaf area ($m^2 kg^{-1}$)
and w_F is the dry weight of foliage ($t\,ha^{-1}$). The factor of 10 enters because
of the units chosen for w_F and σ_F. The assimilation rate (A) can then be
expressed as:

$$A = A_0 \, (1-\exp(-k\,L^\star)) \tag{1}$$

where A_0 represents the assimilation rate attainable by the canopy when all
incident photosynthetically active radiation is absorbed. Dark respiration by
foliage is implicit in equation (1), which treats assimilation as a net process.
The equation effectively assumes that canopy respiration is proportional to
canopy photosynthesis (McCree & Troughton 1966; McCree 1970). This
approach is supported by evidence from agriculture (Gallagher & Biscoe 1978;
Monteith 1977) and forestry (Cromer et al. 1983; Linder 1985) of a linear
relationship between biomass production and radiation interception. In practice, A_0 and the other model parameters vary seasonally and fluctuate with
weather conditions. However, for the purposes of the current analysis, we
assume that A_0 is constant. Let $\eta_F(t)$, $\eta_R(t)$ and $\eta_B(t)$ denote the fractions of

assimilate partitioned to the production of foliage, fine root and wood (including boles, branches and coarse roots), respectively. The partitioning coefficients can vary with time, t. McMurtrie and Wolf (1983) assume that fractions γ_F and γ_B of foliage and stem biomass are lost annually through litterfall and tree mortality, respectively. I assume that both the rate of consumption of assimilate in the maintenance of respiring fine root tissue, and the rate of fine root mortality are proportional to the dry weight of fine roots, w_R. Let γ_R represent the rate of loss of root dry weight in respiration and mortality to obtain a model of the form:

$$\frac{dw_F}{dt} = \eta_F(t)\ YA - \gamma_F w_F \tag{2a}$$

$$\frac{dw_R}{dt} = \eta_F(t)\ YA - \gamma_R w_R \tag{2b}$$

$$\frac{dw_B}{dt} = \eta_B(t)\ YA - \gamma_B w_B - R_B \tag{2c}$$

where w_B represents the dry weight of stemwood, where the parameter Y represents the efficiency of conversion of assimilate to tissue dry weight, and where R_B represents the rate of stem respiration.

The pattern of stand growth generated by this model, illustrated in Figure 1A, is qualitatively consistent with that described by Albrektson (1980) and Cannell (1978). Both w_F and w_R approach asymptotic weights (corresponding to canopy closure), while w_B increases steadily. Simulations are illustrated both for a poor quality site, where it is assumed that the annual dry matter production is partitioned between foliage, wood and fine roots in the ratios 20:20:60, and for a good quality site in which the equivalent partitioning ratios are 30:30:40 ($\eta_F:\eta_B:\eta_R$). Figure 1B summarizes the annual carbon budget at age 40 for the two stands.

Such a difference in partitioning results in a 50% increase in net annual wood production after canopy closure ($2\cdot0$ to $3\cdot0$ t ha^{-1} yr^{-1} at age 40, Fig. 1B). It is interesting that this occurs without any increase in total carbon fixation, and without any increase in harvest increment, which is about 25% at both sites, eg $2\cdot0/(2\cdot0+1\cdot3+4\cdot8)$ at the poor quality site. (See Cannell, this volume, for a definition of harvest increment.) Note that equal proportions of the net dry matter production are partitioned to foliage and wood at both sites (20:20 or 30:30). The greatly increased rate of wood production at the good quality site results mainly from a 36% decrease in the amount of dry matter going to the roots, and a 44% increase in the asymptotic foliage biomass (Fig. 1).

B.   The upper limit to above-ground productivity

The simple model (equations 2a,b,c) is a useful tool for exploring how the fundamental growth processes interconnect to determine forest productivity. The model can be used to derive the partitioning strategy which will maximize

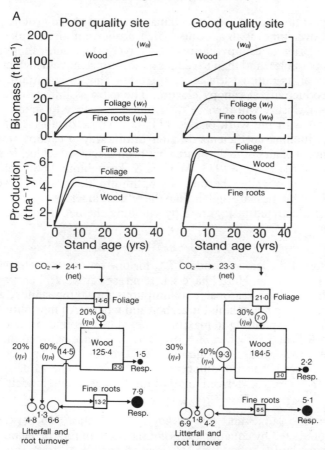

FIGURE 1. Simulated pattern of growth of a coniferous forest on good and poor quality sites (from McMurtrie & Wolf 1983).

A. Predicted changes with time in the biomass and annual production of foliage, fine roots, and wood (stems, branches and coarse roots).

B. Predicted dry matter budgets at the two sites at age 40. Squares: biomass (t ha^{-1}); circles: flux (t ha^{-1} yr^{-1}). The areas of the squares and circles are proportional to the values. The small boxes in the wood biomass square give the annual net increment of wood (2 or 3 t ha^{-1} yr^{-1}).

The parameter values for the model are given by McMurtrie and Wolf (1983) in their Figures 1 and 3. The only difference in parameter values between sites is the partitioning coefficients to foliage, wood and fine roots (η_F, η_B and η_R), which are 30:30:40 for the good site, and 20:20:60 for the poor site. These theoretical budgets may be compared with actual budgets, presented in the same form by Cannell (this volume).

net carbon gain, and hence to determine the upper limit to productivity for a given set of parameter values. Using optimal control theory, McMurtrie (1985) uses a similar model to assess how partitioning will change dynamically in a stand which maximizes net above-ground carbon gain. What emerges is that the 'best' partitioning strategy (which maximizes net above-ground production integrated over time) is to allocate a high proportion of assimilate to foliage production prior to canopy closure (effectively, to reach canopy closure as quickly as possible), and then to reduce η_F to a constant value which maintains the canopy at its optimal leaf area, corresponding to maximum net above-ground productivity at canopy closure. The extra assimilate made available after canopy closure will then be distributed primarily to stems. This result is consistent with the work of Beets (1982), whose data suggest that *Pinus radiata* partitioning coefficients do alter in this way at canopy closure.

The concept of an optimal leaf area has been discussed widely in agriculture (eg Donald 1961; Harper 1977; McCree & Troughton 1966; Robson 1973). At leaf area index values beyond the optimum, the costs of investment in additional leaf biomass are higher than the returns in terms of extra production. This fact is illustrated in Figure 2 by graphing the net above-ground rate of production,

$$Pr = (1-\eta_R)\ YA - \gamma_F w_F \tag{3}$$

as a function of the leaf area index, $L^\star$, for one set of parameter values, with η_R constant over time. Here I have set stem respiration, R_B, and wood losses, $\gamma_B = 0$, which will be reasonable assumptions for young stands, where stem respiration is not a major sink for carbon and where tree mortality is low. The value of $L^\star$ corresponding to maximum net above-ground productivity is 4·6 when $\eta_R = 0·5$, and 5·5 when $\eta_R = 0·2$. The difference between the maximum rates of net above-ground productivity (10·0 versus 18·3 t ha^{-1} yr^{-1}) is much more pronounced than the difference in $L^\star$ values. The value of $L^\star$ at this optimum ($L^{\star 0}$) can be derived analytically for the above model:

$$L^{\star 0} = (\ln\alpha - \ln\beta)/k \tag{4}$$

where $\alpha = (1-\eta_R)A_0 Y$ and $\beta = \gamma_F/(k\sigma_F)$. The relationship between optimal $L^\star$ and k predicted by equation (4) is consistent with the correlations reported by Kawanabe and Okubo (1978) for several species of grass. For the closed canopy[1] to be maintained at the optimum $L^{\star 0}$, a fixed proportion η_F^0 of assimilate must be partitioned to foliage production:

$$\eta_F^0 = (1-\eta_R)(\ln\alpha - \ln\beta)/(\alpha/\beta - 1) \tag{5}$$

and the net rate of above-ground production at the optimum is:

$$Pr^0 = \alpha - \beta(1 + \ln\alpha - \ln\beta). \tag{6}$$

For given values of η_R, A_0, k, σ_F and γ_F, equation (6) predicts the maximum possible net rate of above-ground production at canopy closure. Note that, at canopy closure, the net rate of above-ground production (3) and the rate of stem production are equivalent because foliage mass is constant. Equation (6) could be used to assess the potential for increasing stand productivity by selecting for trees with particular physiological characteristics, such as leaf angle (which affects the value of k) and σ_F (Linder 1985).

Whether optimal leaf area indices actually occur in the real world has been a controversial topic in the botanical literature. The theory of optimal $L^\star$ was posed by Donald (1961). Experimental evidence for the existence of optimal

---

[1] I define canopy closure as occurring when the root and foliage biomasses, w_R and w_F, have achieved a steady state – not when radiation interception is 100%.

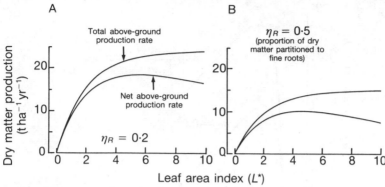

FIGURE 2.   Above-ground production rates as a function of leaf area index (L^*) for two values of the partitioning coefficient to fine roots, η_R. The maximum net above-ground production rate occurs
A. at $L^{*0} = 5\cdot5$ when $\eta_R = 0\cdot2$, and
B. at $L^{*0} = 4\cdot6$ when $\eta_R = 0\cdot5$

The differences between the total and net production curves represent foliage litterfall rates. At canopy closure, foliage production is equal to litterfall, so net above-ground production rate is equivalent to wood production rate. Note that the difference in the rate of net above-ground production (18·3 vs 10·0 t ha^{-1} yr^{-1}) is much more pronounced than the difference in L^{*0} values. (Here $A_0 = 50$ t ha^{-1} yr^{-1}, $k = 0\cdot5$, $\sigma_F = 4$ m^2 kg^{-1}, $Y = 0\cdot6$, $\gamma_F = 0\cdot3$ yr^{-1}, $\gamma_B = 0$, $R_B = 0$, see text.)

L^* has been presented by many authors (see references in McCree & Troughton 1966; Harper 1977), while the case against optimal L^* has been put by McCree and Troughton (1966) who argue that the canopy respiration rate is more directly related to canopy photosynthesis than to total foliage mass, and hence that there is no optimum L^* for the net photosynthetic rate. McCree and Troughton's criticism does not apply to the model (2) where foliage respiration is subsumed in the assimilation model (1). The peak occurs in Figure 2 because of the assumed relationship between litterfall and foliage mass. (See also Linder 1985.) Further, if the relationship between litterfall and foliage mass is nonlinear, eg because leaf longevity declines with L^* (McCree & Troughton 1966), then the peak of Figure 2 will be more pronounced than that illustrated.

Several authors argue that the maximum leaf area index reached at canopy closure generally exceeds the optimal level (eg Black 1965; Donald 1961; Harper 1977). If this is true for forest stands, then it raises the question of whether forest managers should impose thinnings which maintain the canopy close to optimal L^* (eqn 4), where stem productivity is maximized.

The results of Figure 2 can also be expressed as a function of the partitioning coefficients. The rates of stem production at canopy closure resulting from altering the proportion of assimilate allocated to roots, η_R, and foliage, η_F, are illustrated in Figure 3. The effects are dramatic. The rate of stem production is highly sensitive to both η_F and η_R. For instance, if η_F is less than η_F^0 (eqn 5), then L^* will be below its optimum and the forest will not attain its

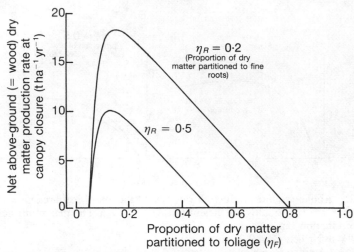

FIGURE 3.   The effects of varying the assimilate partitioning coefficients (η_i) on net above-ground production rates achieved at canopy closure. When $\eta_R = 0 \cdot 5$ the greatest above-ground (= wood) production rate occurs with $\eta_F = 0 \cdot 13$, while when $\eta_R = 0 \cdot 2$ the greatest above-ground wood production rate occurs with $\eta_F = 0 \cdot 15$. The increase in allocation to roots is predominantly at the expense of wood production. Parameter values are the same as in Figure 2.

maximum growth rate. The value of η_F corresponding to the maximum rate of stem production (eqn 5) varies little – from $0 \cdot 13$ to $0 \cdot 15$ while η_R changes from $0 \cdot 5$ to $0 \cdot 2$. These results imply that, if trees adjust their assimilate partitioning to maximize above-ground productivity, then any increase in carbohydrate allocation to roots will be largely at the expense of stem, rather than foliage, production. The ratio, $\eta_B/(\eta_F + \eta_B)$, which is similar to Cannell's harvest increment (see this volume), differs little for the two optima, with values of $0 \cdot 74$ and $0 \cdot 81$, respectively. The relative stability of this ratio as site fertility varies is consistent with Cannell's Table III. This result is also consistent with data from Keyes and Grier's (1981) experiments, where an increase of fine root production from 8% of dry matter production on a fertile site to 36% on an infertile site is achieved by reducing stem production from 58% to 34% with a smaller reduction in foliage production from 18% to 13% (see Cannell's Figure 6B, this volume).

III.   CARBON ALLOCATION VERSUS NUTRIENT CYCLING

A.   The nutrient cycling model

The previous section indicates that dramatic gains in forest productivity might be achieved if it were possible to manipulate assimilate partitioning. However, a major shortcoming of the above model is that roots are assumed to serve no function; the peak productivity in Figure 2 will occur when $\eta_R = 0$. This section describes how the role of roots in nutrient uptake can be incorporated in the above model, and examines how the nutrient status of soils affects growth processes and assimilate partitioning. For a discussion of alternative modelling approaches to this problem, see Reynolds and Thornley (1982) and Charles-Edwards (1982). In the models of Ingestad et al. (1981) and Ågren (1983a,b), the relationship between forest growth and nutrient cycling is considered without explicitly describing the role of roots. In the following simplified model of nutrient cycling, I consider only one dynamic variable: the weight of nutrient stored in tree biomass (N_T). The dependence of assimilation on nutrient availability is represented by the relationship:

$$A = A_0 \ (1 - \exp(-kL^\star)) \ f([N]_F) \tag{7}$$

where $[N]_F$ represents the concentration of nitrogen stored (as distinct from N bound in the structure) in foliage. (We do not consider nutrients other than nitrogen.) The modifying function $f([N]_F)$ takes values between 0 and 1. Retranslocation is implicit in this model; it can be made explicit.

In most natural forests, the major source of nitrogen in soil solution is the decomposition of organic matter, with smaller inputs from throughfall and fixation of atmospheric nitrogen. In this model, there are two mineralization components, one derived from the decomposition of recent litterfall $s_1(t)$ (kg ha^{-1} yr^{-1}) and the other from decomposition of stable organic matter $s_0(t)$. We denote the rate of input of N to the pool of available N in the zone of root production by $s(t)$ ($= s_0(t) + s_1(t)$).

In a stand with a closed canopy, the uptake rate at any time is a function of soil temperature, moisture, root length per unit volume of soil (L_v), the amount of 'plant available' nutrient in the soil solution, and other factors. Uptake by the roots of the trees is expressed as:

$$U = s(t) \ g(w_R) \tag{8}$$

where $g(w_R)$ represents the fraction of mineralized N taken up by tree roots:

$$g(w_R) = \delta w_R / (1 + \delta w_R) \tag{9}$$

This function is of the hyperbolic shape described by Bowen (1985) for the relationship between uptake and L_v. The value of δ reflects the nutrient absorption capacity of tree roots, the specific root length, and the intensity of competition for N from other vegetation and micro-organisms. A more detailed mechanistic model of uptake could be constructed along the lines of Nye and Tinker (1977).

The rate of change of the total quantity of nitrogen stored in biomass is the difference between uptake and its rate of consumption in tissue production (Q):

$$\frac{dN_T}{dt} = U - Q \tag{10}$$

where $Q =$ (rate of tissue production × average nutrient concentration in tissue). Equations (2,10) represent a self-consistent model of the effects of nutrient cycling on the dynamics of forest growth.

B. Upper limit to productivity as a function of nutrient and assimilate availability

The model can now be used to explore the relationship between forest productivity and the assimilate partitioning coefficients, η_i, when the availability of either assimilate or nutrient could be limiting. Assume that values of η_i are independent of t (ie that canopy closure has been achieved) and that $s_0(t)$ is constant. Figure 4, derived from the model, illustrates the relationship between stand productivity at canopy closure and assimilate partitioning for a fixed value of η_B ($= 0.5$) (ie 50% of the assimilates are partitioned to wood). The two sections of the curve in the figure correspond to conditions where growth is limited by the amount of energy absorbed by foliage, and the amount of nutrients absorbed by the roots. Growth is assimilate-limited on the left-hand section at low values of η_F, ie when partitioning to foliage production is relatively low) and is nutrient-limited on the right-hand section (for relatively large values of η_F, ie when partitioning to root production is low).

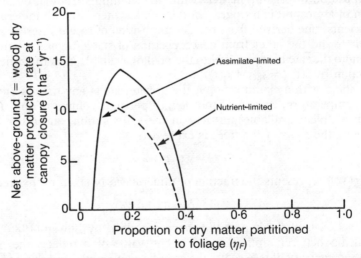

FIGURE 4.   The effects of the mineralization rate for N in soil on stand productivity at canopy closure for the model given in text equations (2) and (10), with half the assimilates partitioned to wood (ie $\eta_B = 0.5$). The left-hand section of the curves corresponds to conditions where growth is assimilate-limited (η_F low, therefore small amount of foliage), and the right-hand sections to conditions where growth is nutrient-limited. The dashed line represents the consequences of a nutrient mineralization rate of $s = 160$ kg N ha^{-1} yr^{-1}, while the unbroken curve assumes $s = 200$ kg N ha^{-1} yr^{-1}. (Here $\gamma_R = 2$ yr^{-1} and $\delta = 0.5$ ha t^{-1}. Other parameter values are the same as in Fig. 2.)

If the model (2,10) is simulated for parameter values where radiation is limiting, but where nutrients are non-limiting (ie on the left-hand section of the curve of Fig. 4), then the amount of nutrient stored, N_T, will accumulate steadily. This implies that nutrient uptake is surplus to requirements and, in terms of the model, that trees have surplus root mass. A net shift of partitioning away from root production results in increased above-ground productivity. In terms of Figure 4, increased net above-ground production can be achieved by increasing η_F to its value at the point of intersection of the nutrient- and radiation-limited sections of the curve.

The model (2,10) allows us to predict the partitioning strategy that will maximize the net rate of above-ground biomass production at canopy closure, and it is interesting to speculate on whether the growth patterns of trees actually tend towards such optima. If so, then the model suggests that the partitioning would shift to an optimum where assimilate and nutrient availability are simultaneously limiting. This hypothesis is worth investigating, although teleological arguments, which assume that plants will adopt a particular strategy, involving maximizing production of particular components, are fraught with danger. Mooney and Gulmon (1979), who develop photosynthetic theories based on maximization of net carbon gain, consider that, because net carbon gain represents a primary component of fitness, deviation from the optima predicted by their model would be maladaptive. An alternative optimization approach is to derive partitioning strategies which maximize reproductive output (Iwasa & Roughgarden 1984, and references therein). A direct correspondence exists between the application of these two optimization criteria; the steady state variable w_B (boles, branches and coarse roots) performs an analogous role in the above model to Iwasa and Roughgarden's (1984) state variable 'accumulated amount of reproductive activity'. A second warning is that there are very good reasons why species adopt relatively conservative, safe strategies in the exploitation of their resources, and why forest managers should not be over zealous in fine-tuning to maximize production, as discussed by Cannell (1979).

Diagrams such as Figure 4 can also be used to explore how both productivity and partitioning might be affected by changes in parameter values. Parameter changes which lift both the right-hand section (eg by increasing the rate of nutrient supply) and the left-hand section (eg by increasing the assimilation rate, A_0, or reducing foliage litterfall, γ_F) will tend to increase productivity for all values of η_F. Any parameter change which lifts only the right section (ie decreases nutrient limitations) will increase maximum productivity and shift the maximum to a higher η_F value. (This is illustrated by the dashed curve in Fig. 4.) Similarly, any parameter change which lifts only the left section (eg by increasing absorbed radiant energy) will increase the maximum productivity but shift it to a lower η_F value. These results are consistent with those obtained in experiments on the response of assimilate partitioning to treatments which vary radiation absorption and the supply of nutrients (Harper 1977; Gulmon & Chu 1981; Brouwer 1983).

It is of interest to consider the relationship between the nutrient supply rate, s, and assimilate distribution. Figure 5 illustrates how the pattern of assimilate distribution which maximizes net above-ground productivity at canopy closure varies as a function of s. This partitioning strategy has been derived by optimizing over all possible combinations of η_F, η_B and η_R. The range of s values illustrated in Figure 5 matches the range of measurements of mineralization rates for N cited by McClaugherty et al. (1982) for temperate

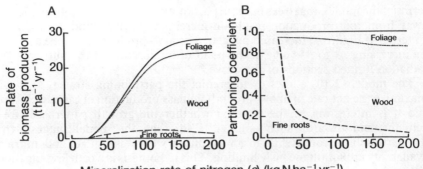

FIGURE 5. The effects of differences in mineralization rate for N in soil on the pattern of assimilate distribution which maximizes net above-ground productivity at canopy closure, for the model given in text equations (2) and (10).
A. The rate of production of foliage, wood and fine root tissue.
B. The partitioning coefficients to foliage, wood and fine roots.
(Here $\delta = 1$ ha t^{-1}. Other parameter values are the same as in Fig. 4, see text.)

forests. The variations in optimal partitioning strategy, and in productivity levels, are striking. According to Figure 5A, mineralization rates below 25 kg ha^{-1} yr^{-1} are too low to permit growth. At low s values, allocation is primarily to roots; but root partitioning declines sharply as s increases (Fig. 5B). Figure 5 suggests that maximum productivity on fertile sites will be achieved with lower values of η_R than on infertile sites. This finding is consistent with the trends observed by Linder and Axelsson (1982) and Keyes and Grier (1981) concerning the proportion of assimilate allocated to roots on nutrient-poor versus rich soils.

The above model provides a framework for considering environments which are uniform over time, whereas real world forests are subject to both seasonal and random environmental fluctuations. If, due to environmental variability, fine root dynamics consists of successive phases of production and root shedding, then partitioning to fine roots is likely to be considerably higher than indicated in Figure 5. This effect is likely to be most pronounced in environments which are subject to extreme climatic variations, and least pronounced where conditions are relatively uniform over time. Iwasa and Roughgarden (1984) discuss how root/shoot partitioning might respond optimally to changes in environmental conditions.

IV. CONCLUSIONS

In this paper, the rate of above-ground biomass production of forests has been shown to be highly sensitive to the pattern of partitioning of assimilate. According to the carbon budget model of Section II, the upper limit to yield for a given environment is achieved by a partitioning strategy where allocation to foliage production is high initially, but declines as the stand approaches canopy closure. Allocation to wood production shows a corresponding increase at canopy closure.

What emerges from the carbon-nitrogen model of Section III is that the rate of tree growth can be limited by the availability of either assimilate or nutrient. Nutrient limitation occurs when the partitioning of assimilate to produce roots is relatively low, while assimilate limitation occurs when partitioning to produce foliage is relatively low. As for the carbon budget model, the rate of wood production is highly sensitive to the partitioning coefficients. The model can be used as a tool to determine the upper limit to productivity, by asking what partitioning pattern will maximize net above-ground productivity. The foliage, stem and root partitioning fractions corresponding to the maximum net rate of above-ground productivity vary dramatically with the values of some parameters, such as the rate of nutrient supply through mineralization of soil N. The model suggests that on relatively fertile sites the upper limit occurs at lower root partitioning coefficients than on infertile sites. This trend is consistent with the field studies of Keyes and Grier (1981) and Linder and Axelsson (1982).

Conceptual models, such as those described here, can be valuable in suggesting general principles governing tree growth. The above model addresses such questions as: what determines the L^* value achieved at canopy closure; how does above-ground productivity depend upon canopy characteristics (k, σ_F, A_0, γ_F), root turnover (γ_R), partitioning coefficients (η_i) and site parameters (eg mineralization rates); what is the upper limit to stand productivity; how does assimilate partitioning change as a forest approaches canopy closure; and how is partitioning related to tree and site parameters. While data are available to support hypotheses generated by the above model (eg Beets 1982; Keyes & Grier 1981; Linder & Axelsson 1982; Linder 1985), the best procedure to test the model rigorously is to focus on the underlying growth processes at a more mechanistic level, using more mechanistic models. The parameters of higher resolution models, which more closely represent the physiological growth processes, can be estimated directly from experimental studies. These detailed process models could then be compared with the simple model.

ACKNOWLEDGEMENTS

I am grateful to Melvin Cannell, Frank Hingston, Joe Landsberg, Sune Linder, Peter Martensz, Marlene Risby and Tony O'Connell for valuable suggestions and assistance, and to Ludek Wolf for guidance with the computing.

REFERENCES

Ågren, G. I. (1983a). The concept of nitrogen productivity in forest growth modelling. *Mitt. forstl. BundesVersAnst Wien*, **147**, 199–210.
Ågren, G. I. (1983b). Nitrogen productivity of some conifers. *Can. J. For. Res.*, **13**, 494–500.
Albrektson, A. (1980). Relations between tree biomass fractions and conventional silvicultural

measurements. In: *Structure and function of northern coniferous forests – an ecosystem study*, edited by T. Persson, 315–327. (Ecological bulletin no. 32). Stockholm: Swedish Natural Science Research Council.

Beets, P. (1982). *Modelling dry matter content of a managed stand of* Pinus radiata *in New Zealand*. Ph.D. thesis, University of Georgia, Athens, Georgia.

Black, J. N. (1965). The ultimate limits of crop production. *Proc. Nutr. Soc.*, **24**, 2–8.

Bowen, G. (1985). Microbial interactions: mechanisms. In: *Research for forest management*, edited by J. J. Landsberg and W. Parsons. Melbourne: CSIRO. In press.

Brouwer, R. (1983). Functional equilibrium: sense or nonsense? *Neth. J. agric. Sci.*, **31**, 335–348.

Cannell, M. G. R. (1978). Improving per hectare forest productivity. *Proc. North American Forest Biology Workshop, 5th*, edited by C. A. Hollis and A. E. Squillace, 120–147. Gainesville, FLA: University of Florida, School of Forest Resources.

Cannell, M. G. R. (1979). Biological opportunities for genetic improvement in forest productivity. In: *Ecology of even-aged forest plantations*, edited by E. D. Ford, D. C. Malcolm and J. Atterson, 119–144. Cambridge: Institute of Terrestrial Ecology.

Charles-Edwards, D. A. (1981). *The mathematics of photosynthesis and productivity*. London: Academic Press.

Charles-Edwards, D. A. (1982). *Physiological determinants of crop growth*. Sydney: Academic Press.

Cromer, R. N., Tompkins, D. & Barr, N. J. (1983). Irrigation of *Pinus radiata* with waste water: tree growth in response to treatment. *Aust. For. Res.*, **13**, 57–65.

Donald, C. M. (1961). Competition for light in crops and pastures. *Symp. Soc. Exp. biol.*, **15**, 282–313.

Gallagher, J. M. & Biscoe, P. V. (1978). Radiation absorption, growth and yield of cereals. *J. Agric. Sci., Camb.*, **91**, 47–60.

Gulmon, S. L. & Chu, C. C. (1981). The effects of light and nitrogen on photosynthesis, leaf characteristics and dry-matter accumulation in the chaparal shrub *Diplacus auranticas*. *Oecologia*, **49**, 207–212.

Harper, J. L. (1977). *Population biology of plants*. London: Academic Press.

Ingestad, T., Aronsson, A. & Ågren, G. I. (1981). Nutrient flux density model of mineral nutrition in conifer ecosystems. In: *Understanding and predicting tree growth*, edited by S. Linder, 61–72. (Stud. for. sueci., no. 160). Uppsala: Swedish University of Agricultural Sciences.

Iwasa, Y. & Roughgarden, J. (1984). Shoot/root balance of plants: optimal growth of a system with many vegetative organs. *Theor. Pop. Biol.*, **25**, 78–105.

Kawanabe, S. & Okubo, T. (1978). Comparison of net assimilation rate and crop growth rate between tropical and temperate grasses. In: *Ecophysiology of photosynthetic productivity*, edited by M. Monsi and T. Saeki, 185–194. (Japanese International Biological Programme no. 19). Tokyo: University of Tokyo Press.

Keyes, M. R. & Grier, C. C. (1981). Above- and below-ground net production in 40–year-old Douglas-fir stands on low and high productivity sites. *Can. J. For. Res.*, **11**, 599–605.

Linder, S. (1985). Potential and actual production in Australian forest stands. In: *Research for forest management*, edited by J. J. Landsberg and W. Parsons. Melbourne: CSIRO. In press.

Linder, S. & Axelsson, B. (1982). Changes in carbon uptake and allocation patterns as a result of irrigation and fertilization in a young *Pinus sylvestris* stand. In: *Carbon uptake and allocation in sub-alpine ecosystems as a key to management*, edited by R. H. Waring, 38–44. Corvallis, OR: Oregon State University, Forest Research Laboratory.

McClaugherty, D. A., Aber, J. D. & Melillo, J. M. (1982). The role of fine roots in the organic matter and nitrogen budgets of two forest ecosystems. *Ecology*, **63**, 1481–1490.

McCree, K. J. (1970). An equation for the rate of respiration of white clover plants grown under controlled conditions. In: *Prediction and measurement of photosynthetic productivity*, 221–229. (Proc. Int. Biological Programme Technical Meeting, Trebon). Wageningen: Centre for Agricultural Publishing and Documentation.

McCree, K. J. & Troughton, J. H. (1966). Non-existence of an optimum leaf area index for the production rate of white clover grown under constant conditions. *Pl. Physiol., Lancaster*, **41**, 1615–1622.

McMurtrie, R. E. (1985). Upper limits to forest productivity in relation to carbon partitioning. In: *The application of computer models in farm management*, edited by D. A. Charles-Edwards, J. R. Childs, J. G. Dingle, M. A. Foale, R. J. Hampson and S. J. Mill. Brisbane: Australian Institute of Agricultural Science, Queensland Branch. In press.

McMurtrie, R. E. & Wolf, L. (1983). Above- and below-ground growth of forest stands: a carbon budget model. *Ann. Bot.*, **52**, 437–448.

Miller, H. G. & Miller, J. D. (1976). Effect of nitrogen supply on net primary production in Corsican pine. *J. appl. Ecol.*, **13**, 249–256.

Monsi, M. & Saeki, T. (1953). Uber den Lichtfaktor in den Pflanzengesellschaften und seine Bedeutung für die Stoffproduktion. *Jap. J. Bot.*, **14**, 22–52.

Monteith, J. L. (1977). Climate and efficiency of crop production in Britain. *Phil. Trans. R. Soc.*, **281B**, 277–294.

Mooney, H. A. & Gulmon, S. L. (1979). Environmental and evolutionary constraints on the photosynthetic characteristics of higher plants. In: *Topics in plant population biology*, edited by O. T. Solbrig, S. Jain, G. B. Johnson and P. H. Raven, 316–337. New York: Columbia University Press.

Nye, P. H. & Tinker, P. B. (1977). *Solute movement in the soil-root system.* Oxford: Blackwell Scientific.

Reynolds, J. F. & Thornley, J. H. M. (1982). A shoot:root partitioning model. *Ann. Bot.*, **49**, 585–597.

Robson, M. J. (1973). The growth and development of simulated swards of perennial ryegrass. II. Carbon assimilation and respiration in a seedling sward. *Ann. Bot.*, **37**, 501–518.

13

PROSPECTS FOR MANIPULATING VASCULAR-CAMBIUM PRODUCTIVITY AND XYLEM-CELL DIFFERENTIATION

R. A. SAVIDGE*
National Research Council Canada, Biological Sciences Division, Ottawa, Ontario, Canada

I. INTRODUCTION

Wood, biologically known as xylem, is one of the principal products of trees, yet our knowledge of the biological processes that occur in the cambial region is rudimentary. There is a pressing need to extend this knowledge in order to manipulate stem development to advantage, both silviculturally and by selection and breeding. Moreover, a new age of genetic manipulation has dawned, which requires a more fundamental understanding of the genes, enzymes and molecular structures contributing to wood development.

With this in mind, this chapter reviews a number of the biochemical and anatomical developments of the cambial region and discusses what is known about their regulation. Recent reviews by Berlyn (1982) and Burley (1982) have dealt with related issues, and a more extensive guide to the literature on

* New address: Department of Forest Resources, University of New Brunswick, Fredericton, NB, Canada, E3B 6C2

the hormonal control of cambial activity and xylem development will be found in Savidge and Wareing (1981b).

II. FACTORS INFLUENCING VASCULAR DEVELOPMENT

Three classes of factors must be considered when attempting to explain any type of multicellular development in eukaryotes (Savidge 1983a). These are (a) genetic factors, which normally originate during meiosis and cause permanent changes in the genetic information available for expression, (b) epigenetic[1] factors, which regulate the sequential and differential expression of genes during development, and (c) physiological factors, which are transient, such as physical or chemical changes that alter enzyme activity. Genetic, epigenetic and physiological factors can act singly, in combination, or at cross-purposes to influence the occurrence of events such as cell division and differentiation.

A. Cambial competence[2] and determination[3]

Procambial development during and following embryo morphogenesis undoubtedly occurs because the genetic information enabling such development is present in the zygote from the moment it originates. However, it is unlikely that procambial development *per se* is coded for in DNA; rather, the several subcellular developments that together add up to procambial development are contained in the genetic code. Because these genes are neither randomly expressed nor expressed among total populations of apical cells (Esau 1965; Larson 1982), it is necessary to enquire into factors eliciting their expression. Similar considerations apply to interfascicular and vascular-cambium development (Catesson 1980; Larson 1982).

Following induction of differing ploidy levels in discrete layers of the shoot apex of fruit trees, cytological studies indicated that vascular cambium originated from both the layer of apical cells serving as pith progenitors and the layer of apical cells serving as cortex progenitors (Dermen 1953). These

---

[1] Epigenesis originally denoted the capacity for, or occurrence of, continuing developmental change in a eukaryotic organism from its beginning as a relatively structureless single cell. The theory of epigenesis, now generally accepted, contrasts with the theory of preformation (see J. W. Saunders, jr. 1982. *Developmental Biology*, pp. 191 and 476, Macmillan Publishers). Modern-day usage of 'epigenetics' refers to orderly physical or chemical changes that occur to the structure or transcribability of genetic information, relative to the zygote's original capacity for gene expression, and that persist through replication and nuclear division.

[2] Competence refers to the capacity of a tissue to respond to an inductive stimulus by following a particular developmental pathway, different from that which it would follow in the absence of induction (Bird et al. 1982).

[3] Determination (or commitment) refers to the genome becoming restricted such that only one differentiation pathway can be followed (Bird et al. 1982; Wareing 1982; Savidge 1983a). In the present context, that pathway is production of vascular tissues.

observations suggest that no strict commitment to vascular development arises in particular cell layers within shoot apices.

Gahan (1981) observed histochemical esterase reactions in some apical cells of dicotyledons before these cells appeared anatomically as procambium. Procambial and cambial cells showed similar reactions. Gahan (1981) proposed that, as procambial and cambial cells originated, they became committed to vascular development. Commitment was suggested to occur in response to auxins, cytokinins, and sucrose. Although a considerable body of evidence has implicated auxins, cytokinins and sucrose in the regulation of vascular development (see Savidge & Wareing 1981b), it remains unclear whether the histochemical reaction described by Gahan (1981) is, in fact, evidence for determination. It may alternatively be interpreted as evidence for competence.

Siebers (1971) observed xylem to develop on the centrifugal[4] side, and phloem to develop on the centripetal[4] side of the cambium in hypocotyl blocks of *Ricinus* after they had been surgically removed and replaced in the inverted position. This reversal of normal phloem-xylem positioning led Siebers (1971) to suggest that the sites of initiation of cambium, and the polarities (ie centrifugal or centripetal) of tissue differentiation from the cambium, were determined in the embryonic shoot. An alternative interpretation, however, is that the reversed polarity occurred in response to factors regulating cambial activity and xylem development (little phloem developed in the inverted blocks of Siebers 1971) in intact tissues adjoining the inverted blocks (Savidge & Wareing 1981a; Lintilhac & Vesecky 1984). In other words, the cells within the inverted blocks may have been competent but not determined to undergo vascular development, an interpretation that agrees with the observation of Gautheret (as cited in Kühn 1971, p. 396) that phloem development in cultured callus occurred positionally associated with an adjacent explant of mature phloem, while xylem development in similar callus occurred positionally associated with mature xylem.

There are additional observations suggesting that cambial cells are competent but not determined for vascular development. In *Pinus contorta*, the vascular cambium disappeared in the absence of a continuing supply of exogenous auxin (Savidge & Wareing 1981b; Savidge 1983b), suggesting physiological rather than epigenetic regulation of vascular cambium structure. Cambial cells appear to be specialized for the polar (basipetal) transport of auxin (Savidge *et al.* 1982; Lachaud and Bonnemain 1984), and the characteristic shapes of fusiform cambial cells therefore may be due to a combination of auxin-promoted polar extension and stress-regulated planes of periclinal cytokinesis[5] (Hertel 1983; Lintilhac & Vesecky 1984). In *Populus*, DeGroote and Larson (1984) suggested that a threshold level of endogenous auxin is required for the vascular cambium to develop.

Because cambial derivatives differentiate into elements of both phloem and xylem, and because there are several types of xylem-cell differentiation possible (Panshin & de Zeeuw 1980), there can be no doubt that cambial derivatives, though competent, are uncommitted to any particular type of differentiation

---

[4] Centrifugal and centripetal are used in relation to the concept of a cylindrical sheath of vascular cambium; centripetal cells are on the pith side and centrifugal cells are on the bark side of the cambium.

[5] Cytokinesis is the division of the cytoplasm following nuclear division.

when they first originate. Because cambial derivatives probably inherit, through mitosis, identical competence to that of their predecessor cambial cells, it can be deduced that cambial cells *per se* must be competent to follow a variety of secondary[6] and terminal[6] differentiation pathways. In agreement with this deduction, entire radial files of the cambial zone have been induced to differentiate as tracheids (Savidge & Wareing 1981a; Savidge 1983b). Moreover, the well-known ability of cells in the cortex and pith of whole plants to differentiate into sieve elements, 'tracheids', and wound-vessel members is additional evidence that differentiation occurs in response to induction by transported factors (Kučera 1978; Gahan 1981; Savidge & Wareing 1981b). It is possible that cambial cells and their derivatives are no more determined than extra-vascular cells to undergo types of vascular differentiation.

B.   Cambial 'initials'[7]

The width and relative volumes of phloem and xylem produced each year can be explained in terms of cells derived from cambial 'initials' departing toward either phloem or xylem sides of the cambium. The assumption here is that centrifugal cambial derivatives are committed to becoming phloem and centripetal cambial derivatives are committed to becoming xylem. Because cambial determination remains an assumption, this reasoning is clearly circular; however, it makes the initial the controlling element in cambial activity, as well as in phloem and xylem production. In other words, the cambial initial, if it exists, must be the cell that most influences the quantity of xylem and phloem produced each year.

Anticlinal divisions commonly occur in fusiform cambial cells that are one to two cells centripetal to differentiating phloem cells, and, because anticlinal divisions *initiate* new radial files, these dividing cells are considered to be initials (Philipson *et al.* 1971). However, anticlinal divisions can occur in more than a single fusiform cambial cell of each radial file. In *Pinus contorta*, Savidge and Farrar (1984) commonly observed two or more spatially separated

---

[6] Savidge (1983a) suggested cells be described as in a state of secondary differentiation when they have ceased cell division and expansion but nevertheless remain capable of cell division, eg when transferred to a sterile nutrient medium; terminally differentiated cells are enucleated, and thus cannot resume cell division activity.

[7] For a recent review of the cambial initial concept, see Timell (1980). 'Initial' refers to a single cambial cell (customarily a *fusiform* cell) of each radial file that has the following characteristics: (a) the initial is the original and the continuing source of all cells within its radial file; (b) following periclinal cytokinesis in the initial, one of the daughter cells remains as an initial and the other becomes a xylem or phloem 'mother' cell with the function of producing elements of xylem or phloem, respectively (whether the mother cell contributes to phloem or xylem production depends on its position; if it is on the phloem side of the initial, it contributes to phloem development; if on the xylem side, it contributes to xylem development); (c) new initials, and thus new radial files, arise by the occurrence of anticlinal cytokinesis in existing initials and (d) within each radial file, the initial is shorter than its derivatives. The cambial initial concept is hypothetical; there is no convincing fine structural, biochemical or physiological evidence that cambial initials actually exist.

fusiform cambial cells of a radial file to be undergoing more or less concomitant anticlinal division (Fig. 1).

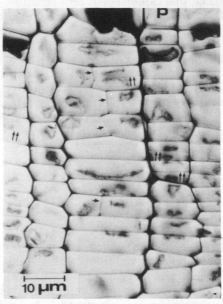

FIGURE 1.   Transverse section through fusiform cambial cells of *Pinus contorta* spp. *latifolia*, showing a radial file with four anticlinal divisions (single arrows) in two locations. Periclinal dividing walls are indicated by double arrows. P = phloem on the centrifugal periphery of the cambial zone.

An alternative to the cambial initial concept is that any cell of the cambial zone receiving the necessary balance of physical and chemical factors will develop and function in the manner traditionally ascribed to the hypothetical initial. Whether a cambial cell divides anticlinally or periclinally, becomes incorporated into xylem or phloem, or remains as a cambial cell may be regulated by factors that shift radially across cells of the cambial zone. Evert (1963), for example, deduced that cambial 'initials' in apple trees were continually shifting their positions both tangentially and radially. In conifers, cell division first occurs in early spring in fusiform cambial cells bordering mature xylem; later, cell division becomes more frequent in more centrifugal cells. Developmental shifts may occur in response to changes in cell pH and in concentrations and compositions of solutes, including hormones, known to differ markedly between the inner and outer peripheries of the cambial zone (Savidge *et al.* 1982).

C.   Fusiform cambial cell activity[8]

Fusiform cambial cells divide in various planes (Philipson *et al.* 1971), cytokinesis possibly following the lines of the principal stress at the moment of cell-plate orientation (Brown & Sax 1962; Lintilhac & Vesecky 1984).

[8] 'Activity' refers to cell division occurring within the cambial zone.

Periclinal divisions increase the number of cells per radial file within the cambial zone. This number appears to be the primary factor underlying the rate of wood formation. The number of fusiform cambial cells per radial file depends on cambial age and the time of year (Philipson *et al.* 1971; Savidge *et al.* 1982; Savidge & Wareing 1984). A single cell per radial file has been encountered only rarely, normally in young cambia during months of cambial inactivity. Following reactivation of older conifer cambia in early summer, the number per radial file commonly exceeds 20 (Savidge & Wareing 1984). The largest number of cambial cells per radial file occurs during the 'grand period' of mitotic activity which, in conifers, immediately precedes the most productive period of xylem formation. By mid-summer, the number of fusiform cambial cells per radial file declines to between two and ten, depending on cambial age. Periclinal cell divisions continue into late autumn in most conifers, while in many hardwoods cambial cells stop dividing earlier in the year (Savidge & Wareing 1981b).

The vascular cambium's continuity around the circumference of a stem is maintained by the initiation of new radial files following anticlinal divisions of cambial cells (Philipson *et al.* 1971), although tangential expansion also occurs, particularly in young cambia. Waves of pseudotransverse anticlinal divisions have been deduced to move both axially and tangentially along stems (Hejnowicz & Romberger 1979). Pseudotransverse anticlinal divisions occur primarily at the time of latewood development and are more than adequate to maintain the continuity of the cambium, with the result that substantial numbers of xylem and phloem elements are shorter than they need be.

In whole trees, many changes in the external environment have been shown to promote or inhibit stem diameter growth. In general, growth is increased in response to any change or management operation that enhances foliage production or prolongs leaf activity, particularly thinning, fertilizing and irrigating. Stem bending, eg by wind action, also stimulates cambial activity, particularly at stem bases. In conifers, cambial activity is promoted on the sides of stems made concave by bending and is inhibited on the convex sides; in hardwoods, the situation is reversed (Büsgen & Münch 1929, p. 174; Wareing *et al.* 1964).

The compositions and concentrations of solutes in xylem and phloem saps, and of reserves in stem tissues and evergreen leaves, surely influence the width and meristematic activity of the cambial zone; however, the quantitative relationships remain to be investigated.

Exogenous auxins, gibberellins and ethylene promote cambial activity in stems of temperate-zone trees, provided the stems are not 'dormant' (see review by Savidge & Wareing 1981b). Exogenous auxin alone promoted cell division in young, but not in 3–year-old, conifer cambia (Savidge 1981, 1983b). Zajączkowski and Wodzicki (1975) presented evidence for an unidentified factor necessary for cambial activity. Some investigators have reported that gibberellins promote cambial activity when applied to stems of intact conifers. However, this is not the case with disbudded-defoliated stem segments of conifers, although it is so for disbudded-foliated stem segments of hardwoods, which respond even more to a mixture of auxin and gibberellic acid (Savidge & Wareing 1981b).

Ethylene appears to have a role in promoting cambial activity in both hardwoods (Phelps *et al.* 1980) and conifers (Barker 1979). Auxin-promoted ethylene biosynthesis may be at least part of the basis for increased cambial activity in response to wind sway, and on the lower sides of conifer branches when compressionwood is formed (Savidge *et al.* 1983).

Exogenous cytokinins are generally less effective than auxins and gibberellins in promoting cell division in fusiform cambial cells, although seasonal changes in endogenous cytokinin (bioassay) activity in *Pinus sylvestris* cambia can apparently parallel the seasonal change of cell division activity (Kubowicz 1979). However, it is unclear whether cytokinins are supplied to the vascular cambium from sources such as roots (Wareing 1980) or are biosynthesized in the cambial region itself (van Staden & Choveaux 1980).

Cambial activity has been promoted by exogenous inositol (Wolter & Skoog 1966; Wodzicki and Zajączkowski 1974). Dikegulac promoted cambial activity, simultaneously inhibiting shoot elongation (Bhattacharjee & Gupta 1984).

Several endogenous growth regulators, including indol-3yl-acetic acid (IAA), zeatin, zeatin riboside, and abscisic acid (ABA), have been positively identified by combined gas chromatography – mass spectrometry (GCMS) in conifer cambia (see Savidge & Wareing 1981b), but it has yet to be established unequivocally that gibberellins are present. The ethylene precursor 1-aminocyclopropane-1-carboxylic acid was identified in active compressionwood cambial regions of *P. contorta* (Savidge *et al.* 1983), and dihydroconiferyl alcohol is present in the active cambium of the same species (R. A. Savidge, unpublished). Also, zeatin ribonucleotide (as estimated by selected-ion monitoring GCMS) appeared to be more abundant than zeatin and zeatin riboside in differentiating xylem of *P. contorta* (I. Scott, pers. comm.).

None of the molecules within the above-mentioned classes of plant growth regulators has been unequivocally identified in the cambium of any hardwood species.

The width of the radial file in the cambial zone is not correlated with endogenous IAA levels in *P. contorta*. Moreover, levels of endogenous IAA, sufficient to support cambial activity in early spring, were associated with inactive cambia during the winter and in mid-summer (Savidge *et al.* 1982; Savidge & Wareing 1982, 1984).

Low temperatures inhibit cambial activity, possibly by affecting microtubule stability (Rikin *et al.* 1983). On the other hand, the cambium may fail to reactivate despite warm periods, such as on the lower sides of roots and at the bases of shaded branches (Büsgen & Münch 1929, pp. 158–160; Farrar 1961; Fayle 1968; Savidge 1981).

Cambial activity is temporarily arrested following wounding (Savidge & Farrar 1984), possibly owing to supra-optimal wound-ethylene levels. Following arrest, cambial activity may increase beyond that of controls, but exogenous plant growth regulators have not promoted healing (eg McQuilken 1950; Fahn *et al.* 1979). Many instances of cambial non-responsiveness to exogenous hormones have been reported, variously attributed to cambial 'dormancy', altered cambial 'sensitivity', inability of the cambium to transport auxin, and substrate shortages (see Savidge & Wareing 1981b).

Growth cessation and dormancy have often been attributed to abscisic acid (ABA), but there is no convincing evidence that endogenous ABA levels increase when cambial activity ceases (Little & Wareing 1981; Savidge & Wareing 1984). ABA may have a role in cryoprotection of cambial cells during the winter (Chen & Gusta 1983; Rikin et al. 1983).

D.   Rays

The amount of ray tissue in the phloem, xylem and the cambial zone influences wood quality and whole tree growth (eg Büsgen & Münch 1929, pp. 353–354; Höll 1975; Larcher 1980, pp. 140–142), but little research has been done on factors regulating cambial ray abundance.

Some stem xylem rays begin as medullary cells close to the pith at the time of primary xylem development and vascular cambium formation (Büsgen & Münch 1929, p. 111; Philipson et al. 1971). In many species, the height of each ray is greatest in the first annual ring of xylem; it then diminishes, increasing again in old age (Büsgen & Münch 1929, pp. 113–115). Increased ray cell number has been noted in response to increased light availability to the tree crown, and ray formation appears to be associated with a tree's ability to accumulate storage reserves (Büsgen & Münch 1929, pp. 115–116).

New rays can arise in the cambial zone in several ways (Philipson et al 1971). Applications of exogenous cytokinin promoted an increase in ray tissue in Picea sitchensis (Philipson & Coutts 1980).

E.   Primary-wall expansion (increase in cell volume)

The lengths of fusiform cambial cells increase with cambial age to a maximum, then remain roughly constant for many years, and finally may decrease in very old cambia (Philipson et al. 1971).

In P. contorta, the extension of particular fusiform cambial cells usually occurs at the expense of other fusiform cambial cells which shorten by undergoing imperfect periclinal divisions (Savidge & Farrar 1984). It has been suggested that the number of ray cells contacting each fusiform cambial cell influences whether the fusiform cell elongates (Gregory & Romberger 1975; Philipson et al. 1971), but Savidge and Farrar (1984) found that fusiform cambial cells without any ray contact could elongate.

Conifer sieve cells and tracheids are approximately the same length as the fusiform cambial cells from which they are derived. The same is true for vessels and sieve elements in hardwoods, but considerable extension may occur in cells that differentiate as fibres or longitudinal parenchyma. Thus, the occurrence of perfect or imperfect planes of cytokinesis in fusiform cambial cells has less effect on the final length of hardwood 'fibres' than it has on conifer tracheids, and the regulation of cell elongation may well be different between hardwoods and conifers.

Factors acting to delimit the peripheries of the cambial zone (ie to establish points where cambial cells cease dividing and undergo radial expansion and elongation) have not been investigated. In older stem regions of P. *contorta*, centripetal cambial derivatives expand radially in spring well before bordered-pits develop (Savidge 1983b; Savidge & Wareing 1981a, b, 1984), so it can be suggested that primary-wall growth is regulated separately from subsequent differentiation. This interpretation agrees with observations that tracheid differentiation can occur without any preceding radial expansion (Savidge 1983b; Savidge & Wareing 1981a, b).

High auxin levels have been found at the centripetal peripheries of cambial zones of both hardwoods and conifers (Sheldrake 1971; Savidge *et al.* 1983). Endogenous dihydroconiferyl alcohol, present in xylem sap, may have a role in determining auxin distribution in the cambial region (Sakurai *et al.* 1975; Lee *et al.* 1981).

It is well known that exogenous auxin promotes primary-wall growth, and endogenous auxin may have this effect in the cambial region. Gibberellins and coumarin also promote primary-wall expansion (eg Stant 1961; Itoh 1976). Little is known of inhibitors of primary-wall growth in the cambial region.

F. Phloem-cell differentiation

Phloem and xylem cells both originate from the vascular cambium. The cellular differences between these two tissues therefore must arise in response to either separate sets, or varied concentrations, of regulatory factors. Auxins, gibberellins and cytokinins promote phloem development both in stems and in callus cultures, but these same exogenous growth regulators also promote xylem development (see Savidge & Wareing 1981b).

Subcellular developments such as bordered-pits and sieve areas initially involve the same type of primary-wall modification; thus, they are probably regulated by the same factors (Savidge 1981). Axial parenchyma and fibres are common to both the xylem and phloem in many species (Panshin & de Zeeuw 1980).

The differentiation of sieve elements can be promoted by high levels of sucrose in sterile cultures (see Savidge & Wareing 1981b), and sucrose levels seem to remain high in the mature phloem of intact stems at all times. However, there is no evidence that changes in sucrose concentration in the cambial region parallel seasonal changes in phloem production.

Instances have been noted where phloem formation occurred in the absence of any associated xylem formation (Büsgen & Münch 1929, pp. 204, 222; Barnett 1971). Larson (1982), working on *Populus* shoots, concluded that protophloem differentiated in response to factors originating in developing leaves, while protoxylem developed in response to factors originating in leaf primordia.

G. Subcellular aspects of xylem-cell differentiation

Wood formation consists largely of the production and precise positioning of insoluble polymers outside the plasma membrane and inside most of the primary wall. Primary-wall dissolution and other modifications can also occur, depending on the cell type which differentiates (Catesson & Czaninski 1979; Barnett 1981; Butterfield & Meylan 1982).

Hemicelluloses and cellulose are biosynthesized by cells of the vascular cambium, by expanding cambial derivatives, and by cells actively differentiating into phloem and xylem. Pectin biosynthesis, on the other hand, is restricted to cells of the cambial zone and to its radially expanding derivatives (Northcote 1982), while lignin biosynthesis normally occurs somewhat later, in cells distantly removed from the cambial zone (Wardrop 1981).

Many enzymes contributing to hemicellulose and lignin biosynthesis have been identified, and presumably the enzymologies of cellulose, hemicellulose and lignin biosynthesis are identical whether the cells differentiate into tracheids, vessel elements or fibres.

The number of chromosomes in a cell has no apparent bearing on differentiation. Haploid, diploid and polyploid cells are capable of differentiating into tracheids (Esau 1965; Armstrong 1982). The possibility that DNA synthesis or mitosis may be necessary for tracheid differentiation to occur has been extensively researched and now appears unlikely. RNA biosynthesis, on the other hand, does appear to be essential and protein biosynthesis is certainly necessary (Northcote 1982; Fukuda & Komamine 1983).

Plant hormones may have several regulatory roles during xylem-cell differentiation, but there has been little biochemical research in this area. Hormones influence the activities of wall-forming enzymes in vivo, but exogenous hormones have not been found to modify enzyme activities in vitro (Northcote 1982). Aseptically cultured cells which normally produce 'tracheids' in response to exogenous auxin and cytokinin lose this ability after several transfers, suggesting that other factors are needed to initiate secondary-wall formation and lignification (Northcote 1982). The factors initiating tracheid differentiation may be derived from mature leaves (Savidge & Wareing 1981a, b). Phillips (1954) presented evidence suggesting the existence of a transported factor that regulated lignification (see also Grand et al. 1982).

The distribution of bordered-pits is highly variable both within individual tracheids and across annual rings (Phillips 1933). The development of bordered-pits and perforation-plates has been observed in situ, and in cultured callus, but the controlling factors are unknown (Barnett & Harris 1975; Catesson & Czaninski 1979; Savidge 1983b). It should be emphasized that, although auxins and cytokinins have clearly promoted 'tracheid' differentiation in sterile culture, varied ratios or concentrations of these hormones have apparently had no effect on bordered-pit or perforation-plate development. Cellulose is probably the first secondary-wall polymer to be produced during tracheid differentiation, because cellulosic rings mark the sites of future bordered-pits (Barnett & Harris 1975; Savidge 1981).

Cambial derivatives which develop lignified secondary walls frequently, but not always, undergo cytoplasmic autolysis (Büsgen & Münch 1929, pp. 177, 355; Dumbroff & Elmore 1977). The exceptions suggest that autolysis is initiated and controlled independently from secondary-wall formation and lignification.

Detailed reviews of protoplasmic and fine structural changes during xylem-cell development have been prepared by, for instance, Catesson (1980), Barnett (1981) and Butterfield and Meylan (1982).

H. Cellular aspects of xylem development

Vessel and tracheid differentiation are promoted in disbudded-defoliated stem segments of hardwoods and conifers when auxins are applied to their apical ends (see Savidge & Wareing 1981b). The vertical distribution of xylem development appears to be influenced by concentration gradients of auxin (Savidge & Wareing 1981b; Wodzicki et al. 1982), and gradients of endogenous auxin have been found in the cambial region (Savidge et al. 1982; Savidge & Wareing 1981b, 1984). In P. contorta stem segments, most new xylem developed close to the site of exogenous auxin application (Savidge 1981, 1983b). In several studies, xylem formation has been localized at the bases of stems, possibly because endogenous regulators accumulated there (Savidge & Wareing 1981b; Savidge 1983a).

Stem girdling prevents the downward movement of polar-transported auxin (Savidge & Wareing 1982), and incomplete differentiation of centripetal cambial derivatives below stem girdles has been observed in both hardwoods and conifers (Evert & Kozlowski 1967; Savidge 1981).

Expansion and secondary-wall formation/lignification occur more rapidly in differentiating vessel elements than in adjacent cambial derivatives (Zasada & Zahner 1969). More rapid differentiation of vessel elements could again be a result of greater influx of substrate due to higher auxin levels, as a result of preferential polar transport of auxin through these cambial derivatives. Applications of exogenous auxin have promoted vessel development in several hardwood species (Savidge & Wareing 1981b; Lachaud 1983; Zakrzewski 1983).

In conifers, high concentrations of exogenous auxin have promoted compressionwood tracheid differentiation (Sheriff 1983). Yamaguchi et al. (1983) observed compressionwood development in conifer stems distal to the sites of morphactin application, while normal wood developed basal to the site of application. Morphactins interfere with polar auxin transport (Schneider 1970), so it can be deduced that high endogenous auxin levels were associated with compressionwood tracheid differentiation.

Several investigators have found that substances that inhibit auxin transport also promote tensionwood development (eg Kennedy & Farrar 1965a); however, ethylene may also be involved (Nelson & Hillis 1978).

Wide-diameter earlywood tracheids followed by narrow-diameter latewood tracheids are common in conifers. In hardwoods, the annual ring patterns can be much more complex (Panshin & de Zeeuw 1980). The cell types, their distributions, and their degrees of differentiation depend on the species, but they can also be altered experimentally, both by exogenous hormone application and by manipulating the environment in which wood is formed.

In conifers, latewood can be formed prematurely in response to short days or forestalled in long days (Savidge & Wareing 1981b). Compressionwood formation occurred in upright stems kept in the dark (Savidge 1983b), in response to stem tilting (Kennedy & Farrar 1965b), and in roots exposed to light (Fayle 1968).

In hardwoods, Bissing (1982) reported changes from ring-porous to diffuse-porous xylem, and *vice versa*, in response to changing soil moisture regimes, while Phillips (1954) observed that the level of illumination influenced the extent of lignification in bands of xylem in *Fraxinus*. Photoperiod has also influenced the type of xylem formed in hardwoods (Savidge & Wareing 1981b). Graaf and Baas (1974) recorded many facets of xylem anatomy which are altered by changing latitude or altitude. Roberts (1983) has detailed the effects of other physical factors on xylem development *in vitro*.

III. HYPOTHESES ON THE REGULATION OF WOOD FORMATION

I would like to propose here a set of related hypotheses that encompass a number of common aspects of secondary xylem development. These hypotheses draw upon the findings reviewed above, but they are not comprehensive, and I do no wish them to initiate poorly supported 'dogma'.

I make two assumptions, namely that (a) cambial cells of all species are 'competent' but not 'determined' to undergo any of a number of diverse types of cellular differentiation, and (b) cambial derivatives do not differentiate into any particular cell type in order to fulfil any subsequent function (such as water conduction, structural support or storage).

The term 'variable', as used below, refers solely to intra-tree variability. The term 'factor' requires loose interpretation; a factor may be more than a single entity and may be in the realm of biophysics as well as biochemistry. Individual components of a factor may have different roles in regulating subcellular developments.

With the above points in mind, the following 12 hypotheses are proposed for the regulation of cellular differentiation during wood formation.

1. The fusiform shape of a cambial derivative is maintained by pressure and polar-transported auxin. In the absence of these factors, the fusiform cambial derivative will divide in the transverse plane, which is a prelude to differentiation of axial parenchyma, septate fibres, strand tracheids, etc.

2. The variable radial diameter attained by a cambial derivative during differentiation is primarily a function of its endogenous auxin concentration.

3. The variable length attained by an elongating cambial derivative is primarily a function of its endogenous gibberellin concentration.

4. The extent of intercellular bonding of differentiating cambial derivatives is regulated by ethylene. High ethylene levels result in cell rounding and intercellular separations such as those found with compressionwood tracheids and vessel elements.

5. The variable mass of secondary-wall material produced by a cambial derivative is primarily a function of its concentration of a tracheid-differentiation factor (TDF). The formation of helical secondary-wall

thickenings (eg in *Pseudotsuga*, *Taxus*, and many hardwood species) interior to the tertiary layer of the secondary wall occurs in response to declining TDF levels.

6. The orientation of microfibrils during secondary-wall formation is regulated by the ethylene concentration.

7. The variable content and composition of lignin produced during the differentiation of cambial derivatives into prosenchyma or water-conducting elements is primarily a function of its endogenous concentration of a lignification factor (LF).

8. The variable number and positioning of bordered-pits produced by a cambial derivative is primarily a function of its endogenous concentration of a bordered-pit factor (BPF). (Similar hypotheses can be formulated for the regulation of other types of pits and wall openings.)

9. The variable occurrence of autolysis in secondary-walled elements is primarily a function of their endogenous concentration of an autolysis factor (AF).

10. A combination of TDF and BPF elicits tracheid differentiation in cambial derivatives. LF and AF may or may not be present.

11. Vessel elements differentiate in response to exceptionally high auxin and ethylene levels. TDF, BPF, LF and AF also contribute. Vessel elements link up as a consequence of basipetally polar movement of auxin through axially adjoining cambial derivatives.

12. When BPF is not available, high TDF concentrations elicit differentiation of libriform fibres in hardwoods and differentiation of 'tracheids' devoid of bordered-pits in both hardwoods and conifers. LF and AF may or may not be present. Parenchyma differentiation occurs in cambial derivative where TDF, BPF, LF and AF are either absent or annulled.

IV. IMPROVING WOOD – RESEARCH NEEDS AND PERSPECTIVES

In the final analysis, rational attempts to manipulate wood quality and quantity depend on whether ideas such as cambial 'determination' and cambial 'initials' are correct. If the cambial genome is committed to producing vascular tissue, it is necessary to be concerned only with factors promoting or inhibiting cambial activity *per se* in order to manipulate wood production. If the vascular cambium is competent but not determined, many more opportunities for manipulating wood formation unfold, but it is important to know the epigenetic/physiological factors initiating and controlling subcellular aspects of xylem-cell differentiation.

Ideas on the regulation of seasonal cambial activity and wood formation have progressed from the time when 'Wuchsstoff' (auxin) was *the* hormone controlling every facet of diameter growth, to the present time when auxins, cytokinins, gibberellins, ethylene and abscisic acid have all been implicated as regulators. However, plant hormones have been discovered using bioassays based on primary growth and development ('primary-differentiation' events – Savidge 1983a). More anatomically based bioassays will be needed before the full spectrum of substances regulating secondary and terminal types of cellular development is known.

Mature conifer and hardwood leaves promote xylem development, apparently by producing an unidentified factor (TDF) that regulates secondary-wall deposition during tracheid differentiation (Savidge & Wareing 1981a). Therefore, the extent of secondary-wall thickening, and the control of early-wood-latewood production may well reduce largely to questions concerning seasonal TDF production, allocation and activity, while cambial productivity and radial expansion in primary-walled cambial derivatives would appear to be largely related to similar questions concerning the regulators of primary growth. This reasoning suggests that genotypes might be selected that are capable of producing thicker secondary walls, regardless of their rates of height growth, auxin production and radial expansion.

In addition to discovering new endogenous regulators, it is important to resolve the question of which regulators are biosynthesized in the cambial region and which are biosynthesized elsewhere. In dicotyledons, the high cambial activity in some stem tumours is probably due to auxin-cytokinin production induced by *Agrobacterium* (Lippincott & Lippincott 1975). In these species, the cambium may be unable to biosynthesize either its auxin and/or its cytokinin requirement.

Genotypes that are exceptional in their ability to produce or respond to plant hormones undoubtedly exist (Sheriff 1983). Our ability to screen rapidly endogenous hormone levels is improving (Weiler & Ziegler 1981), but, because the level of one hormone can influence that of another, and because the environment also influences hormone levels, clones and rigorously controlled growth conditions are needed for such research to be meaningful.

Wood specific gravity is often considered a good measure of wood quality. Cellulose has a density of $1 \cdot 6 \, g \, cm^{-3}$ (Jones 1971), and pectins and hemicelluloses probably have similar values, while lignins have specific gravities near $1 \cdot 3 \, g \, cm^{-3}$ (Stamm 1969). Conifer woods have specific gravities which rarely exceed $0 \cdot 5 \, g \, cm^{-3}$, and temperate zone hardwoods rarely exceed $0 \cdot 8 \, g \, cm^{-3}$ owing to the voids in the xylem. These voids will need to be decreased in order to increase wood specific gravity, by decreasing cell diameter and/or by increasing secondary-wall thickness. However, any decrease in the number or size of bordered-pits or plate-perforations could seriously decrease potential growth rates (Zimmermann 1978), so anatomical research should accompany specific gravity measurements. Moreover, because lignin largely determines the compression resistance of wood, yet polysaccharides exceed lignin in density, it is possible that increased specific gravity and decreased strength could result from genetic selection that ignored the chemical constitution of the wood. Also, it is not merely the quantities of lignin, hemicellulose, and cellulose that determine wood strength but also the types of chemical interactions that occur during cellular differentiation that bond these three classes of polymers together. For example, rubbery apple wood contains as much lignin as normal wood, but is less strong, probably because the lignin is less firmly bound to the polysaccharide framework (Scurfield & Bland 1963).

The cellulose content of wood is approximately 40% and is a variable trait, albeit of generally low heritability. As indicated above, the amount of cellulose produced during xylem-cell differentiation appears to be greatly influenced by factors derived from mature leaves. Identification of these factors may be essential before it is possible to manipulate the polysaccharide content of xylem.

The extent of lignification that occurs during xylem-cell differentiation can also be regulated by extra-cambial factors (eg exogenous hormones and light). A mycoplasma is known that alters lignification during xylem differentiation in fruit trees (Minoiu *et al.* 1980). This mycoplasma might be used to engineer lignification genes genetically; however, the mechanism by which it influences lignification is unknown. Monocotyledons possess mutations that influence xylem-cell lignification (Grand *et al.* 1982), and screening for similar mutants in trees may be of value. However, achieving improved xylem-cell lignification at the expense of decreased resistance to pathogen invasion would not be progress (Vance *et al.* 1980).

The nutritional requirements of whole trees are reasonably well understood, but a knowledge of the inorganic requirements of particular tissues remains rudimentary. Thus, it remains unclear whether fertilizer applications that increase volume production do so by meeting the nutritional requirements of the cambial region directly, or by increasing photosynthesis, cytokinin biosynthesis in the roots, and so forth. Sterile culture methods such as those employed by Zajączkowski and Wodzicki (1975) enable the growth and development of stem tissues to be assessed in response to defined nutritional conditions. These methods might be employed to provide forest managers with a basis for amending soils specifically for improved stem development. In addition, there are traits such as the duration of cambial activity, width of the cambial zone, lengths of the fusiform cambial cells, and frequencies of particular planes of cell division that can be meaningfully compared among genotypes only under stringently controlled conditions, such as those afforded by the sterile culture approach.

In both hardwoods and conifers, it is well established that direct relationships exist between foliage biomass and stemwood production (Kozlowski 1971). Improving photosynthetic 'efficiency' would appear to be the most obvious genetic engineering approach to achieve rapid gains in woody biomass yields (Farnum *et al.* 1983; Larson & Gordon 1969); however, a critical examination of the literature suggests this reasoning may be overly simplistic. Only a small proportion of assimilated carbon is incorporated into stemwood (see Cannell, this volume), and large quantities of photosynthate and nutrients move in xylem and phloem saps, in close proximity to the vascular cambium, without being used in wood formation.

At present, there is little information about how unloading to the cambial region is regulated, about how photosynthate and other substances are channelled into primary-wall material, secondary-wall material, storage reserves, protective substances, or other materials, and about how the extent of secondary-wall deposition during xylem-cell differentiation is regulated.

V. CONCLUSIONS

The well-established intra specific and within-tree variability in anatomical and biochemical characteristics of woody cells strongly suggests that differentiation of each type of xylem cell occurs through independently regulated and cumulative gene expressions. The expression of genes coding for any one aspect of development, such as lignification, does not appear to be tightly coupled to the expression of genes coding for other associated aspects, such as cellulose biosynthesis[1]. In other words, the cambial genome seems to be comprised of very flexible 'biochemical' phenotypes rather than specific 'cell-type' phenotypes. This suggests that it is possible to manipulate cell-type ratios and distributions to advantage and also to encourage the formation of improved types of xylem cells. In addition, the number of dividing cells per radial file in the cambial zone, and the extent to which primary walls expand in cambial derivatives, might be regulated independently of xylem-cell differentiation. In short, it should be possible to manipulate separately the rate of diameter growth and the type of wood that forms.

ACKNOWLEDGEMENTS

I wish to thank J. Burley, R. F. Evert, and P. R. Larson for critically reading the first draft of this manuscript and M. G. R. Cannell for his assistance with the final draft. This chapter was prepared while engaged in postdoctoral research within the National Research Council of Canada, and my thanks are extended to J. R. Colvin for his co-operation and to Margaret Schade, Librarian, NRCC, and her staff for their assistance.

[1] Note added in proof: Smart and Amrhein (*Protoplasma*, **124**, 87–95, 1985) recently provided confirmatory evidence for this conclusion.

REFERENCES

Armstrong, J. E. (1982). Polyploidy and wood anatomy of mature white ash, *Fraxinus americana*. *Wood Fibre*, **14**, 331–339.

Barker, J. E. (1979). Growth and wood properties of *Pinus radiata* in relation to applied ethylene. *N.Z. J. For. Sci.*, **9**, 15–19.

Barnett, J. R. (1971). Winter activity in the cambium of *Pinus radiata*. *N.Z. J. For. Sci.*, **1**, 208–222.

Barnett, J. R. (1981). Secondary xylem cell development. In: *Xylem cell development*, edited by J. R. Barnett, 47–95. Tunbridge Wells: Castle House.

Barnett, J. R. & Harris, J. M. (1975). Early stages of bordered pit formation in radiata pine. *Wood Sci. Technol.*, **9**, 233–241.

Berlyn, G. P. (1982). Morphogenetic factors in wood formation and differentiation. In: *New perspectives in wood anatomy*, edited by P. Baas, 123–150. London: Martinus Nijhoff/Junk.

Bhattacharjee, A. & Gupta, K. (1984). Differential responses of sunflower (*Helianthus annuus* cv. Modern) towards high and low concentrations of dikegulac sodium. *Can. J. Bot.*, **62**, 495–500.

Bird, A. P., Truman, D. E. S. & Clayton, R. M. (1982). Introductory review: the molecular basis of differentiation and competence. In: *Stability and switching in cellular differentiation*, edited by R. M. Clayton and D. E. S. Truman, 61–64. New York; London: Plenum.

Bissing, D. R. (1982). Variation in qualitative anatomical features of the xylem of selected dicotyledonous woods in relation to water availability. *Bull Torrey bot. Club*, **109**, 371–384.

Brown, C. L. & Sax, K. (1962). The influence of pressure on the differentiation of secondary tissues. *Am. J. Bot.*, **49**, 683–691.

224   R. A. Savidge

Burley, J. (1982). Genetic variation in wood properties. In: *New perspectives in wood anatomy*, edited by P. Baas, 151–170. The Hague; London: Martinus Nijhoff/Junk.

Büsgen, M. & Münch, E. (1929). *The structure and life of forest trees*. (Engl. transl. by T. Thomson). New York: Wiley.

Butterfield, B. G. & Meylan, B. A. (1982). Cell wall hydrolysis in the tracheary elements of the secondary xylem. In: *New perspectives in wood anatomy*, edited by P. Baas, 71–84. The Hague; London: Martinus Nijhoff/Junk.

Catesson, A. M. (1980). The vascular cambium. In: *Control of shoot growth in trees*, edited by C. H. A. Little, 12–40. Fredericton, NB: Canadian Forestry Service.

Catesson, A. M. & Czaninski, Y. (1979). Dynamical cytochemistry of wall development during vessel differentiation. *IAWA Bull.*, 1979/2–3, 36.

Chen, T. H. H. & Gusta, L. V. (1983). Abscisic acid-induced freezing resistance in cultured plant cells. *Pl. Physiol., Lancaster*, **73**, 71–75.

DeGroote K. K. & Larson, P. R. (1984). Correlations between net auxin and secondary xylem development in young *Populus deltoides*. *Physiologia Pl.*, **60**, 459–466.

Dermen, H. (1953). Periclinal cytochimeras and origin of tissues in stem and leaf of peach. *Am. J. Bot.*, **40**, 154–168.

Dumbroff, E. B. & Elmore, H. W. (1977). Living fibres are a principal feature of the xylem in seedlings of *Acer saccharum* Marsh. *Ann. Bot.*, **41**, 471–472.

Esau, K. (1965). *Vascular differentiation in plants*. New York: Holt, Rinehart and Winston.

Evert, R. F. (1963).The cambium and seasonal development of the phloem in *Pyrus malus*. *Am. J. Bot.*, **50**, 149–159.

Evert, R. F. & Kozlowski, T. T. (1967). Effect of isolation of bark on cambial activity and development of xylem and phloem in trembling aspen. *Am. J. Bot.*, **54**, 1045–1055.

Fahn, A., Werker, E. & Ben-Tzur, P. (1979). Seasonal effects of wounding and growth substances on development of traumatic resin ducts in *Cedrus libani*. *New Phytol.*, **82**, 537–544.

Farnum, P., Timmis, R. & Kulp, J. L. (1983). Biotechnology of forest yield, *Science, N.Y.*, **219**, 694–702.

Farrar, J. L. (1961). Longitudinal variation in the thickness of the annual ring. *For. Chron.*, **37**, 323–330.

Fayle, D. C. F. (1968). *Radial growth in tree roots*. (Faculty of Forestry technical report no. 9). Toronto: University of Toronto.

Fukuda, H. & Komamine, A. (1983). Changes in the synthesis of RNA and protein during tracheary element differentiation in single cells isolated from the mesophyll of *Zinnia elegans*. *Pl. Cell. Physiol., Tokyo*, **24**, 603–614.

Gahan, P. B. (1981). Biochemical changes during xylem element differentiation. In: *Xylem cell development*, edited by J. R. Barnett, 168–191. Tunbridge Wells: Castle House.

Graaf, N. A. van der & Baas, P. (1974). Wood anatomical variation in relation to latitude and altitude. *Blumea*, **22**, 101–121.

Grand, C., Boudet, A. M. & Ranjeva, R. (1982). Natural variations and controlled changes in lignification process. *Holzforsch.*, **3**, 217–223.

Gregory, R. A. & Romberger, J. A. (1975). Cambial activity and height of unseriate vascular rays in conifers. *Bot. Gaz.*, **136**, 246–253.

Hejnowicz, Z. & Romberger, J. A. (1979). The common basis for wood grain figures is the systematically changing orientation of cambial fusiform cells. *Wood Sci. Technol.*, **13**, 89–96.

Hertel, R. (1983). The mechanism of auxin transport as a model for auxin action. *Z. Pflanzenphysiol.*, **112**, 53–68.

Höll, W. (1975). Radial transport in rays. In: *Transport in plants. I. Phloem transport*, edited by M. H. Zimmermann and J. A. Milburn, 432–450. (Encyclopedia of plant physiology, n.s. vol. 1). Berlin: Springer.

Itoh, T. (1976). Microscopic and submicroscopic observation of the effects of coumarin and colchicine during elongation of pine seedlings. *Pl. Cell Physiol., Tokyo*, **17**, 367–384.

Jones, D. W. (1971). C. X-ray and electron diffraction. C.1. Structure studies. In: *High polymers. Vol. 5: Cellulose and cellulose derivatives, part 4*, edited by N. M. Bikales and L. Segal, 117–150. New York; London: Wiley-Interscience.

Kennedy, R. W. & Farrar, J. L. (1965a). Induction of tension wood with the antiauxin 2–3–5 tri-iodobenzoic acid. *Nature, Lond.*, **208**, 406–407.

Kennedy, R. W. & Farrar, J. L. (1965b). Tracheid development in tilted seedlings. In: *Cellular ultrastructure of woody plants*, edited by W. A. Côté, jr, 419–453. Syracuse: Syracuse University Press.

Kozlowski, T. T. (1971). *Growth and development of trees. Vol. 2: Cambial growth, root growth and reproductive growth.* New York: Academic Press.

Kubowicz, D. B. (1979). The possible relation between cytokinins and secondary xylem formation in *Pinus silvestris*. I. Seasonal correlations. *Acta. Soc. Bot. Pol.*, **48**, 295–303.

Kučera, L. J. (1978). Vascular nodules in the pith of yew (*Taxus baccata* L.). *IAWA Bull.*, 1978/4, 81–85.

Kühn, A. (1971). *Lectures on developmental physiology*, translated by R. Milkman. 2nd ed. Berlin; New York: Springer.

Lachaud, S. (1983). Xylogénèse chez les Dicotylédones arborescentes. IV. Influence des bourgeons, de l'acide β-indolyl acétique et de l'acide gibberellique sur la réactivation cambiale et la sylogénèse dans les jeunes tiges de Hêtre. *Can. J. Bot.*, **61**, 1768–1774.

Lachaud, S. & Bonnemain, J. L. (1984). Seasonal variations in the polar-transport pathways and retention sites of (^{3}H) indole-3-acetic acid in young branches of *Fagus sylvatica* L. *Planta*, **161**, 207–215.

Larcher, W. (1980). *Physiological plant ecology.* 2nd ed. Berlin; New York: Springer.

Larson, P. R. (1982). The concept of cambium. In: *New perspectives in wood anatomy*, edited by P. Baas, 85–122. The Hague; London: Martinus Nijhoff/Junk.

Larson, P. R. & Gordon, J. C. (1969). Photosynthesis and wood yield. *Agric. Sci. Rev.*, **7**, 7–14.

Lee, T. S., Purse, J. G., Pryce, R. J., Horgan, R. & Wareing, P. F. (1981). Dihydroconiferyl alcohol – a cell division factor from *Acer* species. *Planta*, **152**, 571–577.

Lintilhac, P. M. & Vesecky, T. B. (1984). Stress-induced alignment of division plane in plant tissues grown *in vitro*. *Nature, Lond.*, **307**, 363–364.

Lippincott, J. A. & Lippincott, B. B. (1975). The genus *Agrobacterium* and plant tumorigenesis. *A. Rev. Microbiol.*, **29**, 377–406.

Little, C. H. A. & Wareing, P. F. (1981). Control of cambial activity and dormancy in *Picea sitchensis* by indol-3yl-acetic and abscisic acids. *Can. J. Bot.*, **59**, 1480–1493.

McQuilken, W. E. (1950). Effects of some growth regulators and dressings on the healing of tree wounds. *J. For.*, **48**, 423–428.

Minoiu, N., Isac, M., Pattantyus, K., Stirban, M., Cracium, C. & Straulea, M. (1980). Experimental results concerning the apple rubbery woody mycoplasma in Romania. *Acta phytopathol. Acad. sci. Hung.*, **15**, 267–271.

Nelson, N. D. & Hillis, W. E. (1978). Ethylene and tension woody formation in *Eucalyptus gomphocephala*. *Wood Sci. Technol.*, **12**, 309–315.

Northcote, D. H. (1982). Control of enzyme activity during plant cell development. In: *Differentiation in vitro*, edited by M. M. Yeoman and D. E. S. Truman, 49–64. Cambridge: Cambridge University Press.

Panshin, A. J. & de Zeeuw, C. (1980). *Textbook of wood technology.* 4th ed. New York: McGraw-Hill.

Phelps, J. E., McGinnes, E. A. Jr., Saniewski, M., Pieniazek, J. & Smolinski, M. (1980). Some anatomical observations on the effect of morphactin IT 3456 and ethrel on wood formation in *Salix fragilis* L. *IAWA Bull.*, n.s.**1**, 76–82.

Philipson, J. J. & Coutts, M. P. (1980). Effects of growth hormone application on the secondary growth of roots and stems in *Picea sitchensis* (Bong.) Carr. *Ann. Bot.*, **46**, 747–755.

Philipson, W. R., Ward, J. M. & Butterfield, B. G. (1971). *The vascular cambium: its development and activity.* London: Chapman & Hall.

Phillips, E. W. J. (1933). Movement of the pit membrane in coniferous woods, with special reference to preservative treatment. *Forestry*, **7**, 109–120.

Phillips, E. W. J. (1954). Influence of leaf activity on the composition of the wood cell wall. *Nature, Lond.*, **174**, 85–86.

Rikin, A., Atsmon, D. & Gitler, C. (1983). Quantitation of chill-induced release of a tubulin-like factor and its prevention by abscisic acid in *Gossypium hirsutum* L. *Pl. Physiol., Lancaster*, **71**, 747–748.

Roberts, L. W. (1983). The influence of physical factors on xylem differentiation *in vitro*. In: *Tissue culture of trees*, edited by J. H. Dodds, 88–102. Westport, CN: AVI Publications.

Sakurai, N., Shibata, K. & Kamisaka, S. (1975). Stimulation of auxin-induced elongation of cucumber hypocotyl sections by dihydroconiferyl alcohol. Dihydroconiferyl alcohol inhibits indole-3-acetic acid degradation *in vivo* and *in vitro*. *Pl. Cell Physiol., Tokyo*, **16**, 845–855.

Savidge, R. A. (1981). *Regulation of seasonal cambial activity and tracheid differentiation in* Pinus contorta *Dougl.* Ph.D. thesis, University College of Wales, Aberystwyth.

Savidge, R. A. (1983a). The role of plant hormones in higher plant cellular differentiation. I. A critique. *Histochem. J.*, **15**, 437–445.

Savidge, R. A. (1983b). The role of plant hormones in higher plant cellular differentiation. II. Experiments with the vascular cambium, and sclereid and tracheid differentiation in the pine, *Pinus contorta. Histochem. J.*, **15**, 447–466.

Savidge, R. A. & Farrar, J. L. (1984). Cellular adjustment in the vascular cambium leading to spiral-grain formation in conifers. *Can. J. Bot.*, **62**, 2872–2879.

Savidge, R. A., Heald, J. K. & Wareing, P. F. (1982). Non-uniform distribution and seasonal variation of endogenous indol-3yl-acetic acid in cambial region of *Pinus contorta* Dougl. *Planta*, **155**, 89–92.

Savidge, R. A., Mutumba, G. M. C., Heald, J. K. & Wareing, P. F. (1983). Gas chromatography – mass spectroscopy identification of 1-amino-cyclopropane-1-carboxylic acid in compressionwood vascular cambium of *Pinus contorta* Dougl. *Pl. Physiol., Lancaster*, **71**, 434–436.

Savidge, R. A. & Wareing, P. F. (1981a). A tracheid-differentiation factor from pine needles. *Planta*, **153**, 395–404.

Savidge, R. A. & Wareing, P. F. (1981b). Plant-growth regulators and the differentiation of vascular elements. In: *Xylem cell development*, edited by J. R. Barnett, 192–235. Tunbridge Wells: Castle House.

Savidge, R. A. & Wareing, P. F. (1982). Apparent auxin production and transport during winter in the non-growing pine tree. *Can. J. Bot.*, **60**, 681–691.

Savidge, R. A. & Wareing, P. F. (1984). Seasonal cambial activity and xylem development in *Pinus contorta* Dougl. in relation to endogenous indol-3yl-acetic and (S)-abscisic acid levels. *Can. J. For. Res.*, **14**, 676–682.

Schneider, G. (1970). Morphactins: physiology and performance. *A. Rev. Pl. Physiol.*, **21**, 499–536.

Scurfield, G. & Bland, D. E. (1963). The anatomy and chemistry of 'rubbery' wood in apple var. Lord Lambourne. *J. hort. Sci.*, **38**, 297–306.

Sheldrake, A. R. (1971). Auxin in the cambium and its differentiating derivatives. *J. exp. Bot.*, **22**, 735–740.

Sheriff, D. W. (1983). Control by indol-3-acetic acid of wood production in *Pinus radiata* D. Don. segments in culture. *Aust. J. Plant Physiol.*, **10**, 131–135.

Siebers, A. M. (1971). Initiation of radial polarity in the interfascicular cambium of *Ricinus communis* L. *Acta bot. neerl.*, **20**, 211–220.

Stamm, A. J. (1969). Correlation of structural variations of lignins with their specific gravities. *TAPPI*, **52**, 1498–1502.

Stant, M. Y. (1961). The effect of gibberellic acid on fibre-cell length. *Ann. Bot.*, **25**, 453–462.

Timell, T. E. (1980). Organization and ultrastructure of the dormant cambial zone in compression wood of *Picea abies. Wood Sci. Technol.*, **14**, 161–179.

Vance, C. P., Kirk, T. K. & Sherwood, R. T. (1980). Lignification as a mechanism of disease resistance. *A. Rev. Phytopathol.*, **18**, 259–288.

Van Staden, J. & Choveaux, N. A. (1980). Cytokinins in internode stem segments of *Salix babylonica. Z. Pflanzenphysiol.*, **96**, 153–161.

Wardrop, A. B. (1981). Lignification and xylogenesis. in: *Xylem cell development*, edited by J. R. Barnett, 115–152. Tunbridge Wells: Castle House.

Wareing, P. F. (1980). Root hormones and shoot growth. In: *Control of shoot growth in trees*, edited by C. H. A. Little, 237–256. Fredericton, NB: Canadian Forestry Service.

Wareing, P. F. (1982). Determination and related aspects of plant development. In: *The molecular biology of plant development*, edited by H. Smith and D. Grierson, 517–541. (Botanical monograph no. 18). Oxford: Blackwell Scientific.

Wareing, P. F., Hanney, C. E. A. & Digby, J. (1964). The role of endogenous hormones in cambial activity and xylem differentiation. In: *The formation of wood in forest trees*, edited by M. H. Zimmermann, 323–344. New York; London: Academic Press.

Weiler, E. W. & Ziegler, H. (1981). Determination of phytohormones in phloem exudate from tree species by radioimmunoassay. *Planta*, **152**, 168–170.

Wodzicki, T. J., Rakowski, K., Starck, Z., Porandowski, J. & Zajączkowski, S. (1982). Apical control of xylem formation in pine stem. I. Auxin effects and availability of assimilates. *Acta Soc. Bot. Pol.*, **51**, 187–202.

Wodzicki, T. J. & Zajączkowski, S. (1974). Effect of auxin on xylem tracheids differentiation in decapitated stems of *Pinus silvestris* L. and its interaction with some vitamins and growth regulators. *Acta Soc. Bot. Pol.*, **43**, 129–148.

Wolter, K. E. & Skoog, F. (1966). Nutritional requirements of *Fraxinus* callus cultures. *Am. J. Bot.*, **53**, 263–269.

Yamaguchi, K., Shimaji, K. & Itoh, T. (1983). Simultaneous inhibition and induction of compression wood formation by morphactin in artificially inclined stems of Japanese larch (*Larix leptolepsis* Gord.). *Wood Sci. Technol.*, **17**, 81–89.

Zajączkowski, S. & Wodzicki, T. J. (1975). Inhibition and requirement of natural stimulator for cambial xylem production in isolated stem segments of *Pinus silvestris*. *Physiologia Pl.*, **33**, 71–74.

Zakrzewski, J. (1983). Hormonal control of cambial activity and vessel differentiation in *Quercus robur*. *Physiologia Pl.*, **57**, 537–542.

Zasada, J. C. & Zahner, R. (1969). Vessel element development in the earlywood of red oak (*Quercus rubra* L.). *Can. J. Bot.*, **47**, 1965–1971.

Zimmermann, M. H. (1978). Structural requirements for optimal water conduction in tree stems. In: *Tropical trees as living systems*, edited by P. B. Tomlinson and M. H. Zimmermann, 517–532. Cambridge: Cambridge University Press.

14

BRANCHING, CROWN STRUCTURE AND THE CONTROL OF TIMBER PRODUCTION

E. D. FORD*
Institute of Terrestrial Ecology, Bush Estate, Penicuik, Midlothian, Scotland

I. INTRODUCTION

The rate of timber production by a forest is dependent upon the size and functioning of tree crowns. Spacing and thinning, the most widely practised silvicultural operations, influence both total stand volume increment and its distribution between differently sized trees, because they influence tree crown structure and function (Assmann 1970). The empirical relationships on which these silvicultural operations are based have their origins in research initiated over 100 years ago, yet attempts to increase timber yield by selecting and breeding trees with particular crown structures are still in their infancy.

One theory, discussed by both Dickmann and by Kärki and Tigerstedt in

* New address: Center for Quantitative Studies, University of Washington, Seattle, USA.

this volume, is that sparsely branched tree genotypes can produce greater amounts of stemwood than heavily branched genotypes. This hypothesis seems to be counter-intuitive, which highlights our need to understand (a) the interaction between branch growth, crown development and the control of timber production, and (b) intraspecific differences in these interactions, and how they may be exploited.

Three factors complicate the study of these problems. First, there are differences between tree species in crown form, and in the anatomical and morphological processes by which crowns are produced. Second, tree branches perform functions other than the production of stemwood. Natural selection operates through breeding success, and branching structures may have evolved, at least in part, to ensure the efficient display of reproductive organs, or to shade neighbouring plants. Third, branch production and growth are influenced by a wide range of environmental factors, and it can be difficult to isolate their separate influences on stemwood production.

The operation of a complex of factors in controlling branch growth and crown development, and the problems these pose to scientific study, are apparent in the descriptions and classifications which have been made of branching patterns and crown forms. Most frequently, both qualitative and quantitative models have been developed for single aspects of branch growth and function. These models are reviewed here, and are used to interpret empirical evidence on the relationship between crown form and stemwood production in single trees, and to develop a discussion about factors controlling timber production in stands.

II. CLASSIFICATIONS AND DESCRIPTIONS OF BRANCHING AND CROWN FORM

Tree species have been classified into a few crown or morphological types, which suggests that, during evolution, certain morphological and physiological requirements have been met repeatedly in similar ways. Hallé et al. (1978) classified tropical trees into 23 architectural models. They defined architecture as the 'morphological expression of the genetic blueprint', and stressed that this included developmental sequences. Their dichotomous key is based on characters of the primary meristem, such as its lifespan – which determines whether growth is monopodial or sympodial, its pattern of differentiation to sexual or vegetative growth, and its orientation to give plagiotropic or orthotropic shoots.

Brunig (1976) produced a classification of 12 prototype crown architectures based on ecophysiological principles – mainly the aerodynamic properties of leaves and tree shape, which influence the exposure of mature leaves to radiation and wind. The balance between light interception, and the requirement to invest material in branchwood, was also considered. Brunig's classification was based on visual observations of broad differences among tree crowns along vegetational gradients, in both tropical and temperate forests. For example, he described forests growing along a catena, ranging from tall, large-leaved broad crowns on a mesic latosol to short, small-leaved forms on a xeric podsol.

Brunig (1976) considered his classification to be an initial approach. For the precise use of trees as crop plants we need to be able to describe crown form functionally – in relation to its branching structure (how the tree grows) and its efficiency in timber production (how the crown works).

A. Branching morphology

A wide variety of tree crown forms can arise from variation in a few branching rules. This fact has important implications when framing hypotheses about the mechanisms that control branching. Tree crowns are comprised of three basic types of shoot: the main stem, the branches or 'long shoots', which frequently have indeterminate growth, and 'short shoots', which may carry a large proportion of the foliage, but which have little influence on crown form.

Four categories of main stem can develop from terminal and axillary meristems, as illustrated in Figure 1. (a) A single apical meristem may remain active throughout the life of the tree (Fig. 1A). (b) A bifurcating apical meristem may give dichotomous branching with equal branch development, or one branch may develop reproductive organs giving sympodial growth (Fig. 1B). (c) The apical meristem may generate a number of meristems of

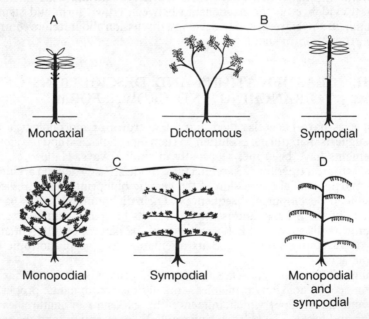

FIGURE 1.   Four categories of main stem branching and development in trees, and their influence on crown shapes.
A.   Only the main stem extends.
B.   Left: bifurcation with equal vegetative axes; right: bifurcation with vegetative and reproductive axes.
C.   Main stems and branches have unequal growth potentials.
D.   Main stems and branches have equal but mixed growth potentials.

unequal growth potential, producing crowns with orthotropic main stems. These can be monopodiums, or sympodiums – where the main stem develops from a lateral shoot either with (proleptically) or without (sylleptically) a period of correlative inhibition (see below) from the apical bud (Fig. 1C). (d) Main stem branches may be produced by multiplication of the apical meristem, giving shoots which, at different times, may become branches or main stems (Fig. 1D). Both monopodial and sympodial types occur. Branch-like (plagiotropic) main stem tips can later become erect by producing reaction wood and, in sympodial types, erect main stems may become plagiotropic.

Lateral shoots originate from meristems in the axils of leaves, or, in a few genera such as *Picea*, from meristems apparently differentiated from internode cortical tissues. *Apical dominance* is the suppression, by the terminal apex, of buds on the current year's shoot, and can occur both before or after a period of branch growth (see Phillips 1975). *Apical control* is the partial or complete inhibition of lateral shoot elongation by the influence of one or more distal apices (Fig. 2) (Brown *et al.* 1967). Broadleaved temperate trees with narrow excurrent crowns, such as *Populus*, have leading shoots with weak apical dominance (over the current year's buds) but strong apical control (over the previous year's shoots), while those with spreading, decurrent crowns have

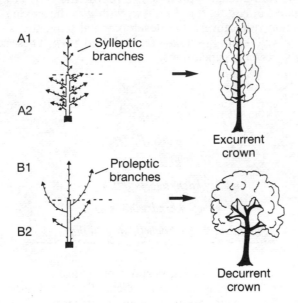

FIGURE 2.   Schematic relationship between apical dominance, apical control, and the development of excurrent and decurrent crowns on broadleaved trees.
A1.   Weak apical dominance of buds on the current year's shoot.
A2.   Strong apical control, restricting the growth of shoots produced in previous years.
B1.   Strong apical dominance, preventing the growth of buds on the current year's shoot.
B2.   Weak apical control, allowing the active growth of buds produced in previous years.

strong apical dominance but weak apical control (Fig. 2). Shoots which are strongly suppressed by apical control, and produce a rosette of leaves with little internode elongation, are called 'short shoots', as are the needle fascicles of pines.

B.   Generation of branching patterns

The shoot apices control branching, by influencing the number of lateral buds produced, the distance from the apex at which the buds develop (apical dominance), and the rate of growth of the lateral shoots relative to the main stem (apical control). Whilst the physiological control through hormonal, nutritional and other metabolic processes is still debated (Trewavas 1981), mathematical descriptions of branch generation have indicated an apparent underlying simplicity, which may be important in understanding both genetic and environmental influences.

Rozenberg and Lindenmayer (1973) used a simple recurrence formula to describe the development of a compound leaf as a branched structure, produced initially from a single apical cell. Suppose the cells of a leaf margin exist in ten states: $b, c, d, e, f, g, h, i, j, k$, with a as the single starting state, and ten transition rules govern the developmental sequence: $a \to bc$, $b \to kd$, $c \to ek$, $d \to gb$, $e \to cf$, $f \to ih$, $g \to hi$, $h \to de$, $i \to k$, and $k \to k$. These rules produce the following successive generations,

a

bc

kdek

kgbcfk

khikdekihk

kdek kgbcfk kdek

kgbcfj khikdekihk khbcfk

khikdekihk kdekkgbcfkkdek khikdekihk

Cells in stage k define non-growing portions of the leaf (notches) and occupy positions between developing adjacent leaflets. The last three generations of this developmental sequence are represented as stages of a developing leaf in Figures 3A, B and C. The centre part of each generation has a string of cells, which generates the entire string of two steps previously, while its left and right portions generate the entire string of three steps before. This can be written as a locally catenative formula for the nth generation, $n > 5$,

$$\alpha_n = \alpha_{n-3}\, \alpha_{n-2}\, \alpha_{n-3} \tag{1}$$

A locally catenative formula, which may have particular relevance to development morphology, has the form $\alpha_n = \alpha_{n-2}\, \alpha_{n-1}$. Starting from a single state, this formula generates strings with lengths which are the consecutive numbers of the main fibonacci series (1, 2, 5, 8, 13, . . .).

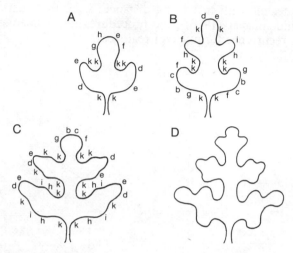

FIGURE 3. The development of a compound leaf, following a theoretical generation system with 10 basic states and 10 transformation rules between states. A, B and C illustrate stages of development to the final leaf form D (see text) (from Rozenburg & Lindenmayer 1976).

A change in just one transition rule can have a dramatic effect on the final pattern. For example, symmetry in the proposed development of the compound leaf is maintained by two of the transition rules, $g > hi$ and $f > ih$. A change in either, to produce just i, generates branches on only one side of the structure. Such dramatic changes in tree architecture do exist in nature (Hallé 1978). The shoots of cassava (*Manihot esculenta*) normally bifurcate dichotomously (as in Fig. 1B), but a sympodial form also occurs. The normal crown forms of *Pinus caribea* and *Hevea braziliensis* are as in the left of Figure 1C, but both species can produce single unbranched stems, termed 'foxtails' and 'lampbrushes', respectively. Hallé and Martin (1968) produced lampbrush trees of *Hevea* by removing most of the leaves when they were young. Hallé (1978) listed 21 architectural 'mutants' which involved substantial changes in branching pattern, although only some of them bred true. He also noted that considerable architectural polymorphism occurs in most taxonomic families, and in some genera, which, from an evolutionary standpoint, implies that within-species genetical varation in branching does occur.

Just as it is possible to represent bud production and orientation in a simple manner, so it is possible simply to describe the growth relationships between lateral branches and their parent shoot. Frijters and Lindenmayer (1976) advanced a simple formulation for 'paracladial' relationships, where branches repeat the inflorescence-like structure of the main axis. Only two variables were required: a delay period before the daughter branch began the repetition, b (akin to a measure of apical dominance), and a proportional growth rate, a akin to a measure of apical control). Repeated application of linear formulae, with constant values of a and b, produced the branching patterns observed in inflorescences, except that branching at the base was more prolific than actually observed (Fig. 4). This process can be improved upon if b, and particularly a, decline with increasing distances from the main stem apex. Frijters and Lindenmayer (1976) gave procedures for estimating the parameters of these recurrence formulae in real trees.

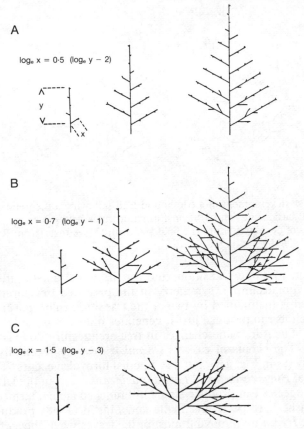

FIGURE 4.   Generation of branched structures, with varying degrees of apical domin ance, approximated by b (the delay in internode position before development starts and apical control, approximated by a (the growth rate of the branch relative to that of the parent stem). In A, $a = 0.5$ and $b = 2$; in B, $a = 0.7$ and $b = 1$; in C, $a = 1.5$ and $b = 3$ (from Frijters & Lindenmayer 1976).

C.   Description of branching as a connected system

The bifurcation ratio, R_b, is a simple descriptive statistic of the branching structure as a connected system. It has been used to show how branching structures vary in a consistent way between broad taxonomic groups, a different positions along an ecological gradient, in different environments, and in different parts of tree crowns.

To calculate R_b, branches are classified according to their order, where terminal sections have order 1 (Strahler 1957; Fig. 5). These join at nodes to give branch sections with order 2, and two order 2 branches join to form branches with order 3, and so on to the main stem. If two branches of different order meet, then the conjoined branch takes the same order as the higher of the two. Segments which form one contiguous branch of the same order are all considered part of the same branch (Fig. 5B). Note that, when applied to a living tree, the ordering system does not necessarily reflect the age of the shoots.

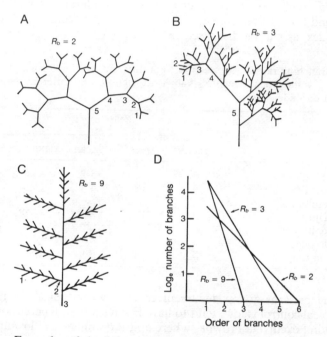

FIGURE 5.   Examples of the bifurcation ratio, R_b, used to describe the branching structures of trees and other plants. In A, B and C, the numbers 1, 2, 3 . . . indicate the orders of branches.

The logarithm of the number of branches in each order, plotted against the order itself, typically gives a linear plot, and the antilog of the slope is the average bifurcation ratio, R_b, of the system; that is, there are R_b times as many branches in each order as in the next higher order, and the minimum value of R_b is 2·0 (Fig. 5). As will be discussed, R_b can vary within individual trees, and most workers have used the formula:

$$R_b = \frac{N - N_{max}}{N - N_2} \qquad (2)$$

where N is the total number of branches of all orders, N_{max} is the number of branches of the highest order (and will be 1 if the system is considered down to the main stem) and N_1 is the number of branches of the first order, that is the endmost branches. Equation (2) averages the value of the bifurcation ratio over the whole system, giving slightly more weight to the more numerous lower order branches (Motomura 1947).

Oohata and Shidei (1971) measured the branching structures of contrasting tree species in Japan, $1 \cdot 5 – 7 \cdot 0$ m tall and 2–10 cm in basal diameter, and found significant differences in R_b between species with different types of leaves, characteristic canopy sizes and foliage durations (Table I). Those with evergreen foliage, expecially those with leaves closely adpressed to the stem, and where the stem was an integral part of the foliage frond, had the highest values of R_b. Deciduous, broadleaved trees had the lowest R_b values. Typically, foliage areas are larger in evergreen, and in coniferous, forests than in deciduous and broadleaved forests. This characteristic seems to be related to their R_b values, as will be discussed below.

TABLE I.   Branching ratios (R_b, see Fig. 5) of different tree life forms, measured in a forest near Kyoto, Japan. Mean R_b values are significantly different with $P < 0 \cdot 05$ (after Oohata & Shidei 1971)

	Numbers of		R_b		
	species	trees	Mean	Maximum	Minimum
Deciduous broadleaved	6	11	3·2	3·7	2·7
Evergreen broadleaved	9	16	4·4	5·9	3·1
Evergreen coniferous needle foliage	5	12	5·1	3·9	6·5
Evergreen coniferous leaves scale-like, adpressed to the stem	5	6	7·8	10·8	5·6

Branching patterns giving decurrent crowns, where apical dominance is high and apical control is low, tend to have low R_b values, whereas branching patterns giving excurrent crowns, where apical dominance is low and apical control is high, tend to have high R_b values (Fig. 2). The difference in R_b values between species broadly parallels their evolutionary advance in complexity of leaf type. For the primitive conifers, with adpressed leaves, Oohata and Shidei (1971) reported that the regression of $\log_e$ (branch number) on branch order could be extended to include the final 'leaf branch', although the numbers of these appeared to be slightly, but consistently, higher than expected in the five species examined. In contrast, for three deciduous species, leaf number was greater than would be predicted by extending the regression of $\log_e$ (branch number) on branch order to zero. However, Barker et al. (1973) reported that the number of winter buds on two deciduous species could be predicted by extrapolating the branching regression.

There is a close relationship between the branching pattern of deciduous, simple-leaved angiospermous trees and their position in the successional sequence of the deciduous forest of eastern North America (Whitney 1976). Four shade-intolerant, early-successional species had higher values of R_b (5·9 standard error 0.95) than three intermediate (4.9 ± 0.85), and three late-successional and very shade-tolerant species (3.9 ± 0.25). Whitney (1976) discussed these differences in relation to the proposal (Horn 1971) that, in early-successional species, the leaves are randomly distributed throughout the crown, while, in late-successional, shade-tolerant species, the leaves are held in non-overlapping monolayers. *Populus tremuloides*, and early-successional species with a large R_b (8.6), has a multiranked branching pattern with a large number of short shoots positioned around large erect branches. By contrast *Fagus grandiflora*, with a low R_b (3.5), has highly forked (tending to bifurcating) branches flattened in the horizontal plane.

The environment in which a tree grows may influence its R_b value; fast-growing trees on good sites may produce more branches, and have larger R_b values, than slow-growing trees on poor sites (Borchert & Slade 1981). However, R_b does provide a useful interpretative statistic in some situations. *Acer saccharinum* was classified by Whitney (1976) as a late-successional species with a relatively low R_b (4.4), but Steingraeber *et al.* (1979) found that open-grown trees had $R_b = 3.2$ whereas understorey trees had $R_b = 7.1$ (significantly different, $P<0.01$). Pickett and Kempf (1980) found that *Acer rubrum*, *Cornus florida* and *Viburnum prunifolium* had significantly larger values of R_b when growing in open fields as opposed to closed forest canopies ($P<0.001$). However, this difference may not exist for all species. Oohata and Shidei (1971) found that R_b was the same on experimentally unshaded and shaded seedlings of *Quercus phillyraeoides*, and Whitney (1976) concluded that open- and shade-grown *Fraxinus americana* had similar R_b values, although Pickett and Kempf (1980) noted that this species was usually under severe stress in closed forests.

Branching structures can vary within tree crowns. In *Betula populifolia*, R_b was 5.1 in the upper part of the crown and 4.2 in the lower part (Whitney 1976). In *Quercus rubra*, while R_b did not differ significantly between 16 m and the top of a 27 m tall tree, the length of both the first-order branches and the petioles was less at 27 m, and the angles which first-order branches made at nodes were more acute (44° compared with 77°).

D.   Crown dimensions and timber yield

Trees growing in stands differ in crown shape, depending on the species and the trees' position within the canopy (Fig. 6A,B). The crowns of coniferous trees (excurrent form, large R_b) are greatest in diameter about two-thirds from the top ($l_o/l = 0.67$, Fig. 6C), whereas the crowns of broadleaved species (decurrent form, small R_b) are broadest nearer the tree top ($l_o/l>0.5$, Fig. 6D).

Trees within fully stocked stands differ, in both their absolute rates of timber production (m³ tree⁻¹), and in their production per unit crown projection area, crown volume and crown surface area. Assmann (1970) summarized analyses for stands of *Pinus sylvestris* and *Quercus petraea*. In all stands, large trees had the largest absolute rates of timber production both between and within three 'social classes' – dominant, codominant and dominated. However, *within* each social class, the smaller trees, which had more

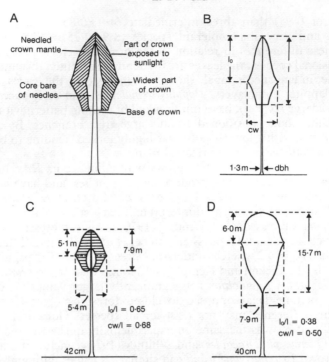

FIGURE 6.   Crown dimensions of forest-grown trees showing typical differences between coniferous and deciduous species.
A. Idealized crown structure of a conifer.
B. Crown dimensions.
C. The structure of an 88-year-old *Pinus sylvestris* tree with a crown volume of 87·3 m³.
D. In contrast to C, the crown volume of an 88-year-old dominant *Fagus sylvatica* tree of similar height (25-30 m) is 356 m³, with the major part of that volume below the widest part of the crown. Note that, despite its smaller crown, the stem diameter of the *Pinus sylvestris* is greater than that of the *Fagus sylvatica*. A hypothesis to explain this difference is described in the text. (Redrawn from Assmann 1970.)

slender crowns and therefore a relatively larger crown surface area per unit of growing space, had generally greater timber production 'efficiencies', in terms of timber produced per unit ground area, crown surface area or crown volume.

With increasing crown width and crown fullness ratio (CW and CW/1, Fig. 6), the relationship between crown surface area and crown volume must change. As a crown grows, an increasing proportion of its volume is occupied by a core of supporting branches which carry no needles. This supporting structure contributes very little photosynthate, but it uses photosynthate both for wood production and respiration. Each branch must continue to thicken along its length in order to support the weight of foliage produced at an increasing distance from the trunk (see below). This demand for photosynthate by the supporting branches may explain the lower efficiency of stemwood production of the larger trees in each social class.

Surface area is the crown parameter which correlates most closely with stemwood volume increment, both in single species (Hamilton 1969), and multistorey mixed species stands (Magin 1959).

III. CONTRIBUTION OF DIFFERENT BRANCHES ON A TREE TO STEM GROWTH

The vertical distribution of trunk thickening, within and below the crowns of stand-grown trees, has been estimated in anatomical studies (Denne 1979) and by pruning living branches (Labyak & Schumaker 1954). Branches contributing most to trunk thickening are at the point of crown interaction and competition for light, and are generally above the position where branches have maximum foliage weight.

The contribution by branches to stemwood increment depends both upon their position in the canopy and their seasonal pattern of export. A comprehensive analysis of this potential has been made in *Populus* in relation to its use in short rotation coppice in the Lake States of the USA (Isebrands 1982). Leaves show a distinct hierarchy, in both photosynthetic performance, and in the destination of exported photosynthate. In two-year-old plants grown from cuttings, leaves on the current year's terminal shoots had a high photosynthetic rate over the whole season, whereas leaves on lateral branches had lower photosynthetic rates which declined in late summer. Two types of lateral shoots were produced: 'short shoots', comprised solely of leaves preformed in the bud, and 'long shoots', which also formed leaves during the current season. Within the mid-crown, shade leaves of long shoots had a higher photosynthetic potential than those of short shoots, mainly because their average leaf age was less – there being a general decline in photosynthetic potential with increasing leaf age during the season (Nelson & Michael 1982).

Very little of the photosynthate produced by leaves on lateral branches of *Populus* was exported to the leader or to other laterals (Isebrands 1982). Prior to bud-set, export was primarily to the main stem internodes below the branch and to the supporting branch itself.

Following bud-set, an increasing proportion went to the roots. Main stem height growth was achieved using photosynthate from the main stem leaves, although after bud-set they too contributed an increasing amount to roots. Differences in the timing of bud-set among lateral branches influenced the pattern of export of photosynthate: in the lower canopy bud-set could be three weeks later than in the upper canopy. However, differences in photosynthetic rate resulted in a larger total contribution to stem growth from upper canopy branches.

IV. SOME MODELS OF BRANCH STRUCTURE AND FUNCTION

The measurements of timber production per unit crown size, reported by Assmann (1970), suggest that *stand* production might be increased, if trees were grown which maximized the ratio of photosynthesizing mantle to non-photosynthesizing cones of supporting branches within the crown. This hypothesis needs to be explored with regard to genetic improvement and stand management. What inherent attributes of branch growth are required to produce efficient crowns? And can improvements in crown 'efficiency' be maintained by management throughout the growth of the stand?

In this section, some models of branch growth are considered, which, to varying degrees, all use the concept of 'optimization of biological structure'. This concept has some disadvantages, which are discussed below, but it also yields useful insights into the relationship between structure and function.

A. R_b and the interception of light

Horton (1945) introduced the concept of R_b to describe the branching networks of rivers. The R_b of river networks in a wide variety of climates and physiographic settings is about 3·5, varying within narrow limits. Also, the length ratio between successive orders of tributaries is fairly constant at about 2·3 (Leopold 1971). As a river grows by the joining of tributaries, its course adjusts to accommodate the increased flow, and Leopold described the steady state of a river branching system as the result of a balance between opposing tendencies for (a) minimum power expenditure in the whole system, and (b) an equal distribution of power throughout the system. By analogy, he suggested that the branching patterns of trees are a balance between minimizing energy expenditure in the production of branches, and maximizing a photosynthetic surface to provide the most efficient interception of sunlight.

Leopold (1971) produced evidence for this theory in a photographic analysis of a sunflower plant. By taking photographs from different sun angles, he found that 51% of the leaf area was exposed to sunlight over a day, compared with 46% of a hemisphere with the same total surface area. The sunflower plant had 21 leaves, supported by 3·8 m of petioles and stems, whereas the length of a second-order branching system needed to support the hemisphere, divided into 21 units, was five metres. Compared with the hemisphere, the sunflower had a greater surface illumination and less branch support, so that the ratios of sunlit hours to stem lengths were 4·5 and 2·8 for the sunflower and hemisphere, respectively.

Tree branching systems do not follow a single branching rule, as river systems appear to do. Neither do they minimize path lengths (stems) to reach a network of points (leaves), in the way in which the bronchial tubes ($R_b = 2·8$), and bronchioles ($R_b = 2·3$) do to reach the alveoli in lungs (which Barker *et al.* 1973 speculated optimizes bidirectional gas flow). Leopold (1971) proposed that small and large values of R_b represented two different ecologically based strategies, in terms of yield output per unit of energy input. In shaded situations, self-shading is avoided by producing the minimum branch length to ensure a regular, non-overlapping leaf distribution; R_b is then small and there is a continuous outward development from many growing points. In more open situations, as occur early in a succession, when typically there is all-round illumination and a requirement for rapid height growth, R_b is large, and there is minimal expenditure on a branch support system between the main stem and the foliage.

Conifer needles have lower maximum photosynthetic rates per unit area or weight than deciduous broadleaves (Ford 1984), but conifer needles are retained for more than one year, and Schulze et al. (1977a) found that 47% of the CO_2 uptake in crowns of Picea abies occurred in needles three to four years old. Thus, for evergreen conifers, there is a premium on producing a branching structure which enables light to penetrate to the older needles, and this is just what a high value of R_b does, at least around the periphery of the crown. This fact also has an important consequence for the shade crown. From the results of simulating the light climate of Pinus sylvestris crowns, Oker-Blom and Kellomäki (1983) suggested that, in most situations, within-plant shading was considerably greater than between-plant shading, and that the light conditions of an individual tree were, to a high degree, determined by its own structure, and particularly by the very clumped nature of foliage. This structure is also a consequence of a high R_b. Schulze et al. (1977a) estimated that, in P. abies, 71% of the annual CO_2 uptake occurred in the sun crown. Also, branches in the shade crown of P. abies contributed considerably less (29%) to seasonal CO_2 uptake than those of Fagus sylvatica (48%).

The development of a branching structure with a low R_b value, and its relationship to light interception, was studied by Fisher and Honda (1979a), who simulated the branch generating process of Terminalia catappa. This tropical species has regularly bifurcating branches, produced in pseudo-whorls along the main stem, which become dorsiventrally flattened with age. Each branch produces a cluster of leaves at its distal end, and one of the new branches of the bifurcation predominates. In successive growth periods, leaves are produced at the distal end of each branch segment so that the leaf positions remain unchanged.

Fisher and Honda (1979b) calculated the total simulated leaf area of each branch, and its horizontal projected area, as branching angles and other structural features were varied. They attempted to determine the structure which maximized the average effective unshaded (non-overlapped) leaf area per leaf cluster, or that which minimized the leaf area produced by a branch or tier of branches to ensure full light interception.

The measured branching angles for Terminalia catappa were $\theta_1 = 24 \cdot 4°$ SE$\pm 0 \cdot 7°$ and $\theta_2 = 36 \cdot 9°$ SE$\pm 0 \cdot 0°$ for the minor axis. (That is, when a branch bifurcated, one went $24 \cdot 4°$ to the left, the other $36 \cdot 9°$ to the right.) The conditions in the simulation model which most closely reproduced these angles were second-order branching and either uniform or mixed symmetry in the tier of branches, ie the first θ_1 was in the same or in mixed directions for successive branches around the pseudo-whorl. Optimum branching angles varied, as both the number of branches in a tier, and the order of branching were increased. Branching angles which produced optimum light interception became increasingly asymmetric (ie the difference between θ_1 and θ_2 increased) as branch order was increased, a situation not found in real trees. Thus, it is possible to design trees which are more efficient in light interception than those which exist! Of course, other aspects of the growth process must be considered. Fisher and Honda (1979a) found that the ratio of branch lengths between the two arms of the bifurcations was considerably lower for measured trees than those giving optimum light interception simulations. They suggested that branch length ratios were more closely related to consider-ations of branch strength than to light interception. Whilst Fisher and Honda (1979a,b) demonstrated the effectiveness of a bifurcating branching system in intercepting light, they also revealed constraints which may have limited the evolution of an optimal structure.

B.   Wood increment and branch support

The role which branch length may play in foliage display must be considered in relation to the weight of the branch itself. A branch deflects under its own weight (Fig. 7A), and the deflection of the tip, Δ, relative to the branch length, depends upon the taper of the branch (McMahon & Kronauer 1976). If we assume that a branch decreases in diameter – moving outwards from the trunk – the imaginary point where the diameter is zero is the virtual origin,

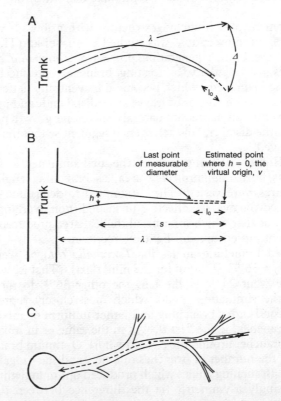

FIGURE 7.   Control of branch deflection by the vertical diameter of the branch. $h = ks^\beta$, where k is a constant; when $\beta = 1\cdot5$, branch deflection under its own weight maintains a constant ratio Δ/λ (see text).

v (Fig. 7B). Then, the taper of the branch in both its vertical dimension, h, and its horizontal dimension, b, (where $h = b$ if the branch is circular) can be expressed by the power laws:

$$h = k_1 s^\beta \quad \text{and} \quad b = k_2 s^\alpha \tag{4}$$

where s is the distance from the virtual origin, v, to the point where the diameter is being considered, and k_1 and k_2 are constants of proportionality. If β (the rate of taper) is $1 \cdot 5$, the branch is elastically self-similar; that is, the deflection of the tip, Δ, divided by its overall length, λ, is a constant, however much λ may vary, and whatever the value of α (Fig. 7B). Note that the deflection depends only upon the rate of taper in the vertical direction, so that a branch in plan view (Fig. 7C) has the same properties of deflection as square or round section cantilevers. For engineering purposes, beams may be designed with different tapers to meet different purposes; for instance, if $\beta = 2$, the beam has uniform stress along both its upper and lower surfaces.

To estimate the relationship between h and s in tree branching systems, McMahon and Kronauer (1976) first had to determine an 'average path length', L_i, from the point where h was measured (distance l_0 from the virtual origin, v) to m end twigs, where:

$$L_i = (s - l_0) = L_i = \frac{1}{m} \sum_{j=1}^{m} l_{ij} \tag{5}$$

A curvilinear relationship is obtained between L and h, with L decreasing more rapidly than h at small sizes. This is because the real measurement of diameter can necessarily only begin at the tip of a twig, and not at the virtual origin. To estimate λ_0 – the distance from the furthest real measurement to the virtual origin – McMahon and Kronauer (1976) used an iterative least squares technique. For the mean of five deciduous trees, they found $\beta = 1 \cdot 50$ with maximum $1 \cdot 66$ and minimum $1 \cdot 37$. To augment these estimates of β, McMahon and Kronauer (1976) used an interesting property of beams – their natural frequency when freely vibrated is related to β. In particular, for $\beta = 1 \cdot 50$, the natural frequency of vibration is proportional to λ^ψ with $\psi = -0 \cdot 50$. McMahon and Kronauer measured the natural frequency of branches of different lengths, and of whole trees, both with and without leaves, and found an average exponent, $\psi = -0 \cdot 59$. They concluded that the taper of vertical branch diameter approximated to the model of 'elastic similarity'. Because vertical branch diameter controls the mechanical properties of branches, trees may have very different R_b values, yet have the same *mechanical* design. They proposed that maintaining a constancy in branch taper ensured that tree crowns maintained their regular form as the tree grew.

C.   Interactions between R_b, branch strength, branch growth and stemwood increment

Whilst, in engineering terms, the bending properties of branches and trunks may be independent of R_b, the requirement that branches should increment a specific amount of wood to maintain a certain taper obviously places a specific demand for photosynthate upon the foliage. The pattern of photosynthate movement in *Populus* described above indicates that, after the first year of

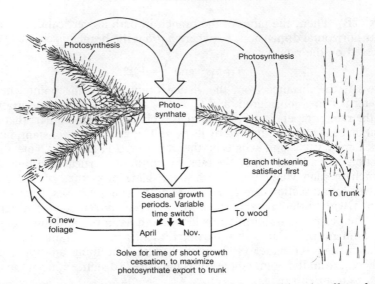

FIGURE 8.   Diagrammatic representation of a model, describing the effect of varying the annual investment in new foliated shoots on branch thickening and photosynthate export to the trunk.

growth, branches do not import photosynthate. If we assume this hypothesis to be generally true, then the investment in new foliage, the requirement for branch thickening, and the export of material to the stem together constitute a dynamic system (Fig. 8). This system was simulated for a conifer branch growing in its second year, where the branching frequency, R_b, the rate of taper in branch diameter, β, and the exponential rate of decline in photosynthetic rate per unit needle weight with age were all varied (Fig. 9). An eight-month growing period was assumed, and the simulation calculated the amount of new foliated branch produced to optimize export to the stem. The optimal branch length was sought, by allowing the 'duration' of shoot extension to vary, during which time all of the photosynthate from the old foliage and 50% of that from the new foliage went to produce new branch length and associated needle weight. New branches were all 'grown' from the distal end of the previous year's branch. During the period after shoot elongation was completed, photosynthate was first allocated to branch thickening – to the diameter required by β using measured constants – and the remaining photosynthate was exported to the trunk. Whilst investment in new branch increased the total photosynthate produced, the additional length obviously placed a greater demand on photosynthate for branch thickening.

As R_b was increased in the simulations, so the material returned to the stem increased, as also did the total length of new shoot produced. That is, it cost less, in terms of branch thickening, to produce new shoot length on many rather than few branches. This is a crucial feature of branch design. The duration of shoot growth which maximized export to the trunk also increased with increase in R_b (ie finely divided branches should grow for longer), because there was less requirement for branch thickening material (Fig. 9). Decreasing β increased the material exported to the trunk.

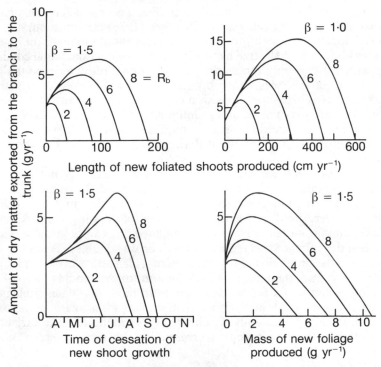

FIGURE 9.   Results of simulations of the effect of varying the bifurcation ratio, R_b, (over the range 2 to 8) and the coefficient of branch diameter thickening, β, on branch growth and the export of photosynthate to the trunk. Values used were those measured on *Picea sitchensis* (Ford 1982a, and unpublished data): initial branch length was 25 cm with 0·05 g needles cm⁻¹, wood density 0·5 g cm⁻³, photosynthetic rate $Pn = 3·5*$ $0·7^{t-1}$, branch diameter at 5 cm from the tip, $d = 0·004v^β$ where v was the 'virtual origin' (see text and Fig. 7).

D.   Are branches optimum structures for stemwood production?

Models of the type described above could be used to develop specifications for the branching structure of an ideotype. However, the use of optimization criteria requires great care.

It may not be valid to assume that branching structures maximize photosynthetic gain per unit investment in branch material. Natural selection operates through breeding success, and features other than simply the growth rate of the plant can influence this factor. Fisher and Honda (1979b) drew attention to Ashton's suggestion that the adaptive value of the pagoda habit in young plants is the ability rapidly to expose new leaf surface in dense layers above competitors (Ashton 1978). Equally, it may not be valid to assume that branching structures develop to optimize light interception, because factors other than light may limit growth. Paltridge (1973) modelled tree growth and structure as a balance between light interception and water stress, which he considered would be likely to increase as trees become taller. This balance was also the underlying rationale of Brunig's (1976) classification.

When modelling branch growth, the criteria should include the selective pressures under which the tree has evolved, and the environmental conditions under which it currently functions. Selective pressures determine the genotype, and so set the rules which branching follows. However, as with any character, there is heterogeneity within populations, and in the broad ecological context there may not be an optimum structure for individuals within a species. Continued breeding success requires sufficient variation between individuals to survive under the differing conditions typical of the species habitat.

There is also evidence that the control of branching is not completely rigorous. Cochrane and Ford (1978) fitted statistical distributions to rules governing branch production, extension and dispersion in *Picea sitchensis*. These rules were used in a simulation model of crown growth (Cochrane 1977). An important feature was that simulated trees were visually 'unreal', both when the variance was reduced to zero or was doubled. A similar result was found in the simulation of rooting patterns (Henderson *et al.* 1983). These findings have important implications for our understanding of biological branching systems, and for our attempts to fit models to data. Biologically, the existence of a significant variance term implies a 'slackness' in the control system under study. Generally, Cochrane (1977) found that the variance for relationships within the canopy increased for the slower, less productive branches.

V. CHANGES IN BRANCHING AND FOLIAGE AMOUNT DURING PLANTATION DEVELOPMENT

The production and growth of branches change as the canopy of a forest plantation passes through different stages of development. These changes may have an important impact on both total timber production and its distribution between individual trees. A crop of *Picea sitchensis* provides an example.

A bud of *P. sitchensis* extends in one year, and in the next year acts as a source of whorl and interwhorl branches (Cochrane & Ford 1978). Each bud may produce a similar sequence of branches, but, as they become submerged in the canopy, branches gradually fail to produce first their own interwhorl, and then whorl branches, and finally they fail to elongate at all (Longman, this volume). Cochrane and Ford (1978) found that, during canopy development, separate rules governed the production, dispersion and extension of branches along the main stem of the tree. However, branch dispersion followed consistent rules from year to year. For instance, whorl branches were always arranged in a spatially regular (not random) fashion around the stem, irrespective of their numbers; interwhorl branches were absent immediately below their distal whorl and above their proximal whorl; and the angles between the vertical main stem and the branches increased from the top of the tree towards the base of the crown, especially for interwhorl branches.

Cochrane and Ford (1978) advanced the hypothesis that there was within-tree competition for resources during the early years of growth, which was related to the numbers of branches produced by a tree on its main stem. There was a marked decrease in the number of whorl branches produced each year after the branches of neighbouring trees met ('foliage overlap', Fig. 10), which was related to an increase in leader growth rates. Prior to year six, leader growth accelerated by some $5 \cdot 2 \, \mathrm{cm \, yr^{-1}}$. Between years seven and ten, the increase in leader increment was $8 \cdot 2 \, \mathrm{cm \, yr^{-1}}$, and over this period annual leader extension was negatively correlated with numbers of whorl branches produced per year. While the leaders certainly exerted apical control over the whorl branches, the whorl branches also influenced leader growth. Individual trees were affected to different extents by this process, because individuals differed significantly in the numbers of whorl, and particularly interwhorl, branches they produced.

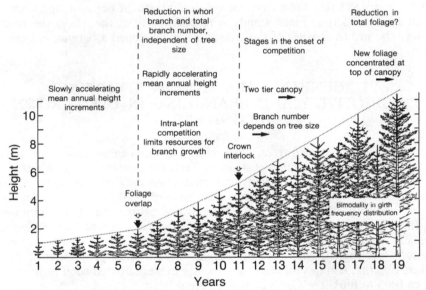

FIGURE 10. Controlling influences on branch growth and canopy function in a developing plantation of *Picea sitchensis* in Scotland.

From year 11 onwards, mean annual height increment stabilized. Large trees produced most branches, and had greatest leader growth, and Cochrane and Ford (1978) suggested that this stage in canopy development ('crown interlock', Fig. 10) marked the onset of between-tree competition. However, whilst this was apparent in the numbers of branches produced at the top of the canopy, competition in terms of trunk diameter increment appeared only at year 16 (Ford 1982a). This delay may reflect the length of time taken for changes in the top whorls of the tree to have an effect on wood production in the trunk.

At year 16, new shoot production shifted from being evenly distributed throughout the crowns to being concentrated at the tops. The canopy changes quite quickly, from being akin to a collection of long but bush-like crowns, to a two-tier mixture of a few dominant trees and many dominated trees. Associated with this change, there was a decrease in leaf area index of 11% between years 16 and 18 (Ford 1982b). Similar decreases have been found in plantations of other coniferous species at the same stage of development – for instance, 24% during two years after attaining a maximum at age seven in *Pinus radiata* (Forest & Ovington 1970) and 23% during the 20 years following a maximum at age 11 in *Cryptomeria japonica* (Kira & Shidei 1967). Isebrands and Nelson (1982) discussed the same effect in short-rotation *Populus*, which they suggested signalled a decline in productivity owing to crown competition.

I suggest that total foliage amount decreases because dominant trees shade smaller neighbours by producing lateral branches, while the centres of their own crowns become increasingly bare. The foliage 'lost' from the canopy, owing to the 'decline' of suppressed trees, is not made up by additional foliage increment on the large trees. Assmann (1970) reported a suggestion made by Metzger in 1893 that the maximum volume increment per unit land area in even-aged coniferous forest stands is reached early in the life of the crop, before the insolated parts of the crowns have developed a bare inner core.

VI. GENETIC VARIATION IN STEMWOOD PRODUCTIVITY AND BRANCHING IN OPEN-GROWN CONIFERS

In young, widely spaced trees, large within-species genetic differences have been found in the production of stemwood relative to branchwood. Matthews *et al.* (1975) estimated that stemwood production on *Pinus virginiana* could be increased by 30%, if family differences in total wood production could be combined with differences in stem/branchwood proportion. They examined open-pollinated progenies, from 20 *Pinus virginiana* parent trees, selected equally from naturally well and poorly pruned trees. At the onset of crown closure (age eight), when branch weights were a large proportion of total wood weights, families differed significantly in stem/branchwood proportion from 0·48 to 0·61 (see Cannell, this volume).

Tallness, sparse branching, and the absence of large basal branches were the most important characters positively correlated with large and efficient stemwood production (per unit of foliage mass or area) in clones of *Pinus contorta* and *Picea sitchensis* (Cannell *et al.* 1983). Seven clones of both species were grown at a lowland 'agricultural' site, and at age eight (before crown closure) the species had similar stem dry weights (2·76 and 2·87 kg tree^{-1}, respectively). However, there were differences between species in branch and foliage structure. *P. sitchensis* had only 56% as much branch weight, and 61% as much foliage weight, as *Pinus contorta*. Within both species, there were significant differences between clones in stem/branchwood proportion and in stemwood production per unit foliage mass and area. The latter (stemwood production per unit of foliage) was *negatively* correlated with percentage needle weight on the tree (ie poorly foliated, sparsely branched trees were relatively 'efficient').

The potential for exploiting these differences depends on how stable they are as the environment changes during stand development. Differences among clones of *P. sitchensis* in stemwood amount may reflect differences in both the overall efficiency of wood production and in the allocation to different tree parts. Four of the *P. sitchensis* clones were also grown at a high-altitude site in a poor soil. At this site, total dry matter production, and foliage amounts were less by different amounts for the four clones than at the lowland site, but for each clone the production of total wood (branches plus stem) per unit of foliage was the same as at the lowland site.

VII.   CAN WE INCREASE PLANTATION YIELD BY GENETIC MANIPULATION OF BRANCH CHARACTERISTICS?

In the study of Cannell *et al.* (1983), the principal morphological characteristic associated with large stemwood production per unit of foliage was sparseness of branching. This characteristic is also considered to be desirable in the ideotypes formulated by Dickmann and by Kärki and Tigerstedt (this volume). If such genotypes were grown in stands, would they give an increase in productivity per hectare?

Crown shape, particularly the ratio of crown surface area to crown volume, greatly influences stand productivity. If this ratio were kept high for longer into the rotation, branch thickening would presumably require less photosynthate and, because the phase of intense crown competition would be postponed, a large foliage area might be maintained for longer. However, to achieve these effects, the trees would have to be close enough to occupy the site. A precise silviculture would have to be worked out. There may be an interesting parallel in the potential for increasing grass yields (Rhodes 1971) or grain yields in maize (Pendleton *et al.* 1968) by growing more erect-leaved genotypes – substantial gains can be achieved, provided that a large enough total canopy is maintained to give high light interception.

I suggest that the possibility of increasing stemwood yields by minimizing branchwood increment will vary between trees of different branching habit and broadly, but not exclusively, between conifers and broadleaved deciduous trees. The essential attribute of the more productive conifer genotypes discussed in the previous section is that they produce less branchwood, so the foliage they grow is closer to the stem. This decreases the requirement for branch thickening, and may reduce self-shading in the crowns. In stands, the canopy would be composed of long columnar crowns, and the strategy should be to increase the longevity of needles and to increase the 'return on investment' in foliage. Illumination levels lower down the tree would increase, but of course other factors, notably nutrition, may also influence needle longevity and canopy structure (Brix 1981).

Late successional broadleaved trees have low values of R_b. This may ensure a spatially more even distribution of foliage throughout the shaded portion of the canopies, but probably implies greater investment in branch thickening per unit length of branch. The growth strategy of these broadleaved trees is different from that of conifers, and probably the strategy for tree improvement should differ also.

In field trials of clonal *Triplochiton scleroxylon*, Leakey and Ladipo (1985) found that, at wide 4·9 m spacings, the trees with fewest branches per unit length of stem were tallest and had greatest stem diameter after 18 months. However, after canopy closure and some branch abscission, there was an even stronger positive relationship between stem diameter and the total number of branches remaining on the trees. Leakey and Ladipo (1985) suggested that, after canopy closure, the ability of branches to survive shading, and not self-prune, became an important determinant of stemwood yield. So, whilst an effective strategy to increase the productivity in conifers might be to concentrate on increasing crown surface area, it might be insufficient in those hardwoods which achieve a substantial proportion of their stemwood increment from branches in the shaded part of the crown.

ACKNOWLEDGEMENTS

I am grateful to Dr R. R. B. Leakey for helpful discussions and access to unpublished manuscripts and to Dr M. G. R. Cannell for helpful editorial comments. I would like to thank Mr R. H. F. Wilson and Mr R. Ford for assistance well beyond the call of duty.

REFERENCES

Ashton, P. S. (1978). Crown characteristics of tropical trees. In: *Tropical trees as living systems*, edited by P. B. Tomlinson and M. H. Zimmermann, 591–615. Cambridge: Cambridge University Press.

Assmann, E. (1970). *The principles of forest yields study*. Oxford: Pergamon.

Barker, S. B., Cumming, G. & Horsfield, K. (1973). Quantitative morphology of the branching structure of trees. *J. theor. Biol.*, **40**, 33–43.

Borchert, R. & Slade, N. A. (1981). Bifurcation ratios and the adaptive geometry of trees. *Bot. Gaz.*, **142**, 394–401.

Brix, H. (1981). Effects of thinning and nitrogen fertilization on branch and foliage production in Douglas fir. *Can. J. For. Res.*, **11**, 502–511.

Brown, C. L., McAlpine, R. G. & Kormanik, P. P. (1967), Apical dominance and form in woody plants: a reappraisal. *Am. J. Bot.*, **54**, 153–162.

Brunig, E. F. (1976). Tree forms in relation to environmental conditions. In: *Tree physiology and yield improvement*, edited by M. G. R. Cannell and F. T. Last, 139–156. London: Academic Press.

Cannell, M. G. R., Sheppard, L. J., Ford, E. D. & Wilson, R. H. F. (1983). Clonal differences in dry matter distribution, wood specific gravity and foliage 'efficiency' in *Picea sitchensis* and *Pinus contorta*. *Silvae Genet.*, **32**, 195–202.

Cochrane, L. A. (1977). *Statistical models for the branching of Sitka spruce*. Ph.D. thesis, Heriot-Watt University, Edinburgh.

Cochrane, L. A. & Ford, E. D. (1978). Growth of a Sitka spruce plantation: analysis and stochastic description of the development of the branching structure. *J. appl. Ecol.*, **15**, 227–244.

Denne, M. P. (1979). Wood structure and production within the trunk and branches of *Picea sitchensis* in relation to canopy formation. *Can. J. For. Res.*, **9**, 406–427.

Fisher, J. B. & Honda, H. (1979a). Branch geometry and effective leaf area: a study of *Terminalia* – branching pattern. 1. Theoretical trees. *Am. J. Bot.*, **66**, 633–644.

Fisher, J. B. & Honda, H. (1979b). Branch geometry and effective leaf area: a study of *Terminalia* – branching pattern. 2. Survey of real trees. *Am. J. Bot.*, **66**, 645–655.

Ford, E. D. (1982a). High productivity in a polestage Sitka spruce stand and its relation to canopy structure. *Forestry*, **55**, 1–17.

Ford, E. D. (1982b). Catastrophe and disruption in forest ecosystems and their implications for plantation forest. *Scott. For.*, **55**, 1–17.

Ford, E. D. (1984). The dynamics of plantation growth. In: *Nutrition of plantations*, edited by G. Bowen and S. Nambiar, 17–52. London: Academic Press.

Forest, W. G. & Ovington, J. D. (1970). Organic matter changes in an age series of *Pinus radiata* plantations. *J. appl. Ecol.*, **7**, 177–186.

Frijters, D. & Lindenmayer, A. (1976). Developmental descriptions of branching patterns with paracladial relationship. In: *Automota languages development*, edited by A. Lindenmayer and G. Rozenberg, 57–73. Amsterdam: North-Holland Publishing.

Hallé, F. (1978). Architectural variation at the specific level in tropical trees. In: *Tropical trees as living systems*, edited by P. B. Tomlinson and M. H. Zimmermann, 209–221. Cambridge: Cambridge University Press.

Hallé, F. & Martin, R. (1968). Etude de la croissance rhythmique chez l'Hevea (*Hevea braziliensis* Mull.-Arg. Euphorbiacae-Crotonoidae). *Adansonia*, **8**, 475–503.

Hallé, F., Oldeman, R. A. A. & Tomlinson, P. B. (1978). *Tropical trees and forests: an architectural analysis.* Berlin: Springer.

Hamilton, G. J. (1969). The dependence of volume increment of individual trees on dominance, crown dimensions and competition. *Forestry*, **42**, 133–144.

Henderson, R., Ford, E. D. & Renshaw, E. (1983). Morphology of the structural root system of Sitka spruce. 2. Computer simulations of rooting patterns. *Forestry*, **56**, 137–153.

Horn, H. S. (1971). *The adaptive geometry of trees.* Princeton, NJ: Princeton University Press.

Horton, R. E. (1945). Erosional development of streams and their drainage basins: hydrophysical approach to quantitative morphology. *Bull. geol. Soc. Am.*, **56**, 275–370.

Isebrands, J. G. (1982). Towards a physiological basis of intensive culture of poplar. *Proc. TAPPI Research and Development Division Conf.*, *1982*, 81–90.

Isebrands, J. G. & Nelson, N. D. (1982). Crown architecture of short rotation, intensively cultured *Populus*. II. Branch morphology and distribution of leaves within the crown of Populus 'Tristis' as related to biomass production. *Can. J. For. Res.*, **12**, 853–864.

Kempf, J. S. & Pickett, S. T. A. (1981). The role of branch length and angle in branching pattern of forest shrubs along a successional gradient. *New Phytol.*, **88**, 111–116.

Kira, T. & Shidei, T. (1967). Primary production and turnover of organic matter in different forest ecosystems of the western Pacific. *Jap. J. Ecol.*, **17**, 70–87.

Labyak, L. F. & Schumaker, F. X. (1954). The contribution of its branches to the main stem growth of loblolly pine. *J. For.*, **52**, 333–337.

Leakey, R. R. B. & Ladipo, D. O. (1985). Selection for improvement in vegetatively-propagated tropical hardwoods. In: *Improvement of vegetatively-propagated plants.* (Proc. Symp. 8th, Long Ashton, England). In press.

Leopold, L. B. (1971). Trees and streams: the efficiency of branching patterns. *J. theor. Biol.*, **31**, 339–354.

Magin, R. (1959). Crown size and increment in multi-storied mixed stands. *Forst- u. Holzwirt.*, **14**, 15.

Matthews, J. A., Feret, P. P., Madgwick, H. A. I. & Bramlett, D. L. (1975). Genetic control of dry matter distribution in twenty half-sib families of Virginia pine. *Proc. Southern Forest Tree Improvement Conf., 13th, Raleigh, NC*, 234–241. Macon, GA: Eastern Tree Seed Laboratory.

McMahon, T. A. & Kronauer, R. E. (1976). Tree structures: deducing the principle of mechanical design. *J. theor. Biol.*, **59**, 443–466.

Motomura, I. (1947). Further notes on the law of geometrical progression in the population density in animal association. *Physiol. Ecol.*, **1**, 55–60.

Nelson, N. D. & Michael, D. (1982). Photosynthesis, leaf conductance and specific leaf weight in long and short shoots of *Populus* 'Tristis no. 1' grown under intensive culture. *Forest Sci.*, **28**, 737–744.

Oker-Blom, P. & Kellomäki, S. (1983). Effect of grouping of foliage on within-stand and within-crown light regime: comparison of random and grouping canopy models. *Agric. Meteorol.*, **28**, 143–155.

Oohata, S. & Shidei, T. (1971). Studies on the branching structure of trees. I. Bifurcation ratio of trees in Horton's Law. *Jap. J. Ecol.*, **21**, 7–14.

Paltridge, G. W. (1973). On the shape of trees. *J. theor. Biol.*, **38**, 111–137.

Pendleton, J. W., Smith, G. E., Winter, S. R. & Johnston, T. J. (1968). Field investigations of the relationships of leaf angle in corn (*Zea mays* L.) to grain yield and apparent photosynthesis. *Agron. J.*, **60**, 422–424.

Phillips, I. D. J. (1975). Apical dominance. *A. Rev. Pl. Physiol.*, **26**, 341–367.

Pickett, S. T. A. & Kempf, J. S. (1980). Branching patterns in forest shrubs and understorey trees in relation to habitat. *New Phytol.*, **86**, 219–228.

Rhodes, I. (1971). The relationship between productivity and some components of canopy structure in ryegrass (*Lolium* spp.). II. Yield, canopy structure and light interception. *J. agric. Sci., Camb.*, **77**, 283–292.

Rozenberg, G. & Lindenmayer, A. (1973). Developmental systems with locally catenative formulas. *Acta Inf.*, **2**, 214–248.

Schulze, E.-D., Fuchs, M. I. & Fuchs, M. (1977a). Spatial distribution of photosynthetic capacity and performance in a mountain spruce forest of northern Germany. I. Biomass distribution and daily CO_2 uptake in different crown layers. *Oecologia*, **29**, 43–61.

Schulze, E.-D., Fuchs, M. & Fuchs, M. I. (1977b). Spatial distribution of photosynthetic capacity and performance in a mountain spruce forest in northern Germany. III. The significance of the evergreen habit. *Oecologia*, **30**, 239–248.

Steingraeber, D. A., Kascht, L. J. & Franck, D. H. (1979). Variation of shoot morphology and bifurcation ratio in sugar maple (*Acer saccharum*) saplings. *Am. J. Bot.*, **66**, 441–445.

Strahler, A. N. (1957). Quantitative analysis of watershed geomorphology. *Trans. Am. Geophys. Un.*, **38**, 913–920.

Trewavas, A. (1981). How do plant growth substances work? *Plant, Cell Environ.*, **4**, 203–228.

Whitney, G. G. (1976). The bifurcation ratio as an indicator of adaptive strategy in woody plant species. *Bull. Torrey bot. Club*, **103**, 67–72.

15

TREES AS PRODUCERS OF EXUDATES AND EXTRACTIVES

J. A. RAVEN
Department of Biological Sciences, University of Dundee, Scotland

I. INTRODUCTION

Man's exploitation of trees has long involved their use as human and animal foods, and as suppliers of timber, fuel and fibres (Howes 1974; Renfrew 1973; West 1977). This paper examines two aspects of this exploitation: the use of naturally occurring, or induced, exudations from trees; and the extraction of particular chemical fractions from detached portions of trees. These two categories overlap, in that substances which exude from trees can also frequently be extracted from detached portions. The consideration of exudates and extractives emphasizes products other than foods and fuels, which are dealt with elsewhere in this volume.

The approach to the 'exudate and extractive' aspect of trees as crop plants which will be adopted here starts by categorizing exudates and extractives chemically, and with respect to their location within the tree. This is followed by consideration of the 'uses' to which the plant puts these products, placing

TABLE I. Chemical constituents of tree extractives and exudates
(from Dell & McComb 1978; Barbier 1979; Harborne 1982; Harrison 1950; Erickson 1976; Friedrich 1976)

Extractive (Ext) or Exudate (Exu)	Occurrence of named constituent in the tree product					
	Carbohydrate	Fatty acids (+esters)	Terpenoids	Flavonoids	Phenolics (& other non-N-aromatics)	Nitrogenous compounds
Xylem sap (spring sap of many temperate deciduous trees) (Exu)	Mono- and di-saccharides	—	—	—	—	Amino-acids Amides Ureides
Phloem sap (from *Fraxinus* spp., many arborescent monocotyledons) (Exu)	Di- and oligo-saccharides	—	—	—	—	Amino-acids Amides
Gums and Mucilages (viscid secretions, exuding naturally or on wounding; soluble in hot or cold water, or forming a gel; insoluble in organic solvents) (Exu)	Acidic poly-saccharides	—	—	—	—	—
Essential Oils (volatile oils recovered from tissue by steam distillation; liquid at ambient temperatures; soluble in organic solvents, immiscible with water) (Ext)	—	Often present (as esters)	Major component	Occasional component (as aglycone; *Populus nigra* buds)	Often present (phenolics; substituted aromatic hydrocarbons)	—
Fatty Oils (not recoverable by steam distillation; liquid at ambient temperatures; soluble in organic solvents, immiscible with water) (Ext)	—	Major component (triglycerides)	—	—	—	—

Latex (colloidal suspension of water-insoluble substances in an aqueous continuous phase; may be released on cutting the plants; typically milky-white) (Exu)	Often present	—	Major component (rubber)	—	eg the proteolytic enzyme ficin
Wax (non-volatile secretion, usually solid at ambient temperatures; insoluble in water, soluble in organic solvents; sometimes harvested in boiling water) (Ext)	—	Major component (long-chain) alcohol esters of long-chain fatty acids; Pentacyclic alkane diols, triterpenes, triglycerides, ketones, aldehydes, may also be present	—	—	—
Resins (non-volatile exudates (external resins) or obtainable by incision or infection (internal resins); insoluble in water, soluble in organic solvents; melt, often at low temperatures, with no sharp melting point) (Exu, Ext)	—	Often major component	Often major component	Often major component	—
Tannins (in vacuoles of living cells, and on walls of dead cells of wood and bark) (Ext)	—	—	—	—	Main component (phenolics and their glycosides)

them into an evolutionary context by pointing out the range of 'non-tree' plants which produce similar compounds. We then turn to the uses to which man has put exudates and extractives, and to the prospects for their use in the future, before presenting some summarizing conclusions.

II. THE CHEMISTRY OF TREE EXUDATES AND EXTRACTIVES

The data summarized in Table I show that tree exudates and extractives are mainly compounds of carbon, hydrogen and oxygen: these substances fulfill their various functions largely without using the potentially growth-limiting element nitrogen, other than in their inheritance and biosynthesis (nucleic acids, proteins). We may categorize these compounds (Table I) as carbohydrates (low M_r,[1] in xylem and phloem sap; polymers in gums and mucilages); derivatives of acetyl units, both straight-chain and isoprenoid derivatives (oils, waxes, rubber); phenolics and other non-nitrogenous aromatic compounds synthesized via the shikimate pathway; the flavonoids, whose two aromatic rings are produced by different pathways (one by the 'normal' shikimate pathway, the other via acetyl units); and the various nitrogenous organic compounds.

The compounds listed in Table I are mainly 'secondary products', that is compounds other than the core of primary metabolites common to all green (in the restricted sense) plants, ie green algae, bryophytes and vascular plants. The exceptions to this generalization are the components of xylem and phloem saps and the fatty oils. It is important to note that the secondary metabolites found in tree exudates and extractives are, in many cases, similar to those found in non-tree vascular plants, and that they have relatively clear biosynthetic relationships to primary metabolites (Bu'lock 1965). The gums and mucilages are similar to the matrix (non-crystalline) components of cell walls; terpenoid secondary products are very similar to terpenoid primary metabolites (eg phytol and carotenoids); the fatty acid and fatty alcohol components of waxes are biosynthetically similar in origin to the fatty acids of polar membrane lipids; and the phenolics are derived from the aromatic amino-acids. In broad chemical terms, it is not easy to find exudates and extractives that are peculiar to trees.

III. LOCATION OF EXUDATES AND EXTRACTIVES WITHIN THE TREE

A. Anatomical scheme

The major criterion used to classify exudates and extractives is whether they are normally found inside or outside living cells. This does not, of course, imply that the compounds found outside living cells were synthesized there:

---

[1] M_r is the relative molecular mass (= molecular weight).

Fahn (1979) discusses the nature of the secretory apparati which are involved in transporting many secondary compounds from their intracellular sites of synthesis to their extracellular sites of storage or activity. Similar considerations apply to the occurrence of extractives in vacuoles and other 'P' phases[2] within the cell: such intracellular spaces are in the same topological relationship to the 'N' phases[2] of cytosol, mitochondrial matrix and plastid stroma as is the extracellular space (also a 'P' phase *sensu* Mitchell 1979).

B. Found within living cells

1. *The vacuoles of relatively unmodified cells*

Matile (1978, 1984) discusses the role of vacuoles in the 'storage' of secondary compounds. Tannins and other phenolics are examples of extractives which are often stored in the vacuole (and invariably in a 'P' phase).

2. *In modified cells: laticifers*

Laticifers are modified cells which ramify through some or all of the plant body in latex-producing plants (Metcalfe 1967; Fahn 1979). 'Articulated' laticifers consist of a number of cells end-to-end, with more or less complete dissolution of the cross-walls (cf sieve tube elements); 'non-articulated' laticifers are single large cells. Laticifers generally grow intrusively between other cells in the plant. The organelle complement of the modified cytoplasm of laticifers frequently includes 'lutoids', 'P' phases with the characteristics of vacuoles or lysosomes (Fahn 1979; Marin *et al.* 1982). Laticifers are turgid and, accordingly, exude latex when injured.

3. *In modified cells: sieve tubes*

Phloem sap is contained in 'super-symplastic' sieve tubes, made up of sieve tube elements in angiosperms, and a few other vascular plants, and of sieve cells in most non-angiosperm vascular plants (Canny 1973; Raven 1977a,b). The high concentrations of sugar alcohol or oligosaccharides (10^4 mol $C m^{-3}$: see Passioura 1976; Lang 1978) in the phloem sap lead to a substantial net C flux along the phloem (some 5 mol C (m^2 sieve tube trans-sectional area)$^{-1}$ s^{-1}), assuming the observed velocity of mass flow of 0·5 mm s^{-1}. Phloem sap also contains nitrogenous and inorganic solutes at lower concentrations than the sugar derivatives.

Phloem differs from laticifers in the nature of the cytoplasmic constituents, and in the occurrence of flow: while laticifers seem to show mass flow only after injury, flow occurs in intact sieve tubes, although it may be hastened by

---

[2] The 'N' and 'P' terminology to categorize intracellular, membrane-bounded compartments was introduced by Mitchell (1979). The basis for the terminology is the electrical potential difference generated by primary active cation (H$^+$, Na$^+$, Ca^{2+}) transporters: such transport renders the 'N' phases electrically negative relative to the 'P' phase, 'N' signifying negative and 'P' indicating positive. 'N' phases have functional nucleic acids, contain a high concentration of protein with hundreds or thousands of different protein species, and have ADP-phosphorylating and ATP-dephosphorylating systems. 'P' phases have a much lower diversity of proteins, lack functional nucleic acids, and cannot phosphorlylate ADP.

injury, provided sealing phenomena do not come into operation (Eschrich 1975; Fisher 1983).

C. Found outside living cells

1. *Within the plant*

(a) *In or on cell walls.* Tannins can occur in or on the walls of dead cells in xylem and bark.

(b) *In lysigenous cavities.* Lysigenous cavities within plants develop primarily by the dissolution of cells, rather than by the separation of cells. Tracheids and vessels in the xylem retain lignified, compression-resistant walls; and mucilage, gum and (in *Eucalyptus* spp.) 'kino' ducts generally have the cell walls torn apart or enzymically removed (Fahn 1979). Lysigenous ducts generally contain hydrophilic polysaccharides in mucilage ducts.

The xylem is generally under tension in a transpiring tree (Pickard 1981), making it difficult to extract the sap (eg Ferguson *et al.* 1983). Furthermore, the concentration of organic solutes in the xylem sap of transpiring plants is generally low, being in the order of $10 \, mol \, m^{-3}$ (see Raven 1983). Positive pressure can occur in tree xylem; it may result from classical 'root pressure' in both conifers and angiosperms (White *et al.* 1958; Davis 1961), but, in terms of extractives, the more important phenomenon is the one responsible for the exudation of a sugary solution from wounds in various north-temperate deciduous trees in the early spring. This mechanism (Tyree 1983) is related to gas behaviour in the xylem when freezing at night alternates with warmer daytime conditions; the sugar and other organic components would, in the unmolested tree, be used for the spring flush of growth (Essiamah 1980).

Mucilage ducts and cavities are constitutive in, for example, the Malvales; traumatic gum ducts are found in the Rosaceae/Prunoideae, and (as 'kino' ducts which also contain polyphenols) in some species of *Eucalyptus* (Fahn 1979).

(c) *In schizogenous cavities.* Schizogenous cavities within plants develop primarily by separation of cells, rather than by dissolution of cells. Examples are the protoxylem canals (= carinal canals of *Equisetum*) formed when the earliest-formed xylem is torn apart by continued elongation of the plant axis; resin ducts; essential oil ducts and cavities; and most of the intercellular gas spaces of vascular plants and bryophytes (Fahn 1979; Sifton 1945, 1957; Roland 1978).

The protoxylem (carinal) canals of *Equisetum* have been shown to function in transpiratory water movement (Bierhorst 1958); the extent to which they can operate under tension is unclear in view of the absence of a compression-resistant wall (Raven 1983). The solute content of such canals is probably similar to that of the xylem of the same plant.

Resin ducts are common in the Pinaceae and the Leguminoseae; the constitutive or traumatic nature of the ducts is variable between genera of the conifers (Fahn 1979).

Essential oil ducts and cavities are present, for example, in the leaves of *Eucalyptus* spp. (Fahn 1979).

(d) *Some conclusions.*   Insofar as generalizations are possible, it would appear that lysigenous cavities most commonly have hydrophilic contents (dilute aqueous solutions in xylem; hydrophilic polysaccharides in mucilage and gum ducts), while schizogenous cavities generally have hydrophobic contents (resin and essential oils; gases, whose presence, under conditions in which cell wall water is not under tension, demands a relatively hydrophobic cell wall surface).

2.   *Outside the plant* (the *plant* surface)

(a) *Waxes.*   It is likely that all *external* cuticle of vascular plants has some wax on its surface (Juniper & Jeffree 1983). Wax is secreted by epidermal cells through the cuticle rather than via special glands (Fahn 1979; Dell & McComb 1978).

(b) *Surface resins.*   These external resins are generally produced by special glands (Fahn 1979; Dell & McComb 1978), analogous to the secretory cells which line the internal resin ducts (see C.1.c above).

(c) *Externalization of products which were originally secreted within the plant.*   The waxes and external resins mentioned above are elaborated by the surface cells of the plant, and are secreted across the plasmalemma of these cells. Many other secondary compounds which are secreted across the plasmalemma of cells within the plant body (internal resins; mucilages) or are contained within specialized cell systems (latex) reach the plant surface, expecially as a result of damage to the plant.

IV.   THE FUNCTIONS OF EXUDATES AND EXTRACTIVES IN TREES

This section is bound to be less rigorous than other parts of the paper, because it is very difficult to establish the role of secondary plant products with the same certitude as attaches, for instance, to the assertion that chlorophyll is essential for photosynthesis. Even if a possible role can be established (eg by demonstrating that a natural product is toxic to phytophages), there remains much complex experimentation to be carried out before it can be shown that the natural product is adaptive in the sense of conferring a selective advantage to the tree in its natural habitat. Osmond *et al.* (1980) point out that a comparison of the fitness (reproductive success) of different genotypes in the same environment is necessary in order to establish that a trait, present in some genotypes but not in others, is selectively advantageous, and even then the results are not immediately transferable to performance in other environments. The generation time of trees is such that they are not ideal experimental material for such investigations. However, it is useful to consider likely functions of secondary metabolites in trees, in order to give some idea of the effects on tree performance of increasing the production of some useful metabolite, or of reducing the production of some undesirable secondary metabolite (eg from the point of view of pulp production).

A.   Modifiers of the physical and chemical environment

1.   Modifications which may be desirable

We may envisage that modifications to the physicochemical environment of the plant could be of some selective advantage, if they enhance its capacity (a) to acquire scarce, growth-limiting resources, (b) to limit the acquisition of resources present in potentially damaging excess, (c) to conserve scarce resources which are already within the plant, and (d) to moderate the effect on the plant of environments which may lead to extremes of plant temperature.

2.   Modifications of the light environment

The effect of exudates here is largely one of *decreasing* the absorption of light in environments with very high photon flux densities, thereby lessening (a) the possibility of photo-inhibition of photosynthesis (Osmond 1981), (b) damaging increases in leaf temperature, and (c) the amount of water transpired per unit carbon fixed (Farquhar & Sharkey 1982). While waxes are most generally thought of in the context of exudates which increase leaf reflectance, resins may also fulfill this important role in some arid zone woody plants (Dell & McComb 1978). Extractives may have a role in absorbing potentially damaging ultraviolet light before it can be absorbed by more sensitive plant components (Caldwell 1979). Exudates and extractives do not appear to have a well-defined positive role in enhancing acquisition of light in low-light environments, for instance within or below the main tree canopy.

3.   Modification of water relations

Enhanced light reflectance can improve the water use efficiency of plants in high photon flux density environments by reducing (a) photo- and thermal inhibition of photosynthesis, and (b) transpiration at a given stomatal conductance. Wax (and resin?) may also serve to reduce cuticular water loss by improving the waterproofing of the leaf. Schönherr and Merida (1981) showed that the water permeability of monolayers of fatty alcohols was *halved* for each ($-CH_2-CH_2-$) unit added in the range $C_{16}-C_{22}$, so that a monolayer of the C_{22} alcohol had as low a water permeability as eight monolayers of C_{16} alcohol in series. This important work confirmed the the *composition* of the wax layer, rather than the quantity per unit area of plant surface, was of great significance for waterproofing plants, and helped to explain why many of the aliphatic components of plant waxes have such long chain-lengths (Juniper & Jeffree 1983).

4.   Modification of nutrient relations

There is a substantial body of evidence showing that nutrient losses (by leaching) from leaves of plants of nutrient-poor environments are lower than those from leaves of plants of nutrient-rich environments, and that this fact is attributable to a difference in the thickness of their cuticles and wax layers (Chapin 1980). In addition to decreasing the permeability of the plant surface to nutrient solutes, surface wax (and resin) may also increase runoff of water (water-repellency, *sensu* Crisp 1963), thus decreasing the time over which surface water is present to act as a sink for nutrient leakage. Runoff of surface water is also important in terms of increasing the potential to acquire the nutrient carbon dioxide (see Raven 1977b).

5. Modification of thermal relations

We have already seen that reflection of very high photon flux densities by exudates can have important effects on leaf temperature. At the other extreme of temperature in the plant habitat, Juniper and Jeffree (1983) point out that water-repellency may, by removing surface water, improve frost resistance in glaucous ecotypes of *Eucalyptus* species. If surface water does remain, frost resistance may be increased by the secretion of antifreeze compounds into this water (eg the afro-alpine *Lobelia keniensis*: see Juniper & Jeffree 1983).

An extreme aspect of the thermal environment is fire. While tree exudates and extractives are probably not very important in *protecting* (by insulating) the organism from the effects of fire, they may be important fuel for fires. Essential oils are present in relatively high concentrations in the atmosphere around many woody plants of arid and sub-arid regions (Juniper & Jeffree 1983), forming explosive mixtures, and the oils still present in the leaves render them more flammable. It is likely that many of the woody (and grassland) communities of seasonally dry habitats (comprised of fire-resistant plants which are also fire-promoters) owe their existence to fires, which prevent the growth of other plants which are less fire-resistant and fire-promoting, but which might out-compete the 'fire' plants in the absence of fairly frequent fires (Mutch 1970; Gill et al. 1981). Could it be that drops of exuded gum or resin act as spherical lenses which ignite dead leaves or bark? It would seem that today's fire-dominated communities of eucalypts and pines (Mutch 1970) could have had analogues at least as far back as the lower Carboniferous, not long after the woody habit evolved in the middle and upper Devonian (Cope & Chaloner 1980; see also Section IV.B.2).

B. Modifiers of the interaction between trees and other biota

1. Modifications which may be desirable

We may envisage that modifications of biotic interactions would be selectively advantageous if they (a) reduced competition with other phototrophs for scarce resources, (b) decreased the extent to which trees were consumed by biophages, unless these were of benefit to the tree (eg mycorrhizal fungi increasing P uptake; rhizobial or actinorhizal associations fixing atmospheric N_2), or (c) modified the activities of necrophages and chemolithotrophs (eg by decreasing the rate of nitrification, thus making ammonium available to the tree).

2. Modification of competition with other phototrophs

The role of exudates and extractives in maintaining fire-dependent woody communities has already been mentioned. The significance of allelopathy, that is the inhibition of growth of a phototroph by exudates or extractives from another phototroph, is still a matter of dispute (Harborne 1982; Newman 1978).

3. *Modification of biophagy*

A major role for secondary plant products as regulators of phytophagy now has widespread support (Rosenthal & Janzen 1979; Harborne 1982). Trees whose 'apparency' (longevity and size) is high, would appear to be particularly at risk from phytophages: however, any cost-benefit analysis of investment of resources in chemical defences must take into account, not only the likelihood of loss of biomass to phytophages in an 'undefended' plant, but also the cost of the defence system in relation to the cost of replacing the lost biomass from scarce resources. If nitrogen is the limiting resource for a tree's growth, and also the nutrient most sought by phytophages, then defence of plant nitrogen with mainly non-nitrogen-containing compounds might well be advantageous in a cost-benefit analysis.

Dell and McComb (1978) recently reviewed the data on antiphytophage activity of internal resins, and concluded that the evidence is most convincing for an anti-insect role for resins: evidence relating to an antifungal or anti-bacterial role is more equivocal. The finding that the production of gum, mucilage, resin and latex is often increased after phytophage (or even mechanical) damage to trees, is consistent with a defence role for these compounds (Dell & McComb 1979; Rosenthal & Janzen 1979; Fahn 1979; Harborne 1982). Recent data (Baldwin & Schultz 1983) show that volatile pheromones, evolved by a wounded tree, can induce the synthesis of putative defence compounds in neighbouring, undamaged trees of the same species. This apparently altruistic behaviour among trees may help to limit overall biophage populations, and hence benefit the tree that issues the warning in the long run. Juniper and Jeffree (1983) discuss the effects of surface wax on biophagy by fungi and insects, and suggest that, while a water-repellent surface is generally a more effective barrier to biophagy than a less water-repellent surface, this effect is not universal.

Turning to the interaction of trees with *beneficial* biophages, we find that the micro-organisms concerned (*Rhizobium* and *Frankia* related to N_2 fixation; *Glomus* and various basidiomycetous fungi associated with enhanced acquisition of P and other nutrients) only infect subterranean plant organs (Raven 1983; Nadkarni 1981). These parts of trees are poorly endowed with such exudates (secretions) as waxes and external resins. This may render infection by the symbiotic organisms easier than would be the case for the better protected aerial parts of the plant: but, alas, this argument also applies to parasitic and grazing biophages! A role for exudates in attracting the symbionts to the plant surface cannot be ruled out at present (Smith & Walker 1981; Walker & Smith 1984), while extractives (eg tannins) may function in delimiting the fraction of the tree's tissue which is accessible to the symbiont (Harley & Smith 1983). Mycorrhizal infection (*Glomus*) of the guayale shrub (*Parthenium argentatum*) increases the latex content, but not the resin content, of the biomass relative to the content of non-mycorrhizal plants (Bloss & Pfeiffer 1984). The explanation of this finding may be significant for latex production.

4. *Modification of the activities of necrophages and chemolithotrophs*

The only point which will be made here relates to the effect of phenolic extractives on the activities of the chemolithotrophic bacteria, which convert the ammonium released by necrotrophs into nitrate. Rice and Pancholy (1972, 1973, 1974) and Rice (1974) have shown that the activities of these nitrifying bacteria (*Nitrosomonas* and *Nitrobacter*) are more inhibited by phenolics than are the necrophages which regenerate ammonium from dead plant (and other organic) material, or the plants which reconvert inorganic nitrogen (ammonium or nitrate) into organic nitrogen in the plant. Accordingly, the occurrence of plant-derived phenolics in 'climax' communities, particularly forests, can short-circuit the nitrification-nitrate assimilation parts of the nitrogen cycle, thus lessening the possibility of leaching nitrogen as nitrate, and eliminating the energy (and, indirectly, water) costs of nitrate assimilation as compared to ammonium assimilation by the plant (Raven 1984a).

C. Phylogeny of exudates and extractives

1. *Taxonomic distribution*

We have already seen (Section II) that the exudates and extractives produced by trees are biosynthetically related to secondary products in other plants, and to the primary metabolic 'core' of phototrophs. The secondary metabolites which are related to tree exudates and extractives have a variety of apparent 'uses' to the plant, some of which differ from the 'uses' of exudates and extractives of trees outlined above. *Xylem* and *phloem* saps appear to have similar functions in all vascular plants. Xylem sap is analogous to the hydrome sap of bryophytes; phloem sap is analogous to the leptome sap of bryophytes and the sap of the phloem-type tissue of many of the larger brown algae (Raven 1977b, 1984b). *Mucilages* are found in many plants: Boney (1981) has succinctly discussed the multitudinous functions of algal mucilages. *Essential oils* are found in many herbaceous vascular plants where, in animal-pollinated herbs as in animal-pollinated trees, they may attract pollinators (Harborne 1982). *Fatty oils* function as food reserves in a very wide range of plants. *Latex* is found in many non-tree vascular plants, including the heterosporous aquatic fern *Regnellidium* (Labouriau 1952); its function in these plants is presumably (as in trees) that of chemical defence (Metcalfe 1967). *Waxes* are found on the surfaces of essentially all terrestrial vascular plants. Non-vascular eukaryotic phototrophs can also produce true waxes (ie long-chain fatty acid esters of long-chain fatty alcohols, as opposed to solid triglycerides). *Euglena* wax functions as an energy and carbon reserve, which is mobilized during dark starvation, or in 'de-etiolation' of chemo-organotrophically grown cells (Rosenberg 1963, 1967; Guehler *et al.* 1964; Rosenberg & Pecker 1964), and as a non-toxic and re-usable fermentation product (Inui *et al.* 1982). *Resins* are found in herbaceous (eg Apiaceae) flowering plants as well as in woody vascular plants (Howes 1974): surface resins are probably commoner in woody plants (particularly those of arid regions) than in herbaceous plants (Dell & McComb 1978).

2. *Evolutionary origin and significance of exudates and extractives*

Here we confine our attention to the secondary plant metabolites.

Gums and mucilages, like other extracellular polysaccharides, may have had their origin in the glycosyl residues on those portions of integral membrane proteins which protrude at the 'P' side of the membrane (the extracellular, apoplastic phase in the case of the plasmalemma). In many lines of phototroph (eg at least thrice in the green algae: Domozych *et al.* 1980) there has been parallel evolution of a plant-type, pressure-resistant cell wall from 'glycocalyx-like' extracellular polysaccharides. Gums and mucilages are related to the matrix, non-crystalline components of these wall polysaccharides (Boney 1981). Among the functions of cell walls in general, and algal mucilages in particular, is protection against phytophages: this is also an important function of tree gums and mucilages.

Essential oils and *latex* contain terpenoids which are biosynthetically related to a range of primary metabolites. An early antibiophage role for terpenoid derivatives may be seen in sporopollenin, a polymerized terpenoid found in pollen and spore walls of bryophytes and tracheophytes, and as an antiphytophage component in the cell walls of some algae, both extant (Gunnison & Alexander 1975) and fossil (350 million years old: Brook & Shaw 1971).

Waxes (long-chain fatty acid esters of long-chain fatty acids) are found internally in some non-vascular phototrophs: the functions of *Euglena* internal wax were discussed in Section IV.D.1. Waxes are also found in chemo-organotrophic prokaryotes and animals (Gurr & James 1971). On terrestrial plants, and on insects, surface waxes have important water-repelling and water-resisting functions (Hadley 1981).

Resins and *tannins*, inasmuch as they contain phenolics, have parallels as antibiophage agents in algae, both as 'exudates' (wall components: Gunnison & Alexander 1975) and as 'extractives' (in vacuoles: Lobban & Wynne 1981). Phenolics may also have been more important in absorbing ultraviolet light, at or near the surface of plants, in times past, when the ultraviolet photon flux density at the earth's surface was greater than it is today, because there was then a less effective ozone shield (Lowry *et al.* 1980, 1983; Swain & Cooper-Driver 1981). Resin ducts have a well-documented fossil history in the conifers. The conifers and their ancestors in Carboniferous, Permian and Triassic strata lacked resin ducts: such ducts are found in some fossil conifer woods from the Jurassic onwards (Jain 1976), and fossil resin (amber) from both conifers and leguminous trees is known (Fahn 1979). Tannins are commoner in 'woodey' than in 'herbaceous' angiosperms, and are also important chemical defence compounds in the 'lower' vascular plants (see Table 5.9 of Harbourne 1982).

D. Conclusions

It is clear from the foregoing that even single chemically defined groups of exudates or extractives can have a multiplicity of effects on the ecology of a tree, and that modifying the quantity or quality of exudates or extractives produced by a tree is likely to have substantial, and largely unpredictable, effects on its growth and pest resistance.

V. USES TO WHICH MAN HAS PUT TREE EXUDATES AND EXTRACTIVES

This summary of the uses to which exudates and extractives have been put by man is based on the compilations by Howes (1974), Erickson (1976), Friedrich (1976), Dell and McComb (1978) and Wang and Huffman (1981).

Xylem and phloem saps are used as sources of food, and may also be used medicinally. *Gums and mucilages* have found a wide range of uses in the food industry as a base for lozenges (eg gum arabic), and as a smoothing agent in ice cream (eg gum tragacanth). Gum arabic is also used as an adhesive, in medicine, and in inks and water colours. *Essential oils* have been used mainly in flavouring, perfumery and medicine. *Fatty oils* have found uses as foods, and industrially as coatings, plasticizers, and lubricants. *Latex* has been used in the food industry and in rubber production. *Waxes* have found uses as coating and lubricants. *Resins* have yielded commercially important coatings. *Tannins* have been used in tanning leather and in drilling oil wells.

There has also been an increased interest in the use of many of these categories of exudates and extractives as substrates (feedstocks) for chemical industries, and as fuels.

For comparison with Section IV, we note that many of the uses to which man has put tree exudates and extractives are related to the 'uses' of these components in plants. Thus, the transport saps (xylem and phloem) and fatty oils are used as 'foods' by the plant as well as by man; the various exudates and extractives, used as coatings by man, also have protective functions in the plant which produced them; tannins (and other polyphenols) have protein-denaturing functions (digestibility reduction) in the plant, which parallels their use in tanning leather; and the flavouring and perfumery uses of essential oils recall their use by plants as animal attractants.

VI. PROSPECTS FOR THE FUTURE OF TREE EXUDATES AND EXTRACTIVES

The first eight decades of the twentieth century have seen increased replacement of tree exudates and extractives by petroleum-based chemicals. For instance, petroleum 'waxes' (hydrocarbons) have been replacing, or extending, the use of vegetable waxes, and synthetic rubber has been replacing natural rubber. Furthermore, petrochemicals have been used in the production of such commodities as plastics, which have uses not covered by tree exudates and extractives. The economics of the use of petrochemicals are now such that alternative chemical feedstocks are being sought, and there is renewed interest in 'botanochemicals' (including, but not limited to, exudates and extractives from trees). We shall, accordingly, deal with the extent to which botanochemicals can replace petrochemicals as chemical feedstocks, as well as consider the potential for increasing yields of tree exudates and extractives.

A. Botanochemicals: tree exudates and extractives as chemical feedstocks

Figure 1 indicates the routes which may be taken from plant constituents, and from petroleum, to various commercial products. It will be seen that there are feasible paths from major plant constituents to all of the major groups of petroleum-derived chemicals and that, with the exception of the polymers (plastics etc), there are relatively direct routes from exudates and extractives to the otherwise petroleum-derived products. Notably absent from Figure 1 are dollars per tonne values appended to the arrows leading to the end products from plants and from petroleum.

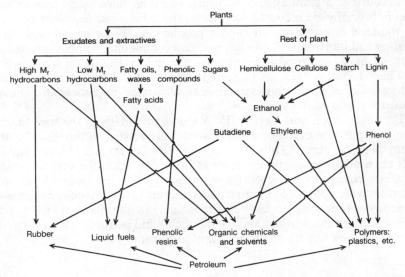

FIGURE 1. Plants and petroleum as sources of commercially important products (modified from Wang & Huffman 1981).

B. Possibilities for increasing yield

The yield of extractives and exudates can be quite high. Simmonds (1982) quotes a mean value of 3.7 kg latex tree^{-1} yr^{-1} from seven *Hevea brasiliensis* clones, whose net biomass increase was 35.8 kg wood tree^{-1} yr^{-1}, while Dell and McComb (1978) show that up to 30% of the leaf dry weight of West Australian woody plant leaves can be surface resin. In analysing the partitioning of photosynthate between wood and rubber in *Hevea*, Simmonds (1982) considers untapped trees whose annual net biomass increase is W_p tonnes of wood per hectare. Tapping rubber from these trees decreases their ability to produce biomass as a result of diversion of assimilate toward rubber and other components removed in the latex, so that the new net biomass increase W (tonne wood ha^{-1}yr^{-1}) is given by:

$$W = W_p(1-k)$$

where k is a constant defined by kW_p (the decrement of wood production attendant on tapping rubber). Simmonds (1982, his Table 1) shows that k typically has a value of about 0·5: that is, a tapped tree has only half the wood increment per year of an untapped tree. The decrement in wood production is related to rubber production as follows,

$$R = kcW_p$$

where R is the rubber yield (tonne ha^{-1}yr^{-1}) and c is a constant, which is essentially the ratio 'synthetic efficiency of rubber production/synthetic efficiency of wood production'; both of the synthetic efficiencies have the units g product (g photosynthate consumed)$^{-1}$ (see Penning de Vries et al. 1974; Penning de Vries 1975). Enhanced rubber yields can be attained by increasing W_p, k or c. Simmonds (1982) points out that the methods available for estimating c include non-rubber components in the latex in the denominator, but not in the numerator (of the definition of c), leading to 'low' c values in the range 0·08–0·13. However, c also includes the effect which the diversion of photosynthates from wood (and foliage) production to latex production has on the capacity for photosynthesis (see Cannell, this volume). The reason for calling the c value 'low' can be seen if we look at the value of c derived from a consideration of biochemical pathways. Following Penning de Vries (1975), 1 g of glucose substrate yields 0·83 g carbohydrate, or 0·47 g lignin, or 0·33 g lipid (including terpenoids such as rubber). For a tree whose wood is half polysaccharide and half lignin, we would predict a c value of 0·51 (ignoring effects of latex removal on tree photosynthetic capacity). Simmonds (1982) points out that more rigorously controlled investigations are needed to define W_p, k and c so that these components of rubber yield (R) can be tackled by rubber breeders (Borlaug 1983; Farnum et al. 1983; Sheppard et al. 1983).

VII. CONCLUSIONS

Tree exudates and extractives have been used by man since before the Neolithic Revolution, which saw the advent of plant and animal domestication. The uses to which the human race has put these tree products have, in general terms, paralleled the uses which plants make of them. Increasing the yield of exudates and extractives to provide 'botanochemicals' as a supplement to, or replacement for, 'petrochemicals' requires more knowledge of the botany of the trees concerned. Whether such improvement is worthwhile is a matter which must be decided in relation to the costs of petrochemicals, and alternative calls (eg for food production) for the resources (land, manpower, fertilizers, pesticides, etc) which are needed to produce botanochemicals from tree exudates and extractives.

ACKNOWLEDGEMENTS

Many of my colleagues in Dundee have helped me to formulate whatever may be construed as novel in this paper: I hereby thank them. Dr M. G. R. Cannell has helped in many ways to improve the text.

REFERENCES

Baldwin, I. T. & Schultz, J. C. (1983). Rapid changes in tree leaf chemistry induced by damage: evidence for communication between plants. *Science, N.Y.*, **221**, 277–279.
Barbier, M. (1979). *Introduction to chemical ecology.* London: Longman.
Bierhorst, D. W. (1958). Vessels in *Equisetum. Am. J. Bot.*, **45**, 534–537.
Bloss, H. E. & Pfeiffer, C. M. (1984). Latex content and biomass increase in mycorrhizal guayale (*Parthenium argentatum*) under field conditions. *Ann. appl. Biol.*, **104**, 175–183.
Boney, A. D. (1981). Mucilage: the universal algal attribute. *Br. phycol. J.*, **16**, 115–132.
Borlaug, N. E. (1983). Contributions of conventional plant breeding to food production. *Science, N.Y.*, **219**, 689–693.
Brook, J. & Shaw, G. (1971). Recent development in the chemistry, biochemistry, geochemistry and post-tetrad ontogeny of sporopollenins derived from pollen and spore exines. In: *Pollen: development and physiology*, edited by J. Heslop-Harrison, 99–114. London: Butterworth.
Bu'lock, J. D. (1965). *The biosynthesis of natural products.* London: McGraw-Hill.
Caldwell, M. M. (1979). Plant life and U.V. radiation: some perspectives in the history of the earth's U.V. climate. *BioScience*, **29**, 520–525.
Canny, M. J. (1973). *Phloem translocation.* Cambridge: Cambridge University Press.
Chapin, F. S. III. (1980). The mineral nutrition of wild plants. *Annu. Rev. Ecol. Syst.*, **11**, 233–260.
Cope, M. J. & Chaloner, W. G. (1980). Fossil charcoal as evidence of past atmospheric composition. *Nature, Lond.*, **283**, 647–649.
Crisp, D. J. (1963). Waterproofing mechanisms in animals and plants. In: *Waterproofing and water-repellancy*, edited by J. L. Moilliet, 416–481. Amsterdam: Elsevier.
Davis, T. A. (1961). High root-pressures in palms. *Nature, Lond.*, **192**, 277–278.
Dell, B. & McComb, A. J. (1978). Plant resins – their formation, secretion and possible function. *Adv. bot. Res.*, **6**, 277–316.
Domozych, D. S., Stewart K. D. & Mattox, R. (1980). The comparative aspects to cell wall chemistry in the green algae (Chlorophyta). *J. mol. Evol.*, **15**, 1–12.
Erickson, R. E. (1976). The industrial importance of monoterpenes and essential oils. *Lloydia*, **39**, 8–19.
Eschrich, W. (1975). Sealing mechanisms. In: *Transport in plants. 1. Phloem transport*, edited by M. H. Zimmermann and J. A. Milburn, 39–56. (Encyclopedia of plant physiology, n.s. vol. 1). Berlin: Springer.
Essiamah, S. K. (1980). Spring sap of trees. *Ber. dt. bot. Ges.*, **93**, 257–267.
Fahn, A. (1979). *Secretory tissues in plants.* London: Academic Press.
Farnum, P., Timmis, R. & Kulp, J. L. (1983). Biotechnology of forest yield. *Science, N.Y.*, **219**, 694–702.
Farquhar, G. D. & Sharkey, T. D. (1982). Stomatal conductance and photosynthesis. *A. Rev. Pl. Physiol.*, **33**, 317–345.
Ferguson, A. R., Eiseman, J. A. & Leonard, J. A. (1983). Xylem sap from *Actinidia chinensis*: seasonal changes in composition. *Ann. Bot.*, **51**, 823–833.
Fisher, D. B. (1983). Year-round collection of willow sieve-tube exudate. *Planta*, **159**, 529–533.
Friedrich, H. (1976). Phenylpropanoid constituents of essential oils. *Lloydia*, **39**, 1–7.
Gill, A. M., Groves, R. H. & Noble, I. R., eds. (1981). *Fire and the Australian biota.* Canberra: Australian Academy of Sciences.
Guehler, P. F., Peterson, L., Tsuchiya, H. M. & Dodson, R. M. (1964). Microbiological transformations. XII. Composition of the wax made by *Euglena gracilis. Archs Biochem. Biophys.*, **106**, 294–298.
Gunnison, D. & Alexander, M. (1975). Basis for the resistance of several algae to microbial decomposition. *Appl. Microbiol.*, **29**, 729–738.

Gurr, M. I. & James, A. T. (1971). *Lipid biochemistry: an introduction.* London: Chapman & Hall.

Hadley, N. F. (1981). Cuticular lipids of terrestrial plants and arthropods: a comparison of their structure, composition and water proofing function. *Biol. Rev.*, **56**, 23–47.

Harborne, J. B. (1982). *Introduction to ecological biochemistry.* 2nd ed. London: Academic Press.

Harley, J. C. & Smith, S. E. (1983). *Mycorrhizal symbiosis.* London: Academic Press.

Harrison, S. G. (1950). Manna and its sources. *Kew Bull.*, **5**, 407–417.

Howes, F. N. (1974). *A dictionary of useful and everyday plants and their common names.* Cambridge: Cambridge University Press.

Inui, H., Miyatako, K., Nakano, Y. & Kitaoka, S. (1982). Wax ester fermentation in *Euglena gracilis. FEBS Lett.*, **150**, 89–93.

Jain, K. K. (1976). The evolution of wood structure in the Pinaceae. *Israel J. Bot.*, **25**, 28–33.

Juniper, B. E. & Jeffree, C. E. (1983). *Plant surfaces.* London: Edward Arnold.

Labouriau, J. G. (1952). *Regnellidium diphyllum* Lindm., a lactescent fern. *Revta bras. Biol.*, **12**, 181–183.

Lang, A. (1978). A model of mass flow in the phloem. *Aust. J. Plant Physiol.*, **5**, 535–546.

Lobban, C. S. & Wynne, M. J., eds. (1981). *The biology of seaweeds.* Oxford: Blackwell Scientific.

Lowry, J. B., Lee, D. W. & Hébant, C. (1980). The origin of land plants: a new look at an old problem. *Taxon*, **29**, 183–197.

Lowry, J. B., Lee, D. W. & Hébant, C. (1983). The origin of land plants: a reply to Swain. *Taxon*, **32**, 101–103.

Marin, B., Crétin, H. & d'Auzac, J. (1982). Energization of solute transport and accumulation at the tonoplast in *Hevea* latex. *Physiol. Vég.*, **20**, 333–346.

Matile, P. (1978). Biochemistry and function of vacuoles. *A. Rev. Pl. Physiol.*, **29**, 193–213.

Matile, P. (1984). Das toxische Kompartiment der Pflanzenzelle. *Naturwissenschaften*, **71**, 18–24.

Metcalfe, C. R. (1967). Distribution of latex in the plant kingdom. *Econ. Bot.*, **21**, 115–127.

Mitchell, P. (1979). Direct chemiosmotic ligand conduction mechanisms in proton motive complexes. In: *Membrane bioenergetics*, edited by C. P. Lee *et al.*, 361–372. Reading, MA: Addison-Wesley.

Mutch, R. W. (1970). Wildland fires and ecosystems – a hypothesis. *Ecology*, **51**, 1046–1051.

Nadkarni, N. M. (1981). Canopy roots; convergent evolution in rainforest nutrient cycles. *Science, N.Y.*, **214**, 1023–1024.

Newman, E. I. (1978). Allelopathy: adaptation or accident? In: *Biochemical aspects of plant and animal coevolution*, edited by J. B. Harborne, 328 342. London: Academic Press.

Osmond, C. B. (1981). Photorespiration and photoinhibition. Some implications for the energetics of photosynthesis. *Biochim. biophys. Acta*, **639**, 77–98.

Osmond, C. B., Björkman, O. & Anderson, D. J. (1980). *Physiological processes in plant ecology: toward a synthesis with* Atriplex. Berlin: Springer.

Passioura, J. B. (1976). Translocation and the diffusion equation. In: *Transport and transfer processes in plants*, edited by I. F. Wardlaw and J. B. Passioura, 357–361. New York: Academic Press.

Penning de Vries, F. W. T. (1975). Use of assimilates in higher plants. In: *Photosynthesis and productivity in different environments*, edited by J. P. Cooper, 459–480. Cambridge: Cambridge University Press.

Penning de Vries, F. W. T., Brunsting, A. M. M. & Van Laar, M. M. (1974). Products, requirements and efficiency of photosynthesis: a quantitative approach. *J. theor. Biol.*, **45**, 339–377.

Pickard, W. F. (1981). The ascent of sap in plants. *Prog. biophys. mol. Biol.*, **37**, 181–229.

Raven, J. A. (1977a). H^+ and Ca^{2+} in phloem and symplast: relation of relative immobility of the ions to the cytoplasmic nature of the transport paths. *New Phytol.*, **79**, 465–480.

Raven, J. A. (1977b). The evolution of vascular land plants in relation to supracellular transport processes. *Adv. bot. Res.*, **5**, 153–219.

Raven, J. A. (1983). Phytophages of xylem and phloem: a comparison of animal and plant sap-feeders. *Adv. ecol. Res.*, **13**, 135–234.

Raven, J. A. (1984a). The role of membranes in pH regulation: implications for energetics and water use efficiency of higher plant growth with nitrate as nitrogen source. In: *Annual proceedings of the Phytochemical Society of Europe*, vol. 24, edited by A. Baudet, 89–98. Oxford: Oxford University Press.

Raven, J. A. (1984b). *Energetics and transport in aquatic plants.* New York: Liss.

Renfrew, J. M. (1973). *Palaeoethnobotany.* London: Methuen.

Rice, E. L. (1974). *Allelopathy.* New York: Academic Press.

Rice, E. L. & Pancholy, S. K. (1972). Inhibition of nitrification by climax ecosystems. *Am. J. Bot.,* **59,** 1033–1040.

Rice, E. L. & Pancholy, S. K. (1973). Inhibition of nitrification by climax ecosystems. II. Additional evidence and possible role of tannins. *Am. J. Bot.,* **60,** 691–702.

Rice, E. L. & Pancholy, S. K. (1974). Inhibition of nitrification by climax ecosystems. III. Inhibitors other than tannins. *Am. J. Bot.,* **61,** 1095–1103.

Roland, J. C. (1978). Cell wall differentiation and stages involved with intercellular air space opening. *J. Cell Sci.,* **32,** 325–336.

Rosenberg, A. A. (1963). A comparison of lipid patterns in photosynthesising and non-photosynthesising cells of *Euglena gracilis. Biochemistry,* **2,** 1148–1154.

Rosenberg, A. (1967). *Euglena gracilis*: a novel lipid energy reserve and arachidonic acid enrichment during fasting. *Science, N.Y.,* **157,** 1189–1191.

Rosenberg, A. & Pecker, M. (1964). Lipid alterations in *Euglena gracilis* cells during light-induced greening. *Biochemistry,* **3,** 254–258.

Rosenthal, G. A. & Janzen, D. H., eds. (1979). *Herbivores: their interaction with secondary plant metabolites.* New York: Academic Press.

Schönherr, J. & Merida, T. (1981). Water permeability of plant cuticular membranes: the effects of humidity and temperature on the permeability of non-isolated cuticles of onion bulb scales. *Plant, Cell Environ.,* **4,** 349–354.

Sheppard, J. F., Bidney T., Barsby, T. & Kemble, R. (1983). Genetic transfer through interspecific protoplast fusion. *Science, N.Y.,* **219,** 683–688.

Sifton, H. B. (1945). Air-space tissue in plants. *Bot. Rev.,* **11,** 108–143.

Sifton, H. B. (1957). Air-space tissue in plants. II. *Bot. Rev.,* **23,** 303–312.

Simmonds, N. W. (1982). Some ideas on botanical research on rubber. *Trop. Agric., Trin.,* **59,** 2–8.

Smith, S. E. & Walker, N. A. (1981). A quantitative study of mycorrhizal infection of *Trifolium*: separate determination of the rates of infection and of mycelial growth. *New Phytol.,* **89,** 225–240.

Swain, T. & Cooper-Driver, G. (1981). Biochemical evolution of early land plants. In: *Palaeobotany, palaeoecology and evolution,* vol. 1, edited by K. J. Niklas, 103–134. New York: Praeger.

Tyree, M. T. (1983). Maple sap uptake, exudation, and pressure changes correlated with freezing exotherms and thawing endotherms. *Pl. Physiol., Lancaster,* **73,** 277–285.

Walker, N. A. & Smith, S. E. (1984). The quantitative study of mycorrhizal infection. II. The relation of rate of infection and speed of fungal growth to propagule density, the mean length of the infection unit, and the limiting value of the fraction of the root infected. *New Phytol.,* **96,** 55–70.

Wang, S. C. & Huffman, J. B. (1981). Botanochemicals: supplements to petrochemicals. *Econ. Bot.,* **35,** 369–382.

West, R. G. (1977). *Pleistocene geology and biology.* 2nd ed. London: Longman.

White, P. R., Schucker, E., Kern, J. R. & Fuller, F. H. (1958). "Root-pressure" in gymnosperms. *Science, N.Y.,* **128,** 308–309.

16

TREES AS PRODUCERS OF FUEL

J. BURLEY and R. A. PLUMPTRE
Department of Forestry and Commonwealth Forestry Institute,
University of Oxford, England

I. INTRODUCTION

The purpose of this paper is (a) to outline the extent to which wood is used as a fuel source, (b) to describe the various types of fuel (firewood, charcoal, liquid and gas) derived from trees, (c) to explain the influence of anatomical and chemical attributes of wood on its heating value, (d) to detail the stages of selection and breeding of fuelwood trees, and (e) to draw attention to the managerial and harvesting characteristics of fuelwood forestry, particularly in developing countries.

II. WORLD USE OF FUELWOOD

The world use of fuelwood may well have increased ever since fire was discovered by man. In recent times, the use of wood as a fuel has steadily increased, despite the use of fossil fuels and nuclear energy. Over the period 1966–80 fuelwood and charcoal consumption increased on average by 0·87% per year and accounted for over half of all wood used globally (Fig. 1).

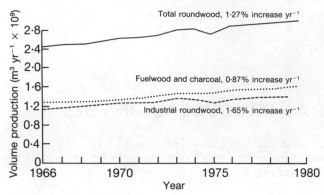

FIGURE 1.   World production of roundwood from 1966 to 1980, showing the proportion used for fuel, as opposed to industrial purposes (data from FAO 1980).

Wood accounts for over 80% of all fuel used in some developing countries,
where it is available in reasonable quantities and where competing fuels are
too expensive. By contrast, in highly industrialized countries, wood seldom
provides more than 10% of the energy used. In general, wherever there is a
subsistence economy based on agriculture, wood is a vital fuel, and it is often
the only fuel available to rural people.

III.   FUELS DERIVED FROM TREES

A.   Wood, bark and foliage

The vast majority of fuelwood is used in solid-wood form. In developing
countries, wood is usually free to local people; it is cut from forests or bush
and is used mainly for cooking, and, in cooler climates, also for heating. The
wood is not always fully dried before burning, and it is often burned in open
hearths or stoves with a very low efficiency of heat capture.

Bark is often burned as kindling, and it is sometimes used to produce power
in woodworking industries. In some parts of the world, leaves are also burned,
and in Kerala, in southern India, dead coconut palm fronds are burned for
cooking, often after they have been used for thatch for two or three years on
houses.

As a fuel, wood has definite advantages over most other natural organic
products, including agricultural residues, in that it is denser, burns more
slowly and gives more heat per unit volume. Unlike agricultural residues,
wood can be stored in living trees and used when required.

B.   Charcoal

Charcoal is obtained by burning wood in a limited supply of air, either in
charcoal kilns, when the only product obtained is charcoal, or in retorts, when

a variety of liquids and gases are obtained by distillation. The theoretical charcoal yield is 33% of the original wood weight, but actual yields vary from 30% in modern portable metal kilns to only 10–15% in earth pit kilns. According to Coombs and Hall (1979), charcoal has about twice the calorific value of air-dry wood, and 1·5 times the calorific value of completely dry wood. Therefore, if wood is burned for charcoal alone (that is, the by-products are not collected) with a 25% efficiency, between half and two-thirds of the energy is lost.

However, because charcoal is only half as heavy as wood per unit of energy, charcoal can be transported over long distances more economically. Charcoal also has the advantages of burning without smoke, of giving a concentrated heat, and of being available in small pieces which can be burned in relatively efficient stoves. Consequently, the energy loss to the user may be considerably less than that suggested by the rough calculation given above.

Charcoal is used in many countries, and in many ways, from cooking to steel smelting. In many countries, the annual consumption of charcoal is over 100,000 tonnes and in Brazil it is 1–2 million tonnes.

C. Comminuted wood residues

Sawdust, planer shavings and bark are produced in quantity by forest industries, and can be used in comminuted form as fuels in especially designed furnaces or stoves. The 'Dutch Oven' is a large industrial furnace designed to burn sawdust, by blowing it into a chamber, and directing an air flow upwards so that the sawdust burns in a free air supply. At the other end of the scale is a small sawdust-burning stove used for cooking in many parts of India; this is made from a tin, which is packed with sawdust leaving a draught up the centre so that the sawdust burns from the centre outwards.

An alternative is to densify, bricquette or pelletize wood residues under pressure, and sometimes heat, possibly with the addition of starch or an adhesive, to give a solid piece of material of desired dimensions. Densification allows the material to be burned in any fire or stove, and makes transport simpler and cheaper. Burning is also much slower and less smoke is produced than by non-densified material. However, the energy used in bricquetting is considerable, and only material of fairly low water content can be used. Also, bricquetting machines are costly, beginning at about £13,000, although work is being carried out to develop cheap hand-operated presses (B. Bryant, University of Washington, Seattle, pers. comm.).

D. Liquid and gaseous fuels

There are four main ways of manufacturing liquid fuels from wood; two use thermochemical processes (pyrolysis and gasification) to give methanol, a third uses hydrogenolysis to produce oil, and a fourth uses a biochemical process of fermentation with yeast to give ethanol (D. Manning, CFI, Oxford, pers. comm.). Ethanol is in some ways a superior fuel, but fermentation is slow and at least 75% of the energy is lost. The main processes used at present are pyrolysis and gasification.

1. *Pyrolysis*

When wood is heated to 500 °C in the absence of air, three products are obtained, with the following theoretical yields: charcoal 33% (as mentioned above), pyroligneous liquid 49% (comprised of water, 28% of the total yield, acetic acid 4%, acetone 1·5%, methanol 2·5%, phenols 0·75% and various other compounds 12%) and gas 18% (comprised of CO, 5% of the total yield, CO_2 11%, alkanes C_1C_4 1·1%, and other compounds 1·2%).

Clearly, the pyroligneous liquid is full of useful chemicals, such as methanol, and so its recovery would be viable if there were a ready market. However, the setting up of expensive retorts to recover the liquid, and the development of further separation methods are not practical in many developing countries, and so the liquid is usually allowed to escape in the interest of charcoal production.

The gas is sometimes referred to as 'producer gas'. It has a calorific value of 1200 cal m^{-3} and can be used in engines to produce shaft and electrical energy. Thus, it can be used in diesel engines (with a small amount of diesel to start up) to give an overall energy yield from wood to electric power of 25%; this is the equivalent of 1 kg of air-dry wood giving 1 kw of electricity. Producer gas was used to power vehicles during the second world war, when petroleum was scarce.

2. *Gasification*

Wood can be totally gasified at temperatures of around 900–1000 °C. The composition of the gas depends on the conditions of gasification. If the wood is gasified in the presence of air, the gas contains N_2 (about 50%), CO, CO_2 and H_2. This gas can be used in the same way as producer gas, but it has a lower calorific value owing to the high content of inert nitrogen. If wood is gasified in the presence of pure oxygen, the gas contains CO (40%), CO_2 (25%), H_2 (24%), alkanes (10%) and other gases (1%).

The standard gasifier has three stages of operation: (a) drying, (b) pyrolysis, and (c) gasification of charcoal and liquids. Design differences occur only in the way in which the air or oxygen is introduced into the reactor; that is, it can be an up-draught, down-draught or across-draught gasifier.

The oxygen-blown gas has a calorific value similar to that of producer gas; however, its value lies in its synthetic potential. If the gas is cleaned and the CO_2 is removed, the remaining gas consists of CO and H_2; this is then called 'synthesis gas', because liquid fuels and other chemicals can be obtained from it.

Methanol is produced from synthesis gas, by adjusting the ratio of CO:H_2 so that their stoichiometric concentrations are in the ratio 1:2, and then reacting the two gases under high pressure and temperature in the presence of a (CuO—ZnO) catalyst, thus:

$$CO + 2H_2 \xrightarrow{\text{CuO/ZnO}} CH_3OH$$

Methanol is a very versatile chemical and fuel. It can be mixed with petrol in a 1:10 ratio and used in a normal petrol engine with no major alterations; in fact, it increases the octane level of the petrol and reduces pollution levels. It can be used in its pure form in especially adapted methanol engines, although it has a lower energy value than petroleum. Methanol can be converted with 90% efficiency to high quality petrol (C_5 to C_{10}) using the Mobil method, in which it is heated under pressure in the presence of a zeolite catalyst. Also, methanol is an important chemical feedstock.

3. *Hydrogenolysis*

Hydrogenolysis is a developing technique for the production of oil from wood. In this process, the wood is directly hydrogenated using CO and/or H_2 as the reducing agent. The technique requires high temperatures (400 °C) and pressures (100–400 Bars) and an alkaline solution of wood pulp or cellulose slurry. So far, about 25% of the wood weight has been converted to high energy oil (similar to crude oil) which has to be fractionated for use as a fuel.

In conclusion, it is clear that wood has a large potential as a fuel source. In southern Britain, a mixture of wood and agricultural residues could be used to produce methanol at a cost per heat unit only 2·3 times greater than that of producing petrol from oil (G. King, AERE, Harwell, pers. comm.). The technologies for wood conversion to fuels should be developed further, so that they are ready for use when supplies of fossil fuels are depleted. Meanwhile, the current uses of charcoal and solid wood should be made more efficient by using well-designed kilns and stoves.

IV.   CHARACTERISTICS OF WOOD AS A FUEL

A.   Carbon/hydrogen ratios and calorific values

The amount of energy or heat that can be obtained from wood, or any organic fuel, depends very largely on the quantities of carbon, hydrogen, oxygen, sulphur and nitrogen contained in the fuel (Bialy 1979). The combination of carbon and hydrogen with oxygen, to give the end products of carbon dioxide and water, is the basic heat-producing reaction, and therefore the carbon/hydrogen ratios determine to a large extent the quantity of heat available from a given quantity of fuel. In general, the larger the percentage of hydrogen, the greater the heat available.

Wood is remarkably consistent in the proportion of hydrogen it contains, ranging from 5·8% to 6·3% (Carman 1950), while the average percentages of carbon and oxygen are 49·5% and 43·5% respectively.

Resin-free softwood contains, on average, 43% cellulose, 29% lignin and 28% hemicellulose, while hardwoods contain 43%, 22% and 35%, respectively (Anderson & Tillman 1977; Doat 1977). The gross calorific value of cellulose is 17·5 MJ kg^{-1}, while for lignin it is 26·7 MJ kg^{-1}, and for resin 34·0 MJ kg^{-1}. It follows, therefore, that the higher percentages of lignin and resins in softwood should give higher calorific values, but, in fact, the values for softwoods and hardwoods overlap, and most species vary between 18 and 21

$MJ\,kg^{-1}$ with outside limits of 15 and 25 $MJ\,kg^{-1}$. Wood, therefore, is relatively constant in the total amount of heat it will give per unit dry weight.

B. Density and water content

The effectiveness of wood as a fuel depends greatly on (a) its density, which affects its rate of burning and general combustibility, as well as the amount of heat produced per unit of wood volume, and (b) its water content, which has a very marked effect on how much heat is produced; wood with a 25% water content (water/dry wood weight$\times 100$) produces only 96% as much heat as dry wood, while wood with a 100% water content (ie half water by weight) produces only 86% as much heat, provided combustion is complete. The rates of burning and the emission of smoke by wood are affected by its water content, as is the completeness of combustion, because wet wood burns at a relatively low temperature, so that smaller quantities of volatiles are combusted and more are driven off with the steam. Earl (1975) quoted heating values of 84% and 66% for wood with 25% and 100% water contents, respectively. Also, wet wood is difficult to ignite. Tillman (1978) stated that wood with a 100% water content needed about six times as much heat to be applied to it for ignition, compared with wood having a 25% water content.

Clearly, with problems of ignition, low heat yield, soot and smoke, there is a strong case for drying wood before it is burned, especially when it is used in open fires in small kitchens. Air-drying of wood to 'fibre saturation point', or just below, gives almost as much benefit as drying to a lower water content.

Wood density affects not only the total amount of heat produced per unit of wood volume (the two are directly related given a constant calorific value), but it also affects (a) the initial green water content of the wood, (b) the rate at which the wood dries out, and (c) the rate of burning at a given water content.

Low-density woods have higher green water contents than high-density woods, but low-density woods normally lose water more quickly when air-dried. When wet, they burn slowly, producing smoke and large quantities of soot and tars, while, when dry, they burn faster at higher temperatures, and with less smoke and tar emission. Dense woods burn more slowly, and drying is probably less critical, because the proportion of wood substance is greater in relation to the total volume.

High-density woods produce strong, hard, charcoal, while low-density woods produce charcoal that is easily crumbled, and may disintegrate during transport to a powder that is not usable in conventional charcoal stoves. Low-density charcoal burns rapidly, and a bag of low-density charcoal may do a great deal less cooking than a similar bag of dense charcoal; hence the strong preference for charcoal made from dense woods in most countries where charcoal is extensively used and sold by the bag. Selling by weight is much more equitable, but even then, rapid burning may release heat too quickly and result in a loss of energy as compared with slow-burning charcoal.

The ratio of surface area to volume varies according to the size of a piece of wood or charcoal, and the higher it is, the faster it burns. A small piece of high-density wood will burn at the same rate as a larger piece of low-density wood.

The packing of pieces of wood or charcoal together during burning also affects their rate of burning. Ignition is more difficult when there are a few large pieces, compared with many small pieces, and combustion on an open fire is probably less complete, because volatiles are driven off at relatively low temperatures from the sides of pieces which are ignited on only one side.

If wood is used for cooking, the method of cooking will affect the type of fuel and stove required to give optimum production of heat. Different conditions are needed for slow, low-temperature simmering compared with rapid, high-temperature frying or roasting. For domestic cooking, freedom from sparking is desirable and this is affected by grain interlocking and fibre bonding. Thus, a large number of factors need to be considered when deciding which species of trees to grow for fuelwood, and how they should be grown and harvested.

V.   GENETIC FACTORS

A.   Species and provenance

The ideal trees to grow for fuelwood are those that grow fast, and produce wood with a medium to high density, a high calorific value, straight grain, no odour or allergenic constituents, and which burns steadily without smoke or sparks. If charcoal is required, an additional advantage is closeness of grain and the presence of small vessels. The desirability of extractives varies, depending on the rate of burning and odour required.

For a site that has not previously carried trees, it is desirable to test a range of species and populations or provenances, which may include locally derived provenances or land races of species that have been deliberately or unconsciously bred elsewhere (see Jones & Burley 1973). There are several stages in this testing. *The species elimination phase* is the mass screening of a large number of possible species in small plots over short periods (1/10–1/5 of the rotation) to determine their survival and promise of reasonable growth. The *species testing phase* is the critical testing or comparison of a smaller number of promising species in larger plots for longer periods (1/4–1/2 of the rotation). The *species proving phase* is designed to confirm, under normal plantation conditions, the superiority of a few promising species. Three similar stages need to be gone through to provenance-test species with a wide natural distribution, namely a *range-wide provenance sampling phase*, a *restricted provenance sampling phase* and a *provenance proving phase*. Because provenance-testing is generally applied to species that are already considered to be promising, the plot sizes and durations of provenance trials can be larger than those used in the comparable phases of species testing.

The ultimate phase is, of course, the complete afforestation project, by which time the source populations will have been reduced to one or two provenances of one or a few species. The importance of using the optimum species and provenance cannot be over-emphasized. There is no standard procedure or time schedule for passage through successive stages of testing; neither is there always a need to use every stage. The above distinct phases may be required either singly (sequentially), or in combination (telescoped), or at the same time (in parallel). Details of the design, analysis and management of trials were given by Burley and Wood (1976) and Huxley (1984).

Where resources for collection and evaluation permit, it is desirable to maintain single parental identities within populations, in a form of provenance/progeny test; this allows intra-population variability to be estimated at an early stage.

For almost any site there are many potential species. In temperate regions, species of the following genera are already under trial for energy plantations – *Alnus*, *Betula*, *Castanea*, *Larix*, *Platanus*, *Populus*, *Quercus*, *Robinia* and *Salix*. In tropical conditions, many more species merit evaluation; a workshop organized by ICRAF, IBPGR and CFI[1] in 1983 recognized some 2000 woody species that have been used for multiple purposes somewhere, most of which yielded fuelwood as one of their products (Burley 1983). Details of several of these species were given in Burley (1980a), Little (n.d.) and NAS (1980, 1983).

It is often difficult to obtain certified material of species for trials, particularly if the species of interest are exotic (not indigenous) and cover a wide natural range. There is great benefit in having centrally co-ordinated research programmes that can (a) explore the natural ranges of species occurring in several countries, (b) evaluate herbarium material taxonomically, (c) collect seed for trials in co-operating countries, (d) provide assistance with the design, assessment and analysis of experiments, and (e) arrange for *in situ* or *ex situ* genetic conservation. Such centrally co-ordinated research has been practised for many years with industrial plantation species in temperate regions, through IUFRO Working Parties and in tropical regions with support from CFI, CSIRO, FAO, ICRAF, NAS and NFTA[1]; information on programmes, seeds available, and results are given in FAO's Forest Genetic Resources Newsletter and in *Leucaena* Research Reports and Nitrogen Fixing Tree Research Reports published by NFTA. Among the hundreds of potential species, several from the following genera are receiving special attention – *Acacia*, *Calliandra*, *Eucalyptus*, *Leucaena*, *Liquidambar*, *Prosopis* and *Sesbania*. Clearly, considerable resources are required to explore and evaluate these groups, and once the best seed sources have been determined, provision must be made to provide seed in bulk. Large supplies may be obtainable from commercial seed dealers, but it is important to obtain details of the genetic history and quality of the parent trees (Jones & Burley 1973). As soon as possible, local seed sources should be established in the form of 'conservation stands' or in breeding populations.

B. Selective breeding

The possibility of breeding trees for use on farms, and in small village plantations, was considered by Burley (1980b), but little has been done beyond

[1] ICRAF, International Council for Research in Agroforestry (Nairobi); IBPGR, International Board for Plant Genetic Resources (FAO Rome); CFI, Commonwealth Forestry Institute (Oxford); NFTA, Nitrogen Fixing Tree Association (Hawaii); NAS, National Academy of Sciences.

species trials, particularly with fuelwood species, except for *Leucaena* in the tropics (see *Leucaena* Research Reports), *Casuarina* and *Prosopis* for dry zones (El-Lakany 1983; Felker 1981), and *Populus* and *Salix* in the temperate zone, such as in Sweden where clonal testing is in progress (Hinrichsen 1983).

When breeding trees for energy production, the breeder must consider the multiplicity of traits outlined above, and those desired in multipurpose trees in general (see Huxley 1984), which involves the assessment of traits not familiar to foresters, and which may require sophisticated assessment techniques and selection indices. For many species, there is little information on the natural breeding system and on population genetic parameters, which must be determined before breeding strategies can be planned.

Genotype evaluation is a major problem in all tree breeding programmes but it will be particularly important in programmes aimed at selecting trees for energy production in rural situations. Progeny or clonal traits evaluated on research stations must be repeated in farm or community situations to determine the yielding ability, stability and acceptability of improved material.

The breeding strategy will also be determined by the kind of propagation method adopted. Even where clonal propagation is used, recurrent selection (see Bridgwater & Franklin, this volume) will be required to provide continued genetic variation and genetic gain (Burley & Plumptre 1984).

VI. MANAGERIAL FACTORS

In industrial plantations, grown for pulp or sawlog timber, the desired tree is usually tall, straight and cylindrical with a small crown and small branches, and large blocks of forest are harvested and transported mechanically. Fuelwood plantings may be in pure blocks (such as village woodlots in Africa and industrial charcoal plantations in Brazil), but are more likely to be as single trees or in strips along roads, railways, canals or farm borders. Some will be in agroforestry mixtures with other tree species, agricultural crops and animals, and most will be harvested by simple, manual methods and transported using animals or human labour. Fuelwood should therefore be small in diameter and length, thornless, and not excessively branchy, and harvest may be taken frequently by coppicing or pollarding.

For any new species, provenance, improved genotype, or environment, considerable research is needed to determine the optimum management method. This includes soil cultural practices, types of planting stock, spacing (possibly with respacing by thinning), weed control, fertilization and irrigation, coppicing or pollarding method and frequency. Reviews of many of these factors as they apply to wood energy plantations and multipurpose trees were given by Anderson *et al.* (1983) and Zsuffa (1984). In general, the highest yields are obtained by planting fast-growing species at less than one metre spacing and harvesting them after rotations of less than five years.

Harvesting in the tropics is often done using poor tools, by women and children who often have to carry headloads of fuel, and cutting tools, over long distances. The optimum lengths and diameters of fuelwood for transport need to be considered. Axes can waste 16–20% of the wood when cross-cutting logs, as compared with saws, unless the chippings are also collected;

very often fuelwood is transported wet, but it can lose 30–60% of its weight if dried before transportation. Wood is easier to cross-cut, by axe or saw, when it is green. However, it is normally easier to split when dry, and it is certainly easier to transport.

REFERENCES

Anderson, H. W., Papadopol, C. S. & Zsuffa, L. (1983). Wood energy plantations in temperate climates. *For. Ecol. Manage.*, **6**, 281–306.

Anderson, L. L. & Tillman, D. A. (1977). *Fuels from waste.* London: Academic Press.

Bialy, J. (1979). Measurement of the energy released in the combustion of fuels. (Occasional paper on alternative technology no. 22). Edinburgh: University of Edinburgh.

Burley, J. (1980a). Selection of species for fuelwood plantations. *Commonw. Forest. Rev.*, **59**, 133–147.

Burley, J. (1980b). Choice of tree species and possibility of genetic improvement for smallholder and community forests. *Commonw. Forest. Rev.*, **59**, 311–326.

Burley, J. (1983). *Global needs and problems of collection, storage and distribution of multipurpose tree germplasm.* (ICRAF/IBPGR/CFI/NAS Planning Workshop, Washington DC). Nairobi: International Council for Research in Agroforestry.

Burley, J. & Plumptre, R. A. (1984). *Species selection and breeding for fuelwood plantations.* (IUFRO Project Group P1–09). Uppsala: International Union of Forest Research Organisations.

Burley, J. & Wood, P. J. (1976). A manual on species and provenance research with particular reference to the tropics. *Trop. For. Pap.*, no. 10.

Carman, E. P. (1950). *Kent's mechanical engineers handbook: power.* 12th ed. New York: Wiley.

Coombs, J. & Hall, D. O., eds. (1979). *Techniques in bioproductivity and photosynthesis.* Oxford: Pergamon.

Doat, J. (1977). Le pouvoir calorifique des bois tropicaux. *Bois Forêts Trop.*, **172**, 33–55.

Earl, D. E. (1975). *Forest energy and economic development.* Oxford: Clarendon.

El-Lakany, M. H. (1983). A review of breeding drought resistant *Casuarina* for shelterbelt establishment in arid regions with special reference to Egypt. *For. Ecol. Manage.*, **6**, 129–137.

Food and Agriculture Organization. (1980). *Forest products yearbook.* Rome: FAO.

Felker, P. (1981). Uses of tree legumes in semiarid regions. *Econ. Bot.*, **35**, 174–186.

Hinrichsen, D. (1983). Swedish energy innovations. *Scient. Am.*, **249**, s2–s28.

Huxley, P. A., ed. (1984). *A manual of methodology for the exploration and assessment of multipurpose trees.* Nairobi: International Council for Research in Agroforestry.

Jones, N. & Burley, J. (1973). Seed certification, provenance nomenclature and genetic history in forestry. *Silvae Genet.*, **2**, 53–58.

Little, E. L., jr. (n.d.). *Common fuelwood crops; a handbook for their identification.* Morgantown, VA: Communi-Tech Associates.

National Academy of Sciences. (1980). *Firewood crops; shrub and tree species for energy production.* Washington DC: NAS.

National Academy of Sciences. (1983). *Firewood crops; shrub and tree species for energy production,* vol. 2. Washington DC: NAS.

Tillman, D. A. (1978). *Wood as an energy resource.* London: Academic Press.

Zsuffa, L. (1984). *Spacing and thinning, with particular reference to the production of biomass for energy.* (IUFRO Planning Workshop, Sri Lanka, 1984, paper 4.1).

17

TREES AS FODDER CROPS

P. J. ROBINSON
Department of Forestry, Commonwealth Forestry Institute, University of Oxford, England

I. INTRODUCTION

The use of trees as a source of fodder is one of those many topics in the natural sciences and agriculture that has been of keen interest in past times, was then forgotten, and has been revived in recent times. The current revival of interest in fodder trees is associated with their important role in agroforestry and sustainable rural development in the tropics (Lundgren & Raintree 1983). In some areas, livestock have been relying successfully on woody perennials for at least part of their fodder for many years, and trees and shrubs can play an important role where there are seasonal shortages in pasture forage and where that forage is of poor quality (Robinson 1983; Torres 1983).

This paper reviews the role of fodder trees in past times and considers their potential value in different farming systems. Naturally occurring trees, which are browsed or lopped, are included as well as 'crop' trees, that are deliberately planted or cultivated, and the term 'fodder' includes leafy shoots, twigs, fruits and pods. Interactions betwen fodder trees and game, as opposed to domestic animals, will be referred to only when they are relevant to farming systems. The role of fodder as a by-product of commercial forestry (Keays

1971, 1975; Young 1976) or of tree crop farming (Hutagalung 1981) is not included if the fodder is processed off the farm, or if the trees are not managed within the farming system (Nelson *et al.* 1984).

II. HISTORICAL PERSPECTIVE

A. Prehistoric evidence

In many parts of the world, fodder trees have played an important role in rural communities since the earliest developments of animal husbandry. In western and northern Europe, it has been suggested that tree fodder was used in about 3000 BC (Simmons & Dimbleby 1974), and palaeobotanic evidence suggests that the livestock of Neolithic man in Europe relied on foliage harvested from *Ulmus*, and perhaps *Tilia, Fraxinus, Ilex aquifolium* (holly) and *Hedera helix* (ivy) (Troel-Smith 1960; Heybroek 1963; Rackham 1980; Linnard 1982).

B. Historical evidence

1. *Classical times*

In ancient China and India, various species and varieties of *Zizyphus*, which have fodder as one of their important products (eg *Z. nummularia*), have been used and grown for the last 4000 years (Mann 1981). *Prosopis cineraria* and *Zizyphus* spp. are mentioned in ancient Indian scriptures dating from before 1000 BC (Khoshoo & Singh 1963; Shanker 1980).

In the Mediterranean region, Amphilochus (an Athenian writer) is said by Pliny (about AD 23–79) to have devoted a whole volume to alfalfa and 'cytisus' (*Medicago arborea*) which was introduced from the Cyclades to Greece, where it was said to have led to a great increase in cheese production.

Problems of livestock feeding were acute in Roman antiquity. Some livestock had to remain on farms to provide manure and power, grazing areas were small and there was a brief pasture growing season. Consequently, many livestock were stall-fed all the year, and much of the fodder was from trees (Cato 234–149 BC; Varro 36 BC; Pliny AD 23–79; Columella AD 64a,b). Tree species were ranked according to the quality of their foliage, fruit and seeds (mast). *Ulmus, Populus, Fraxinus* and *Medicago arborea* were planted specifically for fodder, and nursery techniques were described. Although not the best species for supporting vines, *Ulmus* was nevertheless chosen because of its feed value; further, the 'Atinian' variety of *Ulmus* was often chosen for its more luxuriant leaf growth and better palatability, even though the 'Italian' variety, casting less shade, was more suitable for the vines.

M. arborea took only three years from planting to harvesting, was green for eight months of the year, gave good livestock weight gains even when provided as a sole feed, and was successfully intercropped with garlic and onions. A special name (*frondator*) was given to labourers who lopped or stripped leaves from trees, and some woodlands (*silvae glandiferae*, Devèze 1961) were managed to provide mast for pigs.

2. Middle ages to mid-nineteenth century

In the middle ages, the main reference to fodder trees concerns their value as pasturage for pigs (pannage; Devèze 1961; Rackham 1980). Plaisance (1979) stated that ham from pigs fattened on acorns was renowned for its good quality.

In the UK, before the introduction of improved pasture plants and of liming, and before the increased use of root crops and the enclosure of the commons (spanning the 16th and 17th centuries), winter feed was often desperately short (one beast in five died each winter on Scottish farms even in the 18th century). This shortage resulted in a considerable reliance on palatable evergreen trees and shrubs such as heather (*Calluna vulgaris*), gorse (*Ulex europaeus*) and holly. Both gorse and holly were planted and managed for sheep, cattle and horse fodder (Radley 1961; Spray 1981). Stands of holly within common land often belonged to the lord, and high rentals were sometimes paid for pollarding rights. Holly pollarding seems to have been more prevalent, and to have lasted longer, in areas where winter feed was scarce and which had little early bite. There is also evidence that small-holdings had a higher proportion of holly in their hedgerows than larger farms. Stahl, in Austria, wrote an early treatise on fodder trees in 1765, while Elly (1846), and Burke (1846), for Ireland and Scotland respectively, provided probably the first economic evaluations of a cultivated fodder shrub (gorse), comparing it favourably to more conventional sources of fodder. Elly (1846) included information on the techniques and economics of establishment, on yields, livestock requirements, seasonal variation in feed quality, labour requirements for harvesting, and processing technology (chaffing and crushing). Gorse was often sown on poor land, and, because indigenous gorse was not thought to be as good or luxuriant as the French gorse, germplasm was introduced from France to both Ireland and Scotland (Elly 1846; Fenton 1976). Elly also mentioned two important aspects which are still often neglected: (a) initial palatability is no indication of potential palatability ('Those not used to it, will at first refuse, but after a little starving will prefer it to any other food'), and (b) the feed quality of evergreens can be maintained by frequent cutting.

3. The 1850s to 1950s

More detailed studies on fodder trees, based on experience in the mountainous areas of Europe, appeared in the late 19th and early 20th centuries (eg for Austria, Wessely 1877; Germany, Pässler 1891, 1893; Italy, Anon 1876; Switzerland, Grossmann 1923, and Brockmann-Jerosch 1936. The practice of tree leaf harvesting, prevalent throughout the area before 1800, died out in most areas, apparently because of the introduction of better forage crops. However, the practice continued well into this century in areas where land pressure was severe and during dry years, and can occasionally still be seen today. The central European studies provided data on monthly variations in leaf and twig biomass and chemical composition, and on the digestibility of different plant parts. Results from chemical analyses were found to broadly support traditional lopping regimes. Although not backed up by experimental evidence, recommendations were given for different species concerning cutting cycles, type and time of harvesting (stem lopping, pollarding), storage methods (drying, fermenting) and feed preparation (boiling, mashing). There were considerable regional differences in these techniques and in opinions concerning the relative feed quality of different species. *Castanea vesca* was not valued as fodder in most areas, but it was indispensable in the Cévennes. Harvesting was often carried out by children, and in some parts of the Swiss Jura each fodder tree on common land was numbered and the year's leaf production was auctioned for private harvesting.

European colonization led to further movement of fodder tree germplasm – *Leucaena leucocephala* was introduced to the Philippines from Mexico before 1800 (NAS 1977) – and research was promoted to examine the role of fodder trees in livestock production, and to develop appropriate management strategies for the tree/pasture/livestock complex in different environments (eg Everist 1949, in Australia; Henrici 1935, in South Africa). In the United States, the need to develop sustainable land husbandries in areas which were being severely degraded led to experimentation on trees in the early 1900s, particularly on trees producing fodder for animal feed. Special emphasis was given to hilly regions and areas with shallow soils or low rainfall (Smith 1929), and the opportunities for genetically improving fruit yields and quality, consistency of annual production, and time of fruiting in relation to the availability of other fodder were realized.

In climates with pronounced seasons, information was rapidly being gathered on the chemical composition of fruits and foliage, on certain management aspects, on the importance of fodder trees to livestock nutrition and on traditional patterns of tree ownership and usage rights. For India, these topics were discussed by Gorrie (1937) and Momin and Ray (1943); Laurie (1939) listed 389 species of fodder trees in India and tentatively classified them as 'good', 'medium' or 'poor' according to their popularity with farmers. The increasing realization that probably more livestock obtained food predominantly from associations in which shrubs and trees play an important part than from true grass or grass-legume pastures resulted in a worldwide survey of available information (IAB 1947).

4. Conclusion

This brief survey indicates that for over 2,000 years there have been periods when fodder trees have played an essential role in various agricultural systems. From the survey, it is also possible to identify some important attributes of fodder trees: palatability and quality; coppicing or pollarding ability and resilience to repeated harvesting; leaf retention and quality maintenance during dry and/or cold seasons; regularity of fruit production; ability to produce fodder out of reach of livestock and on sites unsuitable for food or fodder crops; and compatibility with other crops or fodder. The need for appropriate fodder trees has resulted in the deliberate introduction of exotic species. Ownership, usage rights and regulations were often complex reflecting the importance of fodder trees in the rural economy. Management practices at times considered the need to sustain tree production. And, finally, the fact that tree fodder was so commonly harvested (rather than browzed) reflected its high feed value and the low cost of labour needed to harvest it (that is, the high feed value/labour cost ratio).

III. FODDER TREE PRODUCTION AND NUTRITIVE VALUE

A. Introduction

A large body of knowledge concerning various aspects of fodder trees has been gathered over the last decades by foresters, veterinarians, livestock and pasture production scientists, ecologists and anthropologists. Comprehensive lists of fodder tree species used by domestic and wild animals, often including information on chemical composition and palatability to different animals, have been published for Africa (Le Houérou 1980a), the Indian subcontinent (Panday 1982; Singh 1982), Australia (Everist 1969), and elsewhere (IAB 1947; Torres 1983). ICRAF's data base on the feed value of fodder trees currently contains 1,550 records from about 550 species of worldwide origin (Robinson 1984).

Opinions concerning the value of fodder trees range from a view that they are detrimental to livestock production (eg mesquite, *Prosopis* spp. in south-western USA; Martin 1975), to a view that, with genetic improvement, they could 'revolutionize the entire agriculture of the semi-arid tropics' (West 1950, cited by Gray 1970). Also, the same species may be rated differently in different areas or by different people. In India, 46 of the 389 species listed by Laurie (1939) were classed as providing good fodder in some areas but poor or medium-poor fodder in other areas. Neem (*Azadirachta indica*) is apparently ignored by livestock, including goats, in West Africa (NAS 1980), yet in India it is considered to be a good fodder tree and is intensively lopped to feed goats (Singh 1982). Martin (1975) advocated the eradication of *Prosopis* spp. from the semi-desert range areas of south-western USA in order to increase pasture production, while a few Texan farmers find that, with appropriate management, the presence of a certain proportion of *Prosopis glandulosa* var. *glandulosa*, and of other woody legumes, improves livestock and game productivity (Maltsberger 1983, and pers. comm). Some genetic differences between the neems and the mesquites, and between the animals, may help to explain part of these differences in viewpoint. Nevertheless, these and many more contradictions highlight the danger of extrapolating observations from one area to another, or from one management regime to another.

B. Biology and primary productivity

The relevant measure of fodder production from trees is not the average annual production of foliage or pods, but rather the 'feed biomass' available at the time it is browzed or lopped, which is site- and time-specific. However, only a few studies have included phenological descriptions (eg Piot *et al*. 1980; Panday 1982; Singh 1982).

1. Effects of the environment on productivity

Many trees produce fodder in seasons when little herbaceous fodder is available. On the Indian subcontinent, many species are in leaf for a considerable part of the dry season (eg Singh 1982). Leaf production by fodder species in the African tropics and subtropics often begins well before the onset of the rains, and it usually continues long after they have stopped and herbaceous plants have dried. Pod or fruit production also often occurs during or at the end of a dry season. *Acacia albida* and some Capparidaceae (eg *Boscia senegalensis*) start producing foliage towards the end of the rains or in the early part of the dry season (Piot *et al*. 1980; ILCA 1982a).

Estimates of the foliage biomass of trees in the Sahelian zone show a sharp increase from about $60 \, \text{kg} \, \text{ha}^{-1}$ at the 400 mm isohyet (with less than 5% canopy cover) to $1,100 \, \text{kg} \, \text{ha}^{-1}$ at the 1,100 mm isohyet (with about 45% canopy cover) (Penning de Vries & Djitèye 1982). The annual foliage production of several African savanna woodlands has been estimated to be about $1,500 \, \text{kg} \, \text{ha}^{-1}$, and riverine *Acacia xanthophloea* woodland has been estimated to produce $5,000 \, \text{kg} \, \text{ha}^{-1} \, \text{yr}^{-1}$ (Pellew 1980). However, there can be large differences between years. In a severe drought year in the Sahel, the average leaf and fruit biomass on five tree species was only 30% of that in 'normal' years, although considerable differences in the degree of variation occurred between the species (Bille 1980). In Upper Volta (now called Bourkina Fasso), browze species could be grouped into those that were relatively insensitive to changes in environmental conditions (eg *Zizyphus mauritiana*) and those which mirrored the variations in environmental conditions (Grouzis & Sicot 1980). Data from Zambia suggested that within-year variations in the biomass of quasi-evergreen foliage may be considerable in some species (Bille 1980). Nevertheless, the within-year and between-year variations in leaf production by fodder trees are possibly much smaller than those in the herbaceous layer (Torres 1983), and trees often produce fruits in response to adverse climatic conditions (eg *Prosopis glandulosa* var. *glandulosa* in Texas, Maltsberger, pers. comm.).

The proportion of the annual production of foliage and fruits which is actually eaten by livestock and game varies with time of year, stocking density, livestock type, height of the crown, accessibility within the crown, and the availability of water and alternative fodder. Clearly, useful fodder production will often be much less than total production. But, when trees are used to provide fodder only in drought years, their effective productivity is the amount of leaf accumulated without browzing over the non-drought years (eg *Acacia aneura* in Australia; Wilson & Harrington 1980).

2. Effects of tree management on productivity

Based on experiences with other tree crops, Cannell (1983) suggested that fodder trees may respond to management as follows: the removal of old shoots and leaves might result in no decrease in yields and sometimes even in improved yields; the proportion of leaf to stem production should be increased by keeping the trees small and by encouraging branching; regrowth of new shoots following lopping should be less vigorous with increased distance from the roots; however, trees which recover poorly after coppicing might recover better after pollarding because of carbohydrate storage in the stems.

Three Sahelian fodder tree species, *Combretum aculeatum*, *Feretia apodanthera* and *Cadaba farinosa*, responded differently to three leaf-stripping regimes applied during the growing season (Cisse 1980). Most foliage was obtained with no stripping from *Combretum* and *Cadaba*, but with partial stripping every month from *Feretia*. The latter species even outyielded the unstripped control by 30% when it was stripped totally every month, whereas that treatment applied to *Combretum* resulted in a 58% yield reduction over the control. Within a given year, the date of first stripping also influenced the species differently, even taking into account the inherent differences in phenology of the species, rather than calendar dates. Total stripping every 15 days gave the lowest cumulative production in all three species. The depressing influence of monthly stripping during the whole growth period was still felt in *Combretum* and *Cadaba* a year later. However, the effect of such a regime also depended on the time during the previous growing season when stripping began – when it began towards the end of the foliage production period, *Cadaba* did not recover well the following year, whereas *Combretum* recovered so well that it outyielded the control the following year by 99%.

Studies in Libya on the regrowth of a number of shrubs following cropping down to 10–50 cm above the ground showed that autumn/winter cutting resulted in vigorous regrowth, giving almost as much foliage as untreated shrubs, while spring harvesting was detrimental to growth. Furthermore, the regrowth was more palatable than old growth and 20–30% richer in nitrogen (Le Houérou 1983).

In India, circumstantial evidence on several tree species has suggested that several years of rest are necessary between loppings in order to maintain fodder yields (Gorrie 1937). Yet for some species, such as *Prosopis cineraria* (syn. *P. spicigera*) (Khejri), there has been contradictory evidence. *P. cineraria* is traditionally lopped in winter (leaf emergence is in summer), often completely, except for a branch at the top, and in many areas annually (Saxena 1980; Singh 1982). Lopping starts when the tree is about ten years old, and a moderately sized tree is generally reported to yield 25–45 kg of dry leaf forage each year (Bohra & Ghosh 1980; Ganguli *et al.* 1964) (but see below for contradictory evidence). Ganguli *et al.* (1964) stated that *P. cineraria* could withstand recurrent and severe lopping without detriment to its growth or leaf yields, while Saxena (1980) suggested that such treatments harmed the normal growth of the trees and sometimes killed them. However, very few trials have been carried out to determine optimum lopping cycles and intensities.

In Rajasthan, eight trees per treatment of *P. cineraria* were either left intact, were lopped completely except for the leading shoot, or were lopped to remove two-thirds or one-third of the lower canopy (Bhimaya *et al.* 1964). Over four years, the average yield from the completely lopped trees was over twice that from the trees from which the lower two-thirds of the canopy was lopped

(14·7 and 7·1 kg tree^{-1}yr^{-1} of fresh leaf fodder), and the authors suggested that completely lopped trees increased more in stem diameter and height than the trees experiencing either no or only partial lopping (although initial tree diameters and heights were not reported).

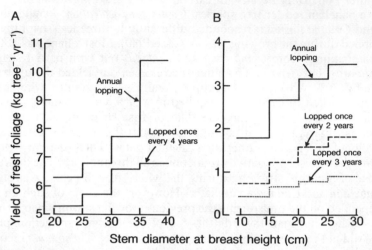

FIGURE 1.   Mean annual fresh weights of leafy fodder harvested from trees of *Prosopis cineraria* in two studies in India, with different harvest intervals.
A. Annual compared with 4–yearly lopping near Jodhpur, Rajastan (26°18′N; *ca* 380 mm rainfall yr^{-1}) (from Bhimaya *et al.* 1964).
B. Annual compared with 2– and 3–yearly lopping near Mohindergarh, Haryana (28°17′N; *ca* 450 mm rainfall yr^{-1}) (from Srivastava 1978).

Bhimaya *et al.* (1964) compared the fodder yields from *P. cineraria* trees which were lopped annually with those lopped after a four-year rest period (Fig. 1A); and Srivastava (1978), working in Haryana, India, recorded the fodder yields of *P. cineraria* trees that were completely lopped annually, or were lopped once every two or three years (Fig. 1B). In both cases, annual lopping gave the greatest yields *per annum*[1]. Also, the difference in mean annual yield between the annually lopped trees and those lopped every four years (Fig. 1A), or every three years (Fig. 1B), was greatest for trees in the largest stem diameter class. This suggests that the largest trees were best able to cope with annual lopping. For the farmer, with large mature trees, annual lopping would provide up to two to four times as much fodder as harvesting on a three- or four-year lopping cycle. It should, however, be noted that the yields in the two studies illustrated in Figure 1 were very different and also, in both studies, the fresh weight yields were considerably less than the dry weight yields of 25 to 45 kg tree^{-1} yr^{-1} considered to be the norm in India (*loc. cit.*).

A lopping trial on *Schima wallichii* near Chautara in Nepal suggested that

---

[1] Bhimaya *et al.*'s (1964) conclusion was that rested trees yielded more than annually lopped trees; however, they appear to have omitted to divide the yield from rested trees by the number of years between loppings to give the annual yield.

the removal of the lower 80% of the crowns resulted in a stem breast height diameter increment of only 20% of that on unlopped trees over the next year (Mohns 1984). In this case, the lopping was done on 12–year-old trees after the leaf flush (the end of the dry season, following local practice).

Several workers have examined the effect of cutting height on the amount of foliage produced by *Leucaena leucocephala*, with conflicting results. Pound and Cairo (1983) suggested that Hawaiian-type varieties could be cut lower than Peru and Salvador cultivars, because the Hawaiian varieties did not hold such a large proportion of their branches high on the plant. They quoted data showing that, out of a range of cutting heights from 0 cm to 76 cm, cuttings at 0·5 cm yielded most fresh material on a Hawaiian-type variety. Others working with Hawaiian types have obtained different results: Pathak *et al.* (1980) showed that the best cutting height was 30 cm (over the range 10 cm to 30 cm, cutting every 40 to 120 days); while Krishna Murthy and Mune Gowda (1982) obtained the greatest yield by cutting at 150 cm (over the range 15 cm to 150 cm, cutting every 40 to 70 days). Pathak *et al.* (1980) suggested that the 30 cm cutting height provided more space on the shoots for branching, leading to increased browze production. Equally variable results have been obtained using Peru varieties: Osman (1981) in Mauritius found that a 90 cm cutting height gave greatest dry matter yields (out of a treatment range of 15 cm to 150 cm, cutting every 90 days), while Mendoza *et al.* (1983) in the Philippines found that a 300 cm cutting height gave the greatest herbage dry weight and crude protein yields per year (over the range 15 cm to 300 cm, cutting every 65 to 110 days).

It has been known for a long time that some shrubs are more susceptible to defoliation than others, and root growth studies may help to explain the differing responses (Hodgkinson & Baas Becking 1977). Also, site characteristics such as soil fertility and soil water regimes are known to have a bearing on the way species respond to different rates of defoliation (eg Jones & Harrison 1980).

3. *Pod production*

Information on pod production is scarce. Some *Prosopis* and *Acacia* species may yield 3–10 t ha^{-1}, depending on the ecological zone (Torres 1983), but there is little information on yearly fluctuations in pod yield, on the contribution of genetic and environmental factors (eg Felker 1983), or on the effects of tree manipulation.

4. *Population trends*

Fodder production over many years depends on changes in the tree population. Factors such as fire frequency and timing, the climate and its variability, grazing and browzing pressures, and so forth, are known to be important. The proportions and densities of different types of livestock and game greatly affect plant community structures, particularly grazer to browzer ratios (eg Staples *et al.* 1942; Lesperance *et al.* 1970; Aucamp 1978; Lange & Willcocks 1980). Natural populations of fodder tree species may regenerate at slower rates than desired or they may die out (eg Chippendale 1963; Seif el Din & Obeid 1971).

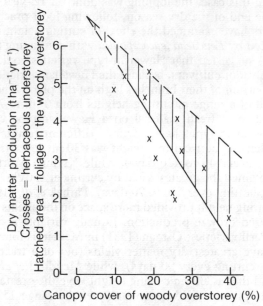

FIGURE 2.   Annual production of herbaceous understorey as a function of the canopy cover of woody species (crosses), and an estimate of the mean foliage production of the trees (hatched area) for an isohyet of 1,100 mm at Satuba in the African Sahel (from Penning de Vries & Djitèye 1982).

5.   Tree-pasture mixes

Fodder tree species differ in their effects on understorey production: some species have a beneficial effect, at least up to certain tree densities and when the canopy is managed appropriately (eg *Hardwickia binata* and *Zizyphus nummularia* in Rajasthan; Bahiti 1981); some species may have a variable influence depending on their age or size; and some species may have a detrimental effect even at very low densities (eg *Acacia aneura* in Australia; Beale 1973). Also, the extent to which trees influence pasture production, and the nature of their influence, can differ between years (eg Walker 1974). Tree foliage production may compensate, in terms of quantity, for the production lost in the pasture component; however, even where it does not (Fig. 2), the quality of forage may often be better (in many pastures there is often a surplus of standing and largely unpalatable herbage biomass during the dry season). Also, in a well-balanced mixed tree-pasture system, the total production may be better distributed over the year (eg Goldson 1973; Kennard & Walker 1973). Thus, some fodder trees can be successfully integrated with pasture production, while others should ideally be grown separately (eg *Acacia aneura* stands for drought reserves; Pressland 1975). Similarly, in cropping systems, some fodder trees can be associated with food or fodder crops without affecting crop yields (eg *Leucaena leucocephala*, *Sesbania sesban*, Venkateswarlu *et al.* 1981; Gill *et al.* 1983), whereas others might need to be manipulated or spatially arranged in ways to minimize negative effects on crop yields.

6. *Conclusions*

The foregoing discussion has highlighted the frequent lack of agreement concerning tree responses to various treatments, even for the species which are supposed to be better understood. This may be due to (a) different site characteristics (which are seldom described in detail), (b) differences in the ways in which individual trees or populations were actually manipulated, even when they appeared to have been manipulated in the same way (eg two-thirds of a canopy can be lopped in very different ways), and (c) the likelihood that many species of fodder trees are genetically variable. Finally, most of the studies investigating the influences of defoliation on subsequent productivity have been carried out over only a few years, and therefore preclude realistic predictions of likely long-term effects.

C. Nutritive value

As much could be said about the problems of evaluating the nutritive value of fodder trees as about the problems of evaluating their productivity; however, because the topic has been well covered elsewhere (eg Wilson 1969; Le Houérou 1980a; Torres 1983), only a brief outline is given here.

The average chemical composition of tree foliage or pods – the measure most frequently given in assessments of feed value – cannot realistically be related to a tree's importance to animal nutrition. The nutritive value of fodder depends on its palatability, intake, chemical composition and on the digestibility of the various chemical constituents. These attributes vary with time in any given species. Generally, we can say that the effective nutritive value depends on a combination of (a) the tree species, (b) changes over time and between parts of a given tree, and (c) the species and breed of animal. Also, the value of any particular feed component in an animal's diet is dependent on the characteristics of all the other components in its diet – including tree-pasture components, feed or mineral concentrates and water. Finally, even for one particular component in a given animal's diet, the interactions between constituent chemicals may affect their useful nutritional value (eg tannins usually decrease the digestibility of crude protein, Lohan *et al.* 1980).

All the above points suggest that the use of standard 'objective' units of nutritional value is highly suspect, in terms of actual value to the animal. Summarizing available information from *in vivo* digestibility studies, Torres (1984) found that the rate of increase in crude protein (CP) digestibility with increasing CP content in woody perennials is lower than that found in herbaceous forage, and the CP digestibility of tree foliage varied from 15·6% to 82·2%. *In vivo* digestibility studies provide the only realistic assessment of the nutritive value of tree fodder, but the cost of such studies is very high.

Nevertheless, we can positively say that, in general, the fodder from good fodder trees has a relatively high CP content, which is maintained during the period when alternative feed sources have low CP contents. Le Houérou (1980b) has reviewed a large number of tree foliar analyses from Africa: the average CP values for all browze species for West and East Africa were 12·5% and 13·3% respectively, compared with 2–11% for most grasses and grain crop residues (Burns 1982; Torres 1983). The average values for Africa for woody legumes and the Capparidaceae were 15·8% and 20·7% respectively. The leaves of some tree species have very high CP contents; for instance, several studies on *Gliricidia sepium* (syn. *G. maculata*) give a range from 18·8% to 30·0% CP (Lindsay Falvey 1982b). Furthermore, livestock can select leaves with much higher CP levels than the average values obtained from hand-collected samples (Wilson 1969).

The foliage of some tree species can be fed to livestock as a sole feed, but the resulting performance of the animals is usually suboptimal (eg *Gliricidia sepium*; Carew 1980). However, several tree species have been found to improve the productivity of stock when their fodder is available as a supplement to a diet which includes otherwise low-quality feeds (eg *Leucaena leucocephala*, Jones 1979; Rosas *et al.* 1981; *Gliricidia sepium*, Chadhokar & Kantharaju 1980). The role of some fodder trees in improving the overall utilization efficiency (both in terms of intake and digestibility) of low-quality herbage and crop residues is therefore particularly important.

IV. LIVESTOCK PERFORMANCE AND NUTRITION

With few exceptions (mainly in the wet tropics), livestock in tropical, subtropical, mediterranean and alpine environments live for considerable periods of the year on sub-maintenance diets (for various regions and ecozones see Dutt 1979; Allden 1982; Crowder & Chheda 1982; ILCA 1979, 1982a,b; Lindsay Falvey 1982a; Mahadevan 1982; Potter 1982; McLean *et al.* 1983). Combined with disease (which can frequently be associated with low nutrition levels), these poor diets result in poor growth rates, delayed reproductive maturity, low birth rates, high adult and immature mortality, low milk production, and a cropping system in which animals are too weak at the end of the dry season to perform their work functions efficiently (Roth & Norman 1978; ILCA 1982b; Raintree 1983).

The minimum CP content of feed required to maintain a ruminant is about 9%, and for lactation and growth it is about 15% (Norton 1982). The nutritive quality of natural swards varies seasonally. The CP content of herbage from a large number of grasslands in the tropics and subtropics during the dry seasons is only 3–4% (eg Hacker 1982; Crowder and Chheda 1982). During the wet seasons, average pasture CP levels, although usually adequate for maintenance and some weight gains, are insufficient for maximum production. Average mineral values are also often well below the animals' requirements, particularly for phosphorus and vitamin A during the dry season. However, in some natural grazing areas, where stocking densities are low enough, within- and between-plant selection by the livestock can enable them to obtain their maintenance requirements during dry seasons (Potter 1982). Nevertheless, several studies of natural grazing conditions have shown that low CP intake is the major factor limiting livestock production (eg Pratchett *et al.* 1977; Torres 1983). In a sub-humid to semi-arid area of West Africa, liveweight changes were shown to be strongly correlated with CP intake ($r = 0.89$; Lambourne *et al.* 1983).

The fodder problem in many mixed farming systems may be due to both a shortage and the low quality of the fodder (Potter 1982; Raintree 1983). In India and Pakistan, the national average shortfalls in meeting livestock nutritional requirements are said to be 40–50%. For Asia and the Far East, the average area of permanent pasture is only 0.12 ha per ruminant livestock unit, and in India the average area devoted to forage crops is 0.033 ha per animal (Mahadevan 1982). Consequently, the main feed in such systems consists of crop residues. In parts of Nepal and northern Nigeria, the yearly contribution of crop residues is about 50% and 80%, respectively (ILCA 1979; Wyatt-Smith 1982). The nutritive value of commonly-grown grain crop residues is low – CP levels ranging from 2% to 6% (Ranjhan & Khera 1976; Sen *et al.* 1978; ILCA 1979; Burns 1982) – and crop residues have low dry matter digestibilities (30–50%) which limit their value as sole feeds (Burns 1982).

The low CP levels of herbage (compared with tree fodder) reduce its digestibility, and hence its energy value, and when there is less than 7% CP less of it is eaten (Crowder & Chheda 1982; Wilson 1982).

Technically, it is possible to improve livestock nutrition and performance by (a) supplementing the diet with mineral licks, urea and protein concentrates, (b) treating the fodder with alkalis to increase its digestibility and palatability, and (c) introducing herbaceous legumes, which have high CP levels and maintain them for longer than the indigenous pastures. However, in developing countries these innovations have usually been uneconomic or unsuccessful (Pratt & Gwynne 1977; ILCA 1979; Potter 1982). Some improvements in livestock nutrition can be achieved in range areas by managing stocking densities, using fire, and varying the proportions of various livestock types (Evans 1982). Dry season 'fodder reserve areas' have traditionally been used by many pastoral societies, but, without a tree fodder component, CP intakes are at sub-maintenance levels, except at very low livestock densities. In mixed farming systems in the sub-humid tropics, the introduction of herbaceous legumes which do not compete with crops, either by being planted on un-utilized areas within crop lands (such as terrace banks), or by relay cropping (eg with various *Stylosanthes* varieties; ILCA 1982b), can also help to improve the nutritional status of livestock.

Natural vegetation could often be used more efficiently by introducing different types and mixes of animals such as camels, giraffes, water buffaloes and other domesticated and non-domesticated species (eg Pellew 1980; NAS 1981, 1983). However, there are a number of technical and social problems impeding their introduction.

V. ACTUAL, POTENTIAL AND FUTURE ROLE OF FODDER TREES

Any attempt to evaluate the place of fodder trees in farming systems must try to answer a number of questions concerning their present, potential and future roles.

First, concerning their present role, what is the nature and extent of their current contribution to the various production and service (eg provision of manure) functions of livestock, and how do fodder trees interact with other aspects of farming systems such as labour demand and food cropping (Roth & Norman 1978; Bernsten *et al.* 1983; Robinson 1983)? In many parts of the world, some farming systems would collapse without fodder trees. Le Houérou (1980c) described a trial in the Sahel in which a group of livestock had no access to fodder trees: the trial had to be discontinued because the livestock would have died. In mixed farming systems, such as those found in many parts of India and Africa, livestock are already on sub-maintenance diets at times of year when tree fodder is a major component of their diet (Dutt 1979; Mohns 1981; Wyatt-Smith 1982; Negi 1983). Figure 3 illustrates the importance of tree fodder in Nepal in the season when crop residue (straw) is almost the only alternative feed.

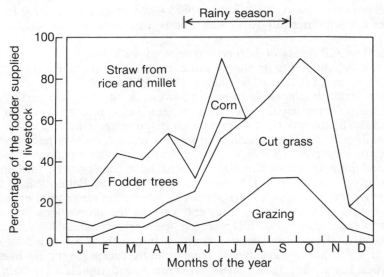

FIGURE 3.   Seasonal variation in the forage supplied to livestock in a hilly area of eastern Nepal (from Mohns 1981, quoting Hager 1978).

Second, concerning their potential role, (a) what are the factors which limit the production and service functions of livestock, (b) what are the attributes of fodder trees which may help to alleviate these limitations and to improve productivity, and (c) what spatial arrangements and management regimes are likely to be most appropriate and how can proposals be implemented?

Third, concerning their future role, (a) what is the likely demand for the various production and service roles of livestock, (b) are there any attributes of fodder trees which can be readily improved, and (c) what changes are likely to take place in other aspects of farming, and how will these influence the value of fodder trees in relation to the efficiency of the whole system?

Although, in developed countries, it has been suggested that we decrease livestock production, in poorer countries the demand for livestock, for food, manure and traction, must increase with human population growth. It is doubtful whether alternative technologies and modes of production can replace livestock in these roles to any significant extent. Draft animal power is already inadequate – the shortage is acute in some areas (eg much of south-east Asia; Mahadevan 1982) – and demand is expected to increase by 0·8% per year (Bernsten *et al*. 1983). The less optimistic of two scenarios investigated to the year 2000 by FAO suggested that there could be an 80% increase in animal production, with an increase in livestock numbers of 15% (FAO 1981). Yet, with few exceptions, increases in animal production over the last 50 years have been mainly due to increased livestock numbers, rather than to improved productivity (Mahadevan 1982). More manure will be needed to sustain crop yields, if fallow cycles shorten further and increasingly more marginal lands are cropped, and this manure may be difficult to supply if the new cropland is taken from areas on which the livestock rely for dry or cold season grazing.

VI. CONCLUSIONS

The trends in agricultural development in developing countries point towards situations where fodder trees could play an increasingly important role. In mixed farming systems, where fodder trees are already in use on croplands, their production is insufficient to meet the demands; more trees are required, but information is needed on which species to grow without decreasing crop yields, and on tree management techniques. In rangelands, the problems of tree establishment are important; a better understanding is required of the factors which create the right conditions for regeneration of appropriate species, and of the livestock types, combinations and stocking densities which promote desirable plant species mixes.

Large dry season 'fodder reserves', which include fodder trees, can successfully be established in pastoral areas, given the will of the pastoralists to do so, and appropriate support from the authorities.

A list of the better fodder tree species for different environmental and management conditions is urgently required so that more detailed investigations can be initiated to resolve the conflicting reports of their responses to various management regimes in different environments. Cheaper and more meaningful methods of determining fodder tree feed values for different animal types would be welcome. Plant breeders have already been assigned to fodder tree improvement projects; but what characteristics are they to select for, and what will be the consequences of selection on other tree characteristics?

The problem of overgrazing in pastoral areas is linked to complex socio-economic and political factors, and these need to be understood and tackled before technical improvements are introduced. Finally, a reductionist research approach, looking at individual components of the complex farming systems which include fodder trees, must go hand in hand with a systems approach; technical solutions must be found to the right problems, and problems will differ in nature in the very different situations encountered.

ACKNOWLEDGEMENTS

I wish to thank the following people who have helped in one way or another towards the production of this paper: Dr J. Burley, Messrs C. E. Hughes, P. S. McCarter, R. H. Neale and Miss M. Mansfield from the Commonwealth Forestry Institute; Mr and Mrs J. A. Robinson, Miss K. Curren; Professor K. D. White, formerly from the Classics Department, Reading University; Dr J. Thirsk, History Department, Oxford University; and Mr B. Mohns, Forestry Department, Australian National University.

This review forms part of a research scheme (R 3720) funded by the UK Overseas Development Administration.

REFERENCES

Allden, W. G. (1982). Problems of animal production from the Mediterranean pastures. In: *Nutritional limits to animal production from pastures*, edited by J. B. Hacker, 45–65. Farnham Royal: Commonwealth Agricultural Bureaux.

Anon. (1876). La foglia dei boschi quale babolo nel Tirolo meridionale *L'Agricolture. Giornale del Consorzio Agrario Trentino e Sui Comizii*. August issue.

Aucamp, A. J. (1978). *The Boer goat – picture of the future.* Stutterheim, S. Africa: Agricultural Research Institute. Mimeograph.

Bahiti, T. K. (1981). Grass-component in silvipastoral system – special reference to Indian arid zone. In: *Agroforestry of arid and semi-arid zones*. Jodhpur: CAZRI.

Beale, I. F. (1973). Tree density effects on yields of herbage and tree components in south west Queensland, Mulga (*Acacia aneura* F. Muell.) scrub. *Trop. Grassl.*, **7**, 135–142.

Bernsten, R. H., Fitzburgh, H. A. & Knipscheer, H. C. (1983). Livestock in farming systems research. *Proc. Annual Farming Systems Symp.*, *3rd*, Keynote address. Kansas State University.

Bhimaya, C. P., Kaul, R. N. & Ganguli, B. N. (1964). Studies on lopping intensities of *Prosopis spicigera*. *Indian Forester*, **90**, 19–23.

Bille, J. C. (1980). Measuring the primary palatable production of browse plants. In: *Browse in Africa*, edited by H. N. Le Houérou, 185–195. Addis Ababa: ILCA.

Bohra, H. C. & Ghosh, P. K. (1980). The nutritive value of Loong (*P. cineraria*) leaves. In: *Khejri (Prosopis cineraria) in the Indian desert – its role in agroforestry*, edited by H. S. Mann et al., 45–50. Jodhpur: CAZRI.

Brockmann-Jerosch, H. (1936). Futterlaubbäume und Speiselaubbäume. *Beitr. Schweiz. Z. bot. Ges.*, **46**, 594–613.

Burke, F. (1846). Note on Furze. *Jl R. agric. Soc.*, 1st ser., **6**, 528.

Burns, J. C. (1982). Integration of grazing with other feed resources. In: *Nutritional limits to animal production from pastures*, edited by J. B. Hacker, 455–471. Farnham Royal: Commonwealth Agricultural Bureaux.

Cannell, M. G. R. (1983). Plant management in agroforestry: manipulation of trees, population densities and mixtures of trees and herbaceous crops. In: *Plant research and agroforestry*, edited by P. A. Huxley, 455–486. Nairobi: International Council for Research in Agroforestry.

Carew, B. A. R. (1980). *Use of Gliricidia sepium as a forage feed in small ruminant production.* (Progress report). Ibadan: ILCA.

Cato, M. P. (234–149 B.C.). De agri cultura. In: *De re rustica*, edited by G. P. Goold, 1979, 1–157. London: Heinemann.

Chadhokar, P. A. & Kantharaju, H. R. (1980). Effect of *Gliricidia maculata* on growth and breeding of Bannur ewes. *Trop. Grassl.*, **14**, 78–82.

Chippendale, G. M. (1963). The effects of grazing on topfeed in central Australia. *Aust. J. exp. Agric. Anim. Husb.*, **3**, 30–34.

Cisse, M. I. (1980). Effects of various stripping regimes on foliage production of some browse bushes of the Sudano-Sahelian zone. In: *Browse in Africa*, edited by H. N. Le Houérou, 211–214. Addis Ababa: ILCA.

Columella, L. J. M. (*c.* A.D. 64 a). *De re rustica*, vols 1, 2 & 3, edited by G. P. Goold (1979). London: Heinemann.
Columella, L. J. M. (*c.* A.D. 64 b). De Arboribus. In: *De re rustica*, edited by G. P. Goold, 1979, vol. 3, 341–411. London: Heinemann.
Crowder, L. V. & Chheda, H. R. (1982). *Tropical grassland husbandry*. London: Longman.
Devèze, M. (1961). *La vie de la forêt francaise au XVIe siècle*, vol. 1. Paris: Imprimerie Nationale.
Dutt, P. (1979). *Preliminary findings and general conclusions on livestock in the KHARDEP area.* (KHARDEP report no. 5). Kathmandu: KHARDEP.
Elly, S. (1846). On the cultivation and preparation of gorse as food for cattle. *Jl R. agric. Soc.*, 1st ser., **6**, 523–528.
Evans, T. R. (1982). Overcoming nutritional limitations through pasture management. In: *Nutritional limits to animal production from pastures*, edited by J. B. Hacker, 343–361. Farnham Royal: Commonwealth Agricultural Bureaux.
Everist, S. L. (1949). Mulga (*Acacia aneura* F. Muell.) in Queensland. *Qd J. agric. Sci.*, **6**, 87–135.
Everist, S. L. (1969). *Use of fodder trees and shrubs.* (Advisory leaflet no. 1024). Brisbane: Queensland Division of Plant Industry, Dept of Primary Industries.
Food and Agriculture Organization. (1981). *Agriculture: toward 2000.* (Economic and social development series no. 23). Rome: FAO.
Felker, P. (1983). Legume trees in semi-arid and arid areas. *Proc. Symp. Nitrogen Fixing Trees for the Tropics.* Rio de Janeiro: PNPBS/EMBRAPA.
Fenton, A. (1976). *Scottish country life.* Edinburgh: John Donald.
Ganguli, B. N., Kaul, R. N. & Nambiar, K. T. N. (1964). Preliminary studies on a few top-feed species. *Ann. arid Zone*, **3**, 33–37.
Gill, A. S., Patil, B. D. & Yadav, C. L. (1983). Intercropping studies in hybrid napier varieties associating *Leucaena* and other leguminous fodder shrubs. *Leucaena Res. Rep.*, **4**, 21.
Golsdon, J. R. (1973). *The effect and contribution of the cashew tree* Anacardium occidentalis *in a cashew – pasture – dairy cattle association on the Kenya coast.* Ph.D. thesis, University of Reading.
Gorrie, R. M. (1937). Tree lopping on a permanent basis. *Indian Forester*, **63**, 29–31.
Gray, S. G. (1970). The place of trees and shrubs as sources of forage in tropical and subtropical pastures. *Trop. Grassl.*, **4**, 57–62.
Grossmann, H. (1923). Das Futterlaub im Jura. *Schweiz. Z. Forstwes.*, **74**, 181–188.
Grouzis, M. & Sicot, M. (1980). A method for the phenological study of browse populations in the Sahel: the influence of some ecological factors. In: *Browse in Africa*, edited by H. N. Le Houérou, 233–243. Addis Ababa: ILCA.
Hacker, J. R., ed. (1982). *Nutritional limits to animal production from pastures.* Farnham Royal: Commonwealth Agricultural Bureaux.
Hager, R. (1978). *Fodder Report, 1978.* (Project report of IHDP). Kathmandu: Swiss Association for Technical Aid.
Henrici, M. (1935). Fodder plants of the broken veld: their chemical composition, palatability and carrying capacity. *Sci. Bull. Dep. Agric. For. Un. S. Afr.*, no. 142.
Heybroek, H. M. (1963). Diseases and lopping for fodder as possible causes of a prehistoric decline of *Ulmus*. *Acta bot. neerl.*, **12**, 1–11.
Hodgkinson, K. C. & Baas Becking, H. G. (1977). Effect of defoliation on root growth of some arid zone perennial plants. *Aust. J. agric. Res.*, **29**, 31–42.
Hutagalung, R. I. (1981). The use of tree crops and their by-products for intensive animal production. In: *Intensive animal production in developing countries*, edited by A. J. Smith *et al.*, 151–184. (Occasional publication no. 4). British Society of Animal Production.
Imperial Agricultural Bureaux. (1947). *The use and mis-use of shrubs and trees as fodder.* (Joint publication no. 10). Aberystwyth: IAB.
International Livestock Centre for Africa. (1979). *Livestock production in the subhumid zone of West Africa.* (ILCA systems study no. 2). Addis Ababa: ILCA.
International Livestock Centre for Africa. (1982a). *Livestock production in Mali.* (ILCA bulletin no. 15). Addis Ababa: ILCA.
International Livestock Centre for Africa. (1982b). *Annual report 1981.* Addis Ababa: ILCA.
Jones, R. J. (1979). The value of *Leucaena leucocephala* as a feed for ruminants in the tropics. *World Anim. Rev.*, **31**, 13–23.
Jones, R. M. & Harrison, R. E. (1980). Note on the survival of individual plants of *Leucaena leucocephala* in grazed stands. *Trop. Agric., Trin.*, **57**, 265–266.

Keays, J. L. (1971). *Complete tree utilization – an analysis of the literature. Part II. Foliage.* (Information report VP–X–70). Vancouver: Canadian Forestry Service, Forest Products Laboratory.

Keays, J. L. (1975). *Recent advances in foliage utilization.* (Western Forest Products Laboratory VP–X–137). Vancouver.

Kennard, D. G. & Walker, B. H. (1973). Relationships between the canopy cover and *Panicum maximum* in the vicinity of Fort Victoria. *Rhod. J. agric. Res.,* **11**, 145–153.

Khoshoo, T. N. & Singh, N. (1963). Cytology of north-west Indian trees. 1. *Zizyphus jujuba* and *Z. rotundifolia. Silvae Genet.,* **12**, 158–174.

Krishna Murthy, K. & Mune Gowda, M. K. (1982). Effect of cutting and frequency regimes on the herbage yield of *Leucaena. Leucaena Res. Rep.,* **3**, 31–32.

Lambourne, L. J., Dicko, M. S., Semenye, P. & Butterworth, M. (1983). Animal nutrition. In: *Pastoral systems research in sub-Saharan Africa,* 183–206. Addis Ababa: ILCA.

Lange, R. T. & Willcocks, M. C. (1980). Experiments on the capacity of present sheep flocks to extinguish some tree populations of the south Australian arid zone. *J. arid Zone,* **3**, 223–229.

Laurie, M. V. (1939). Fodder trees in India. *Indian Forest Leafl.,* no. 82 (Silviculture). Dehra Dun: Forest Research Institute.

Le Houérou, H. N., ed. (1980a). *Browse in Africa: the current state of knowledge.* Addis Ababa: ILCA.

Le Houérou, H. N. (1980b). Chemical composition and nutritive value of browse in West Africa. In: *Browse in Africa,* edited by H. N. Le Houérou, 261–290. Addis Ababa: ILCA.

Le Houérou, H. N. (1980c). Gaps in knowledge and research priorities. In: *Browse in Africa,* edited by H. N. Le Houérou, 479–481. Addis Ababa: ILCA

Le Houérou, H. N. (1983). *Production of shrub regrowth after cutting at Wishtata arboretum.* (FAO/UTFN/LIB/018 Technical paper no. 49). Rome: FAO.

Lesperance A. L., Tweller, P. T. & Bohman, V. R. (1970). Symposium on pasture methods for maximum production in beef cattle: competitive use of the range forage resource. *J. Anim. Sci.,* **30**, 115–121.

Lindsay Falvey, J. (1982a). Factors limiting cattle production in the Thai Highlands. *J. Aust. Inst. agric. Sci.,* **48**, 51.

Lindsay Falvey, J. (1982b). *Gliricidia maculata* – a review. *Int. Tree Crops J.,* **2**, 1–14.

Linnard, W. (1982). *Welsh woods and forests: history and utilization.* Cardiff: National Museum of Wales.

Lohan, O. P., Lall, D., Pal, R. N. & Negi, S. S. (1980). Note on tannins in tree fodders. *Indian J. Anim. Sci.,* **50**, 881–883.

Lundgren, B. O. & Raintree, J. B. (1983). Sustained agroforestry, In: *Agricultural research for development: potentials and challenges in Asia.* The Hague: ISNAR.

Mahadevan, P. (1982). Pastures and animal production. In: *Nutritional limits to animal production from pastures,* edited by J. B. Hacker, 1–17. Farnham Royal: Commonwealth Agricultural Bureaux.

Maltsberger, W. A. (1983). *Statement to the joint meeting of the range and wildlife societies.* (Texas sectors). Austin, Texas. Mimeograph.

Mann, H. S. (1981). Bordi in Indian desert. An overview. In: *Bordi* (Zizyphus nummularia) *a shrub of the Indian arid zone – its role in silvipasture,* edited by H. S. Mann *et al.,* 70–74. Jodhpur: CAZRI.

Martin, S. C. (1975). Ecology and management of south-western semi desert grass-shrub ranges. *Res. Pap. Rocky Mt. For. Range Exp. Stn,* RM–156.

McLean, R. W., McCown, R. L., Little, D. A., Winter, W. H. & Dance, R. A. (1983). An analysis of cattle live-weight changes on tropical grass pasture during the dry and early wet seasons in northern Australia. *J. agric. Sci., Camb.,* **101**, 17–24.

Mendoza, R. C., Altamarino, T. P. & Javier, E. O. (1983). Herbage, crude protein and digestible dry matter yield of Ipil-Ipil (*Leucaena leucocephala* cv Peru) in hedgerows. *Leucaena Res. Rep.,* **4**, 69.

Mohns, B. (1981). *Importance of fodder trees as livestock forage in the hill regions of Nepal.* (Paper RS 652). Fort Collins, CO: Colorado State University, Dept of Earth Resources, Mimeograph.

Mohns, B. (1984). *Layout and first results of a lopping trial on* Schima wallichii *in Central Nepal.* Canberra: Australian National University, Dept of Forestry, Mimeograph.

Momin, S. A. & Ray, S. C. (1943). Tree leaves as cattle fodder. *Indian J. Vet. Sci.,* **13**, 183–190.

National Academy of Sciences. (1977). Leucaena; *promising forage and tree crop for the tropics.* Washington DC: NAS.

National Academy of Sciences. (1980). *Firewood crops.* Washington DC: NAS.

National Academy of Sciences. (1981). *The water buffalo: new prospects for an underutilised animal.* Washington DC: NAS.

National Academy of Sciences. (1983). *Little known Asian animals with a promising economic future.* Washington DC: NAS.

Negi, S. S. (1983). *Foliage from forests – a potential feed resource.* Palampur, H.P.: Indian Veterinary Research Institute. Mimeograph.

Nelson, N. D., Sturos, J. A., Fritschel, P. R. & Satter, L. D. (1984). Ruminant feedstuff from commercial foliage of hybrid poplars grown under intensive culture. *Forest Prod. J.,* **34**, 37–44.

Norton, B. W. (1982). Differences between species in forage quality. In: *Nutritional limits to animal production from pastures,* edited by J. B. Hacker, 89–110. Farnham Royal: Commonwealth Agricultural Bureaux.

Osman, A. M. (1981). The effects of cutting height on the dry matter production of *Leucaena. Leucaena Res. Rep.,* **2**, 37–38.

Panday, Kk. (1982). *Fodder trees and tree fodder in Nepal.* Berne: Swiss Development Corporation.

Pässler, J. (1891). Über Futterwerth und Gerbstoffgehalt des Laubes, der Triebe und schwächsten Zweige der Eiche während der verschiedenen Monate. *Tharandt. forstl. Jb.,* **41**, 172–238.

Pässler, J. (1893). Untersuchungen über den Futterwerth der Blätter, Triebe und schwächsten Zweige verschiedener Laub und Nadelhölzen, sowie eineger anderer Waldgewächse. *Tharandt. forstl. Jb.,* **43**, 212–252.

Pathak, P. S., Rai, P. & Deb Roy, R. (1980). Forage production from Koo-Babool (*Leucaena leucocephala* (Lam.) de Wit). I. Effect of plant density, cutting intensity and interval. *Forage Res.,* **6**, 83–90.

Pellew, R. A. (1980). The production and consumption of *Acacia* browse and its potential for animal protein production. In: *Browse in Africa,* edited by H. N. Le Houérou, 223–231. Addis Ababa: ILCA.

Penning de Vries, F. W. T. & Djitèye, M. A., eds. (1982). *La productivité des pâturages sahéliens.* Wageningen: Centre for Agricultural Publishing and Documentation.

Piot, J., Nebout, J. P., Nanot, R. & Toutain, B. (1980). *Utilisation des ligneux sahéliens par les herbivores domestiques.* Nogent sur Marne: Centre Technique Forestier Tropical.

Plaisance, G. (1979). *La forêt française.* Paris: Denoël.

Pliny. (c A.D. 23–79). Naturalis historia. In: *Natural history,* edited by E. H. Warmington, 1971, vols 4 and 5. London: Heinemann.

Potter, H. L. (1982). Animal feed resources production in semi-arid areas. *Combined Workshop for FAO Dryland Farming Project and USAID Dryland Cropping Project, Embu, Kenya.* Mimeograph.

Pound, B. & Martinez Cairo, L. (1983). Leucaena: *its cultivation and uses.* London: Overseas Development Administration.

Pratchett, D., Copper, B. G., Light, D. E., Miller, M. D., Rutherford, A. S., Rennie, T. W., Buck, N. G. & Trail, J. C. (1977). Factors limiting liveweight gain of beef cattle on rangeland in Botswana. *J. Range Mgmt,* **30**, 442–445.

Pratt, D. J. & Gwynne, M. D. (1977). *Rangeland management and ecology in East Africa.* London: Hodder & Stoughton.

Pressland, A. J. (1975). Productivity and management of Mulga in south-western Queensland in relation to tree structure and density. *Aust. J. Bot.,* **23**, 965–976.

Rackham, O. (1980). *Ancient woodland: its history, vegetation and uses in England.* London: Edward Arnold.

Radley, J. (1961). Holly as a winter feed. *Agric. Hist. Rev.,* **9**, 89–92.

Raintree, J. (1983). *Preliminary diagnosis of land use problems and agroforestry potentials in northern Mbere Division, Embu District, Kenya.* (ICRAF working paper no. 1). Nairobi: ICRAF.

Ranjhan, S. K. & Khera, R. C. (1976). *Feeding farm animals during scarcity.* New Delhi: Indian Council for Agricultural Research.

Robinson, P. J. (1983). The role of silvopastoralism in small farming systems. In: *Agroforestry systems for small-scale farmers,* edited by D. A. Hoekstra *et al.,* 147–169. Nairobi: ICRAF/BAT.

Robinson, P. J. (1984). Data base on fodder tree chemical composition and feed value. *Nitrogen Fixing Tree Res. Rep.,* **2**, 26–28.

Rosas, H., Quintero, S. O., Gomez, J. & Rodriquez, M. (1981). Milk production during the rainy and dry season with arboreous *Leucaena* in the central area of Panama. *Leucaena Res. Rep.*, **2**, 40.

Roth, M. & Norman, D. (1978). Role of animals in the small farm enterprise. *Proc. int. Conf. Integrated Crop and Animal Production to Optimize Resource Allocation on Small Farms in the Developing Countries.* Bellagio.

Saxena, S. K. (1980). Taxonomy, morphology, growth and reproduction of Khejri and its succession in North West India. In: *Khejri* (Prosopis cineraria) *in the Indian desert – its role in agroforestry*, edited by H. S. Mann *et al.*, 4–10. Jodhpur: CAZRI.

Seif el Din, A. & Obeid, M. (1971). Ecological studies of the vegetation of Sudan. IV. The effect of simulated grazing on the growth of *Acacia senegal* (L.) Willd. seedlings. *J. appl. Ecol.*, **8**, 211–216.

Sen, K. C., Ray, S. N. & Ranjhan, S. K. (1978). *Nutritive values of Indian cattle feeds and the feeding of animals.* New Delhi: Indian Council for Agricultural Research.

Shanker, V. (1980). Khejri (*Prosopis cineraria* Macbride) in the Indian Scriptures. In: *Khejri* (Prosopis cineraria) *in the Indian desert – its role in agroforestry*, edited by H. S. Mann *et al.*, 1–3. Jodhpur: CAZRI.

Simmons, I. G. & Dimbleby, G. W. (1974). The possible role of ivy (*Hedera helix* L.) in the mesolithic economy of Western Europe. *J. Archaeol. Sci.*, **1**, 291–296.

Singh, R. V. (1982). *Fodder trees of India.* New Delhi: Oxford IBH Publishing Co.

Smith, J. R. (1929). *Tree crops, a permanent agriculture.* New York: Harcourt, Brace & Co.

Spray, M. (1981). Holly as a fodder in England. *Agric. Hist. Rev.*, **29**, 97–110.

Srivastava, J. P. L. (1978). Lopping studies on *Prosopis cineraria*. *Indian Forester*, **104**, 269–274.

Stahl, J. (1765). Vorschlag von der Ernährung der Thiere durch das Baumlaub. *Allg. Okon. Forstmag.*, **7**, 132–172.

Staples, R. R., Hornby, H. E. & Hornby, R. A. (1942). A study of the comparative effects of goats and cattle on a mixed grass-bush pasture. *E. Afr. agric. J.*, **8**, 62–70.

Torres, F. (1983). Role of woody perennials in animal agroforestry. *Agrofor. Syst.*, **1**, 131–163.

Torres, F. (1984). Protein digestibility in fodder from woody perennials. *International round table on Prosopis tamarugo, June 11–15, Arica, Chile.*

Troel-Smith, J. (1960). Ivy, mistletoe and elm: climatic indicators – fodder plants. *Danm. geol. Unders.*, Rk **4**, 1–32.

Varro, M. T. (*c.* 36 B.C.). Res Rusticae. In: *De re rustica*, edited by G. P. Goold, 1979, 159–543. London: Heinemann.

Venkateswarlu, J., Venkat Reddy, N., Das, R. B. & Rao, U. M. B. (1981). Role of *Leucaena* in intercropping in dryland farming. *Leucaena Res. Rep.*, **2**, 30.

Walker, B. H. (1974). Ecological considerations in the management of semi-arid ecosystems in South-Central Africa. *Proc. int. Congr. of Ecology, 1st*, 124–129. The Hague.

Wessely, J. (1877). *Das Futterlaub: seine Zucht und Verwendung.* Wien: Moritz Perles Buchhandlung Verlag.

West, O. (1950). Indigenous tree crops for Southern Rhodesia. *Rhodesia agric. J.*, **47**, 204–217.

Wilson, A. D. (1969). A review of browse in the nutrition of grazing animals. *J. Range Mgmt*, **22**, 23–28.

Wilson, A. D. & Harrington, G. N. (1980). Nutritive value of Australian browse plants. In: *Browse in Africa*, edited by H. N. Le Houérou. 291–297. Addis Ababa: ILCA.

Wilson, J. R. (1982). Environmental and nutritional factors affecting herbage quality. In: *Nutritional limits to animal production from pastures*, edited by J. B. Hacker, 111–131. Farnham Royal: Commonwealth Agricultural Bureaux.

Wyatt-Smith, J. (1982). *The agricultural systems in the hills of Nepal.* (APROSC occasional papers no. 1). Kathmandu: Agricultural Projects Services Centre.

Young, H. E. (1976). Utilization of forest residues – a segment of the complete tree concept. *Proc. National Convention Society American Foresters, 1975*, 479–484.

Roots, symbionts and soils

18

Roots as a Component of Tree Productivity

G. D. BOWEN

CSIRO, Division of Soils, Glen Osmond, South Australia

I. INTRODUCTION

Tree productivity is often limited by soil resources, yet our knowledge of root biology, the interactions between roots and tops, and the use of soil resources, is fragmentary even for agricultural crop plants. This chapter addresses some current questions about the 'costs' of roots, and how they function in exploiting soil resources and in producing growth factors, highlighting those attributes that might profitably be altered by selection or management.

Tree roots, in contrast to those of annuals, need to function and survive over the full gamut of seasons, and over the annual variations in soil climate during the 12 to 120 years of a rotation. They also change their own environment, by accumulating litter and redistributing nutrients in the profile over time. In such a range of growth conditions, trees must have (a) root systems of great efficiency and plasticity to accommodate changes quickly, and (b) structural roots to form a stable (survival) base. This, I think, is the whole key to effective root function of perennials, and has something both of the r and K phenomena of ecology – stability and resilience.

Trees have usually evolved in mixed ecosystems, in which survival in competitive environments (and not necessarily high productivity) has been the goal. Low-input forestry and horticultural-ley systems often have such competition. High-input monoculture forestry (for high productivity) usually removes competition, and this will have a large impact on how much root it is 'necessary' for a tree to have to obtain adequate soil resources for good growth.

The three main components of the tree root system are: (a) major permanent *structural* roots, usually much larger than the fine roots they produce, (b) a system of *fine roots* 1–2 mm in diameter, consisting of 'long' (exploratory) roots bearing lateral 'short' roots, and when these roots become infected they produce (c) *mycorrhizas*. With several economic forest trees, ectomycorrhizas are the more common, and arise from infection of the short laterals. In the rest of the plant kingdom, vesicular-arbuscular (VA) mycorrhizas are the major type, and occur on both components of the fine root system. The biology and physiology of mycorrhizas have been discussed in detail by Harley and Smith (1983). Although they are caused by quite different fungi, the different mycorrhizal types function in essentially the same way.

II. ROOT DYNAMICS AND COSTS

Data on energy needs, for growth, maintenance and uptake of nutrients, for the structural roots, fine roots and mycorrhizas are sparse. In most cases the amount of assimilate going to roots is considerably greater than the 20–30% suggested by measurements of root biomass at any one time, because (a) there is no cognisance of assimilates lost in exudates and by respiration – in cereals these can account for 20% of the total assimilates, and (b) there is continual turnover of fine roots, largely in response to both environmental fluctuation between and within seasons, and to soil biological activity (see Bowen 1984).

The fine roots occupy a key position in nutrient and water uptake, because, although they may represent only some 5% of root weight (eg in 39-year-old *Pinus sylvestris*, Roberts 1976), they can account for 90% of the root length. Furthermore, they are the sites for mycorrhiza formation. As there can be considerable turnover of fine roots, both the amount of assimilate used in their growth, and the length of roots absorbing nutrients during a season are much greater than suggested by a single sampling (two- to four-fold differences in fine roots recovered over a season are not uncommon – see Bowen 1984), not to mention the difficulties posed by incomplete recovery of fine roots from soil. Problems in the study of fine root production and death have been discussed by Persson (1983). Estimates of assimilate use in fine root production include 36% and 66% of net primary production in 23- and 180-year-old *Abies amabilis*, respectively, some 50% in 15–20-year-old *Pinus sylvestris*, and 8% and 36% of total dry matter production in *Pseudotsuga menziesii* growing on high and low productivity sites, respectively (see Bowen 1984; Cannell, this volume). There is an urgent need to understand factors governing the death and turnover of fine roots. Most conclusions so far are based on correlations with climatic conditions, soil moisture and so on; I suggest that a more experimental approach is necessary.

Vogt *et al.* (1982) calculated the mycorrhizal fungus component of *Abies amabilis* production to be some 3,000 kg ha^{-1}yr^{-1} – about 15% of total primary production – and Fogel and Hunt (1979) calculated that ectomycorrhizas could be 50% of the total root system biomass, when a high percentage of short roots were mycorrhizal. Fine roots, and fine roots plus mycorrhizas, have been calculated to contribute two to four times more N, six to ten times more P and K, and two to three times more Ca to soil than above-ground litterfall (see Bowen 1984). An important question is: how much of the nutrient in senescing fine roots (often a large amount, Bowen 1980b) is translocated to the plant, and how much is returned to the soil to wait the vagaries of decomposition, mineralization and reabsorption by the plant? An increasing body of data indicates little retranslocation from senescing fine roots.

There are few good data on root respiration in the field, and, in carbon balances, the respiratory component due to fine roots is often derived by difference. Linder and Axelsson's (1982) data suggested that the respiration rates of roots of young *P. sylvestris* trees were greater than the respiration rates of above-ground parts. Ectomycorrhizas appear to be intensive sinks for assimilates; Bevege *et al.* (1975) found that ectomycorrhizas of *Pinus radiata* had 15 times as much ^{14}C labelled assimilate as adjacent uninfected laterals 24 hours after exposure to $^{14}CO_2$. Harley and Smith (1983) indicated that respiration rates of ectomycorrhizas were 1·5 to twice those of uninfected roots. With VA mycorrhizas, only some 1–5% of the root biomass is fungus, but Sanders, Martin and Bowen (unpublished) found that the respiration rates of VA mycorrhizal roots on onions were six times those of non-mycorrhizal roots, although much smaller differences have been reported by other workers (see Harley & Smith 1983). Depressions of plant growth, which have sometimes been attributed to the presence of mycorrhizas, may be due to an energy drain, under conditions in which the mycorrhizas are superfluous for nutrient uptake. However, plants often compensate for the 'costs' of mycorrhizas by increasing their photosynthetic rates (Paul & Kucey 1981), possibly associated with increased cytokinin production by the mycorrhizal system (see below).

The structural, permanent, component of the root system is analogous to the structural 'skeleton' of above-ground parts of deciduous trees, in that it gives a base for rapid exploration of the environment (the soil). The cost of maintaining the root system is decreased by sloughing off fine roots when conditions are not conducive to growth. *The rapid production of fine roots and mycorrhizas, and the turnover of fine roots, thus bestows great plasticity on the perennial root system.* The recognition that relatively large amounts of assimilate are used in fine root production inevitably leads to the questions: (a) does the tree need all of these roots, and (b) would an 'ideotype' for maximum above-ground productivity direct less assimilate to roots? The answers to these questions lie in a better understanding of root function in tree growth, but it should be remembered that trees are by no means unique in directing a large amount of assimilate below-ground – the below-ground biomass of several grasses is 35–90% of their total biomass (Marshall 1977).

III.   THE USE OF THE SOIL RESOURCES

The main considerations in the use of soil resources are: the transfer characteristics of the soil for water and nutrients, the 'abundance' of absorbing surfaces (that is, the amount of roots and mycorrhizal hyphae per unit soil volume) and their absorption characteristics.

A.   Root abundance and distribution

Root 'abundance' is usually expressed as L_v (cm root cm^{-3} of soil) or L_A (cm root cm^{-2} soil surface). Table I shows that L_v is often an order of magnitude

TABLE I. Root 'abundance' (length per unit soil volume) of some tree species and of grasses (from Bowen 1984)

Species	Age (yr)	Soil depth (cm)	Root abundance L_v (cm cm^{-3} soil)
Pinus radiata	3–4	0–10	0·13–0·18
		10–20	0·28–0·34
		40–50	0·03
	8	0–10	1·1–2·9
	14–26	0–8	2·0
		25–45	0·8
		91–106	0·4
Pinus sylvestris	30	0–15	5·26
		15–30	1·25
		45–61	0·34
		91–106	0·08
Picea sitchensis	11	surface horizons	1·7–2·8
Eucalyptus marginata		0–10	<8
		50–60	0·2
		1600	0·005
Grasses		0–15	50
Cereals		0–15	5–25
		25–50	4

smaller in forest trees than in cereals and other grasses. Allowing for root turnover during the year, the cumulative L_v of trees would be greater than shown in Table I, but the generality above still holds. For horticultural trees, Atkinson (1980) documented L_A values of 0·8 to 69, compared with 52–320 for herbs and 100–4000 for grasses. The major concentrations of tree roots occur in the surface 15–30 cm of soil (Table I); root concentrations decrease markedly below 30 cm, but a few roots often occur several metres deep (up to 50 m with some species, Taylor & Klepper 1978). Even in surface soils, the distances between tree roots are large compared with those of grasses; for instance, in stands of Pinus radiata, the mean distance between roots in the 'long' and 'short lateral' classes is 9 mm (Bowen 1973). However, soil exploration is supplemented considerably by the growth of mycorrhizal fungi from the roots. In some ectomycorrhizas, aggregations of hyphae (mycelial strands) can permeate the soil between roots and grow into litter up to 12 cm from the mycorrhizas (Skinner & Bowen 1974a). In VA mycorrhizas, some 80 cm of hyphae can be produced for each centimetre of root infected (Sanders & Tinker 1973). Despite the high respiration rates of mycorrhizas, they are relatively cost-efficient: the length/weight ratio of fungal hyphae can be 500 or more times that of fine roots. Factors affecting the growth of mycorrhizal fungi into soil have received scant study, despite the fact that this growth is the main cause of mycorrhizal stimulation of plant growth. Soil factors, such as compaction (Skinner & Bowen 1974b), markedly affect fungal growth into soils, and there is also considerable variation among mycorrhizal fungi in the extent to which they permeate the soil, giving scope for selection of mycorrhizal fungi in this.

B.   Water uptake

Detailed discussions of water uptake in soil-plant systems have been presented by Feddes (1981), Taylor and Klepper (1978), Landsberg and Fowkes (1978) and Passioura (1981). Despite uncertainties about many aspects of root behaviour, and the complexities of the system (Feddes 1981), there is sufficient information to provide guidelines about the relationship between root abundance and water uptake.

The movement of water in soils more moist than $-1\,\mathrm{MPa}$ is usually rapid (the exception being coarse, sandy soils), so transport to the root is normally not a problem. The hydraulic conductivity of suberized parts of fine roots may be 40–70% of that of unsuberized roots (see Bowen 1984). Suberized roots have therefore been assumed to be important in water uptake from soil; this assumption is made in almost all models of water uptake. However, hydraulic conductivity measurements have invariably been made with roots bathed in water, and so they have indicated only the *potential* absorption ability of various parts of the root. There is an urgent need to examine water uptake by various root segments *in soil*, because root-soil contact is a major area of uncertainty. There may be as little as 40% contact as roots traverse soil pores (Atkinson 1980), and root-soil contact can be lessened further by root shrinkage – up to 50% during drying cycles (both diurnally and over longer drying periods). Whilst mucigel exuded by younger parts of roots may ensure significant contact between the soil and root apices, the mucigel thins considerably with cell extension, and is non-existent in suberized areas (R. C. Foster, unpublished). Passioura (1981) pointed out that plants seem to find it more difficult to extract water from soil than from solution.

The hydraulic conductivities of mycorrhizal and non-mycorrhizal roots are often similar (Sands & Theodorou 1981; Sands, Bowen and Sanders, unpublished), although Hardie and Leyton (1981) found that the hydraulic conductivities of mycorrhizal roots of clover plants were 2 to 3 times greater than those of (smaller) non-mycorrhizal roots. Hyphal growth into soil may well facilitate transport of water to the root, especially under drying conditions and in coarse sandy soils. Hyphae could also form a bridge with the soil when root shrinkage occurs, or when the soil/root resistance is large. It has been demonstrated that tritiated water is transported to ectomycorrhizas in mycelial strands (Duddridge *et al.* 1980) and water transport could occur in them either by cytoplasmic streaming (up to $12\,\mathrm{cm\,h^{-1}}$ in VA mycorrhizal hyphae, see Harley & Smith 1983) or by mass flow along dead cells or intracellular spaces (see micrographs by Foster 1981). The relatively small radius of dead hyphae (2–$5\,\mu\mathrm{m}$) suggests that the flow rate in them is much smaller than in tracheids (10–$25\,\mu\mathrm{m}$ radius) (Poiseuilles' Law), but their great abundance may offset this size disadvantage. Critical *quantitative* studies are needed to evaluate the role of mycorrhizas in water transport, bearing in mind that they could have an important role in drying conditions.

Both theory (Barley 1970) and observations on crop plants indicate that an L_v of one to two is sufficient for rapid water uptake in most soils; significant differences between three upland rice varieties, in the removal of soil water from subsoil, occurred when root concentrations were less than $0 \cdot 10 \, \text{mg cm}^{-3}$ ($\equiv L_v$ 1, my conversion) (Mambani & Lal 1983). Table I indicates that there are usually sufficient tree roots for effective water uptake in the surface 15–30 cm of soil, and sometimes possibly an excess of roots, especially if mycorrhizas have a significant role in water uptake.

The L_v of grasses is far in excess of that needed for effective water uptake. However, the sharing of soil nutrient and water resources by competing plants is proportional to their effective rooting lengths, so the much larger L_v of grasses, and some weeds, is a major reason for their strong competitive ability compared with trees (especially tree seedlings) for limited soil water (and nutrient) resources. For example, Sands and Nambiar (1984) reported that failure to control weeds resulted in severe water stress and up to 80% growth reduction in *P. radiata* trees during their first year.

Below 15–30 cm, tree root concentrations are far below those needed to use soil water effectively. For example, in the hot, dry South Australian summer, actual evapotranspiration of *P. radiata* forests is approximately one third to one half of potential evapotranspiration (5–6 mm day^{-1}) and growth is severely limited. Furthermore, with such low subsoil rooting densities, and such a high evaporative demand ($\equiv$ potential high flux into roots), high resistances develop rapidly between the soil and the roots (Williams 1974), thus limiting water uptake even more. The production and growth of cells are inhibited at much lower leaf water potentials (0 to $-0 \cdot 6$ MPa) than are photosynthesis and respiration ($-0 \cdot 5$ to $1 \cdot 0$ MPa, $-0 \cdot 5$ to $-1 \cdot 5$ MPa respectively) (Hsiao *et al.* 1976), and it may be concluded that water absorption by subsoil roots is insufficient to sustain cellular growth, and so is principally directed to tree survival, especially under high evapotranspiration conditions. Subsoil roots are also important in ameliorating competition from grasses in the second and subsequent seasons (Sands & Nambiar 1984).

Apart from selecting for finer roots (having the same L_v with less biomass), the most important attribute of tree roots to manage, or select for, from a water viewpoint, could be their relative distribution with depth. There is a strong case for examination of genetic variation. In parallel with suggestions by Passioura (1981) for wheat, it would be an advantage to reduce extravagant water use by the tree early in the growing season, and to eke out the supply as far into summer as possible, thus prolonging the effective growing season. Water use efficiency (photosynthesis per unit of water transpired) in *P. radiata* increases under mild water stress (Sands *et al.* 1984) (but effects on cell extension must also be considered). A reduction in L_v in the surface soil layers, and complementary increases in rooting below 30 cm, could be of considerable advantage in optimizing photosynthesis and growth for a much longer period. Such genetic differences in root distribution are not uncommon in agricultural species.

C. Nutrient uptake

1. *Absorption*

As for water uptake, there are no good measurements of the inflow of nutrients into different parts of roots in *soil*, although this should not be difficult to measure experimentally, especially using isotopic tracers. Inflow analyses invariably average inflow over the whole root system (Nye & Tinker 1977). In pine, ions can be rapidly absorbed from solution for several centimetres behind the apex (Bowen 1970; Bowen, unpublished), and this often correlates with the distribution of assimilates along the root. Chung and Kramer (1975) found that the suberized parts of *Pinus taeda* roots could have 60% of the potential absorption ability of unsuberized parts, but their measurements were made in solution, so the problem of contact with the soil remains a major question, as with water uptake. Mycorrhizas rapidly absorb ions such as $H_2PO_4^-$ and Zn^{++} from solution (see Bowen 1980a), often at much the same rate per unit of surface area as unsuberized roots (Bowen 1973).

Interspecific and intraspecific differences in ion selectivity almost certainly occur in tree species as in agronomic species (Clark 1983), thus influencing tolerance of toxic ions, such as sodium and chloride, and tolerance of acidic and calcareous soils, such as observed in provenances of *Fagus sylvatica* (Teissier du Cros & Lepoutre 1983).

Quite large differences occur in the rate of absorption of phosphate from solution by different gentoypes of *P. radiata* (Bowen & Theodorou, unpublished) and by different types of ectomycorrhizas (Bowen 1973), and these can be described in terms of Michaelis-Menten kinetics. However, the real question is the extent to which such differences are important in the uptake of phosphate *in soil*. For ions such as $H_2PO_4^-$, Cu^{++}, Zn^{++}, NH_4^+, and to some extent K^+, the limiting factor in uptake is not potential absorption ability, but ion transfer through soil, and it is unlikely, therefore, that selection of genotypes for greater uptake of these ions from solution will be valuable. Genotypic differences in the minimum concentration from which ions can be absorbed (eg $H_2PO_4^-$ and K^+ in maize, Schenk & Barber 1980) may be important, as has been suggested in mycorrhizal function.

Given an *abundance* of highly *mobile* ions such as NO_3^-, SO_4^{--} and Ca^{++} in soil, genetic differences in absorption from solution would be paralleled by differences in uptake from soil. An inflow analysis by Nye and Tinker (1977) suggested that an L_A of 100 cm root cm^{-2} soil surface would be sufficient to supply a crop with 4 kg N ha^{-1} d^{-1} from a continual supply from a 0.5×10^{-3} M nitrogen solution. On this basis, and assuming an uptake of 60 kg N ha^{-1} yr^{-1} (as in *Pinus nigra* var. *maritima* plantations; Miller 1984), the abundance and absorption ability of tree roots is likely to be quite adequate to supply the tree with N, and, in low-input silvicultural systems, N uptake is likely to be limited more by the N supply in the soil than by root absorbing power. However, genotypic differences in absorption rates of nitrate, and many other ions, may be important where sudden flushes of nutrients occur naturally or following the application of fertilizers.

2. *Availability of nutrients*

Some plant species can increase the availability of nutrients in the rhizosphere by producing organic acids (solubilizing phosphates), surface phosphatases and siderophores (which chelate iron). The quantitative aspects of this phenomenon need more research (Bowen 1984) and little is known of genetic variation within species. Most mycorrhizal fungi use essentially the same phosphate sources as higher plants (see Harley & Smith 1983), but there are indications that some VA mycorrhizas can use insoluble mineral phosphates as well (Bolan 1983). Selection for this character may be important.

3. *Use of nutrients in roots*

Variation (with environment and genotype) in the key factor of transport of nutrients from tree roots to shoots, has received little attention. In general, least nutrient is transported to the shoot when plants are under nutrient stress. Jahromi *et al.* (1976) indicated that genotypic differences existed within *Pinus elliottii* in phosphate incorporation in the root, and in translocation to the shoot. Similarly, Gordon and Promnitz (1976) found that clones of *Populus* had consistent and large differences in rates of nitrate reduction, which were correlated positively with field growth. Effects of nutrition on assimilation processes in shoots were discussed by Bowen and Cartwright (1977), and Linder and Rook (1984).

One of the most important aspects of nutrient use by roots is the root's storage function – a phenomenon only poorly developed in annuals, but of potentially great importance in perennials. Most studies have been on fruit trees. Soil temperatures in the autumn, and sometimes in winter, are often high enough to permit some root activity, and Tromp (1983) found that fertilizer nitrogen, applied in autumn, was absorbed and stored in apple roots and root stocks, and could determine the amount of spring growth – supplying at least half of the total N required by the new leaves in spring and summer. Potassium, calcium, and probably several other nutrients, can also be stored in roots, and knowledge of this storage is important in the timing of fertilizer applications. One of the major features of phosphate physiology of both VA mycorrhizas and ectomycorrhizas is their storage of phosphate (and translocation within the fungus) as polyphosphate granules. Other ions such as Ca^{++} are also associated with these granules. The possible ecological roles of such polyphosphate storage were discussed by Harley and Smith (1983).

4. *Root abundance and ion uptake*

In the absence of competition, an L_v of one to two is sufficient for roots to have ready access to ions such as NO_3^-, SO_4^{--} and Ca^{++}, which move to the root principally by convection in water. However, most nutrients are poorly mobile (eg $H_2PO_4^-$, K^+ and NH_4^+) or immobile (eg Cu^{++} and Zn^{++}) in soil. The transfer of such ions through soil to the root is the main factor limiting their uptake, and this transfer is affected by the amount of clay and organic surfaces in the soil, by the soil structure and by soil moisture. In a clay soil, diffusion of phosphate may occur over only a few μm to the root, but in a sandy soil some diffusion may occur over several mm (see Nye & Tinker 1977). Depletion zones around roots for poorly mobile ions are usually quite narrow, and, in these instances, ion uptake increases with increase in root length. For example, in a moist loam soil, an L_v of 6 (much greater than that of most trees) may lead to depletion of only 60% of the soil phosphate (Barley 1970), and for the immobile Cu ion it may be even less than 10%. It is not surprising therefore that (a) trees will often respond to the application of phosphate fertilizers, whereas grasses growing in the same soil, but with a high L_v and well-developed root hairs, do not respond, and (b) genotypic differences in phosphate uptake, and in the ability to respond to added phosphate (in clovers, Caradus 1983; and trees, Goddard & Hollis 1984), are closely related to differences in root length. Nambiar et al. (1982) found that 100% differences occurred among Pinus radiata families in the length per unit weight of regenerating lateral roots, and they concluded that selection for thinner roots (greater L_v for the same biomass) might be advantageous in nutrient uptake. Some tree species, such as some Eucalyptus spp., which are adapted to grow in low nutrient soils, have quite fine roots (Bowen 1980b). Similarly, genotypes with large numbers of laterals per unit root length would have large root lengths per unit root weight, because of the smaller radius of laterals. However, a more effective way to increase L_v may be to promote effective mycorrhizal development.

The very large length per unit weight of fungal hyphae, their extensive penetration into soil and organic matter, their absorption of several ions (including $H_2PO_4^-$, K^+, Zn^{++} and NH_4^+), and their transfer of ions to the root via the hyphae, are the major beneficial attributes of mycorrhizas in plant nutrition. Thus, the influx of phosphate into VA mycorrhizal onion roots was three times that into non-mycorrhizal roots (Sanders & Tinker 1973). The plant response to mycorrhizal infection depends on the soil fertility, the level of infection, and the extent to which the fungal hyphae grow into the soil. Plant growth increases of 50% to several hundred per cent are not unusual compared with uninfected plants (see Bowen 1980a; Harley & Smith 1983). Mycorrhiza production is an important alternate strategy complementary to (and often replacing) fine root production (Bowen 1980a). Marx and Bryan (1971) showed not only that mycorrhizal infection greatly increased the growth of Pinus elliottii var. elliottii trees, but also that infection with some mycorrhizal fungi removed genotypic differences in growth which occurred among uninfected trees. Nevertheless, there are gentoypic differences in tree responses to both ectomycorrhizas and VA mycorrhizas (Goddard & Hollis 1984), due possibly to differences in the numbers of short roots produced (the sites for ectomycorrhizal formation) and to quantitative differences in susceptibility to infection by the fungi.

Mycorrhizas are probably also extremely important in the process of competition between species for soil resources (Bowen 1980a), and therefore in the evolution of mixed communities containing trees. They also give the root the ability to compete with micro-organisms for nutrients released by litter decomposition.

We should not restrict our thinking on mycorrhizas to nutrient-deficient soils. Mycorrhizas will enhance nutrient uptake in many potentially fertile soils in which root growth is poor owing, for instance, to high acidity, high salinity, high soil temperatures or root disease, because hyphal growth will compensate (at least partly) for poor root growth (Bowen 1980a). All that is needed is to select, from the large genome of mycorrhizal fungi, ones which are less susceptible than the roots to a deleterious soil condition. The plant scientist therefore has both plant and mycorrhizal fungus genomes from which to select in order to enhance plant growth.

IV. ROOT-SHOOT INTEGRATION

Models of plant growth usually do not include the important role that roots play as producers of growth-regulating compounds that affect the shoots. Indeed, most treatises on plant growth regulators ignore roots. All known classes of plant growth regulators have been detected in root extracts. Indole-acetic acid and abscisic acid are produced in root cap cells (Bruinsma 1979) and the radial elongation of cortical cells of ectomycorrhizas suggests that they produce indole compounds (see Harley & Smith 1983). Cytokinins are present in high concentrations in root tips, in legume nodules, and in root exudates, and their production is closely related to root tip activity in a range of environments (Bruinsma 1979). Cytokinins are produced by some ectomy-corrhizal fungi in culture, and the enlarged nuclei of plant cortical cells in mycorrhizas, and large increases in the amount of cytoplasm in VA mycor-rhizal cells (see Harley & Smith 1983), suggest that mycorrhizas increase the levels of root cytokinins.

Cytokinins have major roles in leaf longevity (an important component of productivity), in the resistance of plants to stress conditions, and in flower morphogenesis (Bruinsma 1979). Decreases in leaf longevity in response to some nutrient deficiencies may be associated with decreases in cytokinin production in the roots (Bruinsma 1979). The production of zeatin by emerg-ing aerial nodal roots of maize is associated with both an increase in photo-synthesis and a temporary decrease in leaf expansion rate (Ješko 1981), while the breaking of dormancy in *Pseudotsuga menziesii* in spring, and shoot elongation in pear and apple are strongly associated with gibberellin produc-tion in the roots (Bruinsma 1979).

Independent of increased nutrient uptake, some ectomycorrhizal and some VA mycorrhizal fungi have physiological effects which are consistent with cytokinin production by the fungus or the associated plant cells (citrus, Levy & Krikun 1980; grasses, Allen *et al.* 1980; *P. menziesii*, Parke *et al.* 1983). Parke *et al.* (1983) droughted seedlings of *P. menziesii* and found that mycorrhizal seedlings developed much more negative leaf water potentials than non-mycorrhizal seedlings; furthermore, on rewetting, seedlings infected with some mycorrhizal fungi had photosynthetic rates ten times as great as those of non-mycorrhizal seedlings. It may be that judicious selection of mycorrhizal fungi is one avenue for manipulation of growth-regulating substances in the plant.

Growth regulator production by roots deserves increased *quantitative* study, particularly with regard to the breaking of dormancy, water and nutrient stress, and leaf longevity. Is there a quantitative relationship between root apex numbers or total apex volume, growth factor production, and shoot activity? Nambiar *et al.* (1982) showed that two- or three-fold differences existed between *Pinus radiata* genotypes in the numbers of new apices, and in the root length, produced at both 8°C and 11°C in regenerating roots; the implications of such observations for shoot growth, as well as for ion and water uptake, should be examined.

Obviously, a major interaction between roots and shoots is assimilate transfer to roots. Isebrands and Nelson (1983) found that assimilate distribution shifted dramatically in a basipetal direction following bud-set in poplar, and in one clone 60% of the assimilate from mature leaves was translocated to the root. Two clones differed in time of bud-set by four weeks, and they suggested that the larger amount of assimilate transferred to roots in the clone with earlier bud-set (which also produced the larger root/shoot ratio) could explain why it grew well in a wider range of soils.

V.   CONCLUSION

Productivity is often (perhaps usually) limited by soil resources. Although there are increasing numbers of reports on genotype×fertility interactions, it is rare for such phenomena to be dissected with regard to the two cardinal factors: (a) the efficiency of water and nutrient uptake from soil (the subject of this paper), and (b) the efficiency with which these resources are used after they have been absorbed. Both factors need to be addressed.

There is considerable scope for a greater quantitative understanding of roots and mycorrhizas in the use of soil resources, in growth factor production, and in the use of assimilates, before we can have a full understanding of root growth and tree productivity. Genetic variation in the amount of assimilate going to the roots, relative to that going to the harvested product, is worth examining, but the question of how much root a tree 'needs' cannot be divorced from site management considerations. Trees have evolved for persistence in a wide range of conditions, not for productivity – the parameter with which we are concerned when they are grown as crop plants. In general, a relation exists between extensive root growth, adaptability to a wide range of soils, and effective competition with other species. A basic question is whether we should select genotypes which can adapt to a wide range of sites (with increased 'costs' of root production) or whether we should select genotypes specifically for fertile sites, subject to high inputs and intensive management.

I have not dealt with ways of manipulating roots and their functions by employing management practices; instead I have concentrated on exploiting plant genetic and mycorrhizal variation. I suggest that tree species are fairly 'conservative' compared with other species in the amount of assimilate that they divert to root growth, but this does not mean that we cannot select more efficient ideotypes. Trees have evolved two efficient mechanisms giving great flexibility, (a) the production and turnover of fine roots, and (b) mycorrhizas. Genotypic differences probably exist in almost every parameter of root structure and function discussed above, and mycorrhizas provide a large genome from which we may select genotypes that will enhance tree growth in many situations.

REFERENCES

Allen, M. F., Moore, T. S. jr & Christensen, M. (1980). Phytohormone changes in *Bouteloua gracilis* infected by vesicular-arbuscular mycorrhizae: 1. Cytokinin increases in the host plant. *Can. J. Bot.*, **58**, 371–374.

Atkinson, D. (1980). The distribution and effectiveness of the roots of tree crops. *Hortic. Rev.*, **2**, 424–490.

Barley, K. P. (1970). The configuration of the root system in relation to nutrient uptake. *Adv. Agron.*, **22**, 159–201.

Bevege, D. I., Bowen, G. D. & Skinner M. F. (1975). Comparative carbohydrate physiology of ecto- and endomycorrhizas. In: *Endomycorrhizas*, edited by F. E. Sanders, B. Mosse and P. B. Tinker, 149–174. New York; London: Academic Press.

Bolan, N. S. (1983). *Phosphate adsorption by soil constituents and its effects on plant response to both phosphorus application and mycorrhizal infection.* Ph.D. thesis, University of Western Australia.

Bowen, G. D. (1970). Effects of soil temperature on root growth and on phosphate uptake along *Pinus radiata* roots. *Aust. J. Soil Res.*, **8**, 31–42.

Bowen, G. D. (1973). Mineral nutrition of ectomycorrhizae. In: *Ectomycorrhizae*, edited by G. C. Marks and T. T. Kozlowski, 151–205. New York; London: Academic Press.

Bowen, G. D. (1980a). Mycorrhizal roles in tropical plants and ecosystems. In: *Tropical mycorrhiza research*, edited by P. Mikola, 165–190. Oxford: Oxford University Press.

Bowen, G. D. (1980b). Coping with low nutrients. In: *The biology of Australian native plants*, edited by J. S. Pate and A. J. McComb, 33–64. Perth: University of Western Australia Press.

Bowen, G. D. (1984). Tree roots and the use of soil nutrients. In: *Nutrition of plantation forests*, edited by G. D. Bowen and E. K. S. Nambiar, 147–179. London: Academic Press.

Bowen, G. D. & Cartwright, B. (1977). Mechanisms and models of plant nutrition. In: *Soil factors in crop production in a semi-arid environment*, edited by J. S. Russell and E. L. Greacen, 197–223. St Lucia: University of Queensland Press.

Bruinsma, J. (1979). Root hormones and overground development. In: *Plant regulation and world agriculture*, edited by T. K. Scott, 35–47. New York; London: Plenum.

Caradus, J. R. (1983). Genetic differences in phosphorus absorption among white clover populations. *Pl. Soil*, **72**, 379–383.

Chung, H. H. & Kramer, P. J. (1975). Absorption of water and ^{32}P through suberized and unsuberized roots of loblolly pine. *Can. J. For. Res.*, **5**, 229–235.

Clark, R. B. (1983). Plant genotype differences in the uptake, translocation, accumulation and use of mineral elements required for plant growth. *Pl. Soil*, **72**, 175–196.

Duddridge, J. A., Malibari, A. & Read, D. J. (1980). Structure and function of mycorrhizal rhizomorphs with special reference to their role in water transport. *Nature, Lond.*, **287**, 834–836.

Feddes, R. A. (1981). Water use models for assessing root zone modification. In: *Modifying the root environment to reduce crop stress*, edited by G. F. Arkin and H. M. Taylor, 347–390. Michigan: American Society of Agricultural Engineers.

Fogel, R. & Hunt, G. (1979). Fungal and arboreal biomass in a western Oregon Douglas fir ecosystem: distribution patterns and turnover. *Can. J. For. Res.*, **9**, 245–256.

Foster, R. C. (1981). Mycelial strands of *Pinus radiata* D. Don: ultra structure and histochemistry. *New Phytol.*, **88**, 705–712.

Goddard, R. E. & Hollis, C. A. (1984). The genetic basis of forest tree nutrition. In: *Nutrition of plantation forests*, edited by G. D. Bowen and E. K. S. Nambiar, 237–258. London: Academic Press.

Gordon, J. C. & Promnitz, L. C. (1976). Photosynthetic and enzymatic criteria for the early selection of fast-growing *Populus* clones. In: *Tree physiology and yield improvement*, edited by M. G. R. Cannell and F. T. Last, 79–97. London: Academic Press.

Hardie, K. & Leyton, L. (1981). The influence of vesicular-arbuscular mycorrhiza on growth and water relations of red clover. I. In phosphate deficient soil. *New Phytol.*, **89**, 599–608.

Harley, J. L. & Smith, S. E. (1983). *Mycorrhizal symbiosis.* London: Academic Press.

Hsiao, T. C., Acevedo, E., Fereres, E. & Henderson, D. W. (1976). Water stress, growth, and osmotic adjustment. *Phil. Trans. R. Soc.*, **273B**, 479–500.

Isebrands, J. G. & Nelson, N. D. (1983). Distribution of ^{14}C-labelled photosynthates within intensively cultured *Populus* clones during the establishment year. *Physiologia Pl.*, **59**, 9–18.

Jahromi, S. T., Smith, W. H. & Goddard, R. E. (1976). Genotype×fertilizer interactions in slash pine: variation in phosphate (^{33}P) incorporation. *Forest Sci.*, **22**, 21–30.

Ješko, T. (1981). Inter-organ control of photosynthesis mediated by emerging nodal roots in young maize plants. In: *Structure and function of plant roots*, edited by R. Brouwer, O. Gasparíková, J. Kolek and B. C. Loughman, 367–371. The Hague: Martinus Nijhoff/Junk.

Landsberg, J. J. & Fowkes, N. D. (1978). Water movement through plant roots. *Ann. Bot.*, **42**, 493–508.

Levy, Y. & Krikun, J. (1980). Effect of vesicular-arbuscular mycorrhiza on *Citrus jambhiri* water relations. *New Phytol.*, **85**, 25–31.

Linder, S. & Axelsson, B. (1982). Changes in carbon uptake and allocation patterns as a result of irrigation and fertilization in a young *Pinus sylvestris* stand. *Proc. IUFRO Workshop P.I. 07–00* (Ecology of subalpine zones), 38–44.

Linder, S. & Rook, D. A. (1984). Effects of mineral nutrition on carbon dioxide exchange and partitioning of carbon in trees. In: *Nutrition of plantation forests*, edited by G. D. Bowen and E. K. S. Nambiar, 211–236. London: Academic Press.

Mambani, B. & Lal, R. (1983). Response of upland rice varieties to drought stress III. Estimating root system configuration from soil moisture data. *Pl. Soil*, **73**, 95–104.

Marshall, J. K. (1977). Biomass and production partitioning in response to environment in some North American grasslands. In: *The belowground ecosystem: a synthesis of plant-associated processes*, edited by J. K. Marshall, 73–84. Colorado: Colorado State University.

Marx, D. H. & Bryan, W. C. (1971). Formation of ectomycorrhizae on half-sib progenies of slash pine in aseptic culture. *Forest Sci.*, **17**, 488–492.

Miller, H. G. (1984). Dynamics of nutrient cycling in plantation ecosystems. In: *Nutrition of plantation forests*, edited by G. D. Bowen and E. K. S. Nambiar, 53–78. London: Academic Press.

Nambiar, E. K. S., Cotterill, P. P. & Bowen, G. D. (1982). Genetic differences in the root regeneration of radiata pine. *J. exp. Bot.*, **33**, 170–177.

Nye, P. H. & Tinker, P. B. (1977). *Solute movement in the soil-root system.* Oxford: Blackwell Scientific.

Parke, J. L., Linderman, R. G. & Black, C. H. (1983). The role of ectomycorrhizas in drought tolerance of Douglas-fir seedlings. *New Phytol.*, **95**, 83–95.

Passioura, J. B. (1981). Water collection by roots. In: *The physiology and biochemistry of drought resistance in plants*, edited by L. G. Paleg and D. Aspinall, 39–53. New York; London: Academic Press.

Paul, E. A. & Kucey, R. M. N. (1981). Carbon flow in plant microbial associations. *Science, N.Y.*, **213**, 473–474.

Persson, H. Å. (1983). The distribution and productivity of fine roots in boreal forests. *Pl. Soil*, **71**, 87–101.

Roberts, J. (1976). A study of root distribution and growth in a *Pinus sylvestris* L. (Scots pine) plantation in East Anglia. *Pl. Soil*, **44**, 607–621.

Sanders, F. E. & Tinker, P. B. (1973). Phosphate flow into mycorrhizal roots. *Pestic. Sci.*, **4**, 385–395.

Sands, R., Kriedemann, P. E. & Cotterill, P. P. (1984). Water relations and photosynthesis in three families of radiata pine seedlings known to differ in their response to weed control. *For. Ecol. Manage.*, **9**, 173–184.

Sands, R. & Nambiar, E. K. S. (1984). Water relations of *Pinus radiata* (D.Don) in competition with weeds. *Can. J. For. Res.*, **14**, 233–237.

Sands, R. & Theodorou, C. (1981). Water uptake by mycorrhizal roots of radiata pine seedlings. *Aust. J. Plant Physiol.*, **5**, 301–309.

Schenk, M. K. & Barber, S. A. (1980). Potassium and phosphorus uptake by corn genotypes grown in the field as influenced by root characteristics. *Pl. Soil*, **54**, 65–76.

Skinner, M. F. & Bowen, G. D. (1974a). The uptake and translation of phosphate by mycelial strands of pine mycorrhizas. *Soil Biol. Biochem.*, **6**, 53–56.

Skinner, M. F. & Bowen, G. D. (1974b). The penetration of soil by mycelial strands of pine mycorrhizas. *Soil Biol. Biochem.*, **6**, 57–61.

Taylor, H. M. & Klepper, B. (1978). The role of rooting characteristics in the supply of water to plants. *Adv. Agron.*, **30**, 99–128.

Teissier du Cros, E. T. & Lepoutre, B. (1983). Soil×provenance interaction in beech (*Fagus sylvatica* L.). *Forest Sci.*, **29**, 403–411.

Tromp, J. (1983). Nutrient reserves in roots of fruit trees, in particular carbohydrates and nitrogen. *Pl. Soil*, **71**, 401–413.

Vogt, K. A., Grier, C. C., Meier, C. E. & Edmunds, R. L. (1982). Mycorrhizal role in net primary production and nutrient cycling in *Abies amabilis* (Dougl.) Forbes ecosystems in western Washington. *Ecology*, **63**, 370–380.

Williams, J. (1974). Root density and water potential gradients near the plant root. *J. exp. Bot.*, **25**, 669–674.

19

IMPROVING TREE CROPS USING MICRO-ORGANISMS IN DESIGNED SYSTEMS

J. C. GORDON and M. E. AVERY
*School of Forestry and Environmental Studies, Yale University,
New Haven, Connecticut, USA*

I. INTRODUCTION: THE NEED FOR DESIGNED SYSTEMS

Competition for land resources requires silviculturists and land managers to examine seriously ways to improve crop yields, sustain productivity, and to produce a variety of products from each land unit. The trend toward shorter rotations, and the increasing costs of off-site inputs make this requirement particularly evident. There is a need, therefore, for designed systems which incorporate crop mixtures, and which exploit on-site factors (like N_2 fixers) that can provide continuous inputs, rather than for the 'one-shot' single factor approach of our current cultural practices.

Two hypotheses underlie this paper: first, that the biochemical and physiological interactions of microbes and forest crops present a vast and little exploited opportunity to understand sustained forest productivity; and second, that tree crop systems can be designed so that crop requirements – for nutrients, water and protection from pests – are supplied, to a much greater degree than at present, from on-site resources, eliminating or greatly reducing the need for energy and materials from off-site sources.

Most forest researchers will find the first hypothesis credible; few would seriously entertain the second. Nevertheless, we will argue that the genius of forestry and tree crop production generally lies precisely in providing more on-site resources. Under most economic conditions throughout the world, minimization of off-site additions to crops results in cost savings, if yields are maintained. Thus, for example, the substitution of symbiotically fixed nitrogen for commercial fertilizers is attractive in economies where fossil fuels are scarce or expensive (Domingo 1983). In effect, on-site photosynthate is substituted for off-site hydrocarbon with a high 'up-front' cost.

Our purpose here is to explore, from the point of view of silviculturists, some of the diversity of micro-organisms and physiological processes available for inclusion in integrated tree crop systems (Gordon & Avery 1983) and to suggest some ways in which they are, or can be, used to increase yields.

II. BIOLOGICAL DIVERSITY IN TREE-MICROBE SYSTEMS

An enormous variety of microbes and associated higher plants are available for use in constructing crop systems. Here, we will emphasize nitrogen-fixing and mycorrhizal organisms. The broad range of micro-organisms involved in decomposition and nitrogen transformation, and their invertebrate partners, provides an equally rich potential, which we treat only cursorily (Nadelhoffer *et al.* 1983).

A. Free-living nitrogen fixers

Relatively little is known about the occurrence, distribution and importance of free-living, nitrogenase-containing micro-organisms in forest soils. In general, their net input of nitrogen into forest soils is estimated to be low everywhere, and in some places nonexistent (Akkermans & Houwers 1983). Recent research indicates that foliar free-living bacteria contribute less fixed nitrogen to temperate trees than previously thought (Jones 1982). Nevertheless, those free-living organisms, capable themselves of photosynthesis (ie the Cyanobacteria or blue-green algae), or those capable of living in close association with roots (rhizosphere organisms), have the potential to add appreciable quantities of nitrogen to some sites. The overriding limitation on the use of free-living organisms is energy supply (see below). Unless – through selection, mutation or the application of recombinant DNA techniques – free-living nitrogen fixers can be made photosynthetically more effective, or can be given greater access to the photosynthetic capacity of higher plants, their contribution will remain small. Perhaps, in the latter case, trees with roots that 'leak' carbohydrates can be selected or developed to enhance fixation by rhizosphere organisms. Those organisms that are photosynthetic, such as the Cyanobacteria, are handicapped as crop components, because they are restricted to the surface or uppermost layer of the forest floor if they are to intercept light and thus be photosynthetically effective. Nevertheless, if free-living organisms can be adequately supplied with energy, perhaps by direct coupling with decomposers, they have at least two potential advantages for crop improvement: (a) the Cyanobacteria add a large, diverse taxonomic group to the arsenal of crop components, and (b) free-living organisms generally can be easily transported and distributed over a wide range of soils and crops.

B.   Other free-living organisms

Nitrogen, and other plant nutrients are ordinarily not available for uptake by tree crops when in organic combination. Also, partially decomposed organic matter – derived from the sloughing off of plant parts, and acted upon by vertebrate, invertebrate and micro-organism decomposers – strongly affects soil properties by its quantity and kind. Some far-reaching effects have been attributed to decomposition rates; for example, Harrison (cited by Chambers 1983) attributes the prevalence of rural poverty in the tropics to rapid organic matter decomposition rates. In many places, for many cultural purposes, it would be advantageous to speed up or slow down rates of organic matter decomposition, and many cultural techniques now in use (eg clear-cutting, thinning, fertilization, burning and swamp drainage) affect decomposition rates. Little effort, however, has been focused on manipulating micro-organism populations directly to alter organic matter decomposition rates. Nadelhoffer et al. (1983) report that total soil nitrogen was not related to nitrogen mineralization rate, and recommended that increasing the size of the actively cycling nitrogen pool would increase forest productivity. The deliberate decomposition of Fomes-infected stump and root systems, and the addition of decomposers to Pinus contorta slash are operational in pilot-scale experiments.

Similarly, the direct modification of nitrogen-transforming microbe populations in tree crops, to reduce nitrogen volatilization or to affect nitrate supplies, has not been tried on any large scale, although research on environmental influences on soil nitrogen transformation has been extensive (Alexander 1977). Because of the close coupling of decomposition, denitrification, and nitrogen uptake in most forest soils, little improvement is thought to be possible, beyond the acceleration of decomposition in certain temperate and boreal systems (Wollum & Davey 1975). Nevertheless, the slowing or alteration of decomposition may be beneficial in certain tropical and subtropical tree-soil combinations, where the objective is to increase the soil organic matter content, as on mine spoils, or in the rehabilitation of waste lands created by a combination of overcropping and drought.

C.   Mycorrhizal fungi

Mycorrhizas are the result of a symbiotic biotrophy between a fungus and the absorbing organ, usually a root, of a host plant. An enormous array of fungal species, fungus-host combinations and functional inter-relationships occur in nature (Mosse *et al.* 1981). Trappe (1977) estimated that at least 2000 species of fungus form mycorrhizal associations with *Pseudotsuga menziesii* alone. Also, because fungal hyphae extend from mycorrhizas far into soil uncolonized by roots or mycorrhizas, the absorbing capacity of the host can be vastly increased. Thus, a decision to study only roots or mycorrhizas may seriously under-estimate the role of mycorrhizal fungi in nutrient and water uptake (Fogel 1979). Conversely, if carbon allocation from host plant photosynthesis to only mycorrhizas and roots is measured, the carbon uptake related to nutrient and water absorption may also be seriously under-estimated (France & Reid 1983).

Mycorrhizas, and their associated hyphae, absorb and store nutrients, as well as increase nutrient solubility through the release of organic acids, and perhaps through the enzymatic decomposition of soil organic compounds (Reid & Hacskaylo 1982).

The most spectacular effects of deliberate inoculation with mycorrhizal fungi have been in nurseries that (a) were prairie soils (Hacskaylo 1973), (b) were previously used for annual agriculture, or (c) were fumigated to kill pathogens and thus were depleted of beneficial fungi. Field inoculation of highly disturbed soils may promote the establishment of planted seedlings, or may speed revegetation of denuded areas. Several reports indicate that harvesting and site preparation activities can alter naturally occurring levels of inoculum (Mikola 1948; Shaw & Sidle 1983). Currently, inoculum of fungal species, and inoculation techniques are being prepared for use in nursery culture (Marx & Barnett 1974; Molina & Chamard 1983), but studies linking nursery inoculation, tree establishment, and stand performance in defined cultural systems are lacking. Part of the problem is the laboriousness of field studies on mycorrhizal quantity, turnover and function (Fogel 1979). Perhaps an even larger problem is the 'single factor' view , which either focuses entirely on, or completely ignores, the existence of mycorrhizas. Nevertheless, the diversity of associations, functions and species of fungi and hosts promises large rewards, if a systematic effort is made to manipulate mycorrhizal fungi as a component of all tree crop systems.

D.   Symbiotic nitrogen fixation

At least two genera of nitrogen-fixing bacteria are capable of infecting the roots of some woody plants (hosts), with the result that 'nodules' (modified lateral roots harbouring the bacteria) are formed. Within the nodules, the nitrogen-fixing (nif) genes of the bacterium are expressed, and the reduction of N_2 to the level of NH_3 is fueled by photosynthate supplied by the host. The nodules also create conditions under which the nitrogenase enzyme complex is protected from excessive oxygen, and where reduced nitrogen is assimilated into amino acids, which are subsequently transported within the plant. This process allows infected trees to grow and to reproduce with a very small input of exogenous available nitrogen.

The taxonomic diversity of these relationships is, again, enormous. The family Leguminosae, primarily known in agriculture as pulses and pasture crops, is, in reality, primarily a family of tropical woody plants (Becking 1982), with several subtropical and temperate representatives widely used in forestry and horticulture. The legume-*Rhizobium* symbiosis has been studied for agricultural crops, and studies are under way in selected woody species. Indeed, the only known non-legume to be effectively nodulated by a *Rhizobium* species is a woody member of the genus *Parasponia* (*Ulmaceae*). Inoculation with 'superior' strains of *Rhizobium* is common practice in agriculture, but it is as yet rarely done on tree crops. Often, tree legumes are widely planted without knowing the effectiveness or persistence of nodulation, and little is known, for woody species, about competition between inoculated *Rhizobia* and naturally occurring wild types. Nevertheless, nitrogen fixation rates of $50–200\,kg\,ha^{-1}yr^{-1}$ have been reported (Becking 1982), and beneficial effects of leguminous trees on companion crops have been known for a long time.

Less well known are the woody species exhibiting *Alnus*-type, or actinorhizal, symbioses with *Frankia* species. Only in the last 10 years have *Frankia* endophytes been definitively isolated in pure culture (Callaham *et al.* 1978), although the soil-improving qualities of alders have long been recognized. Currently, 20 genera, mostly woody, are known to be nodulated by *Frankia*. Of these, *Alnus* is the most studied and most used in temperate forestry, and the Casuarinas, particularly *Casuarina equiselifolia*, are best known in tropical locations (Bond 1976; Lawrie 1982). Although, with few exceptions, both hosts and endophytes are less well known than legumes and rhizobia, their taxonomic and habitat diversity is greater, and for this reason they may show equal or greater promise in tree crop systems. The greater taxonomic diversity of *Frankia* symbioses, relative to *Rhizobium* symbioses, may also mean that, if attempts are to be made to transfer symbioses to non-nodulating species, it should be first tried with *Frankia* rather than with *Rhizobium*.

Three concerns are paramount in research on nitrogen-fixing trees. First, the available diversity should be captured, catalogued and used before we focus too much on one or a few species. Second, the characteristics of optimum symbioses, for specific systems, should be defined and used to select hosts and endophytes jointly. Third, the costs and benefits of symbiotic nitrogen fixation need to be explored more rigorously, because both are real but unquantified for most systems (Turvey & Smethurst 1983). Economic analysis will undoubtedly temper any euphoria about 'free' nitrogen. The management and energy costs of symbiotically fixed nitrogen are high, and it will be used only in those systems where the use of industrially fixed nitrogen is economically or socially constrained (Gordon 1983).

III. ENERGY RELATIONS IN TREE-MICROBE INTERACTIONS

The governing factor, if there can be said to be one in tree-microbe relations, is the capture and partitioning of energy within the crop. For free-living microbes, the provision of energy from tree to microbe is indirect or non-existent (as in the Cyanobacteria), and is best viewed in the context of ecosystem carbon cycling. The physiology of the host-endophyte, or hostmycosymbiont, interaction is, on the other hand, intimate and complex. The diversion of host photosynthate to nodules or mycorrhizas immediately raises the practical question of whether the investment is worthwhile, or whether the energy would be better used in the economically valuable portion of the crop. To answer this question fully requires a better understanding of host-symbiont physiology than we now have. Here, we attempt a general treatment of the major features of photosynthate production and allocation in infected trees.

A. Photosynthate production

Insofar as symbionts provide trees with additional nitrogen, nutrients and water, they have the capacity to increase dry matter production directly by increasing rates of photosynthesis and leaf areas. Symbionts may also increase photosynthetic rates by providing additional metabolic sinks where photosynthates can be off-loaded (Paul & Kucey 1981). Nodules on *Alnus*, for example, have been calculated to be stronger sinks than the vascular-cambium (Bormann & Gordon 1984). Set against these increases are reductions in net photosynthetic production resulting from (a) the respiration costs of maintaining microsymbiont tissues, as well as tissue produced in the host in response to infection, and (b) the increased absorption and reduction of nutrient compounds. The latter are, of course, particularly severe for nitrogen-fixing symbioses. Most nodulating species will grow more rapidly if kept in the unnodulated state and provided with combined nitrogen, indicating that the energy cost of symbiotic nitrogen is higher than the cost of absorbing combined nitrogen from the soil solution (Dawson & Gordon 1979). Indeed, nitrogen reduction in nodules is ultimately limited by the photosynthetic capacity of the host, as indicated by studies of the effect of enhanced or retarded host photosynthesis on nitrogen reduction rates in nodules (Hardy & Havelka 1976; Gordon & Wheeler 1978). Thus, the enhancement of photosynthetic capacity, by genetic or cultural means (other than by applying combined nitrogen), may enhance growth and dry mass accumulation more in nodulated than in unnodulated plants. An inevitable consequence of enhanced photosynthetic capacity is enhanced nodular nitrogen reduction, if patterns of photosynthate distribution within the plant remain the same (Gordon & Wheeler 1978).

B. Photosynthate distribution

Loomis (1953) proposed a 'growth correlation' model of photosynthate distribution for plants that, with modification, can describe this process in nodulated or mycorrhizal trees. Thus, the apical meristems of the top take precedence over the root apical meristems as sinks for photosynthetic carbon, with the lateral meristems taking lowest priority. Nodules, and by inference mycorrhizas, enhance the ability of roots to attract photosynthates. According to Loomis (1953), if the growth of apical meristems of the top is retarded by some environmental influence, without greatly decreasing the plant's photosynthetic capacity, an 'excess' of photosynthate can be created in the top. If cambial and root metabolic activity persists, a greater proportion of total photosynthate will reach them than before. In these circumstances, nodulated or mycorrhizal plants should allocate more carbon to below-ground dry mass and respiration than uninfected plants. In a study of *Vicia faba* infected by both a vesicular-arbuscular mycorrhizal fungus and a nodule causing *Rhizobium*, Paul and Kucey (1981) found that infection increased both carbon fixation and carbon allocation to roots. Further, infection with both microsymbionts increased nitrogen fixation, in comparison with those plants infected with *Rhizobium* alone. Similar studies should be pursued with woody species, to determine if optimum combinations of symbionts exist that enhance both photosynthesis and nitrogen fixation.

The Loomis model further predicts that root and top growth and dry mass accumulation will be cyclic. Increased allocation to roots should cause greater uptake of nutrients and reduction of nitrogen, which should, in turn, stimulate top growth – unless it is constrained by dormancy processes. Also, nutrient or water stress, which constrain top growth, should bring about a greater allocation of photosynthate to roots, and especially to mycorrhizas and nodules if they form higher order sinks. This hypothesis is consistent with the fact that (a) a greater fraction (40–60%) of total carbon is allocated to tree roots and mycorrhizas on poor than on favourable sites (Keyes & Grier 1981; Vogt *et al.* 1982; Cannell, McMurtrie, this volume), and (b) mycorrhizas and nodules form 'vigorously' on plants in poor soils and in high light environments (Hatch 1937; Björkman 1942).

A paradox arises from the observation that, at least within a species, hosts with the greatest photosynthetic capacity exhibit the greatest nitrogen fixation rates (Gordon & Wheeler 1978; Monaco *et al.* 1982). This paradox results from comparing nodulated plants with other nodulated plants, and merely indicates that those symbioses having the combined properties of 'vigorous' nodules and 'effective' leaves do relatively better as nitrogen fixers.

IV. EXAMPLES OF MANAGEMENT TECHNIQUES

Although the age of fully defined crops has not yet dawned, many examples of the purposeful use of microbes and microbial symbioses exist. A few examples involving trees as a crop component are given here.

A. Mycorrhizal fungi

Most operational applications of mycorrhizal inoculum have been as a single-factor additive, rather than as a portion of a whole designed system. The use of *Pisolithus tinctorius* inoculation of pine seedlings in the nursery, before outplanting on degraded sites (Marx *et al.* 1977), has been successful in increasing field survival and growth, and can be viewed as a system component for growing wood on poor or disturbed sites. The wide distribution of

Pisolithus tinctorius indicates that its use as a system component is potentially worldwide (Marx 1977). Similarly, the inoculation of nursery beds, after fumigation, or to promote the growth of exotic species, has become fairly common (Mikola 1970).

B.   Symbiotic nitrogen fixation

Plants capable of symbiotic nitrogen fixation are used in specialized systems, such as on spoil or dune reclamation sites (Gadgil 1983), in seed orchards (Tarrant 1983), and in forest grazing systems (Giumelli 1978). Funk *et al.* (1979) report that *Juglans nigra* grown in mixture with autumn olive (*Elaegnus umbellata*) was, on average, 82% taller after 9 years in the field, compared with *J. nigra* grown in pure stands. As yet, nitrogen-fixing symbionts have not been used on a large scale to replace commercially prepared fertilizers on 'normal' sites (Turvey & Smethurst 1983), even though most forests respond to added fixed nitrogen with increased growth. N_2 fixers have not been used, for the most part, because (a) species capable of symbiotic nitrogen fixation are either poorly adapted to forest conditions (eg pasture legumes) or are poorly understood (eg *Ceanothus* sp.), (b) it is feared that the N_2 fixers will become weeds, (c) seed or planting stock is poorly available, and (d) there is uncertainty about the costs and benefits (Gordon 1983).

C.   Designed systems

The use of on-site resources to grow tree crops will increase slowly until whole systems are designed and tested with respect to specific production objectives. A convenient device for designing plant production systems, and accounting for their components, is provided by a maximum yield model (Gordon *et al.* 1983) that converts all photosynthetically active radiation intercepted at a site to dry mass by explicit processes, coupled with an assessment of silvicultural objectives (Stoltenberg *et al.* 1970). In this approach, all site factors are related to the biological and physical processes that are directly involved in photosynthate production and distribution, and all economic and social factors are related to the size and quality of the useful portion of the dry mass produced (Gordon & Avery 1983). This 'model' also can be used to accommodate the 'ideotype' approach to plant design, if an 'ideotype' is viewed as an optimal stand participant.

The starting point for this synthesis is the production objective for a given site or class of sites, usually derived by considering larger individual or organizational goals. Potential stand production is then calculated and compared with an estimate of current production in an 'unimproved' system. Strategies (genetic and cultural) for increasing yield (or for maintaining it at lower cost) are then devised using the most basic biological and site information. This approach is particularly useful in the construction of ideotypes which couple both basic plant biology to field performance, and individual plant performance to stand performance. The principal virtue of the approach is that it (a) links all major components of production to the processes governing photosynthesis, and (b) forces accounting of all dry mass produced on the site (Gordon *et al.* 1983). Further, it illustrates the improvability of yields and the role of all components.

Models of this kind are, like all models, abstractions, and are therefore imperfect. Nevertheless, they offer an avenue leading away from the single-factor approach towards yield improvement. Microbes, as symbionts of higher plants and as 'free-livers', should be a significant quantitative part of these models (Fogel & Hunt 1983), as well as a flexible component for genetic and cultural manipulation.

V. INFORMATION NEEDS AND OPPORTUNITIES

Because symbioses represent the closest possible coupling between higher plants and microbes, research on their functioning should receive high priority. A complete inventory of hosts and endophytes should be initiated, and definitive collections of promising host and endophyte material should be assembled at several locations. Hacskaylo (1982) listed several topics of importance in mycorrhizal research: (a) better methods of measuring mycelial extent, (b) detailed information on the formation and development of ecto-mycorrhizas, (c) information on linkages between host carbohydrate supply and mycorrhizal nutrient uptake, (d) the role of growth factors produced by host and fungus, and (e) techniques for the genetic manipulation of fungi, which could be applied with little modification to nitrogen-fixing symbioses. The description of optimum host/endophyte combinations, and the development of methods to screen for them, will be indispensible.

The manipulation and selection of free-living populations of forest fungi and bacteria have hardly begun. Work on organisms found on the forest floor, that play a key role in organic matter decomposition and the nitrogen cycle, will probably pay the greatest cultural dividends. The competitive ability of selected, introduced microbes will, as in agriculture, be a primary determinant of their utility. Also, the vulnerability of both free-living and symbiotic forest microbes to atmospheric pollutants, particularly ozone and acid deposition, should be a subject of concern.

VI. SUMMARY AND CONCLUSIONS

The biological diversity of symbiotic and free-living forest microbes presents a little-explored opportunity for improving the yield of tree crops. Selection of appropriate microbial components, for specific production systems, requires an approach that includes all system parts and their interactions. Fundamental advances in our knowledge of the energy costs and benefits of symbioses and free-living microbes are necessary to be able to describe the whole system, and to be able to design high-yielding plantations that require minimum inputs from sources external to the stand itself.

REFERENCES

Akkermans, A. D. L. & Houwers, A. (1983). Morphology of nitrogen-fixers in forest ecosystems. In: *Biological nitrogen fixation in forest ecosystems: foundations and applications*, edited by J. C. Gordon and C. T. Wheeler, 7–53. The Hague: Martinus Nijhoff/Junk.

Alexander, M. (1977). *Introduction to soil microbiology*. New York: John Wiley.

Becking, J. H. (1982). N_2-fixing tropical non-legumes. In: *Microbiology of tropical soils and plant productivity*, edited by Y. R. Dommergues and H. G. Dicin. The Hague: Martinus Nijhoff/Junk.

Björkman, E. (1942). Conditions favouring the formation of mycorrhizae in pine and spruce. *Symb. bot. uppsal.*, **6**, 1–191.

Bond, G. (1976). The results of the IBP survey of root-nodule formation in non-leguminous angiosperms. In: *Symbiotic nitrogen fixation in plants*, edited by P. S. Nutman, 443–476. Cambridge: Cambridge University Press.

Bormann, B. T. & Gordon, J. C. (1984). Stand density effects in young red alder plantations: productivity, photosynthate partitioning and nitrogen fixation. *Ecology*, **65**, 394–402.

Callaham, D., Del Tridici, P. & Torrey, J. (1978). Isolation and cultivation *in vitro* of the actinomycete causing root nodulation in *Comptonia*. *Science, N.Y.*, **199**, 899–902.

Chambers, R. (1983). *Rural development: putting the last first*. London: Longman.

Dawson J. & Gordon J. C. (1979). Photoassimilate supply and nitrogen fixation in *Alnus*. In: *Symbiotic nitrogen fixation in the management of temperate forests*, edited by J. C. Gordon, C. T. Wheeler and D. A. Perry, 187–195. Corvallis, OR: Oregon State University.

Domingo, I. L. (1983). Nitrogen fixation in southeast Asian forestry: research and practice. In: *Biological nitrogen fixation in forest ecosystems: foundations and applications*, edited by J. C. Gordon and C. T. Wheeler, 295–315. The Hague: Martinus Nijhoff/Junk.

Fogel, R. (1979). Mycorrhizae and nutrient cycling in natural forest ecosystems. In: *Abstracts of the 4th North American Conference on Mycorrhizae*. Fort Collins, Colorado.

Fogel, R. & Hunt, G. (1983). Contribution of mycorrhizae and soil fungi to nutrient cycling in a Douglas-fir ecosystem. *Can. J. For. Res.*, **13**, 219–232.

France, R. & Reid, C. P. P. (1983). Interactions of nitrogen and carbon in the physiology of ectomycorrhizae. *Can. J. Bot.*, **61**, 964–984.

Funk, D. T., Schlesinger, R. C. & Ponder, F. jr. (1979). Autumn-olive as a nurse plant for black walnut. *Bot. Gaz.*, **140**, S110–S114.

Gadgil, R. L. (1983). Biological nitrogen fixation in forestry: research and practice in Australia and New Zealand. In: *Biological nitrogen fixation in forest ecosystems: foundations and applications*, edited by J. C. Gordon and C. T. Wheeler, 317–332. The Hague: Martinus Nijhoff/Junk.

Giumelli, J. (1978). Pasture establishment under native forests. In: *Integrating agriculture and forestry*, edited by K. M. W. Howes and R. A. Rummery, 165–169. Canberra: CSIRO.

Gordon, J. C. (1983). Silviculture systems and biological nitrogen fixation. In: *Biological nitrogen fixation in forest ecosystems: foundations and applications*, edited by J. C. Gordon and C. T. Wheeler, 1–6. The Hague: Martinus Nijhoff/Junk.

Gordon, J. C. & Avery, M. (1983). New frontiers in agroforestry: consequences of pattern in tree and forage systems. In: *Foothills for food and forests* (Proc. int. Hill Land Symposium), edited by D. B. Hannaway. Corvallis, OR: Oregon State University.

Gordon, J. C., Farnum, P. & Timmis, R. (1983). Theoretical maximum phytomass yields as guides for yield improvement. *Proc. North American Forest Biology Conf.*, *7th*, edited by B. Thielges. Lexington, KY: University of Kentucky.

Gordon, J. C. & Wheeler, C. T. (1978). Whole plant studies on photosynthesis and acetylene reduction in *Alnus glutinosa*. *New Phytol.*, **80**, 179–186.

Hacskaylo, E. (1973). Dependence of mycorrhizal fungi on hosts. *Bull. Torrey bot. Club*, **100**, 217–223.

Hacskaylo, E. (1982). Researching the potential of forest tree mycorrhizae. In: *Tree root systems and their mycorrhizae*, edited by D. Atkinson *et al.*, 1–8. The Hague: Martinus Nijhoff/Junk.

Hardy, R. & Havelka, U. (1976). Photosynthate as a major factor limiting nitrogen fixation by field grown legumes with emphasis on soybeans. In: *Symbiotic nitrogen fixation in plants*, edited by P. S. Nutman, 421–439. Cambridge: Cambridge University Press.

Hatch, A. B. (1937). The physical basis of mycotrophy in the genus *Pinus*. *Black Rock Forest Bull.*, **6**, 1–168.

Jones, K. (1982). Nitrogen fixation in the canopy of temperate forest trees: a re-examination. *Ann. Bot.*, **50**, 329–334.

Keyes, M. R. & Grier, C. C. (1981). Above-ground and below ground net production in 40–year-old Douglas-fir stands on low and high productivity sites. *Can. J. For. Res.*, **11**, 599–605.

Lawrie, A. C. (1982). Field nodulation of nine species of *Casuarina* in Victoria. *Aust. J. Bot.*, **30**, 447–460.

Loomis, W. (1953). *Growth and differentiation in plants*. Ames, IA: Iowa State College Press.

Marx, D. (1977). Tree host range and world distribution of the ectomycorrhizal fungus, *Pisolithus tinctorius*. *Can. J. Microbiol.*, **23**, 217–223.

Marx, D. H. & Barnett, J. P. (1974). Mycorrhizae and containerised forest seedlings. *Proc. North American Containerised Tree Seedling Symp.*, edited by R. W. Tinus, W. I. Stein and W. E. Balmer, 85–92. (Great Plains Agricultural Council Publication no. 68).

Marx, D. H., Bryan, W. C. & Cordell, C. E. (1977). Survival and growth of pine seedlings with *Pisolithus* ectomycorrhizae after two years on reforestation sites in North Carolina and Florida. *Forest Sci.*, **23**, 363–373.

Mikola, P. (1948). On the physiology and ecology of *Cenococcum graniforum* especially as a mycorrhizal fungus on birch. *Metsätiet. Tutkimuslait. Julk.* (Commun. Inst. for. fenn.), **36**, 1–101.

Mikola, P. (1970). Mycorrhizal inoculation in afforestation. *Int. Rev. for. Res.*, **3**, 123–196.

Molina, R. & Chamard, J. (1983). Use of the ectomycorrhizal fungus *Laccaria laccata* in forestry. II. Effects of fertilizer forms and levels on ectomycorrhizal development and growth of container grown Douglas fir and ponderosa pine seedlings. *Can. J. For. Res.*, **13**, 89–95.

Monaco, P. A., Ching, K. K. & Ching, T. (1982). Host-endophyte effect on biomass production and nitrogen fixation in *Alnus rubra* actinorhizal symbiosis. *Bot. Gaz.*, **143**, 298–303.

Mosse, B., Stribby, D. P. & LeTacon, F. (1981). Ecology of mycorrhizae and mycorrhizal fungi. *Adv. microb. Ecol.*, **5**, 137–210.

Nadelhoffer, K. J., Aber, J. D. & Mellilo, J. M. (1983). Leaf-litter production and soil organic matter dynamics along a nitrogen-availability gradient in Southern Wisconsin (U.S.A.). *Can. J. For. Res.*, **13**, 12–21.

Paul, E. A. & Kucey, R. M. N. (1981). Carbon flow in plant microbial associations. *Science, N.Y.*, **213**, 473–474.

Reid, C. P. P. & Hacskaylo, E. (1982). Evaluation of plant response to inoculation. B. Environmental variables. In: *Methods and principles of mycorrhizal research*, edited by N. C. Schench, 175–187. St Paul, MN: American Phytopathological Society.

Shaw, C. G. & Sidle, R. C. (1983). Evaluation of planting sites common to a S. E. Alaska clearcut. II. Available inoculum of the ectomycorrhizal fungus *Cenococcum geophilum*. *Can. J. For. Res.*, **13**, 1–8.

Stoltenberg, C. H., Ware, K. D., Marty, R. J., Wray, R. D. & Wellons, J. D. (1970). *Planning research for resource decisions*. Ames, IA: Iowa State University Press.

Tarrant, R. F. (1983). Nitrogen fixation in North American forestry: research and application. In: *Biological nitrogen fixation in forest ecosystems: foundations and applications*, edited by J. C. Gordon and C. T. Wheeler, 261–277. The Hague: Martinus Nijhoff/Junk.

Trappe, J. (1977). Selection of fungi for ectomycorrhizal inoculation in nurseries. *A. Rev. Phytopathol.*, **15**, 203–222.

Turvey, N. D. & Smethurst, P. J. (1983). Nitrogen fixing plants in forest plantation management. In: *Biological nitrogen fixation in forest ecosystems: foundations and applications*, edited by J. C. Gordon and C. T. Wheeler, 233–259. The Hague: Martinus Nijhoff/Junk.

Vogt, K. A., Grier, C. C., Meier, C. E. & Edmonds, R. L. (1982). Mycorrhizal role in net primary production and nutrient cycling in *Abies amabilis* ecosystems in western Washington. *Ecology*, **63**, 370–380.

Wollum, A. G. & Davey, C. B. (1975). Nitrogen accumulation, transformation and transport in forest soils. In: *Forest soils and forest land management*, edited by B. Bernier and C. H. Wingett, 67–106. Quebec: Laval University Press.

20

TREE CROPS AS SOIL IMPROVERS IN THE HUMID TROPICS?

P. A. SANCHEZ, C. A. PALM, C. B. DAVEY, L. T. SZOTT and C. E. RUSSELL
Departments of Soil Science and Forest Resources, North Carolina State University, Raleigh, USA

I. INTRODUCTION

The forests of the humid tropics comprise a valuable resource which it is desirable to conserve, but which also has the potential to provide more land to increase food and fibre production. The productive use of humid tropical ecosystems has aroused a great deal of controversy. It is commonly believed that soils of the humid tropics are fragile and unsuitable for agricultural development. During the last decade, much has been learned about the properties and distribution of soils in the humid tropics (Drosdoff 1972; Sanchez & Buol 1975; IRRI 1980; Cochrane & Sanchez 1982; National Research Council 1982), and considerable advances have also been made in understanding the soil processes involved in sustained management systems for the production of annual crops, pastures, and perennial crops in the humid tropics (Pushparajah & Amin 1977; Serrão *et al.* 1979; Alvim 1981; Greenland 1981; Toledo & Serrão 1982; Sanchez *et al.* 1982, 1983).

Despite these advances, it is commonly believed that trees are the only viable means of producing food and fibre on a sustained basis, because tree stands most closely resemble the natural ecosystem, and because their management would require few inputs. The accumulation of large amounts of biomass on acid, infertile soils – seemingly due to rapid and efficient nutrient cycling – suggests that tropical forests function in a fundamentally different way to annual crops and pastures. It is not known if the same conditions would exist in more artificial production-orientated forests or tree crops.

The purpose of this paper is to examine the available information on the effect of deliberately planted tree crops on soil properties in the humid tropics, and to compare them, whenever possible, with alternative systems such as native forests, annual crops, pastures, or fallows.

II. APPROACH

A. The Lundgren model

A thorough review of the effect of fast-growing tree plantations on soil dynamics in tropical highlands and subtropical regions, by Lundgren (1978), provides a suitable starting point for this paper. Lundgren proposed a conceptual model (Fig. 1) of the dynamics of soil organic matter, nutrients, and bulk density during seven different stages of plantation development. According to the model, soil organic matter content decreases after clearing, burning, and plantation establishment. After canopy closure – the fallow enrichment phase – organic matter increases, but then decreases during the maximum production phase, which terminates with harvest of the first rotation. Organic matter further decreases after felling, logging, burning, and the start of the second rotation. Bulk density follows a pattern opposite to that of organic matter. Mineral nutrients increase after clearing, but then decrease throughout the three stages of the first rotation. Following harvest and burning, prior to the second rotation, nutrient levels increase again. The model does not suggest overall improvements in soil properties with fast-growing tree plantations and, in fact, suggests a general decline in soil properties.

The major conclusions that may be drawn from Lundgren's review are as follows.

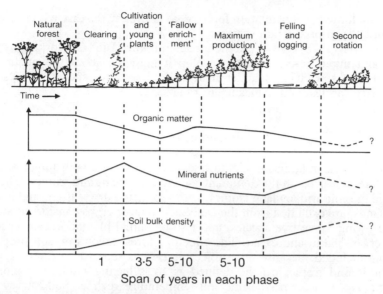

FIGURE 1.   Lundgren's model of the effect of clearing natural forests and growing fast-growing tree plantations on soil properties in the tropics (from Lundgren 1978).

1.   Soil changes invariably occur when natural forests are converted into tree plantations. However, soil differences are reported in the literature, with little indication of the processes involved. Also, spatial variability is often confounded with changes over time, when plantations of different age are sampled at the same time. And soil properties are often confounded with genetic improvement and silvicultural practices.

2.   Beneficial effects of trees on soil properties are found primarily when soils, degraded by poor management, are reafforested.

3.   The establishment of the most commonly used species (pine, *Eucalyptus* and teak) is associated with a relatively pronounced deterioration in soil physical, chemical, and biological properties.

4.   Soil degradation[1] is likely to be faster in lowland humid and sub-humid tropical conditions than the subtropics or tropical highlands.

5.   There is no clear evidence whether the declines in yield that can occur during second rotations are due to soil degradation or to poor silvicultural practices. Decreases in soil organic matter, for example, do not result in immediate yield declines. Nevertheless, soil degradation is widely assumed to be the major culprit.

6.   There is not a single case in the tropics where better growth during the second rotation can be attributed to improved soil properties, unless fertilizers are applied.

7.   Consequently, soil management, including fertilization, will become a

[1] Soil degradation has been defined as the 'result of one or more processes that lessen the current and potential capability of a soil to produce, quantitatively and/or qualitatively, goods or services' (FAO 1977).

necessity for tropical plantation forestry, as is already the case with successful perennial crop production systems.

Lundgren (1978) considered the model in Figure 1 to be a working hypothesis, and urged researchers to develop hypotheses about the quality and direction of soil changes under man-made forests for specific ecosystems, soils, tree species, and management practices.

B.   Focus of this review

We shall use Lundgren's model to assess the effects of establishing tree crops after forest clearing on the dominant soil types of the humid tropics. The sub-humid or semi-arid lowland tropics, with protracted dry seasons, and tropical highlands, are excluded from the analysis. The tree crops considered include fast-growing forest tree species, and also perennial plantation crops such as rubber, oil palm, and cacao. The effects of forest fallows on soil properties are not included, because this subject deserves a separate review.

The humid tropics can be defined as areas having a udic soil moisture regime and an isohyperthermic soil temperature regime (Soil Survey Staff 1975). These terms denote areas with an annual rainfall of 1,500 mm or more, a dry season of less than four months' duration, and a mean annual temperature above 22 °C with little seasonal or diurnal variation (National Research Council 1982). The geographic distribution of the humid tropics according to this definition is shown in Figure 2.

The distribution of the main soils of the humid tropics is now better understood, since the publication of the FAO-UNESCO World Soil Map and

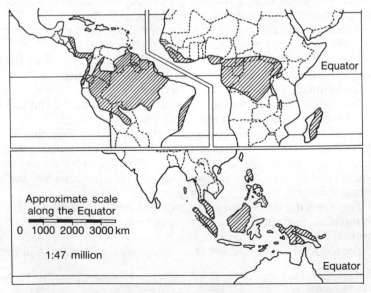

FIGURE 2.   The humid tropics (about 1,500 million hectares).

of many national land resource inventories. A summary of the main soils is given in Table I. Well-drained, acid, inherently infertile soils, classified as Oxisols and Ultisols, cover about 63% of the humid tropics. Moderately fertile, well-drained soils (Alfisols, Vertisols, Andisols, Tropepts, Fluvents, and Mollisols) cover only 15% of the ecosystem. Poorly drained soils (Aquepts) cover 8%, very infertile sandy soils (Psamments, Spodosols) 7%, shallow soils 5%, and organic soils 2%. A significant proportion of the literature on soil-

TABLE I. Simplified description of the major soils in the humid tropics, covering 1,489 million hectares (from Sanchez 1982)

Soil order and Suborder	% of humid tropics	Description and equivalent terminology
Oxisols	35	Highly weathered, deep, red or yellowish, well-drained, acid, low base status soils with generally excellent soil structure. Loamy or clayey textures; no important increases in clay with depth. Other names: Ferralsols (FAO), Sols ferralitiques fortement desaturées (French), Latosols (Brazilian).
Ultisols	28	Similar to Oxisols except for a clay increase with depth. similar chemical limitations. Textures range from sandy to clayey. Other names: Red Yellow Podzolics, Acrisols and Dystric Nitosols (FAO), Sols ferralitiques (French).
Inceptisols:	14	Young soils with A-B-C horizon development but no other diagnostic horizons. Fertility highly variable. Other names: Brown tropical soils, many paddy soils.
Aquepts	(8)	Poorly drained Inceptisols.
Tropepts	(6)	Well-drained Inceptisols (Dystropepts = acid; Eutropepts = high base status).
Entisols:	14	Young soils without A-B-C horizon development. Generally high fertility except for sandy soils.
Psamments	(6)	Sandy (Deep sands, Arenosols, Regosols).
Lithic	(5)	Shallow soils.
Fluvents	(3)	Alluvial.
Alfisols:	4	Higher base status than Ultisols, but similar otherwise. Includes the more fertile tropical red soils. Dominant soils of West African sub-humid tropics and savannas. Other names: Luvisols (FAO), sols ferrugineux (French), Red Earths (Australia): Ochrosols (Ghana).
Histosols	2	Organic soils (>20% organic matter). Peat soils.
Andisols	1	Volcanic soils. Andosols, Andept.
Spodosols	1	Podzols.
Mollisols	0·5	Black soils derived from calcareous materials. Known as Chernozems and Rendzinas.
Vertisols	0·3	Dark heavy clay soils that shrink, crack and swell. Other names: Grumusols, Dark cotton soils.
Aridisols	0·1	Saline soils.

tree relationships is derived from research conducted on less extensive, fertile soils (Alfisols) or on extremely infertile sandy soils (Spodosols). The most extensive constraints to agricultural production, according to the Fertility Capability Classification system, are chemical rather than physical (Table II). The danger of laterite or plinthite formation is not significant enough to be included in this table.

TABLE II.   The most important soil constraints in the humid tropics, according to the Fertility Capability Soil Classification System (Sanchez et al. 1982b,c)

Soil constraint[1]	Million hectares	Percentage of humid tropics
Low nutrient reserves	929	66
Aluminium toxicity	808	57
High phosphorus fixation	550	38
Acid, but not Al-toxic	253	18
Steep slopes (>30%)	240	17
Poor drainage	187	13
Low cation exchange capacity	161	11
Shallow soils (<50 cm)	97	7
Organic soils	27	2
Gravel	14	1
Allophane	10	1
Shrink-swell	9	1
Total area	1,489	100

[1] Deficiencies of N, Mg, S and micronutrients plus temporary drought stress are widespread but cannot be quantified.

C. Methodology

Data used in this analysis were compiled from a literature search, from Chijicke (1980), and from data or soil samples provided by Latin American and south-east Asian colleagues. Attention was given to long-term data sets that included proper soil characterization, so that results could be interpreted in relation to the geographical distribution of soils and their constraints to agricultural production (Tables I and II).

Two types of long-term data sets are available: Type I, where soil dynamics are followed with time on the same site, and Type II, where soils under neighbouring plantations, of known but different ages, are sampled at the same time. Type I data sets are preferred, but they are scarce. Type II data sets confound time with spatial variability, and assume that measured soil differences reflect the effects of time or management and not different initial soil properties. Although the limitation of such experiments are well understood (Andriesse 1977; Lundgren 1978; Ollagnier et al. 1978), they provide the bulk of the available data.

We included, in our analysis, Type II studies which reported little difference in soil particle size distribution with depth between sites. Particle size distribution in the profile is a soil property that is not considered subject to change with management or time, and should therefore be a good indication of whether or not two soils are similar. An example is shown in Table III, from the work of Russell (1983) in Ultisols of Jarí in the Brazilian Amazon. Differences in sand and clay content were small and not statistically significant, so we assumed that the soils were similar. Studies providing data that clearly show major differences in soil texture between sites, and those providing no soil profile data at all, were excluded from this analysis.

TABLE III. Bulk density and texture of the soils at five sandy Ultisol sites sampled in July 1980 at Jarí, Pará, Brazil (from Russell 1983)

Property	Soil depth (cm)	Native forest	0·5 yr Pinus caribaea	9·5 yr Pinus caribaea	8·5 yr Gmelina arborea	8 yr Gmelina +1·5 yr Pinus	Significance
% sand	1	94	93	93	93	91	ns
	30	84	83	81	83	77	ns
	100	79	80	80	82	76	ns
% clay	1	5	5	6	5	7	ns
	30	15	15	16	13	18	ns
	100	20	16	17	16	20	ns
Bulk	1	1·22	0·98	1·23	1·33	1·10	ns
density	30	1·62	1·61	1·58	1·54	1·48	ns
gcc⁻¹	100	1·70	1·76	1·60	1·73	1·61	ns

An example of a data set that was rejected was a study of teak plantations, 0 to 120 years of age, in Kerala, India (Jose & Koshy 1972). Major changes in topsoil organic matter and bulk density with time (plantations of different ages) were reported, and have been widely quoted. Examination of the soil profile data, however, showed considerable differences in the clay and sand contents in the soil profiles at the different sites, supporting the plantations of different ages. Clay content is directly correlated with organic matter content, while bulk density is positively correlated with sand content. It appears very likely, therefore, that the values for organic matter content and bulk density were a function of site differences in soil texture, rather than the effect of teak plantations over time. Some of the comparisons reported by Chijicke (1980) also failed to meet our soil uniformity criteria.

The data sets selected (Type I and Type II) were used to examine soil changes during the five main phases of tree crop development shown in Lundgren's model: forest clearing and crop establishment, fallow enrichment, maximum production, felling and harvesting the first rotation, and the beginning of the second rotation.

III. CLEARING AND CROP ESTABLISHMENT PHASE

Extensive research has been conducted on soil dynamics during land clearing and plant establishment in Oxisols and Ultisols of the humid tropics (Laudelot

1961; Brinkmann & Nascimento 1973; Falesi 1976; Sanchez 1976, 1979; Andriesse 1977; Seubert *et al.* 1977; Ollagnier *et al.* 1978; Silva 1978, 1980, 1982a,b, 1983; Serrão *et al.* 1979; Chijicke 1980; Hecht 1983; Sanchez *et al.* 1983; Pushparajah 1984; Gillman 1984). A summary of the results will be presented here, in addition to details of specific studies. Type I experiments, that monitor soil properties from before clearing tropical rainforests to one to two years after clearing, provide a general trend.

A. Clearing

The general effect of clearing by slash-and-burn techniques can be summarized as follows.

1.   Maximum surface soil temperatures increase.

2.   Rainfall reaching the soil surface increases because there is no tree canopy to intercept and evaporate a significant proportion of the rainfall. Raindrop impact also increases. Evaporation rates from the exposed soil surface are more rapid.

3.   Surface soil compaction, and increased runoff and erosion occur during high intensity rains, if the forest canopy is not replaced by another plant canopy. These effects are likely to be more severe on sloping land, in ustic rather than udic soil moisture regimes, and in Ultisols with sandy topsoil textures rather than in well-granulated loamy or clayey Oxisols.

4.   Topsoil organic carbon decreases and approaches a new equilibrium level, because of higher temperatures, higher rates of decomposition, and lower litterfall. Topsoil total nitrogen also decreases, but at a more gradual rate than carbon. Changes in the subsoil are minor, if any.

5.   The nutrient content of the ash results in a decrease in soil acidity and aluminium saturation, and an increase in the availability of P, Ca, Mg, and K. These effects are reversed with time, but the speed of this reversal varies widely with ash content, initial soil properties, rainfall, and length of dry season. Reversal is generally faster in coarse-textured soils under high rainfall regimes and slower in clayey soils with near ustic soil moisture regimes.

Research conducted on Alfisols of West Africa in the humid and sub-humid (ustic) tropics (Nye & Greenland 1960, 1964; Le Buanec 1972; Lal 1975, 1981; Lal *et al.* 1975, 1985; Juo & Lal 1977; Kang & Lal 1981; Lawson *et al.* 1981) shows similar trends, except that there is a much higher initial supply of nutrients, a less marked decline in fertility, and usually greater deterioration of soil physical properties. In Alfisols with an initial pH of about 6, the production of large amounts of ash may raise the pH too high, inducing micronutrient deficiencies (Lal *et al.* 1975). A similar effect has been recorded in southern Bahía, Brazil, when large quantities of ash were added to an Oxisol (Silva 1982b).

Most mechanized land clearing methods cause immediate negative effects on both chemical and physical soil properties, because much of the topsoil is removed and deposited in windrows away from the field. In addition, the beneficial effects of ash are not realized because the plant biomass is also removed. Severe soil compaction can take place, both in the topsoil and the subsoil.

Comparisons between slash-and-burn and conventional bulldozing techniques show detrimental effects on tree crops similar to that reported for annual crops or pastures (van der Weert 1974; Lal *et al.* 1975; Seubert *et al.* 1977). For example, the growth of *Cordia alliodora* on Oxisols in Surinam in an area cleared by bulldozing was one-third of that measured at an adjacent site cleared by slash-and-burn (van der Weert & Lenselink 1973). The dbh of cacao trees grown for four years in an Oxisol of southern Bahía, Brazil, averaged 8·6 cm in the slashed and burned area but only 1·5 cm in the bulldozed area (Silva 1982). Growth differences were associated with drastic decreases in water infiltration rates, exchangeable bases and organic carbon in the bulldozed areas (Silva 1983). Harmful effects of bulldozer land clearing on *Gmelina arborea* growth have been reported in Jarí, Brazil, and east Kalimantan, Indonesia (Johnson 1976; Russell 1983).

Although the negative effects of mechanized land clearing are nearly universal in the humid tropics, Chijicke (1980) suggests that lands cleared for tree plantations are more adversely affected than those cleared for other uses, because of logging, skid rows, and other disturbances associated with forest harvesting.

Improved mechanical land clearing methods that include the use of a shear blade and burning can largely attenuate the detrimental effects mentioned above (Couper *et al.* 1981; Lal 1981; Alegre *et al.* 1985). Another alternative commonly used in developed countries is to correct the damage immediately using chisel ploughs or other decompacting tools, and to apply fertilizers. It appears more desirable, however, to prevent rather than to correct the damage.

B. Development of a plant canopy

Trees develop a plant canopy that protects the soil surface at a much slower rate than annual crops or pastures (Broughton 1977). Most tropical tree crops require two to five years to close their canopy, whereas annual crops usually provide adequate cover within 30 to 45 days, and pastures within two to six months. However, continuous cultivation of annual crops re-exposes the soil once or several times a year.

An obvious solution to the problem of soil exposure during plantation establishment is to use a managed cover crop. This is routinely done in rubber and oil palm plantations in Oxisols and Ultisols of Malaysia, where the leguminous covers are planted before or at the same time as the trees. The cover crops receive careful management, including fertilization (Watson 1961; Broughton 1977; Chee 1981). Some of the research on rubber (Pushparajah 1984; Type I experiment) shows a significant beneficial effect of the leguminous cover on soil fertility during the first three years after tree establishment (Fig. 3). The legumes are gradually shaded out when rubber develops its own full plant canopy about five years after planting.

Broughton (1977) reviewed research on leguminous cover crops in rubber in Malaysia, and concluded that, when using a mixture of creeping legumes, the initial growth rates of the rubber were faster and the soil generally contained more N, Ca, and Mn than under grass or natural weed cover. Greater nutrient return to the soil was reflected in higher levels of these

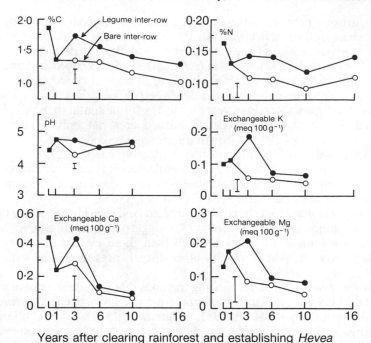

Years after clearing rainforest and establishing *Hevea*

FIGURE 3.   Changes in soil fertility in the topsoil (0–15 cm) after planting *Hevea* rubber with and without legumes in the inter-rows at Sungei Buloh, Malaysia. Time zero shows the value before clearing the rainforest. Vertical bars indicate least significant differences at P = 0·05. The soil was a Typic Paleudult (Ultisol) and was fertilized. This was a Type I experiment, in which changes were monitored with time at one site (adapted from Pushparajah 1984).

elements in the leaves of the rubber trees. Leguminous covers under rubber fixed an average of $150\,kg\,N\,ha^{-1}\,yr^{-1}$ over a five-year period. This, fixed N, coupled with improved soil physical properties, resulted in faster growth rates of rubber trees and increased yield for a 20-year period after the legumes were shaded out. Ninety-six per cent of the economic benefit of leguminous cover was attributed to root proliferation of rubber and 4% to nitrogen fixation. Broughton (1977) suggested research to determine the processes involved in improving root proliferation under a leguminous cover. This suggestion is equally applicable to managed fallows.

Another option for promoting a faster soil cover, while trees develop, is to grow food crops until the tree canopy shades them out. Figure 4 compares the effects of this traditional 'taungya' practice with a leguminous cover (kudzu, *Pueraria phaseoloides*) and normal weeding in an oil palm plantation located on a fertile Alfisol in Benin, Nigeria (adapted from Kowal & Tinker 1959; Tinker 1968; Type I experiment). Intercropping with annual crops, or a kudzu cover, significantly increased topsoil acidity and decreased exchangeable Ca and K, but not organic C and N, compared with a normal grassy cover, during the first five years after planting. These differences gradually

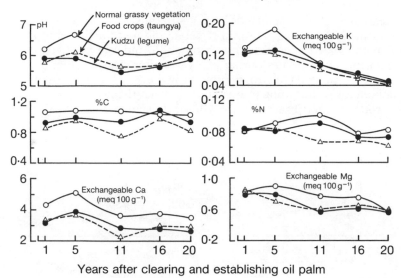

Years after clearing and establishing oil palm

FIGURE 4.   Changes in topsoil (0–15 cm) nutrient dynamics after clearing a 20-year-old secondary forest and establishing oil palm, with a normal grassy vegetation, or a cover of *Pueraria phaseoloides* (kudzu), or food crops intercropped to exhaustion (taungya), at Benin, Nigeria. The soil was a fertile Alfisol. This was a Type I experiment in which changes were monitored at one site (adapted from Kowal & Tinker 1959; Tinker 1968).

disappeared when the oil palms developed a full canopy. In spite of these significant soil chemical changes, the long-term oil palm yields were not affected (7·6 to 7·9 t ha^{-1} yr^{-1} by age 15). The high native fertility of this soil apparently permitted the harvest of corn, yams, cassava, and other crops without affecting tree production. But, would this happen in Ultisols and Oxisols with low nutrient reserves? We were unable to find any solid data from the literature, but would speculate that competition between annual crops and trees for nutrients in Oxisols and Ultisols will decrease tree growth, unless fertilizers are added.

C.   Soil improvement or degradation?

Is the clearing and crop establishment phase soil improving or soil degrading? Variation in the response of the soil to clearing and plant establishment is related to initial soil properties, land clearing methods, the intensity of the burn, rainfall distribution, and post-clearing soil management practices. The type of crop planted, whether an annual crop, a pasture, or a tree crop, is somewhat irrelevant at this stage. The most important factor is the rate at which plants develop a ground cover. If conventional bulldozer clearing is employed, there is little doubt that several soil properties, such as bulk density, water infiltration, organic matter, and available nutrients, are likely to deteriorate. With either slash-and-burn clearing or efficient mechanized land clearing methods that include burning, the answer is likely to be different. The dynamics of a fertile Alfisol in Nigeria, and an acid Ultisol in the Ivory Coast, both cleared and planted with oil palm, indicate no deterioration in topsoil chemical properties during two years after clearing (Fig. 5). In fact, all properties improved relative to pre-clearing levels. Management was excellent in both cases, including proper land clearing, the planting of leguminous cover crops, and fertilization in the Ultisol (Ollagnier *et al.* 1978).

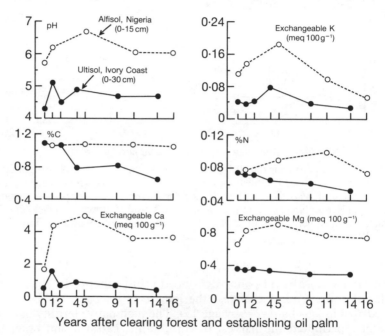

Years after clearing forest and establishing oil palm

FIGURE 5.   Comparison of topsoil dynamics following forest clearing under oil palm plantations in an Alfisol at Benin, Nigeria, and an Ultisol at La Mé, Ivory Coast. The Alfisol was a Type I experiment (see Fig. 4); the Ultisol was a Type II experiment in which plantations of different ages were compared at different sites (adapted from Kowal & Tinker 1959; Ollagnier *et al.* 1978).

The effects of forest clearing and establishing short rotation *Pinus caribaea* plantations in Jarí, Brazil, are shown in Figure 6. Statistically significant differences occur between soil properties under the natural forest and at subsequent stages after clearing and plantation establishment. These differences include decreases in soil acidity and Al saturation, a tripling of exchangeable Ca and a six-fold increase in exchangeable Mg in the topsoil. These changes were still evident in the topsoils 18 months after planting the pines. Exchangeable K tripled after burning, but decreased 18 months after planting. No significant differences were detected in topsoil organic C and available P, or in most subsoil parameters (Russell & Sanchez, unpublished data). Physical properties did not deteriorate either, as shown by the bulk density data presented in Table III.

Effects of forest clearing and establishing *Gmelina arborea* on a fertile

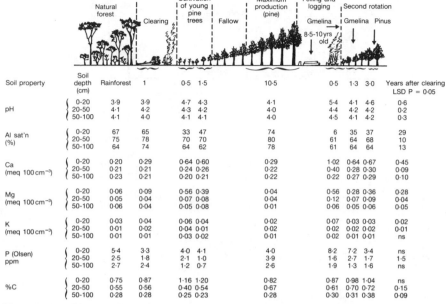

Soil property	Soil depth (cm)	Rainforest	1	0·5	1·5	10·5	0·5	1·3	3·0	Years after clearing LSD P = 0·05
pH	0-20	3·9	3·9	4·7	4·3	4·1	5·4	4·1	4·6	0·6
	20-50	4·1	4·2	4·3	4·2	4·0	4·4	4·2	4·2	0·2
	50-100	4·1	4·0	4·1	4·1	4·0	4·5	4·1	4·2	0·3
Al sat'n (%)	0-20	67	65	33	47	74	6	35	37	29
	20-50	75	78	70	70	80	61	64	68	10
	50-100	64	74	64	62	78	61	64	64	13
Ca (meq 100 cm⁻³)	0-20	0·20	0·29	0·64	0·60	0·29	1·02	0·64	0·67	0·45
	20-50	0·21	0·21	0·24	0·26	0·22	0·40	0·28	0·30	0·09
	50-100	0·23	0·21	0·20	0·21	0·22	0·22	0·27	0·29	0·10
Mg (meq 100 cm⁻³)	0-20	0·06	0·09	0·56	0·39	0·04	0·56	0·28	0·36	0·28
	20-50	0·05	0·04	0·07	0·08	0·04	0·12	0·07	0·09	0·04
	50-100	0·06	0·04	0·05	0·08	0·01	0·06	0·05	0·06	0·05
K (meq 100 cm⁻³)	0-20	0·03	0·04	0·06	0·04	0·02	0·07	0·03	0·03	0·02
	20-50	0·01	0·02	0·04	0·01	0·02	0·02	0·02	0·02	0·01
	50-100	0·01	0·01	0·03	0·02	0·01	0·02	0·01	0·01	ns
P (Olsen) ppm	0-20	5·4	3·3	4·0	4·1	4·0	8·2	7·2	3·4	ns
	20-50	2·5	1·8	2·1	1·0	3·9	1·6	2·7	1·7	1·5
	50-100	2·7	2·4	1·2	0·7	2·6	1·9	1·3	1·6	ns
%C	0-20	0·75	0·87	1·16	1·20	0·82	0·87	0·98	1·04	ns
	20-50	0·55	0·56	0·40	0·54	0·67	0·61	0·70	0·72	0·15
	50-100	0·28	0·28	0·25	0·23	0·28	0·30	0·31	0·38	0·09

FIGURE 6. Changes in soil properties in a sandy Ultisol at Jarí, Pará, Brazil, at different stages of clearing the natural rainforest and growing plantations of *Gmelina arborea* and *Pinus caribaea*. This was a Type II experiment in which samples were taken in July 1981 from stands at different sites (from Russell & Sanchez, unpublished data).

Alfisol of Omo-Ajebandele, Nigeria, are shown in Figure 7 (Chijicke 1980). The differences between the rainforest soils and the soils one and two years after planting are similar to those in the Jarí Ultisol, except for a definite increase in available P and exchangeable K, and a decrease in organic C and total N. Chijicke (1980) did not provide data on soil physical properties other than particle size; therefore, we do not know whether changes in soil physical properties occurred.

The studies examined from the humid tropical locations of Malaysia, Nigeria, Ivory Coast, and Brazil do not support the trends in soil chemical properties proposed by Lundgren (Fig. 1). Soil organic matter did not decrease; soil nutrient levels did not decrease and in some cases increased. Part of the reason is probably the use of appropriate land clearing methods, careful management, and fertilization in the case of rubber in Malaysia (Fig. 3) and oil palm in the Ivory Coast (Fig. 5). Soil deterioration, as suggested by Lundgren, has been quantified in sandy Ultisols of Yurimaguas, Peru, when cleared, burned and planted with annual crops without fertilization, but not when the crops were adequately fertilized (Sanchez *et al.* 1983). The magnitude of changes in soil physical properties is dependent on the soil type, method of clearing, and soil cover. Lundgren's research in Andepts and high elevation Ultisols in Tanzania did not include samplings of plantations less than four years old. Consequently, he did not have an opportunity to examine soil changes during plantation establishment.

Soil property	Soil depth (cm)	Rain-forest	1	2	3	4	5	6	13	Years after clearing
pH	0-10	4.0	6.3	5.6	6.5	6.1	6.6	5.6	5.5	
	10-20	4.1	5.6	4.5	6.3	5.5	5.8	5.3	4.8	
	20-40	4.2	5.0	4.5	5.6	5.6	6.1	4.9	4.8	
Al sat'n (%)	0-10	58	12	12	3	3	5	3	6	
	10-20	66	18	34	6	4	14	4	28	
	20-40	76	23	33	9	5	19	14	38	
Ca (meq 100 g⁻¹)	0-10	1.51	7.53	4.61	4.65	5.41	6.79	4.57	4.02	
	10-20	0.87	2.77	1.43	3.12	3.06	3.05	3.80	2.24	
	20-40	0.55	1.74	1.13	2.18	3.10	2.88	2.13	1.86	
Mg (meq 100 g⁻¹)	0-10	0.38	1.25	1.34	1.18	1.22	1.21	0.85	0.95	
	10-20	0.47	0.63	0.50	0.87	0.82	0.66	0.70	0.44	
	20-40	0.32	0.63	0.54	0.69	0.96	0.66	0.46	0.40	
K (meq 100 g⁻¹)	0-10	0.135	0.320	0.192	0.158	0.131	0.123	0.079	0.092	
	10-20	0.128	0.192	0.115	0.159	0.110	0.009	0.077	0.085	
	20-40	0.007	0.141	0.118	0.192	0.118	0.102	0.079	0.085	
ECEC (meq 100 g⁻¹)	0-10	4.78	10.36	7.00	6.17	6.94	8.54	5.66	5.40	
	10-20	4.39	4.39	3.09	4.43	4.13	4.32	4.78	3.87	
	20-40	3.72	3.25	2.69	3.36	4.42	4.50	3.09	3.81	
P (Bray I) (ppm)	0-10	4.2	36.5	14.1	9.5	10.9	16.8	6.5	3.1	
	10-20	1.2	7.5	7.3	3.1	5.1	6.3	3.6	1.0	
	20-40	0.6	2.0	1.7	2.3	5.7	3.9	1.8	0.9	
%C	0-10	2.40	2.38	2.06	1.26	2.12	1.97	1.89	1.83	
	10-20	1.54	1.36	1.42	1.01	1.84	1.89	1.52	1.27	
	20-40	1.20	1.17	1.06	0.75	1.44	1.42	1.18	1.27	
Total N (%)	0-10	0.384	0.284	0.199	0.181	0.234	0.253	0.325	0.325	
	10-20	0.234	0.156	0.128	0.141	0.173	0.159	0.266	0.194	
	20-40	0.156	0.120	0.094	0.071	0.144	0.135	0.184	0.184	

FIGURE 7.   Changes in soil properties (top 40 cm) in an Alfisol at Omo-Ajebandele, Nigeria, at different stages of clearing the natural forest and growing plantations of *Gmelina arborea*. ECEC = effective cation exchange capacity. This was a Type II experiment in which stands were compared at different sites (adapted from Chijicke 1980).

IV.   FALLOW ENRICHMENT PHASE

The second phase in Figure 1 starts when the trees form a closed canopy and finishes when they approach maximum growth. In fast-growing tree plantations, this period generally lasts for five to ten years. Lundgren (1978) refers to this period as the fallow enrichment phase, because trees cease to act like annual crops and begin to exert their influence on soil properties in a way resembling the fallow phase of shifting cultivation. There are four ways in which trees can have beneficial effects on soil properties: (a) the tree canopy and litter layer can protect the soil surface and thus dampen temperature and moisture fluctuations; (b) tree roots can loosen the topsoils by radial growth, and can improve subsoil porosity when deep roots decompose; (c) trees can capture nutrients from various sources (atmospheric deposition, biological N_2 fixation, weathering of soil minerals and organic matter mineralization) and store them in the biomass; and (d) trees can recycle a proportion of the captured nutrients back to the soil, and pump nutrients from the subsoil that otherwise may have been leached from the rooting zone.

Annual crops and pastures perform similar functions, but not to the same degree or for as long a period of time. It is hypothesized, therefore, that the favourable effects of trees on soils may be related to the long period during which these effects are exerted. Two to three years after clearing, an area planted with trees will still be increasing in biomass and total stored nutrients, whereas a pasture or annual crop would have already attained maximum biomass and nutrient accumulation – at a level below that of the tree crop.

Some possible effects of trees on soil physical properties at this stage include elimination of runoff and erosion, increased infiltration rates and lowered bulk density. The main effects on chemical properties may include an increase in topsoil organic matter content as a result of a high supply of litter, lower maximum soil temperatures, and more uniform moisture supply – which favour the activity of decomposing flora and fauna. Exchangeable bases also increase as leaching virtually ceases, because of the uptake of nutrients by fast-growing roots with their associated mycorrhizal fungi. In addition, available nutrients in the subsoil, if there are any, may be pumped up and added to the surface soil in litterfall.

A.   Runoff and erosion

The elimination of soil losses from runoff and erosion is shown in Table IV for an Ultisol with 7% slope at Adiopodoumé, Ivory Coast. The results of Roose (1970) indicate little difference between the natural forest and oil palm, coffee or cacao plantations with a fully developed canopy. High runoff and erosion losses are reported for cassava. However, the cassava canopy provides less soil cover than other annual crops such as upland rice, maize, grain

TABLE IV.   Effects of ground cover on mean annual erosion, and surface runoff and erosion, in Adiopodoumé, Ivory Coast, on an Ultisol with 7% slope (from Roose 1970, quoted by Ollagnier *et al.* 1978)

Cover	Soil erosion $(t\,ha^{-1}yr^{-1})$	Runoff (% of rainfall)
Bare soil	125	33
Cassava	32	22
Oil palm, coffee and cacao plantations fully developed	0·3	2
Forest	0·1	1

legumes, and yams, so the numbers in Table IV must not be considered representative of annual crops. Lal (1975) reported runoff and erosion losses similar to those from secondary forests, when mulching or minimum tillage was practised with continuous maize production.

The results for the bare soil in Table IV are essentially academic; it is difficult to maintain a soil devoid of some vegetation in the humid tropics. Data on the physical deterioration of soils kept artificially bare by frequent hand weeding (Cunningham 1963) are of agronomic relevance only in situations where clearing by bulldozer leaves a highly infertile subsoil. This is unfortunately the case in some Oxisols and Ultisols of transmigration areas in Indonesia, where patches of Goodland and Irwin's (1975) red desert have been created. Gully erosion is rampant in these areas. Except for this single case, the authors have yet to encounter bare soils in farmers' fields in the humid tropics.

Significant runoff and erosion can occur in plantations of deciduous trees, such as teak, if the litter layer is removed by annual burning. Lundgren (1978) considered litter removal to be the main reason for the 'pure teak problem' described by Laurie and Griffith (1942), Griffith and Gupta (1948), and Cornforth (1970). Apparently, the same situation is occurring in forested Ultisol hillsides of southern China, where farmers remove tree litter to make compost for agricultural crops grown in the valley bottoms (Buol 1983). Thus, the extent to which trees conserve soil properties depends on the extent to which a litter layer, or some other ground cover, is maintained.

B.   Soil structure

Do trees improve the soil structure during the fallow enrichment phase? Lundgren's model suggests that there is a decrease in bulk density and an increase in organic matter content that would improve soil structure and water infiltration. Soil structure, as measured by the size of soil aggregates, for four-year-old plantations, that were cleared either manually or bulldozed, was compared with the original forest, in an Oxisol of southern Bahía, Brazil, by

TABLE V.   Effects, four years after plantation establishment, of two land clearing methods, and different plantation crops, on the percentage of soil aggregates greater than 1 mm in an Oxisol at Barrolandia, Bahía, Brazil (recalculated from Silva 1983)

Treatment		Percentage of soil aggregates >1 mm at soil depth of		
		0–5 cm	5–15 cm	15–30 cm
Virgin forest		61	56	80
Slashed and burned	*Pinus caribaea* (aged 4)	76	73	83
	Oil palm+kudzu[1]	42	57	71
	Rubber+kudzu[1]	51	57	87
Bulldozed	Cacao	33	39	65
	Brachiaria sp. pasture	34	37	40
Least significant difference P = 0·05)		9	3	9

[1] *Pueraria phaseoloides*, a legume

Silva (1983) (Table V). The results indicated that a young *Pinus caribaea* stand significantly improved topsoil structure, compared with the virgin forest, while oil palm and rubber stands, both with leguminous covers, did not. However, all of these stands had a significantly better topsoil structure than soil beneath cacao and pasture that had been planted following clearing using bulldozers. Similar long-term detrimental effects of improper land clearing by bulldozer have been recorded on Ultisols of Yurimaguas, Peru, planted with annual crops (Alegre *et al.* 1985). Outside the humid tropics, Lundgren (1978) detected decreases in bulk density, and increases in total porosity, in topsoils of an Ultisol high in organic matter in a Type II experiment. The available evidence suggests a potential positive effect of the fallow enrichment phase in improving topsoil structure. The effect, however, depends on the type of tree and the management practices.

C. Soil organic matter

The dynamics of topsoil organic C and total N during the fallow enrichment phase have been reported in several studies. No differences were reported under oil palm (Fig. 4) in Alfisols of Nigeria. Slight but gradual declines were detected in Ultisols under rubber in Malaysia (Fig. 3) and oil palm in the Ivory Coast (Fig. 5) and under *Gmelina arborea* in Alfisols in Nigeria (Fig. 7). No clear trends were detected in the Ultisol with high organic matter from the highlands of Tanzania referred to in the previous paragraph (Lundgren 1978). It seems reasonable to assume that the possible improvement in soil structure during the fallow enrichment phase could be attributed to the opening of pores by root pressure and root decomposition, rather than to increases in soil organic matter.

D. Exchangeable bases

Studies show that exchangeable bases can either increase or decrease during the fallow enrichment phase. Exchangeable Ca increased in topsoil layers within two to five years after clearing (a) for oil palm on an Alfisol in Nigeria (Tinker 1968) (Fig. 8), (b) for oil palm and rubber in an Oxisol in Brazil (Silva 1983) (Fig. 9), and (c) for *Gmelina arborea* in an Alfisol in Nigeria (Fig. 7). Exchangeable Ca did not increase during this period in Ultisols of Malaysia under rubber (Fig. 3), or under oil palm in the Ivory Coast (Fig. 5).

The increase in exchangeable Ca in the topsoil is believed to be the result of the slow decomposition of tree trunks and stumps left from the original forest, and is unrelated to the ash effect (Tinker 1968). The large magnitude of these increases in topsoil Ca, and in some cases Mg, is believed to be a consequence of having an established nutrient cycling mechanism capable of returning to the topsoil considerable quantities of bases released by the slowly decomposing tree trunks, roots, and stumps. A similar increase has been detected in the topsoil of an Ultisol in Yurimaguas, Peru, with continuous annual crop production, without fertilization (Sanchez 1979). This increase

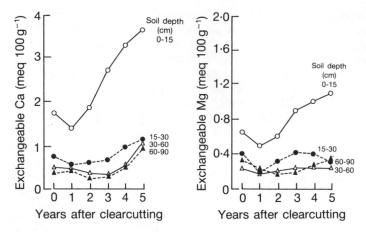

FIGURE 8.   Effects of five years of oil palm plantation establishment on the exchangeable Ca and Mg status in the top 90 cm of an Alfisol at Benin, Nigeria. This was a Type I experiment in which a stand was monitored at one site (adapted from Tinker 1968).

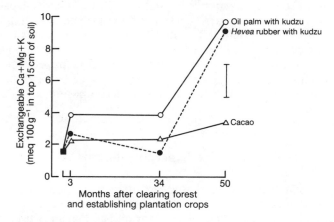

FIGURE 9.   Effects of three perennial cropping systems on the topsoil exchangeable base content of a Haplorthox Oxisol at Barrolandia, Bahía, Brazil. The vertical bar indicates the least significant difference at P = 0·05. This was a Type I experiment. Cacao was established on land cleared by bulldozer, while oil palm and rubber were established after slash-and-burn (adapted from Silva 1983).

took place between the second and third years after clearing, but decreased to pre-clearing levels afterwards. A possible explanation is that, without an effective recycling mechanism, this advantage is lost, but when the tree roots are capable of capturing and recycling the nutrients, the advantage of this flush of Ca and Mg is realized. No increases in Ca were recorded in the Malaysian Ultisol under rubber (Fig. 3). In this case, the flush of Ca and Mg, if any, may have taken place about three years after planting, and, by the time rubber closed its canopy, exchangeable Ca, Mg, and K were all below pre-clearing levels. No flush of Ca and Mg was detected in Ultisols of the Ivory Coast under oil palm (Fig. 5). No clear reasons can be provided, except for the possibility of missing the flush between sampling intervals in both the Malaysian and Ivory Coast studies. Unfortunately, no data for the fallow enrichment period were included in the Jarí study in Figure 6.

The evidence, although inconclusive, suggests that a build-up of exchangeable Ca, and sometimes Mg, in the topsoil can occur during the fallow enrichment phase. This enrichment may result from the slow decomposition of trunks and roots, coupled with efficient nutrient cycling by the trees. This hypothesis is worth testing.

Unlike Ca and Mg, exchangeable K generally decreases or remains the same as under the original forest during this phase, in soils both relatively high or low in this element (Figs 3, 4, 6 and 7). The K recycling mechanism apparently does not increase available K in the topsoil or subsoil during the fallow enrichment phase.

E. Other nutrients

Information regarding available P and micronutrients is very limited. No changes in available P during the fallow enrichment phase were detected in two studies where this parameter was measured, namely in the Nigerian Alfisol under *Gmelina* (Fig. 7) and the Ultisols of northern Trinidad under *Pinus caribaea* (Cornforth 1970). Very little information about micronutrients was found in the literature.

F. Soil improvement or degradation?

The fallow enrichment phase seems to improve certain soil properties. Runoff and erosion are eliminated, provided the litter layer is maintained. Soil structure tends to improve, but the improvement does not appear to be related to the amount of soil organic matter, because this amount remains stable or slowly decreases. A flush of exchangeable Ca, accompanied sometimes by exchangeable Mg, increases topsoil base status, and may be related to tree stump and root decomposition of the previous forest and the trees' capacity to capture such nutrients. Exchangeable K generally declines or remains stable.

V. MAXIMUM PRODUCTION PHASE AND FIRST ROTATION HARVEST

Lundgren (1978) proposed a decrease in organic matter content, and an increase in bulk density, during the last phase of tree growth, because the trees have approached a steady or declining state of activity. Fortunately, several data sets exist for this stage, which enable soil properties before planting to be compared with those near the end of the first rotation, or at the end of the economic life of perennial crops. Some data sets enable different species to be compared at the same site.

A.   Soil physical properties

Mature stands of *Pinus caribaea* (9·5 years old) and *Gmelina arborea* (8·5 years old) on a sandy Ultisol at Jarí, Brazil, did not produce significant differences in soil bulk density at three depths, as compared with the native forest (Table III). Lundgren (1978) did record decreases in bulk density and increases in porosity with *Cupressus lusitanica* by the time of harvest, but he found no trend with *Pinus patula* – both in Ultisols of Shume, in the Tanzanian highlands. Our interpretation of Lundgren's data is that soil physical properties improve as the harvest of the first rotation approaches.

B.   Soil organic matter

No significant differences in soil organic carbon content to 100 cm depth were detected between the native forests and 9·5-year-old *Pinus caribaea* in the Jarí Ultisol (Fig. 6). Total N values in the top metre showed little difference between the mature *Gmelina* and the native forests, but both were higher than in the mature *Pinus caribaea* plantation (Fig. 10). In the case of the Jarí Ultisol, it seems clear that the amount of soil organic matter did not change during the first rotation.

The organic matter dynamics of a 13-year-old *Gmelina arborea* plantation in the Alfisol at Omo-Ajebendele, Nigeria (Fig. 7), indicate a 25% and 30% decrease in topsoil organic C and total N, respectively. Although Chijicke (1980) did not provide a statistical analysis, those decreases may have been significant, but they were unlikely to be depleting because the remaining levels were generally high.

Topsoil organic carbon content increases significantly, compared with that under the native forest, after 10 years of growing laurel (*Cordia trichotoma*) and pão-brasil (*Caesalpinia echinata*), but not after growing the highly valued timber species jacarandá-da-Bahía (*Dalbergia nigra*) on an Oxisol of Brazil (Table VI; Silva 1983).

The dynamics of soil organic matter content toward the end of the productive period of perennial crops show a somewhat different, decreasing, trend. After 16 years of rubber with a leguminous cover in a Malaysian Ultisol, topsoil C and N decreased by 30% and 15%, respectively, in relation to the original forest values (Fig. 3). After 14 years of a well-managed and fertilized oil palm plantation in an Ultisol of the Ivory Coast, topsoil organic Ca and N values were 41% and 28%, respectively, below those of the original forest (Fig. 5). After 16 years of oil palm, in an Alfisol in Benin, Nigeria, topsoil organic C and N did not decrease significantly (Fig. 5).

The decreases in soil organic C and N content in the Malaysia and Ivory

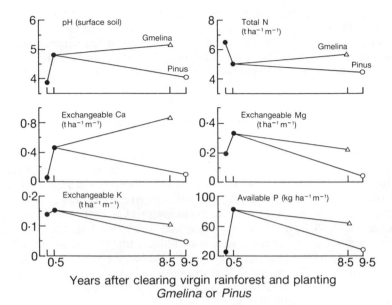

Years after clearing virgin rainforest and planting
Gmelina or *Pinus*

FIGURE 10. Differing effects of *Pinus caribaea* and *Gmelina arborea* plantings on surface soil pH and nutrient content in the top 1 m of a sandy Ultisol at Jarí, Brazil. This was a Type II experiment in which stands were compared at different sites. See also Figure 6 (adapted from Russell 1983).

TABLE VI. Effects of ten years of growth of various timber species on topsoil (0–30 cm) properties of an Oxisol at Porto Seguro, Bahía, Brazil (adapted from Silva 1983)[1]

Forest cover		%C	meq $100\,g^{-1}$ of		
			Ca	Mg	K
Native forest		1·65	0·70	0·50	0·05
10 years old	Cordia trichotoma	2·18	1·70	0·95	0·12
	Caesalpinia echinata	1·40	1·75	1·00	0·13
	Dalbergia nigra	1·92	0·95	0·60	0·07
Least significant difference, P=0·05		0·23	0·90	0·35	0·03
Coefficient of variation (%)		12	35	25	23

[1] These data span the range of values found for a number of plantation species.

Coast studies reflect their intensive management, including the use of leguminous covers and fertilizers. These decreases may reflect the new equilibrium attained between significant yield extraction and large fertilizer inputs. Such decreases are somewhat similar to the 25% and 46% decreases in topsoil organic C and total N, respectively, measured under intensive continuous crop production in an Ultisol of Yurimaguas, Peru (Sanchez *et al.* 1983). The fact that soil organic matter does not change, or in some cases increases, under fast-growing tree plantations probably reflects the fact that nutrients are not extracted from the ecosystem prior to timber harvest.

C.   Soil acidity and nutrient availability

A major difference in soil acidity and base status was observed between mature *Gmelina arborea* and *Pinus caribaea* plantations in the Jarí Ultisol (Fig. 10). The topsoil under *Gmelina* had a pH of 5·2, while that under *Pinus* was about the same as under native rainforest, pH 3·9. The rise in pH under *Gmelina* was accompanied by an actual increase in exchangeable Ca reserves of 860 kg ha^{-1}, compared with 40 kg ha^{-1} in the forest and 100 kg ha^{-1} in the *Pinus* plot. *Gmelina* seemed to act as a calcium accumulator under acid soil conditions, while *Pinus* maintained the rainforest level. *Gmelina* maintained exchangeable Mg, exchangeable K, and total N at pre-clearing levels, while the soil under *Pinus* suffered considerable decreases. *Gmelina* also tripled the available soil P content compared with the original forest or *Pinus*.

Similar positive effects on nutrient availability were recorded in 13-year-old *Gmelina* plantations in a more fertile Alfisol in Nigeria (Fig. 7). Topsoil pH increased from 4·0 to 5·5, and smaller increases were recorded in the subsoil. Aluminium saturation decreased from 58% to 6% in the topsoil, and from 76% to 38% in the 20–40 cm layer. These changes reflected a doubling or tripling of exchangeable Ca at different soil depths, as well as an increase in topsoil exchangeable Mg (Fig. 7). Unlike the Jarí case, Chijicke (1980) detected no change in available P or exchangeable K in comparison with the native forest.

Other fast-growing tree species have also produced increases in exchangeable bases. Silva's (1983) results on an Oxisol in Brazil indicated a doubling or tripling of topsoil exchangeable Ca, Mg, or K after 10 years under *Cordia trichotoma* and *Caesalpinia echinata*, relative to the native forest, but the precious wood species *Dalbergia nigra* did not produce significant increases over the native forest.

In summary, the overall effect of mature fast-growing forest trees on nutrient availability, evaluated over the first rotation, is either highly positive or neutral. Major differences exist among species.

The effect of well-managed perennial plantation crops on acid Ultisols, however, is different. Pushparajah's (1984) data for Malaysian rubber, and Ollagnier *et al.*'s (1978) results for oil palm in the Ivory Coast indicate a stable topsoil pH, but a general decrease in exchangeable bases below pre-clearing levels (Figs 3 and 5). In the more fertile Alfisol at Benin, Nigeria, the results are totally different (Figs 4 and 5). Only K decreased to below pre-clearing levels, triggering K deficiency in oil palm. Topsoil pH, and exchangeable Ca and Mg remained stable throughout 14 years of oil palm growth. The extraction of nutrients as latex or fruits in perennial crops provides, therefore, a different picture from that given by timber species.

VI. THE SECOND ROTATION

The only data set available for the second rotation is for an Ultisol at Jarí where an 8·5 to 10-year-old *Gmelina* plantation was harvested and then burned; changes in soil properties were monitored under a subsequent *Pinus caribaea* planting for three years (Fig. 6). The residual effect of the calcium accumulator, *Gmelina*, plus burning, provided a vastly improved chemical environment for the new pine crop (topsoil pH of 5·4, 6% Al saturation, five times the topsoil Ca, nine times the Mg and twice the exchangeable K compared with the original rainforest). However, these values rapidly decreased during the early growth of pine, before it had the opportunity to establish a complete cover. At three years of age, however, the chemical environment of this second rotation was similar to that of the first (Fig. 6). No significant differences in bulk density were recorded (Table III). It would be most interesting to follow this second rotation and continue to compare it with the first rotation.

VII. MECHANISMS INVOLVED

The soil dynamics through the different stages of tree growth suggest that attention should be given to the several processes proposed in an earlier section of this paper.

A. Protection from erosion

The limited data confirm that the tree canopy and litter layer protect the soil against runoff and erosion. They also underscore the vulnerability of soils under tree crops before canopy closure and, therefore, the desirability of establishing a legume cover, or planting food crops to cover the soil, as quickly as possible.

B. Improvement of physical properties

Reliable information is limited to a few data on bulk density, porosity, and aggregate size. The results show either a positive or a neutral effect of trees on soil physical properties after they have developed a closed canopy. No deterioration of physical properties during the mature phase was detected, based on the limited data; and the suggestion that tree roots loosen the soil and increase the number of continuous air-filled pores in the subsoil appears to be supported.

The main causes of deterioration of soil physical properties are improper mechanical land clearing, and the absence of a soil cover at the early growth stages. Work in southern Bahía indicates that these effects last for several years.

It should be remembered that, with the exception of the bulldozer land clearing example from Bahía, all other data sets came from well-managed trials. In these studies, none of the fast-growing plantations were fertilized, but those perennial crops that needed additional nutrients certainly received them. With poor management, one might expect a deterioration in soil physical properties if the trees fail to develop a complete plant canopy.

C. Nutrient capture and recycling

In none of the fast-growing forest tree plantations examined was there a significant decrease in either the soil organic matter content or the availability of nutrients, relative to pre-clearing levels. In fact, in some studies the availability of nutrients increased above the pre-clearing levels. Decreases in organic matter and nutrient availability did take place with perennial plantation crops, perhaps because of the extraction of nutrients in the harvested part. New equilibrium levels were reached, and, when supplemented with fertilizers, production remained stable.

A most exciting aspect of the results is the potential increase in topsoil exchangeable Ca, Mg, or K within several years after clearing. Some trees apparently are able to capture and recycle nutrients more efficiently than others. The limited information indicates that major species differences occur, particularly in the ability to recycle calcium. *Gmelina arborea* appears to be a calcium accumulator while *Pinus caribaea* is not. At Jarí, this difference was related to the fact that *Gmelina* litter and detritus contained twice as much calcium (0·62% Ca) as the litter and detritus of the virgin forest or mature pine plantation (0·37% Ca). The Mg content of *Gmelina* litter was similar to that of the rainforest's (0·2% Mg) but the *Pinus* litter was only one-third of that value. *Pinus* produced more litter than *Gmelina* so that the actual nutrient inputs in $kg\,ha^{-1}$ were similar for the two species. Therefore, questions about litter quality and quantity should be considered.

The available information is insufficient to explain the mechanisms of base status improvement by certain tree species. The possibility of using particular species as nutrient accumulators is an intriguing one. *Gmelina arborea* is probably a Ca and Mg accumulator. Tergas and Popenoe (1971) found that 10-month-old pure stands of *Heliconia* spp. and *Gynerium* spp. accumulated three to four times as much available phosphorus as mixed fallows of the same age, in P-deficient Inceptisols of the Guatemalan humid tropics. Grass fallows may be K accumulators (Laudelot 1961; Lal *et al.* 1979). A dominant bamboo species appears to be a K accumulator in secondary fallows on Ultisols of Assam, India (Ramakrishnan & Toky 1981). Legume fallows can accumulate N, as indicated by the effect of leguminous covers in Malaysia (Fig. 3) and elsewhere. Whether or not these species indeed accumulate nutrients has to be determined in adequately designed Type I field experiments located on well-characterized soils.

D. Leaching

The fact that nutrient levels do not decrease implies that trees may prevent leaching losses from the soil. The limited evidence available, mainly from

TABLE VII. Annual leaching losses, and net annual gains or losses, of nutrients in forest ecosystems at different stages in the development of tree plantations. Data are for *Pinus caribaea* and *Gmelina arborea* plantations, planted in a sandy Ultisol at Jari, Pará, Brazil (from Russell 1983)

Site	Leaching losses (kg ha^{-1}yr^{-1}) of				Net gains or losses (kg ha^{-1}yr^{-1}) in			
	P	K	Ca	Mg	P	K	Ca	Mg
Rainforest (virgin)	0·04	12·7	16·7	8·1	+0·10	−2	−0·3	−5
Rainforest (logged)	0·08	37·1	39·1	16·1	+0·06	−25	−22	−12
Rainforest (logged and burned)	0·21	199·5	103·7	146·6	−0·06	−181	−84	−137
First rotation { *Pinus* 6 months old	0·16	89·9	89·4	74·7	−0·02	−80	−73	−71
Pinus 10·5 years old	0·05	9·6	12·1	6·1	+0·06	+1	−1	−3
Second rotation { *Pinus* 1·5 years after 8·5 years of *Gmelina*	0·08	9·9	17·5	6·3	+0·09	+1	+1	−3

Brazil, indicates that this is indeed the case after the crop establishment phase, when the trees develop their canopy and begin to recycle nutrients. Russell (1983), working at Jarí, measured negligible losses of P and measurable losses of K, Ca, and Mg at all sites, including the virgin rainforest (Table VII). Large leaching losses of bases occurred after the forest was cleared and burned, and prior to the establishment of tree cover. These losses explain, in part, the decreases in nutrient availability observed in some cases during the establishment phase. Leaching losses during the mature growth stage, and even 1·5 years into the second rotation, were actually lower than those under the rainforest. Consequently, the nutrient cycling mechanism seems to work effectively under *Pinus caribaea*.

Nutrient inputs from atmospheric deposition were also determined by Russell (1983). The balance between atmospheric deposition and leaching is presented in Table VII. This calculation shows a virtual absence of net nutrient losses from the rainforest, the mature pine plantation, and even from the 18-month-old second rotation.

The question of leaching in perennial plantation crops also deserves examination. Santana and Cabala-Rosand (1984) developed a balance between nutrient inputs and outputs in a high-yielding, mature, 17-year-old cacao plantation, with a leguminous tree shade, on a fertile Alfisol in Itabuna, Bahía, Brazil (Table VIII). The balance between inputs (atmospheric and litter) and

TABLE VIII.   Nutrient inputs and outputs in a high-yielding 17-year-old cacao plantation, shaded by *Erythrina fusca*, on a fertile Typic Tropadalf in Itabuna, Brazil (mean of 2 years) (calculated from Santana & Cabala-Rosand 1984)

		\multicolumn{5}{c}{Input or output $(kg\,ha^{-1}\,yr^{-1})$ of}
		N	P	K	Ca	Mg
Inputs	Rainfall	23	3	21	18	12
	Litter	112	13	25	162	53
Outputs	Harvest 1 t ha^{-1} of beans+1 t ha^{-1} of pods	44	10	20	1	3
	Leaching	68	0·5	2	38	63
Balance		+23	+6	+24	+141	−1

outputs (harvest and leaching) is positive for N, P, K, and Ca, and neutral for Mg. The efficiency of this system is outstanding, considering it is operating at very high yield levels. When such plantations are fertilized, N leaching losses decrease; Santana and Cabala-Rosand (1982) attribute this decrease to a stimulating effect of NPK fertilization on the development of cacao rootlets, which presumably absorb more nutrients and prevent them from leaching. The perspective of such efficient use of nutrients under ideal conditions in perennial crop production augurs well for the efficiency of well-managed, well-fertilized forest tree plantations.

VIII. TOTAL NUTRIENT STOCKS

A synthesis of the changes in total nutrient stocks during the course of plantation establishment and growth is presented in Figure 11; data were drawn from Russell's (1983) work at Jarí – the only study in which both biomass and soil data were collected. 'Total nutrient stock' is defined as the sum of all the nutrients in the plant biomass (above-ground, litter, detritus, roots) plus total N, available P (by the Mehlich I method), and exchangeable K, Ca, and Mg in the top metre of the soil. This estimate therefore ignores the total P, Ca, Mg, and K contents of the soil, because it measures only the readily available fractions.

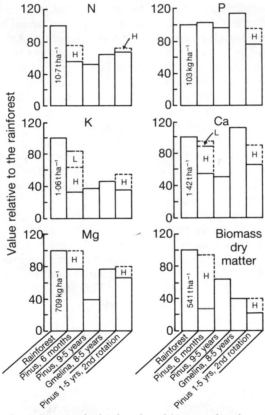

FIGURE 11. Total nutrient stocks in the plant biomass plus the soil (including only the *available* P, Ca, Mg and K) in rainforest, newly planted *Pinus caribaea* (6 months old), *P. caribaea* and *Gmelina arborea* plantations at the end of the first rotation (9·5 and 8·5 years old, respectively), and second rotation *P. caribaea* (1·5 years old). H = harvest loss from trees taken when clearing the rainforest or from the plantations; L = leaching loss. See legend to Figure 10 (calculated using data from Russell 1983).

Total plant biomass decreased to about 40–60% of that in the virgin rainforest at the end of the first rotation of *Gmelina* or *Pinus caribaea*. Most of the losses were quantitatively accounted for by the newly planted trees and the dry matter extracted by harvest.

The plantations, of all ages, contained approximately 60% of the total N stock of the rainforest. Most losses occurred shortly after rainforest clearing, but thereafter the plantations maintained the levels of N. As none of the trees were legumes and no legume cover crops were used, no N build-up occurred. The ecosystem, therefore, lost 40% of its total N, and then reached a new equilibrium level.

A remarkable conservation of P is shown in Figure 11, with nutrient stocks ranging from 76% to 116% of the rainforest values. The decrease in P at the start of the second rotation is largely accounted for by the P removed in the first rotation harvest. The P content in the first harvest is not included, because Russell (1983) described difficulties in methodology. Figure 11 ignores most of the total P in the soil, which is not extracted by the Mehlich procedure. Calculations from total elemental analysis of soils of the Amazon by Marbut and Manifold (1926) indicate an average total P content in the top metre in the order of 60 times the total P stock indicated in Figure 11.

Significant losses of K occur when rainforests are replaced by tree plantations. Potassium stocks decreased to about 32% of that in the forest after land clearing. Most of the losses were accounted for by removal at harvest and the rapid leaching losses recorded during this period. Afterwards, there were slight increases, to about 40% of the rainforest value. The overall stocks and losses of exchangeable K in Figure 11 ($1.06\,t\,ha^{-1}$), however, are small considering that the total K content of these soils is estimated to be $73\,t\,ha^{-1}$ of K (Marbut & Manifold 1926). It is not surprising that research on perennial crops like rubber and oil palm on Ultisols shows rapid depletion of K, and there is a need to fertilize the trees with this element (Figs 3 and 5).

Calcium nutrient stock decreased to about 56% of the rainforest value upon planting the first *Pinus* rotation. The losses were, again, accounted for by the amount removed in the forest harvest and the small amounts leached. This reduced Ca level remained relatively stable with *Pinus*, but increased to above pre-clearing levels with *Gmelina* (Fig. 11). The second rotation started at a lower level, but much of the loss was related to the amount removed in the *Gmelina* harvest. Losses were small compared to the total Ca in the top metre, about $13.6\,t\,ha^{-1}$ of Ca.

The magnesium nutrient stocks decreased with age in the *Pinus* plantations, but mature *Gmelina* plantations maintained a steady level of about 75% of that in the rainforest. The 25% loss appeared to be related to the harvest of the rainforest. Again, the overall losses were small relative to the total Mg content of these soils – about $14.4\,t\,ha^{-1}$ of Mg to 100 cm depth (Marbut & Manifold 1926).

CONCLUSIONS

The evidence presented, drawn only from Type I and II experiments that meet soil uniformity criteria, provides general support for the Lundgren model, except for the decline in organic matter, available nutrients and soil structure during the maximum production phase. Little deterioration of soil properties, relative to the virgin forest, was measured during the establishment phase, particularly when leguminous cover or fertilization was used, and the land was cleared by either slash-and-burn or mechanized land clearing methods that caused little damage to soil properties. Lundgren's model seems more applicable when conventional bulldozer clearing is practised, or when the trees are planted without a legume cover or intercropping.

Some of the beneficial effects of trees on soils after the trees close canopy were unexpected, particularly the maintenance of chemical properties, and the dramatic Ca accumulation properties of *Gmelina arborea*. Many of the advantages of trees, as compared to annual crops, are related to the longer time they protect the soil surface, their larger biomass and nutrient stocks, and their ability to recycle nutrients.

The main deleterious effects of tree crops on soil properties occur during their establishment phase, because forest clearing methods often cause great soil disturbance, and also because the soil is exposed more, and for a longer period of time, than soil under annual crops or pastures.

Despite the potential improvements in soil chemical properties during the fallow phase of tree crops, the extraction of nutrients by harvesting, and the leaching losses incurred prior to canopy closure lead to a depletion of key nutrients, primarily potassium, that must be replaced by fertilization if yields are to be sustained. This is the experience in the cultivation of perennial plantation crops, where fertilization is routine and profitable, even in fertile Alfisols. Coulter (1972) stated that research in Malaysia has shown that the fertility stored in forest soils in areas of highly weathered and leached soils is extremely important for the first planting cycle of rubber and oil palm. The need for additional fertilizers in subsequent cycles has been amply demonstrated. The same is likely to apply to fast-growing forest tree crops. No successful stable crop production system can be based on 'mining' the soil without returning a proportionate amount of what was removed by harvesting. The closed nutrient cycle in tropical forests remains as long as the trees are not harvested.

Many of the observations reported here are speculative, based on comparisons of data from different sites, collected using different methodologies. In order to be definitive about the findings, rigorous comparisons are needed on well-characterized soils. Type I experiments, in which various tree crop systems can be compared with annual crops, pastures, or fallows, are needed to support these observations. Only then can it be demonstrated to what degree trees improve or maintain soil properties in the humid tropics.

ACKNOWLEDGEMENT

This chapter forms Paper no. 9590 of the North Carolina Agricultural Research Service, Raleigh, NC 27695–7619 USA, contribution of NCSU's TropSoils Program supported by the U.S. Agency for International Development.

REFERENCES

Alegre, J. C., Cassel, D. K., Bandy, D. E. & Sanchez, P. A. (1985). Effects of land clearing on soil properties of an Ultisol and subsequent crop production in Yurimaguas, Peru. *Proc. int. Conf. Land Clearing and Development.* Ibadan: International Institute for Tropical Agriculture. In press.

Alvim, P. T. (1981). A perspective appraisal of perennial crops in the Amazon Basin. *Interciencia (Caracas)*, **6**, 139–145.

Andriesse, J. P. (1977). Nutrient level changes during a 20-year shifting cultivation cycle in Sarawak, Malaysia. *Proc. Conf. Classification and Management of Tropical Soils*, 479–491. Kuala Lumpur: Malaysian Society of Soil Science.

Brinkmann, W. L. F. & de Nascimento, J. C. (1973). The effects of slash and burn agriculture on plant nutrients in the Tertiary region of Central Amazonia. *Turrialba*, **23**, 284–290.

Broughton, W. J. (1977). Effect of various covers on soil fertility under *Hevea brasiliensis* and on growth of the tree. *Agro-Ecosystems*, **3**, 147–170.

Buol, S. W. (1983). *China trip report.* Raleigh, NC: North Carolina State University, Dept of Soil Science.

Chee, Y. K. (1981). The importance of legume cover crop establishment for cultivation of rubber (*Hevea brasiliensis*) in Malaysia. In: *BNF technology for tropical agriculture*, 369–376. Cali (Colombia): Centro Internacional de Agricultura Tropical.

Chijicke, E. O. (1980). Impacts of soils on fast-growing species in lowland humid tropics. *FAO For. Pap.*, no. 21.

Cochrane, T. T. & Sanchez, P. A. (1982). Land resources, soils and their management in the Amazon region: a state of knowledge report. In: *Amazonia: agriculture and land use research*, edited by S. B. Hecht, 137–210. Cali (Colombia): Centro Internacional de Agricultura Tropical. (Also in Spanish).

Cornforth, I. S. (1970). Reafforestation and nutrient reserves in the humid tropics. *J. appl. Ecol.*, **7**, 609–615.

Coulter, J. K. (1972). Soils of Malaysia. In: *Soils of the humid tropics*, edited by M. Drosdoff, 205–206. Washington DC: National Academy of Sciences.

Couper, D. C., Lal, R. & Claasen, S. L. (1981). Land clearing and development for agricultural purposes in western Nigeria. In: *Tropical agricultural hydrology*, edited by R. Lal and E. W. Russell, 119–130. New York: Wiley.

Cunningham, R. K. (1963). The effect of clearing a tropical forest soil. *J. Soil Sci.*, **14**, 334–345.

Daud, N. (1977). Soil genesis on shales and its influence on the soil suitability for *Hevea* cultivation. *Proc. Clamatrops Conf.*, 84–91. Kuala Lumpur: Malaysian Society of Soil Science.

Drosdoff, M., ed. (1972). *Soils of the humid tropics.* Washington DC: National Academy of Sciences.

Falesi, I. C. (1976). *Ecosistema de pastagem cultivada na Amazonia brazileira.* (CPATU Bol Tec.1). Belem (Brazil): Centro de Pesquisa Agropecuaria do Trópico Úmido, EMBRAPA.

Food and Agriculture Organization. (1977). Assessing soil degradation. *FAO Soils Bull.*, 34.

Gillman, G. P. (1984). Nutrient availability in acid soils of the tropics following clearing and cultivation. In: *Proc. int. Workshop on Soils*, 39–46. Canberra: Australian Council for International Agricultural Research.

Goodland, R. J. A. & Irwin, H. S. (1975). *Amazon jungle: green hell to red desert?* Amsterdam: Elsevier.

Greenland, D. J., ed. (1981). *Characterization of soils in relation to their classification and management for crop production: examples from the humid tropics.* Oxford: Oxford University Press.

Griffith, A. L. & Gupta, R. S. (1948). Soils in relation to teak with special reference to laterization. *Indian For. Bull.*, no. 141.

Hecht, S. B. (1983). *Cattle ranching in eastern Amazonia.* Ph.D. thesis, Department of Geography, University of California, Berkeley.

IRRI (1980). *Priorities for alleviating soil-related constraints to food production in the tropics.* Los Baños (Philippines): International Rice Research Institute.

Johnson, N. E. (1976). Biological opportunities and fast-growing plantations. *J. For.*, **74**, 206–211.

Jose, A. I. & Koshy, M. M. (1972). A study of the morphological, physical and chemical characteristics of soils as influenced by teak vegetation. *Indian Forester*, **98**, 338–348.

Juo, A. S. R. & Lal, R. (1977). The effect of fallow and continuous cultivation on the chemical and physical properties of an Alfisol in Western Nigeria. *Pl. Soil*, **47**, 567–584.

Kang, B. T. & Lal, R. (1981). Nutrient losses in water runoff from agricultural catchments. In: *Tropical agricultural hydrology*, edited by R. Lal and E. W. Russell, 153–162. New York: Wiley.

Kowal, J. M. L. & Tinker P. B. H. (1959). Soil changes under a plantation established from high secondary forest. *J. W. Afr. Inst. Oil Palm Res.*, **2**, 376–389.

Lal, R. (1975). Role of mulching techniques in soil and water management. *International Institute for Tropical Agriculture, Tech. Bull.*, no. 1.

Lal, R. (1981). Deforestation of tropical rainforests and hydrological problems. In: *Tropical agricultural hydrology*, edited by R. Lal and E. W. Russell, 131–140. New York: Wiley.

Lal, R., Kang, B. T., Moorman, F. R., Juo, A. S. R. & Moomaw, J. C. (1975). Problemas de manejo de suelos y posibles soluciones en Nigeria Occidental. In: *Manejo de Suelos en America tropical*, edited by E. Bornemisza and A. Alvarado, 380–417. Raleigh, NC: North Carolina State University.

Lal, R., Wilson, G. F. & Okigbo, B. N. (1979). Changes in properties of an Alfisol produced by various cover crops. *Soil Sci.*, **127**, 377–382.

Lal, R., Sanchez, P. A. & Cummings, R. W., jr, eds. (1985). *Land clearing and development.* Oxford: Oxford University Press. In press.

Laudelot, H. (1961). *Dynamics of soils in relation to their fallowing techniques.* (Paper 1124661E). Rome: Food and Agricultural Organization.

Laurie, M. V. & Griffith, A. L. (1942). The problem of the pure teak plantation. *Indian For. Rec. (N.S.) Silviculture*, **5**, 1–121.

Lawson, R. L., Lal, R. & Oduro-Afriyie, K. (1981). Rainfed redistribution and microclimatic changes over a cleared watershed. In: *Tropical agricultural hydrology*, edited by R. Lal and E. W. Russell, 141–152. New York, Wiley.

Le Buanec, B. (1972). Dix ans de culture motorisée sur un bassin versant du centre Côte d'Ivoire. Evolution de la fertilité et de la production. *Agron. trop., Nogent*, **27**, 1191–1211.

Lundgren, B. (1978). *Soil conditions and nutrient cycling under natural and plantation forests in Tanzanian highlands.* (Reports on forest ecology and forest soils no. 31). Uppsala: Swedish University of Agricultural Sciences.

Marbut, C. F. & Manifold, C. B. (1926). The soils of the Amazon basin in relation to agricultural possibilities. *Geogrl Rev.*, **16**, 414–442.

National Research Council. (1982). *Ecological aspects of development in the humid tropics.* Washington DC: National Academy Press.

Nye, P. H. & Greenland, D. J. (1960). *The soil under shifting cultivation.* (Technical Communication no. 51). Harpenden: Commonwealth Agricultural Bureau.

Nye, P. H. & Greenland, D. J. (1964). Changes in the soil after clearing tropical forest. *Pl. Soil*, **21**, 101–112.

Ollagnier, M., Lauzeral, A., Olivin, J. & Ochs, R. (1978). Evolution des sols sous palmeraie après defrichement de la forêt. *Oleagineux*, **33**, 537–547.

Pushparajah, E. (1984). *Nutrient availability of acid soils in the tropics following clearing and cultivation with plantation crops.* In: *Proc. int. Workshop on Soils*, 47–51. Canberra: Australian Council for International Agricultural Research.

Pushparajah, E. & Amin, L. L., eds. (1977). *Soils under Hevea in peninsular Malaysia and their management.* Kuala Lumpur: Rubber Research Institute of Malaysia.

Ramakrishnan, P. S. & Toky, O. P. (1981). Soil nutrient status of hill agro-ecosystems and recovery pattern after slash and burn agriculture (jhum) in north-eastern India. *Pl. Soil*, **60**, 41–64.

Roose, E. (1970). Importance relative de l'érosion, du drainage oblique et vertical dans la pédogénèse d'un sol ferralitique de moyenne Côte d'Ivoire. *Cah. ORSTOM Sér. Pedol.*, **8**, 469–482.

Russell, C. E. (1983). *Nutrient cycling and productivity in native and plantation forests in Jari Florestal, Para, Brazil.* Ph.D. thesis, Institute of Ecology, University of Georgia, Athens.

Sanchez, P. A. (1976). *Properties and management of soils in the tropics.* New York: Wiley.

Sanchez, P. A. (1979). Soil fertility and conservation considerations for agroforestry systems in the humid tropics of Latin America. In: *Soils research in agroforestry*, edited by H. O. Mongi and P. A. Huxley, 79–124. Nairobi: International Council for Research in Agroforestry.

Sanchez, P. A. (1982). Soils of the humid tropics. *Stud. Third World Soc.*, **14**, 347–410.

Sanchez, P. A. & Buol, S. W. (1975). Soils of the tropics and the world food crisis. *Science*, *N.Y.*, **188**, 598–603.

Sanchez, P. A., Bandy, D. E., Villachica, J. H. & Nicholaides, J. J. (1982a). Amazon basin soils: management for continuous crop production. *Science, N.Y.*, **216**, 821–827.

Sanchez, P. A., Couto, W. & Buol, S. W. (1982b). The fertility capability soil classification system: interpretation, applicability and modification. *Geoderma*, **27**, 283–309.

Sanchez, P. A., Nicholaides, J. J. & Couto, W. (1982c). Physical and chemical constraints to food production in the tropics. In: *Chemistry and world food supplies: the new frontiers CHEMRAWN II. Perspectives and recommendations*, edited by G. Bixler and L. W. Shemilt, 89–106. Los Baños (Philippines): International Rice Research Institute.

Sanchez, P. A., Villachica, J. H. & Bandy, D. E. (1983). Soil fertility dynamics after clearing a tropical rainforest in Peru. *Soil Sci. Soc. Am. J.*, **47**, 1171–1178.

Santana, M. B. M. & Cabala-Rosand, P. (1982). Dynamics of nitrogen in a shaded cacao plantation. *Pl. Soil*, **67**, 271–281.

Santana, M. B. M. & Cabala-Rosand, P. (1984). Reciclagem de nutrientes em uma platação de cacau sombreada com Eritrina. *Paper int. Cocoa Research Conf.*, *9th, Lomé, Togo*. Itabuna (Brazil): CEPLAC.

Serrão, E. A. S., Falesi, I. C., Veiga, J. R. & Texeira, J. F. (1979). Productivity of cultivated pastures in low fertility soils of the Amazon of Brazil. In: *Pasture production in acid soils of the tropics*, edited by P. A. Sanchez and L. E. Tergas, 195–226. Cali (Colombia): Centro Internacional de Agricultura Tropical.

Seubert, C. E., Sanchez, P. A. & Valverde, C. (1977). Effects of land clearing methods on soil properties and crop performance in an Ultisol of the Amazon jungle of Peru. *Trop. Agric., Trin.*, **54**, 307–321.

Silva, L. F. (1978). *Influencia do manejo de em ecossistema nas propiedades edáficas dos Oxisols de "Tabuleiro"*. Itabuna, Bahia (Brazil): CEPLAC/Centro de Pesquisas do Cacau.

Silva, L. F., ed. (1980). *Projeto Tabuleiro. Relatôrio de ativadades 1974–1979*. Itabuna, Bahia (Brazil): CEPLAC.

Silva, L. F., ed. (1982a). *Projeto Tabuleiro. Relatôrio de ativadades 1980–1981*. Itabuna, Bahia (Brazil): CEPLAC.

Silva, L. F. (1982b). Manejo del ecossistema tropical humédo y sus consecuencias en el complejo suelo-planta-organismos. *Suelos Ecuat.*, **12**, 316–324.

Silva, L. F. (1983). *Influencia de cultivos e sistemas de manejo nas modificacoes edáficas dos Oxisols de tabuleiro (Haplorthox) do Sul da Bahia*. Belem (Brazil): CEPLAC, Departamento Especial da Amazonia.

Soil Survey Staff. (1975). *Soil taxonomy*. (Agricultural handbook no. 436). Washington DC: United States Department of Agriculture.

Tergas, L. E. & Popenoe, H. L. (1971). Young secondary vegetation and soil interactions in Izabal, Guatemala. *Pl. Soil*, **34**, 675–690.

Tinker, P. B. H. (1968). Changes occurring in the sedimentary soils of southern Nigeria after oil palm plantation establishment. *J. W. Afr. Inst. Oil Palm Res.*, **4**, 66–81.

Toledo, J. M. & Serrão, E. A. S. (1982). Pasture and animal production in Amazonia. In: *Amazonia: agriculture and land use research*, edited by S. B. Hecht, 281–310. Cali (Colombia): Centro Internacional de Agricultura Tropical.

Watson, G. A. (1961). Cover plants and the soil nutrient cycle in *Hevea* cultivation. *Proc. Nat. Rubber Research Conf. 1960*, 1–9. Kuala Lumpur, Malaysia.

Weert, van der, R. (1974). Influence of mechanical forest clearing on soil conditions and the resulting effects on root growth. *Trop. Agric., Trin.*, **51**, 325–331.

Weert, van der, R. & Lenselink, K. J. (1973). The influence of mechanical clearing of forest on plant growth. *Surin. Landb.*, **21**, 100–111.

21

EXPLOITING TREE CROP-SYMBIONT SPECIFICITY

J. WILSON
Institute of Terrestrial Ecology, Bush Estate, Penicuik, Midlothian, Scotland

M. P. COUTTS
Forestry Commission, Northern Research Station, Roslin, Midlothian, Scotland

I. INTRODUCTION

The principal symbiotic associations with tree crops are the ectomycorrhizal and vesicular-arbuscular (VA) mycorrhizal associations, and the nodule-forming associations with *Frankia* and *Rhizobium*.

Interest in the uses of mycorrhizal inoculation began with the introduction of exotic tree species. Many papers document the necessity of making parallel introductions of mycorrhizal fungi (Marx 1980; Mikola 1980) and attention has been brought to the requirements for introducing mycorrhizas when revegetating derelict and disturbed sites (Marx 1975; Marx 1977a). In this paper, we outline the potential for matching symbiont species/strains to host tree species/provenances, particularly in relation to forestry.

Although Wilde (1944) was of the opinion 'that 99% of all *practising* foresters will not have to lose any sleep over the problem of mycorrhizal inoculation', research into the role of mycorrhizas and the nodule symbioses in the growth of tree crops has gathered impetus. Following the general appreciation that the formation of any symbiosis is better than none, it is now understood that the effectiveness of symbioses can depend upon the host and symbiont genotype, the climate and soil. There appears to be much potential for exploiting this variation, which at present is put to only limited use.

Forestry generally uses poor land unsuited for other crops and it is in those circumstances that trees are most dependent on their symbionts. Trees grown for other purposes tend to be planted on better sites, are more intensively managed, and receive larger applications of fertilizers.

Excessive use of fertilizers and pesticides produces its own economic and pollution problems (Alexander 1973). Nitrogen fertilizer production is costly in terms of fossil energy, and much phosphate fertilizer that is applied may be bound in unavailable forms in the soil (Dommergues 1978). The use of symbionts provides a *biological* means of improving plant nutrition – mycorrhizas by increasing the rate of nutrient absorption from the soil, with selective absorption of some ions, and nodules by fixation of atmospheric nitrogen. Their use may reduce or eliminate the need for fertilizers and also produce benefits such as increased survival, for which fertilizer application is no substitute.

Mycorrhizas, particularly ectomycorrhizas, can improve plant performance in a number of other ways, including improving tolerance to drought, heavy metals, soil toxins and extremes of pH and temperature. They can also provide protection against fine-root pathogens (Meyer 1974; Marx & Krupa 1978; Harley & Smith 1983).

II. HOST AND MICROSYMBIONT DISTRIBUTION

Nearly all higher plants are mycorrhizal. According to Wilhelm (1966), plants 'do not, strictly speaking, have roots, they have mycorrhizae'. Worldwide, species forming VA mycorrhizas are far more abundant than those forming ectomycorrhizas. According to Meyer (1973), the latter comprise only 3% of phanerogams. Although ectomycorrhizal associations are much less frequent, the host plants are generally long-lived woody perennials, and many of them are important forest trees. Harley and Smith (1983) listed 133 woody genera containing at least one ectomycorrhizal species, distributed among 30 families. Many of those species are forest dominants of the north and south temperate and subarctic regions. An increasing number of ectomycorrhizal species are now being identified in the tropical and subtropical regions. Their distribution in these regions is mainly in areas where vegetative activity is seasonally restricted by rainfall, or at high altitudes (Singer & Morello 1960). However, this is not always so; some of them, including the economically important Dipterocarpaceae, are more widespread (de Alwis & Abeynayake 1980).

VA mycorrhizas occur on all coniferous families except the Pinaceae, and on most other gymnosperms. They predominate on tropical hardwoods and occur on some temperate hardwoods including *Fraxinus*, *Liquidambar*, *Platanus* and *Liriodendron*. Other tree crops with VA mycorrhizas include apple, cacao, coffee, citrus, cherry, rubber and oil palm.

Nodule-forming associations occur with fewer hosts, and are found together on root systems with mycorrhizas. Until quite recently, *Rhizobium* was thought to be exclusively associated with legumes, but it has now been found in association with a non-leguminous tree belonging to the genus *Trema* (Trinick 1973) (now reclassified as *Parasponia*) that is widely distributed in the tropics (Akkermans 1978). *Frankia* forms associations mainly with trees of temperate regions (including *Alnus*) and with tropical genera at high altitudes, but also with the more widespread tropical genus *Casuarina* which is prevalent in coastal areas.

Research effort into these various symbioses with trees has been rather patchy. It has focused on ecto- rather than VA mycorrhizas, and the nodule symbioses have been comparatively neglected. This imbalance may be partly due to the difficulties of culturing VA fungi and, until recently, *Frankia*, *in vitro*.

III. BALANCE OF THE SYMBIOSIS

In the symbiotic relationship, the host plant supplies the microsymbiont with all its carbohydrates, while the mycorrhizas supply the host with phosphate, other soil-derived nutrients, and water, and the nodule symbionts provide nitrogen.

The symbioses impose a significant drain on the host photosynthate, particularly ectomycorrhizas, which produce large fruiting bodies and have considerable quantities of fungal matter in the mantle. In a spruce forest, fruit body production alone could use carbohydrate, equivalent to 10% of potential timber production (Romell 1939), or $160 \, kg \, ha^{-1} yr^{-1}$ of carbohydrate in a *Pseudotsuga menziesii* forest (Fogel & Hunt 1979) and $450 \, kg \, ha^{-1} yr^{-1}$ in an *Abies amabilis* forest (Vogt et al. 1982) (Harley & Smith 1983). Despite the imposition of this large energy drain, in situations where the nutrient supply is limited or other stresses are imposed, the symbiotic associations are essential for survival.

When selecting 'effective' symbionts, we must seek ones that (a) improve the host's carbon balance and enhance the production of marketable parts, and (b) are able to compete with naturally occurring types – bearing in mind that mycorrhizal symbionts are so widespread in nature.

IV. SELECTION OF ECTOMYCORRHIZAL FUNGI

The genotype of the host and fungus, and both edaphic and climatic factors, should be considered when exploiting mycorrhizal symbioses (Bowen 1965; Mikola 1973; Marx 1977a; Molina 1977; Trappe 1977). Moreover, it is now becoming clear that there is the factor of the 'mycorrhizal succession' to be considered, in that, when young trees are grown apart from more mature trees (as occurs in nurseries), only certain of the fungi that are capable of forming mycorrhizas with trees of that species may be able to form mycorrhizas with the juvenile plants (Fleming 1983; Last *et al*. 1983; Mason *et al*. 1983).

Some ectomycorrhizal fungi are rather host-specific, whereas others have a broad host range. *Suillus grevillii*, for instance, occurs only on a few species including *Larix*, while *Pisolithus tinctorius* forms ectomycorrhizas with over 73 species of trees (Marx 1977b). Conversely, some tree species, such as *Alnus*, have only a few ectomycorrhizal associates (Molina & Trappe 1982) while others have many. Although a fungal species may have a broad host range, this does not mean that all isolates are equally effective in forming mycorrhizas with all hosts or in producing beneficial effects.

Lamb and Richards (1970, 1971), working with *Pinus radiata* and *Pinus elliottii* var. *elliottii*, tested a range of inocula isolated from the roots of these two species. They found that, although some isolates would form mycorrhizas with both hosts, the largest growth increments of the hosts occurred with fungi that had originally been isolated from the same host species. Similarly, Reddy and Khan (1972) found that, although *Pinus roxburghii* would form mycorrhizas with soil inoculum taken from beneath that species or beneath *Eucalyptus* or when interplanted with *Pinus patula*, the only significant growth increase occurred with inoculum taken from *P. roxburghii*.

Maronek and Hendrix (1980) found that an isolate of *Pisolithus tinctorius* taken from beneath *Pinus taeda* formed mycorrhizas with most inoculated plants of *Picea abies* and *Tsuga canadensis*, but with only half the plants of *Pinus nigra*. However, the symbiosis increased height growth only in *Picea abies*, although the degree of infection was similar among all successfully inoculated plants. Molina and Chamard (1983), testing an isolate of *Laccaria laccata* with *Pseudotsuga menziesii* and *Pinus ponderosa* at various fertilizer levels, found little effect on plant size although mycorrhizal formation was excellent.

The importance of isolate selection was further demonstrated by the work of Theodorou and Bowen (1970). In glasshouse studies, they inoculated *Pinus radiata* with four different isolates of *Rhizopogon luteolus* and with *Suillus granulatus* and *S. luteus*. All inoculation treatments enhanced growth and, as a group, the *Rhizopogon* isolates were superior to the *Suillus* species. Considerable differences existed among the *Rhizopogon* isolates, the best promoting nearly double the height increment of the worst. Differences between treatments could also be obtained in the field (Bowen *et al*. 1971). Height increments between treatments diverged up to 32 months and then began to converge, apparently as inoculum spread from plot to plot. These data are important, in that they are one of the earliest pieces of evidence for the beneficial effects of mycorrhizal inoculation against an existing mycorrhizal background. However, a similar, repeat experiment failed to show any benefit of inoculation, apparently because there was a large background population of effective mycorrhizal fungi.

Interactions between host genotypes and inoculation treatments were demonstrated by Berry (1982) who tested the growth of *Pinus rigida* and *Pinus taeda* families, and hybrids between these species, on surface-mined coal spoil in Tennessee. Among plants with naturally occurring mycorrhizas (mostly *Thelephora terrestris*), no single family produced a significantly greater stem volume than any other, whereas inoculation with *Pisolithus tinctorius* stimulated the growth of all families, with some responding significantly more than others to the inoculation treatment.

No account of mycorrhizal exploitation would be complete without reference to the extensive work by Marx and others on *P. tinctorius*. As indicated, this fungus can greatly enhance the growth of host plants. It occurs extensively on mining wastes (Schramm 1966) and appears to be ecologically adapted to poor conditions (Marx 1976) where few other ectomycorrhizal fungi can survive (Marx & Krupa 1978). The exceptional ability of *P. tinctorius* to form mycorrhizas at high temperatures may explain its importance on mine wastes (Marx *et al.* 1970). *Pinus taeda* seedlings inoculated with *P. tinctorius* have survived and grown as well at soil temperatures of 40 °C as at 25 °C (Marx & Bryan 1971).

Although *P. tinctorius* is undoubtedly very beneficial to trees under certain circumstances, it is not a panacea for reafforestation problems. Marx *et al.* (1977a) found that five southern pine species responded differently to it at different outplanting sites. In poor soils, *P. tinctorius* had a competitive advantage over other fungi, whereas at better sites it was out-competed by other fungi. Riffle and Tinus (1982) outplanted pre-inoculated *Pinus ponderosa* and *Pinus sylvestris* on a grassland site. After five years, the only treatment which produced a significant increase in biomass was inoculation with pine duff from a 38-year-old *P. ponderosa* stand. None of the other inoculation treatments, including *P. tinctorius*, enhanced growth. Grossnickle and Reid (1982, 1983) found that neither *P. tinctorius* nor *Cenococcum geophilum* was suited to conditions at a high elevation mine site with a harsh climate and short growing season.

Relatively little is known about other symbionts and their preferences for particular types of site. *Cenococcum geophilum* appears to be more tolerant of drought than other species, although it may not be very beneficial to growth (Mikola 1948; Mexal & Reid 1973; Maronek *et al.* 1981). In culture, it is tolerant of sodium chloride concentrations in excess of those found in most salty soils of dry regions, and so it may prove a suitable symbiont for trees in these regions (Saleh-Rastin 1976). Although *C. geophilum* may not enhance growth, Pigott (1982) has found that, in association with *Tilia cordata*, the fungus could withstand desiccation, and it enabled *T. cordata* to maintain an intact absorptive system through periods of drought which could take up water and ions when conditions became favourable.

There is considerable variation in temperature tolerance between strains of ectomycorrhizal fungi (Trappe 1977). *Paxillus involutus* and *Suillus variegatus* are able to grow at low temperatures, which could be an advantage in some nurseries, allowing mycorrhizal formation in early spring, soon after seed germination (Slankis 1974). An ability to adapt to a changed temperature regime at outplanting is also important.

Measurements of the pH optima for the growth of ectomycorrhizal fungi *in vitro* have shown that best growth is obtained in acid conditions (Hung & Trappe 1983). Differences in the optimum pH are as great within as between species, and some isolates have narrow optimal pH bands while others have broad bands. An isolate with a broad optimal band would presumably have wider applications in forestry.

The most successful fungus will be one which is competitive and able to adapt to soil and climatic conditions. This is an important consideration in tree inoculation, because a fungus which is well suited to conditions in the nursery may not be well adapted to conditions at the planting site. Molina (1977) has commented that *Thelephora terrestris*, *Laccaria laccata* and *Inocybe lacera*, that are common in *Pseudotsuga menziesii* nurseries in the Pacific Northwest, are aggressive and well suited to the highly fertile, irrigated nursery conditions, but they may not be well suited to many planting sites. Bledsoe *et al.* (1982) inoculated *P. menziesii* with *Hebeloma crustuliniforme* and *L. laccata* (both common species in seedling nurseries); neither was able to compete with a native fungus on outplanting. Both isolates originated from west of the Cascade mountains and may not have been suited to planting conditions east of the Cascades.

Microsymbionts may be selected to protect host plants from pathogens, and some mechanisms have been postulated (Zak 1964). Marx (1969a) grew five mycorrhizal fungi in agar plate culture with a number of root pathogenic fungi and soil bacteria; he found that the mycorrhizal fungi produced antibiotics and that 44% of the root pathogens were inhibited. *Leucopaxillus cerealis* var. *piceina* was particularly effective against *Pythium* sp., *Phytophthora* sp. and *Rhizoctonia* sp. The antibiotic produced by *L. cerealis* was identified as diatretyne nitrile (Marx 1969b). *Laccaria laccata* stimulates *P. menziesii* seedlings to produce phenols, which may protect them from *Fusarium oxysporum* (Sylvia & Sinclair 1983). In pot culture, Hyppel (1968) found that *Boletus bovinus* could protect *Picea abies* seedlings against *Fomes annosus*, even when no mycorrhizas were formed. The mantle and Hartig net of mycorrhizas may present a physical barrier to infection; thus, Marx (1970) found that the roots of *Pinus echinata* seedlings did not become infected by *Phytophthora cinnamomi* in those parts that had formed mycorrhizas with *Thelephora terrestris* or *Pisolithus tinctorius*.

Recently, Brown (1983) demonstrated that ectomycorrhizal infection can ameliorate zinc toxicity in *Betula*, but little research has been done on the role of ectomycorrhizas in heavy metal tolerance, despite the interest in selecting plants which could be used to reclaim mine waste.

V. SELECTION OF VA MYCORRHIZAL FUNGI

Despite their great importance, comparatively few investigations have been made of the relationships between VA mycorrhizas and tree growth. VA fungal species are much less host-specific than ectomycorrhizal fungi. *Glomus microcarpus*, for instance, can form mycorrhizas with both angiosperms – monocots (*Phleum pratense*) and dicots (*Rubus spectabilis*) – and gymnosperms (eg *Taxus brevifolius*) (Gerdemann & Trappe 1974). Many VA fungal species have a worldwide distribution (Mosse 1973). This wide distribution might suggest that there is less need to inoculate plants with VA fungi than with ectomycorrhizal fungi, but circumstances can still occur where VA fungi are absent. For instance, if they are eliminated from a soil by fumigation, it can take a long time before they are reintroduced naturally, because, unlike the majority of ectomycorrhizal fungi, VA fungi produce their spores below ground so they cannot be dispersed by wind. The fact that certain types of VA fungi predominate in (and perhaps are adapted to) particular regions (Mosse 1973) and soils (Hayman 1975) may indicate that it would be advantageous to introduce particular types when planting new areas. Species of VA fungi are known to differ in tolerance to pH (Green *et al.* 1976), salt (Hirrel & Gerdemann 1980) and temperature (Schenck & Schroder 1974).

As with ectomycorrhizas, not all VA mycorrhizas are equally effective with all hosts. Marx *et al.* (1971) found that *Endogone mosseae* significantly increased the growth of rough lemon, but not sour orange. Infection occurred with both hosts, but the degree of infection was greater (83%) with lemon than with orange (52%). Some citrus cultivars need to form mycorrhizas more than others in order to grow satisfactorily, depending on the fertilizer regime (Menge *et al.* 1978). Schultz *et al.* (1981) experimented with eight hardwood species (*Acer negundo*, *A. saccharum*, *Fraxinus pennsylvanica*, *Juglans nigra*, *Liquidambar styraciflua*, *Platanus occidentalis* and *Prunus serotina*) using a mixed inoculum of *Glomus mosseae* and *G. etunicatus*. Inoculation increased the height growth of all species except *A. saccharum* and *J. nigra*. Species differences in the degree of infection did not correspond with species differences in growth, although the degree of infection has been found to be important in other instances, such as on *Khaya grandifoliola* in Nigeria (Redhead 1975).

Host species can respond differently to different inoculum species. Bryan and Kormanik (1977) inoculated *Liquidambar styraciflua* seedlings with *Glomus mosseae* or naturally occurring inocula from *Liquidambar* soil. *G. mosseae* increased height growth six-fold (compared with an uninoculated control), but the natural inoculum increased height growth eight-fold and was superior to *G. mosseae* in increasing root growth. This experiment was done at high fertilizer levels, comparable to those used in hardwood nurseries, and demonstrated that seedlings have an obligate physiological requirement for VA fungi. Kormanik *et al.* (1982) inoculated the eight hardwood species tested by Schultz *et al.* (1981), with either *Glomus fasciculatus* (GF), a mix of *G. mosseae* and *G. etunicatus* (GM), or a mixture of several *Glomus* and *Gigaspora* species (GG). All tree species were infected, but this did not increase the height growth of *Juglans nigra* in any of the inoculation treatments, and *Acer saccharum* did not respond to GM, which was generally the least effective treatment. The authors commented that the *period* during which a root system is infected with VA fungi is probably more important than the percentage infection at a particular time. Early infection, promoting early growth, is probably very important (Kormanik *et al.* 1981, 1982). Other instances of host species differing in their response to different types of VA fungal inoculum have been reported by Kabre *et al.* (1982) using *Acer pseudoplatanus* and Furlan *et al.* (1983) using *Fraxinus americana*.

Work by Kormanik *et al.* (1977) suggested that there can be ecotypic variation within host species in their response to the same VA fungal inoculum, in that families of *Liquidambar styraciflua* from poor upland sites responded more to inoculation with *G. mosseae* than familes from fertile lowland sites.

Most work with trees has been done using sterilized soils, so that the effects of inoculation have been judged by comparison with controls that lacked a natural endomycorrhizal flora. However, Plenchette *et al.* (1981) recently demonstrated that the growth of apple seedlings growing in an unsterilized phosphate-deficient soil could be enhanced by inoculating the soil with a VA mycorrhizal fungus, and this effect could not be mimicked by applying P fertilizer.

As with ectomycorrhizal fungi, competition between VA fungi may be important when attempting to establish or maintain particular symbioses (Wilson & Trinick 1983; Daft 1983). Evidence for interactions between VA fungi and other soil organisms is somewhat equivocal (Hayman 1978). However, the indications of increased tolerance to root pathogens and resistance to nematodes suggest that this field might be worth exploring.

Evidence for zinc and cadmium tolerance in a strain of *G. mosseae* with clover (Gildon & Tinker 1983) suggests that VA fungal strains differ in heavy metal tolerance – so trees might be 'tailored' with suitable mycorrhizas for particular mine sites.

At present, there is a conspicuous lack of evidence on which to base the rational selection of VA fungi. With the possible exception of the citrus industry, there is little information on which inoculant types might enhance tree growth in different site conditions. More work is needed on the benefits of inoculation against an existing mycorrhizal background, and on the extent to which effects persist after outplanting.

VI.   SELECTION OF *FRANKIA* AND *RHIZOBIUM*

A.   *Frankia*

Frankia strains are markedly host-specific and, indeed, this is used as the basis for the subdivision of the genus (Akkermans 1978). Particular strains may infect species other than their 'own' even in different genera, but the nodules formed are not always effective in fixing N_2.

Poor nodulation may result (a) when exotic species are introduced – for instance, *Ceanothus*, *Coriaria* and *Casuarina* do not normally form nodules with *Frankia* in the UK (Bond 1974), or (b) when there is little inoculum in the soil – as may be the case on sites which have not previously supported the host. However, good nodulation of *Alnus glutinosa* has been recorded on a site which had not supported alders for ten years (Akkermans & Houwers 1979).

Unlike mycorrhizas, *Frankia* nodules are long-lived; on *Alnus* they can live for seven to eight years (Akkermans 1978). Their nitrogenase activity per unit dry weight decreases with increase in nodule size. Unlike ecto- and VA mycorrhizal fungi, *Frankia* cannot grow along the root surface to keep pace with an extending root system; each nodule is induced by a separate point inoculation (Quispel 1954), so that few nodules may be produced if there are low levels of inoculum in the soil.

The importance of good nodule formation prior to outplanting on sites with poor endophyte populations was indicated by Akkermans and Houwers (1979). They grew seedlings of *Alnus cordata*, *A. incana* and *A. glutinosa* in a nursery which had low levels of inoculum, and planted them on a clay polder site which had few nodule-forming *Frankia*. Two years later, many plants were poorly nodulated or lacked nodules, and these plants were significantly shorter than those which were well nodulated.

Evidence for host-genotype×*Frankia*-strain interactions is accumulating for some species. Dawson and Gordon (1979), working with ten clonal lines of *A. glutinosa* growing in nutrient solutions, found significant differences in dry weight and N content among clones when they were not nodulated, but no significant differences among them when they were nodulated. Also, a strong correlation existed between nodule dry weight and growth. Hall *et al.* (1979) tested seedlot×inoculum effects. Three seedlots of *A. glutinosa* and one of *A. rubra* were inoculated with each of four inocula (three from *A. glutinosa* and one from *A. rubra*). Three weeks after inoculation each seedlot, including *A. rubra*, had formed most nodules with the same *A. glutinosa* inoculum, although when growth was measured 13 weeks later a different *A. glutinosa* inoculum gave the best results. Dawson and Sun (1981) used *Frankia* isolates from *Comptonia peregrina* and *A. crispa* to inoculate clones of *A. glutinosa*, *A. cordata* and *A. incana*. Most of the uninoculated plants died. Among the inoculated plants, nodule numbers and dry weights differed significantly with host clone (*A. glutinosa* clones formed most nodules) and there were no significant clone×isolate interactions (in nodule numbers and weights). However, plants inoculated with the *Comptonia* isolate grew more rapidly than the others and measurements of acetylene reduction suggested that the *Comptonia* isolate was more efficient in N_2 fixation. Further evidence for strain differences in *Frankia* was furnished by Hafeez *et al.* (1984), who showed that isolates of the endophyte of *A. nitida* differed 20-fold in their N_2 fixing ability.

B. *Rhizobium*

The potential for selecting *Rhizobium* strains for tree crops has been little studied, despite their importance on poor tropical sites where woody legumes can provide timber and dry season fodder (Döbereiner & Campelo 1977).

Like *Frankia*, *Rhizobium* shows a considerable amout of host-endophyte strain specificity. Effective nodules are formed only when the appropriate *Rhizobium* species invades a particular host species or a taxonomically related species. With other hosts, no nodules are formed or else the symbioses are ineffective (Akkermans 1978).

Considerable intraspecific variation exists; the yield of different cultivars of white clover depends upon the strain of *Rhizobium trifolii* used (Mytton & Livesey 1983). Investigations with tropical trees suggest that specificity is not confined to agricultural crops. Thirteen species of *Acacia* could be categorized according to their ability to nodulate with fast- or slow-growing strains of *Rhizobium*; only four species formed effective nodules with fast-growing strains, six with slow-growing strains, while three could nodulate with both (Dommergues 1981). Under nursery conditions, differences were found in the ability of strains to promote growth; fast-growing strains were the most effective, and produced the greatest quantities of nodules. Although fast-growing strains appear to be the most desirable, work with agricultural crops has indicated that slow-growing strains are more resistant to severe desiccation – a potentially important trait (van Rensburg & Strijdom 1980). Early inoculation is advantageous; good nodulation in the nursery seedbed increased the survival of *Mimosa caesalpiniaefolia* after transplanting from 54% to 94%, and increased growth rates by 60% (Döbereiner & Campelo 1977). Agricultural rhizobia differ in their ability to tolerate temperature extremes (Pate 1961; Lie 1971) and some are effective over wider temperature ranges than others (Roughley & Dart 1969). Also, pH tolerance differs between and within *Rhizobium* species (Graham *et al.* 1982).

As with *Frankia*, evidence exists for host-genotype × *Rhizobium* endophyte-strain interactions. It appears that considerable benefits in growth may accrue from using appropriate host-endophyte combinations, provided the endophyte is selected for the right temperature, drought and pH conditions. Unlike selections for agricultural crops, rhizobia selections for trees must succeed at two locations – the nursery and the planting site. As with mycorrhizas, inoculation may only occasionally be essential, but it may frequently be beneficial, provided that selected strains can compete with naturally ocurring inocula (Parker *et al.* 1977).

VII.   INITIATING AND SUSTAINING THE SYMBIOSES

A.   Features of successful microsymbionts

The tree is a long-lived woody perennial, often with seasonal growth. To be worthwhile, the microsymbiont must remain with the tree for some time.

Seedlings are generally produced in nursery conditions which favour the growth of the host, but may not necessarily favour the growth of the micro-symbiont. The seedlings are then transferred to an outplanting site, where conditions are less favourable for growth, and where opportunities for cultivation are restricted. As they mature, the trees undergo a number of physiological changes, and bring about changes in their own environment – canopy development casts shade, alters soil temperatures and intercepts rain, water and nutrients are removed from the soil, leaf litter is deposited, old roots die and decompose and new ones are formed, and the root system extends to explore new ground.

Clearly, the successful microsymbiont must be adaptable if it is to remain with the host after transplanting and as it matures (or at least for a time), and it must survive during the host's dormancy periods when environmental conditions may be at their most stressful. Also, the microsymbiont must spread to colonize the enlarging root system and must be able to compete with naturally occurring populations of endophytes. Furthermore, for commercial use, the microsymbiont should be cheap to produce, and easily handled, transported and stored. Initiation of the symbiosis should not be a complex procedure.

B. Inoculum production

Traditionally, natural mixed-genotype inocula, present in soil and leaf litter, have been used to initiate symbioses. But if we are to exploit particular strains, ways must be found to produce single-strain inocula of known infectivity.

Techniques have been developed for producing some ectomycorrhizal fungi in bulk liquid culture or vermiculite-peat (Marx & Kenney 1982). VA fungi cannot yet be cultured *in vitro*, but they can be grown on host plants (frequently fibrous-rooted monocotyledonous plants) in glasshouses under clean conditions to produce an inoculum of chopped roots and soil (Menge & Timmer 1982). *Glomus epigaeus* shows great potential for commercial application because it produces sporocarps on the soil surface which can be harvested repeatedly without destroying the pot culture (Daniels & Menge 1981). *Rhizobium* strains may be readily cultured *in vitro* (Date & Roughley 1977) and *in vitro* culture techniques for *Frankia* have been developed quite recently (Callaham *et al.* 1978).

C. Nursery procedures

Special procedures may be necessary to ensure that good symbioses form in the nursery with known types of microsymbionts. At present, most of the information concerns the formation of ectomycorrhizas, but the principles involved probably apply to the other symbioses.

In nurseries where there is a large natural population of 'wild' types, soil fumigation may be necessary to reduce competition for infection sites on the root systems (Marx *et al.* 1976; Lamb & Richards 1978). If the soil is not fumigated, then placement of the inoculum close to the seedlings to allow rapid infection will be critical (Menge & Timmer 1982). The soil conditions and cultural regimes in nurseries seem to create conditions favouring certain species of microsymbiont, such as the ectomycorrhizal fungus *Thelephora terrestris* (Marx 1980). If the chosen microsymbiont is to dominate on the root systems, inoculation must be done soon after germination, allowing infection of new roots as they develop, and conditions must favour the desired symbiosis over one or more seasons (Ruehle 1980).

The levels of fertilizer applied, and the ways they are applied, often greatly affect ectomycorrhizal formation. If large amounts of fertilizer are applied to the soil, this can decrease the sugar content of short roots and limit mycorrhizal formation (Marx *et al.* 1977; Dixon *et al.* 1981). But if the same amounts of fertilizer are applied in a foliar mist, there may be good growth and mycorrhizal formation. Not all systems may be as sensitive; an isolate of *Laccaria laccata* can form good mycorrhizas at a wide range of fertility levels (Molina & Chamard 1983), and VA fungi appear to be less sensitive than ectomycorrhizal fungi to fertilizer application (Kormanik *et al.* 1977; Schultz *et al.* 1981).

For the grower of ectomycorrhizal plants there may be a conflict between the need to produce both large plants and mycorrhizal plants – high fertilizer rates may produce large but poorly mycorrhizal plants, whereas lower rates often produce smaller but mycorrhizal plants, so new methods of grading plants for sale may be needed. This conflict does not appear to arise with VA hardwoods because fertilizer application does not prevent good VA mycorrhizal formation (Schultz *et al.* 1981). It may be possible to use cover crops to build up the inoculum of VA fungi on site (Kormanik *et al.* 1980).

For each proposed microsymbiont-host combination, it will be necesary to optimize nursery conditions – time of inoculation, fumigation treatment, fertilizer and watering regimes should all be investigated.

Having established the desired symbiosis, care with plant handling while lifting, storing and outplanting is essential if benefits are to be maintained, because mycorrhizas and nodules will be vulnerable to inadvertent root pruning and desiccation. The use of container-stock reduces this problem, but, provided bare-rooted stock is handled with reasonable care, sufficient mycorrhizas and nodules should remain to provide benefits after outplanting.

D. Alternative inoculation techniques

Inoculation at the time of outplanting is a possible alternative to nursery inoculation. Nursery procedures would not have to be changed and there would be no risk of losing the desired symbiosis when the trees are lifted. If the symbiont were applied by dipping the tree roots in an inoculum slurry before planting, the inoculum would be well placed to infect newly emerging roots. However, the symbiont would have to survive in the soil until the trees started to grow, and it would have to compete with wild types at the planting site, and with those that had infected in the nursery which would have their food base already established (from the photosynthesizing plant).

Clearly, inoculation at this time would not improve nursery growth and would be unlikely to improve outplanting survival. However, growth benefits might be obtained on sites where there was a low background of natural inoculum.

VIII. PROSPECTS FOR MAINTAINING THE DESIRED SYMBIOSIS

A. Natural succession, competition and dispersal of symbionts

A natural succession of ectomycorrhizal fungi has been observed on *Betula*; that is, different fungi occur as the trees become older (Last *et al.* 1983; Mason *et al.* 1983). Other observations on nursery and outplanted trees also suggest that the range of ectomycorrhizas associated with forest trees alters considerably as the trees age (Mikola 1961; Chu-Chou & Grace 1981; Riffle & Tinus 1982; Malajczuk *et al.* 1982; Danielson 1984). There is no evidence for succession in other symbioses with trees. Spore counts of VA fungi on crops planted annually for six years after clearing woodland do suggest that some systematic changes can occur with particular host plants, but this is a change with time, not with plant age (Schenck & Kinloch 1980).

Succession and competition among microsymbionts will inevitably diminish the effect of any chosen inoculum. On sites which have a poor background inoculum (for which it is essential to establish a good symbiosis before outplanting), competition will probably be no problem, but competition will be a problem on sites where there is a high background of compatible microsymbionts. Evidence suggests that high backgrounds of ectomycorrhizal symbionts may occur on clearcut sites – which have been previously wooded – although this will be affected by the method of site clearance. Slash burning reduced mycorrhizal development on one- and two-year-old naturally regenerated *Pseudotsuga menziesii* seedlings, particularly in the surface layers of soil (Wright & Tarrant 1958). Also, the mycorrhizal inoculum for *P. menziesii* and *Thuja plicata* diminished with time after clear-cutting (Schoenberger & Perry 1982).

Malajczuck *et al.* (1982) raised an interesting point with reference to succession in plantations of ectomycorrhizal exotic tree species. They suggested that, in native stands of eucalypts and *Pinus radiata*, a natural succession of mycorrhizal fungi occurred as the stands matured, and that this succession began with fungi with a broad host range and ended with fungi that were host-specific. This observation has implications for plantation forestry, because host-specific fungi may be absent. Whether or not the lack of late-stage host-specific fungi causes problems is open to question, because the functions of the various fungi are not known.

As mentioned above, it is important for the microsymbiont to be able to spread into the new rooting zone after outplanting. Ectomycorrhizal fungi can produce numerous airborne spores and can grow along the root surface and out into the soil, and so should be well able to infect new roots as they emerge. This ability is one on which selection should be based – fungi which form mycelial strands are likely to be best. Marx *et al.* (1976) found that, in nursery conditions, *Pisolithus tinctorius* mycelium could spread 120 cm in one season. VA fungi can also grow along root surfaces and into the soil. Their spores are not airborne, but they can be moved in soil dust or in water; important vectors include rodents, earthworms, ants, wasps and birds (Janos 1983). *Frankia* and *Rhizobium* cannot spread by growing out into the soil; their spread will depend upon vectors carrying nodule fragments. Thus, of the microsymbionts, the ectomycorrhizal fungi are best able to spread and infect root systems as they develop, and *Frankia* and *Rhizobium* are least able. However, *Frankia* and *Rhizobium* can be very long-lived in the soil and the prospect of 'seeding' the site with resistant propagules should not be dismissed.

B. Persistence of beneficial effects

Few substantial data have been published on how long the beneficial effects of inoculation with mycorrhizas persist after outplanting. Data published by Theodorou and Bowen (1970), Bowen *et al.* (1971) and Riffle and Tinus (1982) suggested that, in *Pinus radiata* and *Pinus ponderosa*, beneficial effects on height growth could persist for at least five years after outplanting and the benefits appeared to be increasing with time (Fig. 1). In *P. radiata*, the differences in heights between inoculated and uninoculated trees could be attributed to a greater height relative growth rate in the inoculated plants

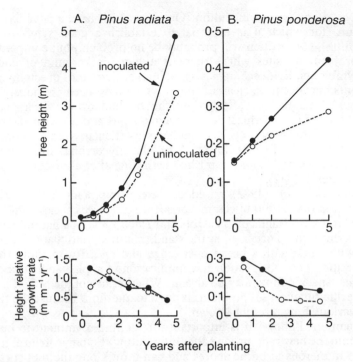

FIGURE 1. Heights, and height relative growth rates, of *Pinus radiata* and *Pinus ponderosa* trees for five years after outplanting, comparing trees that were inoculated with effective mycorrhizal fungi (closed circles, continuous lines) with trees that were not inoculated (open circles, broken lines).

A. The *P. radiata* height data are taken from Theodorou and Bowen (1970) and Bowen *et al.* (1971) who tested four types of inoculum at South Mount Bold, South Australia. Data shown here are for the most effective isolate (*Suillus granulatus*). Height relative growth rates are after Mexal (1980) (with some modification).

B. The *P. ponderosa* height data are from Riffle and Tinus (1982) who tested seven types of inoculum on trees outplanted at a grassland site in North Dakota, USA. Data shown here are for the most effective type (mixed natural inocula from pine duff).

(Because height data were not always collected annually, relative growth rates were estimated from the height graphs.)

only in the year following outplanting, which gave them a long-term height advantage. By contrast, in *P. ponderosa* there was a continuing difference in height relative growth rate between the inoculated and control plants to age five (Fig. 1). However, the *P. ponderosa* trees were growing slowly and they may have been just emerging from 'check' at age five, and so have been equivalent to the *P. radiata* trees at age one to two after planting.

Figure 2 speculates how such differences may continue over the lifetime of a tree crop, comparing the heights of inoculated and uninoculated plants (a) when natural background mycorrhizas are ineffective and not competitive with the introduced inocula, and (b) when uninoculated plants can acquire effective natural mycorrhizas. In both of these illustrations, 'uninoculated'

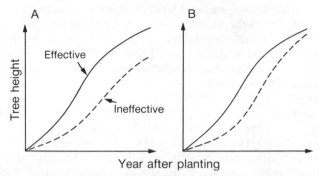

FIGURE 2.   Postulated shapes of height/age curves for trees inoculated with effective (continuous line) or ineffective (broken line) mycorrhizas, and outplanted,
A. on a site with poor natural, background inocula, and
B. on a site with effective natural, background inocula.

is synonymous with 'has mycorrhizas of ineffective, unselected species'. Succession (replacement) with ineffective species would not substantially alter these speculations, because the differences which developed in the first few years after outplanting would persist, although they would represent a small relative difference in height at the end of the rotation. However, in both of these examples, the period during which the sapling is vulnerable to weed competition, frost and browzing damage is decreased, which could be most important.

IX.   PERSPECTIVE: BENEFITS OF SELECTIVE INOCULATION VERSUS GENETIC GAIN

Clearly, inoculation with selected mycorrhizal fungi can give substantial benefits in the nursery and soon after outplanting, but no data are available on which to judge the magnitude of the long-term benefits. We might note that an alternative technique for improving tree growth – genetic improvement of the host – is expected to provide a gain of 10–20% in tree height and stem volume. Except on sites where the benefits of inoculation are 'all or nothing', the long-term benefits of introducing symbioses are unlikely to be greater than this. Also, if genetic improvement is achieved by improving the ability to access nutrients and water, then the benefits of introducing selected mycorrhizas may not be additive with genetic gain. We need to know more about the physiological basis of genetic improvement, and to integrate tree breeding with studies on host responses to mycorrhizal inoculation.

X.   SUMMARY AND DISCUSSION

Mycorrhizal and nodule-forming associations are essential for the growth of tree crops. At present, most research has been done on the ectomycorrhizal and VA mycorrhizal associations. The data obtained demonstrate considerable short-term benefits in the nursery and after outplanting; long-term benefits are a matter for speculation but may be of the same order as those obtained by genetic improvement of the host. There are strong interactions between host and inoculum genotype, and between environment and genotype, which should be taken into account when initiating trials. Although a particular microsymbiont cannot be expected to be equally beneficial in all circumstances, it is necessary to identify 'broad spectrum' microsymbionts, able to perform well in a range of environments. Just as tree provenances/species are grown on particular types of site, so might microsymbiont species/strains also be used on particular tree provenances/species. The ultimate refinements could be in clonal forestry, and in the use of clonal rootstocks in the fruit tree industry, where precise matching of microsymbiont to host could be achieved.

The discovery that a succession of different ectomycorrhizal fungi infect trees with increasing tree age has helped us to select inocula that are suited to the seedling stage, but the existence of succession implies that their beneficial effects may be short-lived. The longevity of a selected symbiotic association will depend upon a number of factors, including the presence or absence of background infective 'wild' inocula, changes in host physiology and the environment, and the ability of the microsymbiont to spread as the root system enlarges after outplanting.

One future development could be the use of mixtures of selected mycorrhizal fungi, which could maintain a physiologically active root system through a range of environmental conditions over time. Powerful combinations of selected N_2-fixing and mycorrhizal associations (on one root system) may be possible for trees that are host to both types of microsymbiont. Furthermore, there are some indications that it may be possible to incorporate N_2-fixing ability into strains of mycorrhizal fungi (Giles & Whitehead 1977). Even without these refinements, symbioses could be exploited much more by identifying and utilizing effective strains. However, we need to assess the costs and benefits of these techniques of tree improvement compared with other methods.

REFERENCES

Akkermans, A. D. L. (1978). Root nodule symbioses in non-leguminous N_2-fixing plants. In: *Interactions between non-pathogenic soil microorganisms and plants*, edited by Y. R. Dommergues and S. V. Krupa, 335–372. (Developments in agricultural and managed-forest ecology no. 4). Amsterdam: Elsevier.

Akkermans, A. D. L. & Houwers, A. (1979). Symbiotic nitrogen fixers available for use in temperate forestry. In: *Symbiotic nitrogen fixation in the management of temperate forests*, edited by J. C. Gordon *et al.*, 23–35. Corvallis, OR: Oregon State University.

Alexander, M. (1973). Microorganisms and chemical pollution. *BioScience*, **23**, 509–515.

Alwis, D. P. de & Abeynayake, K. (1980). A survey of mycorrhizae in some forest trees of Sri Lanka. In: *Tropical mycorrhizal research*, edited by P. Mikola, 146–153. Oxford: Clarendon.

Berry, C. R. (1982). Survival and growth of pine hybrid seedlings with *Pisolithus* ectomycorrhizae on coal spoils in Alabama and Tennessee. *J. environ. Qual.*, **11**, 709–715.

Bledsoe, C. S., Tennyson, K. & Lopushinsky, W. (1982). Survival and growth of outplanted Douglas-fir seedlings inoculated with mycorrhizal fungi. *Can. J. For. Res.*, **12**, 720–723.

Bond, G. (1974). Root nodule symbioses with actinomycete-like organisms. In: *The biology of* *nitrogen fixation*, edited by A. Quispel, 342–378. (Frontiers of biology no. 33). Amsterdam: North-Holland.

Bowen, G. D. (1965). Mycorrhizal inoculation in forestry practice. *Aust. For.*, **29**, 231–237.

Bowen, G. D., Theodorou, C., & Skinner, M. F. (1971). Towards a mycorrhizal inoculation programme. *Proc. Australian Forest Tree Nutrition Conf. Section 2: Biological aspects of nutrition and response to fertilizers*, edited by R. Boardman, 68–80. Canberra Forestry and Timber Bureau.

Brown, M. T. (1983). *Zinc tolerance in* Betula *spp. and mycorrhizal fungi.* Ph.D. thesis, University of Birmingham.

Bryan, W. C. & Kormanik, P. P. (1977). Mycorrhizae benefit survival and growth of sweetgum seedlings in the nursery. *South. J. appl. For.*, **1**, 21–23.

Callaham, D., del Tredici, P. & Torrey, J. G. (1978). Isolation and cultivation *in vitro* of the actinomycete causing root nodulation in *Comptonia. Science, N.Y.*, **199**, 899–902.

Chu-Chou, M. & Grace, L. J. (1981). Mycorrhizal fungi of *Pseudotsuga menziesii* in the North Island of New Zealand. *Soil Biol. Biochem.*, **13**, 247–249.

Daft, M. J. (1983). The influence of mixed inocula on ectomycorrhizal development. *Pl. Soil*, **71**, 331–337.

Daniels, B. A. & Menge, J. A. (1981). Evaluation of the commercial potential of the vesicular-arbuscular mycorrhizal fungus, *Glomus epigaeus. New Phytol.*, **87**, 345–354.

Danielson, R. M. (1984). Ectomycorrhizal associations in jack pine stands in north-eastern Alberta. *Can. J. Bot.*, **62**, 932–939.

Date, R. A. & Roughley, R. J. (1977). Preparation of legume seed inoculants. In: *A treatise on dinitrogen fixation. Section 4: agronomy and ecology*, edited by R. W. F. Hardy and A. H. Gibson, 243–275. New York: John Wiley.

Dawson, J. O. & Gordon, J. C. (1979). Nitrogen fixation in relation to photosynthesis in *Alnus glutinosa. Bot. Gaz.*, **140**, (Suppl.) S70–S75.

Dawson, J. O. & Sun, S-H. (1981). The effect of *Frankia* isolates from *Comptonia peregrina* and *Alnus crispa* on the growth of *Alnus glutinosa, A. cordata* and *A. incana* clones. *Can. J. For. Res.*, **11**, 758-762.

Dixon, R. K., Garrett, H. E., Bixby, J. A., Cox, G. S. & Tompson, J. G. (1981). Growth, ectomycorrhizal development, and root soluble carbohydrates of black oak seedlings fertilized by two methods. *Forest Sci.*, **27**, 617–624.

Döbereiner, J. & Campelo, A. B. (1977). Importance of legumes and their contribution to tropical agriculture. In: *A treatise on dinitrogen fixation. Section 4: agronomy and ecology*, edited by R. W. F. Hardy and A. H. Gibson, 191–220. New York: John Wiley.

Dommergues, Y. R. (1978). Impact on soil management and plant growth. In: *Interactions between non-pathogenic soil microorganisms and plants*, edited by Y. R. Dommergues and S. V. Krupa, 443–458. (Developments in agricultural and managed-forest ecology no. 4). Amsterdam: Elsevier.

Dommergues, Y. R. (1981). Ensuring effective symbiosis in nitrogen-fixing trees. In: *Biological nitrogen fixation for tropical agriculture*, edited by P. H. Graham and S. C. Harris, 395–411. Cali (Colombia): Centro International de Agricultura Tropical.

Fleming, L. V. (1983). Succession of mycorrhizal fungi on birch: infection of seedlings planted around mature trees. *Pl. Soil*, **71**, 263–267.

Fogel, R. & Hunt, G. (1979). Fungal and arboreal biomass in a western Oregon Douglas-fir ecosystem: distribution patterns and turnover. *Can. J. For. Res.*, **9**, 245–256.

Furlan, V., Fortin, J. A. & Plenchette, C. (1983). Effects of different vesicular-arbuscular mycorrhizal fungi on growth of *Fraxinus americana. Can. J. For. Res.*, **13**, 589–593.

Gerdemann, J. W. & Trappe, J. M. (1974). The Endogonaceae in the Pacific Northwest. *Mycol. Mem.*, no. 5.

Gildon, A. & Tinker, P. B. (1983). Interactions of vesicular-arbuscular mycorrhizal infections and heavy metals in plants. II. The effects of infections on uptake of copper. *New Phytol.*, **95**, 263–268.

Giles, K. L. & Whitehead, H. C. M. (1977). Reassociation of a modified mycorrhiza with the host plant roots (*Pinus radiata*) and the transfer of acetylene reduction activity. *Pl. Soil*, **48**, 143–152.

Graham, P. H., Viteri, S. E., Mackie, F., Vargas, A. T. & Palacios, A. (1982). Variation in acid soil tolerance among strains of *Rhizobium phaseoli. Field Crops Res.*, **5**, 121–128.

Green, N. E., Graham, S. O. & Schenck, N. C. (1976). The influence of pH on the germination of vesicular-arbuscular mycorrhizal spores. *Mycologia*, **68**, 929–939.

Grossnickle, S. C. & Reid, C. P. P. (1982). The use of ectomycorrhizal conifer seedlings in the revegetation of a high-elevation mine site. *Can. J. For. Res.*, **12**, 354–361.

Grossnickle, S. C. & Reid, C. P. P. (1983). Ectomycorrhiza formation and root development patterns of conifer seedlings on a high-elevation mine site. *Can. J. For. Res.*, **13**, 1145–1158.

Hafeez, F., Akkermans, A. D. L & Chaudhary, A. H. (1984). Morphology, physiology and infectivity of two *Frankia* isolates An 1 and An 2 from root nodules of *Alnus nitida*. *Pl. Soil*, **78**, 45–59.

Hall, R. B., McNabb, H. S., Maynard, C. A. & Green T. L. (1979). Toward development of optimal *Alnus glutinosa* symbioses. *Bot. Gaz.*, **140**, (Suppl.) S120–S126.

Harley, J. L. & Smith, S. E. (1983). *Mycorrhizal symbiosis.* London: Academic Press.

Hayman, D. S. (1975). The occurrence of mycorrhiza in crops as affected by soil fertility. In: *Endomycorrhizas*, edited by F. E. Sanders *et al.*, 495–510. London: Academic Press.

Hayman, D. S. (1978). Endomycorrhizae. In: *Interactions between non-pathogenic soil micro-organisms and plants*, edited by Y. R. Dommergues and S. V. Krupa, 401–442. (Developments in agricultural and managed-forest ecology no. 4). Amsterdam: Elsevier.

Hirrel, M. C. & Gerdemann, J. W. (1980). Improved growth of onion and bell pepper in saline soils by two vesicular-arbuscular mycorrhizal fungi. *Proc. Soil Sci. Soc. Am.*, **44**, 654–655.

Hung, L-L. & Trappe, J. M. (1983). Growth variation between and within species of ecto-mycorrhizal fungi in response to pH *in vitro*. *Mycologia*, **75**, 234–241.

Hyppel, A. (1968). Effect of *Fomes annosus* on seedlings of *Picea abies* in the presence of *Boletus bovinus*. *Studia for. suec.*, **66**, 1–18.

Janos, D. P. (1983). Tropical mycorrhizas, nutrient cycles and plant growth. In: *Tropical rainforest: ecology and management*, edited by S. L. Sutton *et al.*, 327–345. Oxford: Blackwell Scientific.

Kabre, A., Garbaye, J. & Le Tacon, F. (1982). Influence de la mycorrhization et de la fertilisation sur le comportement de jeunes plants d'erable sycomore (*Acer pseudoplatanus* Link.). *Eur. J. Forest Pathol.*, **12**, 97–103.

Kormanik, P. P., Bryan, W. C. & Schultz, R. C. (1977). Influence of endomycorrhizae on growth of sweetgum seedlings from eight mother trees. *Forest. Sci.*, **23**, 500–506.

Kormanik, P. P., Bryan, W. C. & Schultz, R. C. (1980). Increasing endomycorrhizal fungus inoculum in forest nursery soil with cover crops. *South. J. appl. For.*, **4**, 151–153.

Kormanik, P. P., Bryan, W. C. & Schultz, R. C. (1981). Effects of three vesicular-arbuscular mycorrhizal fungi on sweetgum seedlings from nine mother trees. *Forest Sci.*, **27**, 327–335.

Kormanik, P. P., Schultz, R. C. & Bryan, W. C. (1982). The influence of vesicular-arbuscular mycorrhizae on the growth and development of eight hardwood tree species. *Forest Sci.*, **28**, 531–539.

Lamb, R. J. & Richards, B. N. (1970). Some mycorrhizal fungi of *Pinus radiata* and *P. elliottii* var. *elliottii* in Australia. *Trans. Br. mycol. Soc.*, **54**, 371–378.

Lamb, R. J. & Richards, B. N. (1971). Effect of mycorrhizal fungi on the growth and nutrient status of slash and radiata pine seedlings. *Aust. For.*, **35**, 1–7.

Lamb, R. J. & Richards, B. N. (1978). Inoculation of pines with mycorrhizal fungi in natural soils. III. Effect of soil fumigation on rate of infection and response to inoculum density. *Soil Biol. Biochem.*, **10**, 273–276.

Last, F. T., Mason, P. A., Wilson, J. & Deacon, J. W. (1983). Fine roots and sheathing mycorrhizas: their formation, function and dynamics. *Pl. Soil*, **71**, 9–21.

Lie, T. A. (1971). Temperature-dependent root nodule formation in pea cv. Iran. *Pl. Soil*, **39**, 751–752.

Malajczuk, N., Molina, R. & Trappe, J. M. (1982). Ectomycorrhizal formation in *Eucalyptus*, I. Pure culture synthesis, host specificity and mycorrhizal compatibility with *Pinus radiata*. *New Phytol.*, **91**, 467–482.

Maronek, D. M. & Hendrix, J. W. (1980). Synthesis of *Pisolithus tinctorius* ectomycorrhizae on seedlings of four woody species. *J. Am. Soc. hort. Sci.*, **105**, 823–825.

Maronek, D. M., Hendrix, J. W. & Kiernan, J. (1981). Mycorrhizal fungi and their importance in horticultural crop production. *Hort. Rev.*, **3**, 172–213.

Marx, D. H. (1969a). The influence of ectotrophic mycorrhizal fungi on the resistance of pine roots to pathogenic infections. I. Antagonism of mycorrhizal fungi to root pathogenic fungi and soil bacteria. *Phytopathology*, **59**, 153–163.

Marx, D. H. (1969b). The influence of ectotrophic mycorrhizal fungi on the resistance of pine roots to pathogenic infections. II. Production, identification, and biological activity of antibiotics produced by *Leucopaxillus cerealis* var. *piceina*. *Phytopathology*, **59**, 411–417.

Marx, D. H. (1970). The influence of ectotrophic mycorrhizal fungi on the resistance of pine roots to pathogenic infections. V. Resistance of mycorrhizae to infection by vegetative mycelium of *Phytophthora cinnamomi. Phytopathology*, **60**, 1472–1473.

Marx, D. H. (1975). Mycorrhizae and establishment of trees on strip-mined land. *Ohio J. Sci.*, **75**, 288–297.

Marx, D. H. (1976). Use of specific mycorrhizal fungi on tree roots for forestation of disturbed lands. *Proc. Conf. Forestation of Disturbed Surface Areas, Birmingham, Alabama*, 47–65. USDA Forest Service, State and Private Forestry and International Forest Seed Company.

Marx, D. H. (1977a). The role of mycorrhizae in forest production. *TAPPI Conf. Paper, Annual Meeting, Atlanta, Ga*, 151–161.

Marx, D. H. (1977b). Tree host range and world distribution of the ectomycorrhizal fungus *Pisolithus tinctorius. Can. J. Microbiol.*, **23**, 217–223.

Marx, D. H. (1980). Ectomycorrhizal fungus inoculations: a tool for improving forestation practices. In: *Tropical mycorrhiza research*, edited by P. Mikola, 13–71. Oxford: Clarendon.

Marx, D. H. & Bryan, W. C. (1971). Influence of ectomycorrhizae on survival and growth of aseptic seedlings of loblolly pine at high temperature. *Forest Sci.*, **17**, 37–41.

Marx, D. H. & Krupa, S. V. (1978). Mycorrhizae A. Ectomycorrhizae. In: *Interactions between non-pathogenic soil microorganisms and plants*, edited by Y. R. Dommergues and S. V. Krupa, 373–400. (Developments in agricultural and managed-forest ecology no. 4). Amsterdam: Elsevier.

Marx, D. H. & Kenney, D. S. (1982). Production of ectomycorrhizal fungus inoculum. In: *Methods and principles of mycorrhiza research*, edited by N. C. Schenck, 131–146. St. Paul, MN: American Phytopathological Society.

Marx, D. H., Bryan, W. C. & Davey, C. B. (1970). Influence of temperature on aseptic synthesis of ectomycorrhizae by *Thelephora terrestris* and *Pisolithus tinctorius* on loblolly pine. *Forest Sci.*, **16**, 424–431.

Marx, D. H., Bryan, W. C. & Campbell, W. A. (1971). Effect of endomycorrhizae formed by *Endogone mosseae* on growth of *Citrus. Mycologia*, **63**, 1222–1226.

Marx, D. H., Bryan, W. C. & Cordell, C. E. (1976). Growth and ectomycorrhizal development of pine seedlings in nursery soils infested with the fungal symbiont *Pisolithus tinctorius. Forest Sci.*, **22**, 91–100.

Marx, D. H., Bryan, W. C. & Cordell, C. E. (1977a). Survival and growth of pine seedlings with *Pisolithus* ectomycorrhizae after 2 years on reforestation sites in North Carolina and Florida. *Forest Sci.*, **23**, 363–373.

Marx, D. H., Hatch, A. B. & Mendicino, J. F. (1977b). High soil fertility decreases sucrose content and susceptibility of loblolly pine to ectomycorrhizal infection by *Pisolithus tinctorius. Can. J. Bot.*, **55**, 1569–1574.

Mason, P. A., Wilson, J., Last, F. T. & Walker, C. (1983). The concept of succession in relation to the spread of sheathing mycorrhizal fungi on inoculated tree seedlings growing in unsterile soils. *Pl. Soil*, **71**, 247–256.

Menge, J. A. & Timmer, L. W. (1982). Procedures for inoculation of plants with vesicular-arbuscular mycorrhizae in the laboratory, greenhouse and field. In: *Methods and principles of mycorrhizal research*, edited by N. C. Schenck, 59–68. St. Paul, MN: American Phytopathological Society.

Menge, J. A., Johnson, E. L. V. & Platt, R. G. (1978). Mycorrhizal dependency of several citrus cultivars under three nutrient regimes. *New Phytol.*, **81**, 553–559.

Mexal, J. G. (1980). Aspects of mycorrhizal inoculation in relation to reforestation. *N.Z. J. For. Sci.*, **10**, 208–217.

Mexal, J. & Reid, C. P. P. (1973). The growth of selected mycorrhizal fungi in response to induced water stress. *Can. J. Bot.*, **51**, 1579–1588.

Meyer, F. H. (1973). Distribution of ectomycorrhizae in native and man-made forests. In: *Ectomycorrhizae*, edited by G. C. Marks and T. T. Kozlowski, 79–105. New York: Academic Press.

Meyer, F. H. (1974). Physiology of mycorrhiza. *A. Rev. Pl. Physiol.*, **25**, 567–586.

Mikola, P. (1948). On the physiology and ecology of *Cenococcum graniforme* especially as a mycorrhizal fungus of birch. *Metsätiet. Tutkimuslait. Julk. (Commun. Inst. for. fenn.)*, **36**, 1–104.

Mikola, P. (1961). Mykoritsain Muodostuksen Edistäminen. (Promotion of the growth of mycorrhizae). *Metsätal. Aikakausl.*, **12**, 486–488, 504.

Mikola, P. (1973). Application of mycorrhizal symbiosis in forestry practice. In: *Ectomycorrhizae, their ecology and physiology*, edited by G. C. Marks and T. T. Kozlowski, 383–411. New York: Academic Press.

Mikola, P. (1980). Mycorrhizae across the frontiers. In: *Tropical mycorrhiza research*, edited by P. Mikola, 3–10. Oxford: Clarendon.

Molina, R. (1977). Ectomycorrhizal fungi and forestry practice. In: *Mushrooms and man, an interdisciplinary approach to mycology*, edited by T. Walters, 147–161. USDA Forest Service.

Molina, R. & Chamard, J. (1983). Use of the ectomycorrhizal fungus *Laccaria laccata* in forestry. II. Effects of fertilizer forms and levels on ectomycorrhizal development and growth of container-grown Douglas-fir and ponderosa pine seedlings. *Can. J. For. Res.*, **13**, 89–95.

Molina, R. & Trappe, J. M. (1982). Patterns of ectomycorrhizal host specificity and potential among Pacific Northwest conifers and fungi. *Forest Sci.*, **28**, 423–458.

Mosse, B. (1973). Advances in the study of vesicular-arbuscular mycorrhiza. *A. Rev. Phytopathol.*, **11**, 171–196.

Mytton, L. R. & Livesey, C. J. (1983). Specific and general effectiveness of *Rhizobium trifolii* populations from different agricultural locations. *Pl. Soil*, **73**, 299–305.

Parke, J. L., Lindermann, R. G. & Trappe, J. M. (1983a). Effect of root zone temperature on ectomycorrhiza and vesicular-arbuscular mycorrhiza formation in disturbed and undisturbed forest soils of Southwest Oregon. *Can. J. For. Res.*, **13**, 657–665.

Parke, J. L., Lindermann, R. G. & Trappe, J. M. (1983b). Effects of forest litter on mycorrhiza development and growth of Douglas-fir and western red cedar seedlings. *Can. J. For. Res.*, **13**, 666–671.

Parker, C. A., Trinick, M. J. & Chatel, D. L. (1977). Rhizobia as soil and rhizosphere inhabitants. In: *A treatise on dinitrogen fixation. Section 4: agronomy and ecology*, edited by R. W. F. Hardy and A. H. Gibson, 311–352. New York: John Wiley.

Pate, J. S. (1961). Temperature characteristics of bacterial variation in legume symbiosis. *Nature, Lond.*, **192**, 637–639.

Pigott, C. D. (1982). Survival of mycorrhiza formed by *Cenococcum geophilum* Fr. in dry soils. *New Phytol.*, **92**, 513–517.

Plenchette, C., Furlan, V. & Fortin, J. A. (1981). Growth stimulation of apple trees in unsterilised soil under field conditions with VA mycorrhiza inoculation. *Can. J. Bot.*, **59**, 2003–2008.

Quispel, A. (1954). Symbiotic nitrogen fixation in non-leguminous plants. II. The influence of the inoculation density and external factors on the nodulation of *Alnus glutinosa* and its importance to our understanding of the mechanism of the infection. *Acta bot. neerl.*, **3**, 512–532.

Reddy, M. A. R. & Khan, S. N. (1972). Soil amendments and types of inocula on development of mycorrhiza. *Indian Forester*, **98**, 307–310.

Redhead, J. F. (1975). Endotrophic mycorrhizas in Nigeria: some aspects of the ecology of the endotrophic mycorrhizal association of *Khaya grandifoliola* C. DC. In: *Endomycorrhizas*, edited by F. E. Sanders *et al.*, 447–459. London: Academic Press.

Rensburg, H. J. van & Strijdom, B. W. (1980). Survival of fast- and slow-growing *Rhizobium* spp. under conditions of relatively mild desiccation. *Soil Biol. Biochem.*, **12**, 353–356.

Riffle, J. W. & Tinus, R. W. (1982). Ectomycorrhizal characteristics, growth and survival of artificially inoculated ponderosa and Scots pine in a greenhouse and plantation. *Forest Sci.*, **28**, 646–660.

Romell, L. R. (1939). Barrskogens marksvampar och deras roll i skogens liv. *Svenska SkogsvFör. Tidskr.*, **37**, 238–275.

Roughley, R. J. & Dart, P. J. (1969). Reduction of acetylene by nodules of *Trifolium subterraneum* as affected by root temperature, *Rhizobium* strain and host cultivar. *Arch. Microbiol.*, **69**, 171–179.

Ruehle, J. L. (1980). Inoculation of containerised loblolly pine seedlings with basidiospores of *Pisolithus tinctorius*. *Res. Note S.E. For. Exp. Stn (US)*, SE-291.

Saleh-Rastin, N. (1976). Salt tolerance of the mycorrhizal fungus *Cenococcum graniforme* (Sow.) Ferd. *Eur. J. Forest Pathol.*, **6**, 184–187.

Schenck, N. C. & Kinloch, R. A. (1980). Incidence of mycorrhizal fungi on six field crops in monoculture on a newly cleared woodland site. *Mycologia*, **72**, 445–456.

Schenck, N. C. & Schroder, V. N. (1974). Temperature response of *Endogone* mycorrhiza on soybean roots. *Mycologia*, **66**, 600–605.

Schoenberger, M. M. & Perry, D. A. (1982). The effect of soil disturbance on growth and ectomycorrhizae of Douglas-fir and western hemlock seedlings: a greenhouse bioassay. *Can. J. For. Res.*, **12**, 343–353.

Schramm, J. R. (1966). Plant colonization studies on black wastes from anthracite mining in Pennsylvania. *Trans. Am. phil. Soc.*, **56**, 1–194.

Schultz, R. C., Kormanik, P. P. & Bryan, W. C. (1981). Effects of fertilization and vesicular-arbuscular mycorrhizal inoculation on growth of hardwood seedlings. *Proc. Soil Sci. Soc. Am.*, **45**, 961–965.

Singer, R. & Morello, J. H. (1960). Ectotrophic forest tree mycorrhizae and forest communities. *Ecology*, **41**, 549–551.

Slankis, V. (1974). Soil factors influencing formation of mycorrhizae. *A. Rev. Phytopathol.*, **12**, 437–457.

Sylvia, D. M. & Sinclair, W. A. (1983). Phenolic compounds and resistance to fungal pathogens induced in primary roots of Douglas-fir seedlings by the ectomycorrhizal fungus *Laccaria laccata*. *Phytopathology*, **73**, 390–397.

Theodorou, C. & Bowen, G. D. (1970). Mycorrhizal responses of radiata pine in experiments with different fungi. *Aust. For.*, **34**, 183–191.

Trappe, J. M. (1977). Selection of fungi for ectomycorrhizal inoculation in nurseries. *A. Rev. Phytopathol.*, **15**, 203–222.

Trinick, M. J. (1973). Symbiosis between *Rhizobium* and the non-legume, *Trema aspera*. *Nature, Lond.*, **244**, 459–460.

Vogt, K. A., Grier, C. C., Meier, C. E. & Edmonds, R. L. (1982). Mycorrhizal role in net primary production and nutrient cycling in *Abies amabilis* ecosystems in western Washington. *Ecology*, **63**, 370–380.

Wilde, S. A. (1944). Mycorrhizae and silviculture. *J. For.*, **42**, 290–291.

Wilhelm, S. (1966). Chemical treatments and inoculum potential of soil. *A. Rev. Phytopathol.*, **4**, 53–78.

Wilson, J. M. & Trinick, M. J. (1983). Infection development and interactions between vesicular-arbuscular mycorrhizal fungi. *New Phytol.*, **93**, 543–553.

Wright, E. & Tarrant, R. F. (1958). Occurrence of mycorrhizae after logging and slash burning in the Douglas-fir forest type. *Res. Note Pacif. NW Forest Range Exp. Stn*, PNW–160.

Zak, B. (1964). Role of mycorrhizae in root disease. *A. Rev. Phytopathol.*, **2**, 337–392.

Flowering and fruiting

22

PROMOTION OF FLOWERING IN TREE CROPS: DIFFERENT MECHANISMS AND TECHNIQUES, WITH SPECIAL REFERENCE TO CONIFERS

S. D. ROSS
Research Laboratory, British Columbia Ministry of Forests, Victoria, British Columbia, Canada

R. P. PHARIS
Department of Biology, University of Calgary, Calgary, Alberta, Canada

I. INTRODUCTION

Whereas fruit trees are either regenerated clonally, or have been bred for early and reliable flowering, forest trees still retain variable, and often long, juvenile periods. Forest tree breeders do not wish to select for early abundant flowering, because this might decrease timber production, so they must depend on cultural and growth regulator treatments to hasten the breeding and production of genetically improved seed for use in reafforestation. The control of flowering in forest trees has therefore been extensively, if not intensively, investigated. This progress is summarized in two recent symposia (Bonner 1979; Krugman & Katsuta 1981) and in various reviews (Jackson & Sweet 1972; Puritch 1972; Sweet 1975; Pharis & Kuo 1977; Lee 1979; Ross & Pharis 1982; Ross *et al.* 1983; Pharis & Ross 1985a,b).

Future research may identify new techniques or growth regulators, but the basic treatments that can be used to promote flowering in forest trees are well established. These are water stress, root pruning, girdling, and the application of high temperatures, N fertilizers, and appropriate growth regulator(s). Some workers have attempted to simplify the flowering process and interpret all environmental and cultural influences in terms of a single stimulus. Jackson and Sweet (1972) rejected this simplification because of notable exceptions to every proposed mechanism. Romberger and Gregory (1974) also rejected the single stimulus hypothesis, arguing that woody perennials, unlike annual plants, could not survive if flowering were under the control of a single stimulus. They proposed that numerous biochemical/physiological systems were involved in the control of flowering in woody trees, all of which must be 'permissive' if reproductive structures were to initiate, and subsequently to develop.

In this paper, we review several of the more likely mechanisms by which different treatments may promote flowering, restricting the discussion to the early processes of floral initiation and differentiation. The juvenile phase of woody plants will be considered only indirectly, because this subject has been reviewed recently by Hackett (1985) and Zimmerman et al. (1985), and also by Longman in this volume. Limitations of time and space have also forced us generally to confine our discussion to coniferous forest trees, although we will comment where direct analogies can be made with woody angiosperms.

II. POSSIBLE MECHANISMS INVOLVED IN CONEBUD DIFFERENTIATION

A.   Role of carbohydrates and nutrient diversion

It has long been known that abundant flowering is commonly associated with factors that may be expected to favour either a high rate of photosynthesis (such as high solar insolation, wide spacing or crown 'release' by thinning), an accumulation of assimilates within the shoot, as a result of phloem blockage (induced by girdling or graft incompatibility) or a check on vegetative growth (by water stress, root pruning, etc.) (Jackson & Sweet 1972; Lee 1979). Although this is an attractive hypothesis to explain the action of many diverse types of treatments (Sachs 1977), Jackson and Sweet (1972) pointed out that there is no unequivocal evidence to support the belief that carbohydrates play a direct, or even supportive, role in flower initiation and early differentiation processes in woody plants. Results of shading experiments (Silen 1973; Giertych & Krolikowski 1978) attest to the importance of high solar insolation to abundant flowering, but it appears that the effect of high light intensity may be due as much or more to radiant heating of buds (Dunberg 1979; Giertych & Krolikowski 1978), or to localized water stress (owing to higher evaporative demand), as to the production of photosynthate.

Similarly, it appears that the marked increase in cone production that follows crown 'release' (Matthews 1963; Lee 1979) cannot be attributed exclusively to enhanced photosynthesis or other indirect benefits of high light intensity. Bilan (1960) detected no difference in carbohydrate levels in shoots of *Pinus taeda* trees in thinned and unthinned stands, despite substantially greater cone production by the former. Increased air and soil temperatures, and increased availability of water and nutrients, especially N, also appear to be involved in the flowering response to thinning (Bilan 1960; Schmidtling 1974). This general improvement in site conditions may enhance cone production in the long term, indirectly, through the development of more vigorous crowns with more potential sites for flowering. Thinning may also affect conebud differentiation more directly by creating inductive water stresses, which can occur (even with ample soil water) as a result of increased crown exposure to solar radiation and wind (Sucoff & Hong 1974).

Several studies have failed to demonstrate a positive correlation between (a) the flowering response to girdling (Bilan 1960; Ebell 1971) and other treatments, such as N fertilization and crown 'release' (Bilan 1960; Barnes & Bengtson 1968; Sweet 1979), and (b) the soluble sugar or total carbohydrate content of shoots. It would be unwise, however, to conclude from such studies that assimilate supply is seldom a limiting factor in conebud differentiation. Studies in which current photosynthate was labelled with ^{14}C have shown that gross carbohydrate determinations on entire shoots give inadequate measures of assimilate supplies to the sites of floral determination (Takeda et al. 1980).

Greenwood (1981) has suggested that treatments which promote flowering in Pinus can be divided into two categories: (a) those that hasten the completion of shoot elongation; and (b) those that promote long-shoot (axillary) bud development once the quiescent bud has been set. According to Greenwood, shoots of young seedlings and vigorous older trees continue growing too late into autumn, with the consequence that long-shoot primordia are unable to complete differentiation into seed conebuds before the onset of dormancy in winter. However, it is not clear why this might be a problem in the formation of seed conebuds, but not branch buds, which develop from the same long-shoot primordia. An explanation, perhaps more consistent with reproductive development in other conifers (such as Pseudotsuga and Tsuga) – where early conebud differentiation processes appear to precede, or accompany, shoot elongation, rather than follow it as in Pinus and Picea – is that it is the rate of growth during some critical stage of bud development that is the important factor (Bonnet-Masimbert 1979). The elongating shoot is a strong sink for assimilates relative to developing buds (Dickmann & Kozlowski 1970). Thus, the two treatment effects considered by Greenwood may be different aspects of the same phenomenon, namely diversion of assimilates into potentially reproductive buds and primordia (Sachs 1977).

Treatments that may cause nutrient diversion include water stress, root pruning, bending of shoots, and graft incompatibility. Indeed, most of the effective 'cone enhancement' treatments, including girdling (Hare 1979; Bonnet-Masimbert 1982) and excesses as well as deficiencies of N (Lyr & Hoffmann 1964; Sweet & Will 1965; S. D. Ross, unpublished data), retard shoot elongation, at least temporarily. L. F. Ebell (pers. comm.) examined flowering in seed orchard trees of Pseudotsuga menziesii in response to root pruning in numerous trials in British Columbia and found that this treatment was most effective when it retarded stem elongation by 40–50%.

Results of trials investigating the timing of treatments tend to be rather confusing (as treatments are often related to calendar date rather than to stage of reproductive bud development), but the view emerges that 'stress' treatments are generally more effective when timed to coincide with (or precede) the period of rapid shoot elongation, rather than with the probable period of conebud differentiation (Holst 1959; Ebell 1971, 1972; Ross et al. 1983). Other evidence for this view comes from a recent study (Ross 1985) wherein potted *Picea engelmannii* grafted propagules were subjected to high temperatures or drought stress at different stages of shoot development. Philipson (1983) considered both to be stress treatments, but our results suggested that only drought provided a stress. The optimal time to give high temperatures (30 °C day/20 °C night), to promote conebud differentiation, was during the late stage of slow shoot elongation (when conebud differentiation is known to occur), and this treatment had no discernible effect on shoot growth, which by then was nearly completed. Drought stress at this late stage of shoot development significantly inhibited flowering, as had also been reported for *Picea abies* (Olsen 1978). Responses were reversed, however, when drought and high temperature treatments were applied during the period of rapid shoot elongation, preceding the period of conebud differentiation. In that case, drought stress retarded shoot elongation and promoted flowering, whereas high temperatures accelerated growth and inhibited flowering. Therefore, although both drought stress and high temperature can promote flowering, they may do so by different mechanisms.

Assuming that nutrient diversion accounts (at least in part) for the effectiveness of treatments that retard shoot elongation, how might an increased supply of assimilates to buds favour their subsequent development as reproductive structures? One way might be by allowing the continued development of potentially reproductive primordia that would otherwise abort or remain latent (Sweet 1979; Pharis et al. 1980). However, this does not account for the fact that seed conebuds also differentiate at the expense of vegetative branch buds (Owens & Molder 1979; Pharis et al. 1980). Sachs (1977) suggested that a higher concentration of nutrients was required for buds to differentiate reproductively, as opposed to vegetatively, referring specifically to the possibility that genetically determined events were related to a particular sugar concentration. It has also been postulated (Romberger & Gregory 1974; Tompsett 1978; Sweet 1979) that a vegetative bud's early growth rate is a determining factor in its subsequent development, and that this could be the mechanism by which high nutrient levels influence flowering. We shall consider this hypothesis in more detail below.

B. Role of nitrogen and its metabolites

Nitrogen is the only mineral element which, when applied to the tree as fertilizer, will promote flowering in conifers (Puritch 1972; Schmidtling 1974). However, its role in this regard remains a matter of some controversy. According to Sweet and Hong (1978), the major role of N is to improve tree vigour, increasing crown size and thus the number of sites where conebuds may differentiate when conditions created by other inductive agents are favourable. The other hypothesis is that specific products of N metabolism – amino acids and arginine in particular – play a direct role in the differentiation process (Ebell & McMullan 1970; Schmidtling 1974).

Sweet and Hong (1978) reviewed the literature on flowering responses to N fertilizers in *Pinus*, and noted that N fertilization was most effective on those sites that were naturally deficient in N. It has also been our observation that the flowering response of *Pseudotsuga menziesii* to nitrate-N fertilization is less pronounced in well-fertilized seed orchard and potted trees than in the N-deficient forest stands studied by Ebell (1972). The response to N fertilizer persists for many years after application, and this does appear to result from the general improvement in site conditions, and the associated increase in crown size and number of potential sites for flowering (Ebell 1972; Sweet & Hong 1978).

However, there is fairly conclusive evidence that the positive effect of N on flowering is not strictly related to improved nutrition, but that N in the proper form (ie as NH_4 or NO_3), and at the proper time, can directly affect conebud differentiation (Ebell & McMullan 1970; Ebell 1972; Schmidtling 1974). Nitrate-N, for example, was the preferred source for conebud differentiation in *Pseudotsuga menziesii* (Ebell & McMullan 1970; Ebell 1972), and nitrate-N also synergistically enhanced $GA_{4/7}$ promotion of flowering in both *P. menziesii* and *Tsuga heterophylla* (Ross 1983; Ross *et al.* 1983). The effectiveness of the nitrate ion, relative to the ammonium ion, was correlated with an ability of the former to increase the level of arginine and other guanidines within the shoot, without affecting the total N pool (Ebell & McMullan 1970). Noting that arginine levels were similarly increased by water stress, which also stimulates flowering, Ebell (1972) speculated that arginine, as distinct from other amino acids, may play a regulatory role in conebud differentiation. Barnes and Bengtson (1968) also reported elevated levels of arginine in shoots of *Pinus elliottii* trees induced to flower by NH_4NO_3 fertilizer. In apple propagules, it is the exogenous application of the ammonium, rather than the nitrate, ion that promotes flowering, and here the effect is similarly associated with an accumulation of arginine (Grasmanis & Edwards 1974). Grasmanis and Edwards (1974) also assigned a specific regulatory role to arginine in flowering.

However, there are other studies which show that elevated levels of arginine in the shoot can also accompany non-inductive fertilizer treatments (Sweet & Hong 1978), and that other inductive conditions cause flowering without a concomitant increase in arginine (Ching *et al.* 1973; Lee *et al.* 1979). Furthermore, attempts to promote flowering in conifers by means of exogenously applied arginine have been unsuccessful (Sweet & Hong 1978; Hare 1979; McMullan 1980). It is worth remembering that arginine is an important storage form of N, both in fruit trees (Tromp 1970) and in conifers (van den Driessche & Webber 1977). One might therefore expect arginine to accumulate in shoots under conditions where N uptake exceeds the growth demand. Thus, although the mechanism by which N fertilizers promote flowering remains obscure, it is probably poor N utilization during shoot growth which leads to the accumulation of arginine.

In apples, Grasmanis and Edwards (1974) found that the shoots grew least well in response to that N source (ammonium) that was most conducive to flowering. Although not evident in Ebell's (1972) study, this also generally appears to be the case for *Pseudotsuga menziesii* (van den Driessche & Webber

1977; C. J. Masters, pers. comm.). In unpublished work on this species, we found that the flowering response to increasing amounts of Ca $(NO_3)_2$ was proportional to the inhibition of shoot elongation (relative to unfertilized controls), up to the point where excessive amounts produced overt toxic symptoms. Holst (1959) also speaks of 'fertilizer shock' in relation to the flowering response in conifers to heavy doses of N. Thus, a case can be made that N applications which evoke a specific flowering response constitute a shock treatment. Such an interpretation would resolve the conundrum presented by the fact that starving the plant of N is also an effective cone enhancement treatment for some conifers (Lyr & Hoffman 1964; Sweet & Will 1965).

C. Role of gibberellins

Of the different plant growth-regulating chemicals, only gibberellins (GAs), when applied exogenously, are known to promote flowering in conifers (see Pharis & Kuo 1977; Ross et al. 1983; Pharis & Ross 1985b). In this respect, conifers differ from most woody angiosperms, where exogenous application of GAs (at least GA_3, $GA_{4/7}$, and GA_7) inhibits flowering[1], and high endogenous levels of GAs appear to be associated with the vegetative or so-called juvenile condition (see Hackett 1985). Conversely, chemical growth retardants that promote flowering in woody angiosperms have been ineffective on conifers (Jackson & Sweet 1972), except in two instances where the growth retardant CCC was applied in conjunction with GA_3 (Bleymüller 1976; Chalupka 1979). Similarly, although auxins and cytokinins may enhance or modify the response to exogenous GAs, they are essentially ineffective by themselves (see Pharis & Kuo 1977; Ross et al. 1983).

It has long been known that flowering can be promoted at an early age in conifers within the Cupressaceae and Taxodiaceae by exogenously applying a variety of GAs, of which GA_3 is one of the most effective (see Pharis & Kuo 1977). However, for Pinaceae species, it is the GAs less polar than GA_3, such as GA_4, GA_7 and GA_9, that are most effective (Pharis 1975; Ross & Pharis 1976; Tompsett 1977; Dunberg 1980; Pharis et al. 1980; Greenwood 1982). Ross et al. (1983) noted that successful promotion of flowering, using a mixture of GA_4 and GA_7 ($GA_{4/7}$), has now been reported for at least 16 different species in five of the six genera of Pinaceae, and in over 60 research reports (cited by Pharis & Ross 1985b). It is also worth noting that, in contrast to the usually small interactions reported between different cultural practices (Bilan 1960; Barnes & Bengtson 1968; Ross & Pharis 1982), $GA_{4/7}$ often stimulates flowering synergistically when applied with other cultural treatments (such as girdling, N fertilization, water stress, and root pruning), even under conditions where the cultural practice is ineffective by itself (see Ross & Pharis 1982; Webber et al. 1985).

Some workers have questioned the concept that this response to exogenous GAs reflects an endogenous role for the growth regulators in the flowering of conifers (see Dunberg & Oden 1983). Sweet (1979) and McMullan (1980),

---

[1] See Note, p. 393.

working with *Pinus radiata* and *Pseudotsuga menziesii*, respectively, noted that the amount of exogenously applied $GA_{4/7}$ required to elicit a flowering response was many thousand times greater than the highest level of all GA-like substances detected in shoots and buds. McMullan (1980) suggested that the $GA_{4/7}$ effect was strictly pharmacological; that is, it was the result of a nonspecific physiological stress induced by a massive dosage of the growth regulator. But such calculations do not take into account the fact that only a small proportion of the applied $GA_{4/7}$ will be absorbed by the tree, and that the differentiating primordia have access to only a very small fraction of that small proportion (Ross & Pharis 1982; Pharis & Ross 1985b). Studies on *P. menziesii* using [^{3}H]GA_4 have shown that over 95% of it passes to adjacent stem and needle tissue (see Pharis & Ross 1985b). Additionally, [^{3}H]GA_4 is rapidly metabolized in *P. menziesii* and converted to several [^{3}H]GAs and [^{3}H]GA conjugate-like substances that have a low biological activity (Wample *et al.* 1975).

There is, in fact, a growing body of evidence which leads us to conclude that endogenous GAs of a less polar nature play an important regulatory role in differentiation of conebuds in conifers (see Pharis 1977; Ross *et al.* 1983; Pharis & Ross 1985b). It appears that young, and otherwise vigorously growing, conifers may utilize endogenous GAs preferentially for vegetative growth. Only when environmental conditions, or other factors such as maturation and ageing, restrict vegetative growth (and utilization of GAs), may endogenous GAs become available for a long enough period, and in sufficiently high concentrations, for conebud differentiation to occur. Evidence in support of this hypothesis may be found in Kamienska *et al.* (1973), Pharis (1977), Chalupka *et al.* (1982), Dunberg *et al.* (1983) and Ross (1983), and in several recent reviews (Pharis 1976; Ross *et al.* 1983; Pharis & Ross 1985b); only a brief summary will be given here.

The suggestion has been advanced, and will be considered below, that the flowering response to $GA_{4/7}$ is the result of an enhanced growth rate and/or altered pattern of meristematic activity in vegetative buds during their early development. However, morphologically distinct from this development (Owens *et al.* 1985) is the enhanced elongation of preformed shoots that frequently accompanies the $GA_{4/7}$ promotion of flowering in *Pseudotsuga menziesii* and other Pinaceae family conifers (see Ross 1983; Ross *et al.* 1983). Our studies on *P. menziesii* indicate that these two effects are not causally related, but are independent responses to exogenous $GA_{4/7}$, and, further, that endogenous GAs appear to be limiting both processes. Thus, depending on the timing of $GA_{4/7}$ application, it is possible to influence mainly shoot elongation, mainly flowering, or both, if $GA_{4/7}$ treatment is continued long enough (Ross 1983). In young seedlings of *P. menziesii*, $GA_{4/7}$ preferentially promotes vegetative growth, but with increasing ontogenetic maturity the shoot elongation response to $GA_{4/7}$ decreases and the $GA_{4/7}$ becomes more effective in promoting conebud differentiation (Ross 1983).

The implication here is that older, more 'sexually mature' trees possess high endogenous levels of certain critical less polar GAs – levels that may be adequate for vegetative growth, but are still suboptimal for conebud differentiation. Bioassay results of Crozier *et al.* (1970), comparing shoots from old and young *P. menziesii* trees, seem to support this interpretation. Levels of less polar GA-like substances in *P. menziesii* were also found to increase, relative to more polar GAs, following the inductive treatments of water stress and nitrate-N application (cited in Pharis 1977). In the case of a highly inductive root pruning treatment (Ross *et al.* 1985), the increase in endogenous $GA_{4/7}$-like substances was associated with a slowed conversion of [^{3}H]GA_4 to biologically inactive metabolites (see Pharis & Ross 1985b). Because one effect of root pruning and other stress treatments is to retard shoot elongation (Webber *et al.* 1985), these findings offer reasonable support for our hypothesis that, where less polar GAs are limiting, they (or their polar, biologically active metabolites) are preferentially utilized in vegetative growth. High temperatures (given, for example, by covering the shoots with plastic) are also known to slow the metabolism of [^{3}H]GA_4 (Dunberg *et al.* 1983) and result in higher endogenous levels of less polar GAs within the shoots of *Picea abies* (Chalupka *et al.* 1982). However, this highly effective flower promotion treatment for *Picea* did not inhibit shoot elongation (Philipson 1983; Ross 1985). Hence, the cultural treatment of high temperature may be acting at the biochemical level, to slow the oxidative conversion of active less polar exogenous or endogenous GAs to the inactive (with regard to promotion of flowering) more polar GAs.

D. Bud vigour and differential morphogenesis

Romberger and Gregory (1974) postulated that small changes in the rates and distributions of meristematic activity within embryonic shoots determined whether primordia differentiated reproductively or vegetatively. Such changes (differential morphogenesis) were considered to be the cause, rather than consequence, of floral evocation in conifers. A similar view was advanced by Tompsett (1978), who suggested that the future development of a vegetative bud of *Picea sitchensis* could be predicted from its early growth rate. In this species, as in most conifers, seed cones tend to differentiate from moderately vigorous buds in the upper and outer crown and pollen cones from less vigorous buds in the lower and inner crown, whereas buds of very strong, or very weak, vigour usually remain vegetative (Longman, this volume).

Based on this relationship, and the known ability of exogenous GAs to stimulate supabical meristematic activity in angiospermous plants (see Jones 1973), Tompsett and Fletcher (1979) suggested that GAs may promote flowering in conifers by enhancing the early growth rate of potentially reproductive buds and primordia. This hypothesis has gained some acceptance in recent years (eg Sweet 1979; Chalupka 1980; Greenwood 1981; Philipson 1983), but it is not supported by experimental evidence. Indeed, Owens *et al.* (1985) found that, while $GA_{4/7}$ injected into stems of *Pseudotsuga menziesii* trees could stimulate shoot elongation *per se*, it had no effect on mitotic activity or apical size in the shoot terminal bud or axillary (lateral) bud primordia, prior to the latter undergoing differentiation into conebuds. Ross *et al.* (1984) found a somewhat different response in *Pinus radiata*. Here, topical application of either GA_3 or $GA_{4/7}$ to terminal vegetative buds caused, only eight days later, a significant reallocation of dry matter (and ^{14}C-labelled assimilates) within the buds, from their apical domes and from subtending structural tissues to potentially reproductive lateral long-shoot primordia. Yet only $GA_{4/7}$ significantly promoted flowering, indicating that any benefit from nutrient diversion, and enhanced growth of lateral long-shoot primordia during their early development, was secondary to a direct morphogenetic effect of $GA_{4/7}$ on conebud differentiation.

Owens et al. (1985) concluded that it was a gross over-simplification to suppose that the early growth rate of a bud, or the distribution of mitotic activity within it, determined the bud's subsequent pattern of differentiation. They cited studies on *Pseudotsuga menziesii*, and other conifers within the Pinaceae family, which showed that there was little difference developmentally between probable seed cone, pollen cone and vegetative bud primordia until only shortly before the bud types became anatomically distinct. Thus, the observation that more vigorous buds in the upper tree crown have a higher probability of differentiating seed cones than less vigorous buds in the lower crown (which often form pollen cones) appears not to be related to bud vigour *per se*, but to hormonal, nutritional and environmental gradients within the crown (Schmidtling 1974; Ross et al. 1983; Owens et al. 1985).

There are other findings which are difficult to reconcile with the bud vigour hypothesis (Tompsett 1978). In *P. menziesii* it is unusual for the shoot terminal bud, regardless of its vigour, to differentiate into a seed cone, whereas this is a fairly common occurrence in $GA_{4/7}$-treated trees (Ross 1983). Also, in *P. menziesii*, root pruning and $GA_{4/7}$ treatments each extended the zone of female flowering down the crown to include shoots less vigorous than those that would normally be expected to produce seed cones (Ross et al. 1985), and yet root pruning slowed, and $GA_{4/7}$ had no effect on the subsequent development of the buds (mitotic activity and apical size) prior to their differentiation as seed cones (Owens et al. 1985).

It is not clear how the above results on the effects of root pruning relate to the nutrient diversion hypothesis that has been advanced to explain the action of this and other stress treatments on flowering. By decreasing vegetative growth, stress treatments may also increase the level of endogenous GAs available for reproductive bud development. However, the strong synergistic effect observed between stress treatments and exogenously applied $GA_{4/7}$ (see Ross & Pharis 1982; Ross et al. 1985) implies that other factors are involved in the promotion of flowering. More definitive studies involving ^{14}C-labelled assimilates will be required to determine if increased nutrient availability is involved and, if so, what the role(s) of increased nutrients might be in the initiation, differentiation and early development of reproductive structures.

E. Role of roots

It has been emphasized that many of the treatments which promote flowering in conifers (such as root pruning, drought and flooding of roots, high and low soil temperatures, excesses and deficiencies of N) could halt or diminish root activity. For the most part, we believe these effects on flowering can best be explained by diminished or altered shoot activity, resulting from decreased absorption of water and mineral nutrients. There has, however, been increasing conjecture in recent years (Dunberg 1979; Bonnet-Masimbert *et al.* 1982; Philipson 1983) that roots play a more direct role in conifer flowering, a role that involves the synthesis and export to shoots of substances inhibitory to flowering, as has been suggested for some woody angiosperms (see Hackett 1985).

Perhaps the best studies supporting this hypothesis are Schmidtling's (1969, 1983) showing that rootstock and interstock influences on precocious flowering in *Pinus* are independent of their effect on shoot growth. Lavender *et al.* (1977) proposed that reduced root metabolism, and export of inhibitory substances to shoots, accounted for the promotive effect of low soil temperatures on flowering in potted *Pseudotsuga menziesii* seedlings. It was noted that low soil temperatures affected neither the water nor nitrogen contents of plants, nor the final length of shoots produced that year. However, the same treatment was observed, in another study by these authors (Lavender *et al.* 1973), to significantly delay vegetative bud-burst in spring; hence it may, in fact, have retarded the rate of shoot elongation at a time when conebud differentiation was known to occur. Similarly, when considering Philipson's (1983) suggestion that high soil temperatures promoted flowering in potted *Picea sitchensis* grafted trees (maintained in a warm greenhouse) by reducing root activity, one must bear in mind that high temperatures are also effective when applied only to shoots of trees grown outdoors (Brøndbo 1969).

To our knowledge, only Bonnet-Masimbert *et al.* (1982) have examined the effect of cone induction treatments on the growth both of roots and shoots in a conifer. They found flooding of roots to be more effective than drought stress in promoting flowering in potted *Pseudotsuga menziesii* plants, and they attributed this to the ability of flooding to immediately and reliably arrest root growth, as opposed to any influence on shoot vigour. However, their results (in their Tables 1 and 2) showed what seemed to be a consistent inverse relationship between height increments and flowering response to flooding and drought treatments. Thus we question whether the cessation of root growth can be separated from concomitant effects on the shoot.

We must also ask the question: what kinds of growth regulators and/or metabolites might actively growing roots export to shoots that could inhibit flowering in conifers? In woody angiosperms (such as ivy and blackcurrant), GAs appear to be such a substance (see Hackett 1985). The roots of conifers also export GAs, at least in early spring (Lavender *et al.* 1973), apparently along with cytokinins and various organic nitrogenous compounds (see Wareing 1980; Ross *et al.* 1983). But GAs and cytokinins (when given together with GAs) are known to promote flowering in conifers, and the products of nitrogen metabolism do not, insofar as is known, inhibit flowering. Thus, the evidence for a unique substance, either root or shoot synthesized, that may be inhibitory to flowering in conifers is speculative.

III. CONCLUSIONS

The control mechanisms for flowering in woody perennial angiosperms currently appear to be different from those in conifers, although certain of the same cultural conditions will cause flowering in both groups of trees. Based on evidence to date, the control mechanism in conifers appears to involve endogenous GA concentrations. Just how GAs function in this regard is unknown. However, they appear to have a direct morphogenic role in conebud differentiation that involves only indirectly, if at all, nutrient diversion and/or altered meristematic activity within the developing bud. The evidence also indicates that the GAs which promote flowering in conifers are also used for vegetative growth. An attractive hypothesis is that young and vigorously growing conifers utilize endogenous GAs preferentially for vegetative growth; it is only when environmental or other factors restrict vegetative growth, or otherwise slow the metabolism of endogenous 'effector' GAs, that these are available for a long enough period, at sufficiently high concentrations, for conebud differentiation to take place.

While conebud differentiation in conifers appears to be conditional upon a high concentration of endogenous 'effector' GAs, it is apparent that other factors must also be favourable. We know that the cultural treatments that modify carbohydrate status, or that use N or modify N metabolism, can interact synergistically with GAs in the promotion of flowering in conifers. We also know that these cultural treatments themselves can increase the level of endogenous GAs; yet the addition of extra GAs does not (in the Pinaceae at least) substitute for the cultural treatments in their synergistic interaction with GAs. Logic (and the past literature) tells us that carbohydrates, N and other nutrients must play a role in the flowering of conifers. At the very least, these nutrients are essential substrates, although the possibility cannot be totally discounted that carbohydrates and certain products of N metabolism also play more direct morphogenic roles in the differentiation of conebuds.

Conebud differentiation in conifers involves a continuum of interacting processes that occur over a relatively long period of 4–12 weeeks, depending on the species. A variety of factors – including the concentrations of appropriate GAs, carbohydrates, nitrogenous substances and probably other, as yet undefined, nutrients and growth-regulating compounds – must remain favourable during the entire initiation and differentiation phases. Should one or several of these interacting processes fail or become limiting, the conebud differentiation process is not completed and the end result is a vegetative shoot, or an arrested or aborted reproductive bud. The practical challenge facing us is clear – to obtain sufficient basic understanding of these interacting processes to allow the reliable and cost-efficient control of flowering in conifers.

ACKNOWLEDGEMENTS

The authors gratefully acknowledge financial support from a Natural Sciences and Engineering Strategic Research Council of Canada Grant (G1190) to RPP and J. N. Owens.

[1] Note added in proof: Recent results (Looney, N. E., Pharis, R. P., & Noma, M. 1985. Planta 164. In press) using GA_4 (less than 5% GA_7 contamination) and C-3 epi-GA_4 showed significant flowering of spurs on apple trees (*Malus domestica* Borkh. cv. Golden Delicious) displaying a high degree of alternate-year flowering when the GAs were applied four to seven

weeks after anthesis. Thus, not only are GA$_4$ and C-3 epi-GA$_4$ not inhibitory, they promote flowering in apple trees. Gibberellin A$_4$ (which is native to apple) is now being tested on several woody angiosperms with regard to possible flowering efficacy.

REFERENCES

Barnes, R. L. & Bengtson, G. W. (1968). Effects of fertilization, irrigation, and cover cropping on flowering and on nitrogen and soluble sugar composition of slash pine. *Forest Sci.*, **14**, 172–180.

Bilan, M. V. (1960). Stimulation of cone and seed production in pole-size loblolly pine. *Forest Sci.*, **6**, 207–220.

Bleymüller, H. (1976). Investigations on the dependence of flowering in spruce (*Picea abies* (L.) Karst.) upon age and hormone treatment. *Silvae Genet.*, **25**, 83–85.

Bonner, F. T., ed. (1976). *Proc. Symp. on Flowering and Seed Development in Trees.* Starkville, MS: USDA Forest Service, Southern For. Exp. Stn.

Bonnet-Masimbert, M. (1979). Flowering on lammas shoots of Douglas-fir. *Proc. Symp. Flowering and Seed Development in Trees*, edited by F. T. Bonner, 51–56. Starkville, MS: USDA Forest Service, Southern For. Exp. Stn.

Bonnet-Masimbert, M. (1982). Effect of growth regulators, girdling, and mulching on flowering of young European and Japanese larches under field conditions. *Can. J. For. Res.*, **12**, 270–279.

Bonnet-Masimbert, M., Delanzy, P., Chanteloup, G. & Coupaye, J. (1982). Influence de l'état d'activité des racines sur la floraison induite par des gibbérellines 4 et 7 chez *Pseudotsuga menziesii* (Mirb.) Franco. *Silvae Genet.*, **31**, 178–183.

Brøndbo, P. (1969). Induction of flowering by high temperature treatment in grafts of Norway spruce (*Picea abies* (L.) Karst.). *Meddr. norske SkogsforsVes.*, **27**, 298–311.

Chalupka, W. (1979). Effect of growth regulators on flowering of Norway spruce (*Picea abies* (L.) Karst.) grafts. *Silvae Genet.*, **28**, 125–127.

Chalupka, W. (1980). Regulation of flowering in Scots pine (*Pinus sylvestris* L.) grafts by gibberellins. *Silvae Genet.*, **29**, 118–121.

Chalupka, W., Giertych, M. & Kopcewicz, J. (1982). Effect of polythene covers, a flower inducing treatment, on the contents of endogenous gibberellin-like substances in grafts of Norway spruce. *Physiologia Pl.*, **54**, 79–82.

Ching, K. K., Ching, T. & Lavender, D. P. (1973). Flower induction in Douglas-fir (*Pseudotsuga menziesii* Franco) by fertilizer and water stress. I. Changes in free amino acid composition in needles. *Proc. All-Union Symp. Sexual Reproduction of Conifers, 1st,* 1–14.

Crozier, A., Aoki, H., Pharis, R. P. & Durley, R. C. (1970). Endogenous gibberellins of Douglas-fir. *Phytochemistry*, **9**, 2453–2459.

Dickmann, D. I. & Kozlowski, T. T. (1970). Mobilization and incorporation of photoassimilated ^{14}C by growing vegetative and reproductive tissues of adult *Pinus resinosa* Ait. trees. *Pl. Physiol., Lancaster,* **43**, 284–288.

Driessche, R. van den & Webber, J. E. (1977). Variation in total and soluble nitrogen concentrations in response to fertilization of Douglas-fir. *Forest Sci.*, **23**, 134–142.

Dunberg, A. (1979). Flower induction in Norway spruce. *Proc. IUFRO Working Parties on Norway Spruce Provenances and Norway Spruce Breeding*, 139–157. Escherode, W. Germany.

Dunberg, A. (1980). Stimulation of flowering in *Picea abies* by gibberellins. *Silvae Genet.*, **29**, 51–53.

Dunberg, A., Malmberg, G., Sassa, T. & Pharis, R. P. (1983). Metabolism of tritiated gibberellins A$_4$ and A$_9$ in Norway spruce, *Picea abies* (L.) Karst. *Pl. Physiol., Lancaster,* **71**, 257–262.

Dunberg, A. & Oden, P. (1983). Gibberellins and conifers. In: *The biochemistry and physiology of gibberellins*, vol. 2, edited by A. Crozier, 221–296. New York: Praeger.

Ebell, L. F. (1971). Girdling: its effect on carbohydrate status and on reproductive bud and cone development of Douglas-fir. *Can. J. Bot.*, **49**, 453–466.

Ebell, L. F. (1972). Cone-production and stem-growth responses of Douglas fir to rate and frequency of nitrogen fertilization. *Can. J. For. Res.*, **2**, 327–338.

Ebell, L. F. & McMullan, E. E. (1970). Nitrogenous substances associated with differential cone production responses of Douglas fir to ammonium and nitrate fertilization. *Can. J. Bot.*, **48**, 2169–2177.

Giertych, M. & Krolikowski, Z. (1978). Importance of bud insolation on female flower induction in pine (*Pinus sylvestris* L.). *Arboretum korn.*, **23**, 161–169.

Grasmanis, V. O. & Edwards, G. R. (1974). Promotion of flower initiation in apple trees by short exposure to the ammonium ion. *Aust. J. Plant Physiol.*, **1**, 99–105.

Greenwood, M. S. (1981). Reproductive development in loblolly pine. II. The effect of age, gibberellin plus water stress and out-of-phase dormancy on long shoot growth behaviour. *Am. J. Bot.*, **68**, 1184–1190.

Greenwood, M. S. (1982). Rate, timing, and mode of gibberellin application for female strobilus production by grafted loblolly pine. *Can. J. For. Res.*, **12**, 998–1002.

Hackett, W. P. (1985). Juvenility, phase change and rejuvenation in woody plants. *Hortic. Rev.*, **7**, 109–155.

Hare, R. C. (1979). Promoting flowering in loblolly and slash pine with branch, bud, and fertilizer treatments. *Proc. Symp. Flowering and Seed Development in Trees*, edited by F. T. Bonner, 112–121. Starkville, MS: USDA Forest Service, Southern For. Exp. Stn.

Holst, M. J. (1959). Experiments with flower promotion in *Picea glauca* (Moench) Voss. and *Pinus resinosa* Ait. *Recent Adv. Bot.*, **2**, 1654–1658.

Jackson, D. I. & Sweet, G. B. (1972). Flower initiation in temperate woody plants. *Hort. Abstr.*, **42**, 9–24.

Jones, R. L. (1973). Gibberellins: their physiological role. *A. Rev. Pl. Physiol.*, **24**, 571–598.

Kamienska, A., Pharis, R. P., Wample, R. C., Kuo, C. C. & Durley, R. C. (1973). Gibberellins in conifers. *Proc. int. Conf. Plant Growth Regulators, 8th*, 305–313. Tokyo: Hirokawa Pub. Co.

Krugman, S. L. & Katsuta, M., eds. (1981). *Proc. Symp. Flowering Physiology.* (IUFRO World Congress, 17th, Kyoto, Japan).

Lavender, D. P., Ching, K. K. & Zaerr, J. B. (1977). Effect of soil temperature upon the production of reproductive buds on Douglas-fir (*Pseudotsuga menziesii*) seedlings. *Proc. North American Forest Biology Workshop, 4th*, edited by H. E. Wilcox and A. F. Hammer, 196. Syracuse, NY: New York State University (abstr.).

Lavender, D. P., Sweet, G. B., Zaerr, J. B. & Hermann, R. K. (1973). Spring shoot growth in Douglas-fir may be initiated by gibberellins exported from the roots. *Science, N.Y.*, **182**, 838–839.

Lee, K. J. (1979). Factors affecting cone initiation in pines: a review. *Res. Rep. Inst. For. Genet. Korea*, no. 15, 45–85.

Lee, K. J., Hollis, C. A. & Goddard, R. E. (1979). Strobilus initiation in slash pine in relation to shoot morphology and physiology of the terminal bud. *Proc. Symp. Flowering and Seed Development in Trees*, edited by F. T. Bonner, 359. Starkville, MS: USDA Forest Service, Southern For. Exp. Stn.

Lyr, H. & Hoffmann, G. (1964). Uber den Einfluss der Mineralsalzernährung auf die Frühfruktifikation von *Cryptomeria japonica* (L.E.D.) Don. *Flora, Jena*, **155**, 189–208.

Matthews, J. D. (1963). Factors affecting the production of seed by forest trees. *For. Abstr.*, **24**, 1–13.

McMullan, E. E. (1980). Effect of applied growth regulators on cone production in Douglas-fir, and relation of endogenous growth regulators to cone production capacity. *Can. J. For. Res.*, **10**, 405–422.

Olsen, H. C. (1978). Induction of flowering Norway spruce. *Forstlige ForsVaes., Danm.*, **36**, 231–265.

Owens, J. N. & Molder, M. (1979). The time and patterns of cone differentiation in western North American conifers. *Proc. Symp. Flowering and Seed Development in Trees*, edited by F. T. Bonner, 25–32. Starkville, MS: USDA Forest Service, Southern For. Exp. Stn.

Owens, J. N., Webber, J. E., Ross, S. D. & Pharis, R. P. (1985). Interaction between gibberellin $A_{4/7}$ and root pruning on the reproductive and vegetative process in Douglas-fir. III. Effects on shoot and terminal bud development. *Can. J. For. Res.*, **15**, 354–364.

Pharis, R. P. (1975). Promotion of flowering in conifers by gibberellins. *For. Chron.*, **51**, 244–248.

Pharis, R. P. (1976). Manipulation of flowering in conifers through the use of plant hormones. In: *Modern methods in forest genetics*, edited by J. P. Miksche, 265–282. Berlin: Springer.

Pharis, R. P. (1977). Interaction of native and endogenous plant hormones in the flowering of woody plants. *Proc. Conf. Regulation of Developmental Processes in Plants*, edited by H. R. Schutte and D. Gross, 343–360. Halle: Academy of Sciences.

Pharis, R. P. & Kuo, C. G. (1977). Physiology of gibberellins in conifers. *Can. J. For. Res.*, **7**, 299–325.

Pharis, R. P. & Ross, S. D. (1985a). Progress in hormonal cone induction in Pinaceae conifers. *Proc. Meeting Canadian Tree Improvement Association, 19th*, Part 1, 163–169. Ottawa: Canadian Forestry Service.

Pharis, R. P. & Ross, S. D. (1985b). Hormonal promotion of flowering in Pinaceae family conifers. In: *Handbook on flowering*, vol. 5, edited by A. Halevy. Boca Raton, FL: CRC Press. In press.

Pharis, R. P., Ross, S. D. & McMullan, E. E. (1980). Promotion of flowering in the Pinaceae by gibberellins. III. Seedlings of Douglas fir. *Physiologia Pl.*, **50**, 119–126.

Philipson, J. J. (1983). The role of gibberellin A₄₇, heat and drought in the induction of flowering in Sitka spruce. *J. exp. Bot.*, **34**, 291–302.

Puritch, G. S. (1972). *Cone production in conifers.* (Information report no. BC-X-65). Pacific Forest Research Centre, Canadian Forestry Service.

Romberger, J. A. & Gregory, R. A. (1974). Analytical morphogenesis and the physiology of flowering in trees. *Proc. North American Forest Biology Workshop, 3rd*, edited by C. P. P. Reid and G. H. Fechner, 132–147. Fort Collins, CO: Colorado State University.

Ross, S. D. (1983). Enhancement of shoot elongation in Douglas-fir by gibberellin A₄₇ and its relation to the hormonal promotion of flowering. *Can. J. For. Res.*, **13**, 986–994.

Ross, S. D. (1985). Promotion of flowering in *Picea engelmannii* (Perry) grafts: effects of heat, drought, gibberellin A₄₇ and their timing. *Can. J. For. Res.*, **15**. In press.

Ross, S. D. & Pharis, R. P. (1976). Promotion of flowering in the Pinaceae by gibberellins. I. Sexually mature, non-flowering grafts of Doulas-fir. *Physiologia Pl.*, **36**, 182–186.

Ross, S. D. & Pharis, R. P. (1982). Recent developments in enhancement of seed production in conifers. *Proc. Meeting Canadian Tree Improvement Association, 18th*, edited by D. F. W. Pollard, D. G. Edwards and C. W. Yeatman, Part 2, 26–38. Ottawa: Canadian Forestry Service.

Ross, S. D., Pharis, R. P. & Binder, W. D. (1983). Growth regulators and conifers: their physiology and potential uses in forestry. In: *Plant growth regulating chemicals*, edited by L. G. Nickell, 35–78. Boca Ratan, FL: CRC Press.

Ross, S. D., Bollmann, M. P., Pharis, R. P. & Sweet, G. B. (1984a). Gibberellin A₄₇ and the promotion of flowering in *Pinus radiata*: effects on partitioning of photoassimilate within the bud during primordia differentiation. *Pl. Physiol.*, **76**, 326–330.

Ross, S. D., Webber, J. E., Pharis, R. P. & Owens, J. N. (1984b). Interaction between gibberellin A₄₇ and root pruning on the reproductive and vegetative process in Douglas-fir. I. Effects of flowering. *Can. J. For. Res.*, **15**, 341–347.

Sachs, R. M. (1977). Nutrient diversion: a hypothesis to explain the chemical control of flowering. *HortScience*, **12**, 220–222.

Schmidtling, R. C. (1969). Influence of rootstock on flowering in shortleaf pine. *Proc. Conf. Southern Tree Improvement, 10th*, 17–19. Texas A & M University, College Station.

Schmidtling, R. C. (1974). Fruitfulness in conifers: nitrogen, carbohydrate, and genetic control. *Proc. North American Forest Biology Workshop, 3rd*, edited by C. P. P. Reid and G. H. Fechner, 148–164. Fort Collins, CO: Colorado State University.

Schmidtling, R. C. (1983). Influence of interstock on flowering and growth of loblolly pine grafts. *Tree Plant. Notes*, Winter, 30–32.

Silen, R. R. (1973). First- and second season effect on Douglas-fir cone initiation from a single shade period. *Can. J. For. Res.*, **3**, 528–534.

Sucoff, E. & Hong, S. G. (1974). Effects of thinning on needle water potential in red pine. *Forest Sci*, **20**, 25–29.

Sweet, G. B. (1975). Flowering and seed production. In: *Seed orchards*, edited by R. Faulkner, 72–82. (Forestry Commission Bulletin no. 54). London: HMSO.

Sweet, G. B. (1979). A physiological study of seed cone production in *Pinus radiata*. *N.Z. J. For. Sci.*, **9**, 20–33.

Sweet, G. B. & Will, G. M. (1965). Precocious male cone production associated with low nutrient status in clones of *Pinus radiata*. *Nature, Lond.*, **206**, 739.

Sweet, G. B. & Hong, S. O. (1978). The role of nitrogen in relation to cone production in *Pinus radiata*. *N.Z. For. Sci.*, **8**, 225–238.

Takeda, F., Ryugo, K. & Crane, J. C. (1980). Translocation and distribution of ¹⁴C-photosynthate in bearing and nonbearing pistachio branches. *J. Am. Soc. hort. Sci.*, **105**, 642–644.

Tompsett, P. B. (1977). Studies of growth and flowering in *Piceae sitchensis* (Bong.) Carr. I. Effects of growth regulator applications to mature scions on seedling rootstocks. *Ann. Bot.*, **41**, 1171–1178.

Tompsett, P. B. (1978). Studies of growth and flowering in *Picea sitchensis* (Bong.) Carr. II. Initiation and development of male, female and vegetative buds. *Ann. Bot.*, **42**, 889–900.

Tompsett, P. B. & Fletcher, A. M. (1979). Promotion of flowering on mature *Picea sitchensis* by gibberellin and environmental treatments. The influence of timing and hormonal concentration. *Physiologia Pl.*, **45**, 112–116.

Tromp, J. (1970). Storage and mobilization of nitrogenous compounds in apple trees with special reference to arginine. In: *Physiology of tree crops*, edited by L. C. Luckwill and C. V. Cutting, 143–159. London: Academic Press.

Wample, R. L., Durley, R. C. & Pharis, R. P. (1975). Metabolism of gibberellin A4/7 by vegetative shoots of Douglas-fir at three stages of ontogeny. *Physiologia Pl.*, **35**, 273–278.

Wareing P. F. (1980). Root hormones and shoot growth. In: *Control of shoot growth in trees*, edited by C. H. A. Little, 237–256. Fredericton, NB: Maritimes Forest Research Centre.

Webber, J. E., Ross, S. D., Pharis, R. P. & Owens, J. N. (1985). Interaction between gibberellin A4/7 and root pruning on the reproductive and vegetative process in Douglas-fir. II. Effects on shoot elongation and its relation to flowering. *Can. J. For. Res.*, **15**, 348–353.

Zimmerman, R. H., Hackett, W. P. & Pharis, R. P. (1985). Hormonal aspects of phase change and precocious flowering. In: *Hormonal regulation of development*, 3, edited by R. P. Pharis and D. M. Reid. (Encyclopedia of plant physiology, n.s. vol. 11). Berlin; New York: Springer. In press.

23

VARIABILITY IN FLOWER INITIATION IN FOREST TREES

K. A. LONGMAN
Institute of Terrestrial Ecology, Bush Estate, Penicuik, Midlothian, Scotland

I. INTRODUCTION

Most species of forest trees scarcely qualify as 'crop plants' at present. Among the primary reasons for this are the irregularity in their reproductive behaviour, and our general ignorance about its control, which prevent forest trees from being subjected to the regular improvement by selection and breeding that is routine for the majority of herbaceous and plantation crops. The extent to which forest trees lag behind can be appreciated by imagining the response from farmers if they were offered cereal, root crop or grass seed described only by the geographical region from which it originated.

In the tropics, seed supplies are frequently limited because of sparse flowering and/or short periods of seed viability (eg Dipterocarps, Wycherley 1973; Longman 1984a; *Triplochiton scleroxylon*, Leakey *et al.* 1981; *Agathis* spp., Bowen & Whitmore 1980). Seed-set is often poor in *Pinus caribaea* var. *hondurensis*, giving few viable seeds when the species is grown as an exotic at low elevations between 9°N and 9°S (Gallegos 1981). In Britain, home-produced seed is seldom or never available of *Abies grandis*, *Sequoia sempervirens*, *Metasequoia glyptostroboides* and some *Nothofagus* spp., and this is one factor restricting their use in arboriculture and forestry.

Differences in flowering among provenances and individual trees can cause problems, even where seed supplies are plentiful. For instance, provenances of *Pinus contorta* from south and central interior British Columbia, which are of special interest in the UK, produce heavy seed crops in Britain less regularly than some other less desirable provenances. In general, the progenies of individual forest trees with inherently profuse pollen and ovule production will tend to predominate in seed collected from plantations and seed orchards, so that special steps may be needed to avoid an inadvertent tendency to select profusely flowering trees.

Indeed, without reliable flower induction it is quite difficult to start reaping the benefits of genetic selection of forest trees through seed. Identifying desirable parents is relatively inefficient because it is phenotypically based, and the trees are already too large for easy handling. Even when they have been vegetatively propagated as adult clones, and established at a single site, several years may pass before flowering begins. Variability in the occurrence, timing and sex of flowers adds to the problems, and the flowers become progressively more inaccessible. Because of the long juvenile period, a succession of crosses in a planned breeding programme is out of the question. Not surprisingly, therefore, a high priority has been assigned over the last few decades to the solution of problems concerning flowering.

Progress to date has been slow, but two promising developments may be mentioned, both of which allow substantial miniaturization and standardization of research plant material. First, by using standard horticultural techniques for rooting cuttings, clones can easily be produced of many forest tree species, at least from young trees. Attention can then be concentrated on species and selected clones which flower regularly and early in life. Second, in the Cupressaceae, the initiation of large numbers of male and female cones can be reliably stimulated with gibberellic acid (GA_3) in known positions on the shoots. These two approaches enable forest tree research itself to be 'domesticated', such that the physiology of flowering can now be studied experimentally with known genotypes under defined conditions (Longman 1982; Manurung 1982).

The key steps in floral induction are the initial stages during which an apex is transformed from a vegetative to a reproductive state: once initiation can be obtained at will, later development can be studied relatively easily. Ross and Pharis (this volume) have reviewed the factors affecting flower induction in forest trees. In this paper, I shall review the changes in flowering ability that occur with age, variation in the distribution, timing and sex of flowers, variation between species and genotypes; and I shall suggest approaches to solving problems concerning flowering.

II. CHANGES WITH AGE

The great majority of forest trees do not start flowering until they have grown vegetatively for a number of years (Wareing 1959; Doorenbos 1965; Zimmerman 1972, 1976), and frequent reference is made in the literature to the presence of a juvenile period and to studies with *Hedera* (ivy) which changes abruptly from a juvenile to a mature leaf shape. Tables showing the ages when reproduction usually begins have been produced for forest trees in the UK (Matthews 1955) and USA (Schopmeyer 1974), and for some commonly planted tropical forest trees (Longman 1984a). Various modifications in shoot morphology, growth habit and phenology also occur as a tree becomes older, but these are not necessarily coincident with each other or with the onset of reproductive ability. An example is the 'grass' stage of *Pinus palustris* and *Pinus merkusii*, in which the elongation of the stem (but not of the leaves or roots) is inhibited for several years, starting from germination in *P. palustris* (Brown 1964). In this species, the 'grass' stage persists for much longer than the period of months during which young seedlings produce only primary needles, and is shorter than the time to first flowering, which averages at least 20 years (Krugman & Jenkinson 1974).

A broad distinction may be made between changes that occur with age which can be easily reversed, and those which are relatively permanent. For example, vigorous branches on young seedlings tend to show a progressive decline in growth rate, and in the production of lateral buds, as the number of competing apices increases with time. This process of *ageing* (Wareing 1959) can be reversed, for instance by pruning (Moorby & Wareing 1963), or by detaching the shoots and propagating them as rooted cuttings or grafted scionwood. However, other characteristics which trees attain when they grow older are quite firmly retained after vegetative propagation, suggesting that a process of *maturation* or *phase-change* has taken place. Thus rejuvenation (in its strict sense) of adult or mature tissue is rather uncommon (see, however, Paton *et al.* 1981).

Evidence for ageing may be readily observed in conifers from changes in the number, vigour and type of vegetative shoot on successively older branches. For instance, at the tops of mature *Picea sitchensis* grafts, and on first-order shoots on the main branches, most or all of the terminal buds contain preformed shoots and lateral bud primordia in winter. The total number of buds with preformed shoots per branch increases from the one-year-old branches at the top of the trees to the four-year-old branches below, but below this level the number decreases because an increasing proportion of the buds contain only a living apex and bud scales. Failure to form preformed shoots is particularly true of third- and fourth-order shoots, which are mostly weak and fail to produce lateral bud primordia.

Adult grafts or cuttings of forest trees may not flower for several years, possibly because the shoot apices are close to the roots, or because time is needed to produce the type of branches on which reproduction is possible – the term 'secondary juvenility' has been coined to distinguish this phenomenon from the 'primary juvenility' of young seedlings. Shoots arising near the base of older plants, and especially coppice sprouts, are generally held to have retained much or all of the primary juvenility of the seedling plant (Sax 1962; Doorenbos 1965).

These concepts of ageing and maturation emphasize the difference between plants developing 'ripeness-to-flower' (Klebs 1918), and their response to what might be described as the 'opportunity-to-flower'. In practice, however, it is often difficult to know when the juvenile period has ended, particularly in irregularly flowering species. When a dominant tree flowers, and a suppressed tree does not, both might be mature, but the latter could just be inhibited by competition. Moreover, some fundamental contradictions appear if the classical *Hedera* situation is used as a rigid model for forest trees.

One problem is that certain treatments will induce flowering during the first three years of life in supposedly juvenile seedlings and cuttings. For example, three sexual generations have been achieved in eight years with *Triplochiton scleroxylon* grown in glasshouses in Scotland (Leakey *et al.* 1981), while annual breeding is now practised with rapidly grown *Betula* spp. in polythene shelters in Finland. Perhaps the most striking cases of early flowering are seen following the application of GA_3 in the Cupressaceae and Taxodiaceae (Pharis & Kuo 1977; Longman *et al.* 1982). The induction of a terminal female cone on an eight-month-old *Sequoiadendron giganteum* (Pharis & Morf 1969) demonstrates the problem: does that mean that a tree with a lifespan measured in millenia is already mature in its first year? If so, do juvenile periods exist? Probably, a more useful working hypothesis would be that flowering can take place during the juvenile phase, but becomes progressively easier as the tree matures, implying quantitative rather than qualitative restriction. Many inductive treatments, such as GA_3 application and bark-ringing, may be sufficiently 'powerful' to stimulate reproduction during the juvenile period, without necessarily affecting phase-change.

Experiments with *Thuja plicata* lend some weight to this view. Complete bark-ringing on the main stem of mature cuttings induced 90–100% of them to flower heavily, compared with only 40–50% of the unringed control plants, which also produced fewer cones (Longman 1976). Unringed two-year-old seedlings grown under the same conditions did not flower at all, and only 30% did so when they were ringed, producing relatively few cones. In order to test whether the flowering portion distal to the ring on these plants had been subjected to accelerated phase-change (ie had rapidly become mature), cuttings originating from above and below the ring were rooted. The growth rates and morphology of the two sets of clonal plants were indistinguishable; both produced some primary, linear leaves, and, when given a standard dose of $100 \mu g \, GA_3$, both produced similar numbers of male and female cones. Thus, it was concluded that ringing had promoted flowering, but had not altered phase status (Longman 1976).

The age at which *Betula* and *Larix* trees first produced flowers was greatly decreased by growing seedlings rapidly to a large size, in heated glasshouses under long photoperiods (Longman & Wareing 1959; Robinson & Wareing 1969). Growing plants to a smaller size, through repeated short cycles of growth and dormancy, did not stimulate flowering. To demonstrate conclusively that rapid attainment of a large size induces a phase-change, *two* vegetative propagations are needed. First, a clone has to be produced from a single seedling while it is still very young, and some of the ramets must then be induced to flower. Second, shoots from both the flowering and untreated ramets must be cloned, so they can exist as equivalent plants with only a putative difference in phase between them – independent of differences in plant size, environment and inductive treatment. In species in which adult cuttings can be rooted, material for phase-change research can also be propagated from branches growing at different heights, and from coppice (or epicormic) shoots on the same tree.

III. SPATIAL DISTRIBUTION

In the majority of forest tree species, many buds tend to remain vegetative, even during periods of pronounced reproductive activity. Floral buds may produce cones or inflorescences only, as in *Pseudotsuga, Picea, Larix & Betula* (male) and *Ulmus*, or they can contain leaves as well, as in *Pinus*, *Larix* & *Betula* (female) and *Acer pseudoplatanus*. In several species within the Fagaceae, the female flowers occur in leafy buds, while the male may occur with or without leaves. Segregation of the sexes ranges from nil (strictly hermaphroditic flowers), through bisexual buds, and clearcut female and male zones, to separate male and female trees. It is not generally recognized how widespread is this latter condition: for example, around 20% of the tropical tree species in Central America are dioecious (Baker *et al.* 1983), as are over half of the world's coniferous species (Givnish 1980).

In monoecious conifers, it is typical for the leading shoot, and the apical parts of vigorous upper branches, to be strongly vegetative, for female cones to occur principally in the upper and apical parts of the middle crown, for male cones to occur especially in the middle and apical parts of the lower crown, while the inner, lower crown shows weak vegetative growth (Wareing 1958; Tompsett 1978). Figure 1 shows details of the pattern of cone distribu-

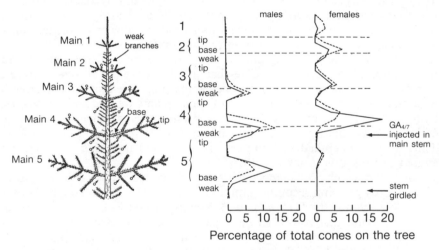

FIGURE 1.   The locations of male and female cones on an 11-year-old adult graft of *Picea sitchensis*, growing in Scotland. The main stem of the tree had been completely girdled two years previously, and injected with 20 mg GA$_{4/7}$ one year previously. There was a total of 1,230 female cones, 1,390 male cones and 360 vegetative shoots on the part of the tree illustrated here.

Dashed lines = lateral buds; continuous lines = terminal buds. The male and female symbols indicate sections of the tree where a high proportion of available sites contained male or female cones. 'Main' branches and 'weak' branches have been called 'whorl' and 'interwhorl' branches, respectively, by other workers.

tion on an adult graft of *Picea sitchensis* that had been induced, by combined bark-ringing and GA$_{4/7}$ injection, to produce over 2,500 female and male cones, leaving only 12% of the shoots vegetative. The female and male zones can be clearly seen, with most of the female cones occurring on the four-year-old branches (and also on younger branches right up to the basal section of the leading shoot), and most of the male cones occurring on the 4- and 5-year-old branches (and also on 3-year-old branches). In the upper part of the tree, both female and especially male cones were found on the weaker branches, between the main pseudowhorl groups, while lower down the tree they chiefly occurred on the main branches. Within a branch, female cones tended to be nearer the tips than the male cones. In both sexes, there was a distinct tendency for cones on more apical, vigorous shoots to be in lateral positions, whereas on less vigorous, more basal sections, terminal cones tended to predominate.

Clearly, position in the crown needs to be taken into account in the layout and analysis of flowering experiments (Bonnet-Masimbert 1982; Marquard & Hanover 1984), and, if certain buds within a tree have a much greater propensity to flower than others (Fig. 1), it may be preferable to apply flower induction treatments directly to the most promising part of the shoot system. Perhaps in some cases seedlings or adult plants may have to produce the 'correct' type of shoot before they can flower (Longman 1970). In addition, analysis of the physiological and structural differences between parts of the tree with high and low reproductive potential might throw new light on the mechanisms of floral morphogenesis.

Most of the male buds of *Larix kaempferi* point horizontally or downwards, generally occupying the underside of horizontal shoots, and occurring on all sides of trailing shoots, which are common in this genus (Longman *et al.* 1965). Male coning can be greatly increased by tying the branches into a horizontal, or especially into a downwardly pointing, position, whereas female coning in *Larix decidua* can be promoted by tying branches into the horizontal position. These gravimorphic effects have been shown to involve the inclination of both the primary and higher order branches, and experimental inter-conversion of male and vegetative positions has been achieved by twisting flexible horizontal shoots of *L. kaempferi* through 180° before the process of cone initiation became irreversible. The genus *Abies* also has numerous male buds confined to the lower side of horizontal shoots, with solitary female cones situated on the upper side, but it is not known whether initiation can be influenced by gravimorphic treatments.

In broadleaved species, a reproductive zone can sometimes be seen on trees that have recently begun to flower, situated in the middle part of the crowns, between distal vigorous and proximal weakly vegetative regions (Bovet 1958). Monoecious species seldom show such a clear separation of the sexes as found in conifers, but in *Fagus sylvatica*, for instance, female flowers always occupy more distal positions than males. Females form especially in the axils of the third foliage leaves in the buds, whereas male inflorescences most commonly form in the axils of the first foliage leaves, or the scale leaves preceding it. Buds containing female flowers contain significantly more leaves than those containing only males, and female buds are more common as terminals on long shoots than on short shoots or laterals. The opposite distribution occurs in *Alnus* and *Corylus*, and also in *Betula*, where male inflorescences are terminal and subterminal on long shoots, and where most female catkins terminate short shoots, as well as some less vigorous long shoots.

Trees with hermaphrodite inflorescences or flowers may also have floral buds occupying particular positions. For example, in *Ulmus americana* the two basal nodes (1 and 2) on one-year-old shoots in winter have very small latent lateral buds, about 0·5 mm long. Flower buds, about 8 mm long, occur with highest frequency at node 3 on shoots of moderate vigour, but can also occur at nodes 4 to 7. Vegetative lateral buds averaging 4 mm in length occupy the remaining lateral and pseudoterminal positions.

Studies on tropical trees, which exhibit a much wider diversity of 'architectural models' than temperate zone woody plants, show that patterns of branching can be closely associated with reproductive activity. For example, *Elaeis guineensis* (the oil palm) belongs to Corner's model (Hallé *et al.* 1978) and has a single, vegetative, terminal shoot apex forming an unbranched main stem – the lateral buds all giving rise to male or female inflorescences. By contrast, in Leeuwenberg's model, shown by *Manihot esculenta* (cassava) and *Tabebuia pallida* (Manurung 1982), the apical bud on the leading shoot becomes reproductive. Two or more lateral buds then grow vegetatively and flower terminally, and the process is repeated to give a highly branched crown. In certain other tropical species, flowers occur on the main stem (as in cacao), on branches, and even on roots or leaf surfaces (Longman & Jeník 1974).

IV. TEMPORAL VARIATION

As already mentioned, the onset and timing of successive events in the reproductive cycle of trees are often extremely variable. Periodicity is the general rule; few woody species flower continuously, even in the tropics (Longman & Jeník 1974). There, flowering can occur (a) regularly every 3 to 4 months, every 6 months, annually or biennially, (b) irregularly during the year, or with longer intervals, (c) gregariously, at intervals of 2 to 8 years, as shown by the Dipterocarps (Longman 1984a), or (d) once in the life cycle, as in some bamboos (Janzen 1976). The popularity of certain widely planted tropical and temperate zone trees, such as *Tectona grandis*, *Terminalia ivorensis* and some *Pinus* spp., may have arisen partly because of their regular annual seed production.

There is also variation in the time at which floral initiation occurs. The shoot apices of trees presumably undergo broadly similar modifications to those that occur in herbaceous plants, in response to environmental and internal stimuli (Lyndon & Battey 1985). However, in trees there is usually an interval of weeks or months before flowering itself occurs, and in many species flower bud dormancy may have to be broken before development proceeds towards female receptivity and pollen shed. These key changes at the apex have seldom been studied, and their nature is poorly understood.

However, observations have been made of the dates when male and female parts first appear in sectioned or dissected buds in several north-west American conifers (Owens & Molder 1979), and in European trees (Lohwag 1910). In both of these groups, floral parts are first seen during the period from late May to early October, in the year previous to flowering, with July and early August the commonest dates. The initial biochemical and cytological steps of floral morphogenesis presumably occur about a month earlier. Exceptions include the five-needled pines, in which the appearance of female cone initials seems to be delayed until March of the flowering year, although the lateral apices in which they occur are formed during the previous summer. In *Tilia argentea*, flower initials are not found until the beginning of May in the year of flowering, whereas in *Pseudotsuga* and *Abies* the earliest stages occur in March of the year before flowering (Owens 1969; Puritch 1972).

Clearly, it is crucial to know at what time of year initiation is possible, if flowering is to be successfully and reliably induced using methods such as those discussed by Ross and Pharis (this volume). Useful test species might include (a) the tree *Ateramnus lucidus* which, in Florida, produces flower buds which for nine months can easily be distinguished from vegetative buds (Tomlinson 1980), and (b) the shrub *Viburnum alnifolium*, which in New England produces flower buds of a recognizable shape by the end of July. Species in the Cupressaceae are also easy to study because the cones are not enclosed within buds, and the same applies to the male inflorescences of *Betula*, *Alnus* and *Corylus*. The minute, red-tipped male catkins of *Betula pendula* and *Betula pubescens* can sometimes be detected in England as early as the end of May, almost a year before pollen is shed.

For many north temperate forest trees with short periods of shoot extension, there may be only a limited 'time-niche' in which floral induction is possible. Once bud-scale initiation has been succeeded by the formation of foliage leaves, it may be impossible for an inflorescence or cone to be formed. There may be more leeway on trees with prolonged or repeated periods of shoot extension; for example, male catkins can sometimes be seen at the ends of both the first and second shoot flushes on vigorous shoots of *B. pendula* and *B. pubescens*, and three such male initiation events have been recorded on grafts grown in long-days in a heated glasshouse. In *Pinus contorta*, there is a difference in the time reported for first appearance of female cones – early October in British Columbia (Owens & Molder 1979) and early July in Scotland (Couper, unpublished data) – which may reflect the capacity of this species to form polycyclic shoots. These shoots can contain two 'tiers' of female cones within the same preformed bud, not necessarily initiated at the same time.

In Scotland, branches of *Thuja plicata* produced male and female cones in response to GA_3 injection at any time from late February to late August, but especially from the end of March to the end of June (Longman 1985). As already mentioned, in *Larix kaempferi* gravimorphic manipulation can induce male cones to initiate a month later than in untreated shoots (Longman *et al.* 1965). This treatment can also cause prospective male buds to revert to the vegetative condition, suggesting that induction does not become irreversible for several weeks after the appearance of distinct changes in bud morphology. In *Thuja plicata*, GA_3-induced female buds, in their early stages of initiation, reverted to vegetative buds when a high dose of 'Ethrel' (2-chloroethylphosphonic acid) was applied (Longman & Manurung 1982).

After initiation has occurred, the rate of male catkin development in *Betula* can be greatly enhanced by short-day treatment, so that by July they can reach the stage normally seen in late August. The next stage – that of flower bud dormancy – has been little studied in temperate zone forest trees, although it has been generally assumed to exist, and to be broken by chilling. Purely floral buds typically flush earlier in the spring than vegetative buds, but it is not clear whether this is due to a smaller chill-unit requirement, or to a lower heat-sum requirement, or both. In south-east USA, *Pinus taeda* buds containing male cones and needles, or only needles, flush normally when transferred to long-days and favourable temperatures without chilling; but buds containing female cones and needles, and also the one-year-old conelets, require chilling to develop normally (Greenwood 1977). The rare male cones of *Metasequoia glyptostroboides* may grow out in warm temperatures in late autumn, but they are then abnormal and shed no pollen, whereas male buds of *Populus* will produce viable pollen in early autumn when grown in a glasshouse after only a brief period of chilling (Seitz 1958).

V. GENETIC DIVERSITY AND THE SOLUTION OF PROBLEMS CONCERNING REPRODUCTION

Large within-species variation in flowering is typically found between clones. For instance, observations over eight years on 25 mature grafts and cuttings of *Picea sitchensis* showed that two clones never flowered, 20 clones flowered occasionally to varying extents, while three clones flowered every year. Also, certain clones produced predominantly one sex, as has been reported for other conifers. Pronounced genetic control of cone production in *P. sitchensis* has also been demonstrated in progeny trials (Longman 1978). Similarly, large differences have been observed among clones of *Betula pendula* – some producing few or no female flowers at age three, while others formed flowers in one-third of their buds.

Some *Pinus* species may start flowering early in life, particularly when used as exotics. Examples include *Pinus contorta* in Britain, *Pinus kesiya* in East Africa and *Pinus caribaea* var. *hondurensis* in Brazil and Indonesia (where some individual trees have flowered 14 months after germination). Ninety per cent of the trees in a plot of *Pinus thunbergii*, planted in Delaware, USA, initiated female cones by the third year after planting, and two-thirds had also started to form male cones by the next year. In these instances, environment as well as genetics may be involved, but these precociously flowering trees may present an opportunity to miniaturize the study of flowering. The seedling progeny of a tree of *Dipterocarpus oblongifolius*, in the Kepong Arboretum in Malaysia, started to flower seven months after germination, when they were less than 0·4 m tall (Srivastava 1977). If clones were raised from such seedlings, and they showed similar precocity, the almost insuperable problems of understanding and stimulating flowering in the large and commercially important Dipterocarp family could be tackled experimentally, perhaps even in small controlled environment cabinets (Longman 1984a).

Striking confirmation of genetic control over the onset of flowering was shown by interbreeding precocious selections of *Betula pendula*. After only three generations, the progeny had virtually no juvenile period, produced inflorescences in every bud, and became effectively annuals or hemicryptophytes instead of trees (Huhtinen 1976). This extreme tendency to flower was even found in plants raised from tissue cultures, suggesting that such systems could even be used for studies on forest tree reproduction.

Thus, clones that are inherently predisposed to flower regularly and heavily as small plants may have a special role to play as research tools to solve the many outstanding problems concerning reproduction in trees, including floral morphology and distribution, factors affecting flower initiation, the timing of flowering, pollination success between matched clone pairs, and so forth. But, unless it can be clearly demonstrated that the net cost of the extra reproductive effort, expressed through their lifetime, is negligible, such genotypes should not be used as parents for plantations or for breeding programmes in tree species grown for timber, firewood or foliage. In trees grown for their fruits, seeds or ornamental flowers, this problem hardly exists; but in forestry the long-term goal for a domesticated tree crop should be a decline in the genetical tendency to flower, corresponding with an increase in our understanding of reproduction, and in our ability to stimulate it at will.

REFERENCES

Baker, H. G., Bawa, K. S., Frankie, G. W. & Opler, P. A. (1983). Reproductive biology of plants in tropical forests. In: *Tropical rain forest ecosystems, structure and function*, edited by F. B. Golley, 183–215. (Ecosystems of the world 14A). Amsterdam: Elsevier.

Bonnet-Masimbert, M. (1982). Effect of growth regulators, girdling and mulching on flowering of young European and Japanese larches under field conditions. *Can. J. For. Res.*, **12**, 270–279.

Bovet, J. (1958). Contribution a l'étude des 'races écologiques' du frêne, *Fraxinus excelsior* L. *J. for. suisse*, **8/9**, 536–546.

Bowen, M. R. & Whitmore, T. C. (1980). Agathis – a genus of fast growing rain forest conifers. *Commonw. Forest. Rev.*, **59**, 307–310.

Brown, C. L. (1964). *The seedling habit of longleaf pine*. Athens, GA: University of Georgia, Georgia Forest Research Council and School of Forestry.

Doorenbos, J. (1965). Juvenile and adult phases in woody plants. *Handb. PflPhysiol.*, **15**(1), 1222–1235.

Gallegos, C. M. (1981). Flowering and seed production of *Pinus caribaea* var. *hondurensis*. (Preliminary results of a world wide survey). *For. Genet. Resour. Inf. (FAO)*, **10**, 17–22.

Givnish, T. J. (1980). Ecological constraints on the evolution of breeding systems in seed plants: dioecy and dispersal in gymnosperms. *Evolution, Lancaster, Pa*, **34**, 959–972.

Greenwood, M. S. (1977). The role of dormancy in the development of male and female strobili of loblolly pine. *Forest Sci.*, **23**, 373–375.

Hallé, F., Oldeman, R. A. A. & Tomlinson, P. B. (1978). *Tropical trees and forests: an architectural analysis*. Heidelberg: Springer.

Huhtinen, O. (1976). Early flowering of birch and its maintenance in plants regenerated through tissue cultures. *Acta Hortic.*, **56**, 243–249.

Janzen, D. H. (1976). Why bamboos wait so long to flower. *Ann. Rev. Ecol. Syst.*, **7**, 347–391.

Klebs, G. (1918). Über die Blütenbildung von *Sempervivum*. *Flora, Jena*, **111**, 128–151.

Krugman, S. L. & Jenkinson, J. L. (1974). *Pinus* L. Pine. In: *Seeds of woody plants in the United States*, edited by C. S. Schopmeyer, 598–638. (Agriculture Handbook no. 450). Washington DC: USDA Forest Service.

Leakey, R. R. B., Ferguson, N. R. & Longman, K. A. (1981). Precocious flowering and reproductive biology of *Triplochiton scleroxylon* K. Schum. *Commonw. Forest. Rev.*, **60**, 117–126.

Lohwag, H. (1910). Beitrag zur Kenntnis der Zeit der ersten Blütenanlage bei Holzpflanzen. *Öst. bot. Z.*, **60**, 369–376.

Longman, K. A. (1970). Initiation of flowering on first year cuttings of *Metasequoia glyptostroboides* Hu and Cheng. *Nature, Lond.*, **227**, 299–300.

Longman, K. A. (1976). Some experimental approaches to the problem of phase-change in forest trees. *Acta Hortic.*, **56**, 81–90.

Longman, K. A. (1978). Control of flowering for forest tree improvement and seed production. *Scient. Hort.*, **30**, 1–10.

Longman, K. A. (1982). Effects of gibberellin, clone and environment on cone initiation, shoot growth and branching in *Pinus contorta. Ann. Bot.*, **50**, 247–257.

Longman, K. A. (1984a). Tropical forest trees. In: *Handbook on flowering*, vol. 1, edited by A. H. Halevy. Boca Raton, FL: CRC Press.

Longman, K. A. (1984b). Physiological studies in birch. *Proc. R. Soc. Edinb.*, **85B**, 97–113.

Longman, K. A. (1985). Effects of growth substances on male and female cone initiation in conifers. *Biologia Pl.* In press.

Longman, K. A. & Jeník, J. (1974). *Tropical forest and its environment.* London: Longman.

Longman, K. A. & Manurung, R. (1982). Manipulation of cone formation in the Cupressaceae. *Annu. Rep. Inst. terr. Ecol. 1981*, 67–69.

Longman, K. A. & Wareing, P. F. (1959). Early induction of flowering in birch seedlings. *Nature, Lond.*, **184**, 2037–2038.

Longman, K. A., Dick, J. & Page, C. N. (1982). Cone induction with gibberellin for taxonomic studies in *Cupressaceae* and *Taxodiaceae. Biologia Pl.*, **24**, 195–201.

Longman, K. A., Nasr, T. A. A. & Wareing, P. F. (1965). Gravimorphism in trees. IV. The effect of gravity on flowering. *Ann. Bot.*, **29**, 459–473.

Lyndon, R. F. & Battey, N. H. (1985). The growth of the shoot apical meristem during flower initiation. *Biologia Pl.* In press.

Manurung, R. M. (1982). *Environment and growth substances affecting gibberellic acid-induced coning of* Thuja plicata *D. Don and flowering of* Tabebuia pallida *Lindl.* Ph.D. thesis, University of Aberdeen.

Marquard, R. D. & Hanover, J. W. (1984). Sexual zonation in the crown of *Picea glauca* and the flowering response to exogenous $GA_{4/7}$. *Can. J. For. Res.*, **14**, 27–30.

Matthews, J. D. (1955). Production of seed by forest trees in Britain. *Rep. Forest Res., Lond., 1953–54*, 64–78.

Moorby, J. & Wareing, P. F. (1963). Ageing in woody plants. *Ann. Bot.*, **27**, 291–308.

Owens, J. N. (1969). The relative importance of initiation and early development on cone production in Douglas fir. *Can. J. Bot.*, **47**, 1039–1049.

Owens, J. N. & Molder, M. (1979). The times and patterns of cone differentiation in western North American conifers. *Proc. Symp. Flowering and Seed Development in Trees*, edited by F. Bonner, 25–32. Starkville, MS: USDA Forest Service, Southern For. Exp. Stn.

Paton, D. M., Willing, R. R. & Pryor, L. D. (1981). Root-shoot gradients in *Eucalyptus* ontogeny. *Ann. Bot.*, **47**, 835–838.

Pharis, R. P. & Kuo, C. G. (1977). Physiology of gibberellins in conifers. *Can. J. For. Res.*, **7**, 299–325.

Pharis, R. P. & Morf, W. (1969). Precocious flowering of coastal and giant redwood with gibberellins A_3, $A_{4/7}$ and A_{13}. *BioScience*, **19**, 719–720.

Puritch, G. S. (1972). Cone production in conifers. A review of the literature and evaluation of research needs. *Can. For. Serv. Inf. Rep.*, BC-X-65.

Robinson, L. W. & Wareing, P. F. (1969). Experiments on the juvenile-adult phase change in some woody species. *New Phytol.*, **68**, 67–78.

Sax, K. (1962). Aspects of ageing in plants. *A. Rev. Pl. Physiol.*, **13**, 489–506.

Schopmeyer, C. S. (1974). *Seeds of woody plants in the United States.* (Agriculture Handbook no. 450). Washington DC: USDA Forest Service.

Seitz, F. W. von. (1958). Frühtreibversuche mit Blühreisern der Aspe. *Silvae Genet.*, **7**, 81–108.

Srivastava, P. B. L. (1977). Precocious flowering (paedogenesis) in Dipterocarpaceae. *Malays. For.*, **40**, 251–253.

Tomlinson, P. B. (1980). *The biology of trees native to tropical Florida.* Petersham: Harvard Forest.

Tompsett, P. B. (1978). Studies of growth and flowering in *Picea sitchensis* (Bong.) Carr. 2. Initiation and development of male, female and vegetative buds. *Ann. Bot.*, **42**, 889–900.

Wareing P. F. (1958). Reproductive development in *Pinus sylvestris*. In: *The physiology of forest trees*, edited by K. V. Thimann, 643–654. New York: Ronald Press.

Wareing, P. F. (1959). Problems of juvenility and flowering in trees. *J. Linn. Soc. Bot.*, **56**, 282–289.

Wycherley, P. R. (1973). The phenology of plants in the humid tropics. *Micronesica*, **9**, 75–96.

Zimmerman, R. H. (1972). Juvenility and flowering in woody plants: a review. *HortScience*, **7**, 447–455.

Zimmerman, R. H., ed. (1976). Symposium on juvenility in woody perennials. *Acta Hortic.*, **56**.

24

REPRODUCTIVE BEHAVIOUR OF FRUIT TREE CROPS AND ITS IMPLICATIONS FOR THE MANIPULATION OF FRUIT SET

G. BROWNING
East Malling Research Station, Maidstone, Kent, England

I. INTRODUCTION

Over the centuries, man has selected and learned how to cultivate a diverse range of fruit tree crop species – domestication having reached the most advanced stage in the temperate and subtropical zones. Most fruit trees are outbreeding, like the majority of timber tree species (Faulkner 1976) and other perennials (Linskens 1983). Many cultivars, chosen for their palatability, fruit size and fruitfulness, have been maintained by asexual propagation, in a manner analogous to inbreeding (Pickersgill & Heiser 1976). Having isolated (often from locally small and slow-moving gene pools) exceptional but highly heterozygous genotypes by vegetative propagation, there can presumably have been little incentive for man to sustain a long process of recurrent progeny selection. Even for the outbreeding seed-propagated fruit tree crops, and for the few inbreeding ones, genetic change will have been slow because of the long generation time and the small size of the tree populations. Therefore, fruit trees have not been subjected, like field crops (Evans 1976), to many generations of direct and indirect selection for morphological and physiological characteristics, often associated with high harvest indices. Nevertheless, the domestication of tree crops has been remarkably successful. The reasons for this success are to be found in the perennial habit of trees and the large size to which they grow. These features have enabled them to be manipulated (by pruning and other horticultural techniques), vegetatively propagated (thereby maintaining rare genotypes), and grafted on to rootstocks (to enhance fruiting, avoid root diseases, etc).

II. TREE FRUITING CHARACTERISTICS

Using horticultural techniques, it is possible to modify many of the natural characteristics possessed by dicotyledonous tree species, which are not desirable in trees grown for their fruits. The most crucial of these characteristics are large size, juvenility (Borchert 1976), irregularity in flower initiation (Monselise & Goldschmidt 1982) and the propensity to flower prolifically but set relatively few fruits because of flower sterility, embryo abortion and fruitlet abscission (Stephenson 1981).

The horticultural techniques developed to manipulate these undesirable characteristics fall into two categories; (a) those that reduce tree size and vigour, and (b) those that directly alter the components of fruit set. In tree crops, variation in fruit numbers, rather than in fruit weights, accounts for most of the variation in yield. Tree vigour and size are reduced by using dwarfing rootstocks, and tree size can be decreased by pruning – which is also used to select wood of differing cropping potential. The techniques used to manipulate fruit numbers directly are supplementary pollination, chemical fruit setting, and fruit thinning.

These various horticultural techniques exploit the fundamental relationships that exist between growth, flower initiation, fruit set and fruit retention – relationships that man has identified empirically through long horticultural experience, but which are incompletely understood. Central to these relationships is an apparent antagonism between vegetative growth and fruiting which is present both in tree species (Kramer & Kozlowski 1979; Spur & Barnes 1980) and in other higher plants (Harper 1977). Flower and fruit development is associated with a depression in cambial activity, shoot extension, leaf and root growth (Woolhouse 1983), consistent with an inhibition of cell division throughout the plant. The commitment by Angiosperms to sexual reproduction – to the generation and placental nurture of new genotypes – appears to impose a stimulus to vegetative senescence. The mother plant may not survive this stimulus, as in the monocarpic annuals and perennials, or it may survive only with difficulty, as in the polycarpic perennials (Molisch 1938). *Coffea arabica*, an inbreeder, sets such an unusually high proportion of its flowers (Leliveld 1938) that many of its youngest shoots become senescent and 'die-back' when the tree crops heavily. Developing fruits appear also to impose this constraint on each other, revealed in fruit trees by the inverse relationship between fruit number and fruit size (Childers 1978) – for which differences in fruit cell number are largely responsible (eg Quinlan & Preston 1968). Developing fruits also affect concurrent floral initiation (Monselise & Goldschmidt 1982) and fruit setting (Stephenson 1981). There is, therefore, an in-built tendency for trees to crop irregularly, stemming from variation in vegetative growth, in flower initiation and in fruit set.

Irregular fruiting in tree crops is further accentuated because of the factors that favour synchronized blossoming. Tree fruits develop over a period of several months. In temperate regions, the development of flowers, which are initiated the previous year, is synchronized by the mechanism of winter dormancy, and climatic conditions permit only one episode of fruiting each year. In tropical conditions, synchronous flowering may be necessary in many tree species to increase the chances of cross-pollination (Opler *et al.* 1976; Browning 1977), and to escape seed predation (Janzen 1971). Physiological mechanisms which serve to synchronize blossoming have been described in *Coffea arabica* (Browning 1977) and *Theobroma cacao* (Alvim 1977). The strong selective pressures favouring synchronous blossoming probably have been reinforced by the existence of mutual competition between flowers at fertilization. Those flowers that are fertilized first appear to exert an inhibitory influence on the fertilization and set of those pollinated later (see Stephenson 1981); consequently, most fruits will probably be produced when all flowers are receptive to fertilization at the same time. Indeed, in selecting for fruitfulness, man might have inadvertently selected for synchronized blossoming and synchronized timing of flower fertility.

The apparent antagonism between vegetative growth and fruiting in fruit trees is expressed in two other ways that are important for horticultural practice. First, actively growing shoot meristems are able to precipitate fruitlet abscission. Thus, the number of fruits that are retained to harvest is increased when shoot tips are removed during the early stages of fruit development, in both pome (eg Quinlan & Preston 1971) and stone fruits (eg Webster & Shepherd 1984), and vegetatively vigorous trees are less likely to retain heavy crops than less vigorous ones (Childers 1978). Second, there is an apparent antagonism between vegetative growth and flower initiation (Jackson & Sweet 1972) displayed in both juvenile and mature trees.

The view is taken here that these antagonisms between vegetative growth and fruiting have two causes. First, they arise from physiological constraints that are fundamental to the manner in which plant growth and development is regulated. In particular, they stem from the way in which vegetative and reproductive meristems compete as sinks, attracting assimilates and other growth factors to themselves at each other's expense (Sachs & Hackett 1969). Second, they reflect physiological and morphological attributes that are more directly linked to the tree habit. In particular, there apparently exists a set of physiological conditions which are necessary for flowering, that are normally met only when the tree (a) has completed an initial 'juvenile' phase of vegetative growth, and (b) then maintains a temporal or physical separation between vegetative and floral meristematic activity. The conditions for floral initiation are such that, as the tree increases in size, the number of meristems suitably placed to become floral greatly increases, and often potentially exceeds the number of fruits the tree can support. Profuse flower production is interpreted here as a direct consequence both of the large size and structural complexity of trees, and of their reproductive strategy. Following the induction of large numbers of flowers, there starts a process of differential flower and fruit survival, exercised through the 'serial sieves'[1] of floral determination, gametogenesis, fertilization, embryo and fruit development. Through this process of 'attrition', there is a progressive reduction in the reproductive burden the tree must bear.

---

[1] The terms 'serial sieve' or 'serial adjustment' are used to mean the cumulative effects, on the numbers of reproductive structures (flowers, cones, fruits) that develop to maturity, of passage through successive critical stages of development. At these stages, the reproductive structures may fail to develop successfully if they do not undergo cytogenetic events or secure resources for their development and growth.

While fruit and seed development is in progress, flower initiation is inhibited by an influence emanating from the seeds. This mechanism interposes a period when fruiting is absent, or is much reduced, accentuating irregular cropping, and enabling the vegetative structure of the tree to recover from the effects of fruiting. For plants embarked on a life strategy (Cole 1954) in which fitness is maximized over a long lifespan, it can be shown that a premium is placed, in constant environments, on mechanisms which favour an absolute temporal separation between growth and reproduction (Cohen 1971). In the variable environments in which trees grow, this separation will not be absolute, but, for efficient resource allocation, there will still be a premium on a negative correlation between vegetative growth and fruiting (Wolgast & Zeide 1983).

III. VEGETATIVE GROWTH CONSTRAINTS

In many respects, trees behave like quasi-colonial structures, consisting of a proliferating population of shoot meristems. Each meristem is potentially an autonomous entity, which has created locally the assimilatory surface, vascular supply and support it needs, and has exploited the reiterated structures established by earlier meristematic activity. Thus regarded, the cambium is a functional extension of each individual shoot meristem, anastomosed throughout the structure of the tree by the system of meristem descent, and driven by the combined activity of the meristems, so that the increment in trunk girth remains closely related to vegetative growth in other parts of the tree (Moore 1978; Causton, this volume). During the early stages of seedling establishment, strong apical dominance exerted by the leading shoot concentrates growth in the vertical direction, enabling the tree to gain dominion over biological space (Ross & Harper 1972). In trees, this upward growth can continue, building up, as lateral buds escape apical dominance, structures of great size and complexity. The differentiation of dead, woody tissues confers long-lived mechanical support for this raised and much expanded structure at minimal respiratory cost (Schulze 1982). The supporting tissues and the cambium are defended from predation and disease by the activity of the phellogen, which also isolates many dormant axillary meristems from the main arteries of vascular supply. Chronological age, size and complexity are thus inextricably linked. As the tree grows, meristems become progressively more dispersed to locations differing in conditions of light, exposure and gravitational orientation, and differing in proximity to the currently active centres of growth and correlative influence (Borchert 1976). Also, with increase in tree size, there is a geometric increase in the mass of tissues intervening between the roots and those shoots that are favourably placed for light interception (Wilson 1970). These distal, well-illuminated shoots must obtain water and nutrients from the roots across distances, despite the withdrawal of these factors by intervening tissues. Presumably, some relief is afforded from these difficulties by apical dominance, especially as an increasing fraction of axillary buds is held quiescent with increase in tree size. But eventually, the respiratory burden of the accumulated tissues approaches the capacity of the light-favoured foliage to supply assimilates (Schulze 1982).

Therefore, it is not surprising that trees generally lose vigour as they age (Wareing 1959), or that it is the shoots nearest to the roots which have the greatest potential for vigour (Maggs 1964; Kaini *et al.* 1984).

Nevertheless, in fruit trees, the proportion of the total annual vegetative growth (roots, stems and foliage) represented by the stems is maintained within narrow limits over a wide range of total growth – growth adjustments occurring principally between the leaves and roots (Avery *et al.* 1979); that is, the shoot meristems act as priority sinks. How this sink priority is achieved remains uncertain (Nooden 1980), but it may result from differential utilization of substrates, directional flow of materials under hormonal control (Seth & Wareing 1967), and differences in the degree of vascularization (Sachs 1975). It might be especially important in trees that vascularization is stimulated as the activity of individual meristems is increased, thereby exercising a 'positive feedback' on sink activity (Jacobs & Morrow 1957). Patterns of vascularization may therefore reflect earlier heterogeneities in growth and supply. Consequently, individual meristems will be differentially advantaged depending on their location and history and, once florally determined, they will be subjected differentially to the influence of other centres of meristematic activity.

These considerations suggest that, in trees, a considerable premium might be placed on vegetative vigour, both to offset the 'physiological burdens' of the woody habit described above, and to confer a competitive advantage during establishment and early growth. Woody plants are generally highly heterozygous (Hamrick 1979), which may confer vigour, and also enable trees to tolerate temporal fluctuations in environmental conditions (Lerner 1954). Polyploidy is thought to be of value in plants because it increases heterozygosity (Bingham 1980), and polyploidy is common among broadleaved tree species (Gustafson & Mergen 1963). The heterozygosity of woody plants, and other long-lived perennials, may be conserved by the fact that these plants take longer than annuals to develop reproductive barriers which isolate subpopulations and lead to ecotypic differentiation (Stebbins 1950; Grant 1971). Also, it seems reasonable to infer that the longevity of trees will increase the risk of disease, which could destroy part of the gene pool, placing a further premium on outbreeding.

IV. REPRODUCTIVE CONSTRAINTS

In order to maintain the needed balance between reproductive and vegetative sinks, mechanisms are required to constrain flower initiation and development. When considering the evidence of how, in fruit trees, this control of flowering is achieved, it is difficult not to impute an important role for the plant hormones. Thus, plant hormones appear to be involved, not only in helping to confer sink strength, but also in preventing, or later aborting, the development of sinks – sinks that are unlikely to develop successfully, yet are still able to impair the continued activity of better established sinks. By preempting or curtailing resource expenditure on unfavourably placed or 'weak' sinks, such mechanisms will increase the functional economy of organogenesis generally, and reinforce the priority of established sinks. These hormonal influences exerted over sink numbers appear to emanate from, and to be entrained to, the activity of existing sinks. The effect, in fruit trees, is to inhibit flower initiation and development within the immediate vicinity of active sinks. Thus, a spatial distancing is imposed between meristems, or a temporal phasing is introduced in the distribution of activity between different types of sink – as occurs when a meristem declines in activity, allowing new meristematic activity within its vicinity.

'Spatial distancing' and 'temporal phasing' would be the roles imputed for auxin in the imposition of apical dominance (Wareing 1977), which, in fruit trees, is a crucial factor in the control of flower initiation. In apple and pear trees, flower buds are initiated from preformed vegetative buds which have accumulated the requisite numbers of leaf primordia (see Buban & Faust 1982). Only when axillary buds are some distance from the centres of apical dominance, or when shoot growth has ceased, will sufficient axillary bud meristematic activity be allowed for floral development to begin. The inhibitory effect of auxin emanating from active apical meristems may, in fruit trees, be reinforced by other hormones, such as gibberellins exported by the shoot tips. Thus, applications of exogenous gibberellins inhibit flower initiation in many fruit trees (Monselise & Goldschmidt 1982), and shoot tips are known to have high gibberellin concentrations (Lang 1965). The latter fact may be the reason why terminal shoot meristems develop flower buds only when extension growth has ceased (see Buban & Faust 1982). Gibberellin, exported by the developing seeds, has also been implicated in the inhibition of flower initiation, which in fruit trees occurs within the vicinity of developing fruits (see Buban & Faust 1982). This local inhibitory influence of the developing seeds has the effect of spatially distancing concurrent flower initiation and fruit development. It also ensures that a period of vegetative recovery, free from fruit competition, can occur immediately after the period of fruit development. In tree species which blossom mainly at the periphery of the canopy, these mechanisms will ensure that, by temporarily separating the phases of growth and fruiting, the two forms of development do not compete simultaneously for the same light-favoured space.

Initials embarked on floral development will continue to be subject to these correlative influences, to the detriment of their later fertility, as rates of shoot growth change and axillary shoots emerge from apical dominance. Flower bud development is affected also by other factors. In temperate regions, flowers initiated late in the season often enter winter dormancy in an immature state, so that their later fertility is uncertain (Luckwill 1974). The gravitational orientation of the immature flower buds is another factor which appears to modify their later fertility (de Maeyer & Deckers 1984). Clearly, of the many flower buds which are initiated during the season, only a proportion achieve full fertility as flowers, a phenomenon expressed horticulturally in the notion of 'flower quality'. Consistent cropping on one-year-old wood is characteristically a feature of the inbreeding, less vegetatively vigorous, fruit tree cultivars and species, such as peach, apricot, and sour cherry. Pear flowers often are present on one-year-old wood, but are unable to set fruit, presumably because of their proximity to the correlative influences emanating from the terminal shoot meristems during flower bud development.

The importance of temporal and spatial separation of vegetative growth and fruiting is revealed in the strategy of fruiting on spurs and short shoots. If, because of stress, or its position on the tree, a shoot loses vigour and apical dominance, a number of its meristems, including most crucially the apical meristem, can become florally determined simultaneously. The loss of centres of apical dominance, and the inhibitory effect of fruiting on further shoot growth, alters the balance of sink activity within the shoot towards continued fruiting. In Rosaceous species particularly, the result is often the development of fruiting spurs and short shoots of intermediate length. Rosaceous spurs are characteristically developed on one-year-old wood, from axillary shoots that are released from apical dominance the year before, but which apparently are unable to undertake rapid extension growth. Instead, floral initiation occurs, the shoots become spurs, and they blossom on the 2-year-old wood. Spur systems are built up by the further tessellation of internodes, which increases vascular supplies to the fruits, and shortens the distance between the fruits and adjacent vegetative buds. Because of this short distance, the developing seeds more effectively inhibit floral initiation of the adjacent axillary ('bourse') buds (Luckwill 1974) and biennial (or alternate) bearing ensues.

On such spur-bearing trees, a primary aim of flower or fruit thinning, and of pruning is to maintain a balance of fruiting and non-fruiting spurs (Jonkers 1979). Also, by decreasing the size of the trees, the fruits are kept in close proximity to a large number of assimilate-supplying leaves. This proximity is important because the rates of phloem translocation needed to maintain the growth of reproductive sinks can occur over only very short distances (Canny 1973). For example, the growth of pome, stone and citrus fruits has been found to depend principally on current photosynthesis (Hansen 1977), by leaves borne on the branches subtending them[2] (Magness 1929; Weinberger & Cullinan 1932; Erickson & Brannaman 1960). Thus, fruiting spurs behave with remarkable functional autonomy, and depend crucially for fruit set (Ferree & Palmer 1982) and flower initiation (Hoad 1979) on their spur leaves. Also, flowers begin to initiate on spurs earlier in the season than on elongated shoots, and are therefore more likely to set fruit (see Buban & Faust 1982). A further advantage of the spur habit might be that it allows light to penetrate further into the tree canopy, and so aids the success of cropping on old wood, away from the distal regions of active shoot growth. An extreme expression of this trend is cauliferous (stem) flowering, found on *Theobroma cacao*, *Artocarpus atilis*, and *Durio zibethinus*.

V. REPRODUCTIVE STRATEGY

Photosynthesis can occur deep in the canopy of fruit trees (Avery 1975), and may not constrain flowering and fruiting, but, as the above discussion indicates, more *local* constraints, in different parts of the tree, are of paramount importance. Flowers initiated at different times, and at different positions in

---

[2] A parallel exists here between the spur habit of fruit trees, and the reduction in the physical separation between reproductive sinks and assimilate sources thought to have been achieved during the unconscious selection of field crops (Evans 1976).

the tree, will be subjected to markedly different conditions of exposure, metabolite supply and correlative influence, and will therefore differ greatly in fertility. For example, shading in apple trees reduces not only flower initiation but also the fertility of the flowers that develop (Jackson & Palmer 1977). By contrast, summer applications of nitrogen to apple can greatly increase the proportion of fertile blossoms the next year (Williams 1965), indicating that some floral initials within the tree are normally starved of nitrogen. Within-tree differences continue to be important at blossoming, and during fruit and seed development, and act on systems already differentially advantaged by their previous history. Hence, many of the floral initials which reach the flowering stage fail to set fruits, even when pollinated, and, of those which are set, a further fraction is lost in successive waves of fruit drop (Stephenson 1981).

A particular question of interest is why trees invest resources in innumerable floral initials that never successfully yield offspring, rather than reduce the competitive load by confining initiation more strictly to regions of the tree where success is more certain. The hormonal or other factors which seem to prevent flower initiation (in the regions where shoots are growing actively, or which are close to developing seeds) may prevent unwanted competition between sinks by physically or temporally distancing them. But, in addition, trees have apparently exploited the strategy of further regulating sink numbers after initiation: they develop more sinks than current resources can support and then allow them to compete. Such a strategy would provide for the 'serial adjustment' of sink numbers with changes in metabolite supply – a particularly important attribute in a perennial – thereby maximizing the number of sinks successfully developed, despite the unpredictable nature of future conditions (Lloyd 1980a). The 'serial adjustment' of reproductive sinks against future uncertainties will be of particular value in deciduous trees, because fruit development occurs in the year after floral initiation, and, on deciduous trees, leaf amounts and durations may be very different in successive years (Harper 1977). Clearly, resources are wasted on those sinks which fail to compete, and hormonal mechanisms may reduce this wastage by accelerating the abortion of failing sinks. These hormonal mechanisms could either be activated from within the sink itself (they could, for example, be entrained to the rate of sink growth) or they could emanate from, and be entrained to, other sinks. The view is widely held that fruitlet abscission is induced by a reduction in auxin export from the fruitlet when its growth rate declines because of competition (Addicott 1982), although unequivocal evidence for such a role of auxin is lacking. There is, as yet, little substantive evidence that an exported senescence factor or inhibitor is important (Woolhouse 1983). A major theoretical benefit of the strategy of 'serial adjustment' in sink numbers is that it should favour the persistence of sinks at positions where resources for later development are most likely to be available – a particularly valuable attribute during the phase of flower initiation in trees. Another theoretical advantage of 'serial adjustment' is the selection of sinks with a high intrinsic competitive ability, if variation in competitive ability exists (Janzen 1977).

The tree habit might conceivably be associated with enhanced dependence on regulating the 'quality', in addition to the number, of offspring. The quality of offspring can be increased by aborting weak or poor embryos. Embryo abortion is a useful life history tactic if (a) the smaller number of seeds remaining after abortion have a higher probability of succeeding, and hence of transmitting parental genes, than the total number of seeds initiated, and/or (b) abortion increases the probability that the maternal parent will reproduce in the future (Stearns 1976). In trees, embryo abortion would satisfy both requirements.

The woody perennial life strategy of competing for biological space over long periods of time is thought to confer advantages in crowded, resource-limited stable habitats. But, in those habitats, establishment is difficult (Harper et al. 1970). Consequently, some tree species in the later stages of succession (ie not pioneer species) produce large seeds (Salisbury 1942) which are dispersed in small numbers by animals (Harper 1961), requiring investment in specialized fruit tissues (Coombe 1976). Fruit tissue development possibly represents the culminating expression of what could be the fundamental reproductive strategy of trees. If it is granted that, in plants, the benefits of sexual recombination exceed the costs (Lloyd 1980b), then the tree habit can be interpreted as a strategy which reduces the numbers of recombinant progeny dispersed in favour of increased individual longevity. The opposite strategy, of dispersing as many seeds as possible in the shortest possible time, is one which is favoured in unstable environments (Woolhouse 1974). In trees, the balance of effort is shifted away from sexual reproduction, towards increased individual longevity, secured through the continuation of vegetative growth (Harper 1961). Through the mechanism of embryo abortion there remain, however, opportunities *before dispersal* for recombinant progeny to survive differentially, which might partially substitute for post-dispersal selection. The selection pressure which operates is competition between the embryos and other sinks.

As the 'serial adjustment' of the less competitively successful seeds proceeds, so the competitive pressure on those remaining presumably decreases, making more resources available, and decreasing the chances that resources will be wasted. Thus, for example, in both stone and pome fruits – which have essentially similar patterns of development (Tukey 1936) – embryo abortion and fruitlet abscission precede the major phase of dry matter accumulation by the fruit and seed tissues (Nitsch 1971). Such temporal demarcation, between the phases when competition is most intense (when abortion and abscission occur) and the phases when an absolute commitment is made to the fruiting load, is made possible by the prolific initial production of sinks. Because of the importance of competition between sinks at an early stage of fruiting, and because the endosperms and embryos (initially minute tissue systems) must establish themselves as sinks, they must presumably exert an inordinately powerful 'specific sink strength'. Accordingly, it is in flowers and fruitlets immediately after.fertilization that the highest concentrations of hormones are found (Goodwin 1978), and it is at the flowering and fruitlet stages that the inhibitory influence of reproductive sinks on vegetative growth is greatest – a compound function of sink number and strength.

In all except the most inbred species, an important force driving competition between embryos will be their genetic differences, one component of which could be hybrid vigour. Desirable nonadditive genetic variance (conferring hybrid vigour) appears to occur in a minority of successful offspring, as evidenced by skewed progeny distributions away from parental means towards low yields (eg Spangelo *et al.* 1971). Presumably, hybrid vigour is possessed by an even smaller proportion of the *total* progeny, including those which fail to survive seed development. If vigour during embryo development is a determinant of sink strength, competition will favour the maturation of large seeds possessing high intrinsic seedling vigour.

Clonal selection of fruit trees stabilizes both additive and nonadditive genetic variances, and fixes varietal differences in genetically determined fertility and susceptibility to embryo abortion. Markedly uneven rates of embryo and endosperm development have been detected in different ovules within the same fruit (Veh 1933; Murneek 1954), especially in varieties possessing some degree of self-fertility (Bryant 1935; Murneek 1954). Accordingly, fruit set in some highly heterozygous varieties might be poor, not only because they possess vigorous shoot growth, but also because they produce embryos which vary greatly in vigour, with many inherently unvigorous embryos. Sterility, and premature degeneration of the female gametophyte are common characteristics of many of the important pome fruit varieties, and are associated with a high frequency of embryo abortion (Dorsey 1930; Howlett 1938; Williams 1970). Such cultivars respond least well to chemical fruit setting agents, both in pome (Dennis 1977) and citrus (Krezdorn 1969) fruits.

In compound fruits, like those in the *Pomoideae*, which are formed from five drupe-like structures enclosed in a fleshy torus of receptacular tissue (Tukey 1936), a further hierarchy is introduced of competitive trade-offs operating through 'serial adjustment' of sinks. The multiple ovules in a compound fruit, and their enclosing fruit tissues, occupy the same advantaged or disadvantaged position on the tree. But not all the ovules in a flower will survive gametogenesis (Sarvas 1968), nor will all fertile embryo sacs be pollinated and successfully fertilized. Because only a small proportion of the ovules in a flower need to be fertilized for fruit development to begin (Tydeman 1944), differences will be established at the outset, between different fruits, in the numbers of embryos they contain. Little information exists concerning competition between embryos within a fruit, nor is it clear what the precise sink effects are of the nucellus or endosperm, but what appears to matter is the combined sink strength of the seeds acting together. Thus, the fruits behave as unitary sinks, and (to a degree, depending on the vigour of the tree, the overall conditions of stress (Zucconi 1981), metabolite supply, and the numbers and seed status of other fruits) fruits set with initially few seeds will abscise with a higher frequency than those set initially with a large number (see Addicott 1982). Later seed loss, through endosperm and embryo abortion, further contributes to the 'serial adjustment' in fruit numbers. Consequently, in most cultivars, it is the fruits with the greatest numbers of fully developed seeds which mature (Ewert 1906; Brittain & Eidt 1933), so maximizing the numbers of seeds dispersed per unit of investment in fruit tissue. The physical proximity of fruits set within the same inflorescence appears to intensify competition between them, but with the fruitlet cluster as a whole behaving as a single sink – of greatest potency perhaps when borne on a spur. Concentrated within the close confines of a fruiting spur, auxin export from the seeds might be a particularly effective stimulus to further local vascularization (Bruinsma 1974).

Using vegetative propagation, man has succeeded in domesticating many cultivars of fruit trees, in particular of citrus, pear and fig, which are to various degrees parthenocarpic – that is, able to set fruits without fertilization, or to complete fruit development despite early seed abortion (Gustafson 1942). In such varieties, there will be no need for cross-pollination and no seeds to exert a competitive effect between fruits and on flower initiation. It is implicit in the ability of parthenocarpic fruits to grow independently of seed-set or development either that they have, for genetic reasons, an enhanced capacity to function as sinks, or that this function is suppressed when seeds are present.

In many fruits, well-marked correlations exist between seed number and final fruit size, and also between the distribution of seeds and the shape of the fruit (Luckwill 1958), and, particularly in parthenocarpic fruits, external applications of hormones increase fruit size (see Goodwin 1978). It has been inferred from these observations that the growth of parthenocarpic fruits reflects an increased capacity for hormone synthesis (Nitsch 1971), but this fact has never been unequivocally demonstrated. In many plants (Gustafson 1942), including fruit tree varieties that are not usually parthenocarpic (eg Goldwin & Schwabe 1975), a small proportion of flowers can be induced to set parthenocarpically by preventing pollination – a response which can also be induced simply by reducing the numbers of flowers (Gustafson 1942). Reduced competition for nutrients and assimilates might be sufficient to stimulate hormone production in a number of flowers. Where mixed populations of parthenocarpic and seeded fruits are present on the same tree, the parthenocarpic ones are more likely to abscise (Ewert 1906), presumably because of the competitive sink effect exerted on them by the seeded fruits (Goldwin & Schwabe 1975). Such a sink effect could, for example, be achieved either by the direction of assimilate and nutrient supplies towards the seeded fruits (Crane 1964), or by the direct suppression of growth in the parthenocarpic fruits by factors emanating from the seeded ones. Decapitated pear flowers that are set parthenocarpically using sprays of gibberellic acid are more likely to be retained to fruit harvest, although many fruits will be small, than normally pollinated flowers given similar sprays (Andrews et al. 1983). This observation suggests that seeds might directly suppress the hormonal capacity of the fruit tissues to prevent pedicel abscission. The production of naturally parthenocarpic fruits in commercial quantities generally requires the initial stimulus of pollination, presumably to stimulate hormone production from the fruit tissues.

There are reasons, also, for suspecting that there is 'parthenocarpic vigour' in the unusually common triploid cultivars of apple and pear (Knight 1963). The exceptional vigour of these cultivars, and of triploid citrus genotypes, has been attributed to increased heterozygosity (Layne & Quamme 1975; Geraci et al. 1975). Triploid vigour is reflected in the production of large fruits and, in the case of the triploid citrus genotypes, in seedlessness. Among apple cultivars grown in England it is the triploid varieties Crispin and Bramley's Seedling which are the most responsive to hormone-induced fruit setting (Modlibowska 1972). The possible relationship, in triploids, between parthenocarpic vigour and fruit size raises the interesting question of whether, by selecting for fruit size, man has inadvertently selected for an increased tendency for parthenocarpy.

VI. IMPLICATIONS FOR THE MANIPULATION OF FRUIT SET

This chapter has sought to identify attributes of the tree habit important for the manipulation of fruit set and the cropping load in fruit trees. Many of the factors which may have influenced tree fruiting strategy can be seen as stemming from the colonial nature of tree structure and development. The long-lived, complex structures that are assembled create a 'physiological habitat' in which individual meristems, both vegetative and reproductive, must compete. The meristems exist in varying conditions of metabolite supply, exposure to light and gravitational orientation, and their growth and development are ordered through the reiterated, correlative (putatively hormonal: Wareing 1977), influences that meristems exert on each other. Crucially important is the need to balance competition between the respectively indeterminate and determinate growth of vegetative and reproductive meristems. This balance is necessary if the tree is to continue to build up its vegetative structure. Equally, the commitment made to vegetative longevity places a heavy evolutionary dependence on being able to maximize the number and quality of offspring which can be dispersed. And these offspring must be produced despite the existence of large within-tree heterogeneities in the potential for successful reproductive development.

This balance in commitment between vegetative growth and fruiting appears to be achieved in three ways, in all of which the horticulturist must intervene. First, competition between active vegetative meristems and reproductive sinks seems to be minimized by physically distancing them – achieved primarily by the mechanism of apical dominance and by concentrating the fruiting points on spurs and short shoots. Second, flower initiation is inhibited within the vicinity of developing fruits, thereby (a) accentuating the temporal alternation between fruiting and vegetative growth that is intrinsic to the polycarpic perennial habit, and (b) giving a period of vegetative 'recovery', when vegetative growth is less impeded by the demands of fruit growth. Third, reproductive sinks are opportunistically initiated, wherever conditions allow, and in numbers which greatly exceed the likely supply of resources for their development, enabling a process of 'serial adjustment' in numbers to proceed, based (a) on heterogeneities in the location of the reproductive sinks, and (b) on the genetic variation exposed as a result of gametogenesis and sexual recombination. In this way, the maximum numbers of fully matured seeds are produced according to the resources available, and some control is exerted over the quality of offspring dispersed. These tactics will clearly be most efficient if physiological mechanisms exist to amplify sink competitive ability.

Given such behaviour, the most fundamental step the horticulturist can take to improve fruit set is to reduce vegetative vigour. He will then decrease vegetative competition and apical dominance, decrease the size of the tree, and provide for the establishment of a structure much reduced in heterogeneities and constraints in metabolite supply. In particular, all areas of fruiting will be nearer to the light-favoured periphery of the structure, and nearer to the root system, and a large proportion of the total volume of the tree will be well illuminated. The tree will accumulate less woody tissues, vegetative recovery after pruning will be decreased, and the exploitation of gravimorphic responses, which alter apical dominance (Wareing & Nasr 1961), will be made easier. The overall effect will be to increase the production of flowers per unit tree size, and for the flowers to develop in better local conditions of illumination and metabolite supply.

In the outbreeding tree crops, a conflict is created between the need to partition resources towards fruiting and the need to retain the hybrid vigour required for flower fertility and fruit size. By contrast, fertility of the naturally inbreeding tree crops, such as peach, appears to be unaffected by inbreeding depression. These tree crops set a much higher proportion of their flowers than the outbreeding ones, presumably because, being more homozygous, there is less possibility of genetic segregation disrupting fruit set and seed development. Self-fertility is also common among many citrus cultivars, tolerated perhaps because of the genetic factors which tend to make them parthenocarpic (Goldschmidt & Monselise 1978). Rootstocks are often, for clonally propagated tree crops, an indispensable adjunct to vegetative propagation, and dwarfing rootstocks have been used to control vegetative vigour in the most successfully domesticated fruit crops. Dwarfing rootstocks restrict the size of the scions, but preserve their heterozygosity; hence the fertility, and ability of outbreeding scions to produce large fruits, is retained. Also, many dwarfing rootstocks possess inherently small root systems and divert less assimilate from fruiting to root growth. Reduced root function is offset by cultivation, irrigation and fertilizer application. The grafting of budwood from mature fruiting trees on to rootstocks also confers, on the grafted tree, greater precocity in flower production and fruit set.

The theoretical advantages of using chemical growth retardants are that (a) they reduce the need for pruning, which stimulates growth at the expense of fruitfulness, and (b) they can temporarily reduce shoot vigour at times favourable for flower initiation and fruit set. Whether growth retardants will enable less dwarfing rootstocks to be used remains to be seen. The main disadvantages of growth retardants appear to be that (a) when they are applied in overall sprays, they can disrupt developmental processes within floral initials, flowers and fruits, and (b) they can alter the functional root/shoot balance towards shoot growth. Also, as with other types of plant growth regulators, their effects are difficult to control with precision under the variable conditions of climate and tree management.

Chemical fruit-setting agents have, so far, worked most successfully on cultivars possessing some degree of parthenocarpy, or which are triploid. The major disadvantages of such agents are that (a) in some cultivars, they cannot overcome inherent infertility in the flower tissues and in the female gametophyte, and (b) by setting an initially large proportion of flowers, competition is increased, and fruitlet abscission arising from differences in seed number is intensified, especially when there is also chemically induced seed abortion.

Perhaps the most effective use of chemical agents has been for flower and fruitlet thinning, to reduce the competitive effect of the cropping load on fruit size and concurrent flower initiation. However, it has been difficult to find chemicals that will discriminate between flowers and fruits that differ in potential for set and fruit growth – particularly as those differences vary unpredictably with season and management.

Clearly, it is in the direction of an improved understanding of the fundamental processes by which sink number and quality are regulated in trees, that the greatest potential for future progress in the manipulation of fruit set and the cropping load will be found.

REFERENCES

Addicott, F. T. (1982). *Abscission*. Berkeley, CA: University of California Press.
Andrews, P. R., Browning, G. & Hedden, P. (1983). Fruit set in Doyenne du Comice and Conference pear. *Rep. E. Malling Res. Stn 1983*, 34–35.
Alvim, P. de T. (1977). Cacao. In: *Ecophysiology of tropical crops*, edited by P. de T. Alvim and T. T. Kozlowski, 279–313. London: Academic Press.
Avery, D. J. (1975). Effects of climatic factors on the photosynthetic efficiency of apple leaves. In: *Climate and the orchard*, edited by H. C. Pereira, 25–31. Farnham Royal: Commonwealth Agricultural Bureaux.
Avery, D. J., Priestley, C. A. & Treharne, K. J. (1979). Integration of assimilation and carbohydrate utilization in apple. In: *Photosynthesis and plant development*, edited by R. Marcelle, H. Ceijsters and M. van Poncke, 221–231. The Hague: Junk.
Bingham, F. T. (1980). Maximizing heterozygosity in autopolyploids. In: *Polyploidy – biological relevance*, edited by W. H. Lewis, 471–490. New York: Plenum.
Borchert, R. (1976). The concept of juvenility in woody plants. *Acta Hortic.*, **56**, 21–36.
Brittain, W. H. & Eidt, C. C. (1933). Seed content, seedling production and fruitfulness in apples. *Can. J. Res.*, **9**, 307–334.
Browning, G. (1977). Environmental control of flower-bud development in *Coffea arabica* L. In: *Environmental effects on crop physiology*, edited by J. J. Landsberg and C. V. Cutting, 321–331. London: Academic Press.
Bruinsma, J. (1974). Hormonal aspects of fruit production. *Acta Hortic.*, **34**, 23–32.
Bryant, L. R. (1935). A study of the factors affecting the development of the embryo sac and the embryo in McIntosh apples. *Tech. Bull. New Hamps. agric. Exp. Stn*, no. 61.
Buban, T. & Faust, R. (1982). Flower induction in apple trees: internal control and differentiation. *Hortic. Rev.*, **4**, 174–203.
Canny, M. J. (1973). *Phloem translocation*. Cambridge: Cambridge University Press.
Childers, N. F. (1978). *Modern fruit science*. (Horticulture publications). New Brunswick, NJ: Rutgers University.
Cohen, D. (1971). Maximizing final yield when growth is limited by time or limiting resources. *J. theor. biol.*, **33**, 299–307.
Cole, L. C. (1954). The population consequences of life history phenomena. *Q. Rev. Biol.*, **29**, 103–137.
Coombe, B. G. (1976). The development of fleshy fruits. *A. Rev. Pl. Physiol.*, **27**, 207–228.
Crane, J. C. (1964). Growth substances in fruit setting and development. *A. Rev. Pl. Physiol.*, **15**, 303–326.
Dennis, F. G. (1977). Physiological control of fruit set and development with growth regulators. *Acta Hortic.*, **34**, 251–260.
Dorsey, M. J. (1930). The relation between embryo sac development and the set of fruit in the apple. *Proc. Am. Soc. hort. Sci.*, **26**, 56–61.
Erickson, L. C. & Brannaman, O. (1960). Abscission of reproductive structures and leaves of orange trees. *Proc. Am. Soc. hort. Sci.*, **75**, 222–229.

Evans, L. T. (1976). Physiological adaptation to performance as crop plants. *Phil. Trans. R. Soc.*, **275B**, 71–83.

Ewert, R. (1906). Die Parthenokarpie der Obstbäume. *Ber. dt. bot. Ges.*, **24**, 414–416.

Faulkner, R. (1976). Timber trees. In: *Evolution of crop plants*, edited by N. W. Simmonds, 298–301. Harlow: Longman.

Ferree, D. C. & Palmer, J. W. (1982). Effect of spur defoliation and ringing during bloom on fruiting, fruit mineral level and net photosynthesis of 'Golden Delicious' apple. *J. Am. Soc. hort. Sci.*, **107**, 1182–1186.

Geraci, G., Esen, A. & Soost, R. K. (1975). Triploid progenies from 2x × 2x crosses of citrus cultivars. *J. Hered.*, **66**, 177–178.

Goldschmidt, E. E. & Monselise, S. P. (1978). Physiological assumptions toward the development of a citrus fruiting model. *Proc. int. Soc. Citriculture, 1977*, **2**, 668–672.

Goldwin, G. K. & Schwabe, W. W. (1975). Parthenocarpic fruit in Cox's Orange Pippin apples obtained without hormones. *J. hort. Sci.*, **50**, 175–178.

Goodwin, P. B. (1978). Phytohormones and fruit growth. In: *Phytohormones and related compounds – a comprehensive treatise*, vol. 2, edited by D. S. Letham, P. B. Goodwin and R. Higgins, 175–214. Amsterdam: Elsevier/North Holland Biomedical Press.

Grant, V. (1971). *Plant speciation*. New York: Columbia University Press.

Gustafson, F. G. (1942). Parthenocarpy: natural and artificial. *Bot. Rev.*, **8**, 599–654.

Gustafson, A. & Mergen, F. (1963). Some principles of tree cytology and genetics. *Unasylva*, **24**, 1–132.

Hamrick, J. L. (1979). Genetic variation and longevity. In: *Topics in plant population biology*, edited by O. T. Solbrig, S. Jain, G. B. Johnson and P. H. Raven, 84–113. New York: Columbia University Press.

Hansen, P. (1977). Carbohydrate allocation. In: *Environmental effects on crop physiology*, edited by J. J. Landsberg and C. V. Cutting, 247–255. London: Academic Press.

Harper, J. L. (1961). Approaches to the study of competition. *Symp. Soc. exp. Biol.*, **15**, 1–39.

Harper, J. L. (1977). *Population biology of plants*. London: Academic Press.

Harper, J. L., Lovell, H. G. & Moore, K. G. (1970). The shapes and sizes of seeds. *Annu. Rev. Ecol. Syst.*, **1**, 327–356.

Hoad, G. V. (1979). Growth regulators, endogenous hormones and flower initiation in apple. *Rep. Long Ashton Res. Stn*, 199–206.

Howlett, F. S. (1938). Factors affecting the rate and course of development of the female gametophyte in apple varieties. *Proc. Am. Soc. hort. Sci.*, **35**, 105–110.

Jackson, J. E. & Palmer, J. W. (1977). Effects of shade on the growth and cropping of apple trees. III. Effects on the components of yield. *J. hort. Sci.*, **52**, 253–266.

Jackson, D. I. & Sweet, G. B. (1972). Flower initiation in temperate woody plants. *Hort. Abstr.*, **42**, 9–24.

Jacobs, W. P. & Morrow, I. B. (1957). A quantitative study of xylem development in the vegetative shoot apex of *Coleus*. *Am. J. Bot.*, **44**, 823–842.

Janzen, D. H. (1971). Seed predation by animals. *Annu. Rev. Ecol. Syst.*, **2**, 465–492.

Janzen, D. H. (1977). A note on optimal mate selection by plants. *Am. Nat.*, **111**, 365–371.

Jonkers, H. (1979). Biennial bearing in apple and pear. A literature survey. *Sci. Hortic. (Neth.)*, **11**, 303–317.

Kaini, B. R., Jackson, D. I. & Rowe, R. N. (1984). Studies on shoot growth patterns on Lincoln Canopy apples. *J. hort. Sci.*, **59**, 141–149.

Knight, R. L. (1963). Abstract bibliography of fruit breeding and genetics to 1960: *Malus* and *Pyrus. Tech. Commun. Commonw. Bur. Hort. Plantn Crops*, no. 29.

Kramer, P. J. & Kozlowski, T. T. (1979). *The physiology of woody plants*. New York: Academic Press.

Krezdorn, A. H. (1969). The use of growth regulators to improve fruit set in citrus. *Proc. int. Citrus Symp., 1st, Riverside, 1968*, **3**, 1113–1119.

Lang, A. (1965). Physiology of flower initiation. In: *Encyclopedia of plant physiology*, edited by W. Ritherland, 1380–1536. Berlin: Springer.

Layne, R. F. C. & Quaumme, H. A. (1975). Pears. In: *Advances in fruit breeding*, edited by J. Janick and J. N. Moore, 38–70. W. Lafayette, IN: Purdue University Press.

Leliveld, J. A. (1938). Vruchtzetting bij koffie. (Fruit setting in coffee). *Archf. Koffiecult. Ned. Jud.*, **12**, 127–161.

Lerner, I. M. (1954). *Genetic homeostasis*. New York: John Wiley.

Linskens, H. F. (1983). Pollination processes: understanding fertilization and limits to hybridization. In: *Strategies of plant reproduction*, edited by W. J. Meudt, 35–49. (BARC symposium no. 6). Ottawa: Allanheld, Osmun.

Lloyd, D. G. (1980a). Sexual strategies in plants. I. An hypothesis of serial adjustment of maternal investment during one reproductive session. *New Phytol.*, **86**, 69–79.

Lloyd, D. G. (1980b). Benefits and handicaps of sexual reproduction. *Evol. Biol.*, **13**, 69–111.

Luckwill, L. C. (1958). Fruit growth in relation to internal and external chemical stimuli. In: *Cell, organism and milieu*, edited by D. Rudnick. New York: Ronald Press.

Luckwill, L. C. (1974). A new look at the process of fruit bud formation in apple. *Proc. int. Hortic. Congr., 19th, Warsaw*, **3**, 237–245.

Maeyer L. de & Deckers, J. C. (1984). Flower bud quality in the pear cultivar Doyenne du Comice: 1982–1983 trials. *Acta Hortic.*, **149**, 153–159.

Maggs, D. H. (1964). Distance from the tree base to shoot origin as a factor in shoot and tree growth. *J. hort. Sci.*, **39**, 298–307.

Magness, J. R. (1929). Relation of leaf area to size and quality in apples. *Proc. Am. Soc. hort. Sci.*, **25**, 285–288.

Modlibowska, I. (1972). The effect of gibberellins and cytokinins on fruit development of Bramley's Seedling apple. *J. hort. Sci.*, **47**, 337–340.

Molisch, H. (1938). *The longevity of plants*. Transl. E. H. Fulling. New York: Fulling, Botanic Gardens.

Monselise, S. P. & Goldschmidt, E. E. (1982). Alternate bearing in fruit trees. *Hortic. Rev.*, **4**, 128–173.

Moore, C. S. (1978). Biometrical relationships in apple trees. *J. hort. Sci.*, **53**, 45–51.

Murneek, A. E. (1954). The embryo and endosperm in relation to fruit development, with special reference to the apple, *Malus sylvestris*. *Proc. Am. Soc. hort. Sci.*, **64**, 573–582.

Nitsch, J. P. (1971). Perennation through seeds and other structures: fruit development. In: *Plant physiology: a treatise*. 6A. *Physiology of development: plants and their reproduction*, edited by F. C. Steward, 413–501. London: Academic Press.

Nooden, L. D. (1980). Senescence in the whole plant. In: *Senescence in plants*, edited by K. V. Thimann, 219–258. (CRC series on ageing). Boca Raton, FL: CRC Press.

Opler, P. A., Frankie, G. W. & Baker, H. G. (1976). Rainfall as a factor in the release, timing and synchronization of anthesis by tropical trees and shrubs. *J. Biogeogr.*, **3**, 321–326.

Pickersgill, B. & Heiser, C. B., jr. (1976). Cytogenetics and evolutionary change under domestication. *Phil. Trans. R. Soc.*, **275B**, 55–69.

Quinlan, J. D. & Preston, A. P. (1968). Effects of thinning blossom and fruitlets on growth and cropping of Sunset apple. *J. hort. Sci.*, **43**, 373–381.

Quinlan, J. D. & Preston, A. P. (1971). The influence of shoot competition on fruit retention and cropping of apple trees. *J. hort. Sci.*, **46**, 525–534.

Ross, M. A. & Harper, J. L. (1972). Occupation of biological space during seedling establishment. *J. Ecol.*, **60**, 77–88.

Sachs, T. (1975). The induction of transport channels by auxin. *Planta*, **127**, 201–206.

Sachs, R. M. & Hackett, W. P. (1969). Control of vegetative and reproductive development in seed plants. *HortScience*, **4**, 103–107.

Salisbury, E. (1942). *The reproductive capacity of plants*. London: Bell.

Sarvas, R. (1968). Investigations on the flowering and seed crop of *Picea abies*. *Metsätiet. Tutkimuslait. Julk. (Commun. Inst. for. fenn.)*, **67**, 1–84.

Schulze, E. D. (1982). Plant life forms and their carbon, water and nutrient relations. In: *Physiological plant ecology* 2, edited by O. L. Lange, P. S. Nobel, C. B. Osmond and H. Ziegler, 615–676. (Encyclopedia of plant physiology, n.s. vol. 12B). Berlin: Springer.

Seth, A. K. & Wareing, P. F. (1967). Hormone directed transport of metabolites and its possible role in plant senescence. *J. exp. Bot.*, **18**, 65–77.

Spangelo, L. P. S., Watkins, R., Hsu, C. S. & Fejer, S. O. (1971). Combining ability analysis in the cultivated strawberry. *Can. J. Pl. Sci.*, **51**, 377–383.

Spur, S. H. & Barnes, B. V. (1980). *Forest ecology*. 3rd ed. New York: Wiley.

Stearns, S. C. (1976). Life history tactics: a review of the ideas. *Q. Rev. Biol.*, **51**, 3–47.

Stebbins, G. L. (1950). *Variation and evolution in plants*. New York: Columbia Press.

Stephenson, A. G. (1981). Flower and fruit abortion: proximate causes and ultimate functions. *Annu. Rev. Ecol. Syst.*, **12**, 253–279.

Tukey, H. B. (1936). Development of cherry and peach fruits as affected by destruction of the embryo. *Bot. Gaz.*, **98**, 1–24.

Tydeman, H. M. (1944). The influence of different pollens on the growth and development of the fruit in apples and pears. II. Fruit size and seed content in relation to fruit drop. *Rep. E. Malling Res. Stn 1943*, 31–34.

Veh, R. von. (1933). Beitrage zur Frage nach den Befruchtungsverhaltnissen der für Deutschland wert vollsten Kern-, Stein- und Beer en Obst-sorten. II. Entwicklungsgeschichtlich – cytologische Untersuchung der Samenanlagen der Apfelsorte 'Schoner V. Boskoop'. *Gartenbauwissenschaft*, **8**, 146–214.

Wareing, P. F. (1959). Problems of juvenility and flowering in trees. *J. Linn. Soc. Bot.*, **56**, 282–289.

Wareing, P. F. & Nasr, T. A. A. (1961). Gravimorphism in trees. I. Effects of gravity on growth and apical dominance in fruit trees. *Ann. Bot.*, **25**, 321–340.

Wareing, P. F. (1977). Growth substances and integration in the whole plant. *Symp. Soc. exp. Biol.*, **31**, 337–365.

Webster, A. D. & Shepherd, U. M. (1984). The effects of summer shoot tipping and rootstock on the growth, floral bud production, yield and fruit quality of young sweet cherries. *J. hort. Sci.*, **59**, 175–182.

Weinberger, J. H. & Cullinan, F. P. (1932). Further studies on the relation between leaf area and size of fruit, chemical composition and fruit bud formation in Elberta peaches. *Proc. Am. Soc. hort. Sci.*, **29**, 23–27.

Williams, R. R. (1965). The effect of summer nitrogen application on the quality of apple blossom. *J. hort. Sci.*, **40**, 31–41.

Williams, R. R. (1970). The effect of supplementary pollination on yield. In: *Towards regulated cropping*, edited by R. R. Williams and D. Wilson, 7–10. London: Grower Books.

Wilson, B. F. (1970). *The growing tree*. Amhurst, MA: University of Massachusetts Press.

Wolgast, L. J. & Zeide, B. (1983). Reproduction of trees in a variable environment. *Bot. Gaz.*, **144**, 260–262.

Woolhouse, H. W. (1974). Longevity and plant senescence. *Sci. Prog. Oxf.*, **61**, 123–147.

Woolhouse, H. W. (1983). Hormonal control of senescence allied to reproduction in plants. In: *Strategies of plant reproduction*, edited by W. J. Meudt. (BARC symposium no. 6). Ottawa: Allanheld, Osmun.

Zucconi, F. (1981). Regulation of abscission in growing fruit. *Acta Hortic.*, **120**, 89–94.

25

SOME ATTRIBUTES OF NUT-BEARING TREES OF TEMPERATE FOREST ORIGIN

R. M. LANNER

Department of Forest Resources, Utah State University, Logan, Utah, USA

I. INTRODUCTION

Before examining the characteristics of nut-bearing trees, it is necessary to define what constitutes a nut. Definitions abound, but I favour the relatively broad ones offered by Steen (1971): (1) an indehiscent, one-seeded, dry fruit usually formed from a compound ovary and typically possessing a hard outer wall or pericarp, like an acorn, hazelnut or chestnut; and (2) one of a number of structures which are not true nuts, like the Brazil nut (a seed) and certain dry drupes after the removal of hard parts, like the almond, coconut, pecan, and walnut. I would further broaden these definitions to include large coniferous seeds enclosed in hard testas. Also, for the present discussion, we must exclude nuts that are inedible to man or his domesticated animals, and very small nuts, like the 'nutlets' of *Nothofagus* and *Betula*.

The criteria of size and edibility have important biological ramifications, because large edible nuts are attractive to many animals, and are too large to be dispersed by the wind. The animals that eat nuts therefore become prime candidates for their dispersal. As we shall see, dispersing animals can, theoretically at least, exert very strong and directed selective pressures on the trees, causing them to evolve in ways advantageous to the dispersing organisms. These pressures can mould such diverse characters as crown form, site specificity and tolerance, and seed crop characters.

II. BOTANICAL NATURE OF NUT TREE GENERA

Using the above criteria, we find that the temperate forest nut-bearers are found in four genera of gymnosperms (Table I) and ten genera of angiosperms (Table II).

TABLE I.   Gymnospermous nut-bearing trees of temperate forests: phylogenetic and geographic occurrence; and economic status for nut and timber production

Genus	Geographic occurrence	Approximate number of nut-bearing species	Species cultivated for food	Value as timber producers
Araucaria	SW Pacific, South America	10[1]	0	minor
Ginkgo	E Asia, culti-vated through-out northern hemisphere	1	0	negligible
Pinus	Europe, Asia, W North America	26	2	major
Torreya	E Asia, W & SE North America	6	0	negligible

[1] Only one species is temperate in origin, the others are subtropical or tropical.

In three of the four gymnosperm genera, one of which is monotypic, all the species are nut-bearers. But in *Pinus*, only about 26 of the approximately 100 species of the genus bear seeds large enough to qualify as nuts. Most of these are in the soft pine or white pine subgenus (*Strobus*), and include, notably, the stone pines (five species) and the piñon pines (eleven species). The use of pine nuts as a food by humans has recently been discussed by Lanner (1981), and there is ample documentation on the consumption of *Torreya* (Burke 1975), *Ginkgo* (Li 1963), and *Araucaria* (Dallimore & Jackson 1961), although these genera have been utilized on a much smaller scale than the pines.

Despite the regional importance of coniferous nuts in many parts of the world, only two species appear to have been *cultivated* for their seed crops. These are the Italian stone pine (*Pinus pinea*), currently an important crop species in the Mediterranean area, and the Siberian stone pine (*P. sibirica*), which is reportedly planted by villagers in the Urals (Pravdin 1963). Because *P. pinea* has been widely planted since antiquity, its natural area of distribution is now impossible to determine (Critchfield & Little 1966). It alone forms the *Pinus* subsection Pineae, and it appears to have no close relatives within the genus. *Pinus sibirica*, on the other hand, ranges widely across northern Siberia, and is one of a complex of five closely related species, the others being *P. albicaulis*, *P. cembra*, *P. koraiensis*, and *P. pumila*. It has frequently been united with *P. cembra* as var. *sibirica*.

TABLE II.   Angiospermous nut-bearing trees of temperate forests: phylogenetic and geographic occurrence, and economic status for nut and timber production

Genus	Geographic occurrence	Approximate number of nut-bearing species	Species cultivated for food	Value as timber producers
Aesculus	Europe, Asia, North America	13	0	minor
Carya	E Asia, North America	16	1 (plus 1 hybrid)	major
Castanea	Europe, Asia, Africa, North America	12	3	major
Castanopsis	Asia, North America	100[1]	0	minor
Corylus	Europe, Asia, North America	15	2	negligible
Fagus	Europe, Asia, North America	10	0	major
Juglans	Europe; Asia; North, South, Central America; West Indies	20	1	major
Lithocarpus	E Asia, North America	100[1]	1	minor
Prunus	SW Asia, cultivated widely	1	1[2]	negligible
Quercus	Europe; Asia; Africa; North, Central America; West Indies	500	0	major

[1] All but a few are subtropical or tropical in origin.
[2] Excluding those cultivated for their fleshy fruits.

Most nut-bearing angiosperms belong to genera in which all species bear nuts. The sole exception is the almond, *Prunus dulcis* (syn. *P. amygdalus*), which differs from its congeners by bearing large and esculent kernels. Surprisingly, few of the nut-bearing angiosperms have been cultivated for their seeds (Table II), even in such genera as *Carya*, *Castanea*, and *Corylus*, whose nuts have exceptional flavour and nutritive value (Westwood 1978; Woodroof 1979). The angiospermous genera tend to be rather large – in the case of *Quercus*, very large indeed – which increases the likelihood of (a) finding species or biotypes adapted to a variety of habitats or cultivation methods, and (b) designing hybrids with adaptations or crop attributes that diverge from those of the parents.

TABLE III. Characteristics of the reproductive systems of the major nut-bearing genera of temperate forests

| Genus | Chromosomes | | Pollination[2] | Sex distri-bution[3] | Self-compatible?[4] |
	Base number	Ploidy[1] level			
Pinus	12	Diploid	wind	monoecious	no
Aesculus	20	Diploid	insect	monoecious	—
Carya	16	Diploid, Tetraploid	wind	monoecious	yes
Castanea	12	Diploid	insect or wind	monecious	no
Corylus	14	Diploid	wind	monoecious	no
Fagus	12	Diploid	wind	monoecious	—
Juglans	16	Diploid	wind	monoecious	no
Prunus (P. dulcis)	8	Diploid	insect	monoecious	no
Quercus	12	Diploid	wind	monoecious	—

[1] Data from Wright (1976), Mehra (1976) and Westwood (1978).
[2] Westwood (1978); USDA Forest Service (1965).
[3] USDA Forest Service (1965) and Bean (1981).
[4] Wright (1976) and Westwood (1978). 'No' may indicate greatly reduced seed-set and non-vigorous offspring.

Most of the nut-bearing genera have relatively simple genetic and reproductive systems (Table III). Nearly all are diploids, with low chromosome numbers (the genus *Prunus* is of course complex, but its complexities do not extend to *P. dulcis*). Most of the angiosperms belong to families in the Amentiferae (Juglandaceae: *Juglans*, *Carya*; Fagaceae: *Castanea*, *Castanopsis*, *Fagus*, *Lithocarpus*, *Quercus*; Betulaceae: *Corylus*). The Amentiferae nut-bearers are all monoecious; and those of the Floriferae have perfect flowers. Nearly all are self-incompatible, at least in having lowered seed-sets or less vigorous offspring as a consequence of self-fertilization. In those genera frequently used in commercial orchards (*Prunus*, *Juglans*, *Corylus*, *Castanea*, *Carya*), the selected cultivars are self-sterile, and it is necessary to interplant them with other cultivars as pollinators. Controlled crosses between walnut cultivars give between 10% and 90% fruit set (Westwood 1978). In the genera *Aesculus*, *Juglans*, *Carya*, *Castanea*, *Quercus* and *Pinus*, hybridization between species either occurs naturally or can be accomplished artificially.

III. CONSEQUENCES OF ANIMAL DISPERSAL OF TREE NUTS

Foresters have become accustomed to the notion that tree seeds are dispersed by wind, because, in most commercially important temperate trees, this is the case. But seeds that qualify as nuts are, almost by definition, too heavy to become airborne, and so must be dispersed by animals.

The animals that disperse nuts are invariably predators on those nuts, and their function as dispersers is incidental to their activities as predators. In the cases pertinent here, nuts are dispersed to a place of *storage*, where they are concealed by the predator-disperser for future consumption. This differs fundamentally from the dispersal of seeds like those of *Juniperus*, which are randomly defecated by birds that have eaten the soft pericarps (Salomonson 1978).

A.   How pine nuts are dispersed

This brief synthesis summarizes results of studies recently concluded in the Swiss Alps (Mattes 1982), Hokkaido (Saito 1983), and the western USA (Balda & Bateman 1971; Vander Wall & Balda 1977; Tomback 1978; Lanner & Vander Wall 1980; Hutchins & Lanner 1982; Lanner 1980, 1982) on the inter-relationships between corvid birds and pines that have large, wingless seeds. Nutcrackers (Corvidae: *Nucifraga* sp.) and jays (Corvidae: *Aphelocoma* sp., *Cyanocitta* sp., *Gymnorhinus* sp.) remove ripened seeds from cones. They fly to the ground, or to caching areas up to 22 km away, carrying one to over 100 seeds in their mouths or distensible esophagi (jays) or in specialized sublingual pouches (nutcrackers). Seeds that are not eaten immediately are placed in the soil in groups of one to 15 or more, at 2–3 cm depth. In a mast year, a single nutcracker may cache about 100,000 seeds. Seeds are retrieved and eaten throughout the fall, winter, and spring, and they are fed to newly hatched young. Unrecovered seeds, which in a mast year constitute a majority of those stored, often germinate and become established. Hutchins and Lanner (1982) showed that regeneration of whitebark pine (*P. albicaulis*) depends upon the services of Clark's nutcracker (*N. columbiana*), as no other animal in the pine's ecosystem exhibits the requisite behaviour. Nutcracker dispersal of *P. albicaulis* and of *P. flexilis* results in a highly clumped pattern of tree dispersal, restricting the pines to areas within the natural range of the nutcracker, and frequently dispersing the seeds to xeric, windswept, rocky sites (Lanner 1980). Furthermore, the mixed age class distribution of stands of these pines has been attributed to the nutcracker's persistence in caching seeds repeatedly in preferred areas (Lanner 1980).

It has been argued that the indehiscent cone of the Cembrae pines (*P. albicaulis, P. cembra, P. koraiensis, P. pumila, P. sibirica*) is a 'package' that is easily 'unwrapped' by nutcrackers, but not by other seed predators, and that this adaptation to the harvesting efficiency of the nutcracker has evolved through natural selection (Lanner 1980, 1982). It is also argued that the crowns of whitebark pine trees function as cone display surfaces, and that their shapes have resulted from nutcracker-mediated natural selection (Lanner 1982). Note that persistent caching of seeds on xeric sites should, through natural selection, result in trees adapted to droughty habitats; and the preferred caching of large seeds should result in selection for large-seeded genotypes. Apparently there is little known about the dispersal ecology of *Araucaria*, *Ginkgo* or *Torreya*.

B.   How acorns and beechnuts are dispersed

Amazingly little has been written about the dispersal of acorns, although oaks are nearly ubiquitous in the north temperate zone, and are of great economic importance. Studies in hardwood forests in Virginia and Wisconsin have indicated that the blue jay (*Cyanocitta cristata*) is the only animal vector that is able to carry oak acorns and beechnuts (*Fagus grandifolia*) over long distances (Darley-Hill & Johnson 1981; Johnson & Adkisson 1985). Squirrels (*Sciurus* sp.) appeared to be important dispersers on a local scale (they are territorial animals that do not stray from their limited home ranges [Stapanian & Smith 1978; Smith & Follmer 1972]), but apparently the Fagaceae species in the study area depended on jays for the establishment of new stands away from the seed source. Harrison and Werner (1984) have also concluded that blue jays are responsible for long-distance (to 400 m) dispersal of acorns into open areas.

Johnson and Adkisson (1985) observed a woodlot containing a number of beech trees, from which about 150,000 beechnuts were dispersed by jays. The jays carried either a single nut, or a bur containing two nuts. These were transported up to 4 km, placed in a cache just below the soil surface, and then concealed with litter. Johnson and Adkisson (1985) considered that jays were essential to maintain populations of beech trees in landscapes where only small tracts of woodland were scattered within a matrix of farmland, and where, according to current concepts of island biogeography, extinction would be likely.

In Holland, the European jay (*Garrulus glandarius*) has been carefully observed in its mutualistic association with pedunculate oak (*Quercus robur*) and sessile oak (*Q. petraea*), as well as with the introduced red oak (*Q. rubra*) (Bossema 1979). In a wide-ranging series of experiments, Bossema established that jays preferred (a) thin-shelled native acorns and beechnuts over the thicker-shelled acorns of introduced oaks, or native hazelnuts, (b) large acorns over small ones, being able to discriminate weight differences of less than 10%, (c) long, narrow acorns for long-distance transport, and (d) ripe to green, sound to damaged, and normal to loose-shelled acorns.

Preferential behaviour of the jays had ecological consequences for the oaks. For example, acorns were cached singly, not in groups, so oak trees were single-stemmed rather than in clumps, as are pines seeded by nutcrackers (Lanner 1980). Acorn-dispersing flights were in all directions from the seed source, and usually exceeded 80 m. Burial sites were not chosen at random, but tended to have specific characteristics. They were seldom under shade, but were more often in the open, especially on edges of 'grass islands' among heather. Soft and rough-textured soil was preferred to hard, smooth soil as a caching substrate, and caches were widely spaced.

The result of these jay behaviour patterns was to disperse the oaks disproportionately to open habitats, where competition was not severe, and to areas with well-drained soils. Trees growing under those conditions should develop full crowns that bear ample acorn crops, a result similar to that predicted for whitebark pines seeded in the open by Clark's nutcracker (Hutchins & Lanner 1982). There is much more to Bossema's complex tale of jay-oak symbiosis, but only one more result will be mentioned here. It seems that jays feed not only on the cotyledons of exhumed acorns, but also on the cotyledons of the hypogeous sprouted seedlings. To do so, they take hold of the stem of first-year seedlings with the bill, and tug with vigour. This action uproots poorly-rooted seedlings quite readily, but leaves strongly taprooted seedlings unharmed. Bossema considered that this tugging behaviour represented a strong selective pressure favouring taproot development in *Quercus*. Thus, as with the pines involved in the mutualisms described above, the ecological consequences of avian seed dispersal are profound for the oaks. There is strong presumptive evidence, in both sets of mutualisms, that the birds and trees have co-evolved, that is, that they have each responded over time to natural selection pressures generated by the other.

C. How squirrels disperse nuts of Fagaceae and Juglandaceae

Squirrels have long been known to bury individual acorns, beechnuts, walnuts, and hickory nuts in a widely scattered pattern ('scatterhoarding'). Typically, they dig a hole, place the nut in it, cover it with soil, compact the soil, and place some grass or litter on top, probably as camouflage. Planting depth may be barely enough to conceal the nut (Cahalane 1942), or up to 10 mm of soil may be placed above the nut (Thompson & Thompson 1980). Nuts of *Aesculus* are also cached by squirrels (Nixon *et al.* 1968; Thompson & Thompson 1980) and it is safe to assume the same is true of *Castanea*, *Castanopsis*, and *Lithocarpus*. (*Corylus* is known to be dispersed in Europe by nutcrackers; *Prunus dulcis* is only known in cultivation, so no disperser of an ancestral type can be identified.) Unlike the wide-ranging corvids, squirrels stay quite close to home, usually within a territory of a few hectares. Therefore, nuts dispersed by squirrels (ie buried and left unretrieved) do not establish new stands but merely augment or extend existing ones. Squirrels commonly carry nuts only about 15 to 30 m from their source before burying them (Smith & Follmer 1972). Stapanian and Smith (1978) showed that the number of nuts buried per unit area of ground affected the probability that those nuts would be eaten by squirrels that did not bury them. They calculated that uniform hexagonal spacing of about 13·4 m between nuts would provide an optimum dispersal from the standpoint of surviving predation. There appear to be no quantitative studies of squirrel caching comparable to those on nutcrackers and jays, so little can be said about the exact role that squirrels play in the regeneration of nut-bearing trees. However, Thompson and Thompson (1980) believed that squirrels were probably necessary for the establishment of horse-chestnut (*Aesculus hippocastanum*), because their seeds were unlikely to survive if they were not buried.

Clearly, animal dispersers are attracted to nut-bearing trees because the trees produce large numbers of highly nutritious nut 'meats' in large seeds. The lipid content of the nuts is especially important in giving them high energetic value (Lanner 1981). It is therefore no surprise that commercially planted nut trees also attract predatory animals, including the species that disperse their seeds in the wild. In the USA, jays prey upon orchards of *Corylus* and *Juglans* (Westwood 1978); and squirrels must be excluded from orchards of all kinds (Funk 1969). Control of nut-eating wildlife would be a necessary part of orchard management if additional species were brought into cultivation.

The crown architecture of deciduous nut trees has never been examined in relation to the needs of seed dispersers, as has that of some nut-bearing pines (Lanner 1980, 1982). The assumption is often made that crown design is optimized to orient leaves properly to the sun (Brunig 1976; Hallé *et al*. 1978). Yet a crown must also place flowers where they can be reached by pollinating insects, birds, or bats, and fruits where they can be reached by dispersers. According to Whitmore (1975), bat flowers and bat fruits are held away from the main foliage of the crown, presumably because this improves the bats' chances of pollinating flowers and dispersing seeds. In other words, it is a characteristic that has been selected for by the bats. In heavily fruited species, where the entire fruit abscises and falls to the ground (eg *Juglans*), fruit presentation may not be a factor. But among those taxa whose nuts are taken by dispersers directly from the tree crowns (eg *Quercus* and *Fagus*), branching habit and other morphological features may be adapted to 'accommodate' disperser behaviour. To the degree that a tree species is dependent on a single dispersing species, that disperser has the opportunity to shape the tree's evolution. But if a number of dispersers, each with its own habits and needs, are effective in establishing the tree, then the tree is less likely to become 'specialized' to suit any one of them. The only tree species for which the available data so far indicate total dependence upon a single disperser species is whitebark pine, as discussed earlier.

IV. POTENTIAL FOR EXPANDED USE OF NUT BEARERS

It is difficult to understand why, with so many nut-bearing species available in temperate forests, so few have been brought into cultivation. Oaks, for example, have historically been important sources of 'mast' for livestock, and of starch for diverse peoples around the world. Yet nowhere does man seem to have cultivated oaks as food-producing trees. Even in eastern North America, where, since settlement by Europeans, the nuts of the black walnut (*Juglans nigra*) have been savoured, and even used commercially, the crop is largely gathered wild, although over 100 cultivars are known (Woodroof 1979). Only in recent years has the economic potential of nut production been recognized, so that the integration of nut and lumber production is being advocated in tree improvement schemes (Funk 1969).

There seems to be no shortage of variability; Tables I and II show that a wide range of genera are available, and most of them have wide geographic distributions. Table IV gives the elevational, latitudinal, and longitudinal range of some North American nut-bearing species, which must be repositories of great stores of adaptive variation. There is also plenty of variability in economic 'crop' traits. For example, nuts of the Japanese chestnut (*Castanea crenata*) are usually smaller than those of the European *C. sativa*, but selected trees yield nuts at least as large as the best European varieties (Bean 1981). The same is true of the under-utilized Chinese chestnut (*C. mollissima*), which

TABLE IV. The wide geographic ranges of representative North American nut-bearing trees, as exemplified by their altitudinal, latitudinal and longitudinal spread, and their occurrence in different hardiness zones[1]

Species	Altitudinal occurrence, meters above sea level	Latitudinal spread °Latitude	Longitudinal spread °Longitude	Hardiness zones occupied[2]
Carya illinoensis	—	15	15	5–9
C. ovata	0–645	35	45	4–9
Fagus grandifolia	0–1935	38	35	3–9
Quercus alba	0–1450	15	26	4–9
Q. macrocarpa	—	24	39	2–9
Juglans nigra	0–1290	16	28	4–9
Pinus edulis	1290–2900	15	20	4–7
P. monophylla	1030–3225	20	18	4–8

[1] Data mainly from Little (1971).
[2] Plant hardiness zones are numbered in reference to mean minimum temperature in degrees Fahrenheit (°F) as follows: Zone 2, −50° to −40°; Zone 3, −40° to −30°; Zone 4, −30° to −20°; Zone 5, −20° to −10°; Zone 6, −10° to 0°; Zone 7, 0° to 10°; Zone 8, 10° to 20°; and Zone 9, 20° to 30°.

has recently attracted some interest in the USA (Payne *et al.* 1983). Within the genus *Fagus*, nuts are usually very small, but *F. englerana*, a native of China, has nuts over half an inch long (Bean 1981). The Japanese walnut (*J. ailantifolia*), esteemed for the fine flavour of its nuts, has a thin-shelled variety, var. *cordiformis*; and the Persian or English walnut (*J. regia*) has a variant with such thin shells (f. *fragilis*) it is called 'titmouse walnut' because its shells are easily pierced by these little birds (Bean 1981). Another form of Persian walnut (f. *macrocarpa*) has nuts twice the normal size, though the kernels are small; and still another (f. *racemosa*) bears clusters of up to 50 nuts each (Bean 1981). Genetic variability in nut characteristics has been documented in beech (Brinar 1974), filbert (Popnikola 1972; Kozlov 1975), almonds (Sykes 1975), walnut (Zarger 1945; Sykes 1975), and even in ginkgo (Stilinovic & Tucovic 1975). Yield characters also vary greatly. While most large, mature, open-grown black walnut trees bear up to 3,000 nuts per year, one tree has borne over 6,000 (Funk 1969). Genetic variation in this species is considerable at individual, regional and racial levels.

A walnut (*J. regia*) improvement programme was recently started in the Jammu and Kashmir districts of India, by gradually replacing seedling trees, which do not bear until they are about 17 years of age, with much earlier-bearing selections. Top-working vigorous trees with selected scionwood has also been practised. The selection programme focused on early-bearing, vigorous trees producing large crops of medium-sized, well-filled kernels (Woodroof 1979). This programme was based on a long-standing native practice of growing scattered walnut trees along roadsides, around farmsteads, and in small groups. Natural selection had probably led to the establishment of an adapted 'land race' in the district. Smith (1977) advocated the use of waste spaces, uncultivatable slopes, and roadsides for many nut bearers worldwide, and has documented the practice in many areas. More formal schemes of agroforestry, like those described by Douglas and Hart (1978), also utilize nut-bearing trees that protect the soil and ultimately produce valuable crops of wood products.

The potential for bringing more wild species of nut-bearing trees into cultivation is illustrated by the recent history of the pecan (*Carya illinoensis*), the only American forest tree that has been domesticated for food production (Woodroof 1979). It is speculated that in pre-Columbian times Indians expanded the natural range of this species by planting nuts at campsites and along travel routes. Its natural range is mainly in the states of Texas, Louisiana, Oklahoma, Arkansas, Missouri, Iowa, Illinois, Indiana, and Mississippi. Late in the nineteenth century, the fine flavour and nutritive qualities of pecan nut were recognized, 'papershell' varieties were discovered, and a new industry began. At first, the only means used to produce pecans was to top-work wild trees and seedling orchards growing within the natural range of the species. But before long, intensive selection led to the creation of about 500 named cultivars, as well as 'hicans', hybrids with *C. ovata*, *C. laciniosa*, and *C. cordiformis*. Many of these varieties are adapted to climatic conditions quite different from those in the natural range of the species. Thus, the state of Georgia, which is outside the natural range, has become the most important pecan-producing state, and large irrigated operations have sprung up in Arizona and New Mexico. By the late 1960s, 100,000 trees were being planted annually in New Mexico. During the 1970s, a large (750 ha) irrigated orchard was planted in New South Wales, Australia, with a projected annual production of $8,400 \, \text{kg} \, \text{ha}^{-1}$ (7,500 lbs acre^{-1}). A total area of 30,000 ha was to be planted in Israel in 1980. Other pecan industries can be found in South Africa and Mexico (Woodroof 1979), as well as in Soviet Georgia (Ramishvili & Lomadze 1975).

The growth of this industry has been explosive. In 1975, production in the United States exceeded 200,000 tonnes valued at over US\$98 million. The present trend is a shift towards Texas, Arizona, and New Mexico, with a concomitant increase in the use of western cultivars. What originated as a cottage industry, utilizing nuts fallen from wild trees, has become a large enterprise increasingly using intensive cultural practices. The large and heterogeneous area that comprises the natural range of this species would seem to ensure that there is no danger of biotype depletion; indeed, its storehouse of genetic variability has been barely sampled.

V. CONCLUSIONS

The nut-bearing trees of temperate forests comprise an enormous potential food resource. As yet, few taxa have been utilized on a commercial scale. Modern selection and breeding methods could be used to exploit a vast reservoir of genetic variability, perhaps repeating mankind's past successes in domesticating the trees we now grow routinely as horticultural crops in profitable well-tended orchards.

REFERENCES

Balda, R. P. & Bateman, G. C. (1971). Flocking and annual cycle of the piñon jay, *Gymnorhinus cyanocephalus. Condor*, **73**, 287–302.

Bean, W. J. (1981). *Trees and shrubs hardy in the British Isles.* 4 vols. 8th ed. New York: St. Martin's Press.

Bossema, I. (1979). Jays and oaks: an eco-ethological study of a symbiosis. *Behaviour*, **70**, 1–117.

Brinar, M. (1974). (Variation in the morphological characteristics of beech fruits in relation to the ecological conditions.) (Slovenian). *Gozd. Vest.*, **32**, 370–386.

Brunig, E. F. (1976). Tree forms in relation to environmental conditions: an ecological viewpoint. In: *Tree physiology and yield improvement*, edited by M. G. R. Cannell and F. T. Last, 139–156. London: Academic Press.

Burke, J. G. (1975). Human use of the California nutmeg tree, *Torreya californica*, and of other members of the genus. *Econ. Bot.*, **29**, 127–139.

Cahalane, H. (1942). Caching and recovery of food by the western fox squirrel. *J. Wildl. Mgmt*, **6**, 338–352.

Critchfield, W. B. & Little, E. L. (1966). *Geographic distribution of the pines of the world.* (Miscellaneous publication no. 991). Washington DC: USDA Forest Service.

Dallimore, W. & Jackson, A. B. (1961). *A handbook of Coniferae including Ginkgoaceae.* London: Edward Arnold.

Darley-Hill, S. & Johnson, W. C. (1981). Acorn dispersal by the blue jay (*Cyanocitta cristata*). *Oecologia*, **50**, 231–232.

Douglas, J. S. & Hart, A. de J. (1978). *Forest farming: towards a solution to problems of world hunger and conservation* (N. Amer. ed.) Emmaus, PA: Rodale Press.

Funk, D. T. (1969). Genetics of black walnut (*Juglans nigra*). (Res. Pap. WO-10). USDA Forest Service.

Hallé, F., Oldeman, R. A. A. & Tomlinson, P. B. (1978). *Tropical trees and forests: an architectural analysis.* New York: Springer.

Harrison, S. & Werner, A. (1984). Colonization by oak seedlings into a heterogeneous successional habitat. *Can. J. Bot.*, **62**, 559–563.

Hutchins, H. E. & Lanner, R. M. (1982). The central role of Clark's nutcracker in the dispersal and establishment of whitebark pine. *Oecologia*, **55**, 192–201.

Johnson, W. C. & Adkisson, S. (1985). Dispersal of beech nuts by blue jays in fragmented landscapes. *Am. Midl. Nat.* In press.

Kozlov, G. V. (1975). (Wild forms of *Corylus avellana* in the basin of the rivers Malaya Laba and Belaya in the Krasnodar region). (Russian). *Byull. Vses. Ordena Lenina i Ordena Druzhby Narodov Instituta Rast. Imeni N. I. Vavilova*, **54**, 47–49. VIR, Leningrad, USSR. (*Pl. Breed. Abstr.*, **47**, no. 3722).

Lanner, R. M. (1980). Avian seed dispersal as a factor in the ecology and evolution of limber and whitebark pines. *Proc. North American Forest Biology Workshop, 6th, Edmonton, Alberta*, 15–48.

Lanner, R. M. (1981). *The piñon pine: a natural and cultural history.* Reno, NV: University of Nevada Press.

Lanner, R. M. (1982). Adaptation of whitebark pine for seed dispersal by Clark's nutcracker. *Can. J. For. Res.*, **12**, 391–402.

Lanner, R. M. & Vander Wall, S. B. (1980). Dispersal of limber pine seed by Clark's nutcracker. *J. For.*, **78**, 637–639.

Li, H. L. (1963). *The origin and cultivation of shade and ornamental trees.* Philadelphia, PA: University of Pennsylvania Press.

Little, E. L., jr. (1971). *Atlas of United States trees, Vol. 1. Conifers and important hardwoods.* (Miscellaneous publication no. 1146). Washington DC: USDA Forest Service.

Mattes, H. (1982). Die Lebensgemeinschaft von Tannenhäher und Arve. *Swiss Fed. Inst. For. Res. Rep.*, no. 241, 1–74.

Mehra, P. N. (1976). *Cytology of Himalayan hardwoods.* (Dept. Bot. Monogr.). Chandigarh, India: University of Panjab.

Nixon, C. N., Worley, D. M. & McClain, M. W. (1968). Food habits of squirrels in southeast Ohio. *J. Wildl. Mgmt*, **32**, 294–304.

Payne, J. A., Jaynes, R. A. & Kays, S. J. (1983). Chinese chestnut production in the United States: practice, problems, and possible solutions. *Econ. Bot.*, **37**, 187–200.

Popnikola, N. (1972). (Selection of *Corylus avellana.*) *Gozd. Vest.*, **30**, 88–98.

Pravdin, L. F. (1963). The selection and the seed production of the Siberian stone pine. In: *Fruiting of the Siberian stone pine in east Siberia*, edited by A. P. Shimanyuk, 1–20. Jerusalem: Israel Program for Scientific Translation. (Translated from Russian).

Ramishvili, G. G. & Lomadze, Ts.A. (1975). (Economic importance of the cultivation of *Carya pecan* (*C. illinoensis*), and its range of distribution). (Russian). *Subtrop. Kul't.*, **3**, 99–102.

Saito, S. (1983). Caching of Japanese stone pine seeds by nutcrackers at the Shiretoko Peninsula, Hokkaido. *Tori*, **32**, 13–20.

Salomonson, M. G. (1978). Adaptations for animal dispersal of one-seed juniper seeds. *Oecologia*, **32**, 333–339.

Smith, J. (1977). *Tree crops, a permanent agriculture.* Old Greenwich, CT: Devin-Adair Co.

Smith, C. C. & Follmer, D. (1972). Food preference of squirrels. *Ecology*, **53**, 82–91.

Stapanian, M. A. & Smith, C. C. (1978). A model for seed scatterhoarding: co-evolution of fox squirrels and black walnuts. *Ecology*, **59**, 884–896.

Steen, B. (1971). *Dictionary of biology.* New York: Barnes & Noble.

Stilinovic, S. & Tucovic, A. (1975). (Morphological variability of the seeds from different mother trees of *Ginkgo biloba* in Serbia during 1971–74). *Sumarstvo*, **28**, 27–39.

Sykes, J. T. (1975). The influence of climate on the regional distribution of nut crops in Turkey. *Econ. Bot.*, **29**, 108–115.

Thompson, D. C. & Thompson, P. S. (1980). Food habits and caching behaviour of urban grey squirrels. *Can. J. Zool.*, **58**, 701–710.

Tomback, D. F. (1978). Foraging strategies of Clark's nutcracker. *Living Bird, 1977*, no. 16, 123–161.

USDA Forest Service. (1965). *Silvics of forest trees of the United States*, compiled by H. A. Fowells. (Agricultural handbook no. 271). Washington DC: USDA Forest Service.

Vander Wall, S. B. & Balda, R. P. (1977). Coadaptations of Clark's nutcracker and the piñon pine for efficient seed harvest and dispersal. *Ecol. Monogr.*, **47**, 89–111.

Westwood, M. N. (1978). *Temperate-zone pomology.* San Francisco: W. H. Freeman.

Whitmore, T. C. (1975). *Tropical rain forests of the Far East.* Oxford: Clarendon.

Woodroof, J. G. (1979). *Tree nuts: production, processing, products.* 2nd ed. Westport, CT: AVI Publ. Co.

Wright, J. W. (1976). *Introduction to forest genetics.* New York; London: Academic Press.

Zarger, C. (1945). Nut-testing, propagation, and planting experience on 90 black walnut selections. *Rep. Proc. Nut Grow. Ass.*, no. 36, 23–30.

Trees in stands

26
FUTURE FRUIT ORCHARD DESIGN: ECONOMICS AND BIOLOGY

J. E. JACKSON
East Malling Research Station, Maidstone, Kent, England

I. INTRODUCTION

Fruit tree orchards have changed dramatically in recent years and are still in a state of rapid evolution and, indeed, of revolutionary development.

The changes have been particularly pronounced in the context of apple growing.

Large, spreading, apple trees, 4–5 m in height, have all but vanished from the commercial scene in western Europe. They have been replaced by ordered hedgerows in which the trees are little more than half of the height of their predecessors, a tenth of their spread, and are planted at up to ten times their density.

Production per hectare has increased greatly. In the Netherlands, the national average yield has risen from 16 to 38 t ha^{-1}yr^{-1} (fresh weight) over the period from 1950 to 1977 (Wertheim 1981). In the United Kingdom, the average yield of Cox, a high quality but hitherto low-yielding apple, more than doubled over the period 1949 to 1975 (Jackson & Hamer 1980).

441

Labour requirements per hectare have been reduced. In the Netherlands, the number of man-hours needed for cultural practices, excluding harvesting, declined from 550 to 175 hours ha^{-1} yr^{-1} over the 1950–1977 period (Wertheim 1981). In England, the Ministry of Agriculture bulletins on apple growing costs and returns gave an average estimate of pre-harvest labour use of 405 hours ha^{-1} yr^{-1} in 1969 and 100 hours ha^{-1} yr^{-1} in 1982.

Similar changes have occurred throughout western Europe. They have not been a result of changes in the genetic material available to the fruit grower. Cox, Bramley and Golden Delicious are very long-established apples and, even though there has been some change in rootstock usage, the dwarfing Malling 9 (M.9) rootstock, which is by far the most widely used in western Europe, has been available for more than 50 years. The advances have been in the overall technology of management of trees and orchards, making use of scientific and technical developments and integrating them into improved production systems.

The potential for further progress in apple growing systems, and for applications to other crops, can best be considered in relation to economic and crop-physiological productivity modelling. First, however, we need to describe recent changes and the present state of affairs in more detail.

II. RECENT AND CURRENT DEVELOPMENTS IN APPLE ORCHARD SYSTEMS

Historically, fruit orchards have taken many different forms, ranging from elaborately trained and pruned dwarf fruit tree cordons in monastery and palace gardens to large, spreading, trees under which farm cattle grazed.

Large trees, planted 10–16 m apart on seedling rootstocks, are still used in some production systems, notably those involving mechanical harvesting (by tree shaking) for processing in the USA and Canada. Within western Europe, which is the major apple producing area of the world, such large trees have almost vanished from commercial production. They were replaced over a period ranging from the 1930s to the 1950s (depending on the country) by trees of medium vigour, on rootstocks such as M.2 and M.4 or even on seedlings, grown to a height of 4–5 m and maintained at this height by careful detailed pruning. The trees were usually either pruned to a round-crowned shape or trained and pruned into hedgerows, such as those of the Italian palmette system. In the former case, the trees were usually spaced at about 7 m×5 m; in the latter they could be in rows 5 m apart with only 4 m between trees within the row.

At the same time that these systems were being introduced, the spindlebush tree form was developed in Germany (Schmitz-Hubsch & Heinrichs 1941). This was a small tree of about 2 m in height with a maximum width of 1·5 m, cropping on horizontal fruiting laterals arising from a central axis (the centre leader) and supported by a tall stake. Originally planted at a spacing of 2·5 m×2·5 m, this tree form, with rather less rigorous training, was widely planted in Holland at spacings of about 4 m×2 m, and a number of different variants developed.

From the 1960s, these spindlebushes were progressively supplemented and replaced by even more compact trees – slender-spindlebushes – at spacings ranging from $3\,m \times 1\,m$ to $4\,m \times 2\,m$. In general, these were still planted in single rows, separated by tractor alleys, but an even more slender variant, the North-Holland spindle, is now widely planted in a design with three rows of trees between adjacent alleys (Flierman & Houter 1976) and a tree population of around 3,000 trees ha^{-1}.

One advantage of the very high density systems is that their yield per hectare can be high within a few years from planting. An alternative approach towards this same objective has been to plant large trees with numerous lateral branches (feathers) at the time of planting. This policy, using Cox on the semi-dwarfing MM.106 rootstock at planting densities of around 600 trees ha^{-1}, has become very popular in England, subsequent pruning of the tree being similar to that of some of the spindlebush systems, with a central leader bearing cropping laterals which may or may not be trained in a fruiting 'table'.

Also, in recent years there have been a number of even more intensive or extreme systems under experimental investigation. The most striking is the meadow orchard (Hudson 1971; Luckwill 1978) where the planting density can be more than 70,000 trees ha^{-1}. This concept, in which the fruit-bearing shoots are harvested by being cut off near ground level and then allowed to regrow from the stumps to crop again, has not proved practical for apple which needs two years to produce its fruits. It is, however, still being actively investigated for peach which bears fruits annually under this system (Erez 1981; Couvillon & Pokorny 1985). An apparently very different thrust, but one which has some underlying conceptual similarities in terms of both plant physiology and economics, is the modification of tall hedgerow systems into simple geometric forms suited to mechanical pruning and mechanically aided picking. The extreme developments of this method are the elaborately trellised systems with the trees, on wire supports, trained to give shallow horizontal or V-shaped canopies with the intention of mechanical harvesting and pruning (Dunn & Stolp 1981; Chalmers *et al.* 1978).

III. BACKGROUND ECONOMICS

A. Structure of costs and returns

The rapid change in orchard production systems has taken place, particularly in recent years, whilst there has been a structural surplus in apple production (Winter & Welte 1985) and an openly competitive market.

In such a competitive environment, new production systems are adopted if they improve the ratio of output, expressed in cash terms, to resources employed. The latter may be defined in different ways, depending on economic and social circumstances, but are usually considered in terms of units of land, of capital and of labour. These resources can all be expressed in cash terms, but they are not fully interchangeable at the operational level, so it is as well to consider them separately as well as in aggregate.

The degree to which land is a limiting factor clearly varies from country to country. In eastern Europe, fruit orchards may be on the Agro-Industrial-Complex scale of thousands of hectares. In the eastern USA, the scale may be similarly vast, especially where the fruits are mechanically harvested for processing from trees which are given little labour input in their management. More typical of the world's temperate fruit production units are those in England, which are average-to-large, and those in the Netherlands, which illustrate small-scale intensive production. In England, approximately 60% of the total orchard area is made up of farms with more than 20 ha of fruit, whereas in the Netherlands the corresponding figure is 8%, with 49% of Dutch orchards being less than 7 ha (Britton 1977; van Oosten 1979). German fruit farms tend to be more similar to the Dutch, with 50% of the orchards in the Elbe valley being between 5 ha and 10 ha (Utermark 1977). Typical Australian orchards are from 6 ha to 12 ha (Hutton 1980).

It is clear that, where farms are small, output value per hectare becomes a dominant consideration because it is essential to ensure an adequate livelihood. Where farms are larger, output value per unit of capital employed may become relatively more important. In any case, land has to be treated differently from other costs because, it is usually assumed, it will be worth at least as much at the end of an orchard's life as it was at the time of planting. The other costs involved in fruit production (Steer 1982) are summarized in Table I for English orchards.

These costs are best subdivided into costs of orchard establishment, which represent a once-and-for-all capital investment in the particular orchard, and costs in a typical production year. Three factors stand out.

(i) The cost of establishment is high, and, when treated as an annual charge over a 20-year orchard life, it is greater than the annual cost of all materials and labour used pre-harvest.

(ii) Pruning accounts for almost two-thirds of the total pre-harvest labour cost.

(iii) Harvesting and post-harvesting costs, which are essentially yield-dependent, are much greater than the pre-harvest costs, which are essentially area-dependent. Assuming a 25 t ha^{-1} crop, the total cost of 'farm overheads', the annual charge arising from the cost of establishment and the total 'growing cost', ie pruning, chemicals, spraying, etc, was equivalent to 10·9 pence kg^{-1} in 1982. Harvesting cost a further 5·1p, storage 5·8p and marketing 11·2p. Thus, out of a total cost equivalent to 33p kg^{-1}, more than 22p are incurred picking the fruits or post-harvest.

With regard to the other side of any economic assessment, the returns, these were primarily dependent on fruit quality. The average of the weekly prices for Cox apples from the 1982 crop was 41p kg^{-1} for Class I apples and 30p kg^{-1} for Class II. A crop of 25 t ha^{-1} of Class I apples would have given £2,000 profit, while the same crop of Class II apples would have given a loss. This is not to say that Class II Cox fruit was not worth producing (its sale price was greater than the costs of harvesting, storage and marketing which came to 22p kg^{-1}), merely that it could make only a small contribution towards recouping area-dependent costs. The quality argument is of even greater importance in relation to production of different varieties: high-quality varieties such as English Cox and Washington-State Red Delicious sell for

TABLE I. The economics of apple production in England in 1982
A. Costs per hectare of an orchard of Cox's Orange Pippin (pounds sterling ha^{-1})

	667 trees ha^{-1}	1,111 trees ha^{-1}
Establishment year		
Trees and stakes	1,868	3,444[1]
Total	3,476	5,265
Production year		
Materials	488	
Pruning	179	
Other labour (pre-harvest)	109	
Harvesting (picking & supervision+materials)	1,275	
Storage (25 tonnes ha^{-1})	1,450	
Marketing	2,800	
Overheads+Interest	1,035	

[1] Pro-rata with density for other tall-stake systems

B. Production year economics of an apple orchard of Cox/M.26 with 667 trees ha^{-1} yielding 25 t ha^{-1}

Costs of production etc[1], pence per kilo		Sale price[2], pence per kilo	
Overheads	4	Class I	41
Establishment	4		
'Growing'	3	Class II	30
Harvesting	5		
Storage	6		
Marketing	11		
Total	33		

[1] From Steer (1982)
[2] Average of weekly figures published in *The Grower*.

much higher prices than the easier-to-grow Golden Delicious, which may be unprofitable irrespective of yield because prices per kilogram do not cover the costs of harvesting, storage and marketing.

B. Integration of costs and returns: the use of discounted cash flows

Orchards are long-term investments, and different orchard systems have different patterns of costs and returns over the years. There is thus need to be able to compare the overall profitability of, for example, an orchard with a low planting cost, but which then does not crop heavily until the eighth or ninth year, with one with a higher initial cost but much quicker returns. Because money spent, or earned, in an early year must be regarded as having had the potential to incur or accrue interest thereafter, all costs and returns over the life of the orchard must be adjusted to take into account this 'time-value change' of money. Thus, a pound earned in the fifth year is 10% more valuable than a pound earned in the sixth year, if the interest rate still being paid on borrowed capital is 10%. The process of adjusting for interest rates is known as discounting, and the result is a discounted cash flow. There are two commonly used investment criteria based on discounted cash flow analysis.

(a) *Net present value* (NPV). This is found by discounting – at the rate at which loan capital is borrowed by the investor – all future cash flows to their present value (investment date) equivalent. Assuming that A is the net cash flow for year i, that is the profit or loss in that year, where the project has a life of n years and r is the project cost of capital, then:

$$P = \sum_{i=1}^{i=n} \frac{A_i}{(1+r)^i} \tag{1}$$

and P is the weighted sum of the annual cash flows.

If C is the initial capital invested, then the NPV is P–C.

(b) *Internal rate of return* (IRR). This is the rate of interest which, if charged to the project, would result in a NPV of zero, that is the highest rate which it could bear without making a loss. It is calculated as r from equation (1) with the value P set equal to C.

Thus, the earlier that costs and returns occur in the life of an orchard, the greater is their effect on NPV and IRR, to an extent determined by the interest rate r.

Another important economic criterion, which is best calculated using the discounting technique, is the time (years) required to break even, that is to pay back the initial capital plus interest. This is particularly important when there is a reasonable prospect of changes in demand for different varieties, or the possibility that a variety will become out-of-date in terms of productivity by the early introduction of successors.

IV. CHANGES IN PRODUCTION SYSTEMS, PRODUCTIVITY AND ECONOMICS

Two major changes need to be examined, the progressive replacement of tall trees on vigorous or semi-vigorous rootstocks with dwarfed trees, and the moves towards even higher densities of planting of dwarfed trees.

A. Production levels

The gross impact of the changes in production systems on production levels may be illustrated by comparing yields from three well-documented English orchards.

The first of these, planted in spring 1946, was the Fernhurst orchard of Imperial Chemical Industries. The trees, Cox plus pollinators on M.2 rootstock, were planted at a density of 330 trees ha^{-1} and grown quickly to their mature size – 4·5 m tall, round-headed bush trees. This orchard was regarded as a model of its kind, and a highly profitable investment (Anon 1965).

The second, planted in winter 1968/69 at East Malling, compared a wide range of densities of planting. It included updated versions of the Fernhurst system, using MM.111 as rootstock instead of M.2, with populations of 299 and 427 trees ha^{-1}, and also 'hedgerow' plantings on the dwarfing M.26 rootstock at densities up to 1,922 trees ha^{-1}. Cox was one of the main varieties studied (Parry 1981).

The third, planted in winter 1972/73 at East Malling, compared two contrasting management systems, with Cox as the main variety. One, on the semi-dwarfing MM.106 rootstock, is at a density of 667 trees ha^{-1} with the trees in hedgerows separated by tractor alleyways; the other has double rows of Cox on the dwarfing M.9 rootstock between adjacent alleyways at a density of 2,000 trees ha^{-1}.

TABLE II.   Yields of fruit (t ha^{-1} fresh weight) from English apple orchards, managed at different intensities (see text), from 2–10 years after planting

Site:	Fernhurst[1]	East Malling Research Station[2]				
Planting date:	1945/46	1968/69			1972/73	
Trees ha^{-1}:	330[3]	299[4]	427[4]	1922[5]	667[6]	2000[7]
Year						
2	0	0	0	0	3	8
3	0	1	1	9	2	7
4	0	1	1	2	10	19
5	2	7	12	26	1	5
6	2	7	12	14	24	30
7	3	11	16	18	33	41
8	4	20	26	24	18	24
9	12	1	0	10	12	25
10	12	17	23	27	18	36

[1] Dessert varieties, mainly Cox.
   Averages in years 11–15 = 20 t ha^{-1} and 16–20 = 26 t ha^{-1}.
[2] Cox
Rootstocks: [3] = M.2, [4] = MM.111, [5] = M.26, [6] = MM.106, [7] = M.9.

Yields are shown in Table II. The Fernhurst orchard, typical of its period (Anon 1958), did not achieve its maximum yield until between 16 and 20 years after planting, and its first heavy crop, of over 20 t ha^{-1}, was not attained until its twelfth year. The delay, compared with the more modern systems, must have been largely a result of the much more severe pruning used. Although Preston (1955) showed that trees on MM.111 do give slightly heavier early crops than those on M.2, the differences are not comparable with those in Table II. Preston (1958) stressed the lack of knowledge about how to induce early cropping of Cox. One very important contribution to earlier cropping in recent years has been the improved technology of producing well-branched trees in the nursery so that they bear fruit on up to 15 or 16 primary branches already present at planting.

In the trial planted in 1968/69, Cox on MM.111 with 299 and 427 trees ha^{-1} attained a 20 t yield in their eighth season, and the much higher density planting on M.26 attained this yield in the fifth season as, no doubt, the 1972/73 planting of 2,000 trees ha^{-1} on M.9 would have done but for a frost. Trees planted at 667 trees ha^{-1} in 1972/73 yielded more than 20 t ha^{-1} in their sixth year.

The changes in yield at maturity were not so great as those in precocity of cropping, but the more modern plantings at the higher densities do seem to have higher plateau levels of yield.

As will be discussed later, part of this change may be due to rootstock effects. When we look at density effects *per se*, resulting from changes in within-row spacing (with between-row spacings constant), we find the following three results in numerous trials, typified by the one reported by Parry (1981). First, in the first cropping year or two, yields per tree are highest at the closest spacings, possibly because they benefit from mutual shelter. Second, in subsequent years, the yield per tree at the closer spacings fails to increase as much as that at wider spacings, so that the yields per hectare move towards a similar level – although yields at the closest spacings tend to remain the highest: even in the last three years of Parry's trial, yield per hectare was always higher the closer the spacing in the row. Third, the fruits tend to be smaller where the trees are grown at higher planting densities, and the fruits have a lower proportion of their surface red-coloured – although a higher proportion of the fruits are free from serious russet and cracking.

Moving to multi-row systems, these tendencies are continued – Wertheim *et al.* (1985) showed that increasing the tree population of Red Boskoop on M.9 from 2,400 to 3,409 trees ha^{-1} (with slender spindles) or from 2,663 to 3,698 trees ha^{-1} (with North-Holland spindles) increased yield over the first six years from 196 to 244 t ha^{-1} and from 179 to 217 t ha^{-1}, respectively (1·1 times the yield per 0·9 ha). The regressions of yield on plant population were statistically significant. Goedegebure (1981) showed yield per hectare increasing with planting density (1,000, 2,000 and 3,000 trees per hectare) up to and including the fifteenth year although, as expected, the benefits were much greater in the earlier years. Other authors, eg Crowe (1985), observed a levelling off of the yield density curve at the highest densities as orchards reached their fifteenth year.

The greatest precocity of cropping to date, with yields of more than 50 t ha^{-1} of fruit in the second year after planting, has been achieved with tree densities of 13,720 trees ha^{-1} on the very dwarfing M.27 rootstock (Preston 1978) and in meadow orchards with 70,000 trees per hectare (Luckwill 1978).

B.   Economics

Some of the changes in costs have resulted from mechanization or the substitution of chemical technology for hand labour (eg for fruit thinning), but others have been system-related.

In the work-study report on the Fernhurst orchard of the 1960s, a harvesting rate of 4 bushels (72 kg) per hour was stated as the target for good pickers. In 1982, UK Ministry of Agriculture estimates of labour costs for harvesting implied a picking rate of $125\,kg\,h^{-1}$ for a semi-intensive production system. In northern Italy, it has been found that pickers average $106\,kg\,h^{-1}$ from large, round-canopy trees, $120\,kg\,h^{-1}$ from tall hedgerows (palmettes) and $185\,kg\,h^{-1}$ from the modern high-density systems on M.9 rootstock (Werth 1978). In the same region, the pruning of a round-crown or palmette orchard requires between 100 and 200 hours per hectare, whereas the dwarf-tree, high-density systems take 60 man-hours. With a pruning season of 500 hours, this means that one man can prune $2\cdot5$–$5\cdot0$ ha of the older-style orchards, but 8–10 ha of the modern systems, with 1,400 to 3,000 trees ha^{-1}. Because pruning dominates the pre-harvest labour inputs this determines how much land one man can manage.

Increase in intensification of planting from 1,000 to 3,000 trees ha^{-1} on M.9 rootstock has very little effect on labour requirements (Goedegebure 1981) and further intensification *per se* is unlikely to increase the orchard area which can be managed by one man. The greatest gain in this aspect of productivity is likely to come from the use of chemical plant growth regulators which, by controlling vegetative growth, can almost halve the time taken in pruning (Anon 1984).

The cost of establishment is markedly system-dependent and has increased dramatically. When each tree costs $£1\cdot80$ and each stake £1 (1982 prices), the cost of establishing a modern 2,000 trees ha^{-1} orchard is £5,600 for trees and stakes alone. This figure is ten times as much as it would cost to plant an older-style orchard with about 300 trees ha^{-1} without need (because of their vigorous, well-anchored rootstocks) for permanent stakes.

In spite of this increased planting cost, the increase in returns early in the life of the more intensive orchard has resulted in much earlier attainment of the 'break-even' point. The Fernhurst dessert apple orchards repaid their costs, including interest at 6%, by 1958, 12 years after planting. In contrast, all of the systems reported on by Parry (1981) were very solidly profitable within 10 years from planting, all giving internal rates of return of more than 23% over that period, and Stephens and Nicholson (1978) found that modern centre-leader Cox orchards on M.9 and MM.106 rootstocks reached 'break-even' in years 4 and 5. Stephens and Nicholson (1978) also used relatively short-run data to show that much earlier pay-back, as well as higher NPVs and rates of return, was obtained from modern centre-leader systems on M.9 and MM.106 than from older-style, more widely spaced, bush trees. Within the modern systems, the high-density systems on M.9 are outstanding in terms of NPV, that is in output value per hectare over the orchard life. The semi-intensive systems on MM.106, which do not need expensive tall stakes and have lower planting costs, because of lower tree numbers, can give as good, or better, returns on capital (Parry 1982; Jackson *et al.* 1985).

One factor which might affect the long-term profitability of the most intensive fruit orchards is loss of fruit quality as the trees mature (Goedegebure 1981; Parry 1981). The evidence on this point is, however, inconclusive and will be discussed further in the section on crop physiology where the apparent contradictions will be resolved.

Taking a broad general view of the changes in production and economics, two points are clear. First, the replacement of large-tree orchards by intensive systems on the dwarfing M.9 rootstock has: (a) greatly increased the yields per hectare in the early years after planting, and consequently over the orchard lifetime (of 15–20 years) though yields at maturity are not necessarily much higher; (b) greatly reduced the labour requirement for picking and pruning, and hence the total labour cost per kilogram of fruit; and (c) achieved (a) and (b) at the cost of much higher capital investment in the form of trees and stakes. The net effect has been to substitute capital for labour and to maximize income per hectare by investing heavily at planting time. Second, further increases in density of planting on M.9 rootstock above the basic level of around 1,000 to 1,250 trees ha^{-1} lead to increases in cropping, especially in the early years, at the expense of higher capital investment, but do not further reduce labour requirements.

V.   CROP-PHYSIOLOGICAL ANALYSIS

The most straightforward approach to assessing the components of system productivity in agronomic (non-economic) terms is to look at (a) the efficiency of solar energy interception, (b) the efficiency with which the energy is used to produce dry matter, (c) the partitioning of dry matter into biological components such as fruits, shoots and roots, and (d) further partitioning of the economic product according to quality grades.

In this review, it is useful to tackle these steps in reverse sequence.

A.   Factors controlling the quality of the harvested economic product

The fruit is the harvested product and its commercial value is determined by (a) its flavour and texture – varieties which are poor in these respects cannot be sold profitably, (b) its storage potential – to give an extended marketing season, and (c) its size, colour and skin finish – to meet consumer demands. These attributes are influenced by many varietal and environmental factors and by cultural practices. The one of greatest relevance to orchard system design is light intensity (Jackson 1980).

Fruit size, proportion of red-coloured skin, soluble solids content, sugar content and acidity are all influenced in a favourable way by high light intensity on the fruits and/or on the adjacent leaves. This influence has been shown both by correlation studies within trees and in artificial shading experiments. For Cox, red colouration, dependent on directly photosensitive anthocyanin production in the apple skin, as well as on available carbohydrate, is reduced by levels of shade which appear to have little effect on fruit size (this latter effect probably being to some extent masked by the concomitant effect of shading on fruit shed).

The reduction in dry matter content, starch and titrateable acid has effects on eating quality which are readily detectable. Fruits from the central, shaded, parts of trees frequently lack the flavour characteristic of the variety.

Light intensity also influences the numbers of fruits produced. The shaded parts of trees produce relatively few flower buds and a relatively small proportion of the buds sets fruits. The net effect is that dry matter production is reduced in shaded parts of trees, a relatively small proportion of the assimilates is partitioned to the fruits, and many of the fruits are of low commercial quality.

Among other system-related factors influencing fruit quality are (a) effects of rootstock on fruit quality – the fact that M.9 increases fruit size more than other rootstocks being particularly important, and (b) the influence of age of fruiting wood on fruit size – fruits borne as axillaries on one-year-old wood and on very old spur systems typically being smaller than those on spurs on 3- and 4-year-old wood.

B. Factors controlling dry matter partitioning

There is ample evidence that rootstocks have a major effect not only on dry matter production by the scion (the dwarfing effect) but also on cropping in relation to growth, that is on partitioning.

In general, fruit trees on the dwarfing rootstocks flower more profusely, and set larger crops of fruit early in their lives, than do trees on the more vigorous rootstocks (Hatton 1927), while at maturity they have a higher proportion of fruit buds to vegetative buds and also improved fruit set. The net effect is typified by the finding of Preston (1958) who noted that the ratio of total accumulated crop to weight of trunk and branches of Cox trees grubbed at 22 years of age was 1·8 for trees on M.16 (vigorous), 4·8 for trees on M.2 (semi-vigorous), and 8·3 for trees on M.9 (dwarfing).

The relative fruitfulness of trees, that is their ratio of fruit crop to vegetative growth, is also increased by (a) exposure to high levels of solar radiation, which increase flowering and fruit set, (b) minimal pruning – heavy pruning essentially stimulates vegetative growth rather than cropping, (c) tying branches down towards the horizontal instead of allowing them to grow upright – horizontal branches grow less vigorously, are more floriferous and set fruits more readily (Champagnat & Crabbe 1974), and (d) using growth retardants, particularly those which interfere with gibberellin biosynthesis and check shoot growth while increasing flower production (Quinlan & Richardson 1984; Williams 1984).

C. Efficiency of solar energy interception

The efficiency and effectiveness with which solar energy is captured are functions of overall orchard geometry, which is defined by the orchard system as well as by the density of the canopy and its foliar characteristics.

The fraction of the available solar energy which is intercepted (F) can be calculated from:

$$F = F_{max} - F_{max}e^{-KL} \qquad (2)$$

where F_{max} is the fraction of the available light which would be intercepted by non-transmitting trees or hedgerows of the same shape and arrangement, K is a light extinction coefficient (0·6 for apple) and L is $(LAI)/(F_{max})$. Details are given by Jackson and Palmer (1979, 1981) and Jackson (1981).

F_{max} can be calculated from knowledge of hedgerow heights and dimensions and solar angles and azimuths for direct light and also for diffuse light distributions (Jackson & Palmer 1972). Where the tree form and arrangement are too difficult to define mathematically, a physical system for measuring F_{max} may be possible.

Values of F_{max} for a wide range of hedgerow dimensions and configurations at different times of year and latitudes have been published by Jackson and Palmer (1972) and Jackson (1981). Values of both F_{max} and of F for a range of canopy densities have been published by Jackson and Palmer (1980) and Palmer (1981).

Given that fruit bud formation, fruit set, size, colour and eating quality are all adversely affected by shade, it is also of interest to calculate the volume of canopy which is, on average, irradiated above specified levels. This calculation can be done by using the equation:

$$L_I = F_{max} [(\ln I)/(-K)] \tag{3}$$

where I is the specified level of irradiance and L_I is the leaf area index of that part of the canopy that is illuminated above the specified level. The volume which is 'well illuminated' can then be calculated, as long as leaf area per unit tree volume is known (Jackson & Palmer 1981; Jackson 1981).

The implications are (a) that both the maximum yield potential and the maximum production of good quality fruits are limited by F_{max} when this is less than unity (continuous cover), and (b) that a given leaf area index (on an orchard basis) will be more efficient in light interception the greater the value of F_{max} with which it is associated. Typical values of F_{max} for hedgerow orchards of differing geometries are shown in Figure 1.

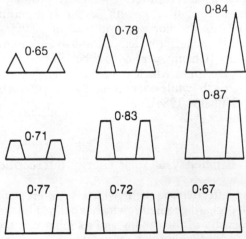

FIGURE 1. Hypothetical north-south orientated hedgerows, showing the fraction of available light (F_{max}) which is intercepted annually at 52°N, assuming that the hedgerows act as solid objects.

D.   Overall implications of the crop-physiological analysis

Evaluation of the recent changes in orchard systems in these crop-physiological terms leads to the conclusion that there has been a significant gain in productivity through the use of dwarfing rootstocks which, in particular, has increased the proportion of assimilates allocated to economic yield. The higher yields of the Cox hedgerow systems on M.26 compared with those of the more vigorous trees on MM.111 (Parry 1981) must have been due to differences in partitioning, because both ground cover and height, and hence potential light interception, were much greater on the latter. The partitioning efficiency or 'harvest index' of trees on M.9 can be very high. Hansen (1980) showed that the fruits represented more than 70% of the total dry matter increment of 4- and 5-year-old trees of Golden Delicious on M.9 rootstocks. Barlow (1971) reported on a long-term study of total dry matter production (fruits, leaves, trunks and branches, prunings and main roots) of trees of the apple cultivar Laxton's Superb. Over the 13 years of the trial, more than 70% of the dry weight of the trees on M.9 rootstocks had been in the fruits, as opposed to 40–50% of that of the trees on M.16. Such high values of partitioning to fruit are not usually attained with Cox, but further progress on assimilate partitioning at the systems level is dependent on finding the appropriate ways forward in terms of systems components – by research on clonal selection, rootstock selection, tree management and plant growth regulator use. For the globally dominant varieties, such as Golden Delicious, there does, however, seem to be little possibility to increase their overall system productivity by further increasing the proportion of assimilates allocated to fruit.

The question is, therefore, whether total potential productivity, in terms of light interception and dry matter production, has been and can continue to be increased.

The answer as far as commercial systems are concerned is that, as a result of the much higher densities of planting, light interception in the early years has been greatly increased. There is, apparently, no published information on light interception by traditional orchards of round-headed trees in their early years, but Jackson and Palmer (1972) reported that 38% of available light was intercepted by trees of Golden Delicious/M.9 planted at 3,780 trees ha^{-1} in single rows in their second year, while at the same age only 11% was intercepted by a (more vigorous) Cox/M.26 and Egremont Russet/MM.106 orchard at 961 trees ha^{-1} (Jackson 1975). Similarly, Verheij and Verwer (1973) showed that a 7-year-old Golden Delicious orchard on M.9 at a spacing of $3\,m\times1\,m$ intercepted 67% of the available light, while an orchard of the same age on M.2 at a spacing of $4\cdot25\,m\times3\cdot50\,m$ intercepted only 55%.

This rapid progress in improving light interception in the early years is being achieved in two ways. The first way is by planting trees which are already tall, with a large number of lateral primary branches, at the time of planting. These branches are available as the result of improved nursery practices, including chemical treatments which temporarily break apical dominance. The second way is by planting these trees at higher densities, either in hedgerows or, more recently, in multi-row systems, so minimizing tractor alleyways and maximizing F_{max}. As is clear from the equations given earlier, F_{max} is greatest per unit of leaf area when the trees are evenly distributed over the orchard surface, and multi-row and bed-systems are a move in this direction.

Much less progress is being made in increasing light interception by orchards at maturity; in fact, the reverse is probably occurring. Jackson and Palmer (1972) reported 81% interception by old-fashioned, round-crown, 5 m tall apple trees, spaced at 5·9 m×5·9 m and overlapping each other over the tractor alleyway. In contrast, good, modern hedgerow orchards generally intercept between 55% and 70% of the available radiation. Verheij and Verwer (1973) concluded that higher values were associated with loss of yield. This loss of yield at high levels of light interception may, however, result from poor tree and orchard design under crowded conditions, with uncontrolled vegetative shoots in the upper parts of the trees shading the fruiting zone excessively. This situation could be rectified by appropriate management. Jackson (1978) showed, for Golden Delicious on M.9, that yield was a linear function of light interception between 20% and 60%, with a yield of about 60 t ha^{-1} at the latter interception levels. Within 'meadow orchards', which have a virtually continuous cropping canopy and hence, presumably, very high light interception, yields of almost 100 t ha^{-1} of Golden Delicious have been achieved at Long Ashton in the cropping year (Luckwill 1978).

The reason that light interception, even in modern multi-row systems (Wertheim *et al.* 1985), is still under 70% is that, under conditions of even moderate shade, fruit quality is reduced, particularly fruit colour, and, under more severe shade, fruit bud initiation and set are decreased. Both of these disadvantages were minimized in the meadow orchards mentioned above because Golden Delicious is a green apple (not requiring light-dependent red colouring) and because the biennial harvesting of all shoots results in fruit bud formation occurring on well-exposed wood – but that system has its own disadvantages of biennial cropping and very high planting costs. When conventional trees are planted at very high densities, shade from the current season's growth, especially that at the top of the tree, becomes excessive. Such growth shades the older, fruiting, zones of the trees, and Jackson (1978) calculated that an orchard of otherwise optimal density with 4,773 evenly-spaced trees ha^{-1} of Golden Delicious/M.9 grown as typical spindlebushes would have a leaf area index of 0·43 above the uppermost fruits. This leaf area would intercept about 18% of the available light before it reached the cropping zone. To meet this problem, there is increasing interest in (a) tying down branches, including current-year's shoots, (b) summer pruning, to remove the current-year's shoots, in ultra-high-density orchards, and (c) the use of plant growth retardants to check shoot extension (Quinlan 1981).

A complementary approach to this removal or suppression of the outer vegetative canopy is to attempt to deepen the productive zone by overcoming the adverse effects of low light intensity on fruit quality and yield. Because red colour formation is the most sensitive of all quality parameters to shade, selection of 'coloured sports' which need less exposure to light is a high priority. There is also a possibility of using plant growth regulators to induce a greater degree of fruit bud initiation under shaded conditions.

Effects of higher densities of planting on fruit size are complex. Substitution of the dwarfing rootstocks, M.9 and M.26, for the more vigorous rootstocks in itself leads to an improvement in fruit size (although moving still further down the vigour scale to M.27 reduces the size of Cox and Golden Delicious fruits). The choice of pruning system, to tailor the trees to a more restricted space, also has an influence because an increase in the proportion of fruits on either one-year-old wood or old spurs reduces fruit size. Shade also reduces fruit size directly but if, as seems almost certain, this is a consequence of reduced carbohydrate supply, then this should be overcome by fruit thinning to bring the ratio of fruits to assimilate supply back in balance. It would appear, therefore, that developments in management techniques should enable fruit size to be retained as density of planting is increased. However, some of the potential treatments may have interactive effects. For example, summer pruning to increase the light available to the fruits and their adjacent leaves, which supply most of their photosynthates (Hansen 1969), also removes a proportion of the total photosynthesizing leaf surface.

VI. THE INTER-RELATIONSHIP BETWEEN CROP-PHYSIOLOGICAL AND ECONOMIC FACTORS *RE* APPLE PRODUCTION SYSTEMS

The evolution of systems which attain high levels of light interception, and hence yield, earlier in their lives than hitherto, not only increases the lifetime productivity of the orchard, but also alters the distribution of output value over time in an economically advantageous way. This is because, following the logic of discounted cash flow analysis, output early in the life of an orchard is more valuable than later output. This point is particularly important at present, given the historically high level of real interest rates. Where, as is generally the case, these earlier returns are obtained by using higher planting densities, the same logic works against the intensive systems, and it is clear that the high cost of trees and stakes is a constraint on further intensification. Research to lower the cost of planting materials is thus of the highest priority. Also, the first step in intensification – the move from large-tree to dwarf-tree orchards – was accompanied by special advantages resulting from use of the M.9 rootstock (giving greater floral bud production, better fruit set and increased fruit size) which contributed to a higher 'harvest index'. Such benefits will not attend further intensification, which must rely solely on density-induced changes in the cropping pattern over time and the final cropping level.

Rapid attainment of a high value of F_{max} with minimal within-tree shading can be obtained by growing tall, thin hedgerows, or trained, angled or horizontal canopies, on vigorous rootstocks, as well as by planting large numbers of potentially small trees. Essentially, F_{max} is determined by the proportion of ground surface directly covered by the trees and by their shadows integrated over the season. It is therefore a function of 'covered ground' plus the proportion of the alleyway surfaces which are shaded, the interception of diffuse light being rather similar to that of direct light in these respects under English conditions (Jackson & Palmer 1972). In order to intercept more than 60% of the light otherwise falling on an alleyway, the flanking hedgerows need to be at least twice as tall as the clear alleyway is wide, if the hedgerows are of the desirable, tapering, cross-section. Even this gives an F_{max} of only around 80%, and it is clear that shorter hedgerow trees, found in most commercial fruit orchards, yield appreciably below the potential level (Jackson & Palmer 1980). Tall hedgerows (such as in the English pillar and the Italian palmette systems) can be much cheaper to establish than high-density, short-tree plantings, and operations on them, such as harvesting, can readily be aided mechanically. The major difficulty with this tree form has always been that of controlling the vigour of the upper part of the trees and preventing excess shade and poor fruiting and branch replacement at the base. The availability of very effective plant growth retardants should make such systems more attractive.

At the more general level, it is clear that, for apple, there has been a massive switch of resources from labour for tree management to capital at planting time. It is questionable, given the currently high real interest rates and availability of labour, whether this trend will continue. The importance of fruit quality, which can be improved by labour-intensive treatments such as summer pruning, may even tend to switch the emphasis back towards more detailed tree management. Further reductions in labour inputs may, however, still be achieved by the use of plant growth regulators to reduce the need for pruning and, possibly, by increased mechanical aid for pruning and harvesting.

VII. RELEVANCE OF APPLE SYSTEMS ADVANCES TO OTHER FRUIT TREE CROPS

Among the other temperate fruits, pears seem very likely to follow the same pattern of movement to intensive systems of production as have apples, with two significant differences. First, pear fruits are less shade-sensitive than apples, so planting at high densities should carry fewer risks and drawbacks. Second, the only truly dwarfing rootstock currently available, Quince C, does not have specific advantages equivalent to those of M.9 for apple. It tends, in particular, to give small fruits in comparison with the semi-dwarfing rootstocks available.

Plums and cherries, particularly cherries, are characterized by very poor partitioning compared with apples. Cherry trees on the standard rootstocks (eg F12/1 and Colt) grow more rapidly than typical, commercially grown, apple trees but cropping levels are much lower. The major development here is likely to be the use of truly dwarfing rootstocks, compact scions or chemical growth control, to permit a move towards hedgerow orchards similar to the apple orchards planted in the 1970s.

Peaches have several characteristics which suit them to a revolutionary change in cropping system. Some of the varieties root well from hardwood cuttings and, if the shoots are cut back after cropping, a new shoot can grow and differentiate flowers in the same season in warm climates (Erez 1981). It is therefore possible to grow them in an annual-cropping meadow orchard system. If the initial commercial ventures succeed, peach or nectarine could well be transformed into a cheaply established high-density crop with an annual cropping cycle. It will therefore have followed cotton as far as the 'rattoon' stage in the progress from a perennial to an annual crop.

VIII. RELEVANCE OF FRUIT TREE SYSTEMS TO OTHER TREE CROPS

Clearly, the concept of high-density planting of high-quality planting material, in order to exploit rapidly the resources of soil and solar radiation, has direct relevance to nut trees and others, such as rubber, which yield an annual harvest. Economic considerations may also be similar for the different crops, although some of the special factors relevant to fruit tree crops may not apply. In particular, the value of dwarf trees, which can be hand-harvested from the ground and easily pruned, is not universally applicable to non-fruit tree species.

The definite stimulus to growth, presumably as a result of mutual shelter, which occurs in the early orchard years as a consequence of close planting may be of wider general relevance.

REFERENCES

Anon. (1958). Apples and pears. *Bull. Minist. Agric. Fish. Fd*, no. 133, 131.

Anon. (1965). *Fernhurst Orchard – a profitable investment in dessert apples.* Haslemere (Surrey): ICI Agricultural Division, Plant Protection.

Anon. (1984). *Paclobutrazol plant growth regulator for fruit.* (Technical data sheet.) Haslemere (Surrey): ICI Plant Protection Division.

Barlow, H. W. B. (1971). Effect of cropping on the growth of the apple tree. *Rep. E. Malling Res. Stn 1970*, 52.

Britton, D. K. (1977). Changes in the structure and performance of British fruit production. *Rep. E. Malling Res. Stn 1976*, 169–176.

Chalmers, D. J., van den Ende, B. & van Heek, L. (1978). Productivity and mechanisation of the Tatura trellis orchard. *HortScience*, **13**, 517–521.

Champagnat, P. & Crabbe, J. (1974). Morphological constraints and training of fruit trees. *Proc. int. Horticultural Congress, 19th, vol. 3*, 125–136.

Couvillon, G. A. & Pokorny, F. A. (1985). Production of inexpensive peach trees from rooted cuttings. *Acta Hortic.*, **160**. In press.

Crowe, A. D. (1985). Effect of density of cropping of Spartan apple trees through 16 seasons. *Acta Hortic.*, **160**. In press.

Dunn, J. S. & Stolp, M. (1981). Mechanical harvesting of apples and raspberries grown on the Lincoln Canopy System. *Acta Hortic.*, **114**, 261–268.

Erez, A. (1981). The fresh market peach meadow orchard: the mechanized and intensive high-yield systems. *Acta Hortic.*, **114**, 285–291.

Flierman, J. & Houter, J. (1976). Alternatieve plantsystemen I en II. *Fruitteelt*, **66**, 1170–1172; 1190–1192.

Goedegebure, J. (1981). Economic aspects of high density plantings in apple growing in the Netherlands. *Acta Hortic.*, **114**, 388–394.

Hansen, P. (1969). [14]C studies in apple trees. IV. Photosynthate consumption in fruits in relation to the leaf-fruit ratio and the leaf-fruit position. *Physiologia Pl.*, **22**, 186–198.

Hansen, P. (1980). Crop load and nutrient translocation. In: *Mineral nutrition of fruit trees*, edited by D. Atkinson *et al.*, 201–212. London: Butterworth.

Hatton, R. G. (1927). The influence of different rootstocks upon the vigour and productivity of the variety budded or grafted thereon. *J. Pomol.*, **6**, 1–28.

Hudson, J. P. (1971). Meadow orchards. *Agriculture, Lond.*, **78**, 157–160.

Hutton, R. J. (1980). Update on the Australian fruit industry – culture, production, marketing and trends. *Compact Fruit Tree*, **13**, 72–87.

Jackson, J. E. (1975). Patterns of distribution of foliage and light. In: *Climate and the orchard*, edited by H. C. Pereira, 31–40. Farnham Royal: Commonwealth Agricultural Bureaux.

Jackson, J. E. (1978). Utilization of light resources by high density planting systems. *Acta Hortic.*, **65**, 61–70.

Jackson, J. E. (1980). Light interception and utilization by orchard systems. *Hortic. Rev.*, **2**, 208–267.

Jackson, J. E. (1981). Theory of light interception by orchards and a modelling approach to optimizing orchard design. *Acta Hortic.*, **114**, 69–79.

Jackson, J. E. & Hamer, P. J. C. (1980). The causes of year-to-year variations in the average yield of Cox's Orange Pippin apple in England. *J. hort. Sci.*, **55**, 149–156.

Jackson, J. E. & Palmer, J. W. (1972). Interception of light by model hedgerow orchards in relation to latitude, time of year and hedgerow configuration and orientation. *J. appl. Ecol.*, **9**, 341–357.

Jackson, J. E. & Palmer, J. W. (1979). A simple model of light transmission and interception by discontinuous canopies. *Ann. Bot.*, **44**, 381–383.

Jackson, J. E. & Palmer, J. W. (1980). A computer model study of light interception by orchards in relation to mechanized harvesting and management. *Sci. Hortic. (Neth.)*, **13**, 1–7.

Jackson, J. E. & Palmer, J. W. (1981). Light distribution in discontinuous canopies: calculation of leaf areas and canopy volumes above defined 'irradiance contours' for use in productivity modelling. *Ann. Bot.*, **47**, 561–565.

Jackson, J. E., White, G. C. & Duncan, C. (1985). Economic appraisal of orchards of Cox's Orange Pippin apple on M.9 and MM.106 rootstocks. *Acta Hortic.*, **160**. In press.

Luckwill, L. C. (1978). Meadow orchards and fruit walls. *Acta Hortic.*, **65**, 237–243.

Palmer, J. W. (1981). Computed effects of spacing on light interception and distribution within hedgerow trees in relation to productivity. *Acta Hortic.*, **114**, 80–88.

Parry, M. S. (1981). A comparison of hedgerow and bush tree orchard systems at different within-row spacings with four apple cultivars. *J. hort. Sci.*, **56**, 219–235.

Parry, M. S. (1982). Cash-flow studies on three orchard systems for Cox. *Rep. E. Malling Res. Stn 1981*, 185–191.

Preston, A. P. (1955). Apple rootstock studies: Malling-Merton rootstocks. *J. hort. Sci.*, **30**, 25–33.

Preston, A. P. (1958). Apple rootstock studies: thirty-five years' results with Cox's Orange Pippin on clonal rootstocks. *J. hort. Sci.*, **33**, 194–201.

Preston, A. P. (1978). A bed system for planting apples on the dwarfing rootstock M.27. *Acta Hortic.*, **65**, 229–235.

Quinlan, J. D. (1981). Recent developments in the chemical control of tree growth. *Acta Hortic.*, **114**, 144–151.

Quinlan, J. D. & Richardson, P. J. (1984). Effect of paclobutrazol (PP333) on apple shoot growth. *Acta Hortic.*, **146**, 105–111.

Schmitz-Hubsch, H. & Heinrichs, P. (1941). *Der Spindelbusch und seine Behandlung beim Pflanzen und Schneiden*. 3. Aufl. Wiesbaden.

Steer, P. (1982). *A quick guide to top fruit costings 1982*. Cambridge: MAFF, Agricultural Development & Advisory Service.

Stephens, C. P. & Nicholson, J. A. H. (1978). The economics of intensive orchards in the United Kingdom. *Acta Hortic.*, **65**, 31–39.

Utermark, H. (1977). Growing and marketing fruit in the Elbe River Valley, Germany. *Compact Fruit Tree*, **10**, 38–48.

van Oosten, H. J. (1979). Current developments in the Dutch fruit industry. *Compact Fruit Tree*, **12**, 34–46.

Verheij, E. W. M. & Verwer, F. L. J. A. W. (1973). Light studies in a spacing trial with apple on a dwarfing and a semi-dwarfing rootstock. *Sci. Hortic. (Neth.)*, **1**, 25–42.

Werth, K. (1978). Economics of high density planting in South Tyrol. *Acta Hortic.*, **65**, 47–52.

Wertheim, S. J. (1981). High-density planting: development and current achievements in the Netherlands, Belgium and West Germany. *Acta Hortic.*, **114**, 318–330.

Wertheim, S. J., de Jager, A. & Duyzens, M. J. J. P. (1985). Comparison of single-row and multi-row planting systems with apple with regard to productivity, fruit size and colour and light conditions. *Acta Hortic.*, **160**. In press.

Williams, M. W. (1984). Use of bioregulators to control vegetative growth of fruit trees and improve fruiting efficiency. *Acta Hortic.*, **146**, 97–104.

Winter, F. & Welte, M. (1985). Trends of production, cultivars and planting systems on apples and pears in western Europe. *Acta Hortic.*, **160**. In press.

27

TRANSPIRATION AND ASSIMILATION OF TREE AND AGRICULTURAL CROPS: THE 'OMEGA FACTOR'

P. G. JARVIS
Department of Forestry and Natural Resources, University of Edinburgh, The King's Buildings, Edinburgh, Scotland

NOTATION

A	total assimilation rate	mol m^{-2} s^{-1}
C	carbon dioxide concentration	μmol mol^{-1}
c_p	molar heat capacity of air at constant pressure	J mol^{-1} K^{-1}
D	water vapour saturation deficit of the air	kPa
D_{eq}	equilibrium saturation deficit of the air (defined by equations 5 and 15)	kPa
D_{imp}	imposed saturation deficit of the air (defined by equation 3)	kPa
E	total transpiration rate	mol m^{-2} s^{-1}
E_{eq}	equilibrium transpiration rate (defined by equations 4 and 13)	mol m^{-2} s^{-1}
E_{imp}	imposed transpiration rate (defined by equations 2 and 14)	mol m^{-2} s^{-1}
E_I	evaporation rate of intercepted water	mol m^{-2} s^{-1}
e	partial pressure of water vapour	kPa
$e^\star$	saturation vapour pressure of water at leaf temperature	kPa

g	surface conductance	mol m^{-2} s^{-1}
P	atmospheric pressure	kPa
R_n	net radiation flux density	J m^{-2} s^{-1}
S	flux density of heat into storage in canopy and soil	J m^{-2} s^{-1}
s	slope of the relation between saturation vapour pressure $e^\star$ and temperature	kPa K^{-1}
Γ	carbon dioxide compensation concentration	μmol mol^{-1}
γ	psychrometric constant ($c_p P/\lambda$)	kPa K^{-1}
λ	molar latent heat of vaporization of water	J mol^{-1}
ε	$s/\gamma = s\lambda/(Pc_p)$	dimensionless
Ω	the 'omega factor' or decoupling coefficient (defined by equations 8 and 16)	dimensionless

subscripts

a	a property of the ambient air outside the leaf boundary layer
as	for the pathway from canopy surface to the independent reference level
b	for the pathway from leaf surface to ambient air
c	a canopy property
i	at the level of instrument placement
l	a leaf surface property
m	a property of the mixed layer of the planetary boundary layer
o	a property of the notional canopy surface
s	for the pathway through the stomatal pores
w	at the mesophyll cell walls

I. INTRODUCTION

We usually understand a crop to be vegetation that is managed by man to produce a particular product. The management usually includes cultivation of the soil, planting, tending in various ways and harvesting, and to facilitate these operations the plants are generally grown in a regular pattern, such as in rows, pure stands or simple mixtures. We are used to talking about agricultural crops and we have a fairly clear idea of what we mean. A number of species of shrubs and trees have also been grown as crops for a very long time in orchards (eg olives, apples, cherries) and in plantations (eg tea, coffee, rubber). Commercial forestry has been moving progressively from exploitation of natural forest, through tending of natural forest, to the intensive management of completely artificial plantations, sometimes on very short rotations.

Plantations of forest species have many similarities with fields of agricultural crops, and recently foresters working with tree plantations have described themselves as tree farmers. Foresters and agronomists share similar management problems, concerning, for example, spacing, fertilizer regime, irrigation and pest control; and these problems concern similar biological issues such as canopy structure and radiation interception, carbon assimilation and allocation, fertilizer requirements, water loss and sensitivity to water stress. We might, therefore, expect substantial rapid advances to be made in our understanding of the functioning of tree crops, and in our identification of individual tree and stand ideotypes, by directly extrapolating many of the ideas and concepts that have been developed by agronomists. As this conference shows, such advances have been made in orchard and plantation crops, perhaps because the development of these crops has generally been in the hands of agronomists. With forest crops, there has, regrettably, been a hold-up in the transfer of information and ideas from agronomy into plantation management, probably largely because foresters and agronomists follow separate educational and career paths. This separation has its roots in the historical origins of the two professions and is largely maintained today by a sense among foresters of the uniqueness of their problems.

Some of the differences between forest and agricultural crops are obvious, and do not have fundamental biological consequences – such as their perennial and annual habit. Other differences *do* have fundamental biological consequences, and, in this chapter, I shall focus on one such difference, namely that trees are tall, whereas most agricultural crops are short (ie less than 1 m in height). To show how tallness affects the functioning of crops, I shall introduce the concept of coupling between leaves and the atmosphere, and the '*omega factor*' (see below). Later I shall show that this concept provides useful insights (a) when extrapolating from experiments – in growth rooms, glasshouses or small plots – to field conditions, (b) when making crops out of plants that may grow as isolated individuals in the wild, and (c) when designing crops made up of mixtures of species.

II. COUPLING BETWEEN LEAVES AND THE ATMOSPHERE

A. The concept of coupling

By reason of its height, tall vegetation generates more turbulence than short vegetation, has a larger roughness length (Szeicz *et al.* 1969), a larger 'low-level' drag coefficient (Jarvis & Stewart 1979) and is said generally to be aerodynamically rough (Thom 1975). Also, because of its height, a tall canopy is in a higher windspeed regime than a short canopy and this, combined with a larger drag coefficient, gives a tall canopy a much lower boundary layer resistance than a short canopy (Stewart & Thom 1973). Consequently, the leaves in a tall canopy experience a more turbulent and faster air-stream than the leaves in a short canopy. In general terms, we may say that the leaves in a tall canopy are well coupled to the air around about them, and that the air within the canopy is well coupled to the atmosphere overhead.

Monteith (1981) defined coupling in the following way: 'Two systems are said to be coupled when they are capable of exchanging force, momentum, energy or mass. – The coupling of an organism to its environment can be described by a set of analogous circuits, each describing the transport of a specific entity – if the resistance between A and B in a circuit is much smaller than the resistance between B and C, then A and B are said to be "tightly coupled"'.

To obtain an intuitive appreciation of what this definition means, consider a leaf in an air-stream (Fig. 1A). If the conditions of temperature, vapour pressure, vapour saturation deficit and carbon dioxide concentration at the surface of the leaf were the same as in the ambient air-stream, there would be perfect coupling between the two. This would be approached if the leaf were extremely well ventilated, so that the boundary layer was very thin, and any fluxes through the leaf surface were very small.

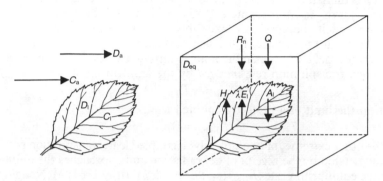

FIGURE 1. A diagram to illustrate A. a perfectly coupled leaf and B. a completely decoupled leaf. D is saturation deficit, and C is carbon dioxide concentration. The subscript l indicates values at the leaf surface, and the subscript a values in the ambient air-stream. R_n is net radiation, Q is photosynthetically useful shortwave radiation, H is sensible heat transfer, λE_l is latent heat transfer and A_l is assimilation of CO_2. The box around the leaf in B isolates it from the air-stream above so that sensible and latent heat are continuously added to, and CO_2 removed from, the enclosed volume.

At the other extreme, consider a leaf completely isolated from the air-stream by an infinite resistance (Fig. 1B). Because of the input of radiation, heat and water vapour will be continuously added to the air around the leaf, and carbon dioxide will be removed from it, so that the temperature and humidity of the air will rise and its CO_2 concentration will fall. This leaf is completely decoupled from the ambient air-stream. In practice, complete decoupling does not occur: there is always some exchange across the walls of the box in Figure 1B, however short and dense the crop and low the windspeed. The degree of coupling or decoupling that occurs in practice can be expressed quantitatively on a scale between these two extremes. To define this scale we consider transpiration from a leaf. By analogy, the same argument may be applied to assimilation by a leaf and to the exchanges of water vapour and CO_2 by a canopy (Monteith 1963).

B. Transpiration from a leaf

Although stomatal conductance, boundary layer thickness, temperature and saturation deficit vary over the surface of a leaf, in the following discussion we shall assume a leaf with uniform properties over its surface. The rate of transpiration from an isothermal, hypostomatous[1] leaf (E_l) is exactly given by:

$$E_l = g_s[e^\star - e_l]/P = g_s D_l/P \tag{1}$$

where g_s is the stomatal conductance per unit area of the surface containing stomata, $[e^\star - e_l]$ is the usual drop in water vapour pressure across the stomatal pores, D_l is the saturation deficit at the surface of the leaf and P is atmospheric pressure (Jarvis & McNaughton 1985). It is useful to work in terms of saturation deficit, because this takes into account both the heat and water vapour fluxes at the surface. For a leaf perfectly coupled to the atmosphere, the saturation deficit of the ambient air is imposed at the leaf surface, so that we define a transpiration rate *imposed* by the ambient air-stream $(E_{l,imp})$ as:

$$E_{l,imp} = g_s D_{l,imp}/P \tag{2}$$

where, in the limit of a perfectly coupled leaf,

$$D_{l,imp} = D_a . \tag{3}$$

At the other extreme, of a completely decoupled leaf, transpiration proceeds at a rate dictated by the receipt of net radiation and approaches the limit often called the equilibrium rate $(E_{l,eq})$ (eg Slatyer & McIlroy 1961; McNaughton & Jarvis 1983). For a hypostomatous leaf with uniformly distributed net radiation (R_n) and boundary layers of equal thickness on its two surfaces:

$$E_{l,eq} = R_n \varepsilon / [(\varepsilon + 2)\lambda] \tag{4}$$

where λ is the molar latent heat of vaporization, and ε is the change of latent heat content relative to the change of sensible heat content of saturated air, defined explicitly in the list of symbols. The saturation deficit at the surface of a decoupled, hypostomatous leaf also approaches an equilibrium value $(D_{l,eq})$ that is given by:

$$D_{l,eq} = \gamma \varepsilon R_n / [(\varepsilon + 2)c_p g_s] \tag{5}$$

where γ is the psychrometric constant and c_p is the molar heat capacity of air at constant pressure (Jarvis & McNaughton 1985).

The transpiration rate normally operates somewhere between the two extremes represented by equations (2) and (4), the saturation deficit at the leaf surface, D_l, expressing the degree of coupling. For all but a perfectly coupled leaf, D_l is clearly not an independent variable. If, for example, the stomatal conductance of all the stomatal pores changes, so that g_s changes significantly, the rates of transpiration and sensible heat flux will change together with the gradients of temperature and vapour pressure across the leaf boundary layers. An increase in g_s, for example, will lead to an increase in humidity, a decrease in temperature, and thus a decrease in D_l at the leaf surface. A wholly independent reference saturation deficit, unchanging with changes in transpiration rate, will only be found further away from the surface, outwith the leaf boundary layer.

We may describe transpiration in terms of the imposed and equilibrium components with the following form of the combination equation:

$$E_l = \Omega_l E_{l,eq} + (1 - \Omega_l)E_{l,imp} \tag{6}$$

and the saturation deficit at the leaf surface by:

---

[1] A hypostomatous leaf has stomata in its under (abaxial) surface only, whereas an amphistomatous leaf has stomata in both its surfaces.

$$D_1 = \Omega_1 D_{1,eq} + (1-\Omega_1)D_a, \tag{7}$$

where Ω_1 is a decoupling coefficient now known as the *'omega factor'*. For a hypostomatous leaf with boundary layers of equal thickness, Ω_1 is defined by:

$$\Omega_1 = (\varepsilon+2)/(\varepsilon+2+2g_b/g_s). \tag{8}$$

Jarvis and McNaughton (1985) also give a set of definitions of D_1, E_1 and Ω_1 for symmetrical amphistomatous leaves.

Ω_1 is a dimensionless factor that can assume values between 0 and 1, depending on the degree of coupling, or, more appropriately, the degree of decoupling. For a perfectly coupled leaf, as in Figure 1A, $\Omega_1 = 0$; for a completely decoupled leaf, as in Figure 1B, $\Omega_1 = 1\cdot0$. It is essentially a weighting factor that describes the extent to which transpiration is made up of the equilibrium and imposed components as shown in Figure 2. When Ω_1 is close to zero and coupling is strong, the transpiration rate is dominated by the imposed component and depends on the ambient saturation deficit and the stomatal conductance. When Ω_1 is close to $1\cdot0$, the transportation rate is dominated by the equilibrium component, and depends on the net radiation receipt, but is not sensitive to the stomatal conductance.

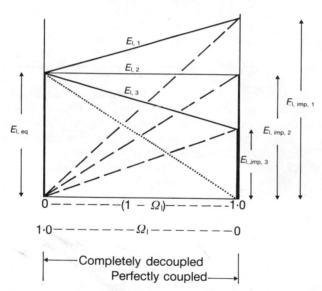

FIGURE 2.   A diagram to show how the equilibrium (.........) and imposed (————) components of transpiration add up to give the total transpiration of a leaf (————). The equilibrium rate on the left ordinate, set by net radiation, is combined with three different imposed rates on the right ordinate, set by saturation deficit and stomatal conductance.

Jarvis and McNaughton (1985) showed that the responsiveness of transpiration to a small, fractional change in stomatal conductance is given by:

$$dE_1/E_1 = (1-\Omega_1)dg_s/g_s. \tag{9}$$

Thus, for perfect coupling ($\Omega_1 = 0$), a small change in g_s results in an equiproportional change in transpiration rate, whereas for complete decoupling a small change in stomatal conductance has no effect on transpiration. At intermediate values of Ω_l, transpiration is controlled by g_s with intermediate effectiveness and shows varying dependence on net radiation and ambient saturation deficit.

The value of Ω_l depends on both the boundary layer and stomatal conductances (see equation 8). A large boundary layer conductance minimizes the gradient of saturation deficit across the boundary layer and results in strong coupling between D_l and D_a. Thus, values of Ω_l are smaller at higher windspeeds than at lower windspeeds, and small leaves have smaller values of Ω_l than large leaves (Table I). Large stomatal conductances, on the other

TABLE I. Some examples of the omega factor for hypostomatous leaves (Ω_l) of different sizes in different windspeeds (for details, see Jarvis & McNaughton 1985). Small leaves, at high windspeeds, are most closely coupled to the atmosphere (ie Ω_l is smallest)

	Leaf width (mm)	Windspeed (m s^{-1})		
		0·2	1·0	5·0
Teak	260	0·97	0·94	0·79
Apple	60	0·50	0·26	0·11
Spruce	2	0·18	0·08	0·03

hand, minimize the gradient of D through the stomata so that D_l tends towards zero. To take an extreme example, for a wet leaf, ie with infinite g_s, D_l is zero, irrespective of the values of D_a or g_b. Thus, the degree of coupling increases with stomatal closure. It is noteworthy, too, that hypostomatous leaves have smaller values of Ω_l than do amphistomatous leaves, other things being equal (Jarvis & McNaughton 1985). It may be significant that most trees have hypostomatous leaves so that, on this account, their transpiration would be more sensitive to change in g_s.

C.   Photosynthesis by a leaf

A parallel set of concepts may be applied to coupling between the concentration of carbon dioxide at the leaf surface (C_l) and that in the ambient air-stream (C_a). Concentration, in this context, is expressed as the molar fraction of CO_2 in air. Over the normal range of ambient CO_2 concentrations, assimilation of carbon dioxide (A_l) increases almost linearly with increase in the average CO_2 concentration at the mesophyll cell walls within the leaf (C_w), as shown in Figure 3A. The locations of the series of CO_2 concentrations across the leaf boundary layer, and through a stomatal pore, are shown in the diagram of the system being considered in Figure 3B. C_w is a pivotal concentration that depends on the fluxes of CO_2 to and from the mesophyll cells and the supply of CO_2 through the stomata. How a particular value of C_w is the result of these fluxes is also shown in Figure 3A. The CO_2 concentration at the leaf surface, C_l, depends on both C_a and C_w. Combining these supply and demand

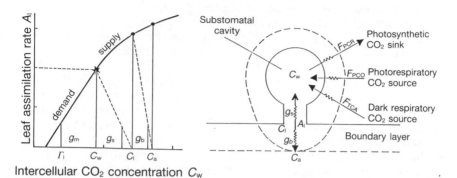

Intercellular CO_2 concentration C_w

FIGURE 3.
A.   The relationship between assimilation rate of leaves of *Picea sitchensis* (A_l) and the average CO_2 concentration at the mesophyll cell walls in the intercellular spaces (C_w). Superimposed are CO_2 concentrations along the pathway from ambient air (C_a) to leaf surface (C_l) to mesophyll wall (C_w), leading to the assimilation rate indicated by $\star$. The supply functions are shown by the dashed lines, the slopes of which give g_b and g_s as shown. The heavy solid line is the demand function, the initial slope of which gives the mesophyll conductance (g_m).
B.   A diagram of the system around a single stoma to show the location of the concentrations, conductances and fluxes.

functions for carbon dioxide with the light requirement of photosynthesis leads to complete models of assimilation (eg Reed *et al.* 1976). As with transpiration, we may derive from such a model parallel expressions for 'imposed' and 'equilibrium' assimilation rates. For a leaf perfectly coupled to the atmosphere (Fig. 1A), the CO_2 concentration of the ambient air is imposed at the leaf surface like D_a. For a leaf completely decoupled from the ambient atmosphere (Fig. 1B), C_l falls to Γ_l and the net influx of carbon dioxide through the stomata becomes zero. The assimilation of carbon dioxide into the photosynthetic carbon reduction (PCR) cycle then equals the evolution of carbon dioxide through the photosynthetic carbon oxidation (PCO) cycle and the concurrent daytime component of 'dark' respiration through the TCA cycle (Fig. 3B). The net influx of carbon dioxide when assimilation is proceeding at the equilibrium rate is zero, but the fixation of carbon dioxide into the PCR cycle continues at a rate that is dependent on radiation and temperature. As with transpiration, the degree of coupling determines the primary driving variables and the effectiveness of stomatal control.

D.   Transpiration from plants in the field

In the field we are concerned with transpiration from individual plants, groups of plants in clumps, and large areas of crops with a continuous canopy. We can regard an individual plant as a collection of the leaves we have just considered, and continue to use the argument so far developed, as long as the ambient saturation deficit is not affected by a change in the transpiration rate. When the foliage is grouped together, it may be necessary to move the reference location further away from the leaf surfaces for D_a to remain independent, and this results in a smaller boundary layer conductance. When a number of plants are grouped together, the saturation deficit in the vicinity of the leaves certainly becomes influenced by a change in g_s and E_1.

If the stomatal conductance of most of the leaves in an extensive crop changes, the consequent changes in the fluxes of heat and water vapour from the individual leaves combine to change the saturation deficit in the vicinity of the leaves. As the scale increases from leaf to plant, to a group of plants and to an extensive canopy, it becomes necessary to move further and further away from the leaf surface to find a reference location where the saturation deficit is again independent of changes in stomatal conductance and transpiration rate.

Let us now consider an extensive crop with a well-developed internal boundary layer extending across the surface layer above (McNaughton & Jarvis 1983) (Fig. 4). With some reservations (see Jarvis & McNaughton

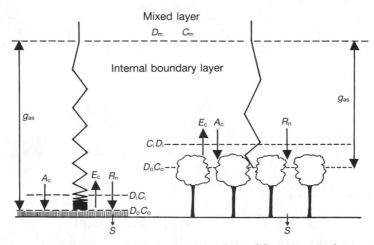

FIGURE 4. A diagram to show the location of the CO_2 concentrations, saturation deficits and conductances referred to in the text. On the left is shown a short agricultural crop, and on the right is a tall tree crop. The notation is given at the beginning of this chapter.

1985), we can treat such an extensive canopy in an analogous manner to an individual leaf with convective heat and water vapour transfer from one side only (the 'big leaf' model), and express transpiration from the canopy as:

$$E_c = g_c D_o/P. \qquad (10)$$

The canopy conductance (g_c) is usually taken as the unweighted total of the stomatal conductances of all the leaves, although this is not without criticism (Jarvis & McNaughton 1985), and D_o is a notional surface saturation deficit within the canopy boundary layer. A reference saturation deficit, (D_m), unchanging with changes in the canopy conductance, is now found in the mixed layer above the surface layer (Fig. 4), and a canopy boundary layer conductance or resistance (r_{as}) is defined from the notional crop surface out to this reference location. McNaughton and Jarvis (1983) showed that about one-third of this resistance may occur *above* the level where instruments are usually sited, with the result that r_{as} is usually substantially under-estimated.

With these definitions, transpiration from the whole canopy can be expressed in an analogous form to the equations for a single leaf as follows:

$$E_c = \Omega_c E_{c,eq} + (1 - \Omega_c) E_{c,imp} \tag{11}$$

and

$$D_o = \Omega_c D_{c,eq} + (1 - \Omega_c) D_m \tag{12}$$

where

$$E_{c,eq} = (R_n - S)\varepsilon/[(\varepsilon+1)\lambda], \tag{13}$$

$$E_{c,imp} = g_c D_m/P, \tag{14}$$

$$D_{c,eq} = \gamma\varepsilon(R_n - S)/[(\varepsilon+1)c_p g_c] \tag{15}$$

and

$$\Omega_c = (\varepsilon+1)/(\varepsilon+1+g_{as}/g_c). \tag{16}$$

The sensitivity of a change in transpiration to a fractional change in canopy conductance is, as before, given by:

$$dE_c/E_c = (1 - \Omega_c)dg_c/g_c. \tag{17}$$

Ω_c is a decoupling coefficient exactly analogous to Ω_1 but always larger than Ω_1, because the total conductance from leaves in a canopy to the unchanging reference above is always smaller than the conductance across the leaf boundary layer alone.

Some typical values of Ω_c are shown in Table II. These are likely to be under-estimates, because of the under-estimation of r_{as} referred to earlier, but they clearly show large differences between tall, aerodynamically rough vegetation and short, smooth crops in the degree of coupling to the air overhead.

TABLE II. Some examples of average values of the omega factor (Ω_c) for vegetation of different heights (for details see Jarvis & McNaughton 1985). Tall canopies are most closely coupled to the atmosphere (ie Ω_c is smallest)

Vegetation	Height	
	(m)	Ω_c
Grassland	0·2	0·8
Wheat	0·5	0·6
Cotton	1·3	0·4
Pine woods	15	0·1

Putting these values of Ω_c into equation (11) shows that transpiration from tree crops is dominated by $E_{c,imp}$ whereas, in complete contrast, transpiration from agricultural crops is dominated by $E_{c,eq}$. Putting appropriate values of

Ω_c into equation (17) shows that a small, fractional change in g_s would be expected to bring about an almost proportional change in the transpiration rate of tree crops, whereas it would have little effect on transpiration from agricultural crops. In other words, transpiration from tree crops is expected to follow the saturation deficit of the ambient air-stream closely and to be sensitively controlled by canopy conductances, whereas transpiration from agricultural crops is expected to follow the net radiation closely and to be relatively insensitive to small changes in canopy conductance.

In support of the first contention, Figure 5 shows transpiration from two adjacent stands of *Pinus sylvestris* increasing with increase in the saturation

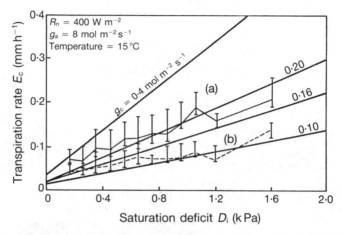

FIGURE 5. The relation between transpiration rate (E_c) and saturation deficit just above the canopy (D_i) for two stands of *Pinus sylvestris* with leaf area indices of (a) 3·1 and (b) 2·4. The four straight lines show the expected transpiration rates at the constant canopy conductances indicated (g_c) (from Whitehead *et al.* 1984).

deficit of the air above the stands. The two stands had similar stomatal conductances most of the time, but rather different canopy conductances because of different leaf area indices. The curves are curvilinear, rather than linear, as implied by equation (14), because the stomatal conductances declined somewhat at the higher saturation deficits. In support of the second contention, Figure 6 shows transpiration from pasture increasing with increase in the net radiation. In another study, Van Bavel (1967) showed that transpiration by alfalfa was quite insensitive to large changes in canopy conductance induced by water stress: a ten-fold increase in canopy resistance only halved the rate of transpiration (see Jarvis & McNaughton 1985). Recently, Baldocchi *et al.* (1983) showed that a five-fold increase in stomatal resistance of soybean reduced transpiration by only one-third, and, as expected, this was associated with a substantial increase in saturation deficit measured just above the crop.

While evidence of this kind can be adduced to support the contentions advanced, this correlative approach has serious limitations (Jarvis 1981). Because saturation deficit is often significantly correlated with net radiation, it is quite possible to obtain significant correlations between the transpiration

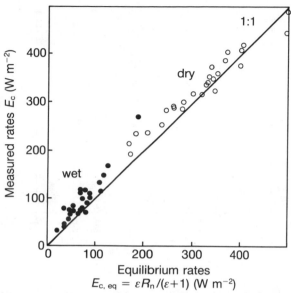

FIGURE 6.   Mean hourly rates of actual transpiration (o) and evaporation (●) from a grazed grass-clover mixture in relation to the equilibrium rate (see McNaughton & Jarvis 1983 for details).

of tree crops and net radiation, and between the transpiration of agricultural crops and saturation deficit. Because stomatal conductance is usually correlated with solar radiation, and hence with net radiation, it is not unusual to obtain significant correlations between the transpiration of agricultural crops and stomatal conductance. Furthermore, because, in many species, stomatal conductance declines at high saturation deficits, good correlations between transpiration rate and saturation deficit or stomatal conductance may not be obtained with particular tree crops. Consequently, the only sure way to determine the contribution of the several variables to the control of transpiration is to estimate Ω_c.

E.   Photosynthesis by a canopy

The concept of coupling between the CO_2 concentration at the leaf surface and that in the ambient air may be extended to leaves in a canopy in a similar manner to the coupling of saturation deficit. When the assimilation rate of many or all of the leaves in a canopy changes, C_a will change as a result. C_a cannot, therefore, continue to be regarded as an independent reference concentration. As previously, an independent reference concentration (C_m) must be found further out in the mixed layer above the canopy, separated from the effective surface of the canopy – where there is a notional surface concentration (C_o) – by the total convective conductance across the surface layer (g_{as}) (Fig. 4). If the canopy is aerodynamically rough, and the windspeed high, or the rate of assimilation (A_c) low, C_o is strongly coupled to C_m: if the

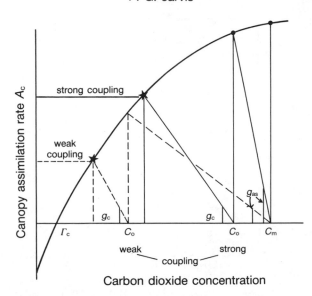

FIGURE 7. A diagram of the relationship between canopy assimilation and CO_2 concentration to show how the fall in carbon dioxide concentrations from the mixed layer (C_m), to the canopy surface (C_o), and to the sites of photosynthesis, affects the assimilation rate, indicated by ⋆. Solid lines: a tall, strongly coupled canopy such as a tree crop; dashed lines: a weakly coupled canopy as in a field crop.

canopy is aerodynamically smooth, and the windspeed is low, or A_c high, C_o is largely decoupled from C_m and will find a value much closer towards the canopy compensation concentration (Γ_c), dependent upon the rate of assimilation.

There is a close parallel between the coupling of C_o and the coupling of D_o to a reference in the mixed layer above a canopy. However, there is a substantial difference in the maintenance of C_m and D_m. Maintenance of D_m in the mixed layer results from encroachment and entrainment of drier air through the capping inversion at the top of an unstable planetary boundary layer, and this follows as a direct consequence of the fluxes of heat and water vapour at the vegetation surface. In contrast, the maintenance of C_m, by addition of CO_2 from above, passively follows the entrainment of heat and water vapour and is not the result of feedback from the surface flux of CO_2.

In a strongly coupled canopy, the CO_2 concentration among the foliage would not depart appreciably from the reference concentration, whereas in a poorly coupled canopy this CO_2 concentration would tend towards Γ_c. Thus, the measured value of C_o could provide a good indication of the degree of coupling. There is, however, a major problem in assessing the degree of coupling by comparison between C_o and C_m or Γ_c. Measurements of C_o are usually compared with concentrations measured only one or two metres above the canopy and are often expressed as a difference from such concentrations. Because a large part of the convective resistance across the surface layer is located above such an upper measurement level (McNaughton & Jarvis 1983), the assumed reference concentration is usually substantially too low and the full extent of the depletion is not evident in the data.

Another consequence of measurement close to the canopy is that wide diurnal fluctuations in CO_2 concentrations, sometimes exceeding $100 \mu mol\,mol^{-1}$, are frequently measured over crops like maize and rice (eg Uchijima et al. 1967; Takasu & Kimura 1978). While very large diurnal variations, of several hundreds of $\mu mol\,mol^{-1}$, generally reflect changes from a stable night-time atmosphere to unstable daytime conditions, large fluctuations in unstable conditions indicate that the so-called reference level is much too close to the canopy.

Concentrations of CO_2 in the atmosphere are known accurately for several locations for the past 25 years. In the northern hemisphere, the average annual concentration at the present time, for example, is ca $343 \mu mol\,mol^{-1}$, with a seasonal variation between summer and winter of about $\pm 6 \mu mol\,mol^{-1}$, depending on latitude. We may, therefore, estimate likely concentrations in the mixed layer, although they do, of course, vary with local conditions and the passage of weather systems. Making use of such information, it seems that carbon dioxide within the canopy may be depleted by $90 \mu mol\,mol^{-1}$ in maize crops (eg Uchijima et al. 1967; Lemon et al. 1969; Uchijima & Udagawa 1978). Smaller, but nonetheless appreciable, depletions of over $60 \mu mol\,mol^{-1}$ have been measured within the canopies of C_3 crops such as red clover (Lemon 1967), rice and soybean (eg Takasu & Kimura 1971, 1972). In contrast, in coniferous forest plantations (eg Jarvis et al. 1976) and in deciduous forest with overstorey and understorey (eg Yabuki et al. 1978), depletions rarely exceed 5 and $10 \mu mol\,mol^{-1}$, respectively. In multistorey tropical rain forest, however, much larger depletions of up to $40 \mu mol\,mol^{-1}$ seem possible (Allen et al. 1972).

Still larger depletions of CO_2 concentrations within field crops have been estimated using a detailed model of carbon dioxide exchange (eg Uchijima 1976; Uchijima & Udagawa 1978). The same model has also been used to show that assimilation by the canopy of field crops should increase with windspeed, essentially because of the stronger coupling to the atmosphere that results, and this is supported by results of Yabuki and Aoki (1978).

How closely a concentration of $240 \mu mol\,mol^{-1}$ in a C_4 crop, or $260 \mu mol\,mol^{-1}$ in a C_3 crop, approaches Γ_c is hard to say. Γ_c for a crop must be much higher than Γ_1 for a single leaf, because of the much larger amount of daytime respiration going on in a crop by the non-photosynthetic, structural and meristematic tissues and by the soil. However, there are no measurements, or even estimates, of Γ_c for crops.

In tree crops, the carbon dioxide concentration in the canopy is strongly coupled to that above, so that assimilation, like transpiration, should be effectively controlled by the canopy conductance, and hence by changes in stomatal resistance. In agricultural crops, however, assimilation is likely to be much less dependent on canopy conductance, because of the feedback between assimilation and C_a. So, in agricultural crops, assimilation, like transpiration, is strongly dependent on radiation. In the soybean crop mentioned earlier (Baldocchi et al. 1983), the five-fold increase in stomatal resistance was associated with only a 50% reduction in assimilation rate. It is noticeable that this reduction was larger than the 30% reduction in transpiration, emphasizing another essential difference between transpiration and assimilation with respect to coupling. In this instance, the increase in stomatal resistance was caused by water stress. The larger effect on assimilation than on transpiration emphasizes the point that the rate of assimilation depends on both the supply and the demand functions for carbon dioxide. As would be expected from physiological experiments, the effect of water stress is to depress the demand function as well as to close stomata. A rigorous treatment of coupling with respect to assimilation does, therefore, require a more complex model than may be used for transpiration.

F. Evaporation of intercepted water

Large amounts of water may be evaporated from wet canopies both during precipitation and after precipitation has ceased. The evaporation of such intercepted water may be a major component of the total loss of water from the vegetation, and may have a major influence on the subsequent availability of water for agronomic and hydrological purposes (Jarvis & Stewart 1979). The saturation deficit at the surface of leaves that have free water on their surfaces is zero, irrespective of the ambient conditions, and is not, therefore, related to the saturation deficit of the air above. Thus, wet leaves are decoupled from the atmosphere above, with respect to the criterion adopted here. However, the saturation vapour pressure at the wet surface depends on the ambient temperature and on the fluxes of net radiation, heat and water vapour at the surface, with the consequence that the evaporation of intercepted water is the simple sum of equilibrium evaporation and a transport component (Monteith 1965), as follows:

$$E_I = \varepsilon(R_n - s)/[(\varepsilon + 1)\lambda] + g_{as}D_m/[(\varepsilon + 1)P]. \tag{18}$$

While there is some variation among crops in net radiation relative to solar radiation, equation (18) shows that the evaporation of intercepted water depends very strongly on the total convective boundary layer conductance, g_{as}, up to the reference saturation deficit, D_m, in the mixed layer. There are few estimates of boundary layer conductance up to such an independent reference. Most estimates extend upwards only as far as instruments placed some metres above the crop and are, therefore, over-estimates of the total conductance (McNaughton & Jarvis 1983). Nonetheless, from the figures available for various crops (see especially Monteith 1976), the boundary layer conductances of tree crops are of the order of 0.1 m s^{-1}, whereas the boundary layer conductances of agricultural crops are one-third to one-eighth of this (Jarvis 1981).

Thus, rates of evaporation of intercepted water from tree crops are likely to be high in comparison with rates of evaporation from agricultural crops (Fig. 8). Although it is usually cloudy and very humid during and immediately after rainfall, rates of evaporation of intercepted water from temperate forest plantations are very similar to the rates of transpiration in good weather – about 0.2 to 0.3 mm h^{-1} in both cases (McNaughton & Jarvis 1983). Comparable data for evaporation rates from agricultural crops are hard to find, perhaps because

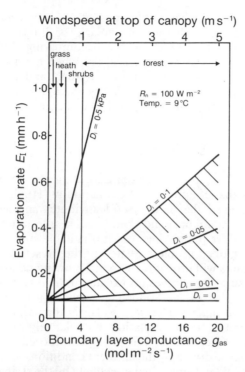

FIGURE 8.   The relation between the rate of evaporation of intercepted water (E_I) and boundary layer conductance (g_{as}), at a range of saturation deficits (D_i). The ranges of likely boundary layer conductances for grass, heath, shrub and forest canopies are shown. The shaded area includes the likely rates of evaporation from wet tree crops (from Jarvis & Stewart 1979).

agronomists don't usually work in the rain or, more likely, because the rates are actually very much smaller (eg Fig. 6). In two much quoted cases (McMillan & Burgy 1960; Waggoner *et al.* 1969), evaporation rates from small areas of a crop on a lysimeter artificially sprinkled with water were measured on a fine sunny day. Such measurements do not, of course, provide realistic estimates of the rates of evaporation of intercepted water to be expected in cloudy weather when the entire immediate landscape has been wetted by rainfall. From evidence like that in Figure 6, rates of evaporation of intercepted water from tree crops are about three times the rates from agricultural crops, because of the big difference in boundary layer conductances.

III.   SOME CONSEQUENCES

Transpiration, evaporation of intercepted water, and assimilation of carbon dioxide, by plants in the field depend on the degree of coupling between the plants and the atmosphere. The degree of coupling determines what are the main driving variables and what are the most effective controls acting on the processes. It follows that an awareness of similarity or differences in the degree of coupling is of great importance (a) when comparing different kinds of vegetation with respect to these processes, (b) when extrapolating from an experimental situation to a field cropping system, and (c) when making changes in the management of a crop. A few examples of the relevance of coupling to particular situations will now be considered.

A. Making new crops

Tropical agroforesters might consider domesticating new crops for semi-arid regions from plants that are growing there naturally (Huxley, this volume). Plants might be selected that have useful attributes and seem to be well adapted to semi-arid conditions, and then brought into intensive cultivation as crops. This procedure has obvious merit if suitable species can be found, but it also carries a hidden problem related to the present considerations.

Likely looking plants will probably be found growing naturally in ones and twos or in small groups. The leaves on isolated individual plants will always be more closely coupled to the atmosphere than leaves on similar plants growing in a crop: the value of Ω_c is always larger than Ω_l for similar leaves. The rates of transpiration and assimilation of a relatively well-coupled plant, growing apart from other plants, are likely to proceed at predominantly imposed rates, and so be driven by the ambient conditions of saturation deficit and CO_2 concentration, and controlled effectively by the stomata. Such plants may well have become adapted to their environment by developing particular stomatal responses to environmental stresses.

When such plants are brought into cultivation and planted close together as crops, transpiration and assimilation will tend towards equilibrium rates and become more dependent on radiation receipt and less on stomatal conductance. In tree crops, such change will be small, and transpiration and assimilation will continue at predominantly imposed rates. In agricultural crops, however, the change may be large: isolated plants may be strongly coupled to the atmosphere whereas plants making up a crop are likely to be largely decoupled. Simply growing plants together as a crop rather than as separate individuals changes the main driving variables and reduces the effectiveness of stomatal control. Adaptations that plants may have acquired to survive as individuals may help them little when they are grown as an extensive crop. A sensitive response of the stomata to, say, saturation deficit may effectively conserve water for isolated plants but have only little influence on transpiration from an extensive crop made up of similar plants. The selection of plants for domestication must, therefore, be based on their performance when grown as a crop rather than as individuals.

B. Experimentation

For the results of an experiment to be applicable to an extensive field crop, coupling in the experiment should be similar to coupling in the crop. This is often not the case and is responsible for the frequent 'discovery' that experimental results may not be applicable to extensive crops in the field. In growth rooms, for example, the saturation deficit and carbon dioxide concentration of the air are set by the operator and imposed on the plants. The feedback loop between the ambient conditions and the fluxes at the leaves is broken – deliberately. Such experiments may well yield relevant results for trees, but they are unlikely to do so for field crops, because transpiration and assimilation are then driven to a large extent by inappropriate variables. A notable case in point is the application of anti-transpirants, which successfully reduce transpiration in growth rooms, but which are ineffective when applied to agricultural crops in the field. In glasshouses, in contrast, transpiration tends towards the equilibrium rate, because ventilation is usually poor, giving the impression that stomata are much less effective than they are in the field, especially in tree crops.

Similar problems can arise with experiments on potted plants in the field. If the potted plants do not form part of a crop, as in the extensive experiments by Briggs and Shantz and their colleagues (eg Briggs & Shantz 1916), the leaves are likely to be much more tightly coupled to the ambient air than if the plants were in an extensive crop. The results obtained will not be representative of performance in an agricultural crop, although they may be a better approximation for a tree crop. Even when potted plants are placed within the crop (eg Denmead & Shaw 1962), the results may be unrepresentative if the experimental plants have transpiration or assimilation rates that differ widely from the rates of the rest of the crop. In a strongly decoupled crop, the saturation deficit and CO_2 concentration within the crop will be largely determined by feedback between the local conditions and the fluxes at the leaves of the *majority* component. This problem arises particularly in experimental arrangements in largely decoupled crops in which a small area of the crop is treated differently from the rest. Examples that are common today include lysimeters, rainfall covers, controlled irrigation treatments, chemical treatments and variety trials. Single plant or tree plots, and small plots of any kind, are particularly likely to give misleading results on this account.

C.   Mixing species

Mixtures of species have been advocated for a number of reasons, including conservation of water. Here, I shall briefly consider mixtures of species of similar habit in agricultural crops, and mixtures of species of widely different habit, as in agroforestry.

In a largely decoupled agricultural crop (with large Ω_c), changes in the transpiration and assimilation rates of one component of a mixture (as a result of water stress, for example) will lead to changes in the rates of transpiration and assimilation of the other components of the mixture. The overall transpiration rate is externally set by the receipt of net radiation: if, for example, the transpiration rate from one species declines a small amount as a result of stomatal closure, the transpiration rate from the other species will increase to compensate for this reduction. The distribution of transpiration among individuals will be changed, but the overall rate will remain about the same. Where roots are differentially distributed through the soil horizons, this process may lead to the most effective use of the soil water, but the overall consequence for the availability of water to the different species is not intuitively obvious. In mixtures of tree crops, on the other hand, where transpiration and assimilation proceed at imposed rates, a reduction in rates by one component of a mixture will not be compensated by increases in rates by the other components, so that, in the case of transpiration, a definite economy of water will result, although whether one component will benefit more than another is, again, not clear.

In agroforestry, the foliage of the different components of the mixture is distributed in the vertical dimension, as is the foliage of herbaceous and woody species in the under- and overstorey in forest plantations. Much more complex, vertically stratified mixtures of species occur in natural woodland, particularly tropical rain forest. In these situations, the overstorey of emergent tree crowns is strongly coupled to the atmosphere above, whereas it seems likely, in most cases, that the understorey is almost completely decoupled, like an extensive field crop. Stanhill (1973) gives an example of this situation in an orange orchard. We would, therefore, expect transpiration from the overstorey to proceed at close to the imposed rate, and transpiration from the ground vegetation, and lower layers of the canopy in multilayered forest, to proceed at close to the appropriate equilibrium rate. Thus, transpiration from the overstorey would increase with increase in leaf area of the tree crowns, and, because this would diminish the penetration of net radiation to lower levels, transpiration from the understorey would be expected to decline (Jarvis 1985). Although there is little information on the distribution of transpiration among components within multilayered mixtures, there is good evidence to suggest that transpiration from forest plantations of variable spacing and with different amounts of understorey is very conservative (Roberts *et al.* 1982; Roberts 1983). It remains to be determined whether this is also the case in agroforestry, but there would seem to be good reasons for supposing that the tree component should not be regarded as a wholly additional drain on the water resources. In short, agroforests may use about the same amount of water in transpiration as would be used by pure stands of the components.

IV. SOME CONCLUSIONS

Tree crops are generally strongly coupled to the atmosphere, whereas agricultural field crops are not. As a result, tree crops have effective stomatal control over their rates of transpiration and assimilation, and they use atmospheric carbon dioxide efficiently.

A major consequence is that there is less risk in extrapolating from most experimental conditions to the field for tree crops than for agricultural crops. However, particular care must be taken when extrapolating from experiments done in glasshouses.

A major question is the depth to which strong coupling extends within multilayered forests, particularly tropical forests, where there are several storeys of tree crowns. The extent to which the ground vegetation is decoupled in forest plantations and in agroforestry plantations also needs resolving.

Because transpiration and assimilation in tree crowns proceed at close to the imposed rate, they depend strongly on the leaf area present. As a result, there is considerable need for demographic studies on leaf recruitment and mortality, and for physiological studies on leaf growth and development in tree canopies. This need is greater for trees than for field crops, but much less work has been done on trees, largely because of the practical difficulties.

REFERENCES

Allen, L. H., Lemon, E. & Müller, L. (1972). Environment of a Costa Rican forest. *Ecology*, 53, 102–111.

Baldocchi, D. D., Verma, S. B., Rosenberg, N. J., Blad, B. L., Garay, A. & Specht, J. E. (1983). Influence of water stress on the diurnal exchange of mass and energy between the atmosphere and a soybean canopy. *Agron. J.*, 75, 543–548.

Briggs, L. J. & Shantz, H. L. (1916). Daily transpiration during the growth period and its correlation with the weather. *J. agric. Res.*, 7, 155–213.

Denmead, O. T. & Shaw, R. H. (1962). Availability of soil water to plants as affected by soil moisture content and meteorological conditions. *Agron. J.*, 54, 385–390.

Jarvis, P. G. (1981). Stomatal conductance, gaseous exchange and transpiration. In: *Plants and their atmospheric environment*, edited by J. Grace, E. D. Ford and P. G. Jarvis, 175–204. Oxford: Blackwell Scientific.

Jarvis, P. G. (1985). Increasing productivity and value of temperate coniferous forest by manipulating site water balance. In: *Forest potentials, productivity and value*, edited by R. Ballard, P. Farnum, G. A. Ritchie and J. K. Winjum, 39–74. (Weyerhaeuser Science Symposium no. 4). Tacoma, WA: Weyerhaeuser Company.

Jarvis, P. G., James, G. B. & Landsberg, J. J. (1976). Coniferous forest. In: *Vegetation and the atmosphere. Vol 2: Case studies*, edited by J. L. Monteith, 171–240. London: Academic Press.

Jarvis, P. G. & McNaughton, K. G. (1985). Stomatal control of transpiration. *Adv. ecol. Res.*, 15, 1–49.

Jarvis, P. G. & Stewart, J. B. (1979). Evaporation of water from plantation forest. In: *The ecology of even-aged forest plantations*, edited by E. D. Ford, D. C. Malcolm and J. Atterson, 327–350. Cambridge: Institute of Terrestrial Ecology.

Lemon, E. (1967). Aerodynamic studies of CO_2 exchange between the atmosphere and the plants. In: *Harvesting the sun*, edited by A. San Pietro, F. A. Greer and T. J. Army, 263–290. New York: Academic Press.

Lemon, E. R., Wright, J. L. & Drake, G. M. (1969). Photosynthesis under field conditions XB. Origins of short-time CO_2 fluctuations in a cornfield. *Agron. J.*, 61, 411–413.

McMillan, W. D. & Burgy, R. H. (1960). Interception loss from grass. *J. geophys. Res.*, 65, 2389–2394.

McNaughton, K. G. & Jarvis, P. G. (1983). Predicting effects of vegetation changes on transpiration and evaporation. In: *Water deficits and plant growth*, edited by T. T. Kozlowski, 1–47. New York: Academic Press.

Monteith, J. L. (1963). Gas exchange in plant communities. In: *Environmental control of plant growth*, edited by L. T. Evans, 95–112. New York: Academic Press.

Monteith, J. L. (1965). Evaporation and environment. In: *The state and movement of water in living organisms*, edited by G. E. Fogg, 205–234. (Symposia of the Society for Experimental Biology no. 19). New York: Academic Press.

Monteith, J. L., ed. (1976). *Vegetation and the atmosphere. Vol 2: Case studies*. London: Academic Press.

Monteith, J. L. (1981). Coupling of plants to the atmosphere. In: *Plants and their atmospheric environment*, edited by J. Grace, E. D. Ford and P. G. Jarvis, 1–29. Oxford: Blackwell Scientific.

Reed, K. L., Hamerley, E. R., Dinger, B. E. & Jarvis, P. G. (1976). An analytical model for field measurements of photosynthesis. *J. appl. Ecol.*, **13**, 925–942.

Roberts, J. (1983). Forest transpiration: a conservative hydrological process? *J. Hydrol. (Amst.)*, **66**, 133–141.

Roberts, J., Pitman, R. M. & Wallace, J. S. (1982). A comparison of evaporation from stands of Scots pine and Corsican pine in Thetford Chase, East Anglia. *J. appl. Ecol.*, **19**, 859–872.

Slatyer, R. O. & McIlroy, I. C. (1961). *Practical microclimatology*. Paris: UNESCO.

Stanhill, G. (1973). Evaporation, transpiration and evapotranspiration: a case for Ockham's razor. In: *Physical aspects of soil water and salts in ecosystems*, edited by A. Hadas, M. Fuchs and B. Yaron, 207–220. Berlin: Springer.

Stewart, J. B. & Thom, A. S. (1973). Energy budgets in pine forest. *Q. Jl R. met. Soc.*, **99**, 154–170.

Szeicz, G., Endrodi, G. & Tajchman, S. (1969). Aerodynamic and surface factors in evaporation. *Wat. Resour. Res.*, **5**, 380–394.

Takasu, K. & Kimura, K. (1971). Microclimate in the field. 2. Diurnal variations of air temperature, humidity and CO_2 concentration in the soybean field. *Nogaku Kenkyu*, **53**, 205–213.

Takasu, K. & Kimura, K. (1972). Microclimate in the field. 3. Diurnal variations of air temperature, humidity and CO_2 concentration in the rice field. *Nogaku Kenkyu*, **54**, 107–120.

Takasu, K. & Kimura, K. (1978). Carbon dioxide microclimate in field crops. In: *Ecophysiology of photosynthetic productivity*, edited by M. Monsi and T. Saeki, 140–144. (JIBP Synthesis vol. 19). Tokyo: University of Tokyo Press.

Thom, A. S. (1975). Momentum, mass and heat exchange of plant communities. In: *Vegetation and the atmosphere. Vol I: Principles*, edited by J. L. Monteith, 57–109. London: Academic Press.

Uchijima, Z. (1976). Microclimate of the rice crop. In: *Climate and rice*, 115–140. Los Baños (Philippines): International Rice Research Institute.

Uchijima, S. & Inoue, K. (1970). Studies of energy and gas exchange within crop canopies. (9) Simulation of CO_2 environment within a canopy. *J. agric. Met., Tokyo*, **26**, 5–18.

Uchijima, Z. & Udagawa, T. (1978). Carbon dioxide environment and CO_2-transfer above and within crop canopies – measurements and simulation. In: *Ecophysiology of photosynthetic productivity*, edited by M. Monsi and T. Saeki, 129–139. (JIBP Synthesis vol. 19). Tokyo: University of Tokyo Press.

Uchijima, Z., Udagawa, T., Horie, T. & Kobayashi, K. (1967). Studies of energy and gas exchange within crop canopies. 1. CO_2 environment in a corn plant canopy. *J. agric. Met., Tokyo*, **23**, 1–10.

Van Bavel, C. H. M. (1967). Changes in canopy resistance to water loss from alfalfa induced by soil water depletion. *Agric. Meteorol.*, **4**, 165–176.

Waggoner, P. E., Begg, J. E. & Turner, N. C. (1969). Evaporation of dew. *Agric. Meteorol.*, **6**, 227–230.

Whitehead, D., Jarvis, P. G. & Waring, R. H. (1984). Stomatal conductance, transpiration and resistance to water uptake in a *Pinus sylvestris* spacing experiment. *Can. J. For. Res.*, **14**, 692–700.

Yabuki, K. & Aoki, M. (1978). The effect of windspeed on the photosynthesis of rice field. In: *Ecophysiology of photosynthetic productivity*, edited by M. Monsi and T. Saeki, 152–159. (JIBP Synthesis vol. 19). Tokyo: University of Tokyo Press.

Yabuki, K., Aoki, M. & Hamotani, K. (1978). Characteristics of the forest microclimate. In: *Biological production in a warm-temperate evergreen oak forest of Japan*, edited by T. Kira, Y. Ono and T. Hosokawa, 55–68. (JIBP Synthesis vol. 18). Tokyo: University of Tokyo Press.

28

THE COMPETITION PROCESS IN FOREST STANDS

D. A. PERRY

Department of Forest Science, Oregon State University, Corvallis, Oregon, USA

I. INTRODUCTION

The design of cropping systems requires that we understand not only the physiology and genetics of individuals, but, because we grow plants in stands, also the nature of interactions among individuals. There are at least three reasons for this requirement. First, although high stocking densities reduce the growth of individuals, low stocking densities may under-utilize the site and therefore reduce yields; for a given combination of species and environment we must know how to balance these two factors. Second, competition has resulted in the evolution of a certain degree of resource allocation among individuals and species; more efficient land use may be achieved by understanding and exploiting such co-evolutionary relationships. Third, yields in genetically heterogeneous stands are likely to be better buffered against pests, pathogens, and climatic changes than those of genetically homogeneous stands; however, economic trade-offs between the short-term gains that we often associate with genetic homogeneity and the yield stability provided by genetic heterogeneity cannot be evaluated until we understand the genetic and environmental factors influencing plant community dynamics.

This paper is divided in two sections, 'Observation and experiment' and 'Theories and models.' In the first, I discuss what we know about the influence of competition on stand structure, the growth and form of individuals, and the growth of stands; I also deal with the ecology and genetics of competition – specifically, the question of resource allocation between species and between genotypes of the same species. In the second section, I briefly discuss some of the ways we go about organizing our observations into models and theories. I deal only with forests; for a discussion of agroforestry systems, see Cannell (1983).

II. OBSERVATION AND EXPERIMENT

'You can learn a lot by just looking' (Yogi Berra, famous American sportsman and philosopher).

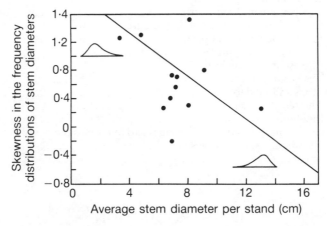

FIGURE 1.   Relationship between average stem diameters and skewness of the dia-meter frequency distributions in 20- to 25-year-old *Pseudotsuga menziesii* stands in the Oregon Cascades (unpublished data). A similar relationship existed for average tree heights.

A.   Competition and stand structure

Even-aged populations of most plant species follow a similar developmental pattern, which can be characterized by (a) the frequency distribution of individual plants sizes within the population, and (b) the relation between size of the average individual and stocking density.

In the early stages of stand development, plant weights are distributed normally, but with time the distribution becomes positively skewed or lognor-mal (ie has a preponderance of small plants, Ford 1975; Mohler *et al.* 1978; Kohyama & Fujita 1981). Diameter and height distributions may move from normal to negatively skewed before eventually becoming positively skewed (Gates 1982). Skewness in the diameter distributions of *Pinus radiata* plantations studied by Gates *et al.* (1983) changed from 0 (normal) to negative and back to positive within 25 years. In 20- to 25-year-old *Pseudotsuga menziesii* stands in the Oregon Cascades, diameter and height distributions tend to positive skewness in stands with relatively small trees and to become progressively more negatively skewed as the average tree size increases (Fig. 1; actual distributions in these stands are shown as insets in Fig. 5). Apparently, rapid early growth by a few individuals (sprinters) in each stand establishes the early positive skewness, but as slower early growers (stayers) catch up the distribution becomes negatively skewed.

It is not necessary to invoke competition to explain the characteristic lognormal size distribution of plant populations: it results from exponential growth of individuals within initially normally distributed populations (Koyama & Kira 1956; Koch 1966). However, competition is likely to reinforce and perhaps to magnify any hierarchy in plant sizes. When mortality reaches about 50%, a bimodal distribution may develop which probably indicates that 'one-sided' competition has occurred – ie large trees have suppressed smaller ones, but small trees have competed very little with larger ones (Ford & Newbould 1970, 1971; Ford 1975). One-sided competition occurs where light is the primary limiting factor (Ford & Diggle 1981); where water and nutrients also are limiting, competitive interactions may become more symmetric.

As competition intensifies during stand development, suppressed plants eventually die, and 'self-thinning' begins. Usually, a constant proportion of the total plants die in any given time period, so that plant numbers decrease exponentially with time, but Kohyama and Fujita (1981) found that, as stands aged, a decreasing proportion of trees died in subalpine *Abies* forests of Japan.

Once self-thinning has begun, the relationship between average plant size and stocking density is characterized by the self-thinning 'law' (reviewed by White 1980; Westoby 1984), stated mathematically as:

$$\log \bar{w} = c - x \log \rho \qquad (1)$$

where $\bar{w}$ is the average plant size (eg weight or volume), ρ is the stocking density, and c and x are constants. The line described by equation 1 represents a ceiling on average plant size at any given stocking density. When a population is self-thinning, any increase in individual plant size is accompanied by a decrease in stocking density; the resulting trajectory, a negatively sloped straight line when expressed on a log-log scale, is the self-thinning line.

The self-thinning law has two remarkable properties. First, although the intercept and slope of the line vary among species, the magnitude of variation is quite small. In White's (1980) tabulation of 36 species, ranging from annuals to trees, slopes (x) varied between $-1·30$ and $-1·80$ (with most between $-1·4$ and $-1·6$), and intercepts (c) varied between $3·06$ and $4·41$. Second, within a given species, there seems to be little site-related variation in the intercept and slope of the self-thinning line. The only significant exception detected so far is that shading can lower the slope of the line.

The intercept of the self-thinning line may tell us something about competitive interactions. For instance, tree species with narrow crowns tend to have larger intercepts than those with spreading crowns (Harper 1977), suggesting that more narrow- than broad-crowned trees of a given size can be packed on to a piece of ground – a very logical proposition.

The slope of the self-thinning line reflects the relationship between mortality and the growth of surviving trees, a steeper (more negative) slope indicating greater growth per unit of mortality than a shallower slope. 'Greater growth' may mean either more total biomass added or more biomass allocated to the plant part measured, such as the bole. Change in total biomass with density may be quite different from that in any single biomass component, and the various biomass components may, in turn, differ from each other (Mohler *et al.* 1978; Hutchings 1979). Self-thinning lines based on leaf weight tend to have slopes close to $-1\cdot0$, which is appreciably shallower (less negative) than those of lines based on total biomass or other biomass components (Mohler *et al.* 1978; Hutchings & Budd 1981). This difference reflects the fact that the maximum leaf area on a given site may be reached relatively early in the self-thinning process; thereafter, although total stand biomass continues to increase, total leaf biomass remains constant (Long & Smith 1984).[1]

What does the slope of the thinning line tell us about the competition process? It is tempting to argue that the growth increment accompanying mortality is a response to reduced competition, and that steeper (more negative) thinning lines reflect more intense competition. However, by the time a suppressed individual dies, its passing is likely to be little noticed by surviving dominants (Ford 1975). West and Borough (1983) demonstrated this fact for stands of *Pinus radiata*, whose self-thinning lines have slopes approaching $-1\cdot5$ only if suppressed individuals are counted as mortality.

In my opinion, the self-thinning trajectory has a great deal to tell us about the dynamics of the competition process; and the message must be read, as all of nature's ciphers, by a combination of theory and experiment through which the underlying dynamic processes are unravelled.

B.   Effect of competition on individual tree growth

Competition influences both the growth of individuals and how this growth is distributed. Much of the direct effect of competition on growth is mediated through its impacts on (a) the amount of carbon fixed per unit leaf area, and (b) crown size and structure. It is well known in agriculture that net assimilation rates (NAR, dry matter production per unit leaf area) decline with increase in leaf area index (LAI); Figure 2 shows this effect for stemwood production of various forest stands in Washington state (Schroeder *et al.* 1982).

As a stand approaches full leaf area, branch production is reduced, and self-pruning causes the base of the crowns to shift upwards (eg Cochrane & Ford 1978). Because of increased internal shading, branch mortality may be greater on large trees than on small ones (Oker-Blom & Kellomäki 1982). Bole increment is often greatest at the crown base (Hall 1965; Brix 1983);

---

[1] A self-thinning slope of -1 means that the weight of an individual changes with density such that the *total* stand weight remains constant. Slopes steeper (more negative) than -1 reflect an increase in total stand weight during self-thinning.

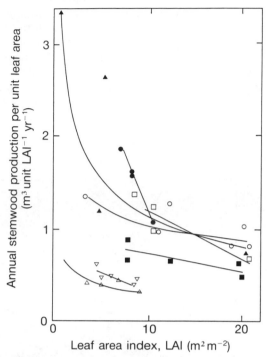

FIGURE 2.   Relationship between (a) stemwood production and (b) leaf area index, in seven conifer stands in eastern Washington (from Schroeder *et al.* 1982).

therefore stem form is likely to be altered during this process as well. Ford (1982) found that the onset of competition in a *Picea sitchensis* plantation was accompanied by a decline in both stand productivity and projected needle area index (from 10–11 at age 16 to 7–8 at age 18).

Trees, like other plants, can compensate somewhat for shading. Shade leaves of *Castanea sativa* have greater surface/weight ratios and more chlorophyll per unit weight than sun leaves (Ford & Newbould 1971). Kellomäki and Hari (1980) found that trees in the lower social positions of *Pinus sylvestris* stands had greater height and radial growth rates than dominants, at least partially because of lower respiration rates and higher leaf area/leaf weight ratios.

What about the trees that are winning the competitive race? Their crowns become larger and broader, which means they accumulate more photosynthetic machinery and are able to fix more carbon. However, respiration by the infrastructure of stems, branches, and roots that accompanies larger crowns usually means decreasing productive efficiency. Maintenance respiration by large trees may be much greater than indicated by studies of woody respiration on small trees, which are relatively efficient at recapturing respired carbon (Waring & Schlesinger 1985). Rook and Carson (1978) found that the respiration rates per unit area of the lower bole of a seven metre tall *Pinus radiata* tree were four times greater than those of an equal surface area of leaves.

Assmann (1970), reviewing European research on coniferous and deciduous tree species, concluded that, within any given social stratum, trees with small- to medium-sized crowns have larger wood increments per unit crown (or ground) surface area than trees with large crowns. The improved light environment of the emerging dominants, however, tends to offset declines due to greater respiration. For instance, in *Pinus sylvestris* plantations there is only a small decline in wood increment per unit crown surface area with increase in tree size among dominant trees, whereas there is a very sharp decline among codominant and dominated trees (Fig. 3). Mayer (1957, cited in Assmann 1970) showed similar relationships in *Quercus petraea* stands.

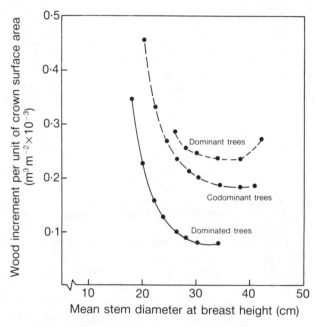

FIGURE 3.   Change in wood increment per unit of crown surface area with increasing stem diameter at breast height, for trees in three social classes within *Pinus sylvestris* plantations (adapted from Assmann's 1970 summary of Badoux 1945).

Trees in thinned stands respond in much the same way as emerging dominants in unthinned stands. The needle/branchwood weight ratio was 1·50 in thinned *Pinus contorta* stands, compared with 2·36 in unthinned stands (Gary 1978), so that the latter had nearly 60% more photosynthetic tissue per unit of respiratory tissue. Trees in 43-year-old *Pseudotsuga menziesii* stands planted at close spacings had larger ratios of crown surface area to crown volume than trees planted at wide spacings (Curtis & Reukema 1970; Fig. 4). Volume increment per unit of crown surface area was 22% greater in heavily thinned than in densely stocked stands of *Picea abies* (Burger 1939, cited in Assmann 1970), but, when increment was measured per cubic metre of crown exposed to direct light, efficiency in the densely stocked stand was nearly twice that in the thinned stand.

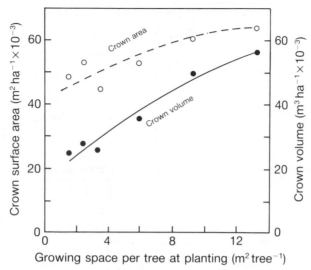

FIGURE 4.   Crown surface areas and crown volumes of trees in 43-year-old *Pseudotsuga menziesii* stands planted at different densities (adapted from Curtis and Reukema 1970).

Despite the range of plastic responses available to dominated trees, high levels of competition reduce growth. Relative growth rates (RGRs) decline sharply with decreasing social status in *Picea sitchensis* (Ford 1975) and *Pinus radiata* (West & Borough 1983) plantations. Figures 5A-D (unpublished data) show the relation between competition levels and the RGRs (2-year basal area growth relative to basal area at the start of the 2-year period) of trees in various size classes in four *Pseudotsuga menziesii* stands in the Oregon Cascades. All are about 20 years old and are mixtures of planted and natural trees. Plots in each stand were thinned three years before measurement, to leave a range of size classes. Competitive levels in unthinned plots were measured as relative density (RD), or stocking density relative to the maximum theoretically attainable at a given mean stand diameter at breast height, the latter taken from Reineke's (1933) maximum density line for *P. menziesii*.

Unthinned plots of the stand shown in Figure 5A have an average RD of 0·22; competition is not severe enough to produce competition-related mortality, small trees have larger RGRs than large ones, and thinning produced no 'release' – ie, despite the strong positive skewness of diameters (inset), no size class is suppressed. The stand shown in Figure 5B is probably in the early stages of competition-related mortality (RD = 0·54). Diameters are negatively skewed, but RGR differs little among social classes and responds only slightly to thinning. Note that diameters are distributed normally in this stand. As I suggested earlier, the greater growth efficiency (larger RGRs) of small trees enables them to catch up with fast early growers. In the stand shown in Figure 5C (RD = 0·75), trees in the lower diameter classes are clearly suppressed and respond strongly to thinning. Note, however, that the RGR

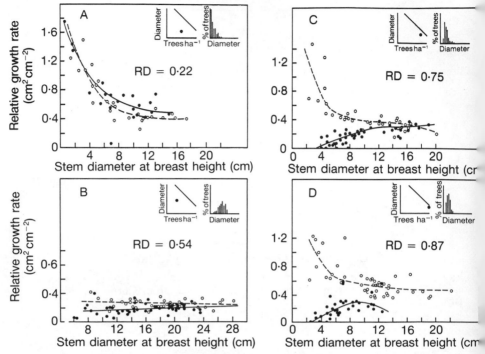

FIGURE 5.   Relative growth rates (RGRs) of *Pseudotsuga menziesii* trees of different stem diameters in thinned (open circles and dashed lines) and unthinned (closed circles and solid lines) plots in four stands of different 'relative densities' (RDs); thinned plots were cut three years before measurement.

RGR = basal area growth over the past two years relative to basal area at the start of the two-year period; RD = actual stocking density relative to the theoretical maximum. Insets show, for the unthinned plots, the diameter-density point relative to the theoretical maximum stocking density (Reineke 1933) and the diameter frequency distributions. The scales on the insets are: 0–20 cm diameter (DBH), 0–8100 trees ha^{-1} and 0–40% of trees.

of trees larger than 12 cm in diameter does not increase following thinning, a clear example of one-sided competition. The stand shown in Figure 5D (RD = 0·87) is probably experiencing competition-related mortality, and manifests the same pattern of suppression in the lower size classes as the stand in Figure 5C. The response to thinning in Figure 5D suggests that, under these superdense conditions, the growth of larger, as well as of smaller, trees may have been reduced; however, stand density before thinning was not as high in the thinned as in the unthinned plot of this stand, so the interpretation is confounded.

Cannell *et al.* (1984) reported changes similar to those shown in Figure 5 in RGR patterns for height in stands of *Pinus contorta* and *Picea sitchensis*. RGR was initially negatively correlated with tree height (cf Fig. 5A), but, as competition intensified, the correlation became positive (cf Figs 5C, D).

C.   Environment and competition

The environment can have profound, and surprising, effects on the competition process. This fact may be illustrated by differences in the response to thinning of 15- to 20-year-old stands of *Pseudotsuga menziesii* growing in varying topographic positions in the Oregon Coast Range (Perry, unpublished). Whereas the RGR of trees growing on steep slopes (50–80%) increases after thinning, RGR actually decreases after thinning on shallow slopes! There are several plausible hypotheses that may explain this phenomenon, including thinning 'shock', increased root rot, decreased mycorrhizal formation, and high water tables. The evidence supports the last hypothesis – that is, the removal of leaf area results in decreased evapotranspiration, a rise in the water tables, and a subsequent reduction in tree growth. Clearly, we must be very careful when extrapolating competitive interactions from one environmental setting to another.

D.   Crown characteristics and competition

The fact that dry matter production per unit leaf area (net assimilation rate, NAR) is a trade-off between photosynthesis and respiration suggests that the degree of competition among individuals, at a given stocking level, depends on their crown characteristics. A simple model illustrates this point. Assume that:

$$\text{NAR} = \frac{P}{\text{LAI}} - R \tag{2}$$

where P is gross photosynthesis per unit leaf area in the absence of competition, LAI is leaf area index, and R is respiration per unit leaf area. As noted earlier (Fig. 2) NAR is inversely related to LAI. It is assumed that R is independent of LAI.

Consider two hypothetical stands (Fig. 6), both with gross photosynthetic rates (P) of $40 \, \text{g m}^{-2} \text{day}^{-1}$, but one consisting of large-crowned individuals with a base respiration rate of $10 \, \text{g m}^{-2} \, \text{day}^{-1}$, the other of small-crowned individuals with a respiration rate of $5 \, \text{g m}^{-2} \, \text{day}^{-1}$ (these numbers are arbitrarily chosen). At any given leaf area, the small-crowned individuals have larger NARs than the large-crowned ones, and, though the absolute difference between the two is a constant $5 \, \text{g m}^{-2} \, \text{day}^{-1}$ (the difference in respiration rate), the relative difference between them increases with increasing LAI. Now, suppose we thinned the small-crowned stand from LAI 4 to 2 (Fig. 6, points A to B). NAR would initially increase, but, as the stand returned to full site occupation (measured by LAI), the NAR would shift toward that of the large-crowned trees. By the time the original leaf area was regained (point C), the trees would, of course, be larger, but they would have smaller NARs than before thinning.

Brix (1983) may have seen this effect in thinned and fertilized plots of *Pseudotsuga menziesii*. Plots were treated in 1970; within one to two years stemwood production per unit leaf area was 30%, 78%, and 135% greater than that of controls in thinned, fertilized, and thinned and fertilized plots,

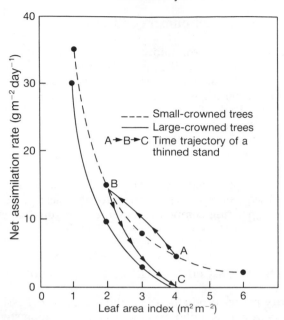

FIGURE 6. Hypothetical relationships between net assimilation rates and leaf area indices for two stands composed of trees with small or large crowns (see text).

respectively. However, stemwood production per unit leaf area subsequently decreased, and by 1977 was at least 20% below that of controls in all treatments. Unfortunately, Brix's data do not allow LAIs to be calculated, so the reason for the decline in stemwood production per unit leaf area cannot be clearly identified.

E. Effects on carbohydrate allocation

Competition has important influences on carbohydrate allocation and tree form other than its effects on crowns. It is a conventional wisdom in forestry that growth in stem diameter is more affected by changes in stand density than growth in tree height. In *Picea sitchensis*, the most dramatic effects on height/diameter ratio occur at the highest initial stocking levels (Jack 1971). Assmann (1970) found that differences in height/diameter ratio among *Picea abies* stands, thinned to different levels, increased with age to a certain point, beyond which they tended to disappear. Thus, competition altered the temporal pattern, rather than the absolute amount, of height relative to diameter growth.

Species differ in the relative response of height and diameter growth to competition. Height growth of *Pinus contorta*, for example, is very sensitive to stocking density (Holmes & Tackle 1962), whereas that of *Larix occidentalis*, its close ecological associate, is little affected (Seidel 1977). In *Pseudotsuga menziesii* stands, trees within the same social class differ greatly in height/diameter ratio, suggesting that considerable genetic diversity exists within species. As I shall discuss later, genotypes within the same population differ in their response to competition.

Competition can influence the chemical composition of trees. Lower photo-synthesis probably results in reduced allocation of photosynthates to those chemical constituents that are most energy-expensive. This effect is likely to differ with species, site, and season, but a rough idea of priorities can be gained from the grams of glucose required to synthesize one gram of various compounds in *Pinus taeda*: lipids, 3·02 g; phenolics, 1·92 g; lignin, 1·90 g; nitrogenous compounds, 1·58 g; organic acids, 1·43 g; and carbohydrates, 1·13 g (Chung & Barnes 1977). The more expensive compounds include important defensive chemicals, such as terpenes and tannins, which have lipid or phenolic precursors. Density stress does, at least in some cases, increase tree susceptibility to insect herbivores (Mitchell *et al.* 1983).

The production of fruits and seeds is likely to be curtailed by stresses of any kind. Flower bud production is sharply reduced by shading in most fruit trees (Cannell 1983; Jackson, this volume). Seeds of some species, such as *Acer saccharinum*, *Quercus rubra*, *Pinus strobus*, and *Pinus palustris*, contain a high proportion of energy-expensive fats and/or proteins (Kramer & Kozlow-ski 1979); thus, unless the situation becomes so severe that stress-related seed crops are produced, seed production may well be one of the first things sacrificed when resources are scarce.

F.   The ecology of competition

1.   *Stand structure and 'competitive tension'*

When we talk about, or attempt to define, competitive interactions, we invariably refer to effects on individuals, but there are also system-level implications. One of the robust general principles of plant ecology is the law of constant final yield – better known in forestry as Langsaetter's relation – which simply states that over a wide range of stocking densities total yields are the same (Kira *et al.* 1953; Harper 1977). Various caveats accompany this statement, including the fact that it is not consistent with the self-thinning law; nevertheless, if we are careful about the time frame within which yields are compared, it is reasonably accurate.

At high plant densities, mutual interference can decrease community yields: this is what foresters call stagnation. But most plant communities do not stagnate because the development of a dominance hierarchy effectively dissi-pates 'competitive tension' – a process much like that in non-equilibrium thermodynamic systems, where structure is created and maintained by the dissipation of energy (Prigogine 1980). Thus, the competition process, through the heterogeneous stand structure it produces, may play a positive role when veiwed in the context of the community. Wood production per unit leaf area in Amazonian forests, for example, is greatest in those stands with the most complex, aerodynamically rough, canopies (Brunig 1983). It is possible that the decline in LAI and productivity sometimes seen in rapidly growing young conifer plantations (Ford 1982) is due to a build-up of 'competitive tension' resulting from inadequate expression of dominance.

2. Resource allocation among species

Plants share the same basic resources and therefore would seem to have fewer options for niche separation than animals, although Tilman (1982) has pointed out that there are far more plant species per limiting 'plant resource' than animal species per limiting 'animal resource'. Most plant species diversity is due to small-scale environmental heterogeneity (Harper 1977), although both the canopy and rooting zone can be vertically stratified (Trenbath & Harper 1973; Yeaton et al. 1977). Of the numerous studies of species mixtures, relatively few have found that yields of mixed species differ significantly from those of pure stands (Trenbath 1974). However, most of these studies have looked at plants of similar stature which share environmental resources over the same time frame (see Cannell 1983). Harper (1977) pointed out that most (a) were conducted in pots with inadequate soil volumes to allow root separation, and (b) used agronomic species bred to grow in low-density monocultures. I would add that they used artificial soil media containing neither the structure nor the microbial richness of natural soils.

Harper (1977) stated that 'a search for "ecological combining ability" is most likely to be successful in species or varieties that have been specifically bred for or evolved naturally toward some degree of niche separation'. But few studies of combining ability in nonagronomic species have been conducted; therefore, our understanding of the relationship between structure and productivity in natural systems remains minimal.

Parrish and Bazzaz (1982) found that species from a late successional community had greater 'ecological combining ability' than species from an early successional community. Turkington et al. (1977) showed that different legumes formed consistent relationships with certain grass species within Ontario grasslands, suggesting that selection had occurred for species-specific neighbours. Both Assmann (1970) and Braathe (1957), reviewing European experience, concluded that mixing shade-tolerant and shade-intolerant trees often resulted in greater productivity than when intolerants were grown alone; in one series of experiments the yield of Pinus sylvestris-Fagus sylvatica mixtures was up to 24% greater than that of pure P. sylvestris (Assmann 1970). The same seems true of Pseudotsuga menziesii-Tsuga heterophylla mixtures in the Pacific Northwest (Wierman & Oliver 1979). The relative advantage of mixtures is likely to vary with site; for instance, the ability of a single species to dominate and exclude others can be greater at high than at low fertility levels (Austin & Austin 1980), and soil pH is an important determinant of yield in Fagus sylvatica-Picea abies mixtures (Assmann 1970). Stand factors also can be important; Vandermeer (1981) showed that, theoretically, the yield of species mixtures relative to monocultures depends on the density at which plants are grown.

In some instances, species packing is increased within plant communities through 'mediators' such as grazers, pathogens, pollinators, or symbionts which act selectively (eg Burdon & Chilvers 1974; Yodzis 1976; Hanley & Taber 1980). The most striking and consistent examples of increased yield in mixtures relative to monocultures are those involving nitrogen-fixing species. When de Wit *et al.* (1966) grew *Panicum maximum* with the legume *Glycine javanica*, they found transgressive behaviour (increased yields in mixtures) only when *Rhizobium*, the nitrogen-fixing symbiont of legumes, was added. Thus, niche separation between the plant species was mediated by the bacterium. Binkley (1983) found that *Pseudotsuga menziesii-Alnus rubra* mixtures were more productive than pure *P. menziesii* stands in soils low in nitrogen, but in soils less limiting in nitrogen this was not the case. In general, where a symbiont can both decrease competition for some limiting factor and act symmetrically (not at the expense of one species), transgressive yields may result. Bowen (1973, 1980, and this volume) suggested that ectomycorrhizas enabled sparsely rooting species, such as trees, to compete more successfully with intensely rooting species, such as grasses, which are not ectomycorrhizal. In that case, alteration of competition by the symbiont (the mycorrhizal fungus) is presumably asymmetric, because trees gain at the expense of grasses. However, if the ectomycorrhizas released organic acids which accelerated solubilization of mineral elements (Graustein *et al.* 1977) or increased the level of antibiosis in the soil, then benefits could conceivably accrue to non-ectomycorrhizal as well as to ectomycorrhizal plants, and competition would become less asymmetric.

3. *Intraspecific competition*

Donald (1968) recognized that stands of less aggressive 'crop' ideotypes were likely to yield more than stands of 'isolation-competition' ideotypes, and the widespread introduction of the former was an important part of the Green Revolution. Ford (1976) and Cannell (1978) have argued the advantages in forestry of using 'crop' ideotypes, which utilize space efficiently and therefore have high yields per hectare in stands. In this section, I deal with a different aspect of the genetics of competition, the allocation of resources among genotypes of a single species.

Intergenotypic competition is probably the most understudied aspect of forest growth dynamics (Libby *et al.* 1969; Adams 1980). Yields in pairwise varietal mixtures of agronomic species are generally either complementary (yield reduction by one variety is balanced by gains in the other) or overcompensatory (yield in mixture is greater than the mean yield of the two monocultures) – which is remarkable, considering that agronomic varieties are bred for high individual yields (or at least were at the time most experiments were conducted), and have no history of co-evolution (see Adams 1980).

One approach to studying intergenotypic competition in forests has been to compare clonal with mixed-genotype stands (Sakai & Mukaide 1967; Sakai *et al.* 1968; Hühn 1969, 1970). Sakai *et al.* (1968) suggested that competition was less in a clonal than in a mixed-genotype forest, but they defined competition as a reduction in the growth of one individual relative to a neighbour, which leads to the absurd conclusion that little competition exists in a stagnated stand. A more relevant measure of competition is growth relative to an open-grown standard (eg Riitters 1985), or growth within a replacement series, in which the proportions of competing genotypes are varied while the total numbers are held constant (de Wit 1960).

I am aware of only three experimental tests of ecological combining ability among genotypes within a single tree species. Adams *et al.* (1973) tested all pairwise combinations of four *Pinus taeda* families; four combinations produced overcompensation, four complementation, two neutrality (no difference between the growth of either genotype in mixture or monoculture), and two undercompensation (the mixture yielded less than the mean yield of the monocultures). There was evidence in this study that related genotypes (half-siblings) were competitively neutral. Adams and Demeritt (unpublished, cited in Adams 1980) found that mixtures of hybrid *Populus* sp. clones were either overcompensatory (2 of 15 pairs), complementary (4 of 15), or neutral. Tauer (1975) showed similar relationships among clones of *Populus trichocarpa*.

With the exception of Adams *et al.* (1973), these studies suffer the same limitation as experiments with agronomic plants: they deal with genotypes which have had no co-evolutionary history. If ecological combining ability is found in even a small percentage of randomly combined clones, the probability is high that it is a significant factor in the growth of natural forests (cf Adams 1980; Hühn 1973). There is evidence supporting this view; the growth of genotypes in stands is often poorly correlated with their performance in the open (Franklin 1979; Panetsos 1980), and half-sibling families of several tree species have been shown to differ greatly in their response to density stress, particularly in shoot growth and shoot/root ratios (Fig. 7; Malavasi and Perry, manuscript in review).

Theoretically, evolution will favour stable mixtures of genotypes which differ in competitive ability only if there is some degree of overcompensation (ie resource allocation) in their competitive interactions (Schutz *et al.* 1968; see also Stern 1969). The selective forces pushing plant populations toward resource allocation are sometimes quite strong. This point was illustrated by Allard and Adams (1969), who showed that wheat cultivars grown in mixtures for eighteen generations evolved so that they yielded better in mixed stands than in monocultures. In my opinion, and particularly in view of our current fascination with clonal forestry, research into the extent and nature of inter-genotypic interactions should be given high priority.

III. THEORIES AND MODELS

'To give an accurate description of what has never occurred is . . . the inalienable privilege of any man of parts and culture' (Oscar Wilde).

A. The self-thinning rule

Theories of the self-thinning rule fall into two general categories: those based strictly on allometry, and those including both allometry and physiology. In their original derivation of the $-3/2$ slope, Yoda *et al.* (1963) simply divided space according to certain rules, namely that: (a) plant weight is a cubic function of some linear plant dimension such as diameter (or height is linearly related to diameter), (b) plant geometry remains constant during self-thinning,

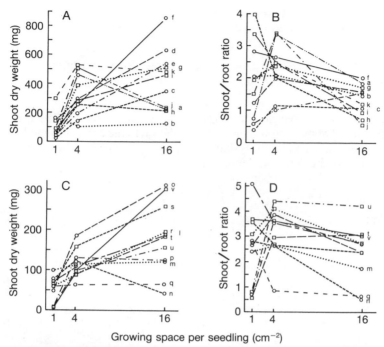

FIGURE 7.   The differing responses, in shoot weight and shoot/root ratio, of one-year-old seedlings of half-sibling families (denoted by different letters) of *Pseudotsuga menziesii* (A and B) and *Tsuga heterophylla* (C and D) to density stress (from Malavasi and Perry, manuscript in review). Seedlings were grown in shade frames at Corvallis. Similar differences were found among half-sibling families of *Abies nobilis* and *Abies amabilis*. All family-density interactions except those for *P. mensiesii* shoot weights (A) were significant at the 0·01 level.

(c) increases in plant size are linearly related to increasing increments of growing space, and (d) the reciprocal of population density is an accurate estimate of the growing space available to the average tree. Various authors have pointed out the inaccuracies of these assumptions (Ford 1975; Mohler *et al.* 1978; White 1981). White (1981) mustered a great deal of data to show that the relationship between height and diameter in trees is rarely linear, and that the relationship between biomass and diameter is not cubic. He used the following allometries:

$$W \propto d^{2\cdot5} \text{ and } C_D \propto d^a$$

where W is individual tree biomass, d is stem diameter at breast height, C_D is crown diameter, and a is a constant, to derive:

$$W \propto \rho^{-2\cdot5/2a} \tag{3}$$

where ρ is stocking density. Equation (3) predicts that trees with wide crowns in relation to stem diameter (ie large values of a) thin along a shallower (less negative) slope than trees with narrow crowns.

An alternative, slightly more general, derivation is based on the following allometries (Perry, unpublished):

$$h \propto G_A^Q \text{ and } W \propto E_V^Z$$

where h is tree height, G_A is ground area per tree, E_V is environmental volume per tree ($= G_A \times h$), and Q and Z are constants. These give:

$$W \propto \rho^{-Z(Q+1)} \qquad (4)$$

where Q measures tree height in relation to ground area (the reciprocal of density), and Z above-ground biomass in relation to the environmental volume that a tree occupies. Values less than 1 for either parameter indicate 'diminishing returns' as the tree gains more space.

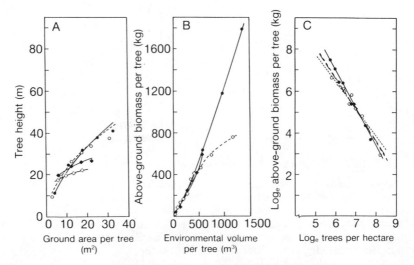

FIGURE 8.   Effect of A. tree height in relation to ground area per tree and B. above-ground tree biomass in relation to the environmental volume occupied per tree (ground area×height) on the slope of the self-thinning line C.

Closed circles: *Pseudotsuga menziesii*: good site (52 m tall at age 100); open circles: poor site (42 m tall at age 100). Closed diamonds: *Pinus ponderosa*: good site (36 m tall at age 100); open diamonds: poor site (24 m tall at age 100).

The *P. menziesii* data were taken from McArdle and Meyer (1961), the *P. ponderosa* data were adapted from Oliver and Powers (1978), and biomass values were calculated from the stem diameters using regressions given by Gholz *et al.* (1979).

Figure 8 illustrates how variation in Q (tree height vs ground area per tree) and Z (above-ground biomass vs environmental volume per tree) affects the slope of the self-thinning line of *Pseudotsuga menziesii* and *Pinus ponderosa*. Height is roughly equal to the square root of ground area per tree for *P. menziesii* but not for *P. ponderosa*. The relation between biomass per tree and its environmental volume (ground area× height) is a nonlinear power function for *P. menziesii* on good sites (52 m tall at age 100) and for *P. ponderosa* on both good (36 m tall at age 100) and poor (24 m) sites; but *P. menziesii* on poorer sites (42 m) is fit more closely by the monomolecular equation $(1 - e^{cE}V)$, where c is constant. Despite very different values of Q for *P. menziesii* on the poorer sites and *P. ponderosa* on the better sites, the slope of the self-thinning line for the two is the same because *P. ponderosa* occupies increasing growing space more efficiently (ie has a relatively high Z value). *P. menziesii* on good sites has high values of both Q and Z and therefore a self-thinning slope more negative than $-1\cdot5$.

Because the efficiency with which a tree occupies space is a function of both its geometry and physiology, theories incorporating both are likely to give the clearest insight into the mechanisms underlying self-thinning. I am aware of only two such theories. Pickard (1983) used elementary relations between available photosynthate and either total plant or crown size in three different approaches, all of which gave slopes close to $-3/2$. Perry (1984) derived a self-thinning relation from Richards' generalized Von Bertallanfy equation (a logistic equation relating growth to photosynthesis and respiration; Richards 1959) which generates some fairly specific and testable hypotheses. For example, for intercepts to be produced within observed ranges, the rate of carbon loss from individuals (maintenance respiration, tissue death, etc) must exceed the individual mortality rate. The model further predicts that the self-thinning slope is determined jointly by the allometric relation between total above-ground biomass and leaf area and by photosynthetic tolerance to density; plants which maintain relatively high leaf areas as they enlarge have relatively steep thinning slopes, and tolerant plants have relatively shallow slopes. These two factors are generally not independent – tolerant plants tend to maintain relatively high leaf areas and *vice versa*; therefore, according to this model, feedback between plant allometry and physiology constrains the self-thinning slope within a relatively narrow range.

B.   Individual tree models

The role of competition in stand structure and growth is most often modelled as the simple linear sum of competitive interactions between individuals. Clearly, the essential ingredient in this approach is an algorithm which successfully predicts how the growth of an individual is influenced by its neighbours. There are two ways to go about formulating such an algorithm; the more direct is to correlate the growth of an individual with some combination of distance to, and size of, its neighbours; the other is to assume logistic growth toward a competition-dependent maximum, for example the self-thinning line or some measure of growing space.

1.   *Distance-size models*

Numerous 'competition indices' have been used in attempts to quantify the influence of neighbours on tree growth. These can be grouped according to the way in which competition is calculated (cf Adlard 1974; Alemdag 1978). Competition can be calculated from: (a) neighbour encroachment into an 'optimum growing space', which is generally defined as the open-grown crown diameter (eg Bella 1971; Gates 1982); (b) the basal area of neighbours (Opie 1968); (c) the available growing space calculated as a polygon, with vertices dependent on the spatial arrangement of neighbours (eg Adlard 1974); (d) the diameters and distances of neighbours (Hegyi 1974); (e) crown surface, volume, etc, in relation to open-grown trees (eg Mitchell 1975); and (f) relative plant sizes or heights, but with competition effects one-sided, that is with trees below a certain relative size having little or no competitive effect (eg Gates 1978; Ford & Diggle 1981).

In general, competition indices by themselves explain a disappointingly small proportion of variation in tree growth, even in stands occupying uniform sites (eg Alemdag 1978; Noone & Bell 1980). Invariably, the most important predictor of how a tree is growing is its own size, independent of its neighbours. Four reasons for this fact come to mind. First, past competitive interactions are integrated in current tree size. Second, variability is introduced because of genotypic differences in response to competition, and because of environmental heterogeneity (cf Cannell *et al.* 1977). Third, as discussed earlier, interactions between individuals can be co-operative rather than competitive. And fourth, where light is limiting, indices based on two-sided competition may not accurately reflect the competition process; in fact, one-sided models have been successful in reproducing the bimodal size distributions which characterize populations with strong dominance hierarchies (Diggle 1976; Ford & Diggle 1981; Gates 1978, 1982).

2. *Logistic-type models*

Logistic growth is simply exponential increase damped by some limiting factor. Of the various ways of writing a logistic equation, one of the more general is:

$$\frac{1}{B}\frac{dB}{dt} = \frac{r(t)}{a}\left[1 - \left(\frac{B}{K(t)}\right)^a\right] \qquad (5)$$

where B is some measure of size, such as biomass, $K(t)$ is the maximum attainable B, $r(t)$ is an 'intrinsic' growth rate, and a is a constant defining the symmetry of the curve.

If plant population growth is to be accurately predicted, r, the intrinsic growth rate, and K, the ceiling on individual plant size, must be variable rather than constant. Earlier I suggested that RGR, which for open-grown trees is the r of equation (5), was roughly proportional to the inverse of plant size. Hozumi (1980) used the density-dependent maximum plant size defined by the self-thinning rule as a K value – an especially nice approach because it links plant growth rate directly to stocking density. Aikman and Watkinson (1980) modified the standard logistic approach by assuming that unconstrained growth was a function of the area occupied by a plant rather than of its size, and that growth constraints (the damping term) were produced by competitive constraints on area. Their model provides for differential competitive ability among individuals – one of the few linking growth dynamics to population structure.

Although rarely used in plant population dynamics, a Lotka-Volterra approach (a set of coupled logistic equations) may be used to model competitive interactions between individuals. This was done by Yamamura (1976), and by Vandermeer (1981), who used his model to derive density-dependent conditions for transgressive yields in species mixtures.

One of the nice things about a mechanistic model, such as the logistic, is that it confers analytical power. Take, for example, the basic logistic, equation 5, with r proportional to B^{-1} and K proportional to ρ^{-x} (from the self-thinning rule):

$$\frac{1}{B}\frac{dB}{dt} \propto \frac{1}{B}\ (1-C_1 B^a \rho^{ax}) \tag{6}$$

Multiplying both sides by ρ, the stocking density, gives an expression for relative growth rate of the stand (RGRS):

$$\text{RGRS} \propto \frac{\rho}{B}(1-C_1 Ba\rho^{ax}) \tag{7}$$

differentiating equation (7) with respect to ρ, setting the resultant equation equal to zero, and solving ρ in terms of B (an elementary maximization technique of the Calculus) gives:

$$\rho_m = \left(\frac{1}{1+ax}\right)^{1/ax}\left(\frac{C}{B}\right)^{1/x} \tag{8}$$

where ρ_m is the stocking density which maximizes stand growth, given an average plant biomass, B. Note that ρ_m varies with a, the parameter determining symmetry, and x, the absolute value of the self-thinning slope. Though such analytical approaches undoubtedly oversimplify the real world, they generate testable hypotheses and provide a foothold in the mechanics of the competition process.

Although logistic equations are typically used to model the time rate of change in a quantity, they can be used in other ways. Westoby (1982), for example, introduced the notion of 'Distribution Modifying Functions' (DMFs), which relate the growth of a plant to its relative size within the community, rather than to its absolute size. He showed that the form of the DMF influenced the size distribution within a population, with a logistic DMF producing the empirically observed bimodal distribution.

C. Holistic models – thermodynamics and Maxwell's ecological demon

The need for holism (synthesis) as well as analysis is self-evident to most scientists (cf Odum 1977); what have been lacking are the tools. Information theory was received enthusiastically by many biologists as, at long last, a theoretical foothold into pattern, but with some notable exceptions (eg Gatlin 1972) it has produced no new biological insights. This is not because the concept of a holistic approach to understanding pattern is a bad one, but rather because biological patterns are much more subtle and complex than simple communication systems (cf Johnson 1970); neither can information theory tell us much about human language, and for the same reasons.

I believe we are on the threshold of a very exciting time in ecology, one in which the theoretical tools of holism will yield new insights into the properties of systems. For example, Axelrod and Hamilton (1981) recently used game theory to investigate the evolution of co-operation, and Wiley and Brooks

(1982) produced a new theory of evolution based on nonequilibrium thermodynamics. In this section, I will discuss one way in which competitive interactions may be interpreted in the context of General Systems Theory.

Laszlo (1972, p. 43) states the principles of self-organization in the following formula:

$$\text{External forcings} \rightarrow \text{Internal constraints} \rightarrow \text{Adaptive self-organization}$$

Earlier I discussed competition in systems which include one nitrogen-fixing species, and pointed out that the competitive interaction between the higher plants was mediated by a third species – the nitrogen-fixing symbiont. In the context of Laszlo's scheme, nitrogen is an internal constraint of this system, and the nitrogen-fixing symbiont the 'external forcing' acting on that constraint. The result, 'adaptive self-organization', is a restructuring of the new, three-species system in niche space (along the nitrogen axis), with a concomitant increase in system productivity.

A related view, with perhaps more potential for quantitative analysis, is in terms of nonequilibrium thermodynamics. Prigogine's (1980) equation for entropy production in a nonequilibrium system is:

$$ds = d_e s + d_i s \tag{9}$$

where ds is total entropy production, $d_e s$ is entropy flow across system boundaries, and $d_i s$ is internal entropy production. Schrödinger (1945) pointed out that organisms maintain structure because they 'import negentropy', that is $d_e s$ is negative. Similarly, the entry of *Rhizobium* into a grass-legume system may be viewed as an importation of negentropy which increases internal structure. In effect, the nitrogen fixer acts as a 'Maxwell's Demon'[2], decreasing the randomness (and therefore the entropy) with which the species occupy niche space.

Analogies between ecological systems and the chemical systems of thermodynamics are perhaps more heuristic than literal. Nevertheless, if there are 'general systems properties', such analogies may bear fruit in ecology (Prigogine 1980). For example, stable, nonequilibrium structures ('dissipative' structures) are characterized by three factors in the theory of nonequilibrium thermodynamics: 'the function, as expressed by the chemical equations; the space-time structure, which results from the instabilities; and the fluctuations, which trigger the instabilities. The interplay between these three aspects:

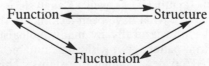

leads to the most unexpected phenomena, including order through fluctuations . . .' (Prigogine 1980, pp. 100–101). If we identify function with productivity, and fluctuation with the flow of negentropy, and generalize space-time structure to niche-space structure, Prigogine's scheme precisely describes the

---

[2] James Clerk Maxwell suggested that the second law of thermodynamics could be violated, in principle, if there existed 'an intelligent being small and agile enough' to sort the molecules in a gas into fast and slow, and thus decrease its entropy. Such an imaginary being came to be known as Maxwell's Demon (quote from Campbell 1982, p. 48).

relationships underlying co-evolutionary interaction within ecosystems, including those which we characterize as competitive. Clearly, the entry of new species (or flows of negentropy) into a pre-existing system does not always increase its structural complexity, or result in a new stable equilibrium containing all the elements of the old system (eg ingestion of carcinogens; introduction of gypsy moth, Dutch elm disease, chestnut blight; spraying Agent Orange). Such an event may be as rare as a successful mutation, but like a successful mutation it could result in an evolutionary advantage to the species-systems.

Some system-level concepts, such as Westoby's (1982) distribution modifying functions, Kikuzawa's (1984) 'stand compactness', and the notion of 'competitive tension' which I discussed earlier, may have predictive potential. On the other hand, the primary advantage gained from holistic models may be new ways of viewing systems. The importance of the latter should not be under-estimated, because it is in the context of our paradigms[3] that we formulate questions, design experiments, and interpret results.

IV. ON PARADIGMS AND LANGUAGES

Although the notion of trees as crop plants says nothing more than that trees can be managed to produce value for humans, it is difficult to avoid associating this concept with the techniques of modern agriculture – in which genetic and structural heterogeneity is eliminated, and the consequent loss in system buffering is replaced by high energy inputs. The way we act on the world is determined by how we view the world: in the words of Barrett (1978), 'Technique has no meaning apart from some informing vision'. It is essential to ask from time to time whether our world view is still appropriate; I believe that we are at such a juncture in both agriculture and forestry.

The development of agriculture was a marvellous statement of human ingenuity; however, it was also a product of ignorance, and its emergence as a modern technology was characterized by both brilliant tactics and questionable strategy. Agriculture was a product of ignorance in that its development assumed the patterns of nature to be chaotic, and its techniques flowed from the logical extension of that assumption, that chaotic systems must be dealt with by reduction to understandable, and therefore manageable, subsystems (individuals). The more we learn about ecosystems, however, the more it becomes obvious that they are far from chaotic. They are, in fact, reminiscent of human language in that, just as communication depends on syntax (the arrangement of words with respect to one another) and on context (the historical setting of the words), so ecosystem function cannot be understood outside the syntactical relationships between organisms and the historical context of co-evolution.

The strategy of modern agriculture assumes that (a) the buffering capacity of natural systems, which is based on information (eg genetic and structural diversity), can be adequately replaced by energy inputs, (b) unlimited supplies

---

[3] A paradigm is an example or pattern of the inflexion of a part of speech; the term is also used to mean a general pattern or model.

of energy will be available for this buffering, and (c) no major climatic changes will occur. It is still unclear whether the first assumption is correct, but the second depends on the development of new energy sources, and the third is manifestly false.

Foresters must not become too enamoured with the techniques of agriculture at a time when agricultural techniques themselves must be seriously re-evaluated. It is very important, in the face of an uncertain future, to keep our options open. This does not mean that we should not manage forests, but rather that we should intensify our efforts to learn the language of nature, so that we can merge with it and produce not only abundance, but security in an uncertain and rapidly changing global environment.

ACKNOWLEDGMENTS

Research was funded by the Long Term Ecological Research Program of the National Science Foundation, and by the Mapleton Ranger District of the Siuslaw National Forest (USDA Forest Service). I thank the following for data collection, analysis, and helpful discussion: Paul Schroeder, Carloyn Choquette, Mark Miller, Betsy Kaiser, Greg Koerper, Jeff Borchers, Emily Semple, and Kyna Perry. Thanks are also due to Melvin Cannell and David Ford for review and editing, and to Carol Rosenblum Perry for teaching me that language is more than words, and knowledge more than analysis.

REFERENCES

Adams, W. T. (1980). Intergenotypic competition in forest trees. *Proc. N. American Forest Biology Workshop, 6th*, edited by B. P. Dancik and K. O. Higginbotham, 1–14. Edmonton: University of Alberta.

Adams, W. T., Roberds, J. H. & Zobel, B. J. (1973). Intergenotypic interactions among families of loblolly pine (*Pinus taeda* L.). *Theor. appl. Genet.*, **43**, 319–322.

Adlard, P. G. (1974). Development of an empirical competition model for individual trees within a stand. In: *Growth models for tree and stand simulation*, edited by J. Fries, 22–37. Uppsala: Royal College of Forestry.

Aikman, D. P. & Watkinson, A. R. (1980). A model for growth and selfthinning in even-aged monocultures of plants. *Ann. Bot.*, **45**, 419–427.

Alemdag, I. S. (1978). Evaluation of some competition indices for the prediction of diameter increment in planted white spruce. *Inf. Rep. For. Manage. Inst. (Ottawa)*, FMR–X–108.

Allard, R. W. & Adams, J. (1969). Population studies in predominantly self-pollinating species. XIII. Intergenotypic competition and population structure in barley and wheat. *Am. Nat.*, **103**, 621–645.

Assmann, E. (1970). *The principles of forest yield study*. Oxford: Pergamon.

Austin, M. P. & Austin, B. O. (1980). Behaviour of experimental plant communities along a nutrient gradient. *J. Ecol.*, **68**, 891–918.

Axelrod, R. & Hamilton, W. D. (1981). The evolution of cooperation. *Science, N.Y.*, **211**, 1390–1396.

Badoux, E. (1945). *Mitt. schweiz. Anst. forstl. VersWes.*, **24**, 405, cited in Assman, E. (1970). *The principles of forest yield study*. Oxford: Pergamon.

Barrett, W. (1978). *The illusion of technique*. New York: Anchor Press/Doubleday.

Bella, I. E. (1971). A new competition model for individual trees. *Forest Sci.*, **17**, 364–372.

Binkley, D. (1983). Ecosystem production in Douglas-fir plantations: interaction of red alder and site fertility. *For. Ecol. Manage.*, **5**, 215–227.

Bowen, G. D. (1973). Mineral nutrition ectomycorrhizae. In: *Ectomycorrhizae*, edited by G. C. Marks and T. T. Kozlowski, 151–205. New York: Academic Press.

Bowen, G. D. (1980). Mycorrhizal roles in tropical plants and ecosystems. In: *Tropical mycorrhizae research*, edited by P. Mikola, 165–1909. Oxford: Oxford University Press.

Braathe, P. (1957). *Thinnings in even-aged stands*. Fredericton, NB: University of New Brunswick.

Brix, H. (1983). Effects of thinning and nitrogen fertilization on growth of Douglas-fir: relative contribution of foliage quantity and efficiency. *Can. J. For. Res.*, **13**, 167–175.

Brunig, E. F. (1983). Vegetation structure and growth. In: *Tropical rainforest ecosystems*, edited by F. B. Golley, 49–75. Amsterdam: Elsevier.

Burdon, J. J. & Chilvers, G. A. (1974). Fungal and insect parasites contributing to niche differentiation in mixed species stands of eucalypt saplings. *Aust. J. Bot.*, **22**, 103–114.

Burger, H. (1939). *Mitt. schweiz. Anst. forstl. VersWes.*, **20**, cited in Assmann, E. (1970). *The principles of forest yield study*. Oxford: Pergamon.

Campbell, J. (1982). *Grammatical man*. New York: Simon & Schuster.

Cannell, M. G. R. (1978). Biological opportunities for genetic improvement in forest productivity. In: *The ecology of even-aged forest plantations*, edited by E. D. Ford, D. C. Malcolm and J. Atterson, 119–144. Cambridge: Institute of Terrestrial Ecology.

Cannell, M. G. R. (1983). Plant management in agroforestry: manipulation of trees, population densities and mixtures of trees and herbaceous crops. In: *Plant research and agroforestry*, edited by P. A. Huxley, 455–487. Nairobi: International Council for Research in Agroforestry.

Cannell, M. G. R., Njuguma, C. K., Ford, E. D. & Smith, R. I. (with appendix by H. M. Ross-Parker). (1977). Variation in yield among competing individuals within mixed genotype stands of tea: a selection problem. *J. appl. Ecol.*, **14**, 969–985.

Cannell, M. G. R., Rothery, P. & Ford, E. D. (1984). Competition within stands of *Picea sitchensis* and *Pinus contorta*. *Ann. Bot.*, **53**, 349–362.

Chung, H. & Barnes, R. L. (1977). Photosynthate allocation in *Pinus taeda*. I. Substrate requirements for synthesis of shoot biomass. *Can. J. For. Res.*, **7**, 106–111.

Cochrane, L. A. & Ford, E. D. (1978). Growth of a Sitka spruce plantation: analysis and stochastic description of the development of the branching structure. *J. appl. Ecol.*, **15**, 227–244.

Curtis, R. O. & Reukema, D. L. (1970). Crown development and site estimates in a Douglas-fir plantation spacing test. *Forest Sci.*, **16**, 287–301.

deWit, C. T. (1960). On competition. *Versl. landbouwk. Onderz. Ned.*, **66**, 1–82.

deWit, C. T., Tow, P. G. & Ennik, G. C. (1966). Competition between legumes and grasses. *Versl. landbouwk. Onderz. Ned.*, **687**, 3–30.

Diggle, P. J. (1976). A spatial stochastic model of inter-plant competition. *J. appl. Probab.*, **13**, 662–671.

Donald, C. M. (1968). The breeding of crop ideotypes. *Euphytica*, **17**, 385–403.

Ford, E. D. (1975). Competition and stand structure in some even-aged plant monocultures. *J. Ecol.*, **63**, 311–333.

Ford, E. D. (1976). Competition, genetic systems, and improvement of forest yield. In: *Tree physiology and yield improvement*, edited by M. G. R. Cannell and F. T. Last, 463–472. London: Academic Press.

Ford, E. D. (1982). High productivity in a polestage Sitka spruce stand and its relation to canopy structure. *Forestry*, **55**, 1–17.

Ford, E. D. & Diggle, P. J. (1981). Competition for light in a plant monoculture modelled as a spatial stochastic process. *Ann. Bot.*, **48**, 481–500.

Ford, E. D. & Newbould, P. J. (1970). Stand structure and dry weight production through the sweet chestnut (*Castanea sativa* Mill.) coppice cycle. *J. Ecol.*, **58**, 275–296.

Ford, E. D. & Newbould, P. J. (1971). The leaf canopy of a coppiced deciduous woodland. I. Development and structure. *J. Ecol.*, **59**, 843–862.

Franklin, E. C. (1979). Model relating levels of genetic variance to stand development of four North American conifers. *Silvae Genet.*, **28**, 207–212.

Gary, H. L. (1978). The vertical distribution of needles and branchwood in thinned and unthinned 80–year-old lodgepole pine. *NW Sci.*, **52**, 303–309.

Gates, D. J. (1978). Bimodality in even-aged plant monocultures. *J. theor. Biol.*, **71**, 525–540.

Gates, D. J. (1982). Competition and skewness in plantations. *J. theor. Biol.*, **94**, 909–922.

Gates, D. J., McMurtrie, R. & Borough, C. J. (1983). Skewness reversal of distribution of stem diameter in plantations of *Pinus radiata*. *Aust. For. Res.*, **13**, 267–270.

Gatlin, L. (1972). *Information theory and the living system.* New York: Columbia University Press.

Gholz, H. L., Grier, C. C., Campbell, A. G. & Brown, A. T. (1979). *Equations for estimating biomass and leaf area of plants in the Pacific Northwest.* (Research paper no. 41). Corvallis, OR: Oregon State University, Forest Research Laboratory.

Graustein, W., Cromack, K. & Sollins, P. (1977). Calcium oxalate: occurrence in soils and effect on nutrient and geochemical cycles. *Science, N.Y.*, **198**, 1252–1254.

Hall, G. S. (1965). Wood increment and crown distribution relationships in red pine. *Forest Sci.*, **11**, 438–448.

Hanley, T. A. & Taber, R. D. (1980). Selective plant species inhibition by elk and deer in three conifer communities in western Washington. *Forest Sci.*, **26**, 97–197.

Harper, J. L. (1977). *Population biology of plants.* New York: Academic Press.

Hegyi, F. (1974). A simulation model for managing jack-pine stands. In: *Growth models for tree and stand simulation,* edited by J. Fries, 74–90. Stockholm: Royal College of Forestry, Dept Forest Yield Research.

Holmes, J. R. B. & Tackle, D. (1962). Height growth of lodgepole pine in Montana related to soil and stand factors. *Bull. Sch. For. Montana St. Univ.*, no. 21.

Hozumi, K. (1980). Ecological and mathematical considerations on self-thinning in even-aged pure stands. II. Growth analysis of self-thinning. *Bot. Mag., Tokyo*, **93**, 149–166.

Hühn, M. (1969). Untersuchungen zur Konkurrenz zwischen verschiedenen Genotypes in Pflanzenbeständen. I. Modifikation der Methode von Sakai zur Schatzung der genetischen-, Umwelt- und Konkurrenzvarianz einer Population. *Silvae Genet.*, **18**, 186–192.

Hühn, M. (1970). The competitive.experiment and its genetic reaction variations. *Proc. meeting IUFRO Working Group on Quantitative Genetics, 2nd,* Section 22, 62–86. New Orleans: USDA Forest Service, Southern Forest Exp. Stn.

Hühn, M. (1973). Populations genetische Untersuchungen zur phänotypischen Selektion in Pflanzenbeständen mit Konkurrenz. *Silvae Genet.*, **22**, 72–81.

Hutchings, M. J. (1979). Weight-density relation in ramet populations of clonal perennial herbs, with special reference to the −3/2 power law. *J. Ecol.*, **67**, 21–33.

Hutchings, M. J. & Budd, C. S. J. (1981). Plant self-thinning and leaf area dynamics in experimental and natural monocultures. *Oikos*, **36**, 319–325.

Jack, W. H. (1971). The influence of tree spacing on Sitka spruce growth. *Irish For.*, **28**, 13–33.

Johnson, H. A. (1970). Information theory in biology after 18 years. *Science, N.Y.*, **168**, 1545–1550.

Kellomäki, S. & Hari, P. (1980). Eco-physiological studies on young Scots pine stands: I. Tree class as indicator of needle biomass, illumination, and photosynthetic capacity of crown system. *Silva fenn.*, **14**, 227–242.

Kikuzawa, K. (1984). Yield-density diagram: Compactness index for stands and stand components. *For. Ecol. Manage.*, **7**, 1–10.

Kira, T., Ogawa, H. & Shinozaki, K. (1953). Intraspecific competition among higher plants. I. Competition-density-yield interrelationships in regularly dispersed populations. *J. Inst. Polytech. Osaka Cy Univ.*, **D4**, 1–16.

Koch, A. L. (1966). The logarithm in biology. I. Mechanisms generating the log normal distribution exactly. *J. theor. Biol.*, **12**, 276–290.

Kohyama, T. & Fujita, N. (1981). Studies on the *Abies* population of Mt Shimagare. I. Survivorship curve. *Bot. Mag., Tokyo*, **94**, 55–68.

Koyama, H. & Kira, T. (1956). Intraspecific competition among higher plants. VIII. Frequency distribution of individual plant weight as affected by the interaction between plants. *J. Inst. Polytech. Osaka Cy Univ.*, **D7**, 73–94.

Kramer, P. & Kozlowski, T. T. (1979). *Physiology of woody plants.* New York; London: Academic Press.

Laszlo, E. (1972). *Introduction to systems philosophy.* New York; London: Gordon & Breach.

Libby, W. J., Stettler, R. F. & Seitz, F. W. (1969). Forest genetics and forest-tree breeding. *A. Rev. Genet.*, **3**, 469–494.

Long, J. N. & Smith, F. W. (1984). Relation between size and density in developing stands: a description and possible mechanisms. *For. Ecol. Manage.*, **7**, 191–206.

Mayer, R. (1957). *Diss. Munich,* cited in Assmann, E. (1970). *The principles of forest yield study.* Oxford: Pergamon.

McArdle, R. E. & Meyer, W. H. (1961). The yield of Douglas-fir in the Pacific Northwest. *USDA Tech. Bull.*, no. 201.

Mitchell, K. J. (1975). Dynamics and simulated yield of Douglas-fir. *Forest Sci. Monogr.*, no. 17.

Mitchell, R. G., Waring, R. H. & Pitman, G. B. (1983). Thinning lodgepole pine increases tree vigor and resistance to mountain pine beetle. *Forest Sci.*, **29**, 204–211.

Mohler, C. L., Marks, P. L. & Sprugel, D. G. (1978). Stand structure and allometry of trees during self-thinning of pure stands. *J. Ecol.*, **66**, 599–614.

Noone, C. S. & Bell, J. F. (1980). *An evaluation of eighth inter-tree competition indices.* (Research note no. 66). Corvallis, OR: Oregon State University, Forest Research Laboratory.

Odum, E. P. (1977). The emergence of ecology as a new integrative discipline. *Science, N.Y.*, **195**, 1289–1293.

Oker-Blom, P. & Kellomäki, S. (1982). Effect of stand density on the within-crown light regime and dying off of branches. *Folia for.*, **509**, 1–14.

Oliver, W. W. & Powers, R. F. (1978). Growth models for ponderosa pine: I. Yield of unthinned plantations in northern California. *Res. Pap. Pacif. SW Forest Range Exp. Stn*, PSW-133.

Opie, F. F. (1968). Predictability of individual tree growth using definitions of competing basal area. *Forest Sci.*, **14**, 314–323.

Panetsos, C. (K) P. (1980). Selection of new poplar clones under various spacings. *Silvae Genet.*, **29**, 130–135.

Parrish, J. A. D. & Bazzaz, F. A. (1982). Competitive interactions in plant communities of different successional ages. *Ecology*, **63**, 314–320.

Perry, D. A. (1984). A model of physiological and allometric factors in the self-thinning curve. *J. theor. Biol.*, **106**, 383–401.

Pickard, W. F. (1983). Three interpretations of the self-thinning rule. *Ann. Bot.*, **51**, 749–757.

Prigogine, I. (1980). *From being to becoming.* San Francisco: Freeman.

Reineke, L. H. (1933). Perfecting a stand-density index for even-aged forests. *J. agric. Res.*, **46**, 627–638.

Richards, F. J. (1959). A flexible growth function for empirical use. *J. exp. Bot.*, **10**, 290–300.

Riitters, K. (1985). *Early genetic selection in Douglas-fir; interaction with drought, shade, and density.* Ph.D. thesis, Oregon State University.

Rook, D. A. & Carson, M. J. (1978). Temperature and irradiance and the total daily photosynthetic production of the crown of a *Pinus radiata* tree. *Oecologia*, **36**, 371–382.

Sakai, K. I. & Mukaide, H. (1967). Estimation of genetic, environmental and competitional variances in standing forests. *Silvae Genet.*, **16**, 149–152.

Sakai, K. I., Mukaide, H. & Tonita, K. (1968). Intraspecific competition in forest trees. *Silvae Genet.*, **17**, 1–5.

Schroeder, P. E., McCandlish, B., Waring, R. H. & Perry, D. A. (1982). The relationship of maximum canopy leaf area to forest growth in eastern Washington. *NW Sci.*, **56**, 121–130.

Schrödinger, E. (1945). *What is life?* Cambridge: Cambridge University Press.

Schutz, W. M., Bruin, C. A. & Usanis, S. A. (1968). Intergenotypic competition in plant populations. I. Feedback systems with stable equilibria in populations of autogamous homozogous lines. *Crop Sci.*, **8**, 61–66.

Seidel, K. W. (1977). Levels-of-growing stock study in thinned western larch pole stands in eastern Oregon. *Res. Pap. Pacif. NW For. Range Exp. Stn*, PNW-221.

Stern, K. (1969). Einige Beiträge genetischer Forschung zum Problem der Konkurrenz in Pflanzenbeständen. *Allg. Forst- u. Jagdztg.*, **140**, 253–262.

Tauer, C. G. (1975). Competition between selected black cottonwood genotypes. *Silvae Genet.*, **24**, 44–49.

Tilman, D. (1982). *Resource competition and community structure.* Princeton, NJ: Princeton University Press.

Trenbath, B. R. (1974). Biomass productivity in mixtures. *Adv. Agron.*, **26**, 177–210.

Trenbath, B. R. & Harper, J. L. (1973). Neighbour effects in the genus *Avena*. I. Comparison of crop species. *J. appl. Ecol.*, **10**, 379–400.

Turkington, R. A., Caners, P. B. & Aarssen, L. W. (1977). Neighbour relationships in grass-legume communities. I. Interspecific contacts in farm grassland communities near Landon, Ontario. *Can. J. Bot.*, **55**, 2701–2711.

Vandermeer, J. (1981). The interference production principle: an ecological theory for agriculture. *BioScience*, **31**, 361–364.

Waring, R. H. & Schlesinger, W. H. (1985). *Forest ecosystems. Concepts and management.* New York; London: Academic Press.

West, P. W. & Borough, C. J. (1983). Tree suppression and the self-thinning rule in a monoculture of *Pinus radiata* D. Don. *Ann. Bot.*, **52**, 149–158.

Westoby, M. (1982). Frequency distributions of plant size during competitive growth of stands: the operation of distribution-modifying functions. *Ann. Bot.*, **50**, 733–735.

Westoby, M. (1984). The self-thinning rate. In: *Advances in ecological research*, edited by A. Macfadyen and E. D. Ford, 167–225. London: Academic Press.

White, J. (1980). Demographic factors in populations of plants. In: *Demography and evolution in plant populations*, edited by O. T. Solbrig, 21–48. Oxford: Blackwell.

White, J. (1981). The allometric interpretation of the self-thinning rule. *J. theor. Biol.*, **89**, 475–500.

Wierman, C. A. & Oliver, C. D. (1979). Crown stratification by species in even-aged mixed stands of Douglas-fir – western hemlock. *Can. J. For. Res.*, **9**, 1–9.

Wiley, E. & Brooks, D. (1982). Victims of history – a non-equilibrium approach to evolution. *Syst. Zool.*, **31**, 1–24.

Yamamura, N. (1976). A mathematical approach to spatial distribution and temporal succession in plant communities. *Bull. Math. Biol.*, **38**, 517–526.

Yeaton, R. I., Trairs, J. & Gilinsby, E. (1977). Competition and spacing in plant communities: the Arizona upland association. *J. Ecol.*, **65**, 587–596.

Yoda, K., Kira, T., Ogawa, H. & Hozumi, H. (1963). Self-thinning in overcrowded pure stands under cultivated and natural conditions. *J. Biol. Osaka Cy Univ.*, **14**, 107–129.

Yodzis, P. (1976). The effects of harvesting on competitive systems. *Bull. Math. Biol.*, **38**, 97–109.

29

FOREST CANOPY DESIGN: BIOLOGICAL MODELS AND MANAGEMENT IMPLICATIONS

D. A. ROOK, J. C. GRACE, P. N. BEETS, D. WHITEHEAD,
D. SANTANTONIO and H. A. I. MADGWICK
Forest Research Institute, Rotorua, New Zealand

I. INTRODUCTION

Forest canopy design concerns the amount and arrangement of foliage within a community of trees. This design is of special interest because it affects the amount and disposition of growth, and because it can be readily manipulated by changing the number and arrangement of trees, by pruning, as well as genetically. Traditionally, the effects of such operations on forest growth have been predicted using graphical methods or empirical regression models. We contend that greater insights can be gained by using dynamic, state-determined models of carbon flow, based on an understanding of the biological processes of crop growth, as has been done in agriculture (eg cotton, Jones *et al.* 1980).

In this chapter, we first review the literature on plant growth models, in order to identify those submodels that might be most appropriate to simulate carbon flow in forest stands, with special reference to *Pinus radiata*. We then use a radiation interception model, and a carbon allocation model, to demonstrate how they can predict differences in photosynthetic production and above-ground biomass allocation within young stands of *Pinus radiata* growing at (a) high stocking densities, (b) medium stocking densities (for sawlog production) and (c) wide spacings (in an agroforestry 'silvopastoral' system). We assume that water and nutrients are not limiting.

II. COMPONENTS OF BIOLOGICAL MODELS TO EXAMINE EFFECTS OF FOREST CANOPY DESIGN

The components of our biological model of carbon flow in a forest stand are illustrated in Figure 1. The rate at which carbohydrates are produced is determined by radiation interception, canopy CO_2 conductance, canopy photosynthesis, and respiration. The carbohydrates are allocated to the growth of foliage, branches, stems, and coarse and fine roots. The disposition of new

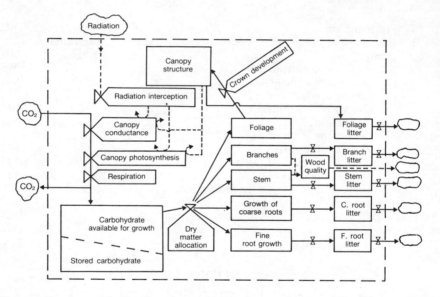

FIGURE 1. A model of carbon flow within a forest, showing the major component models (valve symbols) and state variables (rectangles).

foliage is determined by a crown development model. Carbon flows out of the system in the form of litter from all tree parts. In the case of stemwood, some of the carbon is harvested and its quality characteristics are determined. Changes in forest design will alter the rates of the processes, represented by the valve symbols in Figure 1, as well as the sizes of the state variables, represented by rectangles. Let us now consider each component model in turn.

A.   Radiation interception

A radiation interception model is required to predict, for different seasons, latitudes and slopes, the amount of radiation intercepted by individual trees and by different parts of the crop canopy. Many models of radiation interception have been developed ranging from simple to complex. The main difference is how the canopy structure is treated. The structural variables which are important are, in order of decreasing importance: leaf area index, vertical distribution of foliage, distribution of leaf angles, leaf reflectance and transmittance, clumping of foliage, and the distribution of leaf azimuth angles.

Monsi and Saeki (1953) proposed the first simple theory of radiation interception for a continuous homogenous canopy of horizontal leaves. Thorpe *et al.* (1978) described a model for the distribution of radiation incident on leaves of isolated apple trees, assuming ellipsoidal crown shapes and randomly dispersed foliage. Interception models that consider the clumping of foliage have been written by Norman and Jarvis (1975) for forest canopies, and by Oker-Blom and Kellomäki (1983) for individual trees. Absurd results are produced if it is assumed that the foliage on widely spaced trees is randomly distributed over the whole canopy, but it is adequate to assume random and spherical distributions of foliage within the crowns.

The model that most readily enables one to explore the effects of changes in the spatial arrangement of foliage on radiation interception is that published by Norman and Welles (1983). We have modified this model for our purposes. The model being used allows the latitude, aspect and slope of the site, and the size and location of each tree, to be specified. A crop canopy is approximated by an array of the individual tree crowns arranged in various configurations.

The crown of each tree is assumed to be represented by an ellipsoid and, within this, three other ellipsoids are described forming four shells. The amount of foliage within each shell is specified, and is assumed to be randomly located, with no preferred azimuthal direction and with the inclinations having a spherical leaf angle distribution.

The model calculates, from irradiance above the canopy, the attenuation of irradiance in the visible and near infra-red wavebands, and the irradiance available for photosynthesis in different parts of the crown. The sun and shade crown is normally treated separately with different photosynthetic functions.

B. Crown development

A crown development model is needed to describe changes in the amount and distribution of foliage with time, and in response to treatments. Ideally, we would like to 'grow' a tree, knowing the processes that control the number, growth and senescence of each shoot meristem, but our knowledge is inadequate at this level. Instead we must rely on empirical measurements of crown dimensions (eg Siemon *et al.* 1980), the distribution of foliage biomass within crowns (Beets 1982) and seasonal changes in foliage amounts (Madgwick 1983) measured in different conditions. Empirical, demographic models of leaf populations can be developed when foliage amounts are expressed in terms of the numbers and sizes of leaves according to cohort locations within the crowns (Maillette 1982). There is a need to integrate the fragmentary data available on tree shoot growth and development to construct models of seasonal changes in canopy structure (Landsberg 1981).

C.   Canopy conductance

Photosynthesis by tree canopies may be considered as the sum of photosynthesis of all leaves. For a single leaf, the rate of photosynthesis is often characterized by four parameters: stomatal conductance to CO_2 transfer, mesophyll conductance, quantum yield and CO_2 compensation point (eg Reed *et al.* 1976). When water and nutrients are not limiting, photosynthetic activity can be explained largely by changes in radiation and stomatal conductance. It is desirable to consider the response of stomata to environmental variables in a separate submodel. In conifers, up to 75% of the diurnal variation in stomatal conductance can be accounted for by short-term changes in ambient vapour pressure deficit and radiation, with a secondary effect of low potentials during periods of drought (Whitehead & Jarvis 1982). We might expect these environmental effects to be important when comparing stands with different canopy designs. There are the added advantages that models of stomatal conductance can also be used to estimate crop water use.

Models relating stomatal conductance to environmental variables have recently been classified by Hall (1983) into empirical models using multiple regression analyses (eg Kaufmann 1982) and phenomenological models (eg Jarvis 1976), where least squares regressions have been used to obtain the parameters from data collected in the field, but using the shapes of environmental response curves obtained in controlled conditions. We favour the latter type of model. However, research is needed to determine the effects of thinning and pruning on canopy conductance. Jarvis (1975) indicated that canopy conductance would be halved in a stand where half the trees and leaf area were removed, but Whitehead *et al.* (1984) showed that canopy conductance in an unthinned stand of *Pinus sylvestris* was larger than in a thinned stand by an amount greater than the difference in leaf area index.

D.   Canopy photosynthesis

A canopy photosynthesis model is needed to predict photosynthetic rates of different parts of the crowns of individual trees and of the canopy as a whole. The model will utilize the outputs of the radiation interception, stomatal conductance and crown development models.

There are a great many models of photosynthesis, ranging from the leaf to the ecosystem (Hesketh & Jones 1980; Charles-Edwards 1981; Farquhar & von Caemmerer 1983). Jarvis and Leverenz (1983) described a shoot photosynthesis model at an appropriate level of complexity for our purpose; it depended on inputs of boundary, stomatal and mesophyll conductances for CO_2 transfer, on quantum yields and CO_2 compensation concentrations. To estimate canopy photosynthesis, these photosynthetic parameters were needed for cohorts of foliage of different types in different crown positions. Canopy photosynthesis could than be calculated by summing all cohorts.

Integrations of individual leaf or shoot photosynthesis within an entire forest canopy over a whole year have been carried out in only a few stands

(Jarvis and Leverenz (1983) list studies on *Pinus sylvestris*, *Picea abies* and *Fagus sylvatica*). Data on stomatal conductances and photosynthesis within *Pinus radiata* stands are still too few to attempt such integrations.

E. Respiration

Respiration must be subtracted from the increments in photosynthate to provide an estimate of the carbohydrates available for growth. In conifer stands, respiration losses of 30–50% have been estimated, which could be important in explaining differences in growth between stands with different canopy design (Kinerson *et al.* 1977; Linder & Troeng 1981).

Total respiratory losses depend on the amount, physiological activity and growth rate of the living tissues. Respiration rates of stems, branches and thick roots can be expressed per unit surface area (Jarvis & Leverenz 1983), and surface areas can be derived from biomass measurements (Beets 1982), but information is needed on differences and changes in respiration rates per unit surface area. We favoured the model of Linder and Troeng (1981), in which respiration rates depended on the size class of the stems, branches and roots, and varied with season (growth activity), and air or soil temperature. Also, Linder and Troeng (1980) recognized that at least 25% of the CO_2 respired by thinly-barked parts of stems and branches could be re-assimilated.

Although the respiration rates of coarse roots have been measured on trees in the field (Linder & Troeng 1981; Benecke 1984), fine root respiration rates have been measured only under laboratory conditions using detached roots or potted seedlings (Linder & Troeng 1981). Estimates of root respiration in the field have usually been obtained from the residuals of carbon balances which have varied from 23% of the net annual photosynthetic production in 20–year-old *Pinus sylvestris* to 15–17% in *Nothofagus solandri* and *Pinus contorta* (Linder & Troeng 1981; Benecke & Nordmeyer 1982).

F. Partitioning of growth

A partitioning model is needed to determine the allocation of photosynthates for growth and maintenance of different parts of the tree. Mechanistic models have been constructed to estimate root/shoot partitioning (eg Thornley 1976), but too few data are available to use these models on trees. Lang and Thorpe (1983) proposed a simple phenomenological model, which might prove useful in analysing biomass data for forest trees, but meanwhile we have used an empirical model based on comprehensive data on the distribution of biomass among tree parts at different ages and on different sites (eg Madgwick *et al.* 1977; Beets 1982; Satoo & Madgwick 1982; Cannell, this volume).

Above-ground partitioning affects crown development and radiation interception, and so needs to be estimated every 1 to 2 weeks, depending on previous and current conditions. Empirical methods may be satisfactory, but information is needed on stands of the correct age, stocking density and rate of growth. For instance, young stands often have unusually high foliage masses at canopy closure, and the fraction of dry matter allocated to branches can greatly decrease during canopy closure (Beets 1982; Satoo & Madgwick 1982).

It is recognized that differences in dry matter production in stands are associated with differences in amounts of foliage in the early years of the stand and after thinning (eg Möller 1954; Satoo & Madgwick 1982). No attempt will be made to review the extensive forestry literature on growth responses to lower initial plant numbers and to thinning and pruning, as these are covered in most general forest textbooks (Baker 1950; Assmann 1970). Specific data on the biomass of above-ground components of *Pinus radiata* are given by Madgwick *et al*. (1977) and in response to thinning by Siemon *et al*. (1976), Siemon *et al*. (1980), Shepherd and Forrest (1973) and Beets (1982).

Factors affecting carbon allocation below-ground, and interactions between the root and shoot, are poorly understood, and data on the responses of root systems to silvicultural treatment in particular are extremely limited. Competition below-ground generally starts earlier, and involves many more trees, than competition above-ground, because surface horizontal root systems intermingle before crowns touch (Leaf *et al*. 1971; Fayle 1975).

Theoretically, a model is needed to predict the seasonal carbon requirements of the roots for growth and maintenance, including fine root turnover and respiration. Few data are available, although we know that fine root turnover can account for 8–67% of the net annual dry matter production of trees. The dry matter increment of coarse roots can be 3–17% of net annual production, so that the total dry matter allocated below-ground ranges from 23–78% (Fogel & Hunt 1979; Deans 1981; Keyes & Grier 1981; Vogt *et al*. 1982; Santantonio & Hermann 1985).

G.   Wood quality attributes

It is important that the output of a forest growth model should not be left merely as the flow of carbon out of the system, without regard to the quantity and quality of the products. The kinds of products will depend on the requirements of those marketing and utilizing them.

Although there is a considerable body of data on the anatomical features of wood (eg Denne 1979; Bamber & Burley 1983), which at some stage might be incorporated into a model, our first attempts should be to concentrate on the factors affecting 'log grade', namely log dimensions, taper, and branchiness. Harris (1981) contended that, in general, the effects of silvicultural practices on wood quality were minor compared with effects of tree age and site, but Brazier (1973) presented a more cautious account of the possible effects on wood quality of heavy thinning and pruning practices. Relationships between volume growth and wood quality given by Kellomäki and Tuimala (1981) portray the type of model that might be used to quantify the effects of canopy structure on log grades, and thus on economic returns.

III. SIMULATIONS OF EFFECTS OF FOREST CANOPY DESIGN

So far, we have shown that models that could be used to examine the effects of forest design on wood production are available, or are being developed, with the exception of models for the below-ground allocation of growth. The models being developed are a mix of process-based and empirical relationships. At this stage, it is not possible to construct a complete biological model, but we can illustrate the types of results which can be expected using submodels concerned with (a) radiation interception and photosynthate production, and (b) above-ground dry matter allocation. We shall illustrate differences between 9-year-old *Pinus radiata* stands at (a) high stocking densities, HS, (b) medium stocking densities, MS, and (c) very wide spacings in a 'silvopastoral' agroforestry system, AF.

The first set of simulations shows how much total photosynthate is produced in these forest types, and how it is affected by foliage amount and distribution. The second set of simulations shows how growing conditions affect the relative allocation of resources to stemwood.

A. Radiation interception

The modified Norman and Welles (1983) radiation interception model, together with photosynthesis/photon flux density functions of the foliage, was used to provide daily estimates of photosynthate production by different parts of the crown of individual trees, and per unit area of ground. From the average irradiance above the canopy for each hour of the day, the model predicts the radiation available for photosynthesis in different parts of the crown throughout the day. The photosynthesis/photon flux density functions used were derived from data collected by CO_2 porometry in a 12–year-old stand of *P. radiata* from Nelson province of New Zealand (Lat. 41° 35'S; Long. 17° 45'E). Canopy values of photosynthesis were obtained by using separate curves for sun and shade foliage using data from autumn (April) and winter (June), (ie during periods of high and low photosynthetic activity respectively). The response of photosynthesis (P) to photon flux density (Q) was of the form:

$$P = \frac{Q}{a+bQ} - R_d$$

where R_d was dark respiration (assumed to be constant at $0.5 \, \mu\text{mol m}^{-2}\text{s}^{-1}$) and the parameters a and b were related to the slope and asymptote of P plotted against Q. The estimated values of a and b were as follows:

		a (no dimensions)	$b\left(\dfrac{1}{\mu\text{mol m}^{-2}\text{s}^{-1}}\right)$
Autumn (April)	Sun crown	40·0	0·15
	Shade crown	55·9	0·26
Winter (June)	Sun crown	42·0	0·25
	Shade crown	34·0	0·54

Simulation runs were made for four days in the year, based on radiation data recorded at Puruki, near Rotorua (Lat. 38° 22′S, Long. 176° 10′E). The days selected were clear, sunny days in summer and winter with high direct beam fractions, and cloudy days in summer and winter with low direct beam fractions.

The crown dimensions of each type of forest were measured in stands growing near Rotorua (see Table I). The leaf area index values were obtained by multiplying the number of crowns per hectare by the foliage density per crown (ie the leaf area per crown volume). The latter was found to be $3 \cdot 30 \, m^2 m^{-3}$ at Puruki on 9-year-old trees of $P.$ $radiata$, which, when expressed on a projected leaf area basis, gave a value of $1 \cdot 37 \, m^2 \, m^{-3}$ (cf $0 \cdot 2 - 0 \cdot 4 \, m^2 \, m^{-3}$ quoted for other conifers by Waring 1983).

TABLE I.   Crown dimensions, stocking densities, and leaf area indices of three types of 9–year-old $Pinus \ radiata$ forest

	Crown dimensions width×breadth×height (m)	Stocking density (stems ha^{-1})	Leaf area index[1] (m^2 m^{-2})
High stocking density (HS)	1·4×1·4×7·9	6,944	19·7
Medium stocking density (MS)	4·5×4·5×9·9	499	17·3
Silvopastoral agroforest (AF)	3·6×3·6×6·1	199	2·6

[1] Total foliage surface area; the projected area can be obtained by dividing by 2·4.

The radiation model required information about the structure of the crop (crown dimensions, foliage density, stems ha^{-1}), site location (latitude, slope), characteristics of the foliage (coefficients of reflectance and transmittance) and radiation data (hourly average values of incoming radiation in visible and near infra-red parts of the spectrum).

Figure 2 presents the predicted photosynthetic production of the three forest types (HS, MS and AF) on a sunny summer day (1 January), a cloudy summer day (7 December), and a sunny winter day (7 July). The large crowns of the MS (medium stocking) and AF (agroforest) tree types produced 8 to 12 times as much photosynthate as the small crowns of the HS (high stocking) tree type (Table II). Most importantly, none of the trees produced significant amounts of photosynthate in their inner shells on any day. In winter, and on cloudy summer days, the model predicted a net loss of photosynthates in the lower layers and inner shells of the large-crowned MS trees, although this loss could be the result of a weakness in the present photosynthesis model, which assumes a constant rate of dark respiration.

On a per hectare basis (Table II), the HS forest showed 20–28% greater

TABLE II. Predicted net daily carbon dioxide uptake of *Pinus radiata* trees managed at high stocking densities (HS), medium stocking densities (MS) and as widely spaced trees in a silvopastoral agroforest (AF)

Values are for daylight hours only

		Carbon dioxide uptake		
		per tree (mol d^{-1})	per hectare (mol ha^{-1} d^{-1})	per canopy projection[1] (mol m^{-2} d^{-1})
Sunny summer day	HS forest	2·5	17,360	1·5
	MS forest	29·0	14,470	1·8
	AF forest	19·4	3,860	1·9
Cloudy summer day	HS forest	0·8	5,550	0·5
	MS forest	8·7	4,340	0·5
	AF forest	8·7	1,730	0·9
Sunny winter day	HS forest	0·6	4,170	0·4
	MS forest	6·6	3,290	0·4
	AF forest	6·2	1,230	0·6

[1] Area of canopy projection. HS = 1·6 m²; MS = 15·9 m²; AF = 10·1 m².

rates of CO_2 uptake than the MS forest, and 3·2–4·5 times greater than the tree component of the AF forest. The relative photosynthate production of the different forest types did, however, vary with the radiation conditions; diffuse radiation favoured the productivity of the widely-spaced AF trees. Although the widely spaced trees in the AF forest produced only about one-third, or less, as much photosynthate per hectare as the other forests, their CO_2 uptake was up to 80% more per unit ground area covered by the canopies (Table II).

Halving the foliage densities in the tree crowns, from 3·30 m² m^{-3} to 1·65 m² m^{-3} (total foliage area basis), decreased photosynthate production (eg 6·3 to 4·5 mols d^{-1} in the agroforest, on a sunny winter day), and doubling the foliage density to 6·60 m² m^{-3} increased photosynthate production of the MS and AF forests, but not of the HS forest (the latter produced 0·5, 0·6 and 0·4 mols d^{-1} on a sunny winter day with 1·65, 3·30 and 6·60 m² m^{-3}, respectively).

Figure 3A and Table III show the predicted effects of differences in crown shape on photosynthate production, keeping the crown volumes and foliage densities constant at 37·7 m³ and 3·3 m² m^{-3}, respectively. Predictions are for a sunny winter day with stocking densities of 277 stem ha^{-1} and a leaf area index of 8·2 m² m^{-2}. The tree with the broadest crown produced most photosynthate per tree, but only one-third as much photosynthate per unit ground area covered by the crown as the tree with an elongated crown (0·3 and 0·9 mol m^{-2} d^{-1}). Other workers have also suggested that trees with

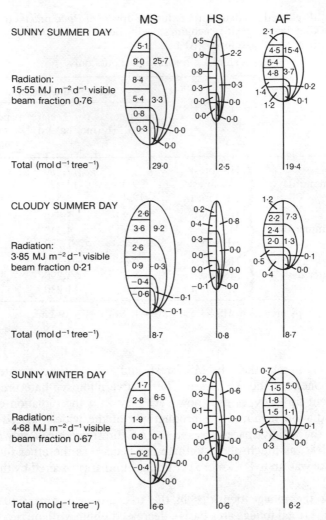

FIGURE 2.   Daily carbon dioxide uptake by 9-year-old trees of *Pinus radiata* within the three different forest types given in Table I, on three different days in New Zealand. Values were predicted using a radiation interception model, and the photosynthesis/radiation functions given in the text. MS = medium stocking density; HS = high stocking density; AF = agroforestry 'silvopastoral' system with trees at wide spacings. Daily photosynthate production (mol d^{-1}) within the shells and layers within the crowns are shown on the right and left of each tree, and the total daily production is expressed per tree.

elongated crowns can be more productive than those with squat crowns (Jahnke & Lawrence 1965; Oker-Blom & Kellomäki 1982). Figure 3B, compared with Figure 3A, shows the effect of increasing the crown volume by increasing the height of the crown, but maintaining the same leaf area index.

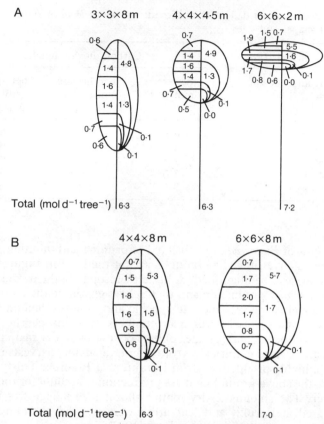

FIGURE 3. Predicted daily carbon dioxide uptake by 9-year-old trees of *Pinus radiata* with different crown dimensions on a sunny winter day in New Zealand. The width × breadth × height of each crown (in metres) is given above each tree. See legend to Fig. 2.

A. Three trees, all with 37.7 m^3 of crown, 3.3 m^2 foliage per m^3 of crown, leaf area index 8.2, and 277 stems ha^{-1}.

B. Two trees with the same leaf area indices as in A, but with increased crown volumes, produced by increasing the crown heights to 8 m.

A 77% increase in crown volume, but with correspondingly reduced foliage density, increased photosynthate production per tree and per unit ground area by 12%.

B. Above-ground dry matter allocation

The allocation of dry matter within trees growing in the MS, HS and AF forest designs defined in Tables I and IV was predicted using the DRYMAT model of Beets (1982). This is a stand model, developed for even-aged

TABLE III.   Predicted net daily carbon dioxide uptake of *Pinus radiata* tree crowns with different shapes and sizes

Crown dimensions (m)	Carbon dioxide uptake		
width × breadth × height	per tree (mol d^{-1})	per hectare (mol $ha^{-1} d^{-1}$)	per canopy projection (mol $m^{-2} d^{-1}$)
3×3×8	6·3	1,750	0·9
4×4×4·5	6·3	1,750	0·5
6×6×2	7·2	1,990	0·3
4×4×8	7·0	1,940	0·6
6×6×8	7·6	2,110	0·3

managed stands of *Pinus radiata* subjected to pruning and thinning, growing on highly productive sites. The model starts at the level in Figure 1 where dry matter flows can be quantified. A basic philosophy of the model is that it generates new foliage production and then relates growth to the crop's foliage mass. The model is species- and site-specific and requires data on (a) stand structure, ie heights, basal areas and numbers of stems per hectare, (b) silvicultural treatments, and (c) rates of net above-ground dry matter production, which are derived empirically from a series of annual harvests in a stand growing on a highly productive site at Puruki, near Rotorua. Thirty per cent was added to the above-ground biomass production to account for root growth and turnover. The amount of dry matter allocated to foliage was based on rates measured at Puruki, and leaf areas were derived assuming specific fascicle weights of 13 to 17 $m^2 kg^{-1}$ (Beets 1982).

The silvicultural details of the three forest types used in the simulations are given in Table IV, and results of the simulations at ages 6 and 10 years are presented in Figure 4. The results of the simulation runs were compared with (a) annual biomass harvests from an HS forest from age 6 to 10 years (Madgwick 1981), and (b) biomass harvests taken from 6-year-old stands on a forest farm with residual stockings of 173 stems ha^{-1} (AF forest) and 600 stems ha^{-1} (MS forest) (Madgwick *et al.* 1983). The same silvicultural conditions were included in the simulations as had been experienced by the harvested stands. All the stands, including that which formed the data base for DRYMAT, were located on the central plateau of the North Island of New Zealand.

There was close agreement between the outputs of the simulations and the field biomass data, for each type of forest, in terms of the proportion of dry matter allocated to above-ground components (Table V) and annual biomass increments. However, for the HS and MS forest the predictions of total biomass were approximately one year behind the actual biomass data, probably because the stands used to develop the DRYMAT model had taken a year longer to become established than the stands that were harvested. The actual field sites for both the HS and MS forests were formerly pastures, and were very favourable for forest growth, and extra care in their establishment might

TABLE IV. Tree heights, thinning and pruning schedules, of three types of *Pinus radiata* stands used in DRYMAT simulations of the allocation of above-ground dry matter

		High stocking density (HS)	Medium stocking density (MS)	Silvopastoral agroforest (AF)
Planted (stems ha⁻¹)		6,700	2,000	500
Age 3	Height (m)	3·8	3·4	3·2
	Thinning (stems ha⁻¹)	Nil	1,000	250
	Pruned height (m)	Nil	1·4	1·4
Age 4	Height (m)	5·6	5·1	4·8
	Thinning (stems ha⁻¹)	Nil	600	200
	Pruned height (m)	Nil	2·4	2·4
Age 6	Height (m)	9·4	8·6	8·1
	Thinning (stems ha⁻¹)	Nil	Nil	150
	Pruned height (m)	Nil	4·4	4·4
Age 10	Height (m)	17·1	15·6	15·0
	Basal area (m²ha⁻¹)	43·7	27·1	18·9

TABLE V. Comparison between measured and simulated allocations of above-ground dry matter in young stands of *Pinus radiata*, managed at high stocking densities (HS), medium stocking densities (MS) or as widely spaced trees in a silvopastoral agroforest (AF). See Table IV

Forest type (age)	Dry matter of field stands as percentage of simulated			Source of field data	Age of simulated stand
	foliage	total branches	stem		
HS forest (6 yrs)	102	74	116	Madgwick (1981)	7 yrs
HS forest (10 yrs)	115	121	121	Madgwick (1981)	11 yrs
MS forest (6 yrs)	41	74	69	Madgwick *et al.* (1983)	6 yrs
MS forest (6 yrs)	97	111	115	Madgwick *et al.* (1983)	7 yrs
AF forest[1] (6 yrs)	48	76	97	Madgwick *et al.* (1983)	6 yrs

[1] The actual stocking density of 173 stems ha⁻¹ was reduced proportionally to be equivalent to a stocking of 150 stems ha⁻¹ used in the simulations.

also have been expected. Foliage production by the AF forest was greatly over-estimated, because the model parameters used for foliage production were derived from measurements on conservatively thinned stands rather than on widely spaced, severely pruned trees.

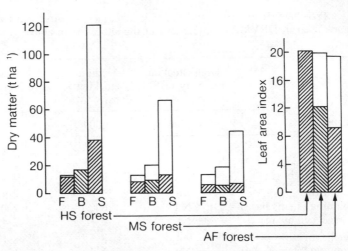

FIGURE 4.   Predicted amounts of biomass of foliage. (F), living branches (B) and stems (S) in 6-year-old (hatched histograms) and 10-year-old (whole histograms) stands of *Pinus radiata*, and their predicted leaf area indices when the trees are grown at high stocking densities (HS), medium stocking densities (MS) and as widely spaced trees in silvopastoral agroforests (AF). The silvicultural schedules for these forests are given in Table IV.

The three main results of the simulations were as follows (Fig. 4). First, a greater proportion of the above-ground biomass was allocated to stem, and correspondingly less was allocated to branches and foliage, in the HS forest compared with the forests with lower stocking densities. Second, the HS forest had about two and three times as much dry matter at age 10 as the MS and AF forests respectively (stemwood biomass was 121, 66 and 44 t ha^{-1} in the HS, MS and AF forests, respectively). Third, at age 10, the predicted leaf area index of all three types of forest was nearly 20, indicating complete site occupancy, in which case, from 10 years onwards, the increment in the HS forest would be spread over 6,700 stems ha^{-1}, whereas that of the AF forest would be concentrated on 150 stems ha^{-1}. In fact, the model consistently over-predicted foliage production of the AF trees, and a leaf area index of near 20 would probably not be attained until 3 years later.

These examples show that a systems model based largely on empirically derived parameters can predict the growth of other stands, provided the site and silvicultural conditions are similar to those incorporated into the model. However, it is necessary to include the lower level processes, of radiation interception, photosynthesis, respiration and submodels of leaf production, if the model is to be applied confidentially to different conditions.

IV.   MANAGEMENT IMPLICATIONS

The simulations presented here reveal only short-term differences between young stands with three very constrasting canopy designs. The results pertain only to the conditions defined in the simulation runs, and the differences could change with age or be modified by other environmental conditions, such as lower nutritional status. However, the simulations do serve to illustrate the uses of this type of approach.

Results of the first set of simulations of light interception (Fig. 2) showed the effects of tree spacing and amount of foliage on photosynthate production. The model could also be used to predict the effects of different spatial arrangements of trees in silvopastoral agroforests (in rows, spaced evenly, or in clumps) on tree growth, and also on the amounts of radiation available for pasture growth.

The radiation interception model was used to examine the effects of crown shape on productivity (Fig. 3). No attempt was made here to define the optimum crown shape, because this depends on the radiation conditions (Oker-Blom & Kellomäki 1982), on the respiratory losses, partitioning between branches and stem, susceptibility to wind damage, and so forth.

Although tall, finely branched, narrow-crowned trees may be highly desirable in many forests, in some conditions there may be a strong economic preference for short thick-stemmed trees with wide crowns, even if there is a loss in total photosynthate production per hectare. Most of the value of a tree is in the butt and second logs (Fenton 1972). The upper parts of the stem have a higher proportion of corewood, are more knotty and of smaller size than the bottom two logs, and they are often damaged when felled. The radiation interception model enables the biological consequences of encouraging a wide sprawling crown above the second log to be examined.

The DRYMAT model simulated above-ground dry matter production and distribution in the three contrasting silvicultural regimes with acceptable accuracy, except for the AF regime where a considerable over-estimation of foliage production and hence growth was noted. The DRYMAT model, which estimates leaf production and leaf area index, would be expected to be more responsive to defoliation treatments than most conventional forest mensurational models, which ignore the foliage.

Another aspect of considerable potential management interest is the large carbon requirement of the roots. A fuller understanding is needed of the impact of silvicultural treatments on below-ground growth and carbon allocation, with the ultimate objective of trying to increase the carbon allocation to stemwood.

These few examples of the value of using biologically based models to evaluate differences in forest design relate directly to output in terms of stem dry matter production. As was mentioned earlier, one of the advantages of biological modelling is that other 'outputs', such as water losses, can also be predicted. Managers are often having to trade gains in one output against losses in another.

ACKNOWLEDGEMENTS

We are grateful to Prof. Paul Jarvis, University of Edinburgh, for initial discussions on our model and to both he and Prof. John Norman, University of Nebraska, for drawing our attention to and discussing appropriate radiation interception models. Messrs M. Carey and G. Oliver are thanked for providing unpublished data, and A. Koehler for silvicultural details of the field trials of the agroforest. The help and support of Dr G. B. Sweet in the project is acknowledged.

REFERENCES

Assmann, E. (1970). *The principles of forest yield study.* Oxford: Pergamon.
Baker, F. S. (1950). *Principles of silviculture.* New York: McGraw-Hill.
Bamber, R. K. & Burley, J. (1983). *The wood properties of radiata pine.* Slough: Commonwealth Agricultural Bureaux.
Beets, P. N. (1982). *Modelling dry matter content of a managed stand of* Pinus radiata *in New Zealand.* Ph.D. thesis, University of Georgia, Athens.
Benecke, U. (1984). Tree respiration in steepland stands of *Nothofagus truncata* and *Pinus radiata.* In: *Establishment and tending sub-alpine forests – research and development,* edited by H. Turner and W. Tranquillini, 61–70. Proc. IUFRO workshop. Birmensdorf: Swiss Federal Institute of Forest Research.
Benecke, U. & Nordmeyer, A. (1982). Carbon allocation and allocation of dry matter by *Nothofagus solandri* and *Pinus contorta* at montane and subalpine altitudes. In: *Carbon uptake and allocation in subalpine ecosystems as a key to management,* edited by R. H. Waring, 9–21. Proc. IUFRO workshop. Corvallis, OR: Oregon State University, Forest Research Laboratory.
Brazier, J. D. (1973). Better softwoods from existing forests. *Commonw. Forest. Rev.,* **52**, 125–132.
Charles-Edwards, D. A. (1981). *The mathematics of photosynthesis and productivity.* London: Academic Press.
Deans, J. D. (1981). Dynamics of coarse root production in a young plantation of *Picea sitchensis. Forestry,* **54**, 139–155.
Denne, M. P. (1979). Wood structure and production within the trunk and branches of *Picea sitchensis* in relation to canopy formation. *Can. J. For. Res.,* **9**, 406–427.
Farquhar, G. D. & von Caemmerer, S. (1983). Modelling of photosynthetic response to environmental conditions. In: *Physiological plant ecology,* edited by O. L. Lange, P. S. Nobel, C. B. Osmond and H. Ziegler, 549–587. (Encyclopedia of plant physiology, n.s. vol. 12D). Berlin: Springer.
Fayle, D. C. F. (1975). Extension and longitudinal growth during the development of red pine root systems. *Can. J. For. Res.,* **5**, 109–121.
Fenton, R. (1972). Economics of radiata pine for sawlog production. *N.Z. J. For. Sci.,* **2**, 313–347.
Fogel, R. & Hunt, G. (1979). Fungal and arboreal biomass in a western Oregon Douglas fir ecosystem: distribution patterns and turnover. *Can. J. For. Res.,* **9**, 245–256.
Hall, A. E. (1983). Mathematical models of plant water loss and plant water relations. In: *Physiological plant ecology. 2. Water relations and carbon assimilation,* edited by O. L. Lange, P. S. Nobel, C. B. Osmond and H. Ziegler, 231–261. (Encyclopedia of plant physiology, n.s. vol. 12B). Berlin: Springer.
Harris, J. M. (1981). Wood quality of radiata pine. *Appita,* **35**, 211–215.
Hesketh, J. D. & Jones, J. W. (1980). *Predicting photosynthesis for ecosystem models.* Vols. 1 and 2. Boca Raton, FL: CRC Press.
Jahnke, L. S. & Lawrence, D. B. (1965). Influence of photosynthetic crown structure on potential productivity of vegetation, based primarily on mathematical models. *Ecology,* **46**, 319–325.
Jarvis, P. G. (1975). Water transfer in plants. In: *Heat and mass transfer in the plant environment,* edited by D. A. de Vries and N. G. Afgan, part I, 369–394. Washington DC: Scripta.
Jarvis, P. G. (1976). The interpretation of the variations in leaf water potential and stomatal conductance found in canopies in the field. *Phil. Trans. R. Soc.,* **273B**, 593–610.
Jarvis, P. G. & Leverenz, J. W. (1983). Productivity of temperate, deciduous and evergreen forests. In: *Physiological plant ecology 4. Ecosystem processes: mineral cycling productivity and*

man's influence, edited by O. L. Lange, P. S. Nobel, C. B. Osmond and H. Ziegler, 234–280. (Encyclopedia of plant physiology, n.s. vol. 12D). Berlin: Springer.

Jones, J. W., Brown, L. G. & Hesketh, J. D. (1980). Cotcrop. A computer model for cotton growth and yield. In: *Predicting photosynthesis for ecosystem models*, edited by J. D. Hesketh and J. W. Jones, 209–241. Boca Raton, FL: CRC Press.

Kaufmann, M. R. (1982). Leaf conductance as a function of photosynthetic photon flux density and absolute humidity difference from leaf to air. *Pl. Physiol.*, **69**, 1018–1022.

Kellomäki, S. & Tuimala, A. (1981). Effect of stand density on branchiness of young Scots pine. (English summary). *Folia for.*, **478**, 1–27.

Keyes, M. R. & Grier, C. C. (1981). Above and below-ground net production in 40-year-old Douglas-fir stands on low and high productivity sites. *Can. J. For. Res.*, **11**, 599–605.

Kinerson, R. S., Ralston, C. W. & Wells, C. G. (1977). Carbon cycling in a loblolly pine plantation. *Oecologia*, **29**, 1–10.

Landsberg, J. J. (1981). The number and quality of the driving variables needed to model tree growth. *Stud. for. suec.*, **160**, 43–50.

Lang, A. & Thorpe, M. R. (1983). Analysing partitioning in plants. *Plant, Cell Environ.*, **6**, 267–274.

Leaf, A. L., Leonard, R. E. & Berglund, J. V. (1971). Root distribution of a plantation grown red pine in an outwash soil. *Ecology*, **53**, 153–158.

Linder, S. & Troeng, E. (1980). Photosynthesis and transpiration of 20-year-old Scots pine. In: *Structure and function of northern coniferous forests*, edited by T. Persson, 165–181. (Ecological bulletin no. 32). Stockholm: Swedish Natural Science Research Council.

Linder, S. & Troeng, E. (1981). The seasonal variation in stem and coarse root respiration of a 20-year-old Scots pine (*Pinus sylvestris* L.). In: *Radial growth in trees*, edited by W. Tranquillini, 125–139. (Mitt. Forstl. BundesVersAnst. Wien no. 142).

Madgwick, H. A. I. (1981). Above-ground dry matter content of a young close-spaced *Pinus radiata* stand. *N.Z. J. For. Sci.*, **11**, 203–209.

Madgwick, H. A. I. (1983). Seasonal changes in the biomass of a young *Pinus radiata* stand. *N.Z. J. For. Sci.*, **13**, 25–36.

Madgwick, H. A. I., Jacksons, D. S. & Knight, P. J. (1977). Above-ground dry matter, energy and nutrient content of trees in an age series of *Pinus radiata* plantations. *N.Z. J. For. Sci.*, **7**, 445–468.

Madgwick, H. A. I., Carey, M. L. & Oliver, G. (1983). *The dry matter and nutrient content above-ground of trees in a 6-year-old forest farm.* (Internal report). Rotorua: Forest Research Institute. Unpublished.

Maillette, L. (1982). Needle demography and growth pattern of Corsican pine. *Can. J. Bot.*, **60**, 105–116.

Möller, C. M. (1954). The influence of thinning on volume increment. *Tech. Publs, N.Y. St. Coll. For.*, **76**, 5–32.

Monsi, M. & Saeki, T. (1953). Über den Lichtfaktor in den Pflanzen-gesellschaften und seine Bedeutung für die Stoffpruduktion. *Jap. J. Bot.*, **14**, 22–52.

Norman, J. M. & Jarvis, P. G. (1975). Photosynthesis in Sitka spruce (*Picea sitchensis* (Bong.) Carr.). V. Radiation penetration theory and a test case. *J. appl. Ecol.*, **12**, 839–878.

Norman, J. M. & Welles, J. M. (1983). Radiative transfer in an array of canopies. *Agron. J.*, **75**, 481–488.

Oker-Blom, P. & Kellomäki, S. (1982). Theoretical computations on the role of crown shape in the absorption of light by forest trees. *Math. Biosci.*, **59**, 291–311.

Oker-Blom, P. & Kellomäki, S. (1983). Effect of grouping of foliage on the within-stand and within-crown light regime. Comparison of random and grouping canopy models. *Agric. Meteorol.*, **28**, 143–155.

Reed, K. L., Hamerly, E. R., Dinger, B. E. & Jarvis, P. G. (1976). An analytical model for field measurements of photosynthesis. *J. appl. Ecol.*, **13**, 925–942.

Santantonio, D. & Hermann, R. K. (1985). Standing crop, production and turnover of fine roots on dry, moderate and wet sites of mature Douglas fir in western Oregon. *Ann. Sci. For.*, **42**. In press.

Satoo, T. & Madgwick, H. A. I. (1982). *Forest biomass.* The Hague: Nijhoff/Junk.

Shepherd, K. R., & Forrest, W. G. (1973). Growth of radiata pine following thinning. *Commonw. Forest. Rev.*, **52**, 133–142.

Siemon, G. R., Wood, G. B. & Forrest, W. G. (1976). Effects of thinning on crown structure in radiata pine. *N.Z. J. For. Sci.*, **6**, 57–66.

Siemon, G. R., Muller, W. J., Wood, G. B. & Forrest , W. G. (1980). Effect of thinning on the distribution and biomass of foliage in the crown of radiata pine. *N.Z. J. For. Sci.*, **10**, 461–475.

Thornley, J. H. M. (1976). *Mathematical models in plant physiology*. London: Academic Press.

Thorpe, M. R., Saugier, B., Auger, S., Burger, A. & Methy, M. (1978). Photosynthesis and transpiration of an isolated tree: model and validation. *Plant, Cell Environ.*, **1**, 269–277.

Vogt, K. A., Grier, C. C., Meier, C. E. & Edmonds, R. L. (1982). Mycorrhizal role in net primary production and nutrient cycling in *Abies amabilis* ecosystems in western Washington. *Ecology*, **63**, 370–380.

Waring, R. H. (1983). Estimating forest growth and efficiency in relation to canopy leaf area. *Adv. ecol. Res.*, **13**, 327–354.

Whitehead, D. & Jarvis, P. G. (1982). Coniferous forests and plantations. In: *Water deficits and plant growth*, vol. 6, edited by T. T. Kozlowski, 49–152. New York: Academic Press.

Whitehead, D., Jarvis, P. G. & Waring, R. H. (1984). Stomatal conductance, transpiration and resistance to water uptake in a *Pinus sylvestris* spacing experiment. *Can. J. For. Res.*, **14**, 692–700.

Economic aspects

30

FUTURE FOREST DESIGN: ECONOMIC ASPECTS

W. R. BENTLEY
The Ford Foundation, New Delhi, India

INTRODUCTION

The purpose of this discussion is to contribute to the synthesis of social science and biology in the context of applied research on the productivity of trees. My examples concern the economics of investments in forest stands, the effects of bioeconomic functions (input–output, quality–price, etc) on the level and distribution of income and wealth, and the uses of economic rationale when designing or planning forestry enterprises – what I call future forest design. The lines of reasoning that I present are applicable to a diversity of research clients and tree crop products or values. A critical first step in the effective design of future forests is to recognize explicitly the clients, be they large multinational corporations or the rural poor, and the products or values, be they fuelwood, fibre and timber; fruit, fodder and other non-wood produce; microclimate influences; or visual amenities.

TABLE I.   A matrix of four kinds of applied research (see text)

	Opportunities for advancement exist	Opportunities for advancement do not exist
Research is in progress	Box 1	Box 3
Research is not in progress	Box 2	Box 4

Based on the oral presentation of Cannell (1979).

A.   Applied tree crop research

Before launching into specifics, two of the conference organizers remind me of illustrations of the travails of applied research. First, there is Gordon's Law, which sounds like John Gordon's brand of wisdom, although he claims not to have stated it first: 'Any research not worth doing, is not worth doing well!' Second, Mel Cannell (1979) pointed out one all-too-common application of Gordon's Law in Box 3 of a whimsical matrix, given in Table I. Box 1 represents most of the research in progress at any time, where more or better results require a sharper focus, a keener or more creative mind, more resources, and so forth. Much of what we are discussing in formal presentations at this conference pertains to Box 1, but our informal moments together are often focused on the missed opportunities in Box 2. Using biological opportunities for advancement in forest yields as examples, Cannell noted that Box 3 is not empty: that is, research is in progress in fields where opportunities for advancement do not exist! One reason is bad science. Another, in my opinion, is the estrangement of applied biology and applied social sciences in the context of agriculture, forestry and other renewable resources. A technically possible biological design, that makes no sense in terms of socio-economics, is no more useful than a desired or imagined socio-economic design that is biologically impossible. Both are found in Box 3, which takes on added importance in tropical forestry and agroforestry, where the issues of poverty and distribution of income, wealth and power are added to the conventional productivity and efficiency concerns of agricultural and forestry research.

B. Topic organization

Economics is useful in (a) evaluating possible tree crop alternatives, (b) selecting the best of the possible alternatives, (c) tracking performance, and (d) assisting designers to specify criteria for, and to develop, more productive patterns for tree crops. In this discussion, I do not dwell on these classic roles for the forest economist, but focus instead on a broader understanding of why research on trees as crop plants makes economic and social sense, especially in the Third World.

My comments are organized around the following six topics:
1. the concept of a 'production function', and its usefulness in organizing managerial information produced by research;
2. the economics of timber scarcity, and the causes of real increases in the price of standing timber (stumpage prices);
3. the evolution toward design-orientated research to create the forests of the future;
4. the implications of timber economics, regarding the distribution of net benefits between this and future generations, and between rich and poor people today;
5. the synthesis of factors affecting efficiency and the distribution of wealth in the context of timber scarcity; and
6. the criteria suggested by these lines of reasoning that might guide the design of future forests.

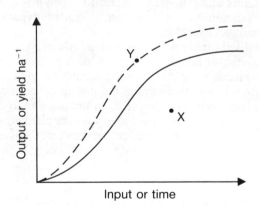

FIGURE 1.   The economic 'production function' is the S-shaped biological growth function that defines the technically most efficient input–output relationship. It separates the possible but technically inefficient (point X) from the technically impossible (point Y).

II.   TREE AND STAND PRODUCTION PROCESSES

The 19th century agronomic experiments at Rothamsted provided the economist with a conceptual linkage to biophysical reality. This was because the S-shaped curve between plant growth and time, and often between yield and an input, is the form of the 'production function' which is the foundation of production economics, and underlies much of what follows about economic supply and macro-relationships between costs and prices (Fig. 1). While as useful empirically today as it was to the emerging agricultural science of 100 years ago, the 'production function' hides a chain of causal relationships inside a simple predictive model. It implies that changes in input levels 'cause' changes in output levels; explicitly it implies that the output resulting from input manipulation by forest managers can be predicted with known levels of precision and accuracy.

A.   Disciplinary concerns

Some of the confusion in communication between economists and biologists results from their approach towards cause and effect.

Economists, as disciplinarians, are concerned with the variety of cause and effect relationships pertinent to why prices for goods and services change, why goods and services are reallocated, why the total sum of goods and services changes, and why societies and the individuals who compose them become richer or poorer as a consequence. Economists often assume that biophysical relationships are stable, or they treat them as if they were exogenous to the causal interactions under consideration. If research and development are key input factors under managerial control, then it is essential to consider the production relationships that are central to the dynamics of prices and quantities of goods and services.

Biologists, as disciplinarians, are searching for more and more fundamental causal relationships, although in applied biology attempts to extend the frontiers of knowledge must be balanced against the practical goal of useful results. Usefulness virtually always is defined in economic terms, although hopefully not as narrowly as is common in financial analysis.

The conjunction between applied biology and applied economics is defined by a central question: how can we improve the design of future forest stands in terms of their economic productivity?

B.   Applied research and production functions

Optimization is a mathematical term which means maximization (or minimization) of a function subject to constraints. A 'production function' describes a basic constraint on the maximization of profit or present net worth, and research produces information which relaxes that constraint.

Managerial intensification really begins when it makes sense to control regeneration – that is, to control the species which is grown, the spacing, level of competition, and so forth. The basic relationships between inputs and benefits are understood for simple forest systems. Most applied silvicultural research is, in effect, the calibration or quantification of equations for specific sites and needs, so that basic standards are established about what is possible.

Once this standard is in place, two rather different research tasks are possible. First, we can diagnose why a given stand is below the possible level (point X in Fig. 1). Second, we can design new alternatives that enable us to raise the production function (point Y in Fig. 1).

The objective of design research is to shift the production function or growth and yield relationships upward. Examples include (a) earlier establishment of new growing stock after harvest, (b) spacing operations to increase stemwood quality, (c) fertilization where early root development or mature photo-synthetic rates are constraints, and (d) redesign of harvest and processing equipment to favour smaller logs and shorter rotations (Brown *et al.* 1982). There is room for considerable refinement in most situations, especially when tree improvement and genetics are part of the total strategy. Physical gains of 200–300% are possible when solid-wood cubic volumes are the objective.

Measurements of production functions and stand productivities require that we define the product of value. The product may be total biomass (dry t $ha^{-1}yr^{-1}$), above-ground biomass (dry t $ha^{-1}yr^{-1}$), above-ground cubic volume to a large top diameter for solid-wood products (m^3 $ha^{-1}yr^{-1}$), fruit or seeds for food, oil, or regeneration purposes (kg $ha^{-1}yr^{-1}$). These different perceptions of production can be defined in terms of stand age and stems per hectare (spacing) as the inputs that are manipulated (Cannell 1983a,b; Huxley, this volume). Obviously, more and more of the total production is ignored (made invisible) as we refine what we consider to be the valuable part of the plant. Because it is difficult to increase total biomass production per hectare, it is usually easier to increase the production of parts of trees and stands that are biologically scarce (like fruits or extractives) than those that are biologically abundant (like leaves and wood).

III.   TIMBER SCARCITY AND PRICE

When we say that something such as trees, fruits or pleasant sylvan environments are scarcer, we mean that it costs more to acquire or rent them than in an earlier time. Scarcity, in other words, is a measure of change, and the index is 'change in real price per unit'. The quality of the index depends upon how well the markets function that determine price, and the time interval involved. Although many markets for fuelwood, timber, various amenities and other forest products are imperfect, over substantial time periods even imperfect price responses give quantitative, if often imprecise, evidence of scarcity.

A.   Supply and demand

Price is the result of interactions between supply and demand. As concepts, both supply and demand are schedules, or functions, that relate quantities to prices in a given time period and market area. Supply is the collective term for the quantities sellers would market at various prices, and demand is the quantities buyers would purchase at various prices. Where both are equal, an equilibrium exists and the market clears. Scarcity occurs whenever demand increases, or 'shifts out', supply decreases or 'shifts back', or both (Fig. 2A).

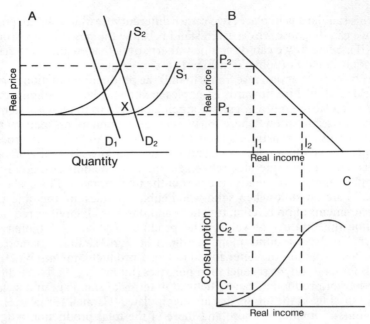

FIGURE 2.
A.   The relationship between the price of goods or services and the quantity of those
     goods or services. A decrease or 'backward shift' in supply from S_1 to S_2, and an
     increase or 'outward shift' in supply from D_1 to D_2, lead to a price increase from
     P_1 to P_2. This price increase is a measure of the scarcity of those goods or services.
     Point X is explained in the text.
B, C. An increase in price from P_1 to P_2 is equivalent to a decrease in income from
     I_2 to I_1, which leads to reduced consumption from C_2 to C_1. The relationship
     between income and consumption, for most goods and services, has a phase
     of increasing rates of consumption per increment of income, followed by
     decreasing rates, and finally a decline in total consumption.

Demand for timber comes from its various end uses such as fuel, pulp,
plywood or lumber. The markets for most of these products have 'demand
functions' that are quite inelastic; that is, a major price change does not have
much effect on the quantity purchased. This is so either because the product
is essential (eg as fuel for cooking) or because it forms a minor part of the
total consumer cost (eg lumber in a new house). Shifts in demand occur with
changes in population size and composition, discretionary income, availability
of mortgage funds, and so forth. With some exceptions, the inelastic demands
for timber-based products are translated into even more inelastic demands for
standing timber.

The supply of timber, in most cases, can vary over a broad range with little
change in price. The price rises as access costs are incurred, which has been
an important factor in the supply of timber from mountainous areas of North
America. At some point (X in Fig. 2A), the capacity to harvest and supply
more timber from a given forest begins to have a negative impact on its future

growth. At this point, a balancing act begins between today and tomorrow, based on rational expectations (Berck 1979; Lyon & Sedjo 1983). Expectations about the future, with regard to increased value resulting from biological growth, quality changes and price changes, are balanced against the perfect certainty of today's values (Bentley *et al.* 1985). Individuals, and collectively the market, attempt to earn the real rate of interest, plus an appropriate 'risk premium' (Sharpe 1981). To do so, thay must anticipate shifts in demand, and shifts in supply, especially those resulting from a decrease in the amount of standing timber.

B. Scarcity

Assuming that the market period is one year (over which biological growth and consequent quality changes are not of major importance), the current supply of timber inventory to the market is the reciprocal of current demand for future inventory (Bentley *et al.* 1985). An equilibrium between supply of, and demand for, inventory is achieved when the rate of value increase is equal to the real rate of interest (about 3%) plus the premium for accepting both biological and market risks, which appears to be 2–5% for timber investments in commercial species. The argument is not that such a market works perfectly, especially as judged after the fact, but rather that there is an understandable and predictable process that rations timber inventories into the marketplace.

Worldwide, timber has been getting scarcer. Berck (1979) estimated that *Pseudotsuga menziesii* timber prices were rising at 5% per year; Bentley *et al.* (1985) found that Connecticut *Quercus rubra* prices for standing timber have increased since 1972 at 8·6% per year; and Bentley (1985) estimated that the general timber prices in India have been rising at 5·8% per year for over a decade. Other investigations of natural resource prices have identified timber to be among the few resources where scarcity is an issue (eg Barnett & Morse 1963; Smith 1979; Skog & Risbrandt 1982). Although the phenomenon of timber scarcity has not been fully explained, prices are rising to yield a rate of growth in investment of 5–9% per year in real terms (after subtracting the effects of inflation). There have been occasional short-term rates of increase that are considerably higher as species enter new markets – for example, *Tsuga heterophylla* and *Populus tremuloides* after World War II, *Q. rubra* in Connecticut over the past decade, and many tropical hardwood species today.

Owners of young, rapidly growing timber stands also benefit from biological growth and increases in bole sizes and wood quality with age. Real rates of return of 10%, to occasionally even 20%, are possible for new investors in timber, if they take advantage of current knowledge and the latest methods for plantation management. At the market level, we can envisage a 'net inventory adjustment' between the increment in growth and the amount harvested. Harvest of inventory, with subsequent reinvestment in protection, regeneration and other inputs, eventually leads to a balancing between growth and removal. At this balance point, there are no changes in the amount of standing timber, so that this factor cannot cause the supply of timber in the current market to decrease. In that case, the price can rise only if demand increases. But when the amount of standing timber increases (ie when growth exceeds removals), then prices will fall, unless demand is increasing faster than supply.

IV. EVOLUTION TOWARDS FOREST DESIGN

Several implications can be drawn from our understanding of timber scarcity that are important in the design of future forests. One is a reinterpretation of the history of forest harvesting and reinvestment. To illustrate these points, I shall consider the Indian subcontinent and North America, which have experienced similar histories of forest exploitation in general terms. Originally, what is now India, Pakistan and Bangladesh was 80% or more forested (Warner 1982). The original percentage forest over North America as a whole was much less than 80%, but there were many regions with 75% or more forest cover (Dana & Fairfax 1980). Starting over 3,000 years ago on the Indian subcontinent, and 350 years ago in North America, forests were deliberately cleared to provide land for cultivated food crops. More or less simultaneously, trees were harvested for construction materials, fuelwood and other purposes. No particular plan guided what was cleared or harvested, or for what purpose. Both land and timber were abundant, and the costs of cultivatable land, fuelwood and construction materials were essentially the costs of the labour required to obtain them.

A. Depletion and conservation

Serious overcutting of forests began in both regions about 1860, usually accompanied by fire, grazing and other ecological factors that retard regeneration and reduce total biomass productivity. Such practices are often described as forest exploitation. However, Ciriacy-Wantrup (1952) defined the shift of use-rates toward the present as 'depletion' and the shift of use-rates toward the future as 'conservation'. When accompanied by explicit objectives, and active reinvestment, both conservation and depletion become resource management. A critical question is why do these shifts occur?

Forests are overcut, in the sense that removal rates exceed timber growth, for four reasons (Bentley et al. 1985). First, overcutting occurs when capital and raw materials are scarce, and when they can be obtained by cutting timber which is abundant (eg in past times). Second, overcutting occurs when a forest is mature and its growth rate is virtually zero, so that the only way to increase growth is to harvest some of the old trees and to replace them with new ones. Third, overcutting occurs when interest rates, which guide investment and liquidation rates, exceed the rate of increase in value of the forests; as a result, the inventory is decreased by cutting older trees, thereby increasing the value growth rate of the remaining forest. Fourth, overcutting occurs when this can make forest assets more 'efficient', in the sense that a given annual growth can be obtained from less standing timber capital or more annual growth can be obtained from the current forest capital. Points one to four are roughly a historical sequence, with forest design becoming an important activity after improvement in the input-output 'efficiency' of timber assets.

B.   Forest management

The first sign of timber scarcity is a concerted effort to protect forests. Clearly, protection makes sense only if what is protected has value, taking into account any expectation of future price increases. About the same time, extensive management begins. This management is most successful if it (a) imitates the natural ecosystem, (b) is a selection, group selection, or 'patch clearcut' system, and (c) requires little initial investment. Hibbs and Bentley (1984), for example, established that spacing is the critical factor to manage with *Quercus rubra*/mixed hardwood stands, established by natural regeneration in southern New England. Extensive management systems, if focused on high-quality logs, can produce competitive real rates of return with virtually no net investment. Unfortunately, many of the early extensive management systems observed were based on faulty ecological and economic premises. The consequences were dramatic shifts in forest composition, often away from the most valuable subclimax species and towards scrubs of one kind or another. This move was especially pronounced in areas where seasonal droughts and grazing combined to make natural regeneration of desired species a slow process, if it occurred at all. Many vivid examples of these shifts following initial harvesting can be observed in the American west and in the semi-arid tropics of India.

The shift towards intensive management is stimulated by scarcity. Intensive management was first practised on a major scale in nations that either had seriously depleted their natural forests (such as Great Britain) or found the native species difficult to utilize (such as Australia and New Zealand). Plantations were established in North America before World War II, but most were the products of public works or soil conservation programmes, not of real concerns about timber scarcity. In the post-War period, demand for house-building and other construction increased the prices of lumber and plywood, and these higher product prices were then translated into higher timber prices. The market has reflected a steady increase in scarcity since the early 1950s.

C.   Research and forest design

It is not by chance that the 1950s was the period of rapid transition toward intensive plantation forestry in the American south and Pacific Northwest, with the concurrent development of forestry research groups in several industrial firms. During this period, tropical forest depletion rates increased dramatically (Gillis 1984). European, North American and Japanese firms were looking for new sources of raw material for conversion (to fibre board, etc), to meet product demands, and to bridge age gaps in their local timber resources. And Third World nations had entered into a period where conversion of natural capital into liquid assets made sense in terms of currently conceived development strategies. Gordon and Bentley (1970) described this shift to intensive plantation forestry as similar to the transition from a 'hunt and gather' economy to a rational and scientifically based agriculture. It is at this point that forest design makes sense.

V. DISTRIBUTION OF WEALTH

There are some implications regarding the distribution of wealth that should not be overlooked in our understanding of this transition. Conservation has often been viewed as a public responsibility. In part, this view reflects the traditional ownership of forests, water, wildlife and many other renewable natural resources by the raj, king or modern nation state. It also represents a response to market failures caused by (a) traditions and institutions, such as common property rights, (b) 'spatial externalities', especially of the upstream/-downstream variety, and (c) low to zero prices (lack of scarcity), which inhibit efficient market function. One reason for public intervention to stop tropical forest destruction is that it may be too late if left until scarcity is recognized and acted upon by the market. Another reason, although seldom stated in these terms, is that the rich want to take benefits from the poor of today and tomorrow.

A. Distribution over time

There are many questions about the optimal balance between conservation and depletion that have yet to be resolved, especially where markets do not reflect critical values. The most obvious omission, of course, is that the unborn cannot vote in the current marketplace. Nonetheless, once markets for timber 'futures' (timber to be delivered at future dates) begin to function, there will be a process that allows actual and potential holders of timber assets to anticipate how future markets might vote, and to act accordingly. At best, this process will be imperfect, but it can only be judged in the light of the alternatives. The performance of public agencies in lieu of the market does not provide much basis, in my opinion, for optimism about administrative non-market mechanisms for allocating between rich and poor, or between present and future generations.

B. The poor as consumers

Foresters and tree scientists should become conscious of the issues concerning the distribution of wealth that are inherent in the flow of forest assets and products between rich and poor, because these issues will be relevant for several decades. The consequences of poverty are most obvious in terms of consumption. The relationship between income and consumption, shown in

Figure 2C, looks a bit like the 'production function' mentioned earlier: a phase of increasing rates of consumption per increment of income is followed by decreasing rates, and finally a decline, in consumption.

Fuelwood provides a useful illustration. The extremely poor cannot acquire adequate fuelwood for cooking or heating, either because their incomes are very low, or because it takes too much time and energy to gather wood in wood-scarce areas. Consequently, increases in real income go disproportionately to acquiring more fuelwood. At some point, basic needs are met. Further increases in income may be used to have more hot water or a bit more comfort in cold weather, but these increased comforts take smaller proportions of the increments in income. Above some level of income, families shift towards more convenient fuels, such as bottled gas, charcoal and coal, and total fuelwood consumption drops. This happened long ago in North America, and the recent return to fuelwood is largely an adjustment to the rapid upward shift in the real price of alternative energy sources. The same phenomenon can be observed in India, where virtually all rural people use fuelwood, leaves, crop residues and dung for cooking and heating. Even in this context, rural families aspire to shift towards other fuels, and do so when their incomes rise (Pendse 1984). City dwellers do so at even lower incomes because of access to lower cost, more convenient fuels. In New Delhi, for example, the fuelwood demand has been cut substantially by this shift to bottled gas and other convenient fuels (Bentley 1985). Given the role that fuelwood harvesting for urban areas plays in forest degradation, this income-driven substitution is helpful, because it gives more time to resolve several critical forestry issues.

C.   The poor as producers

The poor as consumers represent one aspect of the question concerning the distribution of wealth. Another aspect is the poor as suppliers of labour. A simple, but not false, way of looking at poverty is in terms of labour scarcity, especially when considering the plight of people at or below subsistence levels. Just as there is a modest minimum price for timber over a wide quantity range, so there is a modest minimum price for unskilled labour at more or less subsistence wages. Scarcity of such labour occurs when (a) the general economy has a high demand for both skilled and unskilled labour, (b) people invest in their own 'human capital', upgrading their skills and moving into better paid jobs, and (c) wages are driven up by the interaction between increasing demands for labour and decreasing supplies of labour. If increased demand does not cause scarcity of unskilled labour – a not uncommon problem in western nations – a combination of minimum wage laws and various income transfers can lift the minimum income above subsistence levels, but at the price of higher permanent unemployment. In Third World nations, the gap is simply too large to use such schemes; the only possible strategy is to increase the demand for unskilled labour.

One means of increasing the demand for labour is the so-called 'supply-side' or 'trickle down' approach. Basically, 'aggregate economic growth' in terms of total production of goods and services is expanded more rapidly than the population, thereby creating a labour scarcity. Although population growth rates have fallen drastically in India, and in many other tropical nations, there is an enormous challenge to find enough jobs for the currently unemployed and underemployed, and for those who will join the labour force in the next two decades. Economic expansion alone is unlikely to bridge this gap in most Third World countries until well into the next century (eg Krishna 1980).

One of the appeals of 'community forestry', wasteland rehabilitation and similar schemes is that they have high labour/capital ratios, and potentially they use massive amounts of unskilled labour. In fact, some preliminary analyses in India suggest that labour would be a constraint, if there were nationwide schemes for rehabilitation of commonland forests, pastures and wastes (eg Gupta 1978). The obvious additional advantage of such schemes is that capital assets would be produced in the form of 'tree factories' that could be harvested, thinned and spaced, or just left to grow.

D. Institutional issues

There are several institutional and organizational problems that need to be resolved before all the benefits of 'social forestry' and similar schemes can be realized (Bentley 1985). Most of these centre on tenure rights for land, trees and grass (eg Fortmann 1984), and community-based organization of credit, technical knowledge and the like (eg Chowdhry 1982). In time, applied research can contribute greatly to assisting the rural poor. The first step is simply for applied scientists to recognize the poor as one of their clients (Biggs 1982; Chambers 1983).

VI. SYNTHESIS OF EFFICIENCY AND DISTRIBUTION

'Economic efficiency' issues are concerned with the impact on future timber supplies of units of investment, and 'distribution' issues are concerned with who receives the benefits of those supplies.

A. Price effects

The relationships between quantities of goods, prices and incomes (efficiency and distribution) are shown in Figure 2. A supply-demand shift that leads to a higher price (P_1 to P_2) is the same as reducing a consumer's income (I_2 to I_1), other things remaining the same, because the same nominal income will now buy less. The decrease in income is clearly a welfare loss, and it translates into less consumption of certain goods or services (C_2 to C_1). In other words, timber scarcity leads to poor people being worse off as consumers.

B. Income and employment growth

If timber scarcity leads to a major programme of tree planting, and other silvicultural activities that are targeted to hire poor people, the opposite

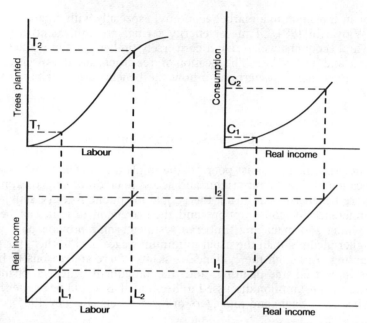

FIGURE 3.   Effect of tree planting on incomes and consumption. An increase in tree planting (T_1 to T_2) requires more labour (L_1 to L_2), which translates into higher incomes (I_1 to I_2), and more consumption of essential commodities such as fuelwood (C_1 to C_2).

sequence can take place (Fig. 3): more tree planting (T_1 to T_2) means that more labour is hired (L_1 to L_2), and then real incomes rise (I_1 to I_2), which enables people to buy more fuelwood and other goods or services (C_1 to C_2). The longer term impact is to increase future supplies (shifting the supply function outwards, S_2 to S_1 in Figure 2A), so that future fuelwood prices decline (or at least do not rise as fast), which further adds to the economic well-being of poor people. The rise in wage rates is more substantial if labour scarcity occurs, whether through increases in demand, or decreases in supply because of 'human capital' development. Consequently, responses to timber scarcity can make poor people better off, as both consumers of forest-based products and as suppliers of labour.

C.   Household economics and intrafamily distribution

Issues concerning the distribution of wealth also occur within many Third World family or clan units, because the household unit is both producer and consumer (eg Bennett 1983). The most striking issues to the outsider are between women (and often children), who are responsible for non-market activities, and men who are more concerned with cash income. These issues may have implications for forest designs, when a village is at the subsistence level, or in transition to a market economy, especially with regard to energy needs (Vidyarthi 1984). Time or energy savings are equivalent to gains in income and economic welfare, and conversely timber scarcity is the same as an income and welfare loss. The location of tree crops, and the species grown, could be important in determining how the benefits are distributed within families.

D.   Asset ownership

Social mechanisms that assist poor people to plant and own trees, especially the allocation of some tenure rights and access to credit or subsidies, may be even more beneficial than hiring the people for public forestry activities. If their preference for consumption, and their aversion to risk, can be dealt with, owning and managing timber investments may provide poor people with higher incomes than the usual minimum wages paid to them for public tree planting. Although the evidence is scanty, there are reasons to believe that the impact on tree planting, and the consequent beneficial changes in incomes and consumption discussed in Section VI B, could be greater if poor people became owners and managers of forest assets (Bentley 1985).

VII.   FUTURE FOREST DESIGN

This review of economic efficiency, and the distribution of wealth, suggests the following nine criteria for forest design. The first four concern productivity and efficiency, and are obvious to anyone who has been concerned with applied research on commercial tree crop production; the other five are of more concern if distributional issues are involved, and may conflict to some degree with the first four.

A.   Design criteria

1. *Area*

Perhaps the single most important criterion for a design is the area over which it can be applied. It is the criterion that gives tree improvement programmes such high reliable pay-offs.

2.   *Time*

The most expensive production expense in forestry is the cost of waiting. A real interest cost of 6% means that costs double every 12 years; current nominal rates of 12% double in 6 years. Planned industrial rotations of *Pseudotsuga menziesii* have declined from over 100 years to 40 or 50 years because of the cost of capital. Intensive systems of growing trees for fuelwood and fibre over rotations of 2 to 6 years are feasible in much of the world with warm, moist growing seasons.

3.   Uniformity

The most critical characteristics affecting timber values are stem uniformity, roundness, straightness and taper. These characteristics obviously increase timber values for solid-wood products, and they also reduce handling costs for low-value products like fuelwood.

4.   Simplicity

The common characteristic of large-scale grain farmers, and of large coffee, tea, fruit and timber plantations worldwide, is simplicity. Simplicity enables managers to avoid the constant choices inherent in complexity, and enables them to focus their operational planning and control.

5.   Sustainability

In its simplest form, a sustainable system never loses productivity. The concept of sustainability is common to many agrarian cultures; forestry's heritage comes from Germany and central Europe (Greeley 1950). The most obvious criteria for sustainable design concern soil stability, water percolation, and nutrient cycling. Simple systems, which often involve single species, may not be sustainable over extended periods in many tropical or near-tropical conditions. Designs that are based on natural balances to control insects and pathogens biologically are likely to be sustainable, but they also are complex.

6.   Flexibility/adaptability

Markets are sure to change, which has been the undoing of many classical sustained-yield designs. Also, the rate at which new biological knowledge is being applied is remarkable. Usually there are trade-offs between the high efficiency and high-risk option of producing a well-defined tree-based product, and the less efficient, lower-risk option of producing multiple products: risk rises as designs become more rigid. 'Flexibility' anticipates that changes will occur, whereas 'adaptability' reflects a positive response after change has occurred.

7.   Subsistence needs

Poor families, especially the women and children, have food and energy needs that are often not recognized by professional foresters and agriculturalists. Fuelwood, leaves, fodder and similar goods do not pass through formal markets in isolated villages. Traditionally, these goods have been free, except for the energy women and children have expended on gathering them. During the transition from subsistence to market economic conditions, desirable design criteria may include (a) those that favour a reduction in the effort needed to gather forest-based non-market goods, and (b) those that favour some effort in growing species that aid subsistence, like *Prosopis* spp., rather than those that yield products with a cash value, such as *Eucalyptus* spp.

8.   Initial investment

For obvious reasons, the poor cannot afford to make high 'front end' investments in agroforestry or forestry. While subsidies, or better access to rural credit, would encourage poor families to use land for social or community forestry, poor people generally prefer to trade their labour (including the farmer as a manager) for capital. By contrast, most corporations favour trading capital for labour, at least up to the point where expected wages equal the expected 'marginal value product' of the labour. One probable reason why poor and corporate forest farmers see this choice differently is that poor farm and family enterprises pay their household members lower wages than corporations pay their employees (eg Galbraith 1979). Consequently, poor families benefit from working for corporations, and corporations benefit from hiring labour from poor farming families.

9. *Risk*

Another substantial difference between poor marginal farmers and corporations (and probably large public forestry agencies) is the nature of the risks that they attempt to minimize. The modern technically based corporation wants predictable cash flows and profits, which it attempts to achieve by substituting capital for labour, and by planning and quality control. By contrast, subsistence farmers have, naturally, an aversion to risks that could bring their food supplies below survival levels.

B.   Social science research

Most of this meeting on 'Trees as crop plants' is concerned with improved applied biological research, but I would like to make a plea for concomitant applied work in the social sciences. My illustrations reflect mainly my own interests in economic issues, but many of the problems discussed cannot be resolved without considerable information on applied anthropology, social psychology and other behavioural sciences. Equity and social justice are values to which many of us subscribe, but the actual needs and responses of the poor are factual matters that should be studied with the same objectivity that we apply to the more affluent consumers and producers in the western economies. This requires more applied social science.

IX.   CONCLUSIONS

The effective design of future forests requires that biological and social sciences be integrated and focused on the needs of particular 'client groups'. This integration serves two purposes; it shifts our attention to new opportunities where research is not in progress, and it helps us to avoid efforts in areas where results are not possible. 'Client groups' are defined as people and organizations that have similar problems. The client focus is a device to assist us in allocating resources to applied research. Applied research, like virtually all other rational activities, is more effective if focused on a few, rather than many, goals, and progress toward those goals is measured over time by results.

In the Third World, we need to consider the distribution of wealth when defining the 'client groups', for both operational and ethical reasons. Many of the current development activities by national and donor organizations recognize that the poorer half of rural societies will not share in economic progress unless programmes are targeted on them. This is the basis for many of the social or community forestry programmes, and some of the applied forestry research programmes in tropical nations, especially those concerned with agroforestry. The underlying issues are ones of equity and social justice. The poor as consumers are more adversely affected by scarcity than are the rich, but they can benefit from activities to alleviate forest resource scarcity as both consumers and as producers of forest-based income and wealth.

The design criteria that emerge from this discussion are orientated towards productivity and efficiency, in the general sense of attempting to maximize the impact on future timber supplies per cost-unit invested. However, some criteria have implications regarding the distribution of wealth. These involve explicit recognition of the distribution of resources between today's and tomorrow's generations (ie sustainability), between the poor and rich of today (eg fuelwood and fodder vs timber), and between the risks that concern the poor (especially food security) and those that concern the rich (stability and predictability of cash flows).

REFERENCES

Barrett, H. J. & Morse, C. (1963). *Scarcity and growth: economics of natural resource availability*. Baltimore: John Hopkins.

Bennett, L. (1983). Preliminary analytical framework for proposed study on the role of women in income production and intrahousehold allocation of resources as a determinant of child health and nutrition. In: *WHO/UNICEF Seminar on Determinants of Infant Feeding Practices, Geneva 1983*. Geneva: WHO.

Bentley, W. R. (1985). *The uncultivated half of India: problems and possible solutions*. (Discussion paper). New Delhi: Ford Foundation. In press.

Bentley, W. R., Hobson, T. C. & Holmes, T. P. (1985). *Price dynamics for Connecticut timber species*. (AERS working paper). Storrs, CT: University of Connecticut, Dept Agric. Econ. & Rural Soc. In press.

Berck, P. (1979). The economics of timber: a renewable resource in the long run. *Bell J. Econ. Manage. Sci.*, **10**, 447–462.

Biggs, S. D. (1982). Institutions and decision making in agricultural research. In: *Economics of new technology in developing countries*, edited by F. Stewart and J. James, 209–224. London: Francis Pinter.

Brown, G. M., Bentley, W. R. & Gordon, J. C. (1982). Developing harvesting systems for the future: linking strategies, biology and design. *Forest Prod. J.*, **32**, 36–41.

Cannell, M. G. R. (1979). Biological opportunities for genetic improvement in forest productivity. In: *The ecology of even-aged forest plantations*, edited by E. D. Ford, D. C. Malcolm and J. Atterson, 119–144. Cambridge: Institute of Terrestrial Ecology.

Cannell, M. G. R. (1983a). Plant management in agroforestry: manipulation of trees, population densities and mixtures of trees and herbaceous crops. In: *Plant research and agroforestry*, edited by P. A. Huxley, 455–487. Nairobi: International Council for Research in Agroforestry.

Cannell, M. G. R. (1983b). Plant population and yield of tree and herbaceous crops. In: *Plant research and agroforestry*, edited by P. A. Huxley, 489–502. Nairobi: International Council for Research in Agroforestry.

Chambers, R. (1983). *Rural development: putting the last first*. London: Longman.

Chowdhry, K. (1982). *Agro-forestry: the rural poor and institutional structures*. Paper presented at the Workshop on Agro-Forestry organized jointly by the United Nations University and the Albert-Ludwigs-Universität, Freiburg i. Br., 1982.

Ciriacy-Wantrup, S. V. (1952). *Resource conservation: economics and policies*. Berkeley, CA: University of California, Div. Agric. Sci.

Dana, S. T. & Fairfax, S. K. (1980). *Forest and range policy.* 2nd ed. New York: McGraw-Hill.

Fortmann, L. (1984). *Land tenure, tree tenure and the design of agro-forestry projects.* Report to the International Council for Research in Agroforestry, Nairobi, Kenya, by Land Tenure Centre, University of Wisconsin.

Galbraith, J. K. (1979). *The nature of mass poverty.* Cambridge, MA: Harvard University Press.

Gillis, M. (1984). Multinational enterprises, environmental and resource management issues in the tropical forest sector in Indonesia. In: *The role of multinational corporations in environment and resource management in developing countries.* Cambridge, MA: Harvard Institute for International Development.

Gordon, J. C. & Bentley, W. R. (1970). Wood fibre production in an industrial society. *For. Res. Notes Wis.*, no. 150.

Greeley, W. B. (1950). *Forest policy.* New York: McGraw-Hill.

Gupta, T. (1978). Nature of the environment for the forestry sector in India. *Indian Forester*, **104**, 787–796.

Hibbs, D. E. & Bentley, W. R. (1984). A growth model and management for red oak in New England. *Can. J. For. Res.*, **14**, 250–254.

Lyon, K. S. & Sedjo, R. A. (1983). An optimal control theory model to estimate the regional long-term supply of timber. *Forest Sci.*, **29**, 798–812.

Krishna, R. (1980). The economic development of India. *Scient. Am.*, **243**, 166–177.

Pendse, D. R. (1984). Dilemmas of energy strategies in India: implications for the third world. *Econ. Polit. Wkly (India)*, **19**, 556–566.

Sharpe, W. F. (1981). *Investments.* 2nd ed. Englewood Cliffs, NJ: Prentice-Hall.

Skog, K. & Risbrandt, C. (1982). Trends in economic scarcity of US timber commodities. *USDA Forest Service Res. Bull. FPL-11.*

Smith, V. K. (1979). *Scarcity and growth reconsidered.* Baltimore: John Hopkins.

Warner, F. (1982). *Indo-Swedish Forestry Programme 2, 1982/83 to 1986/87; background document.* Delhi: Swedish Embassy, Development Cooperation Office.

Vidyarthi, V. (1984). *Energy and the poor in an Indian village.* Sussex: University of Sussex. Institute of Development Studies. Mimeograph.

31

WOOD PROPERTIES, AND FUTURE REQUIREMENTS FOR WOOD PRODUCTS

G. K. ELLIOTT*

Department of Forestry and Wood Science, University College of North Wales, Bangor, Wales

I. INTRODUCTION

In the developed countries, the demands for, and uses of, wood have changed greatly over the last 150 years. The industrial revolution of the 19th century was accompanied by a marked decrease in the use of wood for fuel, and a marked increase in its use in construction and transport, and in the making of furniture, pallets and packaging. Concurrently, improvements in the technologies of pulping and paper-making, combined with increased literacy, resulted in increased demand for wood to make paper of all kinds.

The present century has seen the birth of a non-wood materials revolution, fuelled by cheap energy. Light-weight metals and plastics can be manufactured to defined engineering and design specifications, and this has inevitably changed the overall uses of wood. Only paper and board products have so far remained relatively immune from such competition.

Despite these changes, the world demand for industrial wood has continued to rise, so that present demand – some 1,000 million t yr^{-1} – is equivalent on a weight basis to the annual world production of iron and steel.

II. CHARACTERISTICS OF WOOD

In order to understand current and future developments in the uses of, and demand for, wood, it is useful first to remind ourselves of its major properties

---

* New address: Price and Pierce (Technical Services) Ltd, 51 Aldwych, London WC2B 4AZ, England.

that are valued by man (Dinwoodie 1981). The following ten properties deserve special mention.

1. Wood is a fibrous material. The prosenchymatous nature of the cell, the physical architecture of the secondary cell wall, and the longitudinal alignment of most of the cells combine to make wood an efficient load-bearing material.

2. Wood is a complex chemical material. Although it is characterized by a relatively small number of chemical constituents (45–50% cellulose, 20–25% hemicellulose, 25–30% lignin), it is infiltrated by many so-called extraneous compounds. These compounds add to the variety of colour in grain configurations, they feature prominently in the differentiation between sapwood and heartwood, and, in some species, they have a pronounced effect on wood properties and uses.

3. Sawnwood is a versatile product; that is, it has adequate properties for many uses. This is particularly true when we consider the differences between species, and the ways in which sawnwood properties can be modified by technologies such as drying and preservation.

4. Wood in the comminuted (chipped or pulped) and restructured form (chipboard, etc) can provide a wide range of properties. The flexible nature of the material enables products to be manufactured from fibres, particles, or thin sheets which enhance its performance or value. Wood-based sheet materials, plywood, particle-board and fibre-building-board are examples of such products manufactured to specific design and strength criteria.

5. Wood is anisotropic[1], and the difference in wood properties along and across the grain enables some economies to be made in structural design. Alternatively, if anisotropy is considered to be a disadvantage, wood-based sheet materials of an almost isotropic character can be made.

6. Wood is hygroscopic, because it contains many hydroxyl groups. That is, it absorbs water from an atmosphere wetter than itself, and loses water to an atmosphere drier than itself. This characteristic results in shrinkage or swelling, some loss in dimensional stability, and changes in strength properties. When the hydroxyl groups of freely suspended fibres come within 0.3 nm of each other, a hydrogen bond is formed between them, causing the fibres to cohere without the aid of external adhesives. This cohesive mechanism is the basis of paper production from wood pulp, and distinguishes paper from other sheet materials which owe their integrity to mechanical entanglement or to an adhesive.

7. Wood is combustible, which is clearly a disadvantage when it is used in construction. However, wood retains its strength better than most building materials with increase in temperature.

8. Wood is a variable product, not only between species, but also within them, and within individual trees. The understanding of variation in macro-features, such as colour, grain deviation and knots, and in micro-features, such as fibre dimensions and wood density, and their influence on wood processing and the performance of wood products, is a major part of the Wood Science discipline.

9. Wood is renewable. In an era much concerned with the depletion of

---

[1] With predetermined axes, so that it is influenced in some directions more than others.

the world's resources, the renewable nature of wood as an industrial and energy raw material has increasing appeal.

10.   Wood is aesthetically pleasing. Differences in colour, grain and texture, exposed by judicious choice of cutting pattern and direction, give beauty, warmth and considerable added value to solid wood products.

III.   WOOD AS A STRUCTURAL MATERIAL

The attributes of wood that favour its use as a structural, load-bearing material, and in the mechanical industries, are its toughness, stiffness, tensile strength, its good thermal-insulation properties, its ease-of-working using simple, low energy-consuming tools, and its high strength/weight ratio. Also, wood is readily available, renewable and relatively cheap.

The attributes of wood, as a structural material, that are clearly undesirable are its variability, hygroscopicity, anisotropy, biodeterioration and combustibility. However, the forest products industries have developed a number of technologies to lessen or overcome these disadvantages (see Table I).

TABLE I.   Measures and techniques that have been used to overcome some of the less desirable attributes of wood as a structural material

Undesirable attributes	Improvement techniques
Variability	Grading of wood by machine; removal of defects by finger-jointing; reduction of the effects of variability by lamination; reduction of genetical variation by selection and breeding.
Hygroscopicity	Controlled kiln drying; dimensional stabilization by plastic impregnation; improved coating for timber.
Anisotropy	Production of nearly isotropic board materials.
Biodeterioration	Impregnation of wood with preservatives.
Combustibility	Impregnation with fire retardants.

IV.   WOOD AS A PULP AND PAPER FURNISH

Wood owes its commanding position as the most important raw material for paper-making to the following attributes: (a) it is cellular; (b) non-fibrous constituents such as pith and ray cells can be easily removed; (c) its 'colour' can be removed (and its 'brightness' improved) without too great a loss in 'strength'; (d) the cellulose cell wall can be modified to give a variety of furnishes to make a range of paper grades; (e) a relatively large quantity of paper is yielded per unit of wood pulp compared with other cellulose fibres; and, as before, (f) wood is readily available and relatively cheap.

Both coniferous and broadleaved woods are used in the manufacture of paper products. Coniferous fibres are long and strong, and are used to give good mechanical properties to the sheets. Broadleaved fibres are smaller and fatter, and contribute to the opacity, thickness and smoothness of the sheets.

Secondary additives are used in paper production, such as (a) bright china clay, to improve opacity, brightness and surface smoothness, and (b) waxes, to resist water penetration. Other additives are used to improve optical, mechanical, electrical and chemical properties.

TABLE II. The energy requirements per unit product in the four major forest product industries, and the equivalent amount of fuelwood needed to supply that energy[1]

	Energy used per unit of product (m³ or t)		
Industry and unit of product	Electricity (kWh)	Heat (MJ)	Equivalent wood burnt (t)
Sawmilling (m³)	80	860–4,000	0·16–0·34
Plywood (m³)	200–300	4,600	0·39–0·59
Fibre-board and particle-board (t)	600–650	10,000–12,000	1·2–1·3
Pulp and paper (t)	400–1,100	6,800–18,000	0·8–2·2

[1] It is assumed that wood has a calorific value of 18,200 MJ t^{-1}. Source: Fung (1982).

V. WOOD AS AN ENERGY SOURCE

Wood has a calorific value of about 18,200 MJ t^{-1}, and it is the most important source of energy in the developing countries. Since the 1974 oil crisis, there has been growing interest in the use of wood as a fuel in the developed countries, including the production of 'energy plantations' (Ramsay Smith 1982). In the USA, it has been estimated that a coniferous plantation of 96,000 ha yielding 13 m³ ha^{-1} yr^{-1} could sustain a 400 megawatt power station (Szego & Kemp 1973). Elsewhere, attention has been focused on short-rotation coppicing (Ramsay Smith 1982), or on combining fuelwood production with industrial-wood production. Recent work in the UK has shown that broadleaved 'coppice with standards' with a yield class (maximum mean annual increment) of 8 m³ ha^{-1}yr^{-1}, and a coppice rotation of 15 years, will yield 800 m³ ha^{-1}yr^{-1} over a 45–50 year rotation, 725 m³ of which can be fuelwood. It is beyond the scope of this paper to discuss the potential for fuelwood production in the developed world, except to state that (a) its current importance is probably under-rated, because of the unreliability of statistical information, (b) the production of structural wood and wood fibre is often likely to take priority over fuelwood production, and (c) energy plantations must compete for land with agriculture, water catchment, recreation and conservation.

The most attractive benefits accrue to wood as an energy source within the forest industries themselves. Of the various forest product industries, sawmilling uses the least energy, in the form of electricity and heat, to produce a unit of product (Table II) and this industry also produces the largest proportion of residues. Estimates, based on large sawmills producing 75,000 m^3yr^{-1}, indicate that self-sufficiency in energy would be attained by burning 45–50% of the wood residue. The plywood industry could also become almost self-sufficient, but the wood-based sheet materials industries, notably those producing particle-board and fibre-building-board, use wood residue as their furnish, and so have a negligible amount of wood waste. The pulp and paper industry is the largest energy user per unit of product (Table II); some of that energy can be provided by burning spent pulping liquor, bark and chipper waste, but additional power has to be bought.

Wood can also be converted to methanol or ethanol. Since the 1974 oil crisis, interest has revived in the production of ethanol as a motor fuel, notably as 'gasohol', consisting of a mixture of gasolene with up to 25% ethanol. Use of this fuel mix is mandatory in Brazil, and it is available in the USA, although at present the main source of ethanol is sugar and starch crops rather than wood. Lignocellulosic materials require delignification by acid hydrolysis to release the fermentable sugars (Tomaselli 1982).

VI.   WOOD AS A SOURCE OF CHEMICALS

In addition to alcohols, there are other industrial chemicals which might be derived from trees in the future. Numerous opportunities exist for the production of simple, or discrete, chemical products from wood and/or foliage, such as cattle feed, cosmetics, pharmaceuticals, and products from spent pulping liquors and from ethanol. However, single-product industrial plants rarely operate profitably without the shelter of a protected market. Notable success has been achieved in the use of bark as a source of phenol (derived from tannin) in the formulation of phenol-formaldehyde resin adhesives, which form the cornerstone of the exterior-grade wood-based sheet materials industry. But, elsewhere, considerable research is needed to develop a commercially viable wood-based chemicals industry.

The problems are three-fold. First, low-cost raw materials are required, which means very low prices for the grower, bearing in mind the difficulties of harvesting woody biomass and the high cost of transporting a material with such a low weight/volume ratio. Or, alternatively, the industry would have to be based on residue supplies. Second, the present capital cost of the manufacturing plant required to convert wood to chemical units is twice that required to convert coal to comparable units, and three times that required by petrochemical facilities of comparable capacity. Third, the energy cost of breaking down the complex molecular structure of wood into simple structures, and then rebuilding those structures into monomers and polymers, is very high. Wood is therefore unlikely to provide a generous chemical feedstock, except in those countries with profligate wood supplies and a high technological threshold.

TABLE III. Estimated consumption of (or demand for)[1] wood products in the developed world from 1975 to 2025. Values are given in roundwood raw material equivalents (RRE)×10⁶, recognizing that the paper and board sector will utilize industrial wood residues

Year	1975	1985	2000	2025
Roundwood raw material equivalents×10⁶	RRE(%)	RRE(%)	RRE(%)	RRE(%)
Sawnwood timber	561(55)	583(44)	600(34)	617(25)
Wood-based sheet materials	127(13)	236(18)	386(22)	735(30)
Paper and board	325(32)	500(38)	768(42)	1,100(45)
Totals	1,013(100)	1,319(100)	1,754(100)	2,452(100)

[1] Based on low population growth, low gross domestic production and low income elasticity of demand.
Source: Forestry Commission (1977).

VII. FUTURE REQUIREMENTS FOR WOOD PRODUCTS

Sawn timber is by far the most valuable wood product per tonne, but at present it represents only about 64% of the wood used by industries in the developed world. The remainder is first taken apart and then reconstituted in the form of sheet materials, paper or boards (Table III). Between now and the year 2025, the UK Forestry Commission forecasts that, in the developed world, there will be only a small increase in demand for sawnwood timber, representing a falling percentage of the total wood demand (Table III). In fact, with increasing population, per capita consumption of sawnwood will fall. By contrast, there will be a marked increase in the use of wood-based sheet materials (13–30%, Table III), largely owing to the effect of new technologies. To illustrate the importance of these technologies, Table IV lists just some of the new particle-board products introduced on to the UK market over the past 22 years.

Developments have also occurred in the manufacture of plywood products, such as the use of a honeycomb plastic/metal/carbon-fibre core for certain types of panels, and the manufacture of thick laminar-veneer constructions to standard lumber sizes but with 5–15% enhanced mechanical properties. It is expected that such products will increasingly replace solid wood products in construction, furniture and transport.

Pulp and paper demand is also anticipated to rise dramatically, largely because of greater diversification. The recent success of industrial and reinforced 'structural' papers is an example of a technological advance that has met a highly specific requirement. However, there is a threat to the market in the advances in electronic data transfer. Where instant communication is vital, such as in financial markets and international travel, there is now almost exclusive reliance on electronic data transfer, with decreased paper consump-

TABLE IV. New particle-board products introduced on to the UK market between 1960 and 1982. Particle-board is defined as comminuted (finely divided) particles, pressed together using urea-formaldehyde resin adhesives

1960	Multilayered board with surface properties capable of taking decorative plastic laminates, used for low-cost kitchen furniture and fitments.
1963	High density (>750kg m^{-3}) flooring grade particle-board.
1966	Prefelted bitumen-faced boards, used for roofing.
1969	Graded-density-board, with a single layer, fine surface texture and gravure-printable surface, used for low-cost furniture items.
1970	Low-pressure laminated board, melamine-laminated for kitchen fitments and worktops.
1971	Exterior grade boards, phenol-formaldehyde bonded, used for exterior cladding, signboards, kitchen and bathroom floors and fitments.
1973	Ultra-thin (2–4 mm) 'mende' board, used for low-cost furniture framing and drawer sides.
1977	Cement-bonded exterior board, protected from biodeterioration and fire-proofed, used for exterior cladding.
1980	Orientated structural board (OSB), used as load-bearing members in frame constructions.
1981	Medium-density fibre-board (MDF), that is dry formed fibre-board, bonded and felted to 19 mm thickness, which can be machined, moulded and laminated, used to make quality furniture.
1982	Wafer board, that is large wood flakes bonded with phenol-formaldehyde to exterior-grade specifications, used to make 'concrete' shuttering, exterior cladding and used in construction.

tion. However, to date, microchip technology and television have not decreased the demand for printing and writing papers. There is no evidence to suggest that this pattern will change, but the potential for change is present.

Considering a mature coniferous tree plantation in the southern pine region of the USA, Kulp (1982) considered that the future scenario for the utilization of woody biomass, to achieve the greatest value, would be as follows: 27% to high-value solid wood products (the buttlog and second sawlog); 38% to wood chips (the lighter core-wood and crown-wood chips going to make sheet materials and mechanical pulp, the heavier chips from sawmill residues going to make chemical pulp); and 35% to provide energy to power the processing system, including bark, small branches and stumps.

Speculating on future needs, one can define two possible scenarios. In the first, the highest value per tonne of wood would continue to come from solid wood products. In this case, forest management decisions which affect variation in bole size, tree form and branching within the stand would increase in importance, and research interests would be centred on the value and grade of sawnwood out-turn rather than on volume production ha^{-1}yr^{-1} alone (Fenton 1971, 1972). Also, the processing sector would concentrate on maximum value and volume recovery from the sawlog, and little product innovation would be expected.

In the second scenario, the influence of the process engineer would dominate, through the manipulation of fibres, fibre bundles, and mechanically produced particles and flakes. Here, the technical performance of the end product would be improved, by novel applications of adhesives, water repellents and surface finishes, some of which would probably be derived from wood itself. The forest researcher's attention would be directed more towards uniformity of the raw material (wood fibres), the physiology of cambial activity, and biomass production. Despite the abundant literature on the variation of wood properties within and between trees, little is known about the physiological parameters which govern wood properties (Brazier 1977).

REFERENCES

Anderson, A. B. (1977). Bark extracts as bonding agents for particle board. In: *Wood technology chemical aspects*, edited by I. S. Goldstein, 235–243. (Am. Chem. Soc. symposium series no. 43). Washington DC: American Chemical Society.
Brazier, J. D. (1977). The effect of forest practices on quality of the harvested crop. *Forestry*, **50**, 49–66.
Cibula, E. J. (1980). Trends in timber supply and trade: an information review. *Building Research Establishment Report*. London: HMSO.
Dinwoodie, J. M. (1981). *Timber, its nature and behaviour*. New York: Van Nostrand Reinhold.
Elliott, G. K. (1982). Some other uses of wood. In: *Wood using industries*, 56–69. Edinburgh: Institute of Chartered Foresters.
Evans, R. S. (1974). *Energy plantations – should we grow trees for power plant fuels?* (Inf. rep. VR-X-129). Vancouver: Canadian Forestry Service, Western Forest Products Laboratory.
Fenton, R. (1971). Silviculture and management of *Pinus radiata* for framing timber production. *N.Z. J. For. Sci.*, **1**, 60–73.
Fenton, R. (1972). Economics of radiata pine sawlog production. *N.Z. J. For. Sci.*, **2**, 313–347.
Forestry Commission. (1977). *The wood production outlook in Britain – review*. Edinburgh: Forestry Commission.
Fraser, A. I. (1981). *The role of deciduous woodlands in the economy of rural communities*. Penicuik: International Forest Science Consultants.
Fung, P. V. H. (1982). Wood energy prospects. In: *Energy from forest biomass*, edited by W. Ramsay Smith, 155–170. New York; London: Academic Press.
Kulp, L. (1982). The wood supply and product spectrum of the future. *J. Inst. Wood Sci.*, **9**, 150–155.
Marra, G. G. (1979). Overview of wood. *J. educ. Modules Mater. Sci. eng.*, **1**, 669–707.
Nissan, A. H. (1979). Paper. *J. educ. Modules Mater. Sci. eng.*, **1**, 773–844.
Park, J. C. (1980). A grade index for primed butt logs. *N.Z. J. For. Sci.*, **10**, 419–439.
Ramsay Smith, W., ed. (1982). *Energy from forest biomass*. New York; London: Academic Press.
Szego, G. C. & Kemp, C. C. (1973). Energy forests and fuel plantations. *Chem. Tech.*, May, 275–284.
Tomaselli, I. (1982). Liquidification of wood. In: *Energy from forest biomass*, edited by W. Ramsay Smith, 209–220. New York; London: Academic Press.
Wangard, F. F. (1979). Wood, its structure and properties. *J. educ. Modules Mater. Sci. eng.*, **1**, 437–534.

DISCUSSION OF TREES AS CROP PLANTS

Edited by M. G. R. Cannell

The papers published in this book were discussed on the final half-day of the conference in five discussion groups. The five subjects chosen for discussion were tree breeding, flowering, roots and microbiology, stand design, and light interception. This choice partly reflected the grouping of subjects within the conference, and partly reflected the concerns of the participants. The task given to each group was to highlight the main issues, the main points of contention, and the priorities for future research.

The following reports were drafted by the group chairmen, circulated for comment to contributing members of each group, and then edited to reflect the balance of views within each group. They do, therefore, form a valuable statement of current thinking in tree crop biology.

It is noteworthy that (a) considerable attention was given, by many contributors, to the concept of an ideotype, (b) there was perhaps less attention given to photosynthesis *per se* than to light interception and carbon partitioning, (c) as much attention was given to root functioning and microbiology as to shoot structure, and (d) biological issues were extended to the socio-economics of stand design and agroforestry. There were also many instances where ideas were exchanged between foresters and horticulturists – concerning, for instance, the roles of gibberellins and rootstocks in flowering, models of light interception, the use of clones and dominant gene inheritance in tree breeding, the importance of carbon partitioning to roots, and the roles of root symbionts. However, the meeting inevitably highlighted differences in perspective of people with different research backgrounds and experience; the organizers will be rewarded if these differences are now better understood and the discussion continues.

TREE BREEDING

E. C. Franklin (Chairman), N. W. Simmonds, F. E. Bridgwater, M. R. Rutter, P. M. A. Tigerstedt, K. G. Eldridge, F. H. Alston, R. Timmis, C. G. Williams, G. K. Elliott, H. Y. Yeang.

The largest genetic gains in forestry to date have been the result of species and provenance selection, although these gains are often taken for granted or overlooked entirely. Line breeding (ie population improvement, not inbred line breeding) within adapted provenances has just begun in terms of generations of artificial selection. Nevertheless, there are examples, in various parts of the world, of the application of technology in the production of forest trees, such as mass propagation by rooting cuttings, *in vitro* screening for disease resistance, and the selection and propagation of highly effective mycorrhizas and nitrogen-fixing bacteria for use in forest stands. In addition, the potential of the many genetic manipulation techniques now becoming available should be investigated.

Clonal propagation, as practised on fruit trees, was seen as an excellent way to take advantage of genetic gains in forestry, but line breeding must also be done to advance genetically the base population, and to provide new and better material for cloning or other methods of propagation. An important principle underlying line breeding is to maintain a wide genetic base to provide for genetic advancement as new technology provides new methods of mass propagation, new management and harvesting systems, new processes and uses for wood and other forest products. In general, uniformity was seen as the most important wood property, considering wood as a basic raw material. Uniformity from tree to tree enhances the efficiency of management, harvesting and processing, and uniformity within the tree contributes to processing efficiency and a high net yield of product. It is unrealistic for tree breeders to expect silviculturists or wood technologists to specify the types of trees to be managed and harvested 25 to 75 years from now. Therefore, line breeding for the long term must be directed toward traits of universal value – such as high productivity, uniformity, disease and insect resistance. Some forest tree breeders held the view that it would be the breeder who would specify the silvicultural, harvesting and processing requirements, by the lines which they released for use – the history of forest utilization seemed to bear witness to this trend. Others argued that the breeder must be responsive to silvicultural and market needs.

There was a consensus that research on tree physiology and growth modelling would benefit applied tree breeding programmes. Some group members felt that growth modelling research could provide inputs to current and future tree breeding and testing programmes. Others (a majority of tree breeders) felt that such research would be most beneficial if first done retrospectively, that is if efforts were made to determine the physiological basis of gains already made, rather than to model all the elements of tree growth. It was suggested that genetically defined material should always be used in such research.

The discussion group listed several high-priority topics, relevant to tree breeding, which related directly to tree physiology. These were: (a) the role of light, water and nutrients in competitive interactions between individuals and between families; (b) the lengths of growing periods (diurnal and annual); (c) pure (family or clonal) versus mixed planting strategies; (d) effects of ageing on propagation, flowering and wood quality; (e) pest and pathogen resistance; (f) wood formation; and (g) roots and their associated fungi and bacteria.

There was a general consensus that forestry research in general is underfunded in relation to the rate of progress that could be achieved. Scarce resources are best used when geneticists and physiologists do joint studies, sharing the use of genetically identified plant material, data, and facilities. Such collaboration would also promote better understanding between these two branches of forest science.

FLOWERING

M. P. Coutts (Chairman), E. P. Bachelard, C. Couper, J. Dick, A. M. Fletcher, M. Giertych, V. Koski, R. M. Lanner, K. A. Longman, J. J. Philipson, S. D. Ross, D. T. Seal.

Most of the discussion centred on coniferous forest species, in part reflecting the general interest of members of the group, but also because broadleaved trees have been less intensively investigated with respect to flowering and its control. It was stressed that research on flowering in conifers has been of a largely empirical nature, conducted mainly by applied research institutes, in response to the need to advance tree breeding programmes more rapidly, and to ensure an adequate supply of improved seed for reafforestation. This approach has led to the development of various techniques, such as girdling, water stress, root pruning and the application of nitrogen fertilizers and growth regulators (especially gibberellins), that can be used alone and in combination to promote flowering in many conifers.

However, the empirical approach has yielded little understanding about how the different treatments work, or about the flowering process at a basic level. Members of the group agreed that this basic knowledge is essential if we are to be able to control flowering efficiently and reliably. However, the group could not agree on the best strategy for future research. Some believed that future research should involve modelling, based on detailed observations on physiology and ecology. Others felt that the way forward lay with experimental work in controlled conditions, including whole-plant physiology and biochemistry, and recognized the need for detailed work on morphology and anatomy.

Several areas were identified where further research is especially warranted. One concerned juvenility, and whether conifers undergo a true phase change involving activation/repression of genes controlling flowering, or if the so-called juvenile condition exists, because the rapid vegetative growth during this developmental phase results in essential nutrients and hormones being limiting for reproductive processes. Evidence can be found which supports both hypotheses. The control of sex ratios was considered another important research topic with practical applications for pollen management and hybridization work. Depending on the species, the position of buds (within a branch, and within the crown), and the timing of treatments, photoperiod and growth regulators (especially auxins) can all influence to some degree the ratio of male to female cones produced, but mechanisms involved are poorly understood. The prospects of being able to synchronize flowering times to produce hybrids in seed orchards were also discussed, but it was thought that, in view of the difficulties, it was not a very tractable problem, and alternative approaches, such as the use of pollen collected in previous years, were more worthwhile.

There was much interest and discussion on the specific role, if any, of roots on flowering in conifers. One view expressed was that actively growing roots may export substances inhibitory to conebud differentiation, because many of the cultural treatments (drought, girdling, root pruning) which promote flowering share in common an ability to retard the growth of roots. However, it was noted that none of the substances that roots might be expected to export are known to be inhibitory to flowering in conifers. Furthermore, it appears that the treatments in question invariably also retard shoot elongation and, therefore, may result in an increased availability of essential hormones and nutrients for reproductive development. Several members of the group mentioned that they were working on this problem, but they had no definite results to report.

Related to the role of roots was the possibility of developing specific rootstocks, as in horticulture, both to enhance flowering and to control tree size in conifer seed orchards. Further investigations are required on the use of rootstocks, both to enhance flowering, and as an approach to a better understanding of the role of roots in the flowering process.

The hormonal control of flowering was another topic of great interest to members of the group, several of whom were directly involved in this area of research. Although exogenous applications of certain gibberellins (GAs), most notably a mixture of GA_4 and GA_7, effectively promote flowering in many members of the Pinaceae, questions remain about the endogenous role of gibberellins in flowering, and this area requires further investigation. It was concluded that, despite the apparent importance of GAs, it is highly unlikely that flowering is under the control of a single stimulus. Rather, it appears that conebud initiation and differentiation in conifers involve a continuum of interacting processes – including different growth regulators, carbohydrates and products of nitrogen metabolism – that occur over a relatively long period. Any one, or several, of these processes could become limiting, thus preventing the initiation, differentiation or development of conebuds. As physiologists, our object should be to obtain a basic understanding of these interacting processes sufficient to allow their control in a cost-efficient manner.

ROOTS AND MICROBIOLOGY

D. C. F. Fayle (Chairman), G. D. Bowen, J. G. Torrey, T. T. Kozlowski, T. O. Perry, J. Wilson, L. J. Sheppard, R. Lines, J. D. Deans.

The conference increased the awareness among participants of the importance of root systems and their environment. Roots were discussed in about three-quarters of the presentations, and mycorrhizas were mentioned by one-fifth of the speakers.

The main topics touched on in discussion were assimilate partitioning to roots, root function and activity, competition, allelopathy, genetics and tissue culture.

Tree and stand growth modelling is constrained by inadequate knowledge about the roots. Estimates of the proportion of photosynthates partitioned to roots range from about 20% to 60%; site factors probably play a major role, but the data are meagre. Even less is known about partitioning within the root systems, between cambial growth and elongation. What is the relative importance, functionally, of one gramme of dry matter in one part of the root system as against another?

Inferences made by some speakers, about the above-ground yield of plantations of narrow- vs wide-crowned trees, may well have to be modified when account is taken of root dynamics and below-ground competition. These root aspects need to be studied in single and mixed species plantations, and in mixed cropping systems.

Although quantitative data are needed on such topics as the growth periodicity, abundance, distribution and longevity of coarse and fine roots in relation to environmental factors, we should perhaps attempt to measure root *activity* in terms of actual water and nutrient uptake, and hormonal activities of the root system. There is still disagreement about the relative roles of mycorrhizal hyphae, unsuberized, suberized and secondarily thickened roots in water uptake. Our understanding of the growth regulator function of roots is particularly inadequate. Reference was made to a pertinent volume in press, *viz. New root formation in plants and cuttings*, edited by M. B. Jackson, and published by Martinus Nijhoff, Netherlands (1985).

Technological advancements, such as the use of nutrient mists, may prove valuable in studies of root activity. They may also allow studies of growth in relation to products of decomposition and to allelopathy. Further study is needed on the effects of allelochemicals on root and mycorrhizal growth. The use of horticultural grades of 'Turface' (a commercial mix of montmorillonite prepared for greenhouse use by International Minerals and Chemicals Corporation, USA) can provide a semblance of the soil environment, and permit microtoming of roots in their environment.

Genetics may play a role in the 'design' of root systems for different site and environmental conditions. For example, on certain sites, if root growth could be made to occur at greater depths, moisture availability might be increased. Genetics may also be important in growth regulator activities and in the formation and subsequent growth of root systems from tissue cultures.

STAND DESIGN

D. A. Perry (Chairman), W. R. Bentley, D. A. Rook, L. Kärki, R. R. B. Leakey, R. Faulkner, P. von Carlowitz, D. E. Hibbs, M. Leikola. *

The goal of forestry and agroforestry is to produce value from land in a way that is both efficient and reliable. There are two steps in this process: selection of individual 'ideotypes', and incorporation of individuals into stands. The latter – a marriage of ecology and economics – may be thought of as a kind of 'biological architecture'. (There is a particularly nice symmetry in this view in that ecology and economics both derive from the Greek 'oikos' for house.)

In any given environmental-social-economic setting, the design possibilities will be numerous, ranging from monoclonal forests to intricate patterns in space and time. A critical step in choosing among these possibilities, and a primary goal of the stand architect, is to strike the proper balance between simplicity and complexity. Perry and Bentley pointed out some of the important trade-offs in qualitative terms as follows:

	Simple systems	Complex systems
Inputs		
managerial	low	high
labour	low	high
energy	high	low
capital	high	low to medium
Outputs		
yield	high	(depends on how measured)
yield stability	?	high
Non-market values		
aesthetics	low	high
wildlife	low	high
watershed	high	high

The main issues facing the stand designer relate to how simple and diverse systems differ in inputs (managerial, labour, energy) and outputs (yield, yield stability, nonmarket values). Among the most compelling features of simple systems are the relatively low levels of managerial labour inputs required. Managerial skill is always a scarce commodity; however, computers will continue to make large-scale complexity more manageable. With regard to labour, we must ask whether it makes economic or social sense to design low labour input systems where there is a surplus of unemployed. Energy inputs are better discussed in conjunction with yield stability.

The design of any cropping system must take into account both yield and yield stability. It is generally assumed that yield is maximized in stands containing a single high-yielding ideotype; however, forest researchers are becoming increasingly aware of what agronomists have known for some time – that fast-growing individuals are unlikely to produce the highest stand yields. Further, little is known about the nature of resource allocation in plant communities and, therefore, what yields are attainable in cleverly designed mixtures. Intercropping can sometimes give higher yields than sole cropping in agriculture.

A cropping system must provide immediate yields and insure against future losses. Four factors are of particular concern: pests and pathogens, long-term soil productivity, changes in climate, and changes in markets. No biological system ever was, or will any ever be, robust against all possible perturbations. Nevertheless, natural systems are generally well buffered, owing largely to their genetic and structural diversity (their 'information content'). Historically, farmers incorporated diversity into their systems as a form of insurance. In contrast, the simple system is buffered by energy inputs rather than by internal information. Pests and pathogens are kept in check by using chemicals and/or by conducting an endless race between plant breeders and evolution; and soil productivity is maintained by using fertilizers. Two key questions facing the stand designer are whether energy-intensive buffering strategies (a) are reliable in the long run, and (b) make economic sense in a world with finite free energy sources.

The diversity incorporated into natural ecosystems and traditional agriculture buffers them against what might be termed the paradox of 'certain uncertainty'. Hubris to the contrary, modern humans are not immune to the unpredictability of the future and, in fact, have accentuated it. There is a consensus among climatologists that average global temperature is going to increase from $1 \cdot 5 \,^{\circ}C$ to $4 \cdot 5 \,^{\circ}C$ in the next century, with unpredictable effects on rainfall patterns (the average global temperature at the height of the last glaciation was $5 \,^{\circ}C$ cooler than that today). Thus, the performance of a given ideotype in a given location may be quite different in the future than at present. It is quite possible, for example, that a few degrees' warming will elevate winter temperatures in north-west North America to the point where the chilling requirements of *Pseudotsuga menziesii* are no longer satisfied, and the species would no longer be commercially viable in a large part of its range (D. Lavender, pers. comm.). It is difficult to see how we can cope with 'certain uncertainty', particularly in long-lived crops such as trees, other than to buffer systems through diversity.

Some group members felt there was a need to encourage tropical foresters and farmers to domesticate and grow a wider range of tree species both in simple and complex stand designs.

The group listed the following research needs. (a) Greater understanding is needed of resource allocation among plants in stands. (b) Mechanistic and/or holistic models of stand growth and yield need to be constructed which incorporate ideotype diversity and effects of site quality. (c) Because site quality is an important determinant of stand design, improved methods are needed to classify land capability. (d) We need to identify and preserve genetic diversity, especially that relating to temperature, moisture, CO_2 levels, and acid precipitation. (e) More understanding is needed on the role of community structure in controlling pest populations. (f) Economic models are needed which incorporate nonmarket values (eg water quality), risk, and the irreversibility of some management practices (such as soil degradation and narrowing the gene pool). (g) More consideration should be given to the sociological aspects of land use.

LIGHT INTERCEPTION

P. G. Jarvis (Chairman), J. E. Jackson, P. A. Huxley, M. R. Kaufmann and R. E. McMurtrie.

This group first cleared up a misunderstanding that arose in earlier discussions. They then went on to consider several points relating to management and radiation interception. Next, consideration was given to an integrated strategy of modelling and measurement to evaluate particular ideotypes. Finally, the group considered the consequences of this approach for the organization of research. The main points are listed below.

1. The relationship between growth and leaf area is one of diminishing returns and may even exhibit an optimum leaf area index for growth. Consequently, at a moderate to large leaf area index, some of the foliage can be removed without significant adverse effects on growth. In his paper, Rook pointed out that, in *Pinus radiata*, up to 40% of the foliage could be removed without significant adverse effect, and Jackson

showed that halving the canopy volume of fruit trees reduced light interception by only 10%. Thus, thinning quite heavily, or removing large portions of the canopy, may have little immediate adverse effect on total growth. Indeed, this fact is part of the rationale behind 'respacing', thinning and pruning operations.

2. Maximizing light interception, at least up to about 90%, throughout the life of a crop must be the target for management, if dry matter increment throughout the life of the plantation is to be maximized. Where forest tree thinning is done for commercial purposes, it should not reduce interception much below 90% for too long. The production of fruit buds, and the development of fruits of high commercial quality do, however, depend on high light intensity within the fruiting zone of orchard trees. Their management must, therefore, be aimed at minimizing within-tree shade at critical times, while maximizing effective ground cover and light interception.

3. Putting on more leaf increases the loss of water from tree crops, both by transpiration and interception loss, as well as increasing growth, because of the strong coupling between tall crops and the atmosphere. This paradox is solved in natural stands by the wide spacing between individual trees in areas where water is a scarce resource (eg *Pinus ponderosa* in eastern Washington). In areas where water is limiting, the manager may, therefore, have to modify his approach and settle for less than near maximum light interception to conserve water. His goal would then be the maximum light interception possible without the occurrence of serious stress – both water and nutrients.

4. The interception of radiation by vegetation must be treated at the stand level, but within the stand the growth of individuals is usually important for the production of a particular product. Because it is difficult to measure the distribution of radiation and of the processes that are driven by radiation, we must use *models* of stands comprised of individuals. These models may be poor today for many crops, but even so we must make a start with them, and use them to provide practical guidelines for forest managers and agroforesters. The models can be tested by *measurements* of processes, and these measurements should also lead to the generation of *hypotheses* and to *predictions* of the performance of new genetic ideotypes, such as the narrow-crowned pines and spruces.

5. Using existing models, it is possible to make reasonable predictions of things like E/A (transpiration/assimilation) for stands with different structures, leaf area indices and stresses, integrated over 12 months. These models, even if inexact, will give insight into the importance of likely variables, and may be useful as planning guides in a variety of situations, such as the various types of agroforestry in the tropics.

6. The parameterization and testing of process-based stand models are expensive and need sustained investment in resources, manpower and commitment. It will not be possible to provide adequate large-scale experiments to test models in many places, so collaboration is essential.

SPECIES INDEX

The English common names of most tree species have been omitted from the text, except for apple, cherry, tea, rubber etc., and common names that are not included in the text are not indexed here. However, the authorities of Latin names, which were also omitted from the text, are given here for all higher plants. Thanks are due to Dr L. J. Sheppard for her help in preparing both this index and the subject index.

SUBJECT INDEX

A

Abortion,
  of flowers, fruits, embryos, 176,
    416–418
  (see Abscission)
Abscisic acid (ABA),
  cambial growth, 214, 215
  root origin, 312
Abscission,
  of fruitlets, 410, 411, 413, 416
  (see Abortion)
Absorption,
  capacity of roots, Chapter 18
Acclimatization,
  chloroplasts, 91
  photosynthesis, 84
  (see Adaptation, Frost)
Acetylene reduction, 367
Acid deposition, 324
Acidity,
  of fruits, 450
  of tropical soils, Chapter 20
  (see pH)
Acorns, 283, 431–432
Actinorhizas, 320, Chapter 21
Activation energy, 85
Adaptation,
  branching, Chapter 14
  & competition, 481
  exudates & extractives, 259–263
  multipurpose trees, 16, 17
  suboptimal environments, Chapter 5,
    475, 476
  temperature, Chapter 6
  & thermodynamics, 500
  (see Acclimatization, Evolution)
Additive genetic variance,
  crown form, 106
  defined, 36
  forest tree breeding, Chapter 3
  fruit tree breeding, 51
Adhesive, 265
Adventitious buds, Chapter 9

Aerodynamic roughness, 72,
    Chapter 27
Affinity,
  enzymes to substrate, 85
Agamospermy, 111
Age,
  of leaves and photosynthesis, 239
  effect on partitioning, 182–184
  of tree crops, 6
Ageing,
  & flowering, 399–401
  & ideotypes, 95, 96
  rooting cuttings, 44, 119, 125–127
  vegetative vigour, 412, 413
  (see Longevity)
Agroforestry,
  fodder trees, Chapter 17
  fuelwood trees, 279
  multipurpose trees, 10, 161,
    Chapter 2
  new crops, 11
  nut-bearing trees, 435
  root/shoot ratios, 173
  selection for arid regions, 475, 476
  selection for products, 10
  soil changes, Chapter 20
  tree model, Chapter 29
  transpiration, 477, 478
Agronomic crops,
  canopy properties, Chapter 27
  yield improvement, 90, 91
Alfisols, 331, 334
Algae, 317, 318
Algal mucilage, 264
Aliphatic compounds, 260
Allelopathy,
  exudates & extractives, 261, 262
  root secretions, 19
Alley,
  cropping, 28
  light climate, 30
Allocation (see Partitioning)